PRINCIPLES OF URBAN TRANSPORT SYSTEMS PLANNING

PRINCIPLES OF URBAN TRANSPORT SYSTEMS PLANNING

B. G. HUTCHINSON

Professor of Civil Engineering
University of Waterloo
Waterloo, Ontario

發 行 人：廖 文 遠
出 版 者：楓城出版社
新竹市武昌街42號
劃撥帳號104063
發 行 所：台北市和平東路二段113號2樓
電　　話：(02)7036554
印刷 所：聯和印製廠
行政院新聞局登記證局版台業字第1322號
中華民國七十二年　月

Principles of Urban Transport Systems Planning

2 3 4 5 6 7 8 9 0　KPKP　7 9 8 7 6 5

Library of Congress Cataloging in Publication Data

Hutchinson, B.G.
Principles of urban transport systems planning.

1. Urban transportation policy. 2. Traffic estimation. I. Title.
HE305.H87　388.4　73-20309
ISBN 0-07-031539-6

To Douglas Mary

CONTENTS

PREFACE

The purpose of this text is to provide a contemporary statement of existing approaches to strategic transport-systems planning in urban areas. The book is intended for use by undergraduate students in civil engineering and the other planning professions, postgraduate students, and practicing transport planners.

The book concentrates on the techniques and knowledge that are available for the synthesis, analysis, and evaluation of alternative transport-systems plans. In this book little attention is directed toward the broad urban transport-policy issues, since it is my view that students of transport planning must develop first an intimate understanding of the planning process before attempting to address themselves to the broader policy issues. There has been an unfortunate tendency at many universities in recent years to create an awareness in students of society's problems, without equipping them with the necessary tools and professional perspectives to permit them to contribute to the solution of these problems.

The content of this book has evolved from a sequence of three 13-week-term courses offered by the Department of Civil Engineering at the University of Waterloo to both undergraduate and postgraduate students. The undergraduate and postgraduate courses offerings differ in the extent of the material discussed in connection with each topic.

The first course covers the material presented in Chaps. 1-5, 8, and 9 and the introductory material on economic evaluation in Chap. 10. The objective of this course is to provide students with a detailed understanding of the techniques that can be used to estimate the travel demands that are likely to be created by a specified land-use plan. This first course is presented to undergraduate civil engineering students in the first half of their third year. These students have already been exposed to courses in systems thinking and engineering economic analysis in first and second years, respectively.

The second course in the sequence covers the material presented in Chaps. 6 and 11 on land-use models and their application to regional planning problems. Techniques for population and economic activity forecasting are treated in much greater depth in the course than they are in this book.

The final course covers the material presented in Chap. 10 on economic evaluation as well as the material on welfare economics presented in the Appendix to Chap. 10. There is, in fact, a fourth course in this sequence and this is a course in urban transport-planning case studies which may be taken between the first and second courses. The objective of this course is to illustrate how the transport-planning process has been applied in practical problems.

I would like to acknowledge the contributions made to this book by a number of people. Dr. Douglas T. Wright, former Dean of Engineering at the University of Waterloo and currently Deputy Provincial Secretary for Social Development in Ontario, encouraged the development of a multidisciplinary approach to my earlier work in highway pavement design. This resulted eventually in my current interests in urban transport planning.

Many parts of this book have benefited from the numerous discussions I have had with my colleague Dr. John H. Shortreed, Associate Professor of Civil Engineering at the University of Waterloo. Material has resulted from joint development of courses as well as from the production of a number of coauthored technical papers.

Roberta Taylor has typed and retyped various versions of this manuscript during the past 5 years and her very significant contributions to the preparation of this book are acknowledged gratefully. Iris Woodcock and Lyn Bruce have executed much of the administrative typing required during the preparation of this book.

Nadia Bahar of Engineering Drafting at the University of Waterloo prepared most of the diagrams submitted to the publisher with the remainder being prepared by Diana Rajnovich and Carol Hood.

Approximately 50 percent of the content of this book was developed during my tenure as a C. D. Howe Memorial Fellow in 1968-1969. The support provided by the C. D. Howe Foundation during this period is acknowledged gratefully. Much of the tenure of this Fellowship was spent at the Centre for

Environmental Studies in London, England, where I benefited greatly from my contacts with Professor Alan Wilson, now of Leeds University, and David Bayliss, now of Greater London Council.

My final acknowledgment is to several postgraduate students who studied with the Transport Group at Waterloo. Bill O'Brien read the final draft of the manuscript and identified many errors. The thesis work of John Morrall, Rick Borland, and Andrew Vandertol has been used in parts of the book.

I accept completely the responsibility for any errors that remain after publication. I would appreciate hearing of any errors that still exist.

B. G. Hutchinson

ACKNOWLEDGMENTS

A number of publishers have granted permission to include copyrighted material in this book. Where this permission involves diagrams or tables the permission is noted on the diagrams and tables.

Chapter 1

Harvard University Press for permission to quote from *Design of Water Resource Systems* by A. Maass, M. M. Hufschmidt, R. Dorfman, H. A. Thomas, S. A. Marglin and G. M. Fair. Copyright 1962 by the President and Fellows of Harvard College.

Chapter 9

Her Majesty's Stationery Office for permission to quote from *Traffic in Towns.* Crown Copyright 1963.

Chapter 10

The McGraw-Hill Book Company for permission to quote from *Traffic System Analysis* by Martin Wohl and Brian V. Martin. Copyright 1967 by McGraw-Hill, Inc.

The Johns Hopkins Press for permission to quote from *A Preface to Urban Economics* by Wilbur R. Thompson. Copyright 1965 by the Johns Hopkins Press, Baltimore, Maryland.

Penguin Books Limited for permission to quote from *Analytical Welfare Economics* by D. M. Winch. Copyright by D. M. Winch, 1971.

Material from non-copyrighted publications has also been used and the various sources are identified in the references. In particular, material from the publications of the Highway Research Board and the Australian Road Research Board has been used, and the author wishes to acknowledge the contributions of both of these organizations and the authors who have contributed to their publications.

INTRODUCTION

Planning and design activities in urban areas occur in ordered hierarchies. The transport-planning methods described in this book are directed toward the strategic level of planning. Within the strategic planning level a variety of transport-planning problems are encountered that dictate different requirements from the travel-demand forecasting process.

The greater part of Chap. 1 is devoted to a description of a systems-planning morphology which provides a vehicle for the expansion of the Chicago-type planning framework to include a broader range of impacts. This systems framework is then used to organize the remainder of the book where each phase of this expanded transport-planning process is described in detail.

Chapters 2 to 5 describe the techniques that may be used to estimate the travel demands that are likely to be generated by a given land-use plan. The methods described in these chapters must be regarded as conditional forecasting methods in that they require the specification of a complete land-use pattern.

Chapter 6 describes a family of Lowry-model-based–land-use models that may be used to derive a land-use allocation and the associated transport demands simultaneously. This family of land-use models requires a distribution of basic employment to be specified exogenously to the model along with the broad strategic development and transport policies being contemplated for the future. The models then provide a consistent allocation of population and population-serving employment as well as the associated transport flows.

Chapter 7 describes the trends in different types of travel demands that have been observed in a number of cities throughout the world. The transport demands derived using the methods described in Chaps. 2 to 5 are only as valid as the land-use estimates from which they are derived. It is useful in transport planning to have an historical perspective of the evolution in urban travel demands as well as the demands forecast for the future.

Chapter 8 discusses the properties of urban transport technologies and describes their service and cost characteristics in relationship to the broad classes of travel demand identified in Chap. 7. A set of planning principles that is useful in the development of urban land-use–transport structure concepts are presented in Chap. 9.

The principles of transport investment evaluation are discussed in Chap. 10 while certain elements of welfare theory are presented in the Appendix to Chap. 10.

The transport-systems-planning process enunciated in Chap. 11 is used along with the material presented in Chaps. 2 to 10 to articulate an horizon-year-type–strategic land-use–transport-planning process (described in Chap. 11). Chapter 12 describes some principles of statistical decision theory and illustrates how these principles might be used to develop a sequential-type planning process and to account for the uncertainty involved with the planning of future states of an urban area.

Chapter 13 discusses the sources of data that are normally available for urban areas and explores some of the implications of information systems. Chapter 14 summarizes the present knowledge on urban goods movement. Virtually all of the urban transport studies conducted to date have ignored urban goods movement problems. Finally, Chap. 15 describes some of the major research problems that exist in urban transport planning and summarizes some of the present approaches to these problems.

1 THE PROCESS OF URBAN TRANSPORT PLANNING

Transport-planning studies have been conducted in a large number of urban areas throughout the world during the past 25 years. A process for conducting these studies has developed, and is still evolving, which attempts to provide a systematic method for solving urban transport problems. The planning process that is most commonly used at present had its origins in the studies performed in several cities in the United States during the 1950–1960 period, particularly in Detroit and Chicago. Figure 1.1 shows the principal elements of the process developed for the Chicago Area Transportation Study [1]. While more recent transport studies have made significant contributions to the development of land-use prediction models, travel-demand forecasting methods, and evaluation procedures, most of these studies have been organized within the same type of framework developed for the Chicago study.

The fundamental premise which underlies most transport-planning studies is that some future horizon-year equilibrium condition of an urban area is a meaningful state to attempt to predict and evaluate. In the typical study the most probable pattern of land development is predicted for the horizon year (usually 20 years ahead) and the transport demands created by that land use are

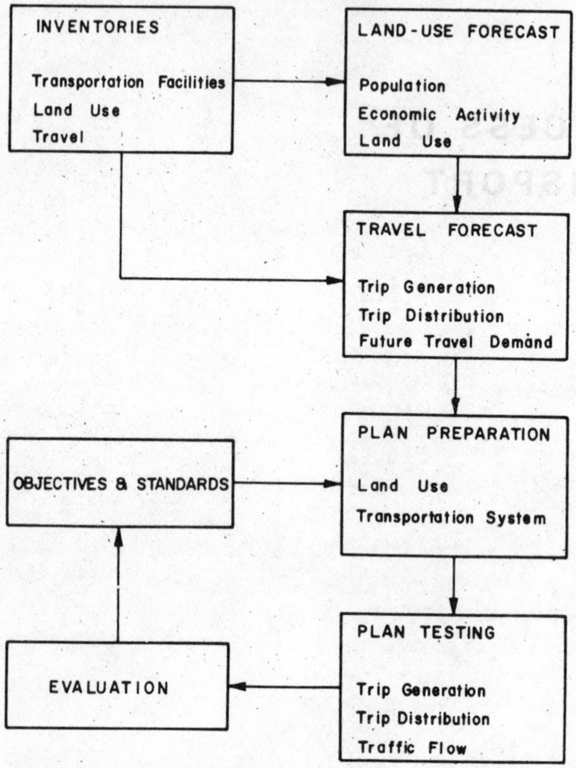

FIG. 1.1. The planning process used in the Chicago Area Transportation Study. This diagram illustrates the processes used in moving from inventories and forecasts to the preparation, testing, and evaluating of a transportation plan. (*Adapted from Ref. 1, Chap. 1.*)

estimated. A set of alternative transport plans is then generated for that horizon year; these plans incorporate varying amounts of highway and public-transport facilities. The operating characteristics of each alternative in the horizon year are then estimated in the form of flows on each link of the horizon-year networks. The usual criterion for choice among the alternatives is that the difference between the collective benefits to users, in the form of reduced travel impedance, and the monetary costs of constructing and maintaining these facilities, should be a maximum. The present planning process implies that there will be an orderly and easily identifiable sequence of public investments that will yield the horizon-year plan selected.

Recent experience in Canada, Britain, Australia, and the United States, with the implementation of plans developed by this type of planning process, has resulted in some disenchantment with the process. A review of a number of public inquiries into transport plans proposed for several metropolitan areas has revealed a similarity in the transport-related issues in these communities.

The dominant transport-related issue in many cities is the adverse environmental impacts of freeways in terms of their use of urban land, their creation of noise and air pollution, their visual impact on adjacent properties, and their interference with community activity patterns. Figure 1.2 suggests that the environmental impact of freeways is the dominant characteristic perceived by the community living in the immediate vicinity of the facility. The information presented in this diagram was obtained from a survey of the impact of a recently constructed urban freeway in Kitchener-Waterloo, Ontario [2]. The scalar values were obtained from a paired comparisons survey of households in the vicinity of the freeway.

A second transport-related issue that has arisen in many cities has to do with the probable impacts on land development patterns of various transport technologies. Many of the groups who have opposed investments in urban freeways have argued that higher residential densities should be encouraged in urban areas and that this end is not realized through freeway building. These groups have argued that centrally focussed rapid-transit facilities promote higher residential densities, and because of this they represent better transport investments. An associated issue in many cities has been the probable impact of transport investments on the growth of activities in the central business districts of these cities. Proponents of both expressways and rapid transit argue that central area development will be inhibited unless there is high accessibility to the central business district (CBD) from all parts of the urban regions.

A third concern with transport plans has been the extent of the travel opportunities supplied to tripmakers who do not have access to a car. In North American cities about 30 to 40 percent of the potential tripmakers in urban areas do not have access to private cars for travel and this includes the young, the poor, the aged, and a growing number of middle-income residents who do not own cars for other than financial reasons. Figure 1.3 shows the number of employment opportunities that may be reached by road and transit from selected residential zones in Metropolitan Toronto [3]. Further evidence of the inadequacies that exist in the typical urban transport system is presented in Table 1.1 [4].

A transport-related issue that has arisen in many cities is the opportunity cost of the capital and the continuing funds required by transport facilities. It is often argued that the resources required for new transport facilities would return higher community benefits if they were invested in other types of urban services. A related issue has to do with the sequence of project investments throughout the planning period required to yield the horizon-year plan. The resources available for transport investment are limited and the benefits which accrue to the community throughout a planning period are sensitive to the particular sequence of project investments followed.

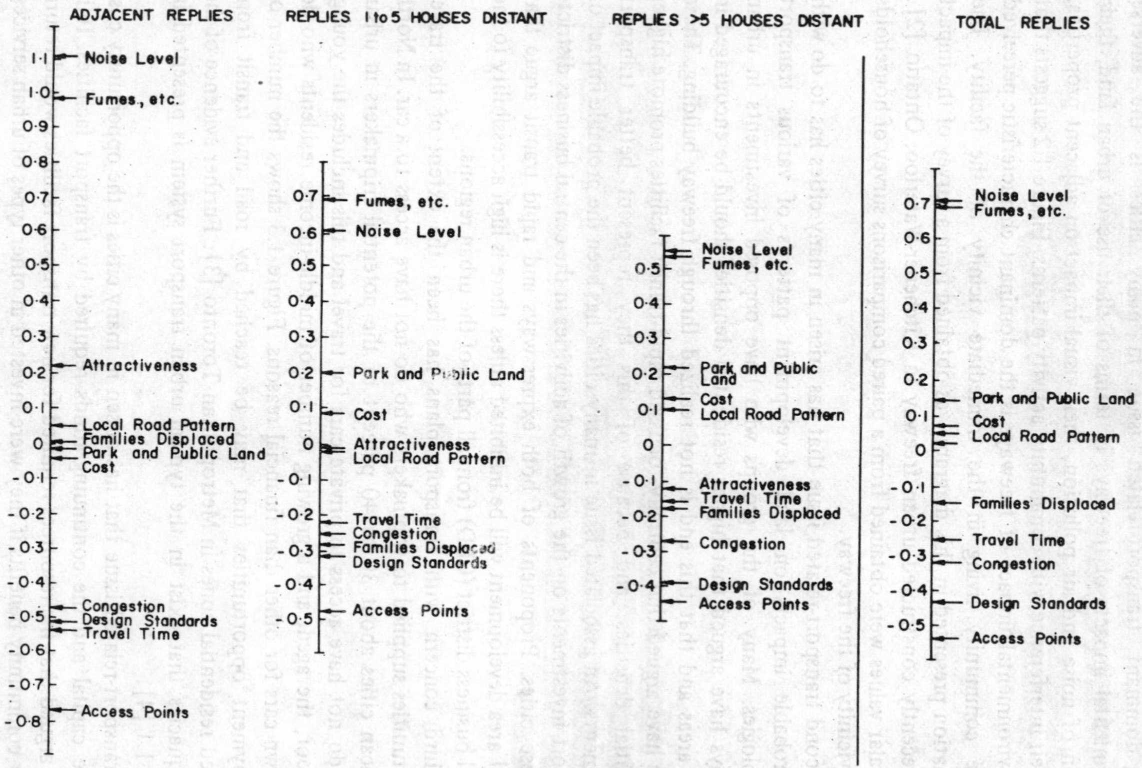

FIG. 1.2. The relative importance of various freeway impacts. (*Adapted from Ref. 2, Chap. 1.*)

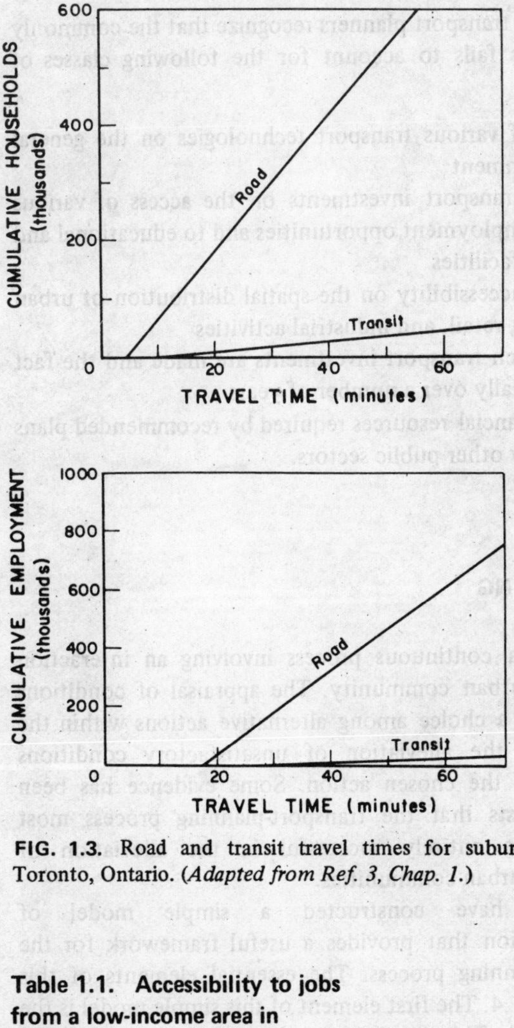

FIG. 1.3. Road and transit travel times for suburban zone in Toronto, Ontario. (*Adapted from Ref. 3, Chap. 1.*)

Table 1.1. Accessibility to jobs from a low-income area in Nashville

Travel time (min)	Percent jobs available by car	Percent jobs available by transit
0–10	50.4	2.6
10–20	30.3	7.0
20–30	13.2	14.0
30–40	6.1	34.7
50–60	0	6.6
Inaccessible	0	26.4

In summary then, most urban transport planners recognize that the commonly used transport-planning process fails to account for the following classes of impact:

1. The differential impact of various transport technologies on the general quality of the urban environment
2. The unequal impacts of transport investments on the access of various socioeconomic groups to employment opportunities and to educational and other types of community facilities
3. The impact of changes in accessibility on the spatial distribution of urban activities such as residential, retail, and industrial activities
4. The uncertainty under which transport investments are made and the fact that they are made sequentially over a number of years
5. The relationship of the financial resources required by recommended plans to the resources required by other public sectors.

1.1 A SIMPLE MODEL OF PUBLIC-SECTOR PLANNING

Urban-transport planning is a continuous process involving an interaction between government and the urban community. The appraisal of conditions within the community leads to a choice among alternative actions within the government and hopefully to the alleviation of unsatisfactory conditions through the implementation of the chosen action. Some evidence has been introduced above which suggests that the transport-planning process most commonly used has not been entirely successful in the alleviation of transport-related issues in many urban communities.

Friend and Jessop [5] have constructed a simple model of government-community interaction that provides a useful framework for the construction of a transport-planning process. The essential elements of this simple model are shown in Fig. 1.4. The first element of this simple model is the perception of the decision field. This involves the development of an initial understanding of what kind of problem it is that the situation in the community creates for the government. The second phase of the process involves the formulation and comparison of alternative courses of action within the decision field. The third step of the process identified in Fig. 1.4, which is still within the government, is the choice of one particular course of action. The final step in this process involves the implementation of the chosen course of action.

This simple four-stage model of public-sector planning provides the basis for the development of the urban transport-planning process described in this chapter. The planning morphology described in the following section represents an extension of the process illustrated in Fig. 1.4.

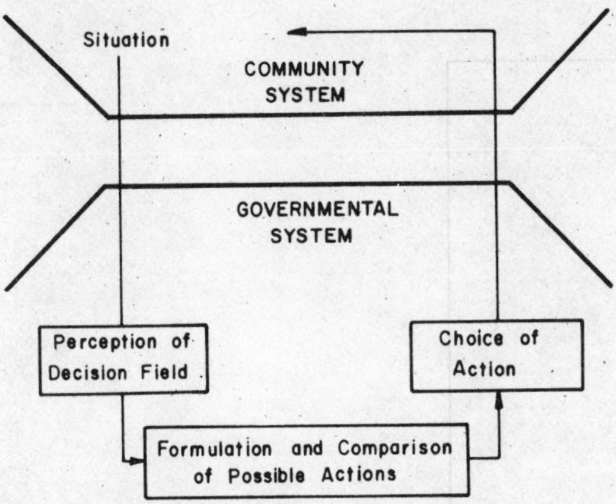

FIG. 1.4. Friend and Jessop's model of public-sector planning. (*Adapted from Ref. 5, Chap. 1. By permission of the publishers.*)

1.2 A TRANSPORT PLANNING MORPHOLOGY

The planning morphology described in this section consists of five principal steps [6,7] which are labeled: (1) problem definition, (2) solution generation, (3) solution analysis, (4) evaluation and choice, and (5) implementation. This morphology is based on certain principles of systems engineering that have been enunciated by Hall [8], and others. The sequence of phases is illustrated in Fig. 1.5.

Before the characteristics of each of the five phases are discussed in detail, it is necessary to introduce the concepts of a system, an environment, and of a system-environment ensemble. In a broad sense, urban transport systems may be thought of as responding to the social and economic forces that exist in urban areas. This urban socioeconomic environment is in turn influenced by the characteristics of the transport system. Different patterns of land development result in different transport demands and require different transport systems to service them. On the other hand, the type of transport system provided also influences the pattern of land development.

A natural system of plant, insect, and animal life will develop at a particular geographic location by constantly interacting with the environment at that location. The environment includes precipitation, temperature, soil type, and so on. In examining this type of system, the botanist and the biologist have found it essential to consider the environment as part of the system. To illustrate this point one need only consider the cycle of vegetation that might occur after the retreat of an Alpine glacier. First, mosses and grasses develop that, in turn, provide the humus necessary for the growth of plants and trees. As forest cover develops, it changes the microclimate by filtering out the sunlight and the

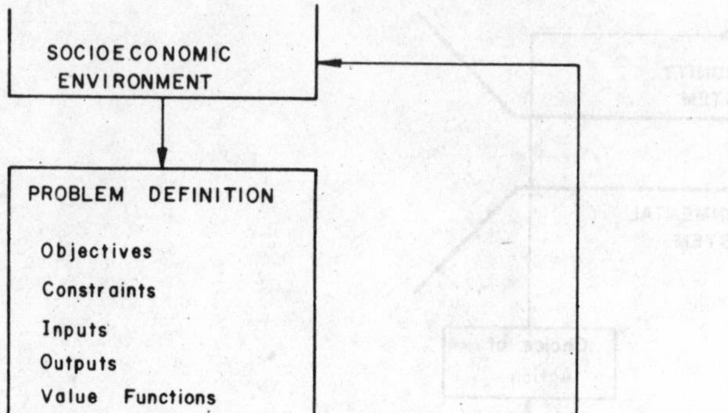

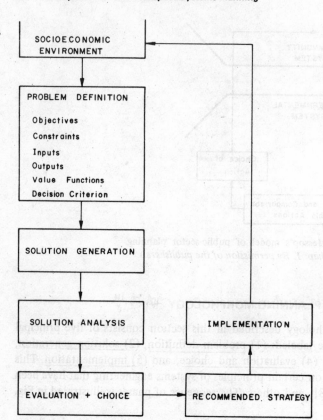

FIG. 1.5. The systems-engineering process.

original plants are replaced by shade-loving plants that find the new environment more hospitable. This changing botanical subsystem will be associated with a changing biological subsystem of birds, animals, and insects. Eventually a condition of quasi-equilibrium will be reached which may exist for a long or short time period.

Changes may occur in both the system and the environment. If these changes are small then the ensemble will maintain this state of quasi-equilibrium, adapting itself to these slow perturbations of the environment. If a major perturbation occurs, the ensemble may not be able to adapt itself to these changes and the ensemble may become unstable and destroy itself. The important characteristic of many natural systems is that they do not exist in an environment, but in conjunction with an environment.

The urban transport system of a community must be conceived of in an analagous manner. The vast changes induced in the urban system through the widespread ownership of private cars is well documented in the literature. Some of the current trends in the interactions between the urban transport system and the broader urban system are described in detail in Chap. 7. Most of the transport-related issues discussed in the introduction to this chapter have arisen because of the lag in the adaptation of the urban system to the private car.

A system may be defined as a set of components that is organized in such a manner as to direct the action of the system under inputs toward specific goals and objectives.

Mechanical and electrical systems, social and governmental systems, water supply and transport systems, are all examples of systems which may be described in the above manner. Each of the systems just mentioned usually consists of a number of components with the interrelationships between the components specified in such a way that the system will respond to the demands placed on it in a desirable manner.

Certain properties of urban areas may be described in terms of the concept of a system. Urban areas consist of parcels of land occupied by various types of physical facilities, or adapted spaces, that house one or more types of human activities. These adapted spaces are serviced by other types of physical facilities such as transport, water supply, and sewage services. The human occupants of the adapted spaces within the urban structure interact within the context of such activity subsystems as the residential-workplace subsystem, the residential-retail trade subsystem, and so on. Changes in the properties of the transport system influence the interaction pattern within these activity subsystems. The activity system of an urban area may be regarded as constituting the environment of an urban transport system.

Figure 1.6 suggests one way in which the urban activity system might be conceived relative to some structure of adapted spaces, and to the role of the transport system. Ideally, the urban activity system should be conceived of as embracing within an urban area all activities and their interactions. However, our present understanding of the urban system is such that it must be planned as a set of quasi-independent subsystems whose interactions are not fully understood. This lack of knowledge concerning many systems has resulted in the use of the concept of a system-environment ensemble.

An environment may be defined as the set of all componets outside a system which both influences the behavior of the system and which in turn is influenced by the behavior of the system.

The distinction between the system and the environment is largely arbitrary. If one examines the short history of urban transport planning one can see that as our understanding of the role of the transport system has increased, the factors included in the transport-planning process have become much more comprehensive. A broader than normal view of urban transport systems planning is presented in Chap. 11 where the transport problem is viewed as a problem in urban spatial organization. The principal challenge in defining an urban transport-planning problem is to define the system-environment interface.

The general notion has been introduced above that systems exist to fulfill certain social and economic goals and objectives that arise in the environment. A

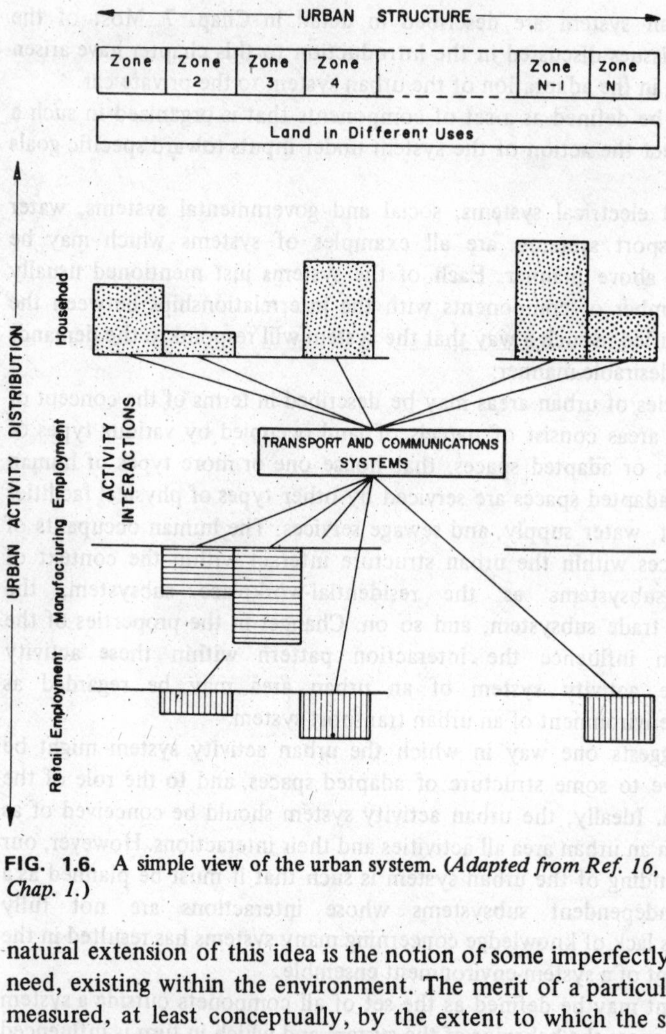

FIG. 1.6. A simple view of the urban system. (*Adapted from Ref. 16, Chap. 1.*)

natural extension of this idea is the notion of some imperfectly satisfied goal, or need, existing within the environment. The merit of a particular system may be measured, at least conceptually, by the extent to which the system fulfills the environmental needs or unsatisfied objectives.

The role of the systems planner may be conceived in a general way as the direction of his efforts to design a system that achieves maximum integration, or "degree to fit," between the system and its environment. The problem-solving morphology described in the following sections provides a framework to guide the planner in his search for an optimal system. Figure 1.7 illustrates the interrelationships of the concepts introduced above.

1.2.1 Problem definition

It is well known that the first step of any problem-solving process is to develop a clear understanding of the problem to be solved. While this may sound like a statement of the obvious, there are many examples in urban transport planning where solutions have been recommended to imperfectly understood and stated problems.

Much of the recent discussion of urban transport problems has been devoted to such issues as the advantages of mass transit, the optimum configuration of the freeway system, and the banning of cars from the central business district. However, most of these discussions have tended to cloud the real issue which is the identification of the urban transport problem in its broadest sense. There is a fundamental difference between refining an existing solution to a problem in an effort to eliminate some of its real weaknesses, and starting with a fundamental and comprehensive problem statement and synthesizing a superior solution to the problem in a systematic fashion. An important principle that should guide the development of the problem definition is that the number of possible solutions to a problem increases with the generality and comprehensiveness of the initial problem definition. Lithwick [9] has made the following observations in a study of urban problems in Canada:

> If our task is to investigate the substance of urban problems, it is necessary at the outset to understand what is meant by the "urban problem." To many, this may appear a ludicrous effort—to them the problems are so obvious that this nit-picking constitutes a diversionary tactic preventing us with getting on with the job. Yet it is precisely because we are not clear about this matter that we have been so unsuccessful in dealing with urban problems. How else can we explain how three levels of government and the vast resources of a wealthy society have failed to make any progress towards solving them? There have

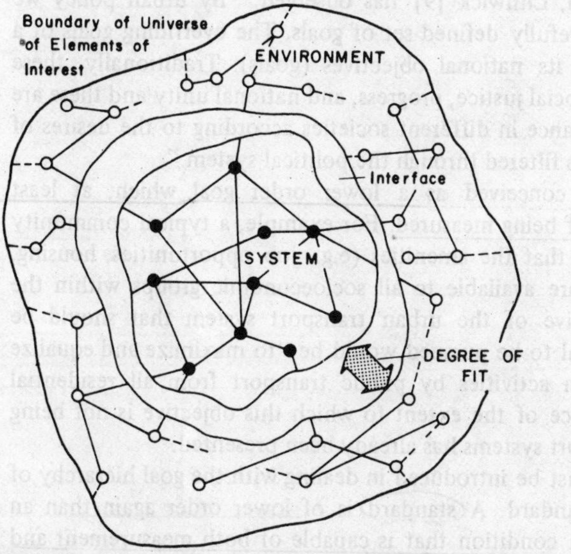

FIG. 1.7. The system environment ensemble.

been major attempts to meet the obvious needs: a substantial flow of resources have been poured into housing, schools, hospitals, transportation improvements, and more recently, into low-income housing and urban renewal. But these policies do not appear to have had any ameliorating effect, and the urban problems grow more serious.

The aim of the problem-definition step is to define the interface between the system and its environment and to identify a rule or criterion which may be used by the planner to identify the optimal system. The pertinent features of a systems problem definition may be developed in a concise and unified form through the use of the following concepts: (1) system objectives, (2) system constraints, (3) system inputs, (4) system outputs, (5) value functions, and (6) decision criterion.

The concept of such a system requires that the system respond in a purposeful manner to inputs arising within in its environment. In the discussion of urban systems it is appropriate to refer to the overall goals of the urban community and to the objectives that must be pursued by a transport system to permit the community goals to be realized. Frequently, the terms *goal* and *objective* are used synonymously, but in this book they are used in the sense in which they are defined below.

A goal may be defined as the end to which a plan trends. In this sense a goal may be conceived as an ideal expressed in abstract terms that is sought after continuously, and not an end state that can be reached. Goals may be thought of as a set of statements that attempt to convey to the planner an image of the ideal system and in this way provide him with overall direction. In his study of urban problems in Canada, Lithwick [9] has observed: "By urban policy we mean the pursuit of a carefully defined set of goals. The overriding goals of a society are contained in its national objectives (goals). Traditionally, these include at least freedom, social justice, progress, and national unity and these are ranked in order of importance in different societies according to the desires of their respective members as filtered through the political system."

An objective may be conceived as a lower order goal which, at least conceptually, is capable of being measured. For example, a typical community goal might be "to ensure that the amenities (e.g., job opportunities, housing, etc.) of the urban area are available to all socioeconomic groups within the community." One objective of the urban transport system that should be fulfilled to permit this goal to be pursued would be "to maximize and equalize the accessibility to urban activities by public transport from all residential areas." Some brief evidence of the extent to which this objective is not being fulfilled by present transport systems has already been presented.

A third concept that must be introduced in dealing with the goal hierarchy of a system is that of a standard. A standard is of lower order again than an objective and represents a condition that is capable of both measurement and attainment. For example, the transport-system objectives stated above may be replaced by a standard such as "the transport system should permit the principal urban activity centers to be reached from each other by public transport services with travel times not greater than 30 minutes."

This distinction between goals, objectives, and standards must be made in order to overcome semantic difficulties as well as to provide information for each of the hierarchical levels of planning referred to later in this chapter. Because of the very subjective nature of goals and objectives, it is very difficult to establish a coordinated and well-structured set of goals, objectives, and standards. These difficulties are well illustrated by the following quotation from an essay by Marglin [10] on the objectives of water resource system development:

> The prime objective of public water resource development is often stated as the maximization of national welfare. That this is a goal to be desired, few would question; that it cannot be translated directly into operational criteria for system design, few would deny. Translation would require not only agreement on a definition for the deceptively simple phrase national welfare, but also some assurance that the defined concept is measurable.
>
> One possibility is to define national welfare as national income. The objective of system design then becomes maximization of the contribution of the system to national income. This definition is measurable, but it has implications for the meaning of national welfare that make us unwilling to accept it as a complete expression of the broad objective. Identifying national welfare with the size of the national income not only excludes non-economic dimensions of welfare but also implies that society is totally indifferent as to the recipient of the income generated by river-development systems, or that a desirable distribution of gains will be made by measures unrelated to the manner in which the system is designed.

The goals and objectives of urban transport investment are discussed in detail in Chap. 10.

A second requirement in formulating goals, objectives, and standards is the development of suitable units of measurement, and the principal concern is with the measurement of objectives. Since the objectives attempt to convey the social and economic aspirations of the community, the appropriate units of measurement will be units of value or utility. Ideally a common unit of value for all objectives would be desirable. If this ideal could be achieved, then the assessments of the relative merits of alternative transport systems would be straightforward.

The development of units of measurement for some objectives is very difficult since no general theory of value exists. At the present time the only operational unit of value is the market value of the good or service. The quotation from Marglin just introduced referred to some of the difficulties in using market values. While some transport objectives may be measured in dollar units, no market mechanism exists whereby appropriate units can be scaled for a number of objectives.

This difficulty in the measurement of the extent to which objectives are fulfilled has resulted in some unfortunate consequences in urban transport-planning studies. There has been a tendency on the part of urban transport planners to neglect those objectives that cannot be measured in monetary units. For example, it is difficult to express the noise and pollution impacts of transport technologies in monetary units, and consequently there has been a tendency to neglect these factors in the evaluation of alternative systems and to concentrate on user benefits.

In discussing goals and objectives many planners refer to the differential importance or weighting of objectives. The concept used in this book to express the relative importance of objectives is the value function. This concept is introduced later in this chapter.

The constraints on a system may be defined as those characteristics of the environment that limit the extent of feasible solutions.

Most of the constraints that arise in connection with the planning of urban transport systems arise because of the necessity of planning systems of limited scope. An example of a constraint is the financial constraint on both the capital and operating expenditures associated with transport systems. Transport investments must compete with investments in other public sectors such as education, water supply, and waste disposal. The financial resources required by many of the urban strategic transport plans developed in recent years have exceeded the available investment resources of the communities involved.

Perhaps some of the most severe constraints on the planning of urban transport systems are those of a political nature. For example, in certain communities it may be necessary to subsidize public transport services out of general property taxation revenues in order to make these services financially viable. This subsidy may be necessary in order to provide non-car-owners with an acceptable level of transport service. However, a government may not accept the principle of direct subsidization of public transport services from general taxation. The transport planner may be forced to find an alternative means of accomplishing this same end which is compatible with the political preferences of the government. Similar comments could be made with respect to road-pricing schemes.

The inputs to a system may be described as those characteristics of the environment that a system must transform into outputs in the light of the system objectives.

The inputs to an urban transport system are the demands for the movements of person and goods between urban activity centers. There are two dimensions of urban travel demand that are of interest and these are: the spatial patterns of travel demand that exist throughout an urban region, and the times throughout the day at which the dominant spatial patterns of travel demand occur.

Figures 1.8 and 1.9 show the spatial patterns of demand for the journey between home and work and for the journey between home and retail trade areas observed in Metropolitan Toronto. Figure 1.10 shows the proportions of various trip types that occur at various times throughout the day. The travel-demand characteristics illustrated in Figs. 1.8–1.10 are shown without

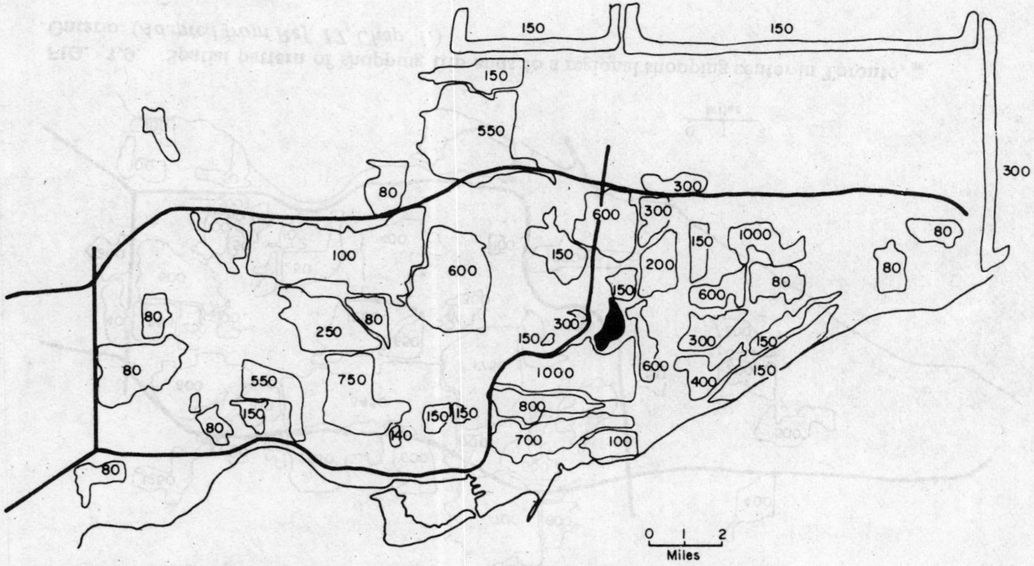

FIG. 1.8. Spatial pattern of work trip ends to an industrial area in Toronto, Ontario. (*Adapted from Ref. 17, Chap. 1.*)

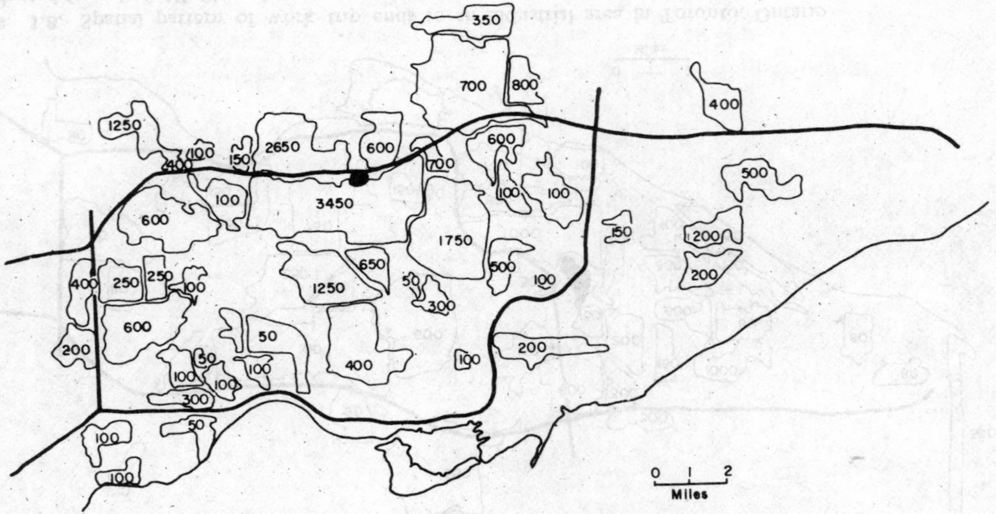

FIG. 1.9. Spatial pattern of shopping trip ends to a regional shopping center in Toronto, Ontario. (*Adapted from Ref. 17, Chap. 1.*)

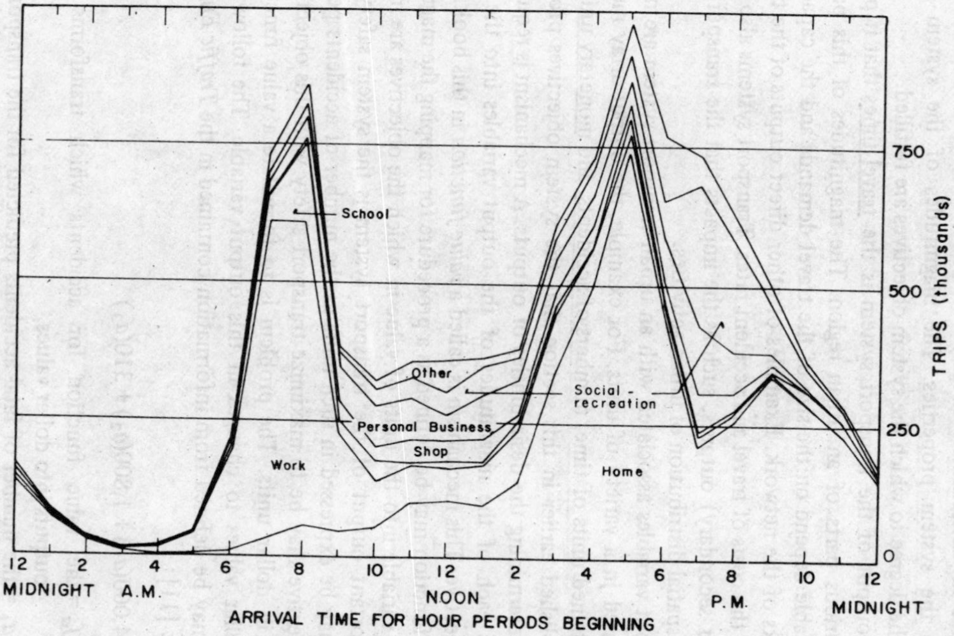

FIG. 1.10. Temporal pattern of trips in Chicago, Illinois. (*Adapted from Ref. 1, Chap. 1.*)

reference to a particular transport system and simply reflect the spatial distribution of land use and the habits of the people within the community. A major portion of this book is devoted to a discussion of methods for estimating future travel demands.

The outputs of a system may be defined as those characteristics of a system that influence its environment directly and that are a function of the system inputs and the system properties. The magnitudes of the system outputs determine the degree to which the system objectives are fulfilled.

A major output of the transport system is the travel times that it produces between various parts of an urban region. The magnitudes of this particular output variable depend on the size of the travel demands and the capacities of various links of the network. Examples of other direct outputs of the transport system are the costs of travel and accident rates. Transport systems also produce indirect (or secondary) outputs, such as the impacts that the transport system has on the spatial distribution of urban activities.

The output variables associated with an urban transport system are measured and expressed in a variety of units. For example, the output array mentioned above contained units of time, numbers of accidents, and monetary units. It has been established earlier in this section that the system objectives provide the basis for determining the desirabilities of outputs. A mechanism is required that transforms each of the magnitudes of the output variables into the relevant system objective. This mechanism is called a *value function* in this book.

A value function may be defined as a procedure for mapping the magnitude of an output variable into the units of value in which the objectives are measured.

An important output of the transport system is the system safety. Safety outputs may be expressed in such units as the number of accidents per day. A stated objective may be to maximize transport safety with this objective being measured in dollar units. The problem is to formulate a value function that assigns dollar values to changes in this output variable. The following value function may be defined from information contained in the *Traffic Engineering Handbook* [11]:

$$f_a = 34{,}000(a_1) + 1{,}800(a_2) + 310(a_3) \tag{1.1}$$

where f_a = the value function for accidents which transforms accident outputs into dollar values,

a_1 = the number of fatal accidents predicted for the transport system,

a_2 = the number of personal-injury accidents predicted for the transport system, and

a_3 = the number of property-damage accidents predicted for the transport system.

The parameters 34,000, 1,800, and 310 represent the monetary values that society is willing to place on deaths, injuries, and property damage, respectively. No attempt will be made to justify the value function presented in Eq. (1.1) since it has been introduced only to illustrate the concept.

The formulation of value functions represents one of the more-difficult activities in the urban transport-planning process. Formal value functions may only be developed for a few of the transport system objectives. The formulation of many of the value functions is a largely subjective operation performed by the planner or achieved through the political process. It is instructive to consider the following statement by Harris [12] at this point:

> Most unfortunately, we find a certain number of planners, whose income is adequate and whose physical needs are well satisfied, who are completely incapable of projecting themselves into the situation and value structures of those less fortunate or different from themselves; they place at the forefront of their pre-occupation those values which they are now striving to satisfy and neglect those which they have already met. More honourable but equally unrealistic are those who have made a too-educated choice and who try to impose their pursuit of the good life on others.

The formulation of transport systems-related value functions is discussed in Chap. 10.

A decision criterion may be defined as a rule that instructs the systems planner how the individual measures of value associated with the system outputs and the financial resources required for the construction and operation of the system should be manipulated in order to arrive at a single index of value for the system in order to allow the optimal system to be identified.

For the ideal (and unrealistic) case in which all of the objectives are measurable in dollar units, the formulation of a decision criterion is straightforward: Select that alternative system with the maximum difference between the net present value of benefits and costs.

The situation normally faced in transport-planning studies is the presence of several objectives which cannot be measured in dollar units and for which formal value functions cannot be developed. The question of values and, therefore, of optimality, must find expression through the political process. One of the principal reasons why many transport plans have not been implemented is because of the unsatisfactory treatment of objectives and values.

Formal conditions cannot be established for identifying the scope of the problem definition in a systems-planning problem, nor its content. The concepts introduced above must be considered only as useful aids to the structuring of the problem to be solved. The adequacy of a problem definition depends on the ability of the planner to perceive the role of a system and its impact on the environment. Figure 1.11 illustrates the interrelation of these six components of the problem definition.

1.2.2 Other phases of the morphology

The second phase of the systems-planning morphology is *solution generation.* The aim of this second phase is to generate an array of solutions that satisfy the previously established objectives to a greater or lesser degree and which do not violate the constraints.

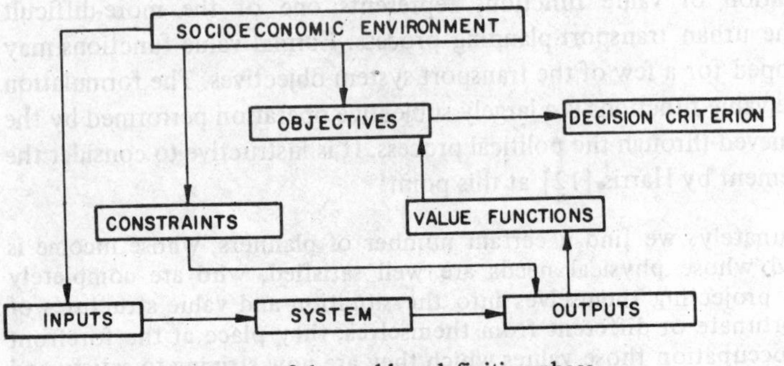

FIG. 1.11. Components of the problem-definition phase.

At the present time no generalized approach to solution generation is available for planning and design problems, although a number of special procedures have been proposed by workers in several fields [13–15]. Some principles useful to the generation of alternative urban transport systems are discussed in Chap. 9.

The third phase of the planning morphology is known as *solution analysis.* The objective of this step of the planning framework is to predict the probable operating state of each of the alternative systems generated in the previous phase, given expectations about the state of the environment.

In terms of the systems terms introduced previously, the planner must predict the magnitudes of the output variables given the input magnitudes and the

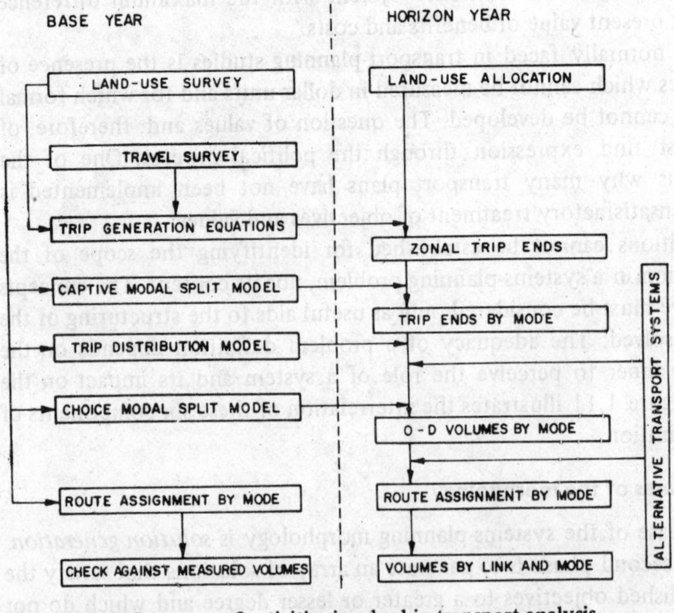

FIG. 1.12. Sequence of activities involved in transport analysis.

system properties. In urban transport planning, the input magnitudes and the behavior of alternative systems are estimated normally through the use of a four-phase process consisting of trip-generation analysis, modal split analysis, trip-distribution analysis, and traffic-assignment analysis. The usual flow of activities involved in this analysis is presented in Fig. 1.12. The structure of this transport analysis process is discussed in more detail in Sec. 1.3.

The fourth phase of the planning process is known as *evaluation and choice*. The aim of this fourth step is to identify the alternative system that satisfies the objectives to the greatest extent.

The data required for this step are the output variable magnitudes predicted in the systems analysis step, the value functions, and the decision criterion identified in the problem-definition step. Methods of evaluation and choice appropriate to urban transport systems are presented in Chap. 10.

The final phase of the systems morphology is known as *implementation*. The optimum system for the horizon year is identified in the previous phase and the aim of this phase is to formulate a strategy for implementing the chosen system throughout the planning period.

1.3 TRAVEL-DEMAND FORECASTING PROCESS

The sequence of activities involved in urban travel-demand forecasting has been illustrated in Fig. 1.12. The detailed structure and content of each of the activities identified in Fig. 1.12 are discussed in Chaps. 2 to 5, inclusive. The aim of this section is to define the content of each of these activities in general terms and to establish in a broad way the interrelationships between the activities.

Figure 1.12 illustrates that the basic set of models is first calibrated to some base-year condition and the calibrated models are then used to predict the travel-demand implications of an horizon-year land-use allocation. The basic premise of the analysis process shown in Fig. 1.12 is that there is a stable relationship between transport-demand properties and the distribution and intensity of urban activities. The analysis process assumes that the properties of the transport system alternatives considered will not influence the horizon-year land-use allocation. The material on land-use models presented in Chap. 6 demonstrates how this assumption may be relaxed. In addition, the travel-demand forecasting methods used currently assume that the total amount of travel is unaffected by the quality of the transport services provided. The implications of this assumption and possible approaches to the relaxation of the assumption are discussed in Chap. 15.

The purpose of the trip-generation analysis phase is to develop equations that allow the trip ends of a particular trip type generated by a traffic-analysis zone to be estimated from a knowledge of the land-use properties of those zones. The technique used most commonly for the development of these prediction equations is multiple-regression analysis. Typical examples of the trip-generation equations developed in this phase are:

$$\text{Work-trips produced} = 9.3 + 0.32\,(\text{population in zone}) \tag{1.2}$$

$$\text{Work-trips attracted} = 43.7 + 0.83\,(\text{employment in zone}) \tag{1.3}$$

The purpose of the captive modal split analysis phase is to develop relationships that allow the trip ends estimated in the trip-generation phase to be partitioned into two groups of trip ends: trips by persons captive to public transport and trips by persons who have a choice between using public transport and a private car. Captive tripmakers are defined as those persons without access to a car for a particular trip. Captive tripmakers are normally identified by certain socioeconomic characteristics such as age and income. The following equations are typical examples of captive modal-split relationships:

$$\%\ \text{Work-trip productions by public transport} = 50.4 - 0.0059\,(\text{average household income of zone}) \tag{1.4}$$

$$\%\ \text{Work-trip attractions by public transport} = -2.3 + 0.3241\,(\%\ \text{nonindustrial employment of zone}) \tag{1.5}$$

In Canadian cities, the majority of tripmakers captive to public transport are females employed in offices and institutions. Equation (1.5) is simply a reflection of this observation.

The purpose of the trip-distribution analysis phase is to develop a procedure that synthesizes the trip linkages or interchanges between traffic zones for both transit captive and noncaptive tripmakers. The technique used most commonly to synthesize these trip linkages is the gravity model which is discussed in detail in Chap. 4.

The purpose of the choice modal split analysis phase is to develop a procedure that simulates the manner in which choice tripmakers traveling between an origin and destination pair will choose between the use of a car and public transport for the trip. Typically, the proportion of public-transport tripmakers is related to some function of the costs of traveling by the competing modes.

The purpose of the route-assignment analysis phase is to develop a technique that simulates the way in which the car and transit trips between each origin and destination pair distribute over the links of their respective networks.

Figure 1.12 illustrates that a knowledge of the properties of the alternative horizon-year transport systems is required for the trip distribution, choice modal split, and route-assignment phases. The principal outputs of this travel-demand forecasting process for each alternative network are: (1) the travel demand

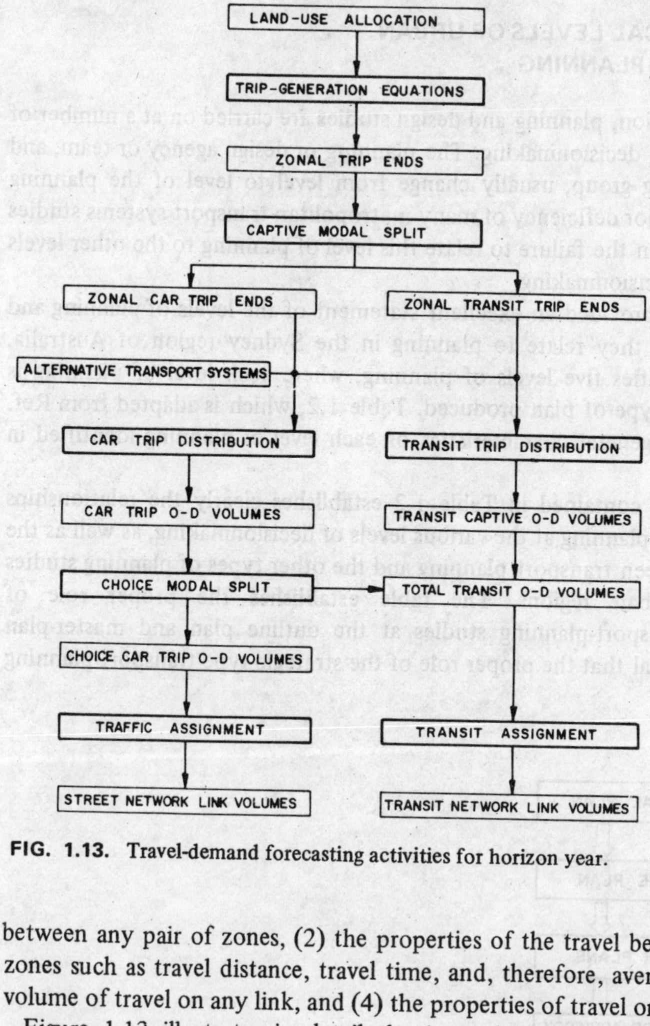

FIG. 1.13. Travel-demand forecasting activities for horizon year.

between any pair of zones, (2) the properties of the travel between any pair of zones such as travel distance, travel time, and, therefore, average speed, (3) the volume of travel on any link, and (4) the properties of travel on any link.

Figure 1.13 illustrates in detail the interrelationships between each of the activities for horizon-year analysis. This diagram shows more specifically the way in which mode-specific origin and destination matrices are developed for each alternative horizon-year transport network tested. It should be noted at this point that the choice modal split analysis phase is not always included in urban transport-planning studies. In many medium and small cities with relatively primitive transit systems, and in which major transit investments are not contemplated for the future, virtually all of the present and future transit patronage will consist of captive riders. Under these circumstances a choice modal split analysis is not warranted. In other situations, a choice modal split analysis may be justified in only one or two of the centrally focussed corridors.

1.4 HIERARCHICAL LEVELS OF URBAN TRANSPORT PLANNING

In any urban region, planning and design studies are carried on at a number of levels of detail and decisionmaking. The planning or design agency or team, and the decisionmaking group, usually change from level to level of the planning hierarchy. One major deficiency of many metropolitan transport systems studies in the past has been the failure to relate this level of planning to the other levels of planning and decisionmaking.

Smith [18] has provided an excellent statement of the levels of planning and decisionmaking as they relate to planning in the Sydney region of Australia. Figure 1.14 identifies five levels of planning, where each level of planning is identified by the type of plan produced. Table 1.2, which is adapted from Ref. 18, identifies the general characteristics of each level of planning identified in Fig. 1.14.

The information contained in Table 1.2 establishes clearly the relationships between transport planning at the various levels of decisionmaking, as well as the relationships between transport planning and the other types of planning studies conducted in urban regions. The table establishes the proper role of strategic-type transport-planning studies at the outline plan and master-plan stages. It is essential that the proper role of the strategic-type transport-planning

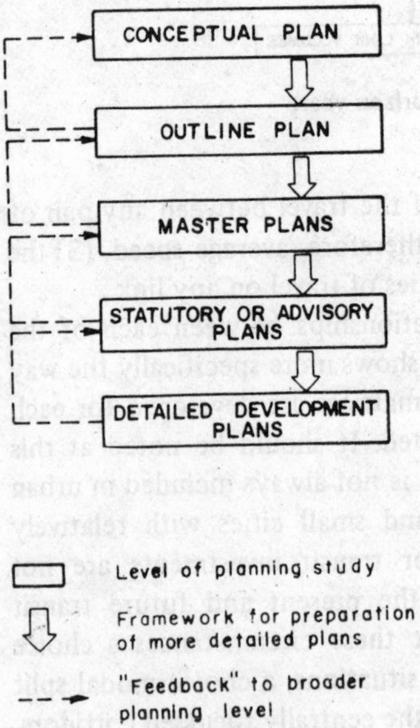

FIG. 1.14. Interrelationship of different levels of planning studies.

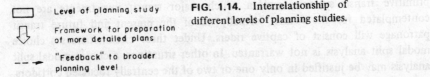

Table 1.2. Comparison of general characteristics of different levels of planning

General Characteristic	Conceptual plan	Outline plan	Master plan	Statutory plan	Detailed plan
Purpose	Establishment of plan objectives for the desirable form and function of the region and development of plan with most viable application of these objectives	Establishment of plan objectives at the sector scale from the regional objectives and development of plan with most viable application of these objectives	Establishment of plan objectives at the district scale from the sector objectives and development of plan with most viable application of these objectives	Establishment of plan objectives at the local scale from district objectives and development of local plan with most viable application of these objectives	Formulation of detailed land-use control plans, development and redevelopment plans, design and implementation schemes
Plan period	30–40 yr and at least one intermediate horizon of 20 yr	20 yr and at least one intermediate horizon of 10 yr	20 yr and at least one intermediate horizon of 5 yr	10 yr and intermediate programming periods of 1 yr	1 yr and up depending on specific proposal
Study area system	Sectors with a future population of 200,000–500,000	Districts with a future population of 50,000–200,000	Neighborhood subdivided into homogeneous zones of 5,000–10,000	Zones, street blocks and/or major property subdivisions	Street blocks and detailed allotment subdivisions
Basic data analysis	Prepare indicative forecasts of major concentrations of land use, population, employment, etc., based on broad understanding of existing conditions	Simplified forecasts of land use, population and employment and other relevant factors by district	Comprehensive forecasts of zonal parameters including population, employment, etc.	Detailed special forecasts depending on problem	(No activities)

Table 1.2. Comparison of general characteristics of different levels of planning (*Continued*)

General Characteristic	Conceptual plan	Outline plan	Master plan	Statutory plan	Detailed plan
Economic studies	Consideration of appropriate economic principles compatible with regional scale	Benefits and costs of major components of government investment	Benefits and costs of major land uses considering government and private investment	Benefits and costs of detailed zoning and design alternatives	Benefits and costs of specific development proposals
Plan details	General types of land use shown in diagrammatic form	Major land-use areas outlined using generalized land-use classifications	Major land-use areas defined using generalized land-use zones	Detailed zoning and preliminary design proposals	Detailed plans
Travel demand forecasts	Indicative estimates of future travel demand by major transport corridor	Estimates of future travel demand on major transport routes using simplified transport models in conjunction with the land-use models	Estimates of future travel demand on all significant routes using comprehen- transport models in conjunction with land-use models	Estimates from preceding planning stage supplemented by detailed travel analysis for specific design problems	Additional forecasts not required

Table 1.2. Comparison of general characteristics of different levels of planning (*Continued*)

Future route locations and characteristics	Described as transport corridors in which major highway and public transport routes could be located	Based on locational studies of major transport routes	Based on functional design studies of major transport routes and locational studies of minor facilities	Based on preliminary design studies which then provide basis for preparing implementation plans	Based on implementation plans for specific proposals
Right-of-way definition	Not applicable	Broad land reservations defined giving consideration to major land	Property affected generally defined as a basis for land reservations	Property acquisition lines defined to nearest 5–10 ft	Accurate definition of property acquisition lines for specific proposals
Cost estimates	Not applicable	Cost/route mile basis	General unit cost per area, volume and length basis for major elements	Detailed unit cost basis for major elements	Detailed cost estimates for specific proposals

Note:–Heavy lines indicate that analytical techniques described in book are directed toward these cells.

process be established clearly, since in the past the process has been used at levels of planning and decisionmaking for which it was not intended. For example, some agencies have used horizon-year-type travel simulations to estimate directional movements at intersections, and so on.

1.5 INTERRELATIONSHIP OF TRANSPORT PROBLEMS AND TRANSPORT MODELS

It has been established in Sec. 1.2 that the most critical component of any systems-planning process is the problem-definition phase. The manner in which a problem is defined conditions the remainder of the process. Earlier in this chapter it has been pointed out that the principal thrust of most urban transport-planning studies performed to date has been one of dimensioning the capacity requirements of transport networks geared to trend-type land-use prognostications. This direction was compatible with the perception of the urban transport problem that existed during the 1950s and early 1960s. Martin [19] has noted in connection with the London Transport Study that:

> In the 1950s the problem was defined in the rather restricted terms of congestion on city streets. How can this congestion be removed and provision be made for future growth of traffic? This was certainly a major consideration in defining the initial objectives of the London studies in 1960. Car ownership was expected to increase rapidly, but there was no basis to estimate how large the increase in road traffic would be and how the nature and pattern of travel would be influenced.

Some of the deficiencies of this view of the urban transport problem have been outlined in the first part of this chapter. Urban transport planners now recognize

Table 1.3. Interrelationship between type of transport-planning problem and requirements of travel-demand forecasting process

Type of transport-planning problem	Requirements of travel-demand forecasting process
Environmental impacts of transport facilities	Ability to provide more-detailed estimates of travel demands at specific points in order to estimate noise levels, air pollution impacts, etc.
Strategic land-use-transport-public utilities planning	Ability to model interaction between urban activity distribution and transport system properties and to interface with housing demand and public utilities planning models
Public-transport planning	Ability to model travel demands by each socio-economic group with emphasis on interaction between housing, employment, and community opportunities

that there is not a unique urban transport problem, but a set of subproblems of different scales and scopes. Table 1.3 lists some of these problems along with the requirements of the travel-demand forecasting process necessary to assist in the solution of these problems.

The study of the environmental impacts of transport systems requires a relatively microscopic view of the transport system. Estimates of the traffic volumes that are likely to occur in various hourly periods throughout the day are required along with the probable speed characteristics and vehicle-type mix. In contrast, problems of strategic development planning require a relatively coarse view of the probable impact of transport-system properties on land development. On the other hand, public transport planning requires a view of an urban area in terms of the activity patterns of a number of separate socioeconomic groups. While the broad groups of information required for each of these planning problems is similar, the amount of detail required will vary significantly between the problem areas. The set of activities shown in Fig. 1.12 may be applied to each of the problem areas identified in Table 1.3. However, the detailed structure of each activity will vary from problem to problem. Environmental impact studies may require the traffic-assignment phase to be conducted in much finer detail. Strategic development planning may require little emphasis on modal split analysis, whereas modal split analysis will assume a major role in public-transport planning.

SUMMARY

Most of the urban transport-planning studies conducted to date have been concerned with dimensioning the capacity requirements of urban transport networks geared to serving trend-type land-use prognostications. This approach to urban transport planning developed during the 1950s and early 1960s when car ownership and travel demands were increasing dramatically.

During the past few years many of the freeway plans developed by this type of planning process have been abandoned. The principal reasons for these actions include the adverse environmental impacts of freeways, poor accessibility provided to non-car-owners, and their excessive consumption of financial resources.

Urban transport planning is a continuous process involving an interaction between government and an urban community. The systems engineering morphology provides a useful technique for organizing this process of community-government interaction. The most critical element of this problem-solving process is the problem-definition phase, since the manner in which a problem is defined conditions the remainder of the process.

An important part of the transport-systems-planning morphology is the travel-demand forecasting process. This process consists of five stages which are: trip-generation analysis, captive modal split analysis, trip-distribution analysis, choice modal split analysis, and traffic-assignment analysis. A basic assumption of this travel-demand forecasting process is that there is a stable relationship between transport demand and the urban activity system. The process assumes that the differences in the properties of the alternative transport networks being analyzed will not influence the land-use distribution.

REFERENCES

1. Chicago Area Transportation Study, *Study Report,* vols. 1–3, Chicago, Illinois, 1969.
2. Borland, L. R., *A Method for Optimizing the Functional Design of an Urban Expressway,* M.A.Sc. thesis, Department of Civil Engineering, University of Waterloo, Ontario, 1970.
3. Morrall, J. F., *Work Trip Distribution and Modal Split in the Metropolitan Toronto Region,* Ph.D. thesis, Department of Civil Engineering, University of Waterloo, Ontario, 1971.
4. Voorhees, A. M., "The Changing Role of Transportation in Urban Development," *Traffic Quarterly,* Vol. 23, no. 4, pp. 527–536, 1969.
5. Friend, J. K., and W. N. Jessop, *Local Government and Strategic Choice,* Tavistock Publications, London, 1969.
6. Hutchinson, B. G., "A Planning Morphology for Transportation Systems," *Traffic Quarterly,* Vol. 20, no. 3, pp. 347–360, 1966.
7. Hutchinson, B. G., W. A. McLaughlin, and J. H. Shortreed, *Planning Urban Transportation Systems,* Proceedings, Australian Road Research Board, Melbourne, Australia, pp. 83–130, 1966.
8. Hall, A. D., *A Methodology for Systems Engineering,* D. Van Nostrand, Princeton, New Jersey, 1962.
9. Lithwick, H., *Urban Canada: Problems and Prospects,* Central Mortgage and Housing Corporation, Ottawa, Ontario, 1971.
10. Marglin, S. A., "Objectives of Water-Resource Development: A General Statement," in A. Maass (ed.), *Design of Water Resource Systems,* Harvard University Press, Cambridge, Massachusetts, 1966.
11. Institute of Traffic Engineers, *Traffic Engineering Handbook,* Washington, D.C., 1975.
12. Harris, B., *Problems in Regional Science,* Papers and Proceedings, Regional Science Association, Vol. 21, pp. 7–16, 1968.
13. Manheim, M. L., et al., *Search and Choice in Transport Systems Planning, Summary Report,* Report No. R68–40, Department of Civil Engineering, Massachusetts Institute of Technology, June, 1968.
14. Jantsch, E., *Technological Forecasting in Perspective,* Organization for Economic Cooperation and Development, Paris, 1967.
15. Kahn, H., and A. J. Wiener, *The Year 2000: A Framework for Speculation on the Next Thirty Years,* MacMillan Company, New York, 1967.
16. Wilson, A. G., "Models in Urban Planning: A Synoptic Review of Recent Literature," *Urban Studies,* Vol. 5, no. 3, pp. 249–276, 1968.
17. DeLeuw Cather and Company of Canada Limited, *A New Procedure for Urban Transportation Planning,* Toronto, Ontario, 1970.
18. Smith E. A., *Organizing for Effective Transport Planning,* Proceedings, Australian Road Research Board, Melbourne, Australia, pp. 406–422, 1970.
19. Martin, B. V., *Transport Planning Models: The London Experience,* Highway Research Record No. 309, Highway Research Board, Washington, D.C., 1970.

2 TRAVEL-DEMAND FORECASTING: TRIP-GENERATION ANALYSIS

The first stage of the travel-demand forecasting process described in Chap. 1 has been identified as trip-generation analysis. It has been pointed out that the principal task of the trip-generation analysis phase is to relate the intensity of tripmaking to and from land-use parcels to measures of the type and intensity of land use.

Two types of trip-generation analysis are carried out and these are normally referred to by the terms *trip production* and *trip attraction*. The term *trip production* is reserved for trips generated by residential zones where these trips may be trip origins or trip destinations. The term *trip attraction* is used to describe trips generated by activities at the nonhome end of a home-based trip such as employment, retail services, and so on. Typical trip-generation equations have been described in Chap. 1.

The first part of this chapter identifies the various trip types that occur in urban areas and notes their relative importance. The principles of regression analysis are then reviewed briefly and their application to the development of trip-generation prediction equations is described. An alternative method of trip-generation analysis, usually referred to as *category analysis*, is then described.

2.1 TRIP CLASSIFICATION

Urban travel demands are made up of a number of different trip types that have specific spatial and temporal characteristics. The first activity in travel-demand forecasting is to identify the various trip types important to a particular transport-planning study. The trip types studied in a particular area depend on the types of transport-planning issues to be resolved. The first level of trip classification used normally is a broad grouping into home-based and non-home-based trips. Home-based trips are those trips that have one trip end at a household. Typical home-based trips are the journey to work, shopping, and school. Examples of non-home-based trips are trips between work and shop and business trips between two places of employment. Table 2.1 provides information on the percentage of home-based trips in a number of study areas; that percentage varies from 80 to 90 percent of total travel.

Trip classifications that have been used in major urban transport-planning studies for home-based trips are: (1) work trips, (2) school trips, (3) shopping trips, (4) personal business trips, and (5) social-recreational trips.

The relative importance of the above-mentioned trip types in a number of urban areas is shown in Table 2.2 [1]. A daily time profile of the various trip types has already been presented in Chap. 1 for one major urban area.

A larger or smaller number of trip classes than identified above may be appropriate for a particular urban area depending on its size, the purpose for which the demand forecasts are to be used, the dominance of particular trip types in the area, and so on.

In large metropolitan areas it might be appropriate to classify work trips into trips by several economic classes in order to isolate the important spatial

Table 2.1. Percent of total internal person trips between home and all destination purposes

City	Year of study	Percent
Charlotte, N.C.	1958	83.9
Chicago, Ill.	1956	86.8
Detroit, Mich.	1953	87.0
Houston, Tex.	1953	91.0
Kansas City, Mo.	1957	88.2
Nashville, Tenn.	1959	85.5
Phoenix, Ariz.	1957	85.3
Pittsburgh, Pa.	1958	87.0
St. Louis, Mo.	1957	91.3
Washington, D.C.	1955	91.6

Table 2.2. Percent of total home-based internal trips between home and destination purposes

City	Purpose of destination					
	Work	Business	Shop	School	Social and recreational	Other
Charlotte, N.C.	32.2	8.0	15.6	6.6	23.8	13.8
Chicago, Ill.	37.5	9.7	18.9	4.0	22.8	7.1
Detroit, Mich.	41.6	8.6	13.9	6.3	20.1	9.5
Houston, Tex.	33.1	8.9	17.3	10.8	18.6	11.3
Kansas City, Mo.	33.4	8.8	17.2	6.0	22.7	11.9
Nashville, Tenn.	30.3	8.5	16.9	7.4	23.9	13.0
Phoenix, Ariz.	25.2	10.2	19.7	11.6	20.0	13.3
Pittsburgh, Pa.	37.7	21.6	14.9	12.0	13.8	–
St. Louis, Mo.	37.5	8.1	17.3	6.4	21.5	9.2
Washington, D.C.	43.1	9.6	14.2	9.4	12.5	11.2

characteristics of the cities. In other cities it might be necessary to isolate weekend recreational trips as a separate trip type, rather than aggregating this trip type with other social and recreational trips. In cities with several major retail shopping centers in addition to the central business district, it may be necessary to classify shopping trips into convenience-goods and durable-goods shopping trips. In small cities of less than 200,000 population, urban travel is dominated by the journey to work and it may be sufficient to isolate the work trip.

The specific trip classifications used for non-home-based trips in a particular city will depend on the planning issues to be resolved. In large cities, business trips and trips by taxi might be forecast along with trips to and from the airport.

2.1.1 Factors influencing trip production

Many of the earlier studies of trip generation in urban areas attempted to relate trip productions and attractions to a wide range of explanatory land-use variables. Most of these studies were restricted to using variables that had been collected for other purposes rather than using variables which had a causal relationship with trip generation. Many trip-generation studies have been performed since these earlier transport-planning studies and the variables influencing trip generations are now much more clearly understood.

It has been pointed out in the introduction to this chapter that the term *trip production* is reserved for trips generated by households, whether they be origins or destinations. Households may be characterized in many ways but a large number of trip-production studies have shown that the following variables are the most important characteristics with respect to the major trip types such as work and shopping trips: (1) the number of workers in a household, and (2) the

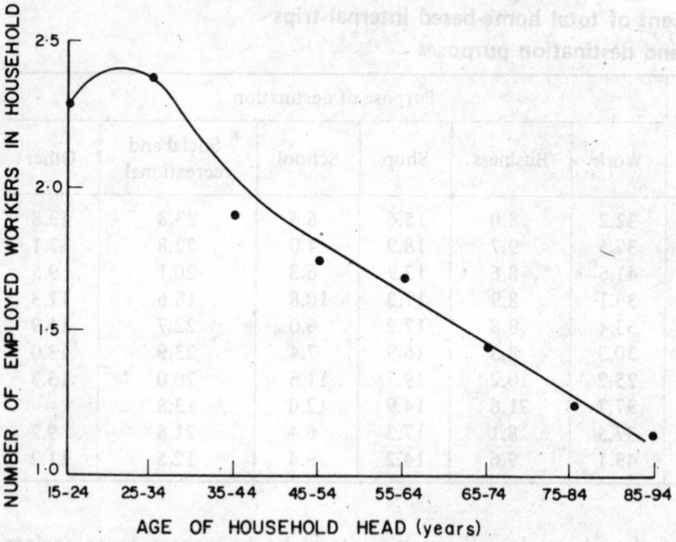

FIG. 2.1. Number of workers per household vs. age of household head.

household income, or some proxy of income, such as the number of cars per household.

A number of studies have shown that the number of workers per household and the age of the household head are related. Figure 2.1 shows a relationship between these two variables for Kitchener-Waterloo, Ontario [2]. This relationship shows that there is a slight increase in the number of workers for household heads in 25–34 age range; this increase simply reflects the high proportion of working wives in families of this age group.

Table 2.3 shows the effect of the occupation of the household head (a proxy for income) on trip production for various-sized households [3]. The decrease in trip production for a given household size with decreasing income is clearly demonstrated by both sets of survey data. Table 2.4 shows similar information on household trip generation for two San Diego subdivisions [4].

2.1.2 Factors influencing trip attraction

Many of the earlier trip-attraction equations were developed in terms of floor areas. Harper [5] developed the following regression equation for trips attracted to the Vancouver central business district:

$$\text{Zonal trips} = 1{,}560 + 14.322\,X_1 + 10.534\,X_2 + 3.670\,X_3 \tag{2.1}$$

where X_1 = thousands of square feet of retail floor area

X_2 = thousands of square feet of service and office floor area

X_3 = thousands of square feet of manufacturing and wholesaling floor area

Equation (2.1) shows that retail floor area attracts trips at a rate 50 percent higher than office space and about four times greater than manufacturing and wholesaling floor area.

There have been difficulties in using floor area as the independent variable since the floor area consumed per employee varies between establishments and with time. Surveys in the Toronto central business district have shown that the office space per employee has varied from an average of 150 square feet in 1960 to as high as 300 to 350 square feet per employee in buildings constructed in 1968.

Table 2.5 shows the car trip-attraction rates for some suburban industrial developments. Rates are given in terms of land area developed, floor area, and employment [6].

The factors that influence other types of trip attractions, such as social and recreational trips, are not as well understood.

Table 2.3. Trip production by occupation and size of family for one-car households

Occupation of head of household	No. persons per household					
	1	2	3	4	5	6
Chicago Area Transportation Study, 1956						
	Trips per household					
Professional	3.58	5.52	6.69	7.88	8.22	13.30
Manager	3.00	5.19	6.84	7.36	6.53	8.32
Sales	3.83	7.19	6.32	8.52	9.71	8.50
Craftsman	2.45	4.29	5.24	5.74	6.73	7.95
Operative	2.35	4.33	5.09	5.28	6.01	7.37
Clerical	3.23	4.57	5.40	6.61	6.91	8.19
Service	3.15	4.53	5.96	6.08	6.11	8.15
Laborer	2.00*	3.79	4.83	6.41	4.80	7.83
Puget Sound Regional Transportation Study, 1961						
	Trips per household					
Professional	4.51	7.02	8.25	9.15	11.37	12.18
Manager	5.09	6.79	9.43	10.01	12.49	13.05
Sales	5.25	7.61	10.69	10.58	11.90	12.04
Craftsman	3.73	6.11	7.72	9.34	10.56	12.25
Operative	3.70	6.49	7.44	9.30	10.24	10.33
Clerical	3.87	6.94	8.30	9.60	11.17	12.90
Service	3.53	6.16	9.36	9.15	8.55	13.26
Laborer	3.21	5.32	7.64	8.08	9.25	9.80

*Represents fewer than 10 observations.

Table 2.4. Resident trip generation per dwelling unit impact on metropolitan area

Trip description	Area and type dwelling unit						Combined average
	Allied Gardens	Clairemont					
	Single family	Single family		Duplex	Apartment	Average	
	Medium value	Medium value	High medium value				
5-day							
All	10.63	10.89	11.53	8.33	8.32	10.00	10.21
Auto driver	6.96	5.83	6.74	4.45	4.82	5.54	6.01
Auto-truck driver	7.39	6.47	6.79	4.62	4.82	5.83	6.33
Auto-truck passenger	3.02	4.15	4.39	3.26	3.17	3.83	3.56
Mass transit passenger	0.20	0.28	0.33	0.41	0.30	0.33	0.29
7-day							
All	10.61	11.90	12.21	8.42	8.34	10.59	10.58
Auto driver	6.56	6.05	7.12	4.69	4.82	5.78	6.04
Auto-truck driver	7.14	6.70	7.21	4.85	4.82	6.08	6.44
Auto-truck passenger	3.29	4.99	4.69	3.24	3.27	4.23	3.92
Mass transit passenger	0.17	0.21	0.32	0.32	0.25	0.27	0.24
Saturday							
Auto-truck driver	7.93	6.29	8.00	6.83	4.40	6.54	7.05
Sunday							
Auto-truck driver	4.42	8.18	9.78	4.17	5.20	7.19	6.28

Table 2.5. Car trip-attraction rates of some suburban industrial developments

Factor	Volume generated					
	Average morning			Average evening		
		Peak			Peak	
	30 min	1 hr	2 hr	30 min	1 hr	2 hr
Developed land area (sq ft)	per 10,000 sq ft			per 10,000 sq ft		
0–100,000	3.0	4.5	6.0	3.8	5.3	6.7
100,000–500,000	2.5	3.9	5.2	1.7	2.8	4.2
Over 500,000	1.8	2.9	3.9	2.4	3.8	5.1
Total mean	2.4	3.8	5.2	2.6	4.1	5.5
Building area (sq ft)	per 10,000 sq ft			per 10,000 sq ft		
0–30,000	10.5	15.6	19.4	10.4	15.6	20.8
30,000–100,000	6.2	8.6	11.5	6.3	7.5	11.4
Total mean	6.5	10.0	12.8	6.7	10.1	13.5
Employment	per employee			per employee		
0–100	0.17	0.25	0.35	0.20	0.31	0.39
100–500	0.24	0.37	0.48	0.20	0.31	0.47
Over 500	0.19	0.32	0.32	0.25	0.42	0.55
Total mean	0.21	0.32	0.42	0.22	0.34	0.46

2.2 MULTIPLE REGRESSION ANALYSIS

The majority of trip-generation studies performed to date have used multiple regression analysis to develop the prediction equations for the trips generated by various types of land use. Most of these regression equations have been developed using a stepwise regression analysis computer program.

Table 2.6 shows a set of trip data and land-use information of the type normally available to the transport planner. Stepwise regression-analysis programs allow the analyst to develop and test a large number of potential regression equations using various combinations and transformations of both the dependent and independent variables. The planner may then select the most appropriate prediction equation using certain statistical criteria. In formulating and testing various regression equations, the analyst must have a thorough understanding of the theoretical basis of regression analysis.

2.2.1 Review of regression-analysis concepts

A complete treatment of regression theory may be found in the literature [7].

The purpose of this section of Chap. 2 is to review briefly some of the fundamental principles of regression analysis.

The principal assumptions of regression analyses are:

1. The variance of the Y values about the regression line must be the same for all magnitudes of the independent variables.
2. The deviations of the Y values about the regression line must be independent of each other and normally distributed.
3. The X values are measured without error.
4. The regression of the dependent variable on the independent variable is linear.

Assume that observations of the magnitude of a dependent variable Y have been obtained for N magnitudes of an independent variable X and that an equation of the form $Y_e = a + b\,X$ is to be fitted to the data. The subscript e refers to the fact that Y_e is an estimate magnitude rather than an observed value Y. Reference [7] shows that for the least-squares criterion the magnitude of the parameters a and b may be estimated from:

$$b = \frac{\Sigma xy}{\Sigma x^2} \tag{2.2}$$

$$a = \bar{Y} - b\bar{X} \tag{2.3}$$

Table 2.6. Land-use and trip data

Zone no.	Employment: Total (X_1)	Manufacturing (X_2)	Retail and service (X_3)	Other (X_4)	Peak-hour trips attracted
1	9,482	6,820	2,547	115	9,428
2	2,010	111	1,899	0	2,192
3	574	228	87	259	330
4	127	0	127	0	153
5	3,836	2,729	813	294	3,948
6	953	101	773	79	1,188
7	223	165	58	0	240
8	36	6	30	0	55
9	2,223	1,550	499	174	2,064
10	272	0	166	106	280
11	50	0	48	2	52
12	209	36	173	0	230
13	410	140	7	263	420
14	11,023	10,932	63	28	9,654
15	527	188	325	14	450
16	183	123	59	1	130

where $x = X - \bar{X}$,
$y = Y - \bar{Y}$, and
$\bar{X}, \bar{Y}$ = the means of the X and Y observations, respectively.

It can also be shown that [7]:

$$\Sigma y^2 = \Sigma y_d^{\,2} + \Sigma y_e^{\,2} \tag{2.4}$$

where Eq. (2.4) states that the total sum of squares of the deviations of the Y observations about the mean value is equal to the sum of the squares of the deviations of the Y observations from the regression line plus the sum of the squares of the deviations of the estimated Y_e magnitudes about the mean value.

The residual sum of squares $\Sigma y_d^{\,2}$ provides a measure of the variability of the observations about the regression line. If $\Sigma y_d^{\,2}$ is small, then the regression equation may be considered to fit the observed data well. The ratio of the sum of squares explained by the regression to the total sum of squares is known as the *coefficient of determination* and is usually denoted by the symbol r^2:

$$r^2 = \frac{\Sigma y_e^{\,2}}{\Sigma y^2} \tag{2.5}$$

This ratio r^2 may assume a magnitude between 0 and 1. For a regression equation for which $r^2 = 1$ there would be no variation remaining that is unexplained by the independent variable used in the regression equation. When $r^2 = 0$, the independent variable used would not explain any of the observed variation in the dependent variable. The square root of the coefficient of determination is usually termed the *correlation coefficient.*

A second useful measure of the validity of a regression line is the standard error of the estimate which is estimated from:

$$s_e = \sqrt{\frac{\Sigma y_d^{\,2}}{(N-2)}} \tag{2.6}$$

where the denominator $(N-2)$ is called the *number of degrees of freedom* associated with the sum of the squares $\Sigma y_d^{\,2}$.

The number of degrees of freedom may be determined by subtracting from the number of observations N, the number of statistics that had to be calculated from the sample in order to obtain the sum of squares. For a simple regression equation with one independent variable, the mean of the dependent variable and the regression coefficient b have to be estimated before the deviations y_d may be calculated.

The standard error of the estimate may be interpreted in the following manner. Of the original observations 68.3 percent may be expected to fall within a band plus and minus one standard error either side of the regression line; or, 95 percent of the observations may be expected to fall within plus and minus two standard errors either side of the regression line, and so on.

The regression coefficient b is a statistical estimate and is therefore subject to error. The standard error is the concept used to convey the magnitude of this error and is estimated from the following expression:

$$s_b = \frac{s_e}{s_X} \sqrt{N} \tag{2.7}$$

where s_e has been defined in Eq. (2.6) and s_X is the standard deviation of the independent variable.

Statements about the confidence that might be placed in an estimated regression coefficient may be derived from the standard error defined in Eq. (2.7). The t test may be used to determine whether an estimated regression coefficient is significant by forming the following ratio:

$$t = \frac{\text{regression coefficient}}{\text{standard error of the regression coefficient}} \tag{2.8}$$

Details of the t test may be found in Ref. [7].

In some instances the analyst may be interested in developing a linear equation which passes through the origin with an equation of the following form:

$$Y_e = bX \tag{2.9}$$

$$b = \frac{\Sigma XY}{\Sigma X^2} \tag{2.10}$$

Equations (2.2) to (2.8) have dealt with the simple regression equation in which there is only one independent variable. A partial or multiple regression equation has the form:

$$Y_e = a + b_1 X_1 + b_2 X_2 + \cdots + b_p X_p \tag{2.11}$$

where there are p independent variables and the regression coefficients b_1, $b_2, \ldots, b_p$, are usually referred to as *partial regression coefficients.*

The equations equivalent to Eqs. (2.5), (2.6), and (2.7) for the multiple regression equations are given below:

$$R^2 = \frac{\Sigma(Y_e - \bar{Y})^2}{\Sigma(Y - \bar{Y})^2} \tag{2.12}$$

where R^2 is known as the *coefficient of multiple determination* and R is known as the *multiple correlation coefficient.*

$$s_e = \frac{\Sigma {y_e}^2}{[N - (p + 1)]} \tag{2.13}$$

$$s_b = \frac{{s_e}^2}{[s^2_{X_i} N(1 - R^2_{X_i})]} \tag{2.14}$$

where s_{X_i} is the standard deviation of the independent variable X_i and R_{X_i} is the coefficient of multiple correlation between X_i and all other independent variables.

2.2.2 The stepwise approach

The stepwise approach to regression analysis may be illustrated by the use of the data contained in Table 2.6. Regression equations may be developed through the following sequence of steps.

Step 1: Examine the relationships between the dependent variable and each of the independent variables in turn in order to detect nonlinearities; if nonlinearities are detected, the relationship must be linearized by transforming the dependent variable, the independent variable, or both.

Figure 2.2 illustrates several types of transformations that may be used to linearize nonlinear relationships. Most computer regression-analysis programs have a number of options for linearizing data sets before the regression analysis is performed.

Step 2: Examine the simple correlation matrix in order to detect: (1) those independent variables which have a statistical association with the dependent variable, and (2) potential sources of collinearity between pairs of the independent variables.

Table 2.7 shows the simple correlation matrix for the data presented in Table 2.6. This simple correlation matrix demonstrates that zonal total employment has a very high degree of association with the dependent variable in that $r = 0.996$. Manufacturing employment also has a high degree of association with the

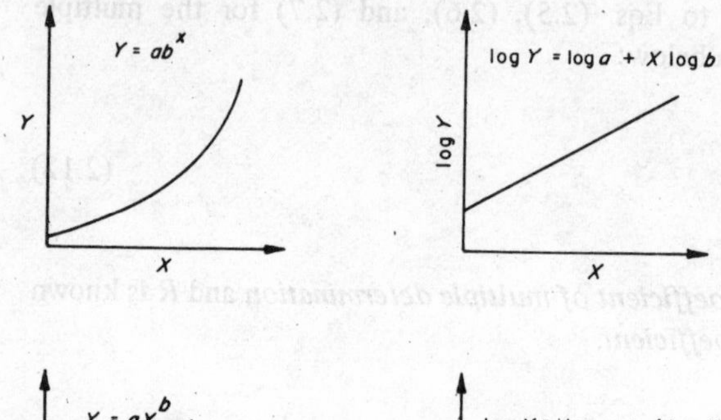

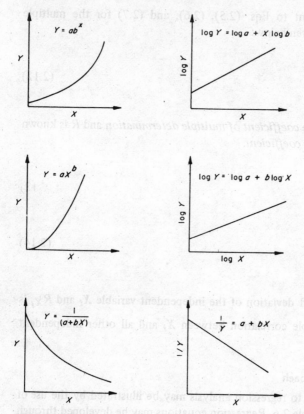

FIG. 2.2. Examples of linearization of relationships through transformation of the variables.

dependent variable ($r = 0.958$) and the other two components of employment are not as highly associated with the dependent variable. The simple correlation matrix also indicates a high degree of association between total employment and manufacturing employment which is simply a reflection of the fact that manufacturing employment is the most important component of total employment. Since total employment and manufacturing employment are largely measures of the same underlying variable they should not be included in the same regression equation. In this problem the analyst has the option of the following regression equations:

$$Y = a + b\,X_1 \qquad \text{(A)}$$
$$Y = a + b\,X_2 \qquad \text{(B)}$$
$$Y = a + b_1\,X_2 + b_2\,X_3 \qquad \text{(C)}$$
$$Y = a + b_1\,X_2 + b_2\,X_3 + b_3\,X_4 \qquad \text{(D)}$$

Step 3: Estimate the parameters of each of the potential regression equations and conduct the following tests:

1. What is the magnitude of R^2?
2. Do the partial regression coefficients have the correct sign and are their magnitudes reasonable?
3. Are the partial regression coefficients statistically significant?
4. Is the magnitude of *a* reasonable?

The four regression equations listed above [Eqs. (A)-(D)] were fitted to the data contained in Table 2.6 with the following results.

$$Y = 61.4 + 0.93X_1 \tag{A}$$

Standard error of estimate = 288.4
Coefficient of determination = 0.992
t value of regression coefficient = 42

$$Y = 507.7 + 0.98X_2 \tag{B}$$

Standard error of estimate = 935.9
Coefficient of multiple determination = 0.921
t value of regression coefficient = 14

$$Y = 25.8 + 0.89X_2 + 1.29X_3 \tag{C}$$

Standard error of estimate = 199.4
Coefficient of multiple determination = 0.996
t values of partial-regression coefficients = 51, 17

Table 2.7. Simple correlation matrix

	X_1	X_2	X_3	X_4	Y
X_1	1.000	0.978	0.486	0.110	0.996
X_2		1.000	0.297	0.068	0.958
X_3			1.000	0.073	0.552
X_4				1.000	0.124
Y					1.000

X_1 = Total employment
X_2 = Manufacturing employment
X_3 = Retail and service employment
X_4 = Other employment
Y = Peak-hour trips attracted

$$Y = -69.9 + 1.26X_2 - 0.37X_3 + 0.02X_4 \qquad \text{(D)}$$

Standard error of estimate = 142.6
Coefficient of multiple determination = 0.998
t values of partial-regression coefficients = 3.7, 1.1, 0.06

Inspection of Eq. (A) indicates that the R^2 magnitude is close to 1.000, the sign and magnitude of the regression coefficient (+ 0.93) are satisfactory, and the t value is significant at the 1 percent level of significance; there are 16 − 2 = 14 degrees of freedom associated with the estimated b and the t distribution magnitude at 1 percent is 2.98.

Equation (B) shows that the use of manufacturing employment instead of total employment does not yield as valid a prediction equation. The R^2 magnitude is lower and the magnitude of a is not reasonable.

Equation (C) which incorporates two independent variables, manufacturing and retail employment, is a slightly better equation statistically than Eq. (A). The standard error of the estimate is smaller for Eq. (C) and both of the partial-regression coefficients are statistically significant ($t = 3.01$ for 13 degrees of freedom at the 1 percent level of significance). The constant term is closer to 0 for Eq. (C), indicating that there would be less overestimation of trips from zones with low employment. Equations (C) and (A) are roughly comparable in terms of their statistical validity. The choice of a prediction equation is then dependent upon the availability of data and the ease with which the independent variables can be forecast. In this case, Eq. (A) would probably be selected since it is the simpler of the two equations.

It is important to review as well the characteristics of Eq. (D). The R^2 magnitude for this equation is the highest of the four equations tested. However, the equation has attributes which prevent it from being selected as the prediction equation for trip attractions. First, the coefficient of X_3 is −0.37 which is irrational. If the retail and service employment of a zone were increased by 100 then this equation suggests that the work-trip attractions would decrease by 37 trips. For 12 degrees of freedom $t = 3.06$ at the 1 percent level of significance and $t = 2.68$ at the 5 percent level of significance. Therefore, the partial-regression coefficient of X_2 is the only coefficient that is statistically significant. Equation (D) demonstrates quite clearly the danger of using R^2 as the only criterion of validity of regression equations.

The stepwise approach to the development of trip-generation prediction equations has frequently been used improperly in transport-planning studies. The errors in most studies have arisen because of two faults which are: (1) the use of the coefficient of multiple determination as the only criterion of statistical validity of the equation, and (2) the inclusion of collinear independent variables in the regression equation.

The concept of collinearity between independent variables requires elaboration since it is probably the most common error. The following equation was developed and used in one major Canadian transport planning study:

$$\text{Zonal peak-hour work trips produced} = 0.3036\ (\text{zonal households}) + 0.5638\ (\text{zonal population}) \qquad (2.15)$$

In this study the equation was selected in preference to either of the simple regression equations because Eq. (2.15) possessed a large R^2 value. Inspection of the simple correlation matrix for this regression analysis revealed that the simple correlation coefficient between the two independent variables, households and population, was 0.998. This indicates that the two variables are collinear and that one variable may be derived from a linear transformation of the second variable. That is, the number of households in a zone and the population of a zone may be regarded as measures of the same underlying variable, the labor force in a zone; and both variables should not be included in a regression equation.

Transport planners frequently reject these statistical arguments and claim that because an equation, such as Eq. (2.15), reproduces the base-year observations better, then the equation should be accepted as the prediction equation. The population of a zone and the number of households in a zone are related by the average persons per household. If this ratio remains constant then errors in work-trip productions estimated by Eq. (2.15) will not occur. However, this ratio is changing and if it changes significantly over the planning period, errors will occur in the forecasts which are due to the inclusion of collinear independent variables in the prediction equation.

The magnitudes of the partial-regression coefficients also become irrational when collinear independent variables are included in the prediction equation. The magnitude of a partial-regression coefficient is interpreted in the following way. The size of the coefficient represents the change in magnitude of the dependent variable induced by a one-unit change in the independent variable when the other independent variables are held at their mean values. Equation (2.15) states that a unit change in the number of households in a zone will only produce 0.3 work trips. Empirical evidence indicates that the true rate is about 0.9 work trips per household.

Finally, perhaps the most important test of a trip-generation regression equation is to establish whether there is a causal basis to the apparent dependency between variables. The relationship between travel demand and the intensity of land-based human activities is quite direct and the validity of trip-generation equations may be assessed easily. In many studies, very complicated trip-generation equations have been developed which are difficult to justify from a causal point of view in spite of an apparent statistical validity. For example, consider the following trip-attraction equation developed in one transport-planning study:

Other home-based trips attracted
= 0.465 (industrial and manufacturing employment)
+ 4.310 (retail and service employment)
+ 0.288 (population) + 4.524 (other employment) (2.16)

It should be noted in connection with Eq. (2.16) that work, shopping, and social-recreational trips attracted had already been accounted for by other regression equations.

2.2.3 Stability of regression equations

Trip-generation equations are developed in order that trip productions and trip attractions associated with the estimated horizon-year land use may be calculated. To be useful for forecasting, the regression coefficients associated with the independent variables must be invariant with respect to time. Consider the following trip-attraction equation developed above:

Peak-hour trip attractions = 61.4 + 0.93 (employment)

The regression coefficient of 0.93 implies that 93 percent of the employees within a zone arrive at work during the peak hour. The remainder represents employees who travel to work outside of the peak hour, employees absent from work, and on vacation. Trends in office and manufacturing functions suggest that during the next 20 years most employees will move toward a 4-day workweek, while the industry or office continues to operate on a 5-day workweek. If total employment were still used as the independent variable, this coefficient of 0.93 would overestimate the peak-hour trip.

The magnitude of this coefficient could also be influenced by continued improvements in communications. It is reasonable to expect that certain types of employment will be located in the household with access to central offices being provided by communications facilities.

Greater instabilities might be expected in the regression coefficients of prediction equations that have to do with non-work trips such as social and recreational trips. Increasing affluence of urban populations and shorter working hours will probably result in greatly increased rates of non-work-tripmaking. While it is difficult to forecast exactly the potential instabilities in regression coefficients, the analyst must explore them to the best of his ability. The uncertainties associated with future travel forecasts are explored more formally in Chap. 12.

2.3 CATEGORY ANALYSIS

Most traffic-analysis zones tend to contain a mixture of social and economic classes. The use of regression equations based on zonally aggregated measures of the zonal characteristics tend to submerge important characteristics of the travel demand. If the aggregation of data used in zonal-regression equations is to be effective, it is important to have as much homogeneity within the units of aggregation as possible. It should be recalled that the purpose of a regression equation is to explain the variation in tripmaking between zones in terms of a number of independent variables.

Table 2.8 shows the results of an analysis of variance of the trips produced by households in an urban area for various areal units of aggregation of these households [8]. The analysis of variance demonstrates that the greatest amount of variation in tripmaking is found within the various areal units rather than between units. For the data on which Table 2.8 is based, a zonal regression equation for predicting total trips would deal with a little over 20 percent of the total variation in tripmaking from households, with the remainder of the variation being lost to aggregation. A number of transport planners have proposed that this difficulty may be overcome through the use of households, rather than traffic zones, as the basic unit of tripmaking.

One technique which is based on the household and its characteristics is known as *category* or *cross-classification analysis* [8, 9]. Category analysis is simply a technique for estimating the trip-production characteristics of households which have been sorted into a number of separate categories according to a set of properties that characterize the household. Category analysis may also be used to estimate trip attractions.

Table 2.9 shows the results of a category analysis of work-trip productions by household in Metropolitan Toronto [10]. The households have been classified in terms of two variables, persons per household and cars per household. The trip-production matrix of Table 2.9 was prepared by sorting all households interviewed in the travel survey into one of the 18 cells. The number of trips produced by all households in a cell and the number of households in a cell were then summed. The trip rate for each cell was then established by dividing the number of trips by the number of households.

Table 2.8. An analysis of variance of tripmaking

Area units (No. of units)	Total SS*	WSS†	Percent	BSS‡	Percent
Sectors (10)	213,936	192,895	90.2	21,041	9.8
Rings (16)	213,936	192,968	90.2	20,968	9.8
Census tracts (52)	213,936	180,226	84.2	33,710	15.8
Districts (57)	213,936	184,864	86.4	29,072	13.6
Zones (247)	213,936	170,270	79.6	43,666	20.4
Dwelling units (5,255)	213,936			213,936	100.0

*Sum of squares.
† Within (area unit) sum of squares.
‡Between (area unit) sum of squares.

Table 2.9. Work-trip production category analysis

Cars		Persons/household 1	2	3	4	5	6+	Total
0	A*	255	1,231	1,149	1,111	827	1,081	5,654
	B†	828	1,341	652	549	389	443	4,202
	C‡	0.308	0.92	1.76	2.03	2.13	2.44	1.35
1	A*	301	4,844	5,781	7,466	4,956	4,879	28,227
	B†	344	2,793	2,472	3,092	2,046	1,889	12,636
	C‡	0.875	1.73	2.34	2.41	2.42	2.58	2.23
2+	A*	8	644	2,220	3,231	2,424	3,002	11,521
	B†	5	294	717	1,022	726	870	3,634
	C‡	1.6	2.16	3.10	3.16	3.34	3.45	3.17
Total	A*	564	6,719	9,150	11,808	8,207	8,962	45,410
	B†	1,177	4,428	3,841	4,663	3,161	3,202	20,472
	C‡	0.48	1.52	2.38	2.53	2.60	2.80	2.215

*Trip productions of households in category.
†Number of households in category.
‡Trip productions per household in category.

Information of the type contained in Table 2.9 may be translated easily into zonal trip-production estimates. The number of households within each traffic-analysis zone that are expected to fall within each cell of the matrix are estimated and multiplied by the appropriate trip rate and these products are summed:

$$p_i^q = \Sigma h_i(c) tp(c) \tag{2.17}$$

where p_i^q = the number of trips produced by zone i by type q people
$h_i(c)$ = the number of households in zone i in category c
$tp(c)$ = the trip-production rate of household category c (the summation is over all categories of type q people)

Zonal trip attractions may be estimated in a similar manner by the following expression:

$$a_j = \Sigma b_j(c) ta(c) \tag{2.18}$$

where a_j = the number of work trips attracted by zone j
$b_j(c)$ = the number of employment opportunities in category c
$ta(c)$ = the trip attraction rate of employment category c

and the summation is over all employment types if work-trip attractions are being estimated.

2.3.1 Variability of category-analysis trip rates

The statistical tests that normally accompany regression analyses allow the analyst to comment on the reliability of the partial-regression coefficients. It has been pointed out in Sec. 2.2.2 that the t test may be used to test whether the magnitudes of the partial-regression coefficients are statistically significant. The transport planner should also be interested in the reliabilities of the trip rates within each cell of a category-analysis matrix.

In transport-planning studies a sample of n households out of total of N households within the study area is selected. The transport planner is interested in estimating a mean trip rate within some band of confidence. For large samples, in which $n > 30$, the confidence interval of the true mean is given by:

$$\bar{x} \pm z\sigma_{\bar{x}} \tag{2.19}$$

where $\bar{x}$ = the mean trip rate,
$\sigma_{\bar{x}}$ = the standard error of sample means, or the standard error of the estimate, and
z = a coefficient which varies with the particular level of confidence desired.

The standard error of sample means is given by:

$$\sigma_{\bar{x}} = \frac{\sigma}{\sqrt{n}} \tag{2.20}$$

where σ = the standard deviation of the population trip rates for households.

Equation (2.20) is for populations of infinite size which may be corrected in the following way for populations of finite size N:

$$\sigma_{\bar{x}} = \frac{\sigma}{\sqrt{n}} \sqrt{\frac{N-n}{N}} \tag{2.21}$$

From Eq. (2.21) the margin of error is given by:

$$d = z\sigma_{\bar{x}} = z\sigma \sqrt{\frac{1}{n} - \frac{1}{N}} \tag{2.22}$$

Vandertol [2] has examined the margins of error associated with trip-generation-category analyses of travel data for Hamilton, Ontario. In this analysis, households were stratified into categories of workers per household and zonal economic levels. The following information was obtained for households with two workers per household and households located in low-income areas:

Number of work trips observed/household	Observed frequency within sample
0	12
1	26
2	29
3	2
4	1

The following statistics were calculated from this information:

Average trip rate = 1.343 trips per household
Standard deviation of trip rate = 0.849 trips per household
Margin of error at 95% confidence level = 0.198 trips per household

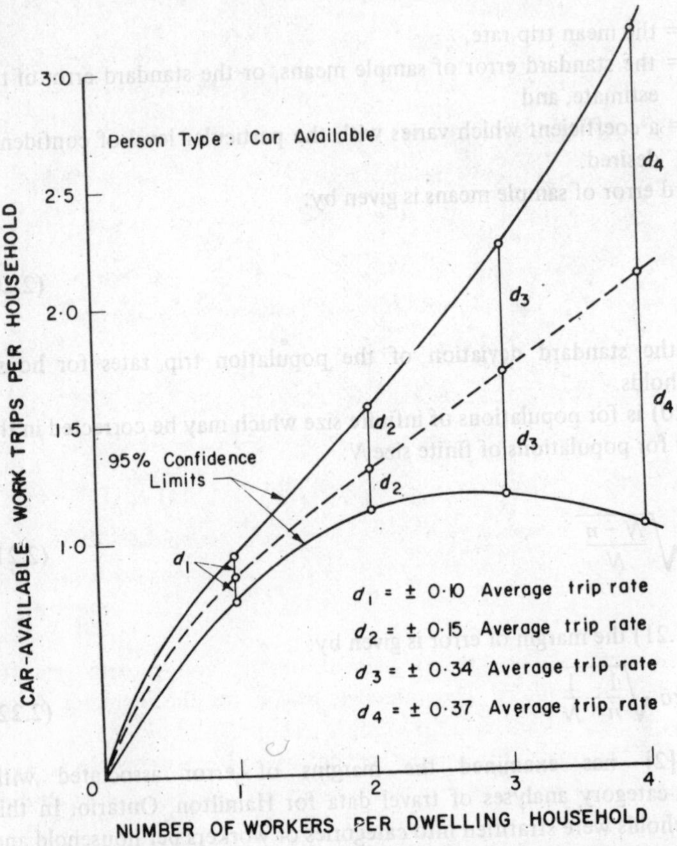

FIG. 2.3. Variations in margin of error of car available trip rates for lower income zones.

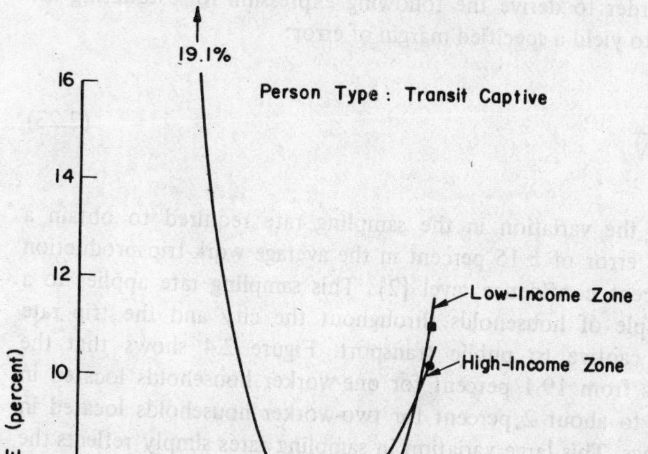

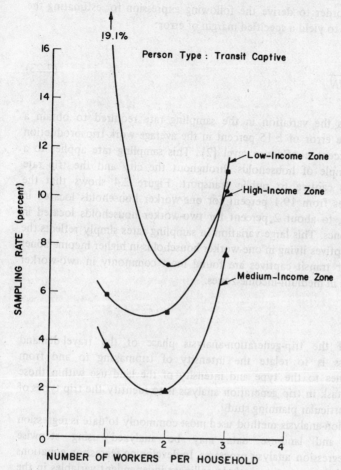

FIG. 2.4. Variations in sampling rates across categories.

Figure 2.3 shows the variation in the margin of error calculated by Vandertol for households within various categories of workers per household for households located in zones of the lower economic category. It is interesting to note that the margin of error varied from 10 percent of the average trip rate for households with one worker, to 37 percent of the average trip rate for households with four workers. The principal reason for the increases in the percentage error are the decreases in the number of households within a category in the sample of households. The sample size decreased from 183 households in the one-worker-per-household category to 6 households in the four-workers-per-household category.

More-stable trip rates in the various household categories may be obtained through increases in the sampling rate for a given category. Equation (2.22) may be manipulated in order to derive the following expression for estimating the sample size required to yield a specified margin of error:

$$n = \frac{z^2 \sigma^2}{d^2 + (z^2 \sigma^2)/N} \tag{2.23}$$

Figure 2.4 shows the variation in the sampling rate required to obtain a maximum allowable error of ± 15 percent in the average work-trip production rate at the 95 percent confidence level [2]. This sampling rate applies to a simple random sample of households throughout the city and the trip rate applies to persons captive to public transport. Figure 2.4 shows that the sampling rate varies from 19.1 percent for one-worker households located in high-income zones, to about 2 percent for two-worker households located in medium-income zones. This large variation in sampling rates simply reflects the fact that transit captives living in one-worker households in higher income zones are rare; and, that transit captives are found most commonly in two-worker households located in medium-income zones.

SUMMARY

The purpose of the trip-generation-analysis phase of the travel-demand forecasting process is to relate the intensity of tripmaking to and from traffic-analysis zones to the type and intensity of the land use within those zones. The initial task in trip generation analysis is to identify the trip types of importance to a particular planning study.

The trip-generation-analysis method used most commonly to date is regression analysis. Travel and land-use data may be analyzed using stepwise computer-based regression analysis programs. In developing regression equations the analyst must be sure not to include collinear independent variables in the equations. The coefficient of determination of a regression equation should be used only as a broad indicator of the overall statistical validity of the equation. The most important test of statistical validity is to determine if the magnitudes of the partial-regression coefficients are statistically significant. The parameter magnitudes and signs of a regression equation should be subject to simple empirical appraisals to ensure that they are reasonable.

A second method of trip-generation analysis is category analysis. Category analysis is simply a technique for estimating the trip-production rates for households which have been sorted into a number of separate categories according to a set of properties that characterize the households. The number of observations within any cell of a category matrix that are required to produce estimates of the mean trip rates within a specified margin of error may be estimated from sampling theory. The sampling rate may vary from 2 to 20 percent depending upon the frequency with which a given household category is represented within an urban area. The high sampling rates for the rare household types may be reduced through stratified random sampling.

REFERENCES

1. Wilbur Smith and Associates, *Transportation and Parking for Tomorrow's Cities*, Automobile Manufacturers Association, Detroit, Michigan, 1966.
2. Vandertol, A., *Transit Usage Estimates from an Urban Travel Demand Model*, M.A.Sc. thesis, Department of Civil Engineering, University of Waterloo, Waterloo, Ontario, 1971.
3. Walker, J. R., *Social Status of Head of Household and Trip Generation from Home*, Highway Research Record No. 114, Highway Research Board, Washington, D.C., 1966.
4. Hall, E. M., *Travel Characteristics of Two San Diego Subdivision Developments*, Bulletin No. 203, Highway Research Board, Washington, D.C., 1958.
5. Harper, B. C. S., and H. M. Edwards, *Generation of Person Trips by Areas within the Central Business District*, Bulletin No. 253, Highway Research Board, Washington, D.C., 1960.
6. Alroth, W. A., *Parking and Traffic Characteristics of Suburban Industrial Developments*, Highway Research Record No. 237, Highway Research Board, Washington, D.C., 1968.
7. Wine, R. L., *Statistics for Scientists and Engineers*, Prentice-Hall, Englewood Cliffs, New Jersey, 1964.
8. Bureau of Public Roads, *Guidelines for Trip Generation Analysis*, U.S. Department of Transportation, Washington, D.C., 1967.
9. Wootton, H. J., and G. W. Pick, "A Model for Trips Generated by Households," *Journal of Transport Economics and Policy*, Vol. 1, pp. 137–153, 1967.
10. Ma, V. C., *Trip Generation in the Toronto Area Regional Model Study*, Proceedings, Workshop on Toronto Region Travel Demand Forecasting Model, Transport Group, Department of Civil Engineering, University of Waterloo, Waterloo, Ontario, 1971.

3 TRAVEL-DEMAND FORECASTING: MODAL SPLIT ANALYSIS

The second stage of the travel-demand forecasting process described in Chap. 1 has been identified as captive modal split analysis. A second stage of modal split analysis was identified as occurring after the trip-distribution analysis phase. This two-stage-type modal split analysis is required because of the existence in urban areas of essentially two separate submarkets for public-transport services. These two submarkets have been labeled *captive transit riders* and *choice transit riders* in Chap. 1.

The aim of the captive modal split analysis phase is to establish relationships that allow the trip ends estimated in the trip-generation phase to be partitioned into "captive" transit riders and "choice" transit riders. The origin and destination patterns of the two groups of tripmakers are then synthesized separately. The purpose of the choice modal split analysis phase is to estimate the probable split of choice transit riders between public transport and car travel given measures of the generalized cost of travel by the two modes.

The ratio of captive to choice tripmakers using a public transport system varies from 9 to 1 in small cities with poorly developed public transport systems to as high as 3 to 1 for very large cities with well-developed systems. The many studies of modal transport choice have demonstrated that the major determinants of public transport patronage are

the socioeconomic charactersitics of the tripmakers, and
the relative cost and service properties of the trip by car and the trip by public transport.

The characteristics of the tripmakers that influence their modal transport choice decisions are those which determine car availability to the tripmakers, and therefore captive or choice status. Variables which have been used to identify this status at the household level are:

1. Household income, or car ownership directly
2. The number of persons per household
3. The age and sex of household members
4. The purpose of the trip

Transport studies have shown that choice tripmakers consider a number of characteristics of both the trip by car and the trip by transit in making a modal transport choice decision, and these include the in-vehicle travel time; the travel time outside of the line haul vehicle, usually called *excess travel time*; the out-of-pocket costs including the vehicle operating costs, parking charges and transit fares; and the reliability, comfort and convenience of the transport modes.

This chapter describes typical examples of the modal split models developed in earlier transport studies. These models accomplished modal split estimation in one stage and contained socioeconomic characteristic variables and transport mode service variables in an aggregated model. The second part of the chapter describes the structure of modal split models developed in more recent years which are based on certain hypotheses regarding individual choice behavior. The final part of the chapter describes examples of two-stage modal split models.

3.1 EARLIER MODAL SPLIT MODELS

The earlier modal split models were used either before or after the trip-distribution analysis phase of the travel-demand forecasting process. Modal split models which have been used before the trip-distribution phase are usually referred to as *trip-end modal split models.* Modal split models that have followed the trip distribution phase are normally termed *trip-interchange modal split models.* Figure 3.1 illustrates the differences in the roles of these two types of modal split models.

In transport planning studies performed to date in medium- and smaller-sized cities, trip-end modal split models have normally been used. Figure 3.1 demonstrates that with this type of model the potential patronage of each transport mode is determined following the trip-generation phase. The basic

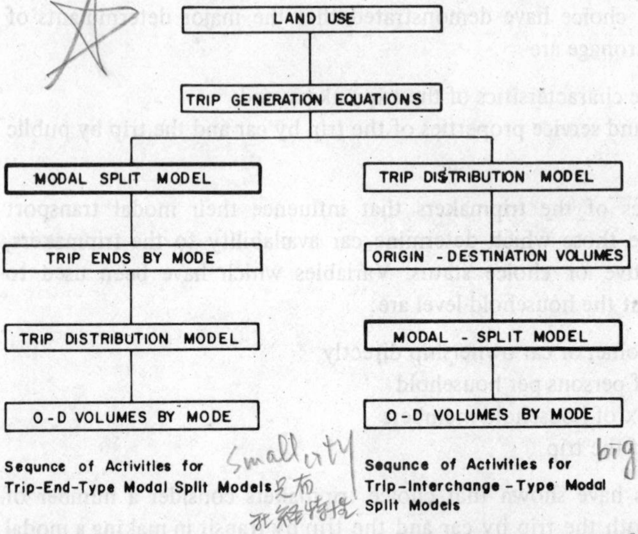

FIG. 3.1. Differences between modal split model types.

assumption of the trip-end-type models is that transport patronage is relatively insensitive to the service characteristics of the transport modes. Modal patronages are determined principally by the socioeconomic characteristics of the tripmakers.

Transport studies performed in larger urban areas, where the public-transport system is well developed, or where significant improvements in the public-transport system are contemplated, have usually employed trip-interchange modal split models. Most of the trip-interchange modal split models that have been developed, incorporate measures of the relative service characteristics of competing modes, as well as measures of the socioeconomic characteristics of the tripmakers.

Typical examples of these two types of model are described next. These examples show that the trip-end-type models place a great deal of emphasis on identifying transit captives, whereas the trip-interchange-type models emphasize choice transit riders. It will be seen as the chapter progresses that the dichotomy just introduced is somewhat arbitrary and that the two types of model should be linked so to produce a two-stage modal split model of the type identified in Chap. 1.

Fertal [1] provides an excellent summary of nine modal split models that might be termed *first-generation modal split models.* These models were developed prior to about 1964. Only two of these models are described in this book in order to convey the basic principles underlying them. The modal split model developed during the southeastern Wisconsin transportation study [2] is used as an example of the trip-end-type model. It does have some of the characteristics of a trip-interchange-type model in that a measure of the relative highway and public-transport service to a zone is incorporated in the model. The modal split model developed and used in two major transport studies in Toronto [3,4] is used as an example of the trip-interchange-type modal split model. This model was also used in Washington, D.C. [5].

3.1.1 Southeastern Wisconsin model

The modal split model developed in this study consisted of seven estimating surfaces that related the percentage of trip ends that will use transit services from a particular traffic analysis zone to the following variables: trip type, characteristics of the tripmaker, and characteristics of the transport system.

Four trip purposes were used to stratify the trips made on public-transport services and these were home-based work trips, home-based shopping trips, home-based "other" trips, and non-home-based trips. Only the surface developed for home-based work trips is discussed in this book.

The socioeconomic characteristics of tripmakers were defined on a zonal basis in terms of the average number of cars per household in a zone. Figure 3.2 shows the relationship that was observed between the zonal percent transit usage and the zonal average number of cars per household for the journey to work in the Milwaukee region.

The characteristics of the transport system relative to a given zone were defined by an accessibility index calculated from the following equation:

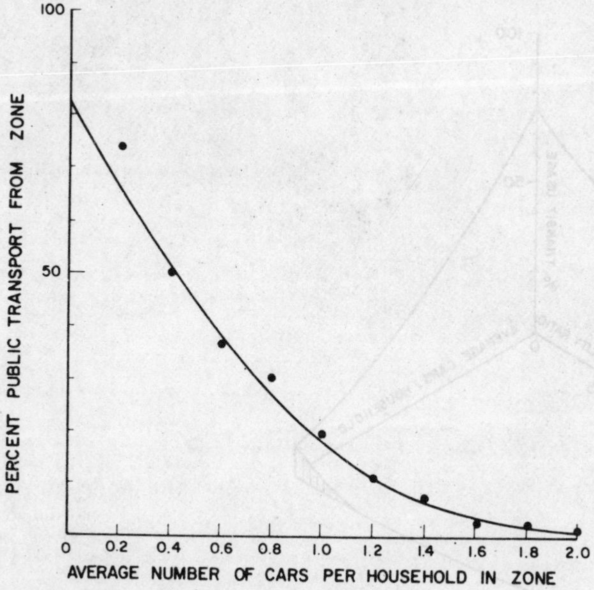

FIG. 3.2. Percent transit usage vs. zonal average number of cars per household.

$$acc_i = \sum_{j=1}^{n} a_j f_{ij} \tag{3.1}$$

where acc_i = accessibility index for zone i

a_j = number of attractions in zone j

f_{ij} = travel time factor for travel from zone i to zone j for the particular mode being considered

The transport service provided to a particular zone by the two modes was characterized by the following accessibility ratio:

$$\text{Accessibility ratio} = \frac{\text{highway accessibility index}}{\text{transit accessibility index}} \tag{3.2}$$

The modal split surface developed for work trips in the Milwaukee region is shown in Fig. 3.3 in which the percent transit usage from a zone is plotted against the accessibility ratio and the zonal average number of cars per household. This modal split surface demonstrates quite clearly the rapid decline in transit use with decreasing level of transit service for the higher income groups. In contrast, the zones with lower per household car ownership were relatively insensitive to changes in transit levels of service.

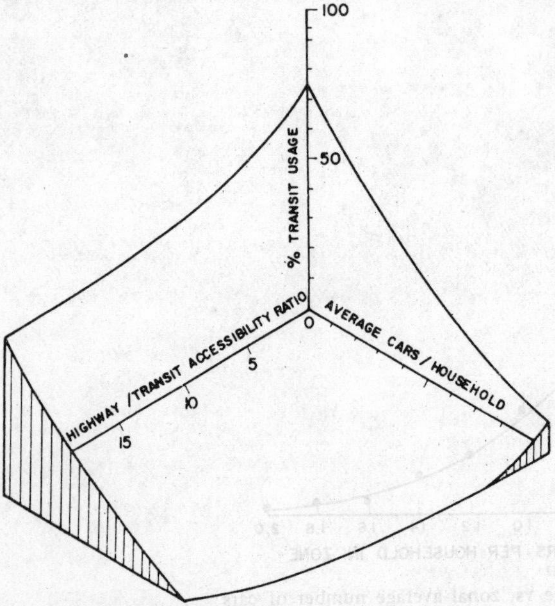

FIG. 3.3. Modal split surface for work trips.

3.1.2 Toronto modal split model

The basic hypothesis underlying the modal split model developed for Metropolitan Toronto has been stated as follows [3]:

The total number of people moving between an origin-destination pair constitutes a travel market and the various modes compete for this market and secure a portion of it in relation to their relative competitive positions which are expressed in terms of: relative travel time, relative travel cost, relative travel service, and the economic status of the tripmaker.

The relative travel time by competing modes was expressed by the ratio of door-to-door travel time by public transit and car as follows:

$$TTR = \frac{a + b + c + d + e}{f + g + h} \tag{3.3}$$

where a = time spent in the transit vehicle
b = transfer time between transit vehicles
c = time spent waiting for transit vehicle
d = walking time to transit vehicle
e = walking time from transit vehicle
f = car driving time
g = parking delay at destination
h = walking time from parking place to destination

The relative travel cost was defined by the ratio of out-of-pocket travel costs by public transit and car as follows:

$$CR = \frac{i}{(j + k + 0.5l)/m} \tag{3.4}$$

where i = transit fare
j = cost of gasoline
k = cost of oil changes and lubrications
l = parking cost at destination
m = average car occupancy

The relative travel service was characterized by the ratio of the excess travel times by transit and car. The excess travel time was defined as the amount of time spent outside the vehicle during a trip. The service ratio was defined as follows:

$$SR = \frac{b + c + d + e}{g + h} \tag{3.5}$$

Figure 3.4 shows part of the modal split curves developed for the journey to work in Metropolitan Toronto. The economic status of tripmakers was characterized by four salary classifications and the boundaries of each of these salary classes are shown in the diagram.

The Toronto modal split model was used as follows. Total person trips by all modes were forecast and distributed using the gravity model for the highway network. The travel time, cost and service ratios, and the income levels were then used to estimate percent transit usage from the diversion curves. The total person trips between the origin-destination pair were then multiplied by this percentage to obtain the transit trips. The car-person trips were then factored by the car occupancy rate to determine the number of car trips between the origin-destination pair. Each group of trips was then assigned to the appropriate network.

While the two models described above have been assigned to different categories, their underlying model structures exhibit many similarities. Both

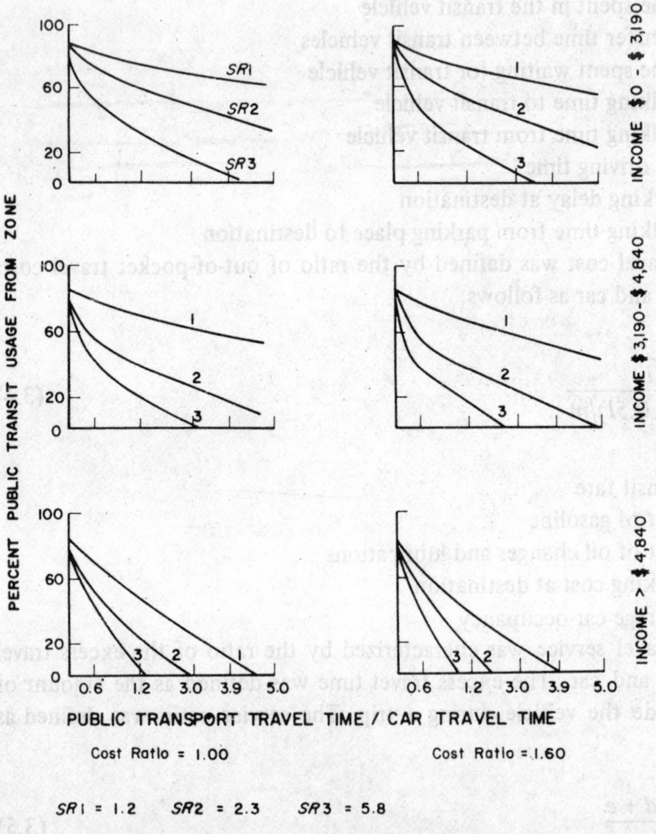

FIG. 3.4. Modal split curves developed for Toronto, Ontario.

contain a measure of the socioeconomic characteristics of tripmakers as well as a measure of the relative service provided by the different transport modes. The essential difference is in the extent to which the two types of variables dominate the model. In the southeastern Wisconsin model the service characteristics of the transport system are introduced in a macroscopic way through the ratio of the accessibility indices. In the Toronto model the service characteristics are introduced very directly in the form of such factors as the travel-time ratio, and so on.

3.1.3 Some limitations of earlier modal split models

Perhaps the principal limitation of these models is that captive and choice transit riders have not been identified and represented separately in the models. For this reason the models do not reflect adequately the manner in which choice transit riders react to changes in transport system characteristics. The transit patronage data used to calibrate the models have contained both captive and choice riders. In addition, the patronage data have been of a zonally aggregated nature. Some evidence was introduced in Chap. 2 which demonstrated that in the typical traffic-analysis zone there is a great deal of within-zone variability in tripmaking which tends to submerge important differences in tripmaking behavior.

Transport service-sensitive modal split relations can only be developed if tripmakers are first segregated into various socioeconomic categories, and diversion curve-type relationships are then constructed for each of these categories.

3.2 MODAL SPLIT MODELS WITH A BEHAVIORAL BASIS

A number of modal split models have been proposed which incorporate various hypotheses about the modal choice behavior of individuals. The focus of these models is on individual behavior rather than on zonally aggregated modal choice behavior. Central to these methods is the concept of trip disutility or the generalized cost of using different modes of transport.

3.2.1 Generalized cost of travel

The concept of generalized travel cost is derived from the notion that tripmaking has a number of characteristics which are unpleasant to tripmakers and that the magnitudes of this unpleasantness depend on the socioeconomic characteristics of the tripmaker. The generalized cost, or disutility of a trip may be estimated from:

$$z_{ij}^{m} = a_n x_{nij}^{m} + b_w u_w + c \quad n = 1, \cdots, n, \quad w = 1, \cdots, w, \tag{3.6}$$

where $z_{ij}{}^m$ = the generalized cost of travel between zones i and j by mode m

$x_{nij}{}^m$ = the nth characteristic of mode m between zones i and j which gives rise to the costs of travel by mode m

u_w = the wth socioeconomic characteristic of a tripmaker

c = constant

a_n, b_w = coefficients that reflect the relative contribution that system and tripmaker characteristics make to the generalized cost of travel

For a binary modal choice situation the following generalized cost difference may be calculated from Eq. (3.6)

$$z_{ij}^* = a_n \Delta x_{nij} + b_w u_w + c \qquad n = 1, \cdots, n \qquad w = 1, \cdots, w \tag{3.7}$$

where z_{ij}^* = the difference in generalized costs of traveling between zones i and j

Δx_{nij} = the difference in the nth system characteristic between the two modes

If tripmakers are stratified into a number of socioeconomic groups, then Eq. (3.7) may be expressed as:

$$z_{ij}^* = a_n \Delta x_{nij} + c \qquad n = 1, \cdots, n \tag{3.8}$$

If z_{ij}^* is the difference in cost between transit and car travel then c may be regarded as a mode penalty reflecting the inferior convenience and comfort of transit relative to the car.

Wilson and his associates [6] have reported the following generalized cost relationship from studies performed in England:

$$z_{ij}{}^m = 0.66 d_{ij}{}^m + 1.32 e_{ij}{}^m + a_3 s_{ij}{}^m \tag{3.9}$$

where $z_{ij}{}^m$ = the generalized cost of traveling between zones i and j by modes m in pence

$d_{ij}{}^m$ = the in-vehicle travel time in minutes by mode m between zones i and j

$e_{ij}{}^m$ = the excess travel time in minutes by mode m between zones i and j

$s_{ij}{}^m$ = the distance in miles by mode m between zones i and j

a_3 = 2.00 for car travel,
= 3.18 for train travel, and
= 3.06 for bus travel.

Archer and Shortreed [7] developed the following generalized cost functions for travel in Kitchener-Waterloo, Ontario:

$$z_{ij}^{*} = \left\{ f - \frac{1}{CO}(0.5p + ms_2) \right\} + tc \left\{ (e_1 - e_2) + 60\left(\frac{s_1}{v_1} - \frac{s_2}{v_2} \right) \right\} \tag{3.10}$$

where z_{ij}^{*} = transit-car generalized cost in dollars
f = transit fare
CO = average car occupancy
p = parking cost per day (in CBD only = \$0.50)
m = out-of-pocket car costs (\$0.04/mile)
s_1, s_2 = trip distances in miles for transit and car, respectively
tc = travel time cost (\$0.02/minute)
v_1, v_2 = network travel speeds in miles/hour for transit and car, respectively
e_1, e_2 = excess travel times in minutes for transit and car, respectively

It should be noted from Eq. (3.9) that excess travel time is valued at twice the value of in-vehicle travel time. A number of studies of the generalized cost of travel have noted this higher valuation of excess travel time by tripmakers.

It is useful to explore the relative importance of each of the components of the generalized costs of travel for two typical work trips within an urban area. Table 3.1 shows the costs of home-based work trips to a suburban location and to a CBD location. The costs have been estimated from the following generalized cost relationships:

Transit cost = 2 (in vehicle minutes) + 5 (excess time in minutes)
1 (fare) + 15

Table 3.1. Generalized costs of travel for two work trips

Item	Suburban trip		CBD trip	
	Transit	Car	Transit	Car
Trip length (miles)	5	5	5	5
Average speed (mph)	12	30	10	15
Trip time (min)	25	10	30	20
Excess time (min)	10	2	10	4
Time costs	\$1.00	\$0.30	\$1.10	\$0.60
Trip costs	.20	.20	.20	.20
Parking costs	–	–	–	1.00
Comfort costs	.15	–	.15	–
Total	\$1.35	\$0.50	\$1.45	\$1.80

Car cost = 2 (in vehicle minutes) + 5 (excess time in minutes)
+ 0.5 (parking charges)

The 15 cents in the transit-cost equation represents a mode penalty for transit reflecting its inferior comfort and convenience characteristics relative to the car.

For the suburban work trip the generalized cost of travel by transit is some 2.5 times higher than the cost by car. One would conclude that choice transit riders would not use public transport, a characteristic observed in most cities. For the CBD work trip the generalized cost of travel by car is higher than the transit cost because of the parking-charge component of the generalized cost. If the costs of travel by different modes are displayed in the manner shown in Table 3.1, then the transport planner is in a position to explore easily the effectiveness of different policies aimed at improving, say, public transport patronage.

3.2.2 Binary choice stochastic modal split models

A number of modal split models have been developed that estimate the probability of modal patronages given a knowledge of the generalized costs of travel for competing modes. Three types of mathematical concepts have been used to construct stochastic modal choice functions for individual behavior and these are discriminant analysis, probit analysis, and logit analysis.

The basic premise of the discriminant analysis approach is that the choice of tripmakers in an urban area may be classified into two groups according to the modes of transport used. The objective is to find a linear combination of explanatory variables, such as Eq. (3.6), in order that the distributions of the explanatory variables for the two groups of tripmakers possess little overlap.

Figure 3.5 illustrates the essence of this method graphically. The diagram shows the frequency distributions of the values of z for the users of the two transport modes being observed. The best estimate of the probability of a tripmaker with a given z magnitude, say z', of choosing mode 2, is the ratio of

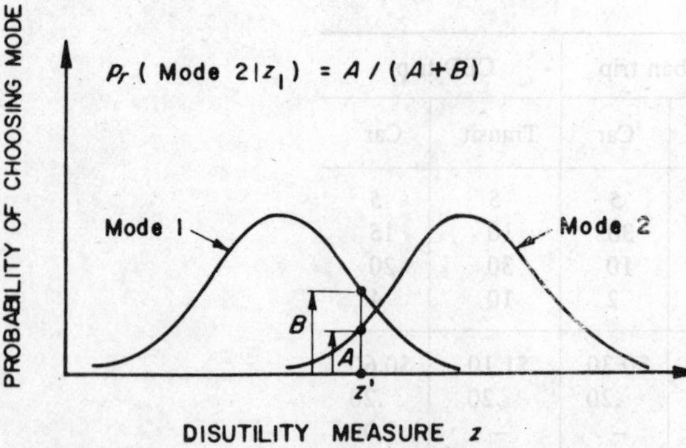

FIG. 3.5. Discriminant function method of estimating modal choice.

the ordinate of the mode 2 distribution at z' to the sum of the ordinates of the mode 1 and mode 2 ordinates at z'. The best discriminant function is the one that minimizes the number of misclassifications of tripmakers to their observed transport modes.

Quarmby [8] has used the discriminant analysis technique to develop the following relationship for estimating car-bus modal split for work trips to central London:

$$pr(c|z) = \frac{2.26e^{1.04(z-0.431)}}{1 + 2.26e^{1.04(z-0.431)}} \tag{3.11}$$

$pr(c|z)$ = the probability of choosing the car mode–given that the travel disutility is z

The disutility measure was developed as a function of differences in total travel time, excess travel time, costs and income-related variables.

Talvitie [9] has shown that if z is assumed to be normally distributed, the following expressions may be developed for estimating the probability of modal patronage in a binary choice situation:

$$pr(m = 1|ij) = \frac{e^{z+1n(x/y)}}{1 + e^{z+1n(x/y)}} \tag{3.12a}$$

$$pr(m = 2|ij) = \frac{1}{1 + e^{z+1n(x/y)}} \tag{3.12b}$$

where $pr(m|ij)$ = the probability that an individual will use mode m given that the trip is between zones i and j

x,y = the a priori probabilities of membership in groups $m = 1$ and $m = 2$, respectively

Warner [10], Lisco [11], and Lave [12] have developed binary modal choice models using a statistical analysis technique known as *probit analysis.* This concept is based on the premise that as choice tripmakers are subjected to changing magnitudes of relative trip costs, the proportion of the tripmakers that respond by choosing a particular mode of transport will follow the type of relationship illustrated in Fig. 3.6. This diagram is a hypothetical representation of the proportions of tripmakers that would use private cars as the difference in the generalized cost of using public transport and car transport varied.

Lave [12] has developed the following equation for estimating the probability of bus-car modal patronage from a set of 1956 data for the Chicago area using probit analysis:

$$Y = -2.08 + 0.00759kW\Delta T + 0.0186\Delta C$$

$$-0.0254IDC_c + 0.0255A \tag{3.13}$$

$$R^2 = 0.379$$

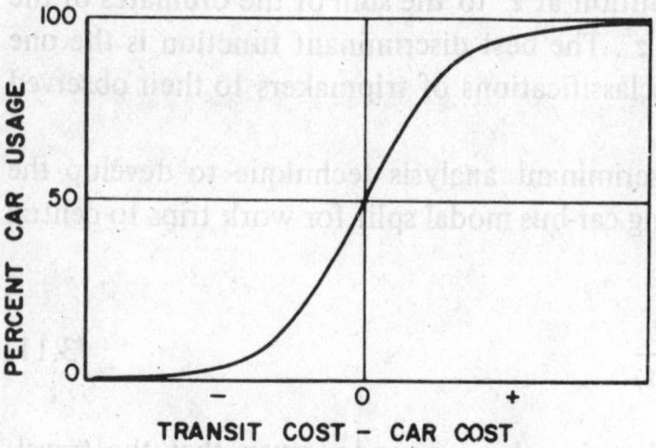

FIG. 3.6. Probit-type modal split function.

where Y = binary variable with positive magnitudes denoting transit riders and negative magnitudes denoting car riders

$kW\Delta T$ = the time difference between the modes multiplied by the tripmaker's wage rate and his marginal preference for leisure time

IDC_c = a binary valued comfort variable multiplied by income and trip distance

A = age of tripmaker

Stopher [13] has used a technique known as *logit analysis* to construct a stochastic modal split function. The logit model has the following form:

$$pr(m = 1|ij) = \frac{e^{z_{ij}^*}}{1 + e^{z_{ij}^*}} \tag{3.14a}$$

$$pr(m = 2|ij) = \frac{1}{1 + e^{z_{ij}^*}} \tag{3.14b}$$

where z_{ij}^* = some function of the generalized costs of travel by modes $m = 1$ and $m = 2$

In Eq. (3.7), z_{ij}^* has been defined as a difference in generalized costs; but z_{ij}^* might also be defined as ratios of generalized costs or as logarithms of generalized cost ratios.

Stopher [13] has proposed a modal split model of the following form:

$$pr(m = c) = a(c_1 - c_2) + b(t_2 - t_1) + d \tag{3.15}$$

where $pr(m = c)$ = the probability of using a car for tripmaking

c_1, c_2 = the out-of-pocket costs of travel by car and public transport, respectively

t_1, t_2 = the travel times by car and public transport, respectively

a, b = parameters determined empirically with the ratio b/a representing the implied value of travel time

Stopher has reported the following equations for trips to two employment locations in central London:

$$pr(m = c) = 0.0076(c_1 - c_2) + 0.00529(t_2 - t_1) + 0.331 \qquad (3.16)$$

$$pr(m = c) = 0.0057(c_1 - c_2) + 0.00599\,(t_2 - t_1) + 0.291 \qquad (3.17)$$

Stopher has pointed out that the linear model in Eq. (3.15) can yield probabilities greater than 1 or less than 0 for very large magnitudes of the cost and time differences. Stopher has shown that the equation of the logistic curve given in Eq. (3.14a) may be transformed as follows:

$$\log_e \left[\frac{pr(m = c)}{1 - pr(m = c)}\right] \quad z^* = a'(c_1 - c_2) + b'(t_2 - t_1) + d' \qquad (3.18)$$

If it is assumed that the value of time remains unaltered in this transformation, that is $b'/a' = b/a$, then $a' = \log_e\,[d/(1 - d)]$. Figure 3.7 shows the linear and logistic models developed by Stopher for travel to the County Hall in London by employees.

It should be noted that each of the models produce S-shaped relationships of the type illustrated in Fig. 3.6. Both Talvitie [9] and Stopher and Lavender [14] have conducted comparative studies of these three methods.

Talvitie concluded from his study that: "The methods of estimation, commonly used in probabilistic modal choice models, probit, logit, and discriminant analyses, all yielded comparable results. Any of them can be used with equal success."

On the other hand, Stopher and Lavender concluded from their study that: "It was found that discriminant analysis was clearly inferior to either probit or logit

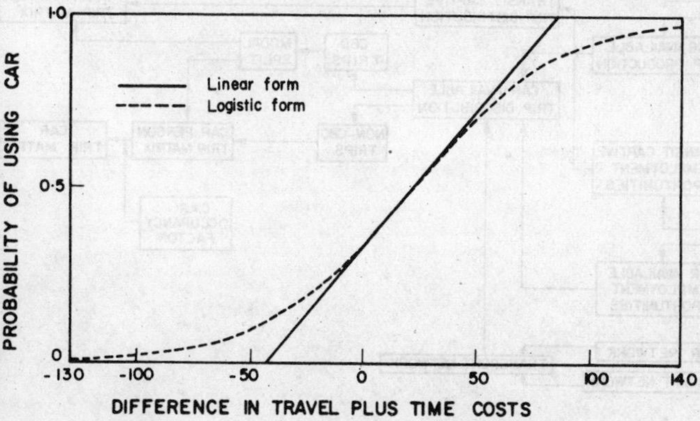

FIG. 3.7. Stopher's linear and logistic modal split models.

analysis. However, there was no distinction between probit and logit, based upon the statistics reported here. Since probit analysis requires a more time-consuming calibration procedure than logit analysis, and yields a more cumbersome model, the authors recommend that logit analysis be considered as the preferred technique for these models." The conclusions of these comparative analyses must be qualified because of the limited amount of data available to the investigators.

3.3 TWO-STAGE MODAL SPLIT MODELS

Vandertol [15] and his associates [16] have developed a simple two-stage modal split model which recognizes explicitly the existence of both captive and of choice transit riders. The broad flow of activities embodied in this modal split model are shown in Fig. 3.8. The model proceeds by first identifying both the production and attraction trip ends of transit captives and choice transit riders separately. The two groups of tripmakers are then distributed from origins to destinations. The choice transit riders are then split between transit and car according to a choice modal split model which reflects the relative characteristics of the trip by transit and the trip by car.

Figure 3.9 illustrates a general relationship that has been developed and that relates the proportion of captive and choice transit riders in an urban area to the population of the area [17]. The principal reason for the increase in transit ridership of choice riders in the very large cities is that it is only in these cities that efficient and comprehensive transit systems exist. It is interesting to note

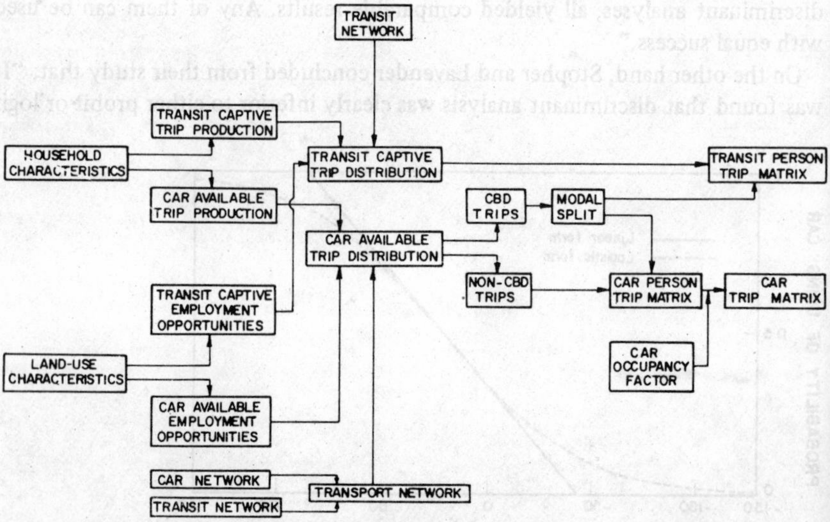

FIG. 3.8 Flow diagram for two-stage modal split model.

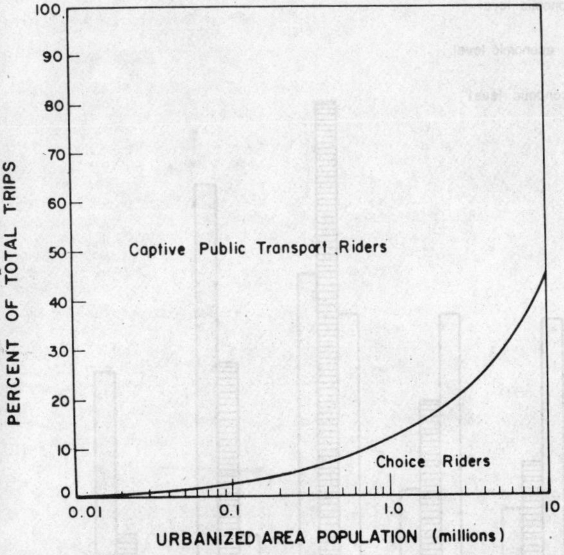

FIG. 3.9. Proportions of captive and choice transit riders vs. population of urban area.

from Fig. 3.9 that even in cities within the 1- to 2-million population range, captive riders represent 85 to 95 percent of the transit ridership.

In most cities, the transit captive is severely restricted in the choice of both household and employment locations. Figure 1.3 has provided some evidence of the extent to which transit captives are limited in their choice of household and employment locations in Metropolitan Toronto. Studies in a number of cities have shown that the trip ends of transit captives tend to be clustered in zones that are well served by public transport. The challenge in developing a two-stage modal split model is to formulate a technique that uses information normally available in urban areas and that may be forecast readily for future years.

Zonal work-trip productions disaggregated by captive and choice transit riders may be estimated from:

$$p_i{}^q = h_i tp^q \tag{3.19}$$

where $p_i{}^q$ = the number of work trips produced in zone i by type q tripmakers, q = 1 = captive transit rider, q = 2 = choice transit rider

h_i = the number of households in zone i

tp^q = the work-trip production rate for tripmaker group q which is a function of the economic status of a zone and the average number of employees per household

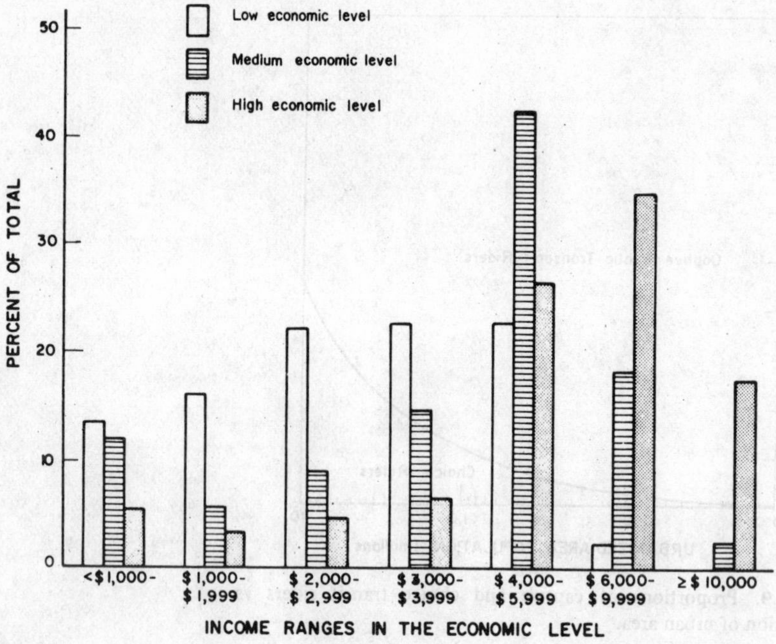

FIG. 3.10. Income distributions of males–Hamilton, Ontario.

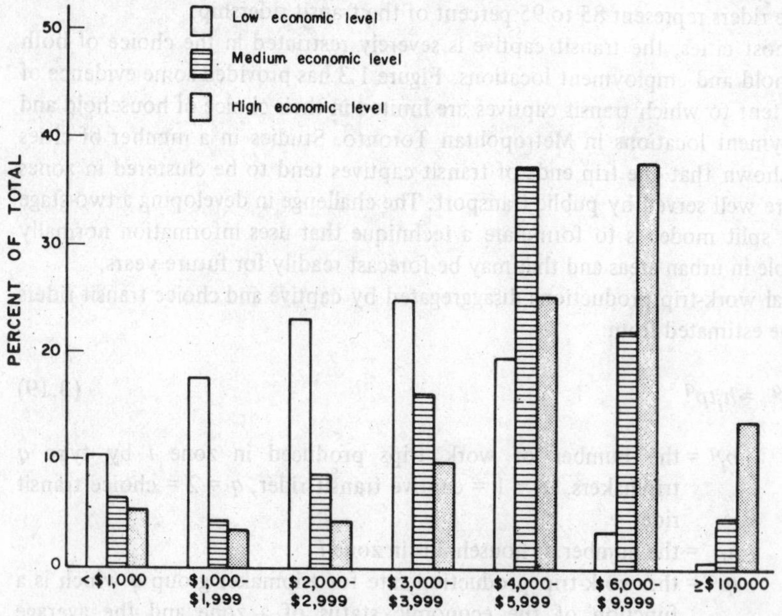

FIG. 3.11. Income distributions of males–Ottawa, Ontario.

Zones may be classified into broad economic classes depending on the income distribution of the heads of households within a zone. Figures 3.10 and 3.11 show the income distributions of males in three traffic analysis zones from the cities of Hamilton and Ottawa, Ontario. The three traffic analysis zones in each city were judged as belonging to three broad groups of low, middle and high economic levels. In many of the earlier modal split models, the economic status of a zone was expressed as an average zonal income which in most Canadian cities is not a sufficiently sensitive indicator. For the 1961 income information that is summarized in Figs. 3.10 and 3.11, the income ranges of less than $3,000, $3-6,000, and greater than $6,000 appear to be important in describing the income distributions for each of the three economic levels mentioned previously. Using the income distribution available for each of the economic levels from these two cities of approximately the same population size, the characteristic income distributions shown in Table 3.2 were derived.

Vandertol used travel data collected in the *Hamilton Area Transportation Plan* [18] to establish home-based work-trip production rates for the two groups of tripmakers. Traffic analysis zones were grouped into one of the three economic levels mentioned above and the work-trip production curves shown in Fig. 3.12 established. The transit captive curves are not particularly reliable because of the small sample size of transit captives available from this study. The choice-rider trip-production curves are much more regular and illustrate the variation in trip-production rates with changes in zonal economic status and with changes in the number of employees per household. Sample sizes required to produce reliable trip rates in a category analysis matrix of this type have been discussed in Chapter 2.

The type of employment available in a zone influences the income distribution of the jobs in that zone. The industry classifications used by Vandertol are shown in Table 3.3 where these classifications have been aggregated from Statistics Canada industry classifications. Figure 3.13 shows the 1961 income distributions for each of the eight most important occupation categories in Hamilton. Vandertol found that the income distributions shown in Fig. 3.13

Table 3.2. Characteristic income distributions

Income range	Income level classification of zone		
	Low	Medium	High
	Percent		
< $3,000	60–35	30–10	20–0
$3,000–6,000	40–50	50–60	40–30
> $6,000	0–15	20–30	40–70

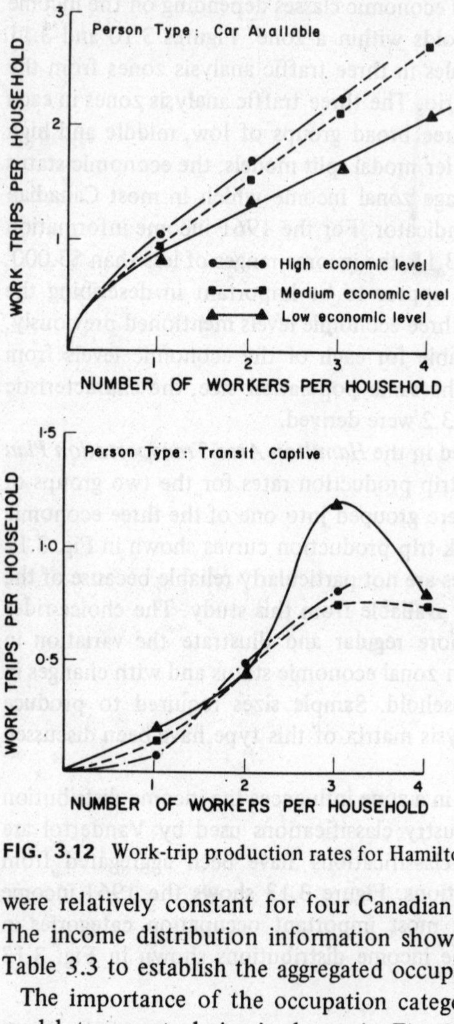

FIG. 3.12 Work-trip production rates for Hamilton, Ontario.

were relatively constant for four Canadian cities of a size similar to Hamilton. The income distribution information shown in Fig. 3.13 was used along with Table 3.3 to establish the aggregated occupation categories shown in Table 3.4.

The importance of the occupation category as a predictor of attraction end modal transport choice is shown in Fig. 3.14. In this diagram, the modes of transport used by tripmakers grouped into the aggregated occupation categories of Table 3.4 are illustrated. It should be noted from Fig. 3.14 that almost twice as many persons in the clerical-sales occupations are captive to public transport as in the other occupation categories.

Vandertol has suggested that the occupation category distribution of each industry type may be expressed in terms of a tripmaker probability vector of the following type:

$$[pr^q] = [pr_1{}^q, pr_2{}^q, \cdots, pr_c{}^q] \tag{3.20}$$

where $pr_c q$ = the probability of a person with a job in occupation category c being of tripmaker type $q, q = 1$ = transit captive, $q = 2$ = choice rider; $c = 1$ = primary occupation category, $c = 2$ = professional-managerial occupation category, $c = 3$ = clerical-sales occupation category, $c = 4$ = labor-service occupation category.

Table 3.5 shows the distribution of occupation categories for each industry type observed in the 1961 Canada census. It should be noted from this table that there is about a 14 percent chance of a manufacturing industry employee being in the clerical-sales occupation category and that this probability increases to 49 percent for commercial establishments.

The work trips attracted to each zone j by tripmaker type q may be estimated from:

$$a_j^q = [pr_c^q]\ [r_{ct}]\ [e_{tj}] \tag{3.21}$$

where a_j^q = the number of work trips of type q tripmaker attracted to zone j

$[pr_c^q]$ = a row vector of the probability of tripmaker type q being in occupation category type c

$[r_{ct}]$ = a $c \times t$ matrix of the probabilities of an occupation category c being within an industry type t

$[e_{tj}]$ = a $t \times j$ matrix of the number of jobs within each industry type t in each zone j

Table 3.3. Aggregation of the Statistics Canada industry types

Industry no.	Industry type used in model	Statistics Canada industry type
1	Primary	1. Agriculture 2. Forestry 3. Fishing and trapping 4. Mines, quarries, and oil wells
2	Manufacturing	1. Manufacturing
3	Service	1. Community, business, and personal service 2. Finance, insurance, and real estate 3. Public administration and defense 4. Transportation, communication, and other utilities
4	Commercial (retail)	1. Trade
5	Other	1. Construction 2. Unspecified or undefined

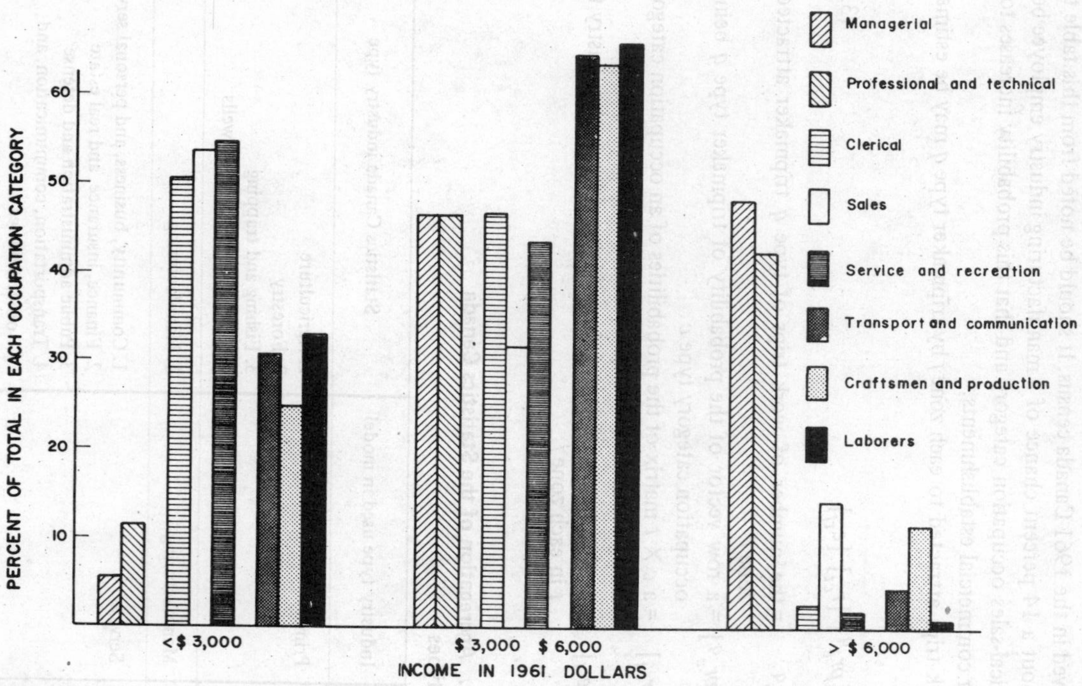

FIG. 3.13. Relationship between income and occupation for Hamilton, Ontario.

Table 3.4. Aggregation of the Statistics Canada occupation categories

Occupation no.	Occupation category used in model	Statistics Canada occupation categories
1	Primary	1. Farmers, farm workers 2. Loggers, related workers 3. Fishermen, trappers, hunters 4. Miners, quarrymen, related workers
2	Professional-managerial	1. Managerial 2. Professional, technical
3	Clerical-sales	1. Clerical 2. Sales 3. Service, recreation
4	Labor-service	1. Transport, communication 2. Craftsmen, production process 3. Laborers

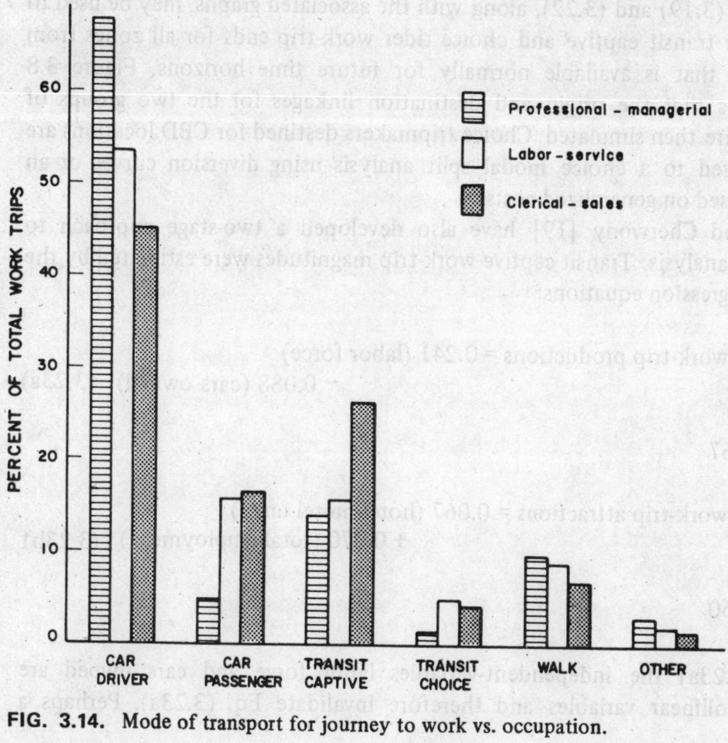

FIG. 3.14. Mode of transport for journey to work vs. occupation.

Table 3.5. Occupation-industry matrix

Occupation type	Industry type				
	Primary	Manufacturing	Service	Commercial	Other
Primary	0.692	0.009	0.009	0.003	0.008
Professional-managerial	0.058	0.102	0.244	0.126	0.053
Clerical-sales	0.066	0.189	0.508	0.558	0.059
Labor-service	0.184	0.700	0.239	0.313	0.880

Source: 1961 Canada census.

The information contained in Fig. 3.14 and Table 3.5 may be substituted into Eq. (3.21) to yield the following:

$$a_j^{\,1} = [0.14 \;\; 0.26 \;\; 0.16] \begin{bmatrix} 0.10 & 0.20 & 0.11 & 0.11 \\ 0.14 & 0.56 & 0.49 & 0.11 \\ 0.76 & 0.24 & 0.40 & 0.78 \end{bmatrix} [e_{tj}]$$

$$= [0.17 \;\; 0.21 \;\; 0.21 \;\; 0.17] \;\; [e_{tj}] \qquad (3.22)$$

Equations (3.19) and (3.22), along with the associated graphs, may be used to estimate the transit captive and choice rider work-trip ends for all zones from information that is available normally for future time horizons. Figure 3.8 demonstrates that the origin and destination linkages for the two groups of tripmakers are then simulated. Choice tripmakers destined for CBD locations are then subjected to a choice modal split analysis using diversion curves or an approach based on generalized costs.

Ferreri and Cherwony [19] have also developed a two-stage approach to modal split analysis. Transit captive work-trip magnitudes were estimated by the following regression equations:

$$\text{Captive work-trip productions} = 0.241\,(\text{labor force}) - 0.088\,(\text{cars owned}) \qquad (3.23a)$$

$$R^2 = 0.67$$

$$\text{Captive work-trip attractions} = 0.067\,(\text{hotel-motel units}) + 0.070\,(\text{total employment}) \qquad (3.23b)$$

$$R^2 = 0.60$$

In Eq. (3.23a) the independent-variables labor force and cars owned are probably collinear variables and therefore invalidate Eq. (3.23a). Perhaps a more-meaningful independent variable would have been labor force minus cars owned, or one in which car ownership was expressed as the average number of cars per household. As the simple correlation matrix has not been provided in Ref. [19] more-definitive statements about the above equations cannot be advanced.

Figure 3.15 shows the choice modal split relationship developed by Ferreri and Cherwony [19]. In this diagram the percentage of choice riders using transit *between an origin and destination pair* is plotted against the transit-to-car travel time ratio for two different employment densities. This diagram illustrates that the increased public-transport patronage is no doubt due to the significant parking charges levied in the zones with higher employment densities. The effect of parking charges on modal patronage has been illustrated in Table 3.1.

Morrall and Morasch [20] have also developed a two-stage modal split model based on the captive and choice transit rider dichotomy for Calgary, Alberta. The following captive transit work-trip production and attraction equations were developed

$$\text{A.M. peak transit captive work trip} = -45.3 + 0.097\,(\text{households}) \qquad (3.24a)$$

$R^2 = 0.77$

$$\text{A. M. peak transit captive work-trip productions to CBD} = -39.0 + 0.082\,(\text{households}) \qquad (3.24b)$$

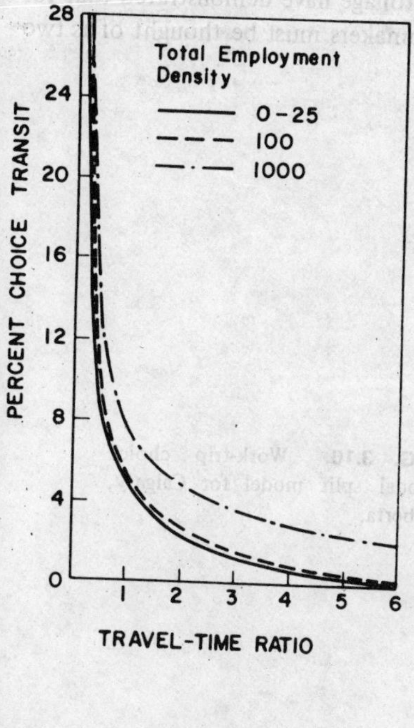

FIG. 3.15. Work-trip choice modal split model for Miami, Florida.

$R^2 = 0.64$

A. M. peak transit captive work-trip attractions

$$= -99.2 + 0.115\,(\text{employment}) \quad (3.24c)$$

$R^2 = 0.94$

Figure 3.16 shows the choice modal split relationship developed by Morrall and Morasch for trips to the Calgary CBD for the 7:00 A.M.-9:00 A.M. peak period. The similarity between the Calgary diversion curve and the Miami curve shown in Fig. 3.15 should be noted. The broken line shown in Fig. 3.15 is the diversion curve developed by Morrall and Morasch for all transit destinations. Comparison of this diversion curve with the curve for trips destined to the CBD also illustrates the influence of parking charges on choice-rider public-transport patronage.

Figure 3.17 shows the 1971 relationship developed by Morrall and Morasch for choice riders alone and for choice and captive transit riders combined. This diagram illustrates clearly the differences in sensitivity to changes in transport system variables that are obtained when choice transit riders are treated separately.

SUMMARY

Many studies of urban-transport-mode patronage have demonstrated that for the purposes of modal choice estimation tripmakers must be thought of as two

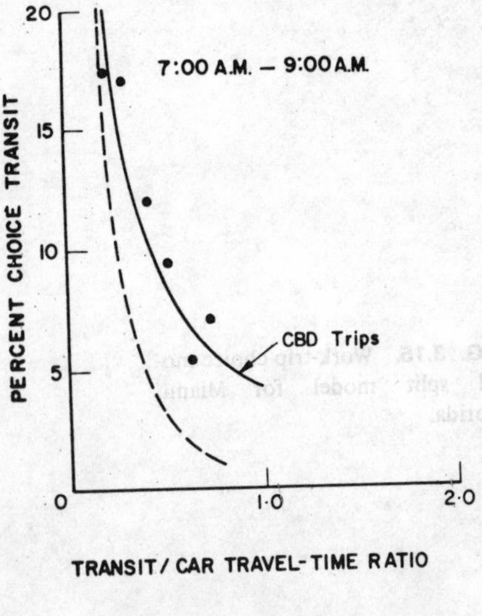

FIG. 3.16. Work-trip choice modal split model for Calgary, Alberta.

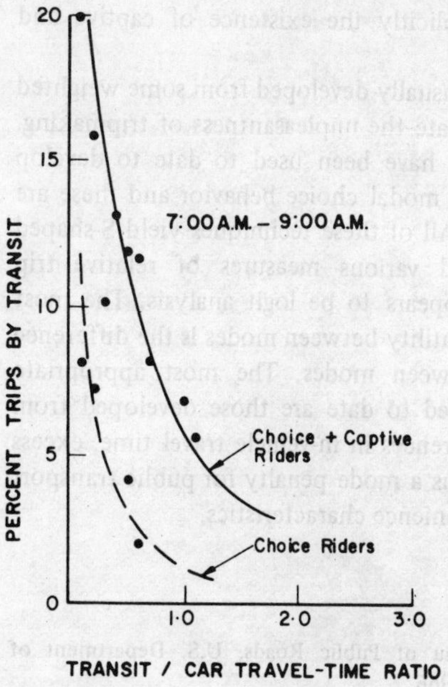

FIG. 3.17. Work-trip modal split models–Calgary, Alberta, 1971.

separate groups which have been referred to in this chapter as *captive transit riders* and *choice transit riders*. Captive transit riders are defined as those tripmakers who do not have access to a car for the particular trip being studied. Choice transit riders are defined as those tripmakers who may choose freely between public transport and priva e car for a particular journey.

Captive or choice status is governed by the income, sex, and age of tripmakers. In making modal transport choice decisions, tripmakers are influenced by the relative service properties of competing transport modes such as in-vehicle travel times, excess travel times, out-of-pocket costs and the overall convenience of travel.

The earlier modal split models were of two types and have been referred to as *trip-end* and *trip-interchange models*. Trip-end models are used between the trip-generation and trip-distribution phases while the trip interchange-type models are used between the trip-distribution and traffic-assignment phases. These earlier modal split models did not distinguish clearly between the captive and choice transit riders. Trip-end-type modal split models tend to emphasize captive riders while trip-interchange models focus principally on choice riders.

A number of observers have pointed to the lack of sensitivity of the earlier modal split models as well as to the absence of any sound behavioral basis to the models. An improved basis for modal split estimation is provided by the concept of the generalized cost of travel in combination with a binary choice stochastic modal split model. More-sensitive modal split models are provided by two-stage modal split models which recognize explicitly the existence of captive and choice transit riders.

Generalized travel-cost relationships are usually developed from some weighted linear combination of the factors that create the unpleasantness of tripmaking. Three different mathematical techniques have been used to date to develop stochastic models of individual transport modal choice behavior and these are discriminant, probit, and logit analyses. All of these techniques yield S-shaped relations between modal patronage and various measures of relative trip disutility. The most useful technique appears to be logit analysis. The most significant measure of the relative trip disutility between modes is the difference in the generalized costs of travel between modes. The most appropriate generalized travel cost functions developed to date are those developed from some weighted combination of the differences in in-vehicle travel time, excess travel time, out-of-pocket travel costs, plus a mode penalty for public transport that reflects its inferior comfort and convenience characteristics.

REFERENCES

1. Fertal, M. J., et al., *Modal Split,* Bureau of Public Roads, U.S. Department of Commerce, Washington, D.C., December, 1966.
2. Weiner, E., *A Modal Split Model for Southeastern Wisconsin,* Technical Record, vol. II, no. 6, Southeastern Wisconsin Regional Planning Commission, August-September, 1966.
3. Hill, D. M., and H. G. Voncube, *Development of a Model for Forecasting Travel Mode Choice in Urban Areas,* Highway Research Record No. 38, Highway Research Board, Washington, D.C., 1964.
4. Metropolitan Toronto and Region Transportation Study, *Calibration of a Regional Traffic Prediction Model for the A.M. Peak Period,* Toronto, Ontario, 1967.
5. Dean, T. B., et al., *Application of a Modal Split Model to Travel Estimates for the Washington Area,* Highway Research Record No. 38, Highway Research Board, Washington, D.C., 1964.
6. Wilson, A. G., et al., "Calibration and Testing of the SELNEC Transport Model," *Regional Studies,* vol. 3, no. 3, 1969.
7. Archer, E., and J. H. Shortreed, *Potential Demands for Demand Scheduled Buses,* Highway Research Record No. 367, Highway Research Board, Washington, D.C., 1971.
8. Quarmby, D. A., "Choice of Travel Model for the Journey to Work," *Journal of Transport Economics and Policy,* vol 1, pp. 273–314, 1967.
9. Talvitie, A., *Comparison of Probabilistic Modal-Choice Models: Estimation Methods and System Inputs,* Highway Research Record No. 392, Highway Research Board, Washington, D.C., 1972.
10. Warner, S. L., *Stochastic Choice of Mode in Urban Travel: A Study in Binary Choice,* Northwestern University Press, Evanston, Illinois, 1962.
11. Lisco, T. E., *The Value of Commuters' Travel Times: A Study in Urban Transportation,* Ph.D. dissertation, Department of Economics, University of Chicago, Chicago, Illinois, 1967.
12. Lave, C. A., "A Behavioural Approach to Modal Split Forecasting," *Transportation Research,* vol. 3, pp. 463–480, 1969.

13. Stopher, P. R., *A Probability Model of Travel Mode Choice for the Journey to Work,* Highway Research Record No. 283, Highway Research Board, Washington, D.C., 1969.
14. Stopher P. R., and J. O. Lavender, *Disaggregate, Behavioural Travel Demand Models: Empirical Tests of Three Hypotheses,* Proceedings, Transportation Research Forum, Oxford, Indiana, pp. 321–336, 1972.
15. Vandertol, A., *Transit Usage Estimates from an Urban Travel Demand Model,* M. A. Sc. thesis, Department of Civil Engineering, University of Waterloo, Waterloo, Ontario, 1971.
16. Vandertol, A., B. G. Hutchinson, and J. H. Shortreed, *Two Stage Modal Split Models,* Paper submitted to American Society of Civil Engineers, New York, March, 1973.
17. Wilbur Smith and Associates, *Transportation and Parking for Tomorrow's Cities,* Automobile Manufacturers Association, Detroit, Michigan, 1966.
18. Hamilton Area Transportation Study, *Hamilton Area Transportation Plan,* Hamilton, Ontario, 1963.
19. Ferreri, M. G., and W. Cherwony, *Choice and Captive Modal Split Models,* Highway Research Record No. 392, Highway Research Board, Washington, D.C., 1972.
20. Morrall, J. F., and L. H. Morasch, *Transit Planning Models for Calgary,* Paper presented at Canadian Transportation Research Forum, April, 1973.

4 TRAVEL-DEMAND FORECASTING: TRIP-DISTRIBUTION ANALYSIS

The third phase of the travel-demand forecasting process outlined in Chap. 1 has been identified as trip-distribution analysis. The purpose of the trip-distribution analysis phase is to develop a procedure that synthesizes the trip linkages between traffic zones for both transit captive and choice tripmakers. Figures 1.12 and 1.13 have shown that at the beginning of this phase of the transport-analysis process, the zonal trip ends for both groups of tripmakers are available. Figure 1.12 has shown also that a knowledge of the properties of the alternative horizon-year transport networks is required for the trip-distribution analysis phase. From this stage in the transport-planning process, the results of the analyses are specific to a particular transport system being contemplated for the horizon year. Trip distribution and the subsequent analysis phases correspond to the solution-analysis phase identified in Fig. 1.5.

Figure 4.1 illustrates in a general way the properties of the trip-distribution matrices that are synthesized during this phase of the travel-analysis process. Trip-distribution matrices are required for the two groups of tripmakers which satisfy the following constraint equations:

$$p_i^q = \sum_j t_{ij}^q \tag{4.1}$$

$$a_j^q = \sum_i t_{ij}^q \tag{4.2}$$

where p_i^q = the number of trips produced in zone i by type q tripmakers that have been estimated for a given land-use allocation, trip generation, and captive modal split analyses

a_j^q = the number of trips attracted to zone j by type q tripmakers that have been estimated during the previous phases, and

t_{ij}^q = the number of trips produced in zone i and attracted to zone j by type q tripmakers

Several methods for synthesizing horizon-year trip-distribution matrices have been developed and used in urban transport-planning studies. In many of the earlier studies, growth-factor techniques were used. This chapter describes briefly the Fratar growth-factor procedure. The majority of urban transport-planning studies performed during the past 20 years have used a version of the gravity model. The second part of this chapter describes the gravity model and its calibration in some depth. The final parts of the chapter

ORIGIN ZONES	DESTINATION ZONES 1	2	3			n	Σ
1	t_{11}	t_{12}	t_{13}			t_{1n}	p_1
2	t_{21}	t_{22}				t_{2n}	p_2
3	t_{31}	t_{32}					p_3
n	t_{n1}					t_{nn}	p_n
Σ	a_1	a_2	a_3			a_n	

Σ_{columns} = Trip productions Σ_{rows} = Trip attractions

FIG. 4.1. Properties required of synthesized trip-distribution matrices.

describe the intervening and competing opportunities trip-distribution models as well as an approach based on the transportation problem formulation of linear programming.

4.1 FRATAR GROWTH-FACTOR METHOD

The Fratar growth-factor method is described in detail in references [1] and [2], while other growth-factor techniques are described in Ref. [3]. The Fratar growth-factor method uses the following expression to synthesize horizon-year trip-interchange magnitudes:

$$t_{ij}^{h} = t_{ij}^{b} f_i f_j \left(\frac{l_i + l_j}{2} \right) \tag{4.3}$$

where t_{ij}^h = the number of vehicle trips between zones i and j in the horizon year

t_{ij}^b = the number of vehicle trips between zones i and j observed in the base year

f_i, f_j = the growth factors for zones i and j which reflect the growth in trip productions and trip attractions expected between the base and horizon years where

$$f_i = p_i^h / p_i^b \text{ and } f_j = a_j^h / a_j^b$$

l_i, l_j = the locational factors where

$$l_i = p_i^b \Big/ \sum_{j=1}^{n} t_{ij}^b f_j \text{ (and } l_j \text{ is derived from a similar expression)}$$

The basic premise of the Fratar method defined in Eq. (4.3) is that the distribution of horizon-year trips from a zone is proportional to the base-year trip-distribution pattern modified by the growth factors of the zones under consideration. The locational factors defined above are the reciprocals of the average attracting forces of all of the surrounding zones.

If the constraint equations (4.1) and (4.2) are violated by a trip-interchange matrix synthesized by Eq. (4.3), then the procedure must be reiterated using the following expressions:

$$t_{ij}^{h*} = t_{ij}^{b*} f_i^* f_j^* \left(\frac{l_i^* + l_j^*}{2} \right)$$

$$f_i^* = \frac{p_i^h}{\sum_j t_{ij}^h} \qquad f_j^* = \frac{a_j^h}{\sum_i t_{ij}^h} \tag{4.4}$$

$$L_i^* = \sum_{j=1}^{n} \frac{t_{ij}{}^b}{\sum\limits_{j=1}^{n} (t_{ij}{}^b f_j^*)}$$

$$L_j^* = \sum_{i=1}^{n} \frac{t_{ij}{}^b}{\sum\limits_{i=1}^{n} (t_{ij}{}^b f_i^*)} \qquad (4.4)\ (\textit{Cont'd.})$$

where the * identifies the new parameters to be used in successive iterations of the trip distribution equations until f_i^* and f_j^* approach 1; or, in other words, the constraint equations (4.1) and (4.2) are satisfied when f_i^* and f_j^* are both equal to 1.

The Fratar growth-factor technique is not used normally for estimating intraurban trip interchanges except for smaller cities or for cities in which significant changes in urban structure are not expected. The technique is used frequently to estimate future through trips in urban studies and for extrapolating origin-destination matrices over short time horizons of up to 5 years. A number of North American highway departments use the Fratar method for estimating both future intercity highway travel and future rural highway demands. The principal deficiency of the technique for estimating intraurban travel demands is that it is not sensitive to changes in the properties of transport networks. In addition, a basic premise of the procedure is that future urban trip interchanges will be simply an extrapolation of the existing trip patterns. Also, changes in the behavior of tripmakers in forming linkages between various types of land-based activities cannot be reflected in this trip-distribution model.

4.2 STOCHASTIC TRIP-DISTRIBUTION MODELS

Three trip-distribution models have been developed and used in urban transport studies that may be classified as stochastic trip-distribution models; these are the gravity model, the intervening-opportunities model, and the competing-opportunities model. The basic structure of these models may be expressed in the following way:

$$T = PB \qquad (4.5)$$

where $T = n \times n$ square matrix of the trip interchanges t_{ij}
$P = n \times n$ diagonal matrix of the zone specific trip productions
$B = n \times n$ square matrix of the probabilities b_{ij} that a trip produced in zone i will be attracted to zone j

If the trip-interchange matrix T is to satisfy the constraint equations (4.1) and (4.2), then the following conditions must be satisfied:

$$\sum_{j} b_{ij} = 1.0 \tag{4.6}$$

$$A = PB \tag{4.7}$$

where $A = 1 \times n$ matrix of trip attractions
$P = 1 \times n$ matrix of trip productions

Consider the following four-zone example:

$$T = \begin{bmatrix} 100 & \cdots & \cdots & \cdots \\ \cdots & 150 & \cdots & \cdots \\ \cdots & \cdots & 50 & \cdots \\ \cdots & \cdots & \cdots & 200 \end{bmatrix} \begin{bmatrix} .4 & .3 & .2 & .1 \\ .2 & .4 & .2 & .2 \\ .1 & .2 & .4 & .3 \\ .2 & .2 & .2 & .4 \end{bmatrix} = \begin{bmatrix} 40 & 30 & 20 & 10 \\ 30 & 60 & 30 & 30 \\ 5 & 10 & 20 & 15 \\ 40 & 40 & 40 & 80 \end{bmatrix}$$

$$A = \begin{bmatrix} 100 & 150 & 50 & 200 \end{bmatrix} \begin{bmatrix} .4 & .3 & .2 & .1 \\ .2 & .4 & .2 & .2 \\ .1 & .2 & .4 & .3 \\ .2 & .2 & .2 & .4 \end{bmatrix} = \begin{bmatrix} 115 & 140 & 110 & 135 \end{bmatrix}$$

Normally the trip productions and trip attractions are estimated exogenously to the models in the prior phases of the analysis process. The trip-distribution models provide procedures for estimating the elements of the B matrix. The procedures differ from each other in the way in which these elements are estimated from empirical information. The calibration techniques used for each of the models are discussed in subsequent sections of this chapter.

4.3 THE GRAVITY MODEL

The gravity model is an heuristically derived expression for synthesizing trip interchanges. The basic premise of the gravity model used in urban transport studies is that the trip-interchange magnitude between two zones i and j is directly proportional to the number of trips produced in zone i, the number of trips attracted to zone j, and inversely proportional to some function of the spatial separation of the two zones. This premise may be expressed algebraically as:

$$t_{ij} \alpha p_i a_j \left[\frac{1}{f(d_{ij})} \right] \tag{4.8}$$

where the terms have all been defined previously.

The expression (4.8) may be rewritten in the following way where the denominator may be regarded as the constant of proportionality:

$$t_{ij} = p_i \frac{a_j f_{ij}}{\sum_j a_j f_{ij}} \tag{4.9}$$

where f_{ij} = some function of the spatial separation of zones, d_{ij}, and referred to normally as the *travel-time factor function,* and sometimes called the *friction factor.*

The travel-time factor may be regarded as a measure of the deterrence that travel time has on tripmaking patterns.

The form of the gravity model defined in Eq. (4.9) will yield a trip-interchange matrix that satisfies the constraint equation (4.1) but which will not necessarily satisfy the constraint equation (4.2). The following may be developed from Eq. (4.9) to show that Eq. (4.1) is satisfied by (4.9):

$$b_{ij} = \frac{a_j f_{ij}}{\sum_j a_j f_{ij}}$$

$$\sum_j b_{ij} = \frac{\sum_j a_j f_{ij}}{\sum_j a_j f_{ij}} = 1.0$$

$$\sum_j t_{ij} = \sum_j p_i b_{ij} = p_i \sum_j b_{ij} = p_i$$

In most applications of the gravity model the constraint equation (4.2) is satisfied by the following iterative procedure:

$$a_j^{*2} = a_j \frac{a_j^{*1}}{\sum_i t_{ij}} \tag{4.10}$$

where a_j^* = the trip-attraction magnitudes substituted into Eq. (4.9) for successive iterations of the model.

In using Eq. (4.9) to estimate future trip interchanges, the problem is to establish the nature of the function which relates the travel-time factor f_{ij} to the measure of spatial separation d_{ij}. Travel time is normally used as the measure of spatial separation of zones in the gravity model and the following functional forms have been used to derive the travel-time-factor magnitudes from travel times:

$$f_{ij} = \text{some polynomial function of } d_{ij} \tag{4.11a}$$

$$f_{ij} = \exp(-w_{ij} d_{ij}) \tag{4.11b}$$

$$f_{ij} = \exp(-n_{ij} \log d_{ij}) = d_{ij}^{-n_{ij}} \tag{4.11c}$$

$$f_{ij} = \exp(-w_{ij}d_{ij})d_{ij}^{-1} \tag{4.11d}$$

Figure 4.2 illustrates the nature of the functional forms defined in Eqs. (4.11a)-(4.11d). These functional forms are normally assumed to be averages of the influence of travel time on the travel-time factor for the entire study area. It should be noted that Eqs. (4.11b)-(4.11d) admit the possibility that the parameters n and w may be i-j pair specific. In some applications of the gravity model the parameters are assumed to be row specific. The techniques which may be used to estimate the various functional forms defined previously are described later in this section.

4.3.1 Formal derivation of the gravity model

Wilson [4] has advanced an approach to the construction of spatial interaction models, such as the gravity model, that is based on the entropy-maximization principle of information theory. The entropy-maximization approach attempts to provide a rationale for describing the state of a system when the analyst has limited information that describes the macroscopic behavior of the system.

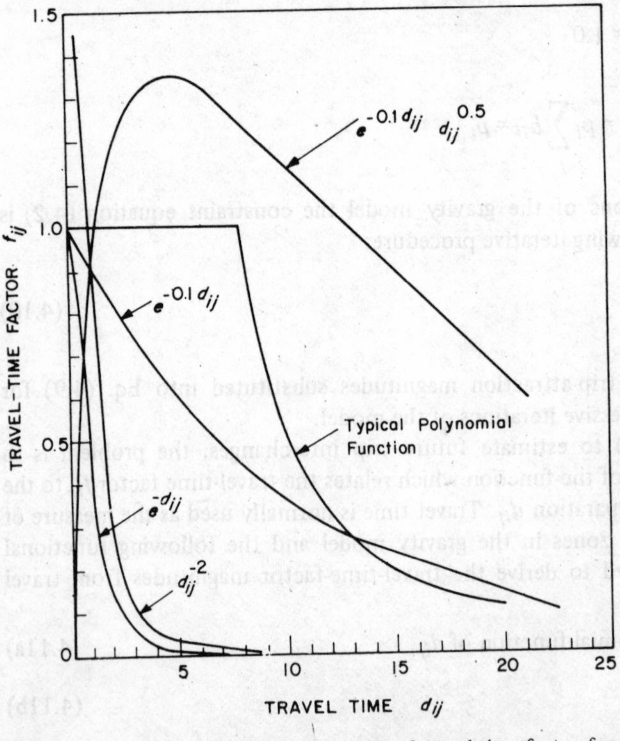

FIG. 4.2. Alternative functional forms of travel-time-factor function.

Wilson assumes that travel within an urban area involves a set of homogeneous tripmakers embarked on a single trip purpose. A state of this system of travel is defined as one particular matrix of t_{ij} magnitudes. Wilson argues that this travel system, therefore, has an extremely large number of possible states, each having a different t_{ij} matrix. A set of the t_{ij} states, denoted by $\{t_{ij}\}$ then defines a distribution of possible trip states.

A trip distribution by the gravity model must satisfy the constraint equations (4.1) and (4.2) and Wilson has introduced a third constraint equation which is:

$$\sum_{i}^{n} \sum_{j}^{n} t_{ij} z_{ij} = Z \tag{4.12}$$

where z_{ij} = the generalized cost of traveling from zone i to zone j
Z = the total amount spent on travel in the region at a particular point in time

Wilson has shown that the most probable t_{ij} matrix that satisfies the three constraints mentioned above is given by the following form of the gravity model:

$$t_{ij} = k_i k_j p_i a_j \exp(-\beta z_{ij}) \tag{4.13a}$$

where

$$k_i = \left[\frac{1}{\sum_j k_j a_j \exp(-\beta z_{ij})} \right] \tag{4.13b}$$

$$k_j = \left[\frac{1}{\sum_i k_i p_i \exp(-\beta z_{ij})} \right] \tag{4.13c}$$

Wilson's derivation of the gravity model using the entropy-maximizing approach yields a gravity model with a negative exponential travel-time-factor function. The terms k_i and k_j are normally referred to as *balancing factors* that ensure that the trip-end constraint equations are satisfied.

4.3.2 Bureau of Public Roads calibration procedure

The most widely used technique for calibrating the form of the gravity model defined in Eq. (4.9) is that developed by the Bureau of Public Roads [5]. The purpose of the calibration procedure is to establish the relationship between f_{ij} and d_{ij}, or in some instances between f_{ij} and z_{ij}, for base-year conditions. This function is then used along with Eqs. (4.9) and (4.10) to develop a trip-interchange matrix that satisfies the constraint equations (4.1) and (4.2). The Bureau of Public Roads calibration procedure is directed toward the

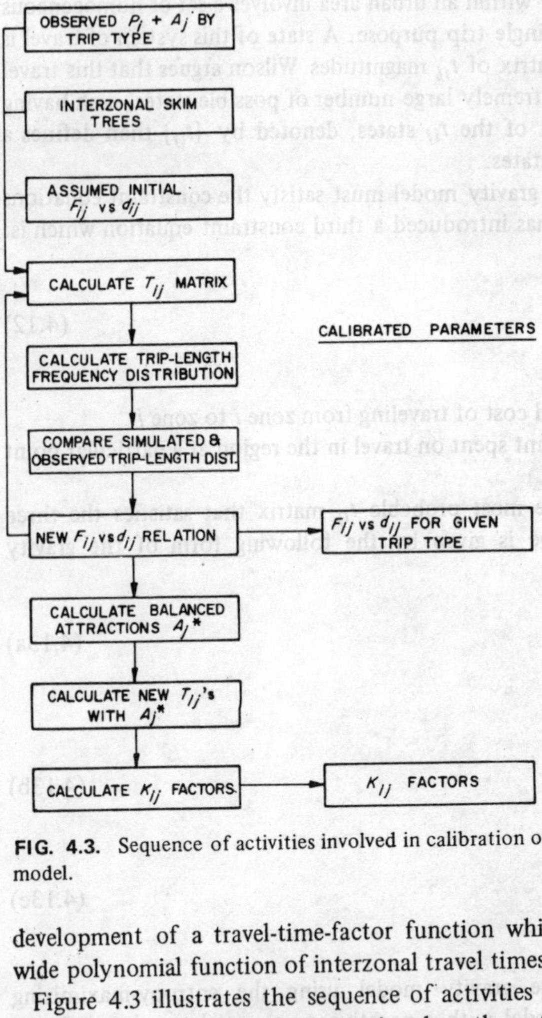

FIG. 4.3. Sequence of activities involved in calibration of a gravity model.

development of a travel-time-factor function which is assumed to be an area wide polynomial function of interzonal travel times.

Figure 4.3 illustrates the sequence of activities involved in the calibration of the gravity model. The first step involves the estimation of the intercentroid travel time for each centroid pair. Figure 4.4 shows a simple street plan overlayed by a street network map. The network map is simply a technique for expressing the major features of the street system in a form that may be used for computer analysis. The network is coded in terms of centroids, nodes, and links. The centroids are a representation of the points of trip production and trip attraction for the traffic-analysis zones. The nodes are representations of the intersections between the links of the street system.

If the travel time on each link of the network is known, then the minimum travel-time paths between any centroid pair may be established. The minimum path tree for centroid 3 is shown in Fig. 4.5. Network coding and techniques for

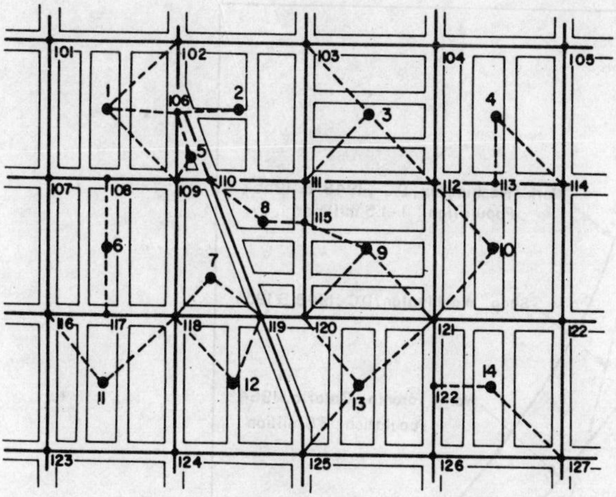

1–14 = Centroids
101–127 = Nodes
----- = Dummy links connecting centroids to street system

FIG. 4.4. Street plan coded as a network of centroids, nodes, and links. Local streets are not shown.

building minimum path trees are described in detail in Chap. 5. The intercentroid travel times, usually called *skim trees,* may be derived from the minimum path trees.

It has been pointed out previously that travel times are incorporated into the gravity model through the travel-time factor and that the relationship between the two is unknown initially. An initial estimate of the relationship is established most effectively from relationships determined in studies in other cities. Figure 4.6 shows typical relationships for different cities and various trip types. This diagram demonstrates that tripmakers are less sensitive to travel-time changes in

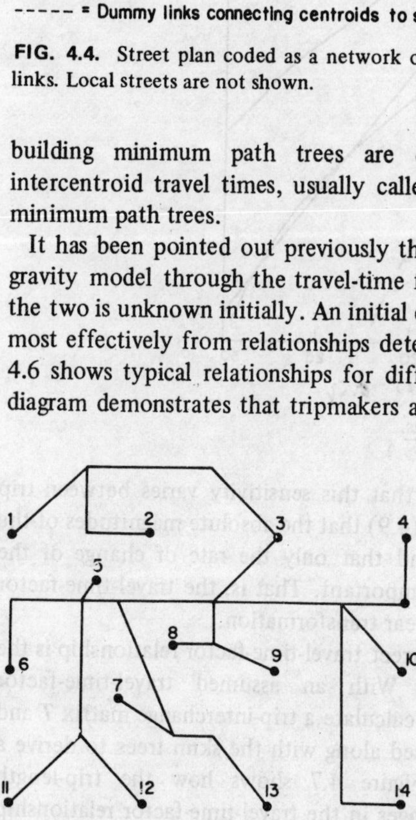

FIG. 4.5. Minimum travel-time tree for centroid 3.

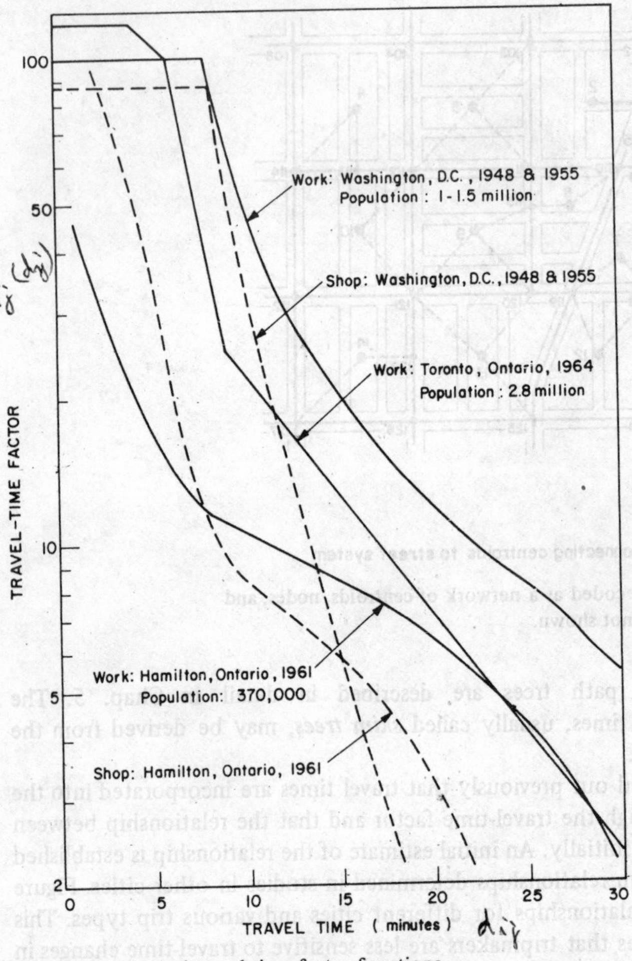

FIG. 4.6. Typical travel-time factor functions.

larger cities than in smaller cities and that this sensitivity varies between trip types. It should also be noted from Eq. (4.9) that the absolute magnitudes of the travel-time factors are unimportant and that only the rate of change of the travel-time factor with travel time is important. That is, the travel-time-factor function may be transformed by any linear transformation.

The criterion used to identify the correct travel-time-factor relationship is the trip length frequency distribution. With an assumed travel-time-factor relationship, Eq. (4.9) may be used to calculate a trip-interchange matrix T and this set of trip interchanges may be used along with the skim trees to derive a trip-length frequency distribution. Figure 4.7 shows how the trip-length frequency distribution varied with changes in the travel-time-factor relationship for one study. The key to the calibration of the gravity model is to vary the travel-time-factor relationship until the trip-length-frequency distribution simulated by the gravity model approximates that actually observed for the city being studied.

Reference [5] suggests that the gravity model simulated and observed trip-length-frequency distributions should exhibit the following two characteristics: (1) the shape and position of both curves should be relatively close to one another when compared visually, and (2) the difference between the average trip lengths should be within ± 3 percent.

If the trip-length-frequency distribution produced by the gravity model does not meet these criteria, then a new set of travel-time factors may be estimated from the following expression:

$$f' = f \times \frac{OD\%}{GM\%} \tag{4.14}$$

where f' = the travel-time factor for a given travel time to be used in the next iteration

f = the travel-time factor used in the calibration just completed

$OD\%$ = the percentage of total trips occurring for a given travel time observed in the travel survey

$GM\%$ = the percentage of total trips occurring for a given travel time simulated by the gravity model

The travel-time factors developed using Eq. (4.14) are then plotted against their corresponding travel times as illustrated in Fig. 4.8 and a smooth curve is then drawn through the points and a new set of travel-time factors is read from the graph. This sequence of activities is repeated until the synthesized and observed trip-length-frequency distributions agree.

The trip interchange matrix simulated by a gravity model which has been calibrated in the manner just described will not necessarily satisfy constraint equation (4.2). The second phase of the calibration procedure developed by the Bureau of Public Roads involves an application of the attraction trip-end balancing procedure defined in Eq. (4.10). A new trip interchange matrix is then calculated using the revised trip attractions, the initial trip productions and the travel-time factors established previously.

The final phase of the Bureau of Public Roads calibration procedure is to calculate the so-called *zone-to-zone adjustment factors* k_{ij}. These factors are calculated from the following expression:

$$k_{ij} = r_{ij}\left[\frac{(1 - x_i)}{(1 - x_i r_{ij})}\right] \tag{4.15}$$

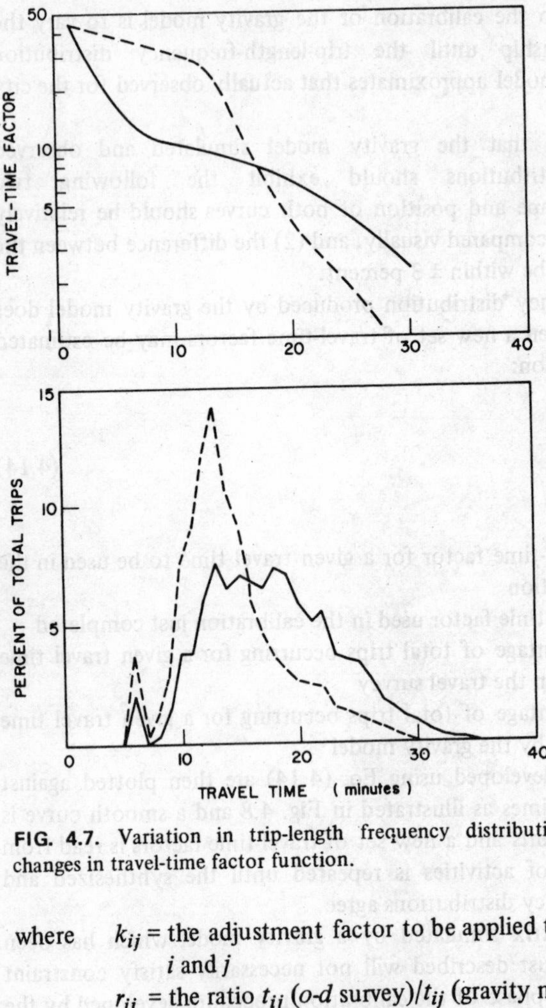

FIG. 4.7. Variation in trip-length frequency distribution with changes in travel-time factor function.

where k_{ij} = the adjustment factor to be applied to movements between zones i and j

r_{ij} = the ratio t_{ij} (o-d survey)/t_{ij} (gravity model)

x_i = the ratio t_{ij} (o-d survey)/p_i

The final gravity model simulated trip-interchange matrix is given by:

$$t_{ij} = p_i \frac{a_j^* f_{ij} k_{ij}}{\sum_j a_j^* f_{ij} k_{ij}} \tag{4.16}$$

An horizon-year trip interchange matrix is calculated from Eq. (4.16) with the following inputs: (1) the horizon-year trip-production and trip-attraction rates, (2) the horizon-year intercentroid skim trees, (3) the base-year travel-time factor–travel-time function, and (4) the k_{ij} magnitudes that are expected to hold for the horizon year. The trip-interchange matrix calculated initially is then subject to attraction trip-end balancing until Eq. (4.2) is satisfied.

4.3.3 A simple example

Figure 4.9 shows a simple five-zone city along with the trip productions, trip attractions, and the trip-length-frequency distribution for the base year. A gravity model of the type defined in Eq. (4.9) may be calibrated for this simple city.

Figure 4.10 shows the relationship between the travel-time factor and the travel time assumed for the first iteration of the model. It should be noted for this simple city that there are only two origin zones, numbers 3 and 5. Table 4.1 shows the calculations required by the first iteration of the model. The entries in lines 1, 2, 6, and 7 of Table 4.1 are obtained directly from the information provided in Figs. 4.9 and 4.10. The sums of $a_j f_{ij}$ products in lines 3 and 8 are the

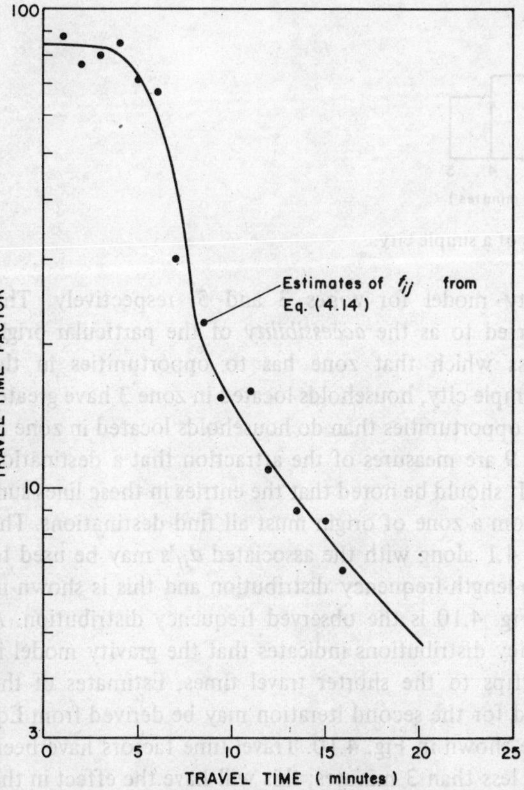

FIG. 4.8. Determination of travel-time factor function for successive iterations of gravity model.

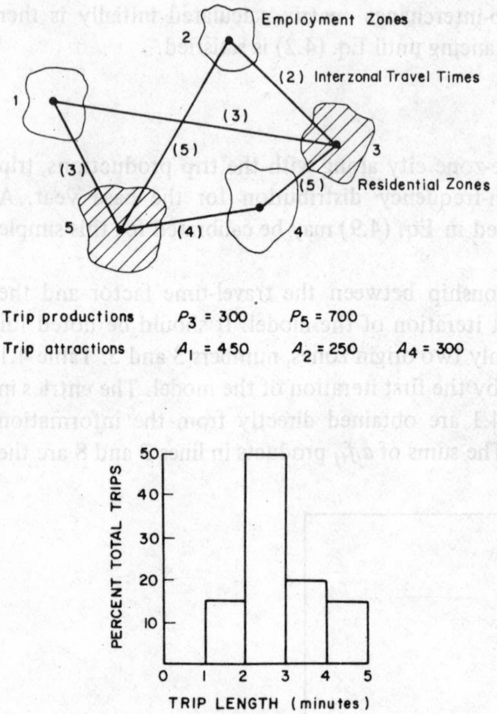

FIG. 4.9. Travel characteristics of a simple city.

denominators of the gravity model for zones 3 and 5, respectively. This denominator is usually referred to as the *accessibility* of the particular origin since it conveys the access which that zone has to opportunities in the destination zones. For this simple city, households located in zone 3 have greater accessibility to employment opportunities than do households located in zone 5.

The entries in lines 4 and 9 are measures of the attraction that a destination zone has to an origin zone. It should be noted that the entries in these lines sum to 1.00 since productions from a zone of origin must all find destinations. The six t_{ij}'s calculated in Table 4.1 along with the associated d_{ij}'s may be used to construct the simulated trip-length-frequency distribution and this is shown in Fig. 4.10. Also shown on Fig. 4.10 is the observed frequency distribution. A comparison of these frequency distributions indicates that the gravity model is not distributing sufficient trips to the shorter travel times. Estimates of the travel-time factors to be used for the second iteration may be derived from Eq. (4.15) and the estimates are shown in Fig. 4.10. Travel-time factors have been increased for travel times of less than 3 minutes; this will have the effect in the gravity model of distributing a larger number of trips to destinations with shorter travel times. The calculations presented in Table 4.1 could now be repeated with the new f_{ij} magnitudes and a second trip-length-frequency distribution calculated with the process being continued until the simulated and observed distributions converge.

The additional components of the calibration procedure described in Eqs. (4.10) and (4.15) will not be demonstrated by this simple city as the exercise would not be particularly meaningful.

4.3.4 Limitations of the calibration procedure

The calibration procedure described in the previous section requires that two criteria be satisfied by a base-year calibration. These two criteria are: agreement between observed and simulated trip-length-frequency distributions and satisfaction of the attraction trip-end constraint equation. A principal difficulty with this calibration procedure is that the travel-time-factor function and the associated trip-length-frequency distribution are assumed to be constant for each zone of a study area. Edens [6] has shown that this assumption is not valid for Quebec City and that significant variations occur throughout the area. This spatial variation of the travel-time-factor function has also been observed by others.

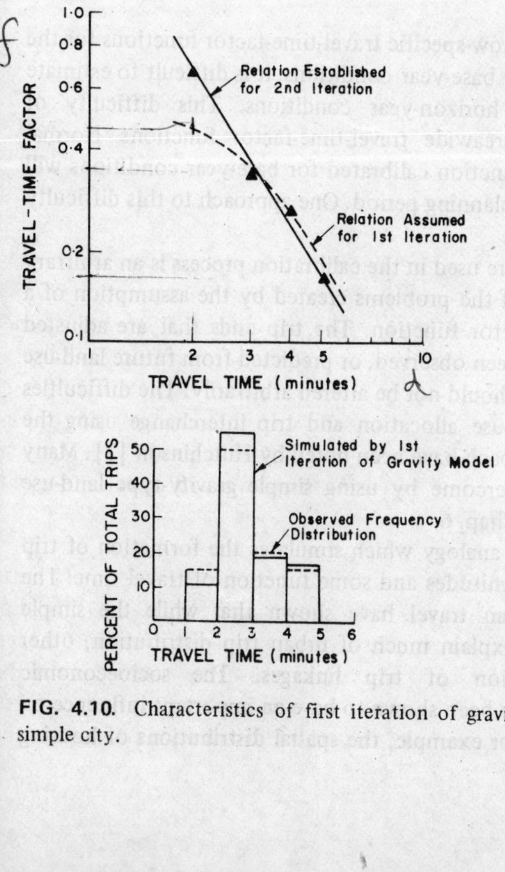

FIG. 4.10. Characteristics of first iteration of gravity model for simple city.

Table 4.1. Calculations required for first iteration

Calculations	Destination zone 1	2	4	Σ
Attractions a_j	450	250	300	
Origin 3 300				
1. Travel time d_{ij}	3	2	5	
2. Travel-time factor f_{ij}	0.36	0.45	0.18	
3. $a_j f_{ij}$	162	112	54	328
4. $a_j f_{ij}/\Sigma a_j f_{ij}$	0.50	0.34	0.16	1.00
5. $t_{ij} = p_i a_j f_{ij}/\Sigma a_j f_{ij}$	150	102	48	300
Origin 5 700				
6. Travel time d_{ij}	3	5	4	
7. Travel-time factor f_{ij}	0.36	0.18	0.25	
8. $a_j f_{ij}$	162	45	75	282
9. $a_j f_{ij}/\Sigma a_j f_{ij}$	0.57	0.16	0.27	1.00
10. t_{ij}	399	112	189	700

While it is possible to calibrate row-specific travel-time-factor functions for the B matrix defined in Eq. (4.5) for base-year conditions, it is difficult to estimate the appropriate functions for horizon-year conditions. This difficulty of forecasting exists as well for areawide travel-time-factor functions. Normal practice is to assume that the function calibrated for base-year conditions will remain invariant throughout the planning period. One approach to this difficulty is described in Sec. 4.3.5.

The trip-end balancing procedure used in the calibration process is an arbitrary approach to overcoming some of the problems created by the assumption of a common areawide travel-time-factor function. The trip ends that are adjusted represent magnitudes that have been observed, or predicted from future land-use allocations, and these trip ends should not be altered arbitrarily. The difficulties in obtaining a compatible land-use allocation and trip interchange using the conventional gravity model approach have been noted by Hutchinson [7]. Many of these difficulties may be overcome by using simple gravity-type land-use models of the type described in Chap. 6.

The gravity model is a simple analogy which simulates the formation of trip linkages in terms of trip-end magnitudes and some function of travel time. The many empirical studies of urban travel have shown that while the simple premises of the gravity model explain much of urban trip distribution, other factors influence the formation of trip linkages. The socioeconomic characteristics of tripmakers have been shown to have an important influence on the spatial patterns of travel. For example, the spatial distributions of housing and job opportunities that are compatible with lower income groups are not simply linear transformations of the distributions of total housing and job opportunities.

Several studies have shown that if the activities compatible with the various socioeconomic groups are stratified and trips are distributed separately within each strata, then the gravity model is capable of explaining the bulk of tripmaking behavior. It should be recalled that this disaggregated view of urban tripmakers is central to the two-stage modal split model advanced in Chap. 3. The use of the so-called *socioeconomic adjustment factors* k_{ij} to achieve this purpose is unsuitable since it is almost impossible to estimate their magnitudes for future conditions.

4.3.5 Alternative approaches to calibration

Ashford and Covault [8] have observed that home-based work-trip travel-time-factor relationships may be expressed by Pearson, type I distributions which are described by:

$$f_{ij} = A^{C_1/m_1+m_2+1}\,\beta(m_1, m_2)\,(t-c)^{m_1}\,[A-(t-c)]^{m_2} \tag{4.17}$$

where m_1, m_2, A = shape parameters
c = shift parameter
C_1 = a constant
t = travel time
$\beta(m_1, m_2)$ = the beta function with parameters m_1, m_2

Ashford established statistical relationships between the parameters of the Pearson distribution and characteristics of the urban area such as home-based work trips per 1,000 population, total trips per car, cars per person, and total trips per 1,000 population.

Morrall [9] has proposed a method for calibrating the gravity model which is based on certain fairly coarse measures of land use. Figure 4.11 shows the elements of this calibration procedure. This calibration procedure was developed for data collected in Metropolitan Toronto in 1964.

The calibration procedure begins by identifying two distinct groups of tripmakers: group 1, choice work tripmakers; and group 2, transit captive tripmakers. The first step of the procedure involves the estimation of the trip ends of both groups in each traffic analysis zone. The concept of an opportunity function is used to split the production and attraction trip ends into groups.

The opportunity functions shown in Fig. 4.12 show the cumulative household or employment opportunities about a zone by road or transit in a given travel time. Opportunity functions are shown in Fig. 4.12 for a central area zone and a suburban zone located near the eastern boundary of Metropolitan Toronto. The relationships illustrate quite clearly that the intensity of opportunities available to group 1 tripmakers is much greater than for the group 2 tripmakers with the exception of short trips near the central business district.

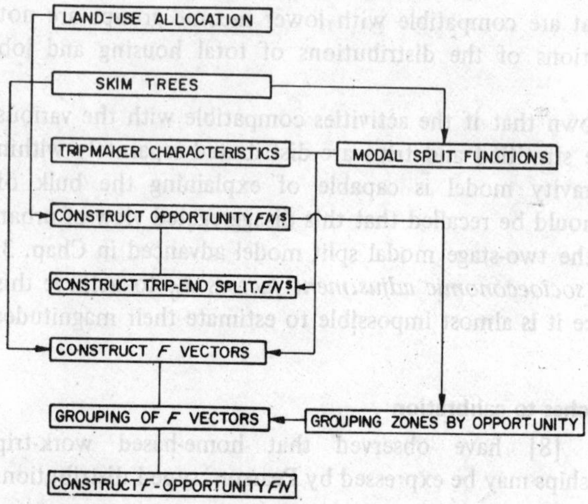

FIG. 4.11. Morrall's calibration procedure.

Figure 4.13 shows the function developed to split trip ends at the work end into trip ends by the two groups. The percentage of group 1 tripmakers in a zone is a function of the difference in dwelling unit opportunities by road and transit in a 30-minute travel-time interval. Figure 4.14 shows the relationship developed to split trips at the home-based end of the trip. This function shows that the percentage of group 1 tripmakers in a zone is a function of the difference in employment opportunity by road and transit in a 30-minute travel time.

The opportunity function has also been used to develop a relationship for estimating travel-time-factor functions. Figure 4.15 shows the relationship that has been observed between the index of the exponential travel-time-factor function and the number of opportunities surrounding a zone. If this relationship is invariant with time, then future exponents of the travel-time function can be estimated directly from a knowledge of land use.

The sequence of activities outlined in Fig. 4.11 may be used to estimate the spatial patterns of travel given certain assumptions about the horizon-year land-use and transport system.

4.3.6 Other forms of the gravity model

Heuristically derived gravity models exist in other forms, and Wilson [4] provides a summary of some of the more important forms. One form of the gravity model which has been used in transport planning studies is the multiterm model in which the productions and attractions are raised to a power. This model is normally referred to as the *abstract mode model* [10] since it was originally used in an attempt to simulate modal transport choice in the Northeast Corridor Transportation Project.

The abstract mode model, or multiterm gravity model, has the following form:

$$t_{ij}{}^{m} = ap_i{}^{b}p_j{}^{c}q_i{}^{e}q_j{}^{f}f(d_{ij}{}^{m})f(z_{ij}{}^{m}) \tag{4.18}$$

where $t_{ij}{}^{m}$ = the trip interchange between zones i and j by mode m

p,q = measures of the intensities of activities in zones i and j such as population and employment

$d_{ij}{}^{m}$ = the relative travel time by mode m between zones i and j

$z_{ij}{}^{m}$ = the relative travel cost by mode m between zones i and j

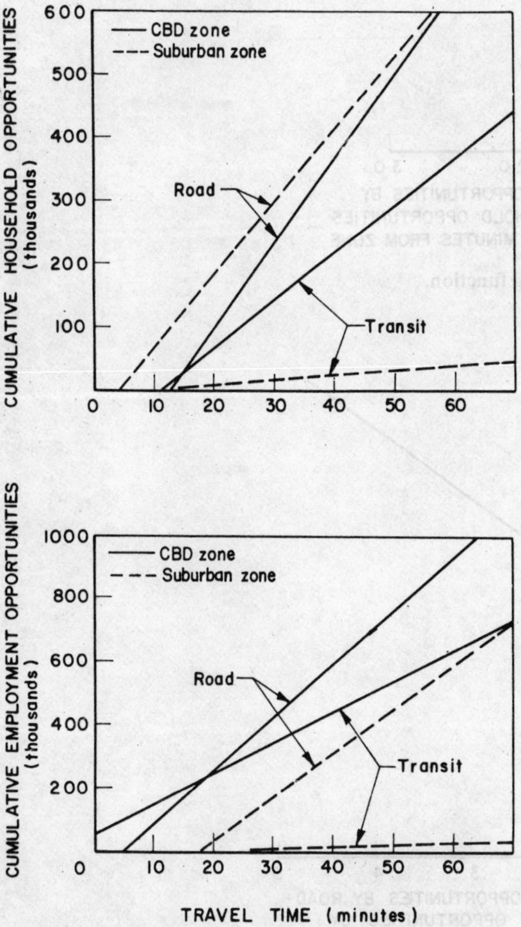

FIG. 4.12. Opportunity functions for two zones in Metropolitan Toronto.

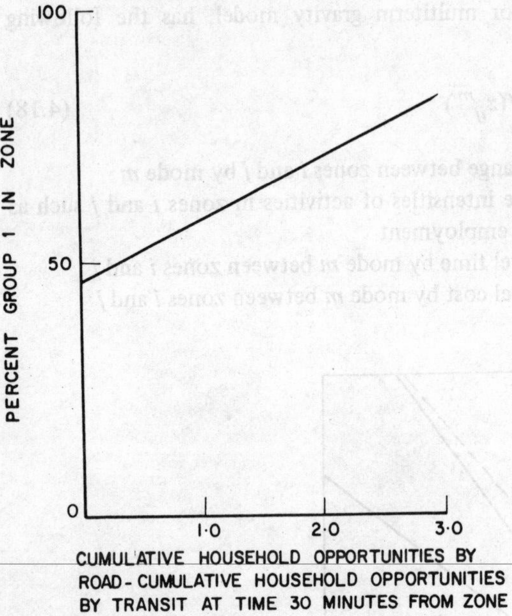

FIG. 4.13. Work-trip end splitting function.

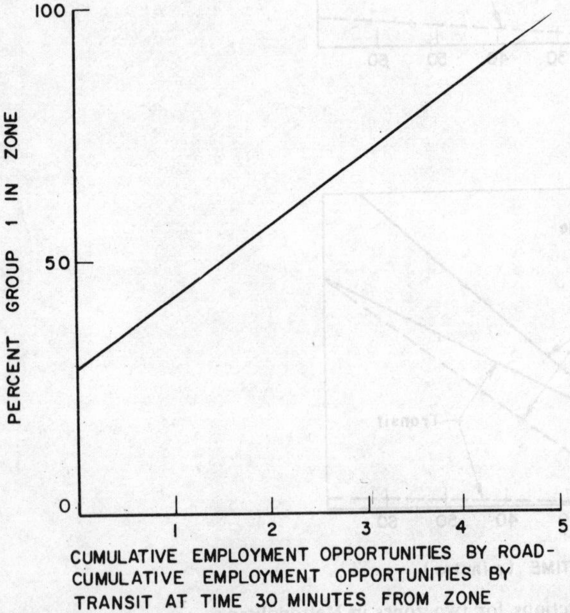

FIG. 4.14. Home-trip end splitting functions.

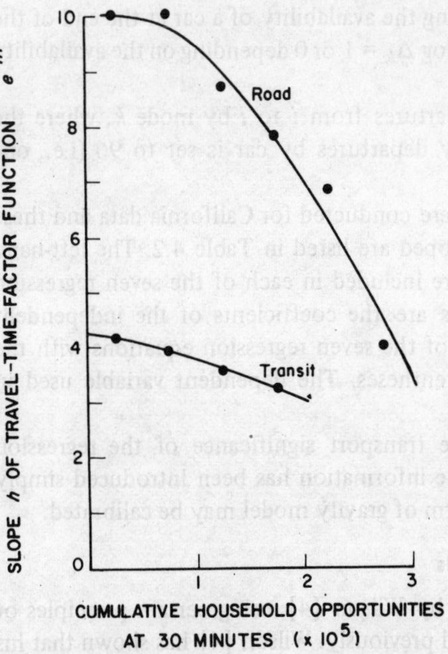

FIG. 4.15. Slope of travel-time-factor function vs. number of household opportunities at 30 minutes.

Equation (4.18) is linear in the logarithms of the variables and the parameters *a,b,c,e,* and *f* may be estimated from empirical data by multiple regression analysis. A variety of variables and indices may be used in expressions of the type shown in Eq. (4.18).

The principal advantages claimed for this model over the more traditional gravity models are: (1) the effect on existing transport modes of the introduction of a new mode of travel can be estimated; (2) it allows a new mode of travel to be introduced in terms of its cost, travel time, and departure frequency characteristics; and (3) total travel demand and modal choice magnitudes are forecast jointly and not independently as is the case with the techniques described earlier in this chapter.

Quandt [11] has used this model in an attempt to simulate intercity travel between 16 city pairs in California and for three modes of travel: air, bus, and automobile. Forecasting equations were developed using the following variables:

$T_{ij}{}^k$ = trip interchange between *i-j* city pairs by mode *k*
P_i = population in millions of the *i*th city
Y_i = per capita income in the *i*th city
D_i = per capita bank deposits in the *i*th city
M_i = percent of employment in manufacturing in the *i*th city
W_i = percent of employment in white collar occupations in the *i*th city

A_k = a dummy variable indicating the availability of a car at the end of the trip if one takes mode k; $\log \Delta_k = 1$ or 0 depending on the availability of a car

F_{ij}^{kr} = relative frequency of departures from i to j by mode k, where the number of potential daily departures by car is set to 96 (i.e., one every 15 minutes).

A number of regression analyses were conducted for California data and these regression equations that were developed are listed in Table 4.2. The left-hand column shows the variables that were included in each of the seven regression equations. The numbers in the cells are the coefficients of the independent variables that were included in each of the seven regression equations with the corresponding t values shown in parentheses. The dependent variable used in each regression equation was $\log T_{ij}^k$.

The reader is left to interpret the transport significance of the regression equations presented in Table 4.2. The information has been introduced simply to demonstrate how this particular form of gravity model may be calibrated.

4.3.7 Gravity-type modal split models

A derivation of the gravity model by Wilson [4] using certain principles of statistical mechanics has been outlined previously. Wilson [4] has shown that his approach to the derivation of the gravity model may be extended to develop a model of transport mode choice. The following notation is used for this development:

t_{ij}^{mq} = the number of trips produced in zone i and attracted to zone j by mode m for person type q

p_i^q = the number of trips produced at zone i by person type q

z_{ij}^m = the generalized cost of traveling from zone i to zone j by transport mode m

t_{ij}^{*q} = the total number of trips between zones i and j by type q people where * represents a summation over all modes of transport

pr_{ij}^{mq} = the proportion of tripmakers of class q who use mode m between zones i and j, which equals t_{ij}^{mq}/t_{ij}^{*q}

The following constraint equations have been suggested by Wilson [4] for the modal choice model:

$$\sum_j \sum_m t_{ij}^{mq} = p_i^q \tag{4.19}$$

$$\sum_i \sum_q \sum_m t_{ij}^{mq} = a_j \tag{4.20}$$

$$\sum_i \sum_j \sum_m t_{ij}^{mq} z_{ij}^m = Z^q \tag{4.21}$$

Table 4.2. Calibration of the abstract mode model

Variable	Regression						
	1	2	3	4	5	6	7
Constant	-31.91	-28.04	-40.71	-33.82	-36.57	-32.56	28.73
	(-.95)	(-1.14)	(-.69)	(1.45)	(-1.62)	(-1.37)	(-1.25)
$\log P_i$	.95	.92	.94	.93	.91	.95	.88
	(5.88)	(4.44)	(3.71)	(6.99)	(7.40)	(7.54)	(6.95)
$\log P_j$	1.08	1.14	1.14	1.12	1.14	.99	.88
	(5.14)	(6.20)	(6.37)	(6.38)	(6.95)	(6.41)	(5.47)
$\log Y_i$	1.75	4.59	3.32	2.64			
	(.53)	(1.30)	(.33)	(1.05)			
$\log Y_j$	3.71	3.11	3.02	3.72			
	(.99)	(1.01)	(.99)	(1.43)			
$\log D_i$	.67						
	(.57)						
$\log D_j$	(.17)						
	(.19)						
$\log W_i$			-.36				
			(-.05)				
$\log W_j$			2.38				
			(.76)				
M_i		-.73					
		(-.53)					
M_j		-.96					
		(-1.15)					
$\log \left(\frac{Y_i + Y_j}{2}\right)$					6.83		
					(2.35)		
$\log C_{ij}^{b}$	-.99	-.61	-1.20	-1.12	-.62	-.57	
	(-1.19)	(-.70)	(-1.69)	(-1.68)	(1.04)	(-.99)	
$\log C_{kij}^{r}$	-3.17	-3.15	-3.18	-2.62	-3.17	-3.15	-2.34
	(-11.40)	(-11.51)	(-11.48)	(3.59)	(11.82)	(-11.62)	(-4.54)
$\log H_{ij}^{b}$	-.32	-.92	-.59	.15	-.20	-1.19	-1.20
	(-.21)	(-.59)	(.36)	(-.12)	(-.16)	(-1.17)	(-1.23)
$\log H_{kij}^{r}$	-2.04	-2.01	-2.05	-1.73	-2.04	-2.01	-1.75
	(-5.45)	(-5.45)	(-5.51)	(-3.23)	(-5.66)	(-5.51)	(-4.59)
$\log F_{kij}^{r}$							.44
							(1.83)
$\log A_{ij}$				.66			
				(.81)			
$\log \frac{P_i Y_i + P_j Y_j}{P_i + P_j}$						6.33	5.82
						(2.08)	(1.96)
R	.9355	.9376	.9360	.9361	.9350	.9331	.9386

where Z^q = the total expenditure on travel by person type q

The set of constraint equations introduced above imply that the trips generated from zone i on each transport mode are a function of person type q, whereas tripmakers from all person types compete for the same attractions. Using the entropy maximizing technique, Wilson [4] developed the following set of equations:

$$t_{ij}^{mq} = k_i^q k_j p_i^q a_j \exp(-\beta^q z_{ij}) \tag{4.22}$$

where
$$k_i^q = \frac{1}{\sum_j \sum_m k_j a_j \exp(-\beta^q z_{ij})} \tag{4.23}$$

$$k_j = \frac{1}{\sum_i \sum_q \sum_m k_i^m p_i^q \exp(-\beta^q z_{ij})} \tag{4.24}$$

Equation (4.22) represents a set of gravity models with an exponential travel-time factor for each m-q category. This set of gravity models is linked through the constants k_i^q and k_j which are equivalent to the balancing constants k_i and k_j of the gravity model derived in Sec. 4.3.1.

If Eq. (4.22) is summed over the modes m and person types q and divided into Eq. (4.22) summed over q, the following modal split expression is obtained:

$$pr_{ij}^{mq} = \frac{\exp(-\beta^q z_{ij}^m)}{\sum \exp(-\beta^q z_{ij}^m)} \tag{4.25}$$

If a two-transport-mode situation exists then Eq. (4.25) may be used to develop the following expression for the modal split by person type q:

$$pr^{1q} = \frac{1}{1 + \exp[-\beta^q(z_{ij}^2 - z_{ij}^1)]} \tag{4.26}$$

In Eq. (4.26) the coefficient β^q is a measure of the sensitivity of type q persons to the travel cost differences between modes. If β^q is large, then Eq. (4.26) indicates that the majority of type q people would travel by the cheaper mode. If β^q is small, then the importance of the travel price difference is low. The differences in sensitivity of various person types to transport service characteristics has already been illustrated in Chap. 3.

Wilson [4] has also derived additional modal split relationships which are based on different sets of assumed constraint equations, and these relationships are described in detail in Ref. [4]. References [12] and [13] describe the calibration of the gravity-type modal split models for two urban areas.

4.4 THE INTERVENING OPPORTUNITIES MODEL

The original form of the intervening opportunities model was proposed by Stouffer [14]. The basic hypothesis of this model is that the number of trips from an origin zone to a destination zone is directly proportional to the number of opportunities at the destination zone and inversely proportional to the number of intervening opportunities. This hypothesis may be expressed as:

$$t_{ij} = k \frac{a_j}{v_j} \tag{4.27}$$

where a_j = the total number of destination opportunities in zone j
v_j = the number of intervening destination opportunities between zones i and j
k = a proportionality constant to ensure that all trips with origins at zone i are distributed to destination opportunities

Schneider [15], Golding and Davidson [16] have proposed extensions to the initial Stouffer hypothesis, and these are described in the section that follows.

4.4.1 Derivation of the model.

Schneider [15] has proposed the following modification of the Stouffer hypothesis. The Schneider hypothesis states that the probability that a trip will terminate in some volume of destination points is equal to the probability that this volume contains an acceptable destination times the probability that an acceptable destination closer to the origin of the trips has not been found. This hypothesis may be expressed as:

$$pr(dv) = [1 - pr(v)]\ l dv \tag{4.28}$$

where $pr(dv)$ = the probability that a trip will terminate when dv destination opportunities are considered
$pr(v)$ = the cumulative probability that a trip will terminate by the time v possible destinations are considered
v = the cumulative total of the destinations already considered
l = a constant probability of a destination being accepted if it is considered

Figure 4.16 illustrates the intent of Eq. (4.28) graphically. In connection with Fig. 4.16, Eq. (4.28) may be restated as: the probability of locating within the dv opportunities being considered, is equal to the product of the probability of not having located within the v opportunities already considered, and the

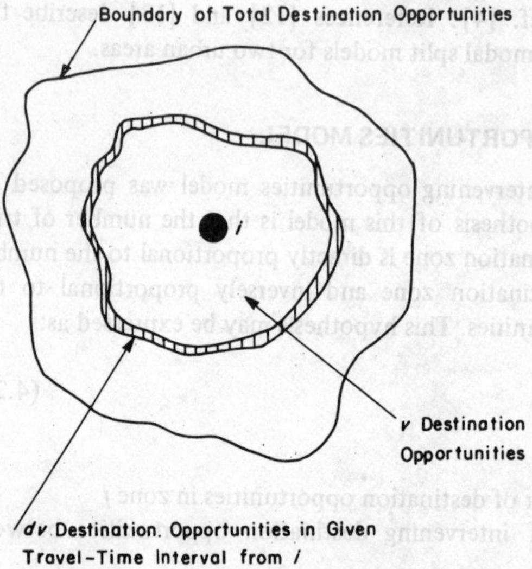

$pr(dv) = [1 - pr(r)]\ l\,dv$

FIG. 4.16. Structure of intervening opportunities model.

probability of finding an acceptable location within dv opportunities, given that a location has not already been found.

Schneider [15] has shown that the solution to Eq. (4.28) is given by:

$$pr(v) = 1 - k_i \exp(-lv) \tag{4.29}$$

where k_i = a constant for zone i to ensure that all the trips produced at zone i are distributed to zone i, or, that the constraint equation (4.1) is satisfied

The trip interchange between an i-j pair is given by:

$$t_{ij} = p_i \text{ (probability of trip terminating in zone } j)$$

$$= p_i\,[pr(v_{j+1}) - pr(v_j)] \tag{4.30}$$

where $pr(v_j)$ = the probability that a trip will have found a suitable destination in the opportunities already considered up to zone j

$pr(v_{j+1})$ = the probability that a trip will have found a suitable destination in the cumulative opportunities considered up to and including zone j

Equation (4.30) may also be written in the following form by using the identity given in Eq. (4.29):

$$t_{ij} = k_i p_i [\exp(-lv_j) - \exp(-lv_{j+1})] \tag{4.31}$$

Equation (4.29) may be expressed in the linear form: $-lv = \ln[1 - pr(v)] - \ln k_j$. Figure 4.17 shows the relationship between v and $[1 - pr(v)]$ reported by Ruiter [17] for journeys to home from the central zone of Chicago. Equation (4.29) should exhibit a linear form on this graph with slope l but the information presented in Fig. 4.17 does not exhibit a linear relationship.

A similar observation has been made by Swerdloff and Stowers [18] in connection with the distribution of residential locations of central business district employees in Greensboro, North Carolina. Figure 4.18 shows the information reported by Swerdloff and Stowers and indicates that two straight lines of different slopes must be used to represent the household distribution.

Golding and Davidson [16] have provided an interesting extension of the intervening opportunities model in an attempt to overcome the shortcomings of the assumption of a constant l magnitude. They propose the following modification of Eq. (4.28) in which the constant l magnitude is replaced by a probability density which is a function of the accumulated destination opportunities considered:

$$pr(dv) = [1 - pr(v)]\, f(v)dv \tag{4.32}$$

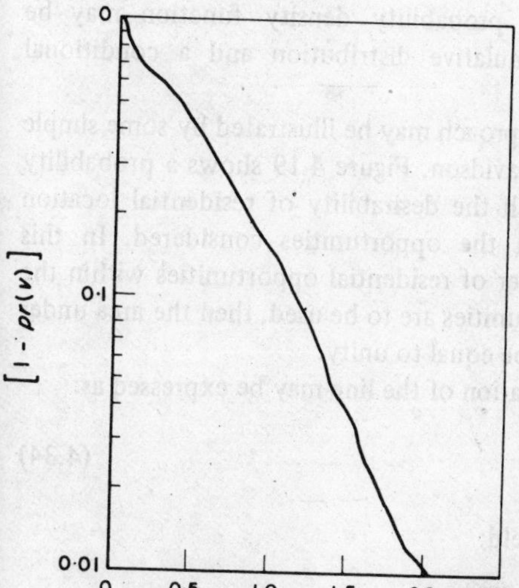

FIG. 4.17. $[1-pr(v)]$ vs. subtended volume for long residential trips for Chicago CBD.

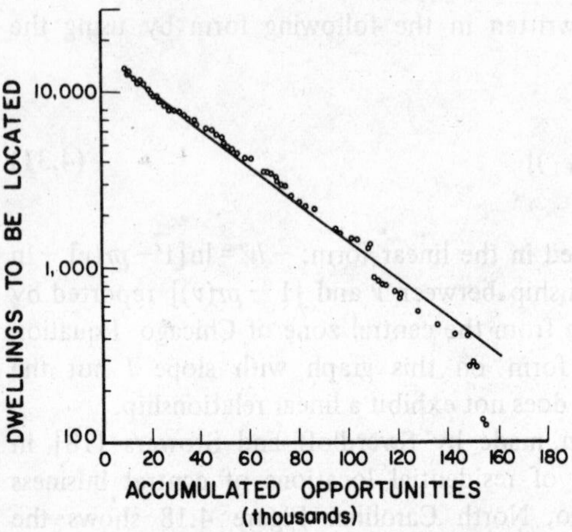

FIG. 4.18. Household location opportunity functions for Greensboro, North Carolina.

Golding and Davidson show that $pr(dv) = dpr(v)$ and that Eq. (4.32) may be rewritten as follows:

$$dpr(v) = [1 - pr(v)]\, f(v)\, dv$$

$$\frac{d}{dv}\, pr(v) = [1 - pr(v)]\, f(v)$$

$$pr'(v) = [1 - pr(v)]\, f(v) \tag{4.33}$$

Equation (4.33) illustrates that the probability density function may be expressed by the product of a cumulative distribution and a conditional probability.

Some of the characteristics of this approach may be illustrated by some simple examples described by Golding and Davidson. Figure 4.19 shows a probability density function for the case in which the desirability of residential location declines uniformly with increases in the opportunities considered. In this diagram $a = v_T$ and v_T = total number of residential opportunities within the region. If all of the destination opportunities are to be used, then the area under the probability density function must be equal to unity.

$(ak)/2 = 1$ or $k = 2/a$ and the equation of the line may be expressed as:

$$pr'(v) = \frac{2}{a} - \left(\frac{2v}{a^2}\right) = \frac{2}{a}\ \frac{a-v}{a} \tag{4.34}$$

and Eq. (4.34) may be integrated to yield:

$$pr(v) = 1 - \left(\frac{a-v}{a}\right)^2 \tag{4.35}$$

Golding and Davidson suggest the following general form of Eq. (4.35) in which b is the calibration parameter:

$$pr(v) = 1 - \left(\frac{a - v}{a}\right)^b \tag{4.36}$$

Figure 4.20 shows the variation in $pr(v)$ for various values of b for $a = 40{,}000$ destination opportunities.

The probability of a trip finding a destination opportunity in zone j is given by

$$pr(dv) = pr(v_{j+1}) - pr(v_j)$$

$$= \left[\frac{a - v_j}{a}\right]^b - \left[\frac{a - v_{j+1}}{a}\right]^b$$

$$t_{ij} = p_i \left\{ \left[\frac{a - v_j}{a}\right]^b - \left[\frac{a - v_{j+1}}{a}\right]^b \right\} \tag{4.37}$$

Using the terminology of Eq. (4.5):

$$b_{ij} = \left[\frac{a - v_j}{a}\right]^b - \left[\frac{a - v_{j+1}}{a}\right]^b$$

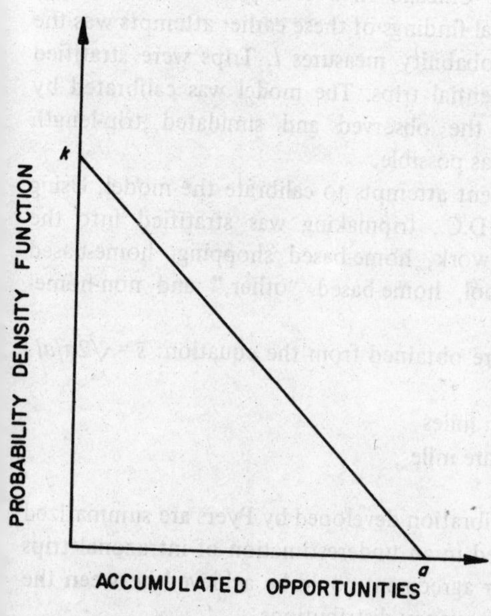

FIG. 4.19. Probability density function.

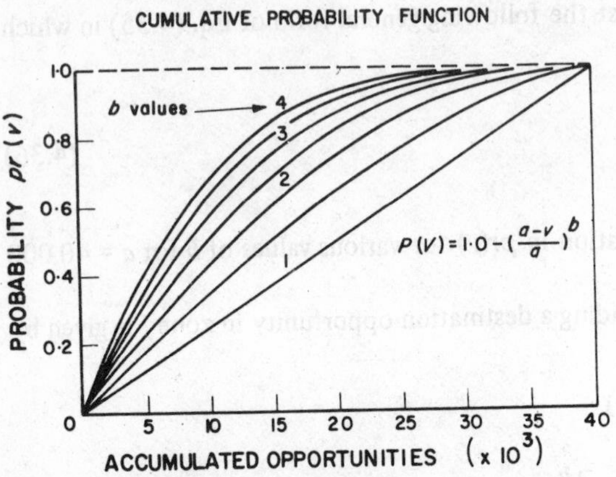

FIG. 4.20. Variation in *pr* (*v*) with index *b*.

It has been shown previously that in the gravity model the b_{ij} magnitudes are calculated from the product of the number of destination opportunities in a zone and some function of the travel time to that zone. In the intervening opportunities model, the b_{ij} magnitudes are calculated from a knowledge of the number of intervening destination opportunities considered prior to reaching a zone.

4.4.2 Calibration of the model

Most of the initial attempts at calibrating the intervening opportunities model were conducted by the staff of the Chicago Area Transportation Study and reported by Ruiter [17]. The principal findings of these earlier attempts was the need to use multiple conditional probability measures l. Trips were stratified into long residential and short residential trips. The model was calibrated by adjusting the l magnitudes until the observed and simulated trip-length frequency distributions were as close as possible.

Pyers [19] has reported more recent attempts to calibrate the model. Using 1948 travel data for Washington, D.C., tripmaking was stratified into the following trip types: home-based work, home-based shopping, home-based social-recreational, home-based school, home-based "other," and non-home-based.

Initial estimates of the l values were obtained from the equation: $\bar{s} = \sqrt{2}\pi/al$.

where $\bar{s}$ = the average trip length in miles
a = trip end density per square mile

The characteristics of the final calibration developed by Pyers are summarized in Table 4.3. The calibration resulted in an underestimation of intrazonal trips by about 55 percent and only poor agreement could be achieved between the simulated and observed trip-length frequency distributions.

A second calibration technique was attempted by Pyers in which the trip classifications used in the Chicago studies were employed. Table 4.4 summarizes the results of this second calibration attempt. While generally good agreement was obtained between the observed and simulated average trip lengths, only very poor correspondence was achieved between the two trip-length frequency distributions.

4.5 THE COMPETING OPPORTUNITIES MODEL

Tomazinis [20] proposed the competing opportunities model of trip distribution. The form of this model may be described as follows:

$$t_{ij} = p_i b_{ij} = p_i (pra_j)(prs_j) \tag{4.38}$$

where pra_j = the probability of attraction to zone j

= the destination opportunities in zone j divided by the sum of the destination opportunities available in time bands up to and including m

$$= \frac{a_j}{\sum_{x=1}^{m} a_x}$$

prs_j = the probability of trip end allocation satisfaction in zone j

= 1 − the sum of the destination opportunities available in time bands up to and including band m divided by the sum of the total destinations in the study area

$$= 1 - \frac{\sum_{x=1}^{m} a_x}{\sum_{x=1}^{n} a_x}$$

x = any time band

m = time band into which zone j falls

a_x = the destination opportunities available in time band x

n = the last time band as measured from an origin zone i

Table 4.3. Characteristics of the calibration of the opportunity model for six trip classes

Trip type	$\bar{s}$ (min)	$l \times 10^{-6}$
Home-based		
Work	20.7	2.85
Shopping	15.6	67.13
Social-recreational	17.8	16.16
School	16.1	93.65
Miscellaneous	17.6	21.50
Non-home-based	16.8	15.76

Table 4.4. Characteristics of the calibration of the opportunity model for three trip classes

Trip type	$\bar{s}$ (min)		$l \times 10^{-6}$	Interzonal trips	
	Observed	Model		Observed	Model
Long residential	21.0	21.0	3.88	4,369	2,042
Long nonresidential	21.1	21.1	2.96	4,117	1,618
Short	15.9	16.0	9.75	54,616	27,494

Figure 4.21 illustrates the structure which underlies the competing-opportunities model.

The competing-opportunities model is calibrated by varying the width of the attraction time bands until the trip-length characteristics of the simulated trips agrees with the observed trip-length frequency distribution. Heanue and Pyers [21] have described an attempt to calibrate this model to tripmaking behavior in Washington, D.C. They concluded that the model is very difficult to calibrate and that it produced results that were clearly inferior to both the gravity and intervening-opportunities models.

Bell [22] has described an attempt at calibrating the model to tripmaking behavior in Sydney, Australia. This analysis showed that the method simulated trip interchange magnitudes reasonably well. However, some large discrepancies did occur and Bell concluded that an attraction trip-end balancing procedure

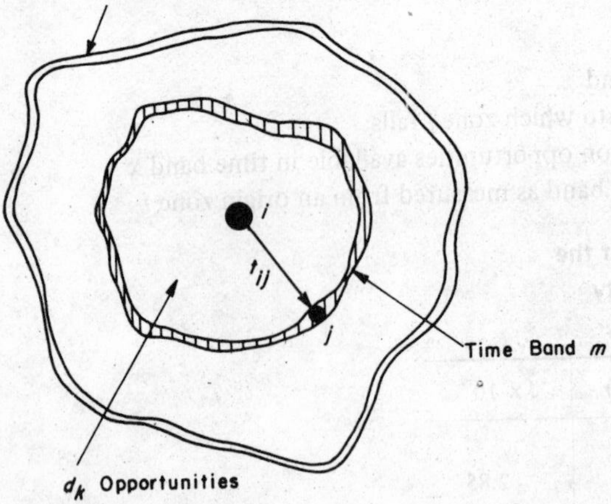

$$t_{ij} = p_i \left(d_j / d_k\right)\left[1 - \left(d_k / d_n\right)\right]$$

FIG. 4.21. Structure of competing opportunities model.

similar to that used in the calibration of the gravity model would have improved the accuracy of the simulation.

4.6 COMPARATIVE STUDIES OF STOCHASTIC TRIP DISTRIBUTION MODELS

The most comprehensive comparative evaluation of the capabilities of the three stochastic-type trip-distribution models is that reported by Heanue and Pyers [21]. Figure 4.22 shows observed and estimated trip-length frequency distributions reported for the calibration of each of the three trip-distribution models to Washington, D.C., data in 1948. The variations in the observed

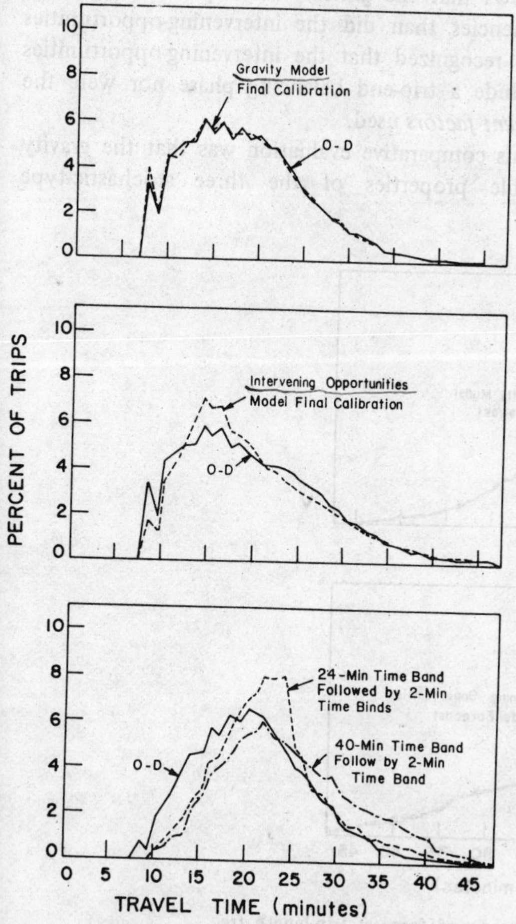

FIG. 4.22. Comparison of calibrations for three models.

trip-length frequency distributions between graphs is due to the way in which the research was conducted. From this study, Heanue and Pyers concluded that:

> As expected, the gravity model had the best agreement through most portions of the trip length frequency curves because of the refined degree of adjustment made during the calibration phase. Both the gravity and intervening opportunities models produced good duplication of the total hours of travel and average trip length. Even though the two curves for the competing opportunity model have some agreement, no rational method could be found to adjust toward a more satisfactory model.

The gravity and intervening-opportunities models calibrated to a 1948 base year were then used to simulate 1955 conditions in Washington, D.C., and Fig. 4.23 shows a comparison of the simulated and observed trip-length frequency distributions. This diagram shows that the gravity model provided a better simulation of trip-length frequencies than did the intervening-opportunities model. However, it should be recognized that the intervening-opportunities model simulation did not include a trip-end balancing phase nor were the so-called *socioeconomic adjustment factors* used.

The general conclusion of this comparative evaluation was that the gravity model has the most desirable properties of the three stochastic-type trip-distribution models tested.

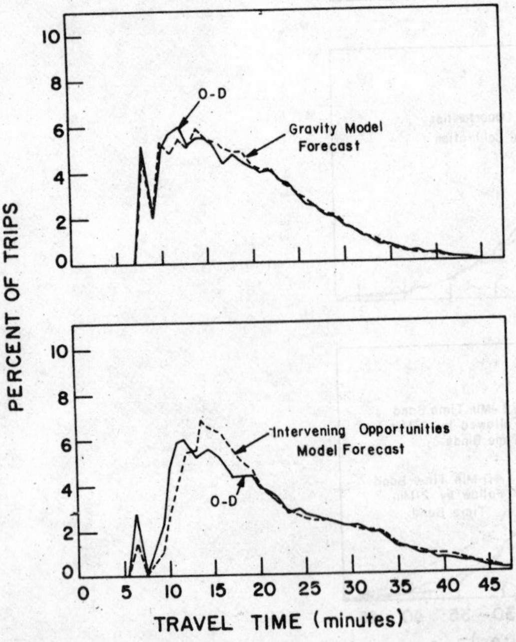

FIG. 4.23. Comparison of observed and forecast trip-length frequency distributions–Washington, D.C., 1955.

4.7 LINEAR PROGRAMMING APPROACH TO TRIP DISTRIBUTION

Blunden [23] and Colston and Blunden [24] have illustrated the use of linear programming techniques for urban trip-distribution modeling. They argue that in attempting to predict the equilibrium trip-distribution state for a given land-use allocation and a particular transport network, a realistic objective is to minimize the total amount of travel time of tripmakers in moving between origin and destination pairs. They have formulated the trip-distribution problem in the following way:

$$\text{minimize} \quad Z = \sum_i \sum_j d_{ij} t_{ij} \tag{4.39a}$$

subject to the trip end constraint equations introducted earlier in this chapter

$$\sum_j t_{ij} = p_i \tag{4.1}$$

$$\sum_i t_{ij} = a_j \tag{4.2}$$

$$\text{and} \quad \sum_i p_i = \sum_j a_j \tag{4.39b}$$

$$t_{ij} \geqslant 0, p_i \geqslant 0, a_j \geqslant 0 \tag{4.39c}$$

References [23] and [24] illustrate how the above problem may be solved using the classical transportation problem solution of operations research.

The validity of the linear programming approach rests on the assumption that urban tripmakers select origin and destinations pairs for a particular trip type so as to minimize collectively the total amount of travel time spent on the transport system. Empirical observations of urban tripmaking show clearly that tripmakers do not act collectively in this way. The trip linkages that form in an urban area are influenced significantly by the socioeconomic characteristics of tripmakers in that there are only certain sets of job and housing types that are compatible with the various socioeconomic groups. The use of the linear programming approach along with trip ends which had been stratified by socioeconomic group would no doubt provide a more valid approach.

Blunden [23] has provided a comparison of the results of the gravity model and the linear programming approach in simulating home-based work trips in

Sydney, Australia. A generally similar desire line pattern was observed and the trip-distribution state estimated by the linear program involved 367,000 trip hours, that estimated by the gravity model possessed 477,000 trip hours compared with an observed 421,000 hours.

SUMMARY

The purpose of the trip-distribution analysis phase is to develop a procedure that synthesizes the trip linkages between traffic analysis zones for both transit captive and choice tripmakers. Any trip-distribution matrix which is synthesized during this phase of the travel-demand forecasting process must satisfy the production and attraction trip-end constraint equations. At the production end, the sum of the trip interchanges to all attraction zones must be equal to the trip-production magnitude estimated during the trip generation and captive modal split analyses for all zones. At the attraction end, the sum of the trip interchanges from all production zones must be equal to the trip-attraction magnitude estimate during the previous phases for all zones.

The Fratar growth-factor method estimates an horizon-year trip-interchange matrix by assuming that this trip matrix is proportional to the base-year trip matrix modified by the trip-end growth patterns of the zones under consideration. The technique is useful for estimating through trips and for updating trip matrices over short time periods. The principal deficiency of the technique is that the trip matrices estimated by the technique are not sensitive to changes in the properties of transport networks.

Three trip-distribution models are available which may be classified as stochastic trip-distribution models. These models estimate trip-distribution patterns by synthesizing a matrix containing the probabilities that a trip produced in a given origin zone will find an attraction opportunity in a specific destination zone. These probabilities are derived from a knowledge of the distribution of attraction opportunities in an urban area and the travel-time properties of the area. Each of the three stochastic-type trip-distribution models calculates these probabilities in a different way.

The gravity model calculates the relative attractivity of a zone from the product of the number of opportunities in a zone and the travel-time factor to that zone divided by the sum of this product for all of the zones of potential attraction. The critical element of this calculation procedure is the identification of the travel-time-factor function which reproduces the observed trip-length frequency distribution. Areawide travel-time-factor functions are used normally, and because of this, an attraction trip-end balancing procedure must be used to produce a trip-interchange matrix which satisfies the trip-end constraint equations. Improved trip-interchange estimates are achieved if the gravity model is used in conjunction with trip ends which have been disaggregated into a number of socioeconomic groups.

The intervening-opportunities model calculates the relative attractivity of a zone from the product of the cumulative probability that a trip has not found a satisfactory destination after a set of destination opportunities has already been considered, and a conditional probability that a satisfactory destination opportunity will be found in the set of opportunities within the zone being considered. The Schneider formulation of the model assumes that the model conditional probability referred to above remains constant. The Golding and Davidson formulation assumes that this conditional probability decreases as additional attraction trip ends are considered.

Most attempts at calibrating the model have shown that the conditional probability varies as additional attraction trip-end opportunities are reached. The calibration procedure for the intervening opportunities model is not as well developed as that for the gravity model. However, a number of studies have demonstrated that calibration using multiple conditional probability magnitudes and a criterion of agreement between observed and estimated trip-length frequency distributions, produces generally satisfactory results.

The attraction trip-end probabilities in the competing opportunities model are calculated from the product of two probabilities known as a *probability of attraction* and a *probability of satisfaction.* The probability of attraction to a given zone is equal to the number of attraction opportunities in a zone divided by the total number of attraction opportunities in time bands up to and including the time band in which the zone is located. The probability of satisfaction in a given zone is equal to one minus the total number of attraction opportunities already considered divided by the total attraction opportunities in the study area. A generally satisfactory method of calibrating the competing-opportunities model has not been developed.

The transportation problem formulation of linear programming has also been used for trip-distribution analysis. The objective function which has been used is to minimize for tripmakers the total amount of travel time in moving between origin and destination pairs. The distribution of trips is subject to the two trip-end constraint equations referred to earlier in this summary.

Most comparative studies of the alternative trip-distribution techniques indicate that the most reliable technique is the gravity model. It is simple to calibrate and use, and experience gained in a large number of studies has allowed some generalizations of the parameters in terms of the broad properties of urban areas. However, for certain special types of trip-distribution problems the other techniques might be more useful.

REFERENCES

1. Fratar, T. J., *Forecasting Distribution of Inter-Zonal Vehicular Trips by Successive Approximations,* Proceedings, Highway Research Board, Washington, D.C., vol. 33, 1954.

2. Brokke, G. E., *Evaluating Trip Forecasting Methods with an Electronic Computer,* Bulletin No. 203, Highway Research Board, Washington, D.C., 1958.
3. Martin, B. V., F. W. Memmott, and A. J. Bone, *Principles and Techniques of Predicting Future Demand for Urban Area Transportation,* Massachusetts Institute of Technology Press, Cambridge, Massachusetts, 1961.
4. Wilson, A. G., *Entropy in Urban and Regional Modelling,* Pion Limited, London, 1970.
5. Bureau of Public Roads, *Calibrating and Testing a Gravity Model for Any Sized Urban Area,* U.S. Department of Commerce, Washington, D.C., 1965.
6. Edens, H. J., "Analysis of a Modified Gravity Model," *Transportation Research,* vol. 4, 1970.
7. Hutchinson, B. G., "Transport Analysis of Regional Development Plans," *Journal, Urban Planning and Development Division,* American Society of Civil Engineers, vol. UP1, March, 1973.
8. Ashford, N., and D. O. Covault, *The Mathematical Form of Travel Time Functions,* Highway Research Record No. 283, Highway Research Board, Washington, D.C., 1969.
9. Morrall, J. F., *Work Trip Distribution and Modal Split in the Metropolitan Toronto Region,* Ph.D. thesis, Department of Civil Engineering, University of Waterloo, Waterloo, Ontario, 1971.
10. Quandt, R. E., and W. J. Baumol, "The Demand for Abstract Transport Modes: Theory and Measurement," *Journal of Regional Science,* vol. 6, 1966.
11. Quandt, R. E., "Estimation of Modal Splits," *Transportation Research,* vol. 2, no. 1, pp. 41–50, March, 1968.
12. Wilson, A. G., et al., "Calibration and Testing of the SELNEC Transport Model," *Regional Studies,* vol. 3, no. 3, pp. 337–350, 1969.
13. Archer, E., and J. H. Shortreed, *Potential Demands for Demand Scheduled Buses,* Highway Research Record No. 367, Highway Research Board, Washington, D.C., 1971.
14. Stouffer, S. A., "Intervening Opportunities: A Theory Relating Mobility and Distance," *American Sociological Review,* vol. 5, no. 6, pp. 845–867, 1940.
15. Schneider, M., *Panel Discussion on Inter-Area Travel Formulas,* Bulletin No. 253, Highway Research Board, Washington, D.C., 1960.
16. Golding, S., and K. B. Davidson, *A Residential Land Use Prediction Model for Transportation Planning,* Proceedings, Australian Road Research Board, Melbourne, pp. 5–25, 1970.
17. Ruiter, E. R., *Improvements in Understanding, Calibrating and Applying the Opportunity Model,* Highway Research Record No. 165, Highway Research Board, Washington, D.C., 1967.
18. Swerdloff, C. N., and J. R. Stowers, *A Test of Some First Generation Residential Land Use Models,* Highway Research Record No. 126, Highway Research Board, Washington, D.C., 1966.
19. Pyers, C. E., *Evaluation of the Intervening Opportunities Trip Distribution Model,* Highway Research Record No. 114, Highway Research Board, Washington, D.C., 1965.
20. Tomazinis, A. R., *A New Method of Trip Distribution in an Urban Area,* Bulletin No. 347, Highway Research Board, Washington, D.C., 1962.
21. Heanue, K. E., and C. E. Pyers, *A Comparative Evaluation of Trip Distribution Procedures,* Highway Research Record No. 114, Highway Research Board, Washington, D.C., 1965.
22. Bell, G., *The Distribution of Work Trips in Urban Areas: Some Considerations,* Proceedings, Australian Road Research Board, Melbourne, pp 126–153, 1970.
23. Blunden, W. R., *The Land-Use/Transport System,* Pergamon Press, Oxford, England, 1971.
24. Colston, M., and W. R. Blunden, *On the Duality of Desire Line and Land Use Models,* Proceedings, Australian Road Research Board, Melbourne, pp. 170–183, 1970.

5 TRAVEL-DEMAND FORECASTING: ROUTE ASSIGNMENT ANALYSIS

The final phase of the travel-demand forecasting process described in Chap. 1 has been identified as route assignment analysis. The purpose of the route assignment analysis phase is to develop a technique that simulates the way in which the car and transit trips between each origin and destination pair distribute over the links of their respective networks. The principal concern of this chapter is with traffic assignment methods, as route assignment for the public-transport network is not normally a problem, except in very large cities with complex public-transport systems.

The earliest attempts at developing traffic assignment methods were made during the initial period of urban freeway building in the early 1950s. These methods were two-path, or diversion-curve techniques. They attempted to forecast the amount of traffic that would be diverted to a freeway from the arterial street system. Descriptions of these two-path methods may be found in Refs. 1-4.

These two-path traffic assignment methods were found to have a number of disadvantages. Their principal disadvantage was that they were unable to simulate the behavior of traffic on the entire network of major streets.

Single-path network assignment methods were developed in an attempt to improve the traffic assignment process. These methods attempt to simulate the behavior of an entire network with the restriction that there is only one preferred path between each origin and destination pair.

More recently a number of multipath traffic assignment procedures have been developed. These procedures allow for a number of potential paths through the street system for traffic traveling between an origin and destination pair.

5.1 NETWORK ASSIGNMENT METHODS

Network assignment methods allocate car travel demands between each origin and destination pair to the entire systems of streets exclusive of the local street system. A number of network assignment procedures have been developed [5–7] and all of these techniques contain the following three components: (1) a driver route-selection criterion, (2) a tree building technique which selects vehicle routes through a network of streets, and (3) a method of allocating vehicle trip interchanges between these routes.

The most fundamental element of any traffic assignment technique is to select a criterion which explains the choice by a driver of one route between an origin-destination pair from among the number of potential paths available.

Wardrop [8] has identified two criteria that might be used to predict the paths that might be taken between an origin and destination pair by motorists and these are: (1) the trip times on all the routes actually used are equal and less than those which would be experienced by a single vehicle on any unused route, and (2) the average journey times of all motorists is a minimum which implies that the aggregate vehicle hours spent in traveling is a minimum. It is useful to quote directly from Wardrop's original article to elaborate on these two criteria:

> The first criterion is quite a likely one in practice, since it might be assumed that traffic will tend to settle down into an equilibrium situation in which no driver can reduce his journey time by choosing a new route. On the other hand, the second criterion is the most efficient in the sense that it minimizes vehicle-hours spent on the journey. In practice, of course, drivers will be influenced by other factors, such as the state of the roads, and the comfort or discomfort of driving in general. However, it is clearly difficult to allow for these psychological factors.

Figure 5.1 shows two relationships between travel time and traffic volume reported by Wohl and Martin [9] for central London roads. The relationship labeled "average travel time" shows the variation in the average travel time faced by individual vehicles as the traffic volume increases. For example, when the traffic volume is 2,000 vehicles per hour, each vehicle will experience an average travel time of 5.0 minutes per mile. When the volume is 3,000 vehicles per hour, then each vehicle will experience an average travel time of 15.0 minutes per vehicle. The second relationship in Fig. 5.1, labeled "marginal travel time,"

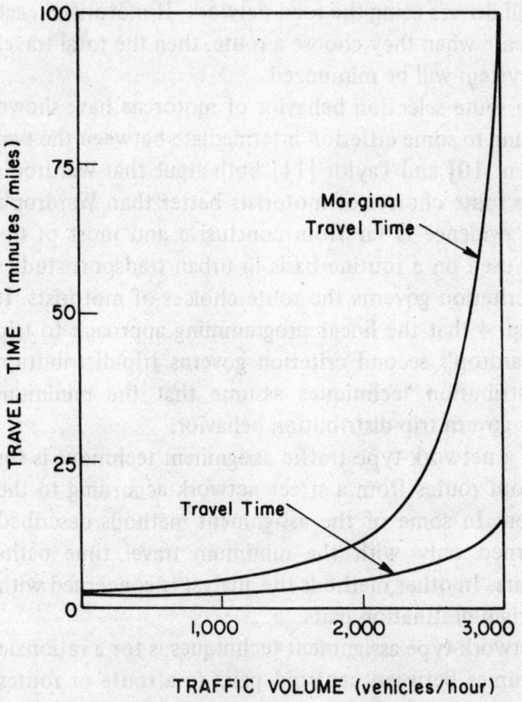

FIG. 5.1. Travel time vs. traffic volume. (*From Martin Wohl and Brian V. Martin, "Traffic System Analysis for Engineers and Planners," McGraw-Hill Book Company, New York,* 1967.)

shows the increase in the aggregate travel time experienced by all vehicles as traffic volume increases. At low traffic volumes, the marginal or additional total travel time contributed to all vehicles by an additional vehicle entering the traffic stream is small. At a volume of 3,000 vehicles per hour the average travel time per vehicle is 15 minutes. The marginal travel time imposed on the set of vehicles by one additional vehicle is 105 minutes. The extra vehicle would actually experience a travel time only slightly above 15 minutes, the other 3,000 vehicles would have their aggregate travel time increased by 90 minutes.

Wardrop's first criterion is equivalent to the notion of average cost pricing of economic theory. Drivers might be regarded as acting selfishly in that they consider only their own individual travel times in making route choice decisions, and not the manner in which their route choice influences the aggregate travel time experienced by all motorists. That is, they base their route choice decisions on the average travel time relationship of Fig. 5.1.

Wardrop's second criterion implies that motorists select their routes according to the marginal cost criterion of economic theory. Drivers are thought of as acting as though they are aware of the way in which their route choices influence the travel times of all drivers using the road network. If motorists react to the marginal costs they create when they choose a route, then the total travel time of all vehicles using the system will be minimized.

A number of studies of the route selection behavior of motorists have shown that motorists behave according to some criterion intermediate between the two mentioned previously. Blunden [10] and Taylor [11] both argue that Wardrop's second criterion describes the route choices of motorists better than Wardrop's first criterion. However, this evidence is far from conclusive and most of the traffic assignment techniques used on a routine basis in urban transport studies assume that Wardrop's first criterion governs the route choices of motorists. It should be recalled from Chap. 4 that the linear programming approach to trip distribution assumes that Wardrop's second criterion governs trip-distribution behavior. The other trip-distribution techniques assume that the minimum individual average travel times govern trip-distribution behavior.

The second requirement of a network-type traffic assignment technique is for an algorithm which searches out routes from a street network according to the driver route selection criterion. In some of the assignment methods described below the analyst is concerned only with the minimum travel time paths between origin-destination pairs. In other methods the analyst is concerned with the "*n*-best" paths between origin-destination pairs.

The final requirement of network-type assignment techniques is for a rationale to assign trip-interchange volumes between centroid pairs to a route or routes between the centroid pair. The various methods may be classified into one of the following groups: all-or-nothing assignment, capacity-restrained assignment, and multipath assignment.

With the all-or-nothing assignment method the trip-interchange volumes are assigned to the minimum path tree independently of the traffic capacities of the links that make up the minimum path tree. Several network assignment procedures have been developed that attempt to recognize that as a traffic system is loaded with vehicles, the travel-time characteristics of the system change. The capacitated assignment techniques attempt to achieve compatibility between the volume of vehicles using a road link and the travel time on that link. The multipath assignment techniques incorporate the fact that there are normally a number of potential routes between a centroid pair and they assign the trip interchanges among these potential routes.

5.2 TRAFFIC FLOW CHARACTERISTICS

Traffic flow along a link of a street network may be described in terms of three fundamental variables which are: volume or flow (v), density or concentration (d), and speed (u).

The volume or flow of vehicles is defined as the number of vehicles passing a point in unit time and is usually expressed in terms of vehicles per hour. The density or concentration of vehicles is defined as the number of vehicles within a unit length of road and is normally expressed in terms of vehicles per mile. The speed of a traffic stream is defined as the distance traveled by vehicles in unit time and is usually expressed in terms of miles per hour.

In characterizing traffic flow it is useful to identify two distinct measures of speed and these are usually termed the *space mean speed* and the *time mean speed.* The space mean speed $\bar{u}_s$ is defined as the mean of the speeds of vehicles traveling over a given length of road. The time mean speed $\bar{u}_t$ is defined as the arithmetic mean of the speeds of vehicles passing a point during a given time interval.

The following relationship exists between these fundamental variables of traffic flow:

$$v = \bar{u}_s d \tag{5.1}$$

5.2.1 Fundamental diagram of traffic flow

Figure 5.2 shows the fundamental diagram of traffic flow between flow and density that has been established from empirical observations of traffic behavior. The essential properties of this diagram are: (1) at zero density flow will be zero, (2) at maximum (jam) density flow will also be zero, and (3) maximum flow is obtained at some density intermediate between these two extremes, and this maximum flow is usually termed the *capacity* of a link.

Capacity may be defined more explicitly as the maximum number of vehicles that can reasonably be expected to pass over a given section of a lane of a roadway in one direction during a given time period under prevailing roadway and traffic conditions.

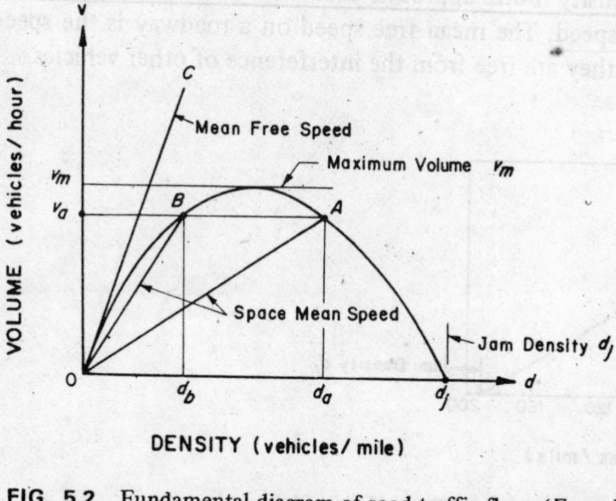

FIG. 5.2. Fundamental diagram of road traffic flow. (*From Martin Wohl and Brian V. Martin, "Traffic System Analysis for Engineers and Planners," McGraw-Hill Book Company, New York,* 1967.)

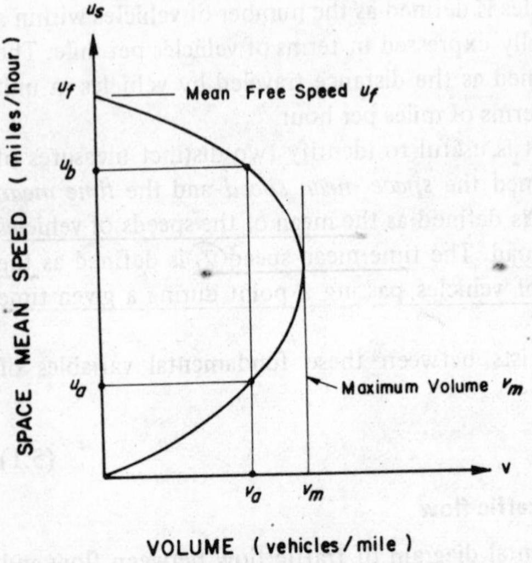

FIG. 5.3. Space mean speed vs. volume. *(From Martin Wohl and Brian V. Martin, "Traffic System Analysis for Engineers and Planners," McGraw-Hill Book Company, New York,* 1967.)

From Eq. (5.1) the space mean speed is equal to the flow divided by the density. The slope of OA in Fig. 5.2 represents the space mean speed corresponding to a volume v_a and density d_a. The diagram demonstrates that for a flow v_a there is another possible speed defined by the slope of OB which corresponds to the density d_b. At jam density d_j the space mean speed is zero and as the flow and density both approach zero the space mean speed will approach the mean free speed. The mean free speed on a roadway is the speed drivers will assume when they are free from the interference of other vehicles.

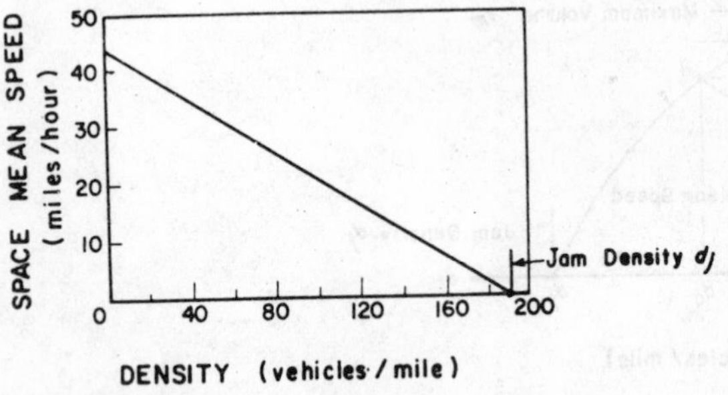

FIG. 5.4. Space mean speed vs. density. *(From Martin Wohl and Brian V. Martin, "Traffic System Analysis for Engineers and Planners," McGraw-Hill Book Company, New York,* 1967.)

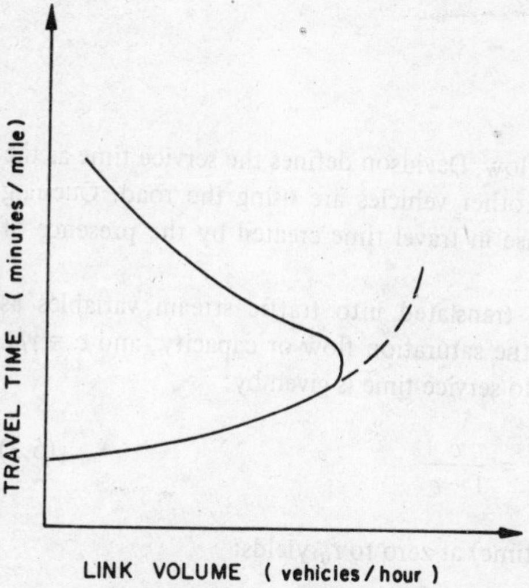

FIG. 5.5. Travel time vs. link volume.

Figure 5.3 may be constructed from Fig. 5.2 and it shows the relationship between the space mean speed and flow. As the flow of vehicles increases, the space mean speed decreases and the travel time along the link will increase. If the volume of vehicles demanding movement along the link approaches ν_m, the dynamics of traffic flow may cause the flow to decrease to say, ν_a. This will reduce the speed to $\bar{u}_a$ and cause a corresponding increase in travel time.

Figure 5.4 shows the third relationship between the variables that describe a traffic stream and this is the relationship between space mean speed and density.

Of importance to traffic assignment techniques is the relationship between the unit travel time on a link and the volume of vehicles using that link. Figure 5.5 shows such a relationship and this relationship has been derived from Fig. 5.3. The backward-bending effect may occur in certain freeway situations but does not normally occur on roads that are not controlled access roads. In fact for transport-planning purposes the broken-line relationship is the one that is used because the conditions on the backward bending portion of the curve are highly unstable and are normally not sustained for any significant length of time.

5.2.2 Flow-travel time relationships

Davidson [12] has developed a flow-travel-time relationship which has its basis in queuing theory and which provides a better basis for developing the appropriate relationships. The delay in a queue for random arrivals and random service is given by:

$$w_\nu = \frac{c^2}{h(1-c)} \tag{5.2}$$

where w_v = the delay per vehicle
h = the arrival rate
u = the service rate
$c = h/u$

In applying this model to traffic flow, Davidson defines the service time as the travel time of a vehicle when no other vehicles are using the road. Queuing delays are considered as the increase in travel time created by the presence of other vehicles on the road.

The terms in Eq. (5.2) may be translated into traffic stream variables as follows: $h = v$ = the flow; $u = s$ = the saturation flow or capacity; and $c = v/s$. The ratio of the delay in the queue to service time is given by:

$$\frac{w_v c}{1/u} = \frac{c^2 u}{h(1-c)} = \frac{h^2}{u^2}\,\frac{u}{h}\,\frac{1}{1-c} = \frac{c}{1-c} \tag{5.3}$$

and setting service time (i.e., travel time) at zero to t_0 yields:

$$\frac{w_v}{t_0} = \frac{c}{1-c} \tag{5.4}$$

Davidson observes that road traffic flow is not truly a single continuous queuing situation. Delay is caused by a succession of queuing situations such that a varying amount of the total service time is subject to queuing delays. Davidson has modified Eq. (5.4) as follows:

$$w_v = t_0 J \frac{c}{1-c} \tag{5.5}$$

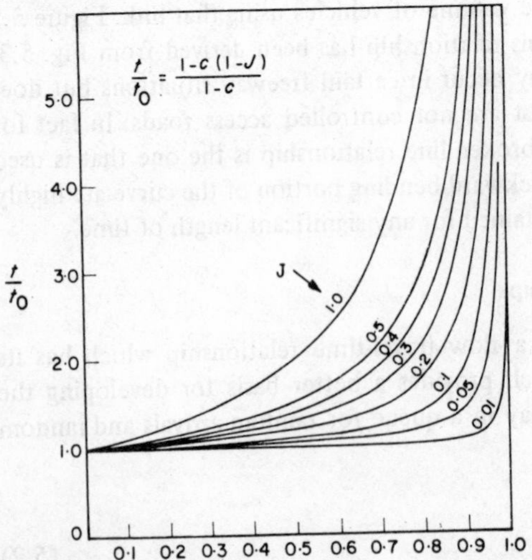

FIG. 5.6. Graphical expression of Eq. (5.6).

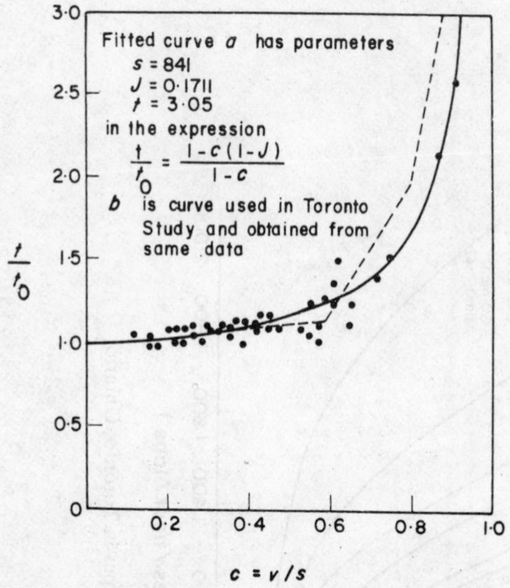

FIG. 5.7. Comparison of Eq. (5.6) with Toronto data.

where J = a factor that varies with road type and the frequency of delay-producing situations along its length and modifies the delay produced by a single queuing case.

The total travel time is made up of the delay w_v and the service time (travel time at zero flow) t_0. The total travel time may be expressed as:

$$t = t_0\left(1 + J\,\frac{c}{1-c}\right) = t_0\,\frac{1-c(1-J)}{1-c} \qquad (5.6)$$

Equation (5.6) is plotted in Fig. 5.6. Figure 5.7 shows Eq. (5.6) fitted to data available from Toronto. The data is for streets with a prevailing speed of 30 miles per hour and three signalized intersections per mile. The best fit line had the following parameters: s = 841 passenger-car units per hour, J = 0.117, and t_0 = 3.05 minutes per mile which is equivalent to a speed of 19.6 miles per hour. Insufficient information is available to allow J to be estimated directly from a knowledge of road type.

Figure 5.8 shows the relationships between travel time and volume per hour per lane developed for Toronto. These relationships were used for the capacitated assignment analyses conducted in the Metropolitan Toronto and Region Transportation Study [13].

A recent study [14] of speed-flow relationships on suburban main roads in Great Britain provided the following relationship:

$$v = v_0 + s\left[\frac{q-300}{1{,}000}\right] \qquad (5.7)$$

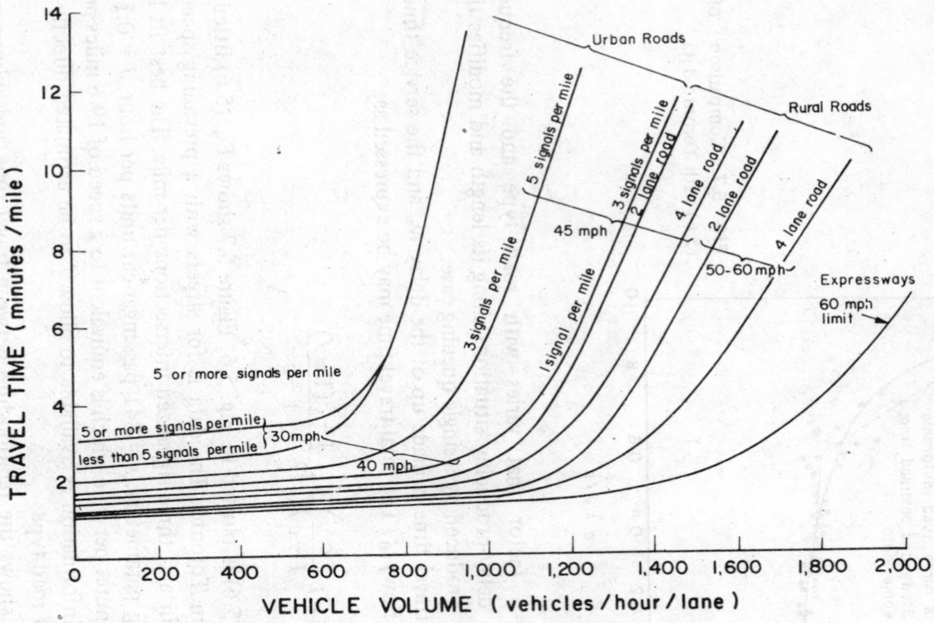

FIG. 5.8. Travel time vs. vehicle volume for various road types in Toronto, Ontario.

where v = the journey speed in kilometers/hour
q = the one-way flow of vehicles/hour/lane
v_0 = the free speed which is the speed of the traffic stream when q = 300 vehicles/hour/lane
s = the slope of the linear relationship between v and q

The slope s may be estimated from the following expression:

$$s = -25 - \frac{4}{3}[v_0 - (50 + 0.1d)] - 30(i - 0.8) - 0.4(b - 65) \tag{5.8}$$

where d = the proportion of dual carriageway expressed as a percentage
i = the density of major intersections expressed as intersections per kilometer
b = the proportion of the roadside that is developed (the average of both sides) expressed as a percentage

5.3 ROUTE-BUILDING ALGORITHMS

The coding of transport networks for computer simulation was discussed briefly in Chap. 3. It is pertinent to describe further the way in which networks are coded for the purposes of traffic assignment. Figure 5.9 shows portions of an urban transport network coded in terms of links, nodes, and centroids. All links are read into the computer in a one-way form. For example, link 315-316 is also entered as link 316-315 since it is a two-way street. On the other hand, link 315-318 only is entered since it is a one-way street.

A number of algorithms [15-17] have been developed for searching out minimum path trees for centroids. The classical work on the shortest path through a network is that by Moore [15]. Most of the available algorithms are similar in principle and differ only in the way in which they keep track of the calculations. For each origin centroid, the aim of this algorithm is to assign a label to each node in the network of the following form: node j label = $[i, d(j)]$.

where i = the node nearest to zone j which is on the minimum travel-time path back to the origin
$d(j)$ = the minimum travel time from node j back to the origin centroid

Initially, each node is assigned a $d(j)$ magnitude which is very large, say 999, with the exception of the origin node where it is set to 0. As the tree is built out from the origin, the following sum is formed for each node: node j sum = $[d(i) + l(i,j)]$.

where $d(i)$ = the travel time from the origin to node i which has just been connected to the origin
$l(i,j)$ = the travel time along the link which connects node j to node i

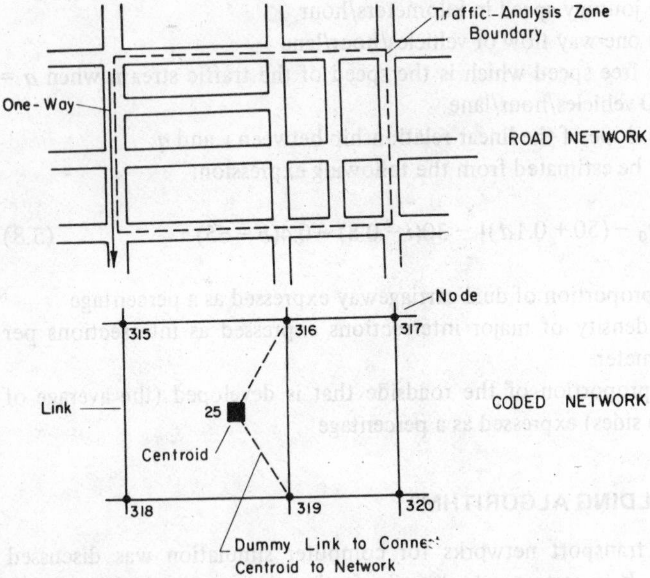

Node From	Node To	Distance (miles)	Speed (mph)
315	316	0·7	20
315	318	0·6	25
316	315	0·7	20
316	317	0·5	20
317	316	0·5	15
317	320	0·6	20
318	319	0·7	20
319	318	0·7	20

COMPUTER DESCRIPTION

FIG. 5.9. Computer coding of road network.

If the sum just formed is greater than the $d(j)$ already recorded for node j, then the node is bypassed. If the sum is less than the existing $d(j)$, then the $d(j)$ is replaced by the newly formed sum and the i is changed in the label to reflect the new connecting link for node j back to the origin. New sums are formed for all of the nodes adjacent to the nodes just connected to the origin and these sums are tested against the $d(j)$ magnitudes recorded for the nodes. This process is continued until all nodes have been reached. The label numbers for each node show the minimum travel time back to the origin as well as the node which is the next nearest on the minimum travel-time path back to the origin. This tree building process must be carried out for each origin centroid in turn. Figure 5.10 illustrates this algorithm with a simple example.

Shortreed and Wilson [18] have modified the original Moore algorithm and have produced a computationally more-efficient tree building algorithm. The improved efficiency results from the manner in which the node labels are stored and updated. This algorithm uses three concepts which are known as the *tree table,* the *link table,* and the *list.* The tree table shows, for a given origin centroid, the sequence of nodes that define the minimum path from any particular centroid back to the origin centroid. The link table defines all of the links in the network in terms of other nodes at either end and the travel time along the link. The list is simply a table in which all of the links emanating from a specified node are entered along with the travel times on the links.

The algorithm is best explained through the use of a simple example network. Figure 5.11 shows a simple street network and the following example will show how the algorithm can be used to build the minimum path tree for centroid 15.

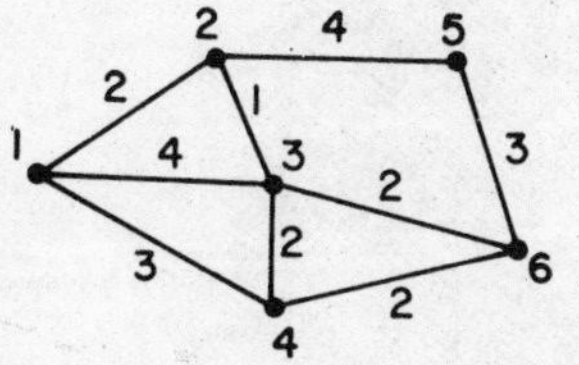

Origin node 1
node 1 label = [–,0]

node 2 sum = 0 + 2 = 2
2 < 999 node 2 label = [1,2] node 2 connected to 1

node 3 sum = 0 + 4
4 < 999 node 3 label = [1,4] node 3 connected to 1

node 4 sum = 0 + 3 = 3
3 < 999 node 4 label = [1,3] node 4 connected to 1

node 3 sum = 2 + 1 = 3
3 < 4 node 3 label = [2,3] node 3 connected to 2

node 5 sum = 2 + 4 = 6
6 < 999 node 5 label = [2,6] node 5 connected to 2

node 4 sum = 4 + 2 = 6
6 > 3 node 4 label = [1,3] node 4 connection remains

node 6 sum = 4 + 2 = 6
6 < 999 node 6 label = [3,6] node 6 connected to 3

node 6 sum = 3 + 2 = 5
5 < 6 node 6 label = [4,5] node 6 connected to 4

node 6 sum = 6 + 3 = 9
9 > 5 node 6 label = [4,5] node 6 connection remains

FIG. 5.10. Example of minimum path tree building algorithm.

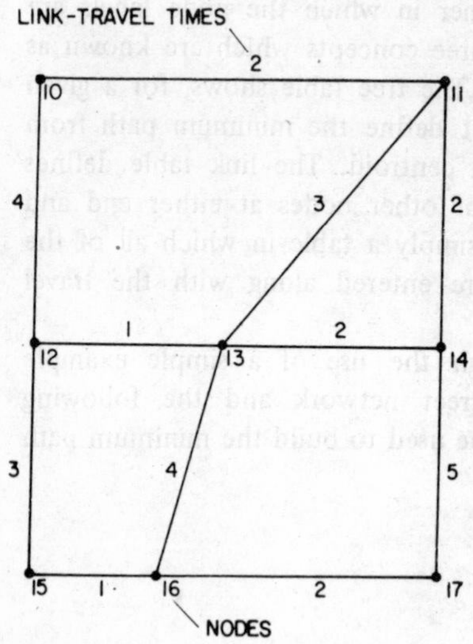

FIG. 5.11. Simple street network.

Table 5.1. Link table for simple network

Node From	Node To	Travel time
10	11	2
10	12	4
11	10	2
11	13	3
11	14	2
12	10	4
12	13	1
12	15	3
13	12	1
13	11	3
13	14	2
14	13	2
14	11	2
14	17	5
15	12	3
15	16	1
16	15	1
16	13	4
16	17	2
17	16	2
17	15	5

Table 5.2. Initialized tree table

Node To	Total time	Node From
10	999	0
11	999	0
12	999	0
13	999	0
14	999	0
15	0.0	0
16	999	0
17	999	0

Table 5.3. Revised tree table

Node To	Total time	Node From
10	999	0
11	999	0
12	3	15
13	999	0
14	999	0
15	0.0	
16	1	15
17	999	0

The link table for the network of Fig. 5.11 is shown in Table 5.1. The minimum path tree is constructed by the following sequence of operations:

1. Initialize the tree table with all the total times equal to 999 with the exception of the origin node which is set equal to 0.0 and this activity is shown in Table 5.2.
2. Add to the list all nodes connected to the nodes just added to the tree table.
3. Test all entries in the list to determine if "Node To" + "Total Time from Origin" travel time is less than the "Total Travel Time" in the tree table and if so enter it in the tree table.
4. Return to step 2 and repeat the process until the list is empty.

The sequence of steps for the simple network of Fig. 5.11 is given below.

Step 2:	LIST	Node From	Node To	Time
		15	12	3
		15	16	1

Step 3: TEST Is Node To + Total Time from Origin $<$ Tree Table Total Travel time?

$0.0 + 3 < 999$ Add 12 to Tree Table

$0.0 + 1 < 999$ Add 16 to Tree Table

The revised tree table is shown in Table 5.3.

Step 2:	LIST	Node From	Node To	Time
		12	10	4
		12	13	1
		16	13	4
		16	17	2

Step 3: TEST

$3 + 4 < 999$ Add 10 to Tree Table

$3 + 1 < 999$ Add 13 to Tree Table

$1 + 4 \nless 4$ Do not add to Tree Table

$1 + 2 < 999$ Add 17 to Tree Table

The revised tree table after this second iteration is shown in Table 5.4.

This process may be repeated until the list is empty and the tree table in Table 5.5 would result. The minimum path tree for centroid 15 can easily be read from the tree table and this minimum path tree is shown in Fig. 5.12. If the row from the origin-destination matrix for centroid 15 is that shown in the lower part of Fig. 5.12, then the volumes on the links due to trips from centroid 15 would be as shown in Fig. 5.12.

5.4 CAPACITY-RESTRAINED ASSIGNMENT TECHNIQUES

The Wayne State arterial assignment method [5] is one of the earlier capacity restrained assignment methods. The basic approach of this method is

Table 5.4. Revised tree table

Node To	Total time	Node From
10	7	12
11	999	0
12	3	15
13	4	12
14	999	0
15	0.0	
16	1	15
17	3	16

Table 5.5. Final tree table

Node To	Total time	Node From
10	7	12
11	7	13
12	3	15
13	4	12
14	6	13
15	0.0	
16	1	15
17	3	16

to assign traffic to the various routes between an origin-destination pair such that the travel times on these routes are all equal, and any route between the origin-destination pair with zero flow will have a larger travel time. The sequence of steps involved in this traffic assignment method are:

1. Minimum path trees are constructed for all origin zones based on travel times computed from average speeds under typical urban conditions.
2. Interzonal volumes are assigned to the minimum path tree on an all-or-nothing basis.
3. Link travel times are recalculated using the following expression:

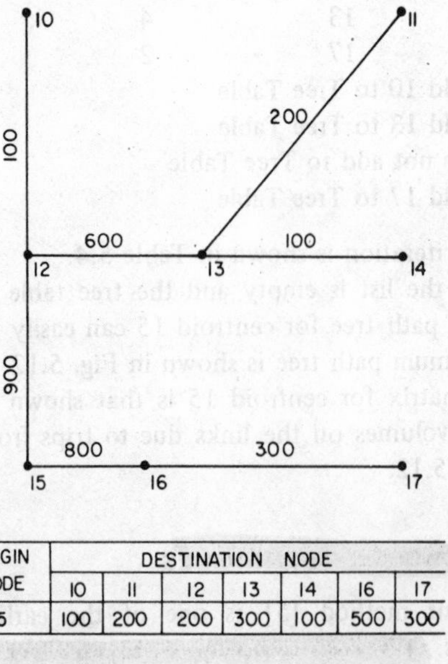

FIG. 5.12. Minimum path tree for node 15.

ORIGIN NODE	DESTINATION NODE						
	10	11	12	13	14	16	17
15	100	200	200	300	100	500	300

$$v_n = e^{(r_n - 1)} v_0, \tag{5.9}$$

where v_n = travel time on a link for the nth iteration
r_n = ratio of the average of the volumes assigned in previous iterations to the capacity of the link
v_0 = original travel time on the link.

4. New minimum path trees are constructed using the new travel times calculated in the previous step.
5. Interzonal trip interchanges are then assigned on an all-or-nothing basis to the new minimum path trees.
6. Return to step (3) until equilibrium occurs or until some predetermined cutoff point is reached.

Mosher [19] and Tomlin [20] have both formulated traffic assignment analysis as a linear programming problem. These formulations assume that Wardrop's second criterion is valid. The trip interchanges are assigned to the paths in the traffic network such that the aggregate travel time on the network is minimized subject to the condition that no link capacity is exceeded and to the condition that all journeys leaving an origin must reach their destination.

The linear program is usually expressed in the following way:

minimize

$$z = \sum_{k,j,i} l(i) a(i,j,k) v(j,k)$$

subject to

$$\sum_{k,j} a(i,j,k) v(j,k) < c(i)$$

and

$$\sum_{j} v(j,k) = t(k) \tag{5.10}$$

where $l(i)$ = travel time on link i
$a(i,j,k)$ = 1 if link i is in path (j,k) (0 otherwise)
$v(j,k)$ = flow on path (j,k) between kth origin-destination pair
$t(k)$ = trip interchange between kth origin-destination pair
$c(i)$ = capacity of link i

The objective function of Eq. (5.10) is the minimization of the product of all link volumes and link travel times over all paths between all centroid pairs.

A third capacity restrained assignment procedure is that developed by Traffic Research Corporation [6,7] which is part of a nest of models involving trip distribution, modal split and traffic assignment. The sequence of steps involved in this method are:

1. Minimum path trees are constructed for all origins on the basis of free-speed link travel times.
2. Travel-time factors are calculated from the travel times between origin-destination pairs and a trip table is generated by the gravity model for a given set of trip generations.
3. The modal split is estimated for each origin-destination pair using a set of diversion curves.
4. Trip interchanges are then assigned to the minimum path trees on an all-or-nothing basis and link volumes are accumulated; the functions shown in Fig. 5.8 are then utilized to revise the link travel times and new minimum time paths are constructed along with a new trip table and modal splits.

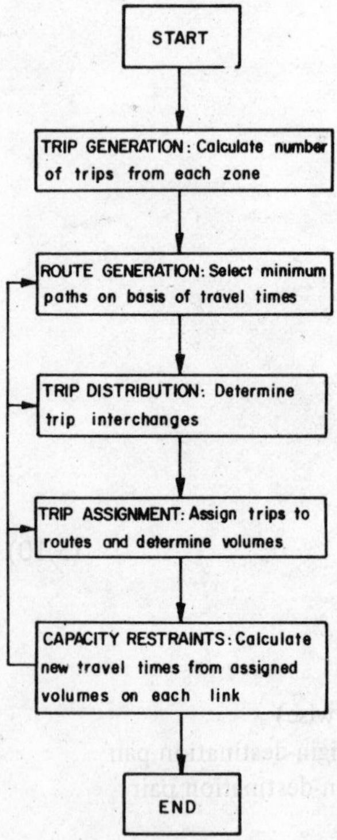

FIG. 5.13. Sequence of activities in traffic simulation model.

This sequence of steps is repeated until equilbrium conditions are established. The sequence of activities involved in this method is shown in Fig. 5.13.

Other methods of single-path network-type route assignment methods exist but the three methods presented above are typical of the methods. The Wayne State method incorporates a capacity restraint feature that attempts to simulate the manner in which equilibrium traffic flows are established in reality. The capacity restraint function used in this assignment method is extremely sensitive. At low-link traffic volumes the travel times tend to change too rapidly while at volumes near link capacity they change too slowly. These characteristics of the restraint function result in the development of minimum path trees and assignments to these paths that would not normally carry any traffic for a particular interzonal interchange. By averaging the assignments for each iteration, these routes will ultimately disappear, but the technique may require many iterations.

5.5 MULTIPATH ASSIGNMENT TECHNIQUES

McLaughlin [21] developed one of the first multipath traffic assignment techniques. A driver route selection criterion is used by McLaughlin which is a function of travel time, travel cost, and accident potential. The minimum resistance paths between each origin and destination pair are calculated with all the link resistances set to values which correspond to a zero traffic volume. The minimum resistance value between an origin and destination pair is increased by 30 percent. All the paths between the origin and destination pair with resistance values less than this maximum value are identified.

McLaughlin used certain principles of linear graph theory to accomplish the multipath assignment. Using an electrical analogy it is possible to identify a through variable y that corresponds to current, or traffic flow. An across variable x may be identified that corresponds to potential difference, or traffic pressure.

Two postulates from linear graph theory may be introduced that are known as the *vertex* and *circuit postulates.* At any vertex

$$\sum_{i=1}^{e} a_i y_i = 0 \tag{5.11}$$

where e = the number of oriented terminal graphs, or elements
y_i = the through variable of the ith element
a_i = 0 if the ith element is not connected to V
= 1 if the ith element is oriented away from V
= −1 if the ith element is oriented toward V

For any circuit,

$$\sum_{i=1}^{e} b_i X_i = 0 \tag{5.12}$$

where X_i = the across variable of the ith element
b_i = 0 if the ith element is not in the jth circuit
= 1 if the ith element orientation is the same as the jth circuit
= −1 if the ith element orientation is opposite to the jth circuit

A subgraph is then established for each origin and destination pair with these representing two vertices. The connecting elements are the acceptable paths between the vertices plus one flow driver element that corresponds to the car travel demand between the origin and destination pair. The travel demand is assigned among the potential paths in accordance with the path resistance values calculated during the path building phase. The traffic assigned to each path must be such that the alternative paths have an equal across variable value.

The across variable X, the resistance value $R(y)$ and the through variable y for each path are assumed to be related as follows:

$$X = R(y)y \tag{5.13}$$

Equation (5.13) is analagous to Ohm's law in that the potential is equal to the resistance times the flow. In this case the resistance along a path is assumed to be a function of the flow along that path.

Figure 5.14 is the way McLaughlin [21] illustrated the assignment method. A schematic two-way street system is shown along with the link descriptions and the trip table. Minimum path trees were determined for all origin-destination pairs using the resistance function for zero flow, and these are given in Table 5.6. The minimum path resistance values were multiplied by 1.3 and the paths whose resistance values were less than this higher value were determined and these paths are also given in Table 5.6.

The trip table inputs were assigned directly for those origin-destination pairs with only one path. Subgraphs were formed for the remaining trip table inputs and solved by the chord formulation of linear graph theory. Figure 5.15 shows the subgraph for origin 1 and destination 3.

The circuit equations may be represented in the general form as:

$$\begin{bmatrix} B_{11} & B_{12} & u & 0 \\ B_{21} & B_{22} & 0 & u \end{bmatrix} \begin{bmatrix} X_{b-1} \\ X_{b-2} \\ X_{c-1} \\ X_{c-2} \end{bmatrix} = 0 \tag{5.14}$$

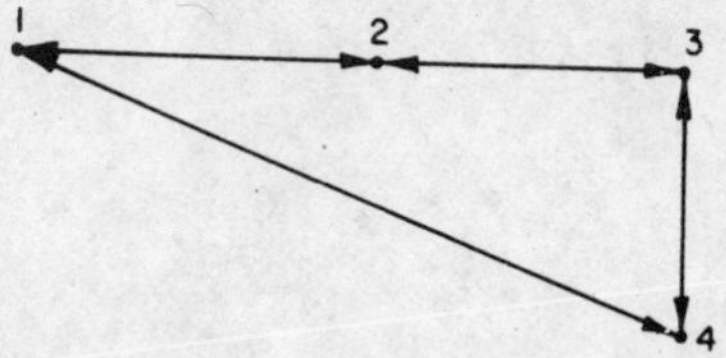

LINK CHARACTERISTICS

No.	Link	Length (miles)	Maximum capacity (vehicles/hour)	Free speed (mph)
1	1 - 2	1·0	1200	40
2	1 - 4	2·0	4000	50
3	2 - 1	1·0	1200	40
4	2 - 3	0·5	1000	30
5	3 - 2	0·5	1000	30
6	3 - 4	0·5	1000	30
7	4 - 1	2·0	4000	50
8	4 - 3	0·5	1000	30

TRIP TABLE

Origin	Destination			
	1	2	3	4
1		100	100	2500
2	300*		100	800

* Passenger cars/hour.

FIG. 5.14. Multipath assignment example problem.

Table 5.6. Paths for multipath example

Origin	Destination	Minimum* path	Diversion* path	Minimum† path	Diversion† path
1	2	1,2	–	1,2	–
	3	1,2,3	1,4,3	1,2,3	–
	4	1,4	–	1,4	1,2,3,4
2	1	2,1	–	2,1	–
	3	2,3	–	2,3	–
	4	2,3,4	–	2,3,4	–

*Based on the resistance function = $s(p)t(p)$

†Based on the resistance function = $S(p)$

where $s(p)$ = travel cost (operating, accident, and comfort) as a function of the volume-to-capacity ratio p

$t(p)$ = travel time as a function of the volume-to-capacity ratio p

$S(p)$ = travel cost (operating, accident, comfort, and time) as a function of the volume-to-capacity ratio p

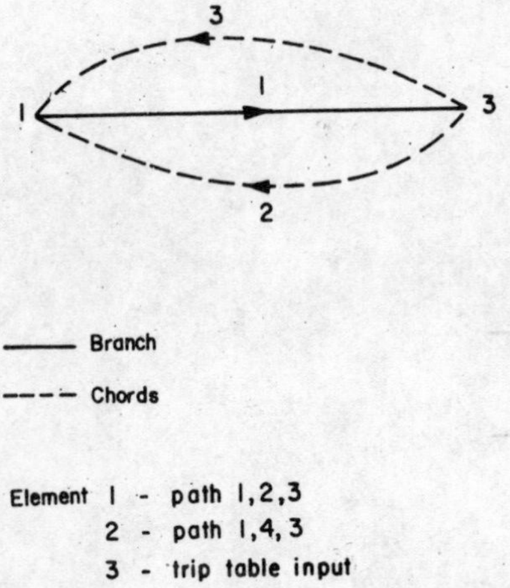

FIG. 5.15. Subgraph of origin 1 and destination 2.

where $B_{11}, \ldots$ = coefficient matrices corresponding to the branches
u = a unit matrix corresponding to the chords
$X_{b-1}, \ldots$ = the column matrices of the branches
$X_{c-1}, \ldots$ = the column matrices of the chords

The first term is nonexistent in this system and the circuit equations are:

$$\begin{bmatrix} B_{12} & u & 0 \\ B_{22} & 0 & u \end{bmatrix} \begin{bmatrix} X_{b-2} \\ X_{c-1} \\ X_{c-2} \end{bmatrix} = 0 \tag{5.15}$$

The terminal equations of the street components may be represented by:

$$\begin{bmatrix} X_{b-2} \\ X_{c-1} \end{bmatrix} = \begin{bmatrix} R_{b-2} & 0 \\ 0 & R_{c-1} \end{bmatrix} \begin{bmatrix} Y_{b-2} \\ Y_{c-1} \end{bmatrix} \tag{5.16}$$

where R_{b-2} = the sum of the link resistances corresponding to branch paths
R_{c-1} = the sum of the link resistances corresponding to chord paths
Y_{b-2} = flow on the branch paths
Y_{c-1} = flow on the chord paths

For the demand assignment:

$$\begin{bmatrix} X_1 \\ X_2 \end{bmatrix} = \begin{bmatrix} 9.51 & 0 \\ 0 & 12.17 \end{bmatrix} \begin{bmatrix} y_1 \\ y_2 \end{bmatrix} \qquad (5.17)$$

The subgraph fundamental circuit equations are then substituted into the chord formulation set of equations:

$$\begin{bmatrix} 0 \\ u \end{bmatrix} X_{c-2} + \begin{bmatrix} B_{12} & u \\ B_{22} & 0 \end{bmatrix} \begin{bmatrix} R_{b-2} & 0 \\ 0 & R_{c-1} \end{bmatrix} \begin{bmatrix} B_{12}{}^T & B_{22}{}^T \\ u & 0 \end{bmatrix} \begin{bmatrix} Y_{c-1} \\ Y_{c-2} \end{bmatrix} = 0$$

$$(5.18)$$

where B_{12} = a column matrix with coefficients equal to −1; the number of rows in this matrix correspond to the number of nondriver chords in the subgraph; or it corresponds to the number of paths less 1 between an origin-destination pair

B_{22} = +1, corresponding to the driver or trip table input

Y_{c-1} = the unknown flows for the nondriver chord elements

Y_{c-2} = the through driver, or trip table input

The specific formulation of Eq. (5.18) for this example is:

$$\begin{bmatrix} 0 \\ 1 \end{bmatrix} X_3 + \begin{bmatrix} -1 & 1 \\ 1 & 1 \end{bmatrix} \begin{bmatrix} 9.51 & 0 \\ 0 & 12.17 \end{bmatrix} \begin{bmatrix} -1 & 1 \\ 1 & 0 \end{bmatrix} \begin{bmatrix} y_2 \\ 100 \end{bmatrix} = 0$$

Taking the first set of the above equations the solution is y_2 = 44 vehicles per hour, and the flow on element 1 is solved by subtraction; y_1 = 100 − 44 = 56 vehicles per hour. The results of the demand assignment are presented in Table 5.7.

In McLaughlin's assignment procedure, new link and path resistance values are calculated for the capacity restraint assignment that correspond to the flows obtained from the demand assignment. The procedure described above is employed again to calculate the restrained volumes. If these volumes are within tolerable limits of the demand volume then the restraint assignment is complete, otherwise an iterative approach is required. The results of the first restraint solution to the above problem are shown in Table 5.7 as y_2. Inspection of Table 5.7 shows that iteration is not required for this example.

Table 5.7. Link volumes for multipath example

No.	Link	R_0	Y_1	R_1	Y_2	Y_3	Y_4
1	12	4.90	156	4.98	138	1,290	625
2	14	7.56	2,544	8.42	2,562	1,410	2,075
3	21	4.90	300	5.00	300	300	300
4	23	4.61	956	16.40	938	2,090	1,425
5	32	4.61	0	4.61	0	0	0
6	34	4.61	800	5.80	1,890	1,890	1,225
7	41	7.56	0	7.56	0	0	0
8	43	4.61	44	4.61	62	0	0

An iterative solution is achieved by averaging the link volumes according to the following expression:

$$\bar{y} = \sum_{i=1}^{n} \frac{y_i}{n} \tag{5.19}$$

where $\bar{y}$ = the average assigned volumes
y_i = the trips assigned to the links during the ith iteration of the linear graph procedure including the demand assignment
n = the number of linear graph iterations

A more-detailed example of this multipath assignment procedure is provided in Ref. 21.

Burrell [22] has proposed a technique for generating multiple paths through a traffic network. This method assumes that the user does not know the actual travel times on links but associates a supposed travel time on each link that is drawn at random from a distribution of times. It assumes that the user finds and uses a route which minimizes the sum of the supposed link times.

Burrell assumes that a group of trips originating from a particular zone have the same set of supposed link times and consequently there is only one tree for each zone of production. A rectangular distribution that could assume eight separate magnitudes was assumed and the ranges of the distributions for each of the links were selected so that the ratio of the mean absolute deviation to actual link time was the same for all links. The demand or capacity restrained assignments are then made to the paths selected in the above manner.

Another multipath assignment technique has been proposed by Dial [23]. With this technique each potential path between a particular origin and destination pair is assigned a probability of use which then allows the path flows to be estimated. This technique is described in detail in Ref. 23.

SUMMARY

Network-type traffic-assignment techniques used in urban transport-planning studies are of three types which are: (1) all-or-nothing assignment to the minimum travel time paths between origin-destination pairs, (2) capacity restrained assignment to the minimum travel-time paths between origin-destination pairs, and (3) multipath traffic assignment.

A fundamental decision in connection with all traffic assignment techniques is the identification of a criterion which is used by motorists in selecting one path from among the potential paths available between an origin-destination pair. Wardrop has suggested two criteria. The first is that motorists act selfishly and attempt to minimize their individual travel times through a network. This criterion is equivalent to the average cost-pricing principle of economic theory. The second criterion suggests that motorists act so as to minimize the total travel time spent by all motorists on the network. This implies that individual motorists are aware of the way in which their choice of route influences the change in the total travel time experienced by all motorists. This second criterion is equivalent to the marginal cost-pricing principle of economic theory. Some limited empirical testing of these two criteria has been performed and the evidence available would suggest that motorists behave according to some intermediate criterion.

Link-travel times vary with the volume of vehicles using a link and the capacity restrained assignment techniques require an understanding of the relationship between the two. Link traffic flow may be described in terms of three fundamental variables: flow, density, and speed. Traffic flow is equal to the product of density and space mean speed. Flow along freeway-type links exhibits a parabolic relationship between flow and density as well as between flow and volume, while the relationship between speed and density is linear. Flow along links with delays created by signals and intersections is better explained in terms of queuing theory.

A number of algorithms exist for building minimum paths between nodes in a network. These algorithms assign a label to nodes; the label indicates the node next nearest to the node under consideration on the way back to the origin as well as the total travel time from the node to the origin by the minimum path.

The all-or-nothing assignment rationale assigns the trip interchange between an origin-destination pair to the minimum travel-time path between the centroid pair. Implicit to this approach is the notion that the travel time on each link is compatible with the traffic volume that is ultimately assigned to the link. Or, alternatively, the traffic volume that is assigned to a link will be served by a road of adequate capacity.

The capacity restrained assignment techniques involve a sequence of all-or-nothing minimum path assignments where the sequence is iterated until the traffic volumes assigned to each link are compatible with the link-travel times assumed in the minimum path tree building phase.

The Wayne State traffic assignment technique yields an allocation of traffic that satisfies Wardrop's first criterion. Trip interchanges are assigned to routes so that the travel times on all routes that are used between an origin-destination pair are equal and that any route with zero traffic volume will have a larger travel time.

The linear programming approach to capacity restrained traffic assignment employs Wardrop's second criterion. Trip interchanges are assigned to the network so that the aggregate travel time of all tripmakers is minimized subject to the constraints of link capacities.

Several multipath assignment techniques have been proposed that assign trip interchanges between origin-destination pairs among a number of paths between the centroid pairs. McLaughlin used certain principles of linear graph theory to assign trip interchanges to a set of paths. Traffic is assigned to the alternative paths so that the resistance to traffic flow times the flow is equal for all paths. Other multiple path techniques have been developed that use certain probabilistic concepts to achieve the assignment to multiple paths.

Few systematic and exhaustive comparative studies of traffic assignment techniques have been performed. The principal reason is that the collection of sufficient data on motorists' path selections is very expensive. Some studies have compared assigned traffic volumes with measured traffic volumes, but this is not a very suitable comparison. There are a number of potential sources of error in this type of comparison and these include: (1) errors in the origin-destination matrix assigned to the traffic network, (2) errors due to oversimplifications of the coded networks, (3) errors in the assignment technique, and (4) errors in the observed traffic volumes.

The potential errors in the origin-destination matrix arise because the matrix entries are obtained from the expansion of a limited sample of trips, usually about 5 percent. Major errors may occur due to the simplified way in which the street network is coded for computer use. Only the major routes and intersections are normally coded and all trips are assumed to begin or end at a point. Network simplifications may produce large errors on some links of the network. Errors may also be present in the measured volume.

At the present time there seems to be a feeling among transport planners that the traffic assignment phase of the travel forecasting process is only of marginal use in resolving strategic transport planning issues. There is also a feeling, largely undocumented, that the all-or-nothing assignment technique provides adequate information for transport planning that is undertaken for conditions expected some 20 years ahead. The more-sophisticated traffic assignment technqiues can probably be justified for shorter-run traffic engineering problems.

REFERENCES

1. May, A. D., and H. L. Michael, *Allocation of Traffic to Bypasses,* Bulletin No. 61, Highway Research Board, Washington, D.C., 1955.
2. Trueblood, D. L., *Effect of Travel Time and Distance on Freeway Uses,* Bulletin No. 61, Highway Research Board, Washington, D.C., 1955.
3. Campbell, E. W., and R. S. McCorgar, *Objective and Subjective Correlates of Expressway Use,* Bulletin No. 119, Highway Research Board, Washington, D.C., 1956.
4. Moskowitz, K., *California Method of Assigning Diverted Traffic to Proposed Freeways,* Bulletin No. 130, Highway Research Board, Washington, D.C., 1956.
5. Smock, R. B., *An Iterative Assignment Approach to Capacity Restraint on Arterial Networks,* Bulletin No. 347, Highway Research Board, Washington, D.C., 1962.
6. Irwin, N. A., N. Dodd, and H. G. Von Cube, *Capacity Restraint in Assignment Programs,* Bulletin No. 297, Highway Research Board, Washington, D.C., 1961.
7. Irwin, N. A., and H. G. Von Cube, *Capacity Restraint in Multi-Travel Mode Assignment Programs,* Bulletin No. 347, Highway Research Board, Washington, D.C., 1967.
8. Wardrop, J. G., *Some Theoretical Aspects of Road Traffic Research,* Proceedings, Institution of Civil Engineers, London, part II, vol. 1, 1952.
9. Wohl, M., and B. V. Martin, *Traffic Systems Analysis,* McGraw-Hill Book Company, New York, 1967.
10. Blunden, W. R., *Some Applications of Linear Programming to Transportation and Traffic Problems,* Institute of Traffic and Transportation Engineering, University of California at Berkeley, 1956.
11. Taylor, W. C., *Optimization of Traffic Flow Splits,* Highway Research Record No. 230, Highway Research Board, Washington, D.C., 1968.
12. Davidson, K. B., *A Flow-Travel Time Relationship for Use in Transportation Planning,* Proceedings, Australian Road Research Board, Melbourne, vol. 3, pp. 183–194, 1966.
13. Metropolitan Toronto and Region Transportation Study, *Calibration of a Regional Traffic Prediction Model for the A.M. Peak Period,* Toronto, Ontario, 1967.
14. Freeman Fox and Associates, *Speed/Flow Relationships on Suburban Main Roads,* Road Research Laboratory, Department of the Environment, London, 1972.
15. Moore, E. F., *The Shortest Path Through a Maze,* Proceedings, International Symposium on the Theory of Switching, Harvard University, Cambridge, Massachusetts, 1963.
16. Minty, G. J., "A Comment on the Shortest Route Problem," *Operations Research,* vol. 5, no. 5, pp. 724–728, 1957.
17. Whiting, P. D., and J. A. Hillier, *A Method for Finding the Shortest Route Through a Road Network;* Research Note RN/3337, Road Research Laboratory, Ministry of Transport, London, 1958.
18. Shortreed, J. H., and J. Wilson, *A Minimum Path Algorithm,* Unpublished report, Department of Civil Engineering, University of Waterloo, Waterloo, Ontario, 1968.
19. Mosher, W. W., *A Capacity Restraint Algorithm for Assigning Flow to a Transportation Network,* Highway Research Record No. 6, Highway Research Board, Washington, D.C., 1963.

20. Tomlin, J. A., *A Linear Programming Model for the Assignment of Traffic*, Proceedings, Australian Road Research Board, Melbourne, pp. 263–269, 1966.
21. McLaughlin, W. A., *Multi-Path System Traffic Assignment Algorithm*, Research Report No. RB 108, Department of Highways, Ontario, 1966.
22. Burrell, J. E., *Multiple Route Assignment and its Application to Capacity Restraint*, Proceedings, 4th International Conference on the Theory for Traffic Flow, Karlsruhe, Germany, 1968.
23. Dial, R. B., "A Probabilistic Multipath Traffic Assignment Model Which Obviates Path Enumeration," *Transportation Research*, vol 5, no. 2, pp. 83–111, 1971.

6 TRANSPORT-RELATED LAND-USE MODELS

Chapters 2 to 5 have described a set of travel-demand forecasting models that require as input a complete specification of land-use activities for the year being studied. The purpose of this chapter is to describe a family of land-use models that may be used to estimate a land-use allocation and the associated travel demands simultaneously. These models require much less information to be specified exogenously to the model. In addition, the models are sensitive to some of the major development policy variables that may be manipulated by governments.

A variety of transport-planning-related land-use models have been developed and used to date. Most of these models were developed originally to prepare land-use inputs to the transport models described in earlier chapters. References 1–4 provide excellent reviews of the characteristics and capabilities of most of the land-use models developed to date.

Until about 1966 virtually all research and development in land-use models had been conducted in the United States. At about this time land-use models gained a bad reputation with decisionmakers in urban affairs. In a number of regional planning and transport studies the model-building efforts became so cumbersome and time consuming that they diverted planning agencies from their main purpose. This purpose is not to build computer models but to provide plans for development control. This same criticism is also valid for some of the earlier transport-planning studies. Much of the effort of the study teams was devoted to transport model-building rather than to transport planning.

The majority of the recent practical applications of land-use models have been in countries outside the United States. Most of these studies have used some form of the Lowry model [5]. The original Lowry model was published in 1964 and since that time several important extensions of the original model have been advanced and applied to practical planning problems.

This chapter describes the Lowry land-use model and some of its variants in detail. The first part of the chapter describes the basic conceptual structure of the Lowry model as well as a form of the Lowry model developed by Garin [6]. Certain dynamic and disaggregated extensions of the model are then introduced. The final part of the chapter describes several practical applications of the Lowry family of land-use models to planning problems.

6.1 THE LOWRY MODEL

Lowry's *Model of Metropolis* [5] views the principal spatial properties of an urban area in terms of three broad sectors of activity which are: (1) employment in basic industries, (2) employment in population-serving industries, and (3) the household or population sector.

Basic employment is defined as employment in those industries whose products or services depend on markets external to the region under study. The important assumption with respect to basic employment, however, is that its location within a region is independent of the population and service employment distribution of that region. On the other hand, the location of service employment is dependent upon the population distribution of a region. Typical of the industries that might be considered as basic are the various primary industries, manufacturing, national financial institutions, and university employment. Retail trade and personal services are typical of the population-serving industries, as well as elementary school and high school employment.

With the Lowry model, the spatial distribution of basic employment is allocated exogenously to the model, and the spatial distributions of households and population-serving employment are calculated by the model. The zonal allocation rules for both households and population-serving employment are specified within the model structure. In addition, the constraints on the maximum number of households for each zone and the minimum population-serving employment thresholds for any zone are specified. The basic structure of the Lowry model is illustrated in Fig. 6.1.

The Lowry model may be regarded as a static equilibrium-type model based on the concept that interactivity accessibilities are the major determinants of the

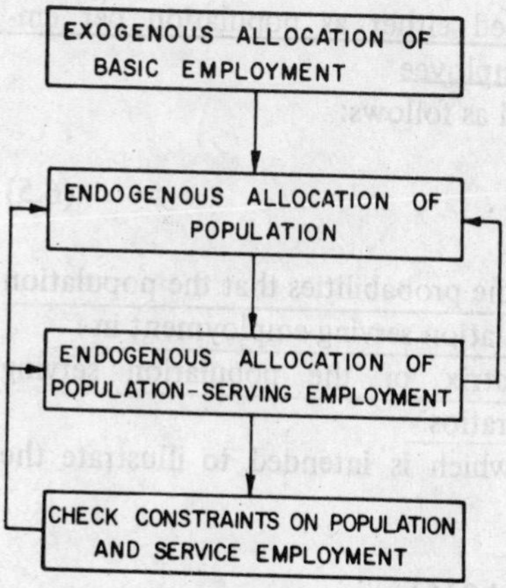

FIG. 6.1. Sequence of activities in Lowry model.

equilibrium distribution of activities. Future states forecast by the Lowry model must be regarded only as conditions of quasi-equilibrium in that they do not reflect the development history of the urban system under study.

6.1.1 The equation system

The Lowry model structure shown in Fig. 6.1 may be expressed in terms of the following system of equations:

$$p = eA \tag{6.1}$$

$$e^s = pB \tag{6.2}$$

$$e = e^b + e^s \tag{6.3}$$

where p = a row vector of the population or households within each of the n zones
e = a row vector of the total employment in each zone
e^s = a row vector of the population-serving employment in each zone
e^b = a row vector of the basic employment in each zone
A = an $n \times n$ matrix of the workplace-to-household accessibilities
B = an $n \times n$ matrix of the household-to-service center accessibilities

The A accessibility matrix may be expanded as follows:

$$A = [a'_{ij}]\ [a_j] \tag{6.4}$$

where $[a'_{ij}]$ = an $n \times n$ square matrix of the probabilities of an employee working in i and living in j
$[a_j]$ = an $n \times n$ diagonal matrix of the inverses of the labor

participation rates, expressed either as population per employee, or households per employee

The B accessibility matrix may be expanded as follows:

$$B = [b'_{ij}]\ [b_i] \tag{6.5}$$

where $[b'_{ij}]$ = an $n \times n$ square matrix of the probabilities that the population in j will be serviced by population serving employment in i

$[b_i]$ = an $n \times n$ diagonal matrix of the population serving employment-to-population ratios

Consider the following simple example which is intended to illustrate the properties of Eqs. (6.1)-(6.5):

Total employment vector $e = [126,177,64,216]$
Basic employment vector $e^b = [100,150,40,200]$

Journey to home function: $[a'_{ij}] = \begin{bmatrix} 0.35 & 0.30 & 0.20 & 0.15 \\ 0.25 & 0.35 & 0.20 & 0.20 \\ 0.15 & 0.10 & 0.35 & 0.40 \\ 0.10 & 0.25 & 0.20 & 0.45 \end{bmatrix}$

Journey to shop function: $[b'_{ij}] = \begin{bmatrix} 0.50 & 0.25 & 0.10 & 0.15 \\ 0.30 & 0.45 & 0.15 & 0.10 \\ 0.15 & 0.20 & 0.40 & 0.25 \\ 0.20 & 0.25 & 0.35 & 0.20 \end{bmatrix}$

Labor participation rate: $[a_j]$ (households/employee) $= \begin{bmatrix} 0.8 & 0 & 0 & 0 \\ 0 & 0.8 & 0 & 0 \\ 0 & 0 & 0.8 & 0 \\ 0 & 0 & 0 & 0.8 \end{bmatrix}$

Service employment ratio: $[b_i]$ (service employment/household) $= \begin{bmatrix} 0.2 & 0 & 0 & 0 \\ 0 & 0.2 & 0 & 0 \\ 0 & 0 & 0.2 & 0 \\ 0 & 0 & 0 & 0.2 \end{bmatrix}$

With the information provided, the A and B matrices may be determined, using Eqs. (6.4) and (6.5):

$$A = \begin{bmatrix} 0.28 & 0.24 & 0.16 & 0.12 \\ 0.20 & 0.28 & 0.16 & 0.16 \\ 0.12 & 0.08 & 0.28 & 0.32 \\ 0.08 & 0.20 & 0.16 & 0.36 \end{bmatrix} \qquad B = \begin{bmatrix} 0.10 & 0.05 & 0.02 & 0.03 \\ 0.06 & 0.09 & 0.03 & 0.02 \\ 0.03 & 0.04 & 0.08 & 0.05 \\ 0.04 & 0.05 & 0.07 & 0.04 \end{bmatrix}$$

The household vector may be calculated from Eq. (6.1):

$$[126,177,64,216]\begin{bmatrix}0.28 & 0.24 & 0.16 & 0.12\\ 0.20 & 0.28 & 0.16 & 0.16\\ 0.12 & 0.08 & 0.28 & 0.32\\ 0.08 & 0.20 & 0.16 & 0.36\end{bmatrix} = [95,128,101,142]$$

The service employment vector may be calculated from Eq. (6.2):

$$[95,128,101,142]\begin{bmatrix}0.10 & 0.05 & 0.02 & 0.03\\ 0.06 & 0.09 & 0.03 & 0.02\\ 0.03 & 0.04 & 0.08 & 0.05\\ 0.04 & 0.05 & 0.07 & 0.04\end{bmatrix} = [26,27,24,16]$$

Equation (6.3) may be used to check if the household and employment allocations are internally consistent

Original total employment vector $e = [126,177,64,216]$
$e^b + e^s = [100,150,40,200] + [26,27,24,16] = [126,177,64,216]$

which indicates that the codistribution of employment and households is in equilibrium.

The example just described used a basic employment vector and a total employment vector that were both specified exogenously to the model. Figure 6.1 has illustrated that in the Lowry model the basic employment is allocated exogenously and that the population-serving employment vector is calculated internally within the model. An iterative procedure for calculating a stable codistribution of population and employment is described next.

6.1.2 The allocation functions

The a'_{ij} elements of the A matrix may be estimated empirically in the following way:

$$a'_{ij} = \frac{h_i f_{ij}{}^w}{\sum_j h_j f_{ij}{}^w} \tag{6.6}$$

where h_j = a measure of the attractivity of zone j for household location
$f_{ij}{}^w$ = the travel-time factor between zones i and j which reflects the manner in which the spatial separation of zones influences the residential location choices of employees

Equation (6.6) will be recognized as a gravity-type accessibility expression.

The alternative functional forms of $f_{ij}{}^w$ that have been used in the gravity model have been described in Eq. (4.11). Similar functional forms have been used in practical applications of the Lowry model and the particular forms which have been used are described later in this chapter.

The b'_{ij} elements may be estimated empirically in a manner similar to that described above for a'_{ij}. It is useful to disaggregate service employment into r types where the expression analagous to Eq. (6.6) becomes:

$$b'^{r}_{ij} = \frac{s_i^r f_{ij}^{sr}}{\sum_i s_i^r f_{ij}^{sr}} \tag{6.7}$$

where s_i^r = a measure of the attractivity of zone i for satisfying the service-type r needs of the households

f_{ij}^{sr} = the travel time factor between zones i and j which reflects the manner in which the spatial separations of zones influences the type r service location choices of households

6.1.3 The zonal constraints

The distribution of activities produced by the above set of equations should be such that the following constraint equations are satisified:

$$p \leqslant p^c \tag{6.8}$$

$$e^{sr} \geqslant e^{sr\min} \tag{6.9}$$

where p^c = a row vector of the population-holding capacities of each of the n zones

$e^{sr\min}$ = a row vector of the population-serving employment thresholds for the r service employment types considered to be viable for any zone

If Eqs. (6.8) and (6.9) are violated, the new accessibility matrices must be developed and the equation set (6.1) to (6.3) solved again using the new matrices. One approach to this problem of developing a distribution of activities that satisfies the constraints (6.8) and (6.9) is to use an approach similar to the attraction trip-end balancing procedure of the gravity model.

$$a_{ij}^* = \frac{h_j^* f_{ij}^w}{\sum_j h_j^* f_{ij}^w} \tag{6.10}$$

$$h_j^* = h_j\left(\frac{h_j}{p_j}\right) \tag{6.11}$$

$$b_{ij}^{*r} = \frac{s_i^{*r} f_{ij}^{sr}}{\sum_i s_i^{*r} f_{ij}^{sr}} \tag{6.12}$$

$$s_i^{*r} = s_i^r \text{ for zones in which } e_i^{sr} \geqslant esr\text{min}$$
$$= 0 \text{ for zones in which } e_i^{sr} \leqslant esr\text{min}$$

in which a_{ij}^* and b_{ij}^{*r} are the new estimates of a'_{ij} and b'^r_{ij} to be used in the next iteration of the model.

6.1.4 Travel demands

The home-based work-trip matrix for any time period (say the peak hour) may be estimated from:

$$T^w = WA' \tag{6.14}$$

where T^w = an $n \times n$ square matrix of home-based work trips where the elements t_{ij}^w represent the number of work trips between zones i and j

W = an $n \times n$ matrix diagonal of the work-trip generation rate per employee during the time period under consideration

A' = an $n \times n$ square matrix of the work-to home accessibilities, a'_{ij}

The home-based service-trip matrices for any time period may be calculated in an analogous way:

$$T^{sr} = RB'^r \tag{6.15}$$

where T^{sr} = an $n \times n$ square matrix of the home-based service-trip interchanges t_{ij}^{sr} to type r population-serving employment opportunities during the time period under consideration

R = an $n \times n$ diagonal matrix of the type r service trip generation rate per household (or person) during the time period under consideration

B'^r = an $n \times n$ square matrix of the home-to-type r service accessibilities b'^r_{ij}

6.1.5 Iterative solution of equations

Batty [7,8] has proposed an iterative approach to the solution of the Lowry model equations (6.1) to (6.3) which is described in this section. Figure 6.2 illustrates the sequence of activities involved in this approach. The urban spatial system is divided into four sets of zones that differ with respect to the constraints imposed and these four sets are:

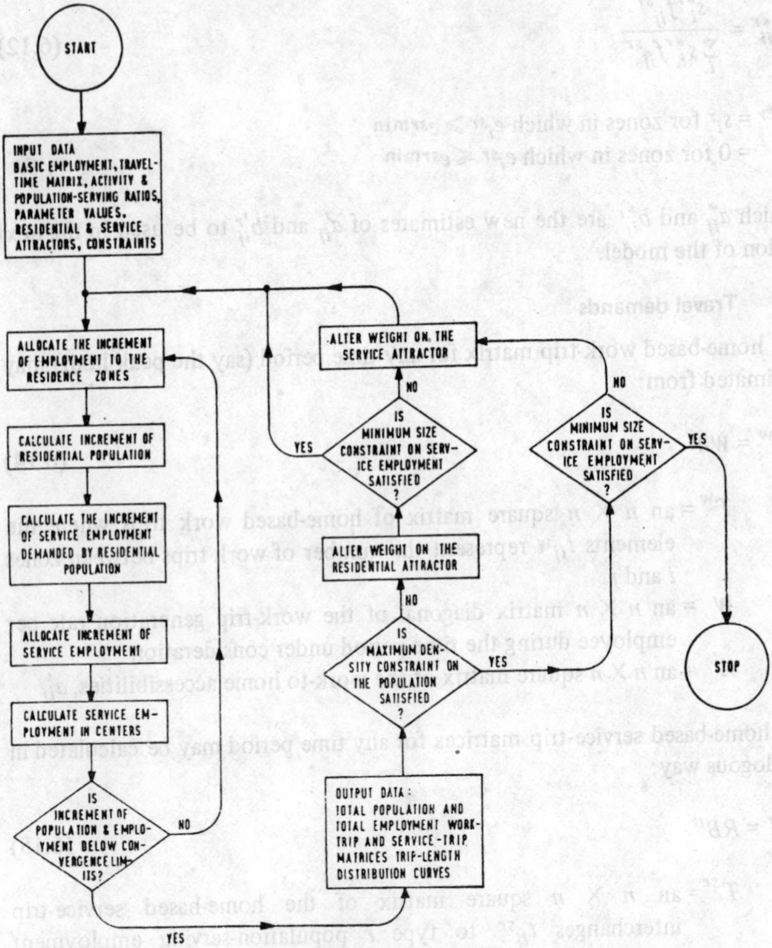

FIG. 6.2. Batty's version of the Lowry model. (*From* Michael Batty *"Design and Construction of a Sub-Regional Land Use Model," Socio-Economic Planning Sciences,* Vol. 5, *Pergamon Press,* 1971. *By permission of publishers.*)

1. Z_1 is the set of zones in which there are no locational constraints.
2. Z_2 is the set of zones in which there are only residential constraints.
3. Z_3 is the set of zones in which there are only service constraints.
4. Z_4 is the set of zones in which there are both residential and service constraints.

In the following equation set, the index m refers to the inner iterations of the model which ensure that the zonal constraints are satisfied. The index n refers to the outer iterations of the equation set to ensure that the population and employment codistributions are stable.

At the start of the model's operation, $m = 1, n = 1$, and it is important to note that $Z = Z_1$, where Z = total set of zones, and the total employment in zone $e_i(1,n)$ is set equal to the basic employment e_i^b. Basic employees $e_i(1,n)$ are distributed to the residential zones by:

$$w_{ij}(m, n) = k_i(n)k_j(n)e_i(m, n)f_{ij}^w \qquad i, j, \epsilon Z \tag{6.16}$$

$$k_i = \left[\frac{1}{\sum_j k_j(n)f_{ij}^w}\right] \tag{6.17}$$

$$k_j = \left[\frac{1}{\sum_i k_i(n)f_{ij}^w}\right] \tag{6.18}$$

where w_{ij} = the number of workers employed at i and living at j

k_i = a balancing factor which ensures that all employees are distributed to residential locations

k_j = a balancing factor which ensures that the number of employees allocated to a zone is equal to the housing opportunities available in that zone which is equal to 1 at the start

The population living in zone j is obtained by summing Eq. (6.16) over all employment zones i:

$$p_j(m, n) = a_j \sum_i w_{ij}(m, n) \qquad i, j \epsilon Z \tag{6.19}$$

The number of service employees demanded $s_j(m,n)$ by the population in zone j is given by:

$$s_j(m, n) = b_j p_j(m, n) \qquad j \epsilon Z \tag{6.22}$$

The service employees demanded by the population in zone j may be distributed to workplaces by:

$$s_{ij}(m, n) = k_j^s(n)s_j(m, n)k_i^s(m, n)f_{ij}^s \quad i, j \epsilon Z \tag{6.23}$$

$$k_j^s(n) = \left[\frac{1}{\sum_i k_i^s(n)f_{ij}^s}\right] \tag{6.24}$$

$$k_i^s(n) = \left[\frac{1}{\sum_j k_j^s(n) f_{ij}^s}\right] \tag{6.25}$$

The service employment at zone i may be estimated from:

$$e_i(m+1, n) = \sum_j s_{ij}(m, n) \quad i, j \epsilon Z \tag{6.26}$$

At this stage of the model, the first increments of population and service employment have been calculated and the service employees must be allocated to residential zones. This allocation is achieved by substituting $e_i(m+1,n)$ for $e_i(m,n)$ in Eq. (6.16). Equations (6.16)–(6.26) are reiterated until:

$$\sum_i e_i(m+1, n) \leqslant Z_e \tag{6.27}$$

$$\sum_j p_j(m, n) \leqslant Z_p \quad j \epsilon Z \tag{6.28}$$

where Z_e and Z_p are the limits below which further increments of service employment and population are small enough to ignore.

The total population and employment predicted by the model may be calculated from:

$$p_j(n) = \sum_m p_j(m, n) \quad j \epsilon Z \tag{6.29}$$

$$e_i(n) = \sum_m e_i(m, n) \quad i \epsilon Z \tag{6.30}$$

The summations of Eqs. (6.16) and (6.23) over m will yield the trip matrices for home-based work trips and home-based service trips, respectively.

The constraints on population and service employment are tested as follows:

if

$$p_j(n) \geqslant p_j^c \quad j \epsilon Z \tag{6.31}$$

then

$$p_j(n) \epsilon Z_2, Z_4 \tag{6.32}$$

and if

$$[e_i(n) - e_i^{\,b}] < e^{s\min} \qquad i \epsilon Z \tag{6.33}$$

then

$$[e_i(n) - e_i^{\,b}] \in Z_3, Z_4 \tag{6.34}$$

If the constraints (6.31) and (6.33) are not satisfied, then the following balancing factors are calculated:

$$k_j(n+1) = \begin{cases} \dfrac{k_j(n) p_j^{\,c}}{p_j(n)} & j \epsilon Z_2, Z_4 \\ 1 & j \epsilon Z_1, Z_3 \end{cases} \tag{6.35}$$

$$k_i^{\,s}(n+1) = \begin{cases} 0 & i \epsilon Z_3, Z_4 \\ 1 & i \epsilon Z_1, Z_2 \end{cases} \tag{6.36}$$

which is effectively a restatement of the approach described in Eqs. (6.10) to (6.13).

The new estimates of the balancing factors obtained from Eqs. (6.35) and (6.36) are then substituted into Eqs. (6.16) and (6.23) and the whole system of equations reiterated until the constraint equations (6.31) and (6.33) are satisfied.

Travel-time factor functions of the following form were used by Batty:

$$f_{ij}^{\,w} = \exp(-\alpha d_{ij}) \tag{6.37}$$

$$f_{ij}^{\,s} = \exp(-\beta d_{ij}) \tag{6.38}$$

6.1.6 The Garin solution of the equations

Garin [6] has proposed a formulation of the Lowry model which obviates the need for the iterative solution to the equations described in the previous section. Using the matrix notation of Sec. 6.1.1 the following sequence of equations may be written.

$$p^b = e^b A$$

$$e^{s(1)} = p^b B = e^b (AB) \tag{6.39}$$

Equation (6.39) calculates the population-serving employment required to serve the households supported by basic employment, and the superscript (1) identifies that it is the first increment of service employment.

$$p^{s(1)} = e^{s(1)} A = e^b (AB)A$$
$$e^{s(2)} = p^{s(1)}B = e^{s(1)}(AB) = e^b(AB)(AB) = e^b(AB)^2$$

and successive iterations will yield the additional employment and population in the xth iteration of:

$$e^{s(x)} = e^b(AB)^x$$
$$p^{s(x)} = e^b(AB)^x A$$

Total employment and total population vectors are given by:

$$e = e^b + e^{s(1)} + \cdots + e^{s(x)} + \cdots$$
$$= e^b [I + AB + (AB)^2 + \cdots + (AB)^x + \cdots]$$
$$p = p^b + p^{s(1)} + \cdots + p^{s(x)} + \cdots$$
$$= e^b [I + AB + (AB)^2 + \cdots + (AB)^x + \cdots] A$$

Garin [6] has shown that under certain conditions on the product matrix AB the above matrix series will converge to the inverse of the matrix $(I - AB)$ which yields the following expressions:

$$e = e^b(I - AB)^{-1} \tag{6.40}$$
$$p = e^b(I - AB)^{-1} A \tag{6.41}$$

where I = the identity matrix

The condition on the product matrix AB is that $(AB)^x$ must tend to zero which will occur if the sum of the elements in each row of AB is less than unity. Garin argues that if this were not the case then an infinite amount of population-serving employment would be generated by a finite amount of basic employment, which is a phenomenon not observed empirically.

Equations (6.40) and (6.41) allow the total employment vector and the population vector to be derived for an exogenously defined basic employment vector once the A and B matrices have been determined.

The Garin-Lowry model may be illustrated by an extension of the simple example given in Sec. 6.1.1. The following product matrix AB may be calculated from the A and B matrices specified earlier:

$$AB = \begin{bmatrix} 0.0520 & 0.0480 & 0.0340 & 0.0260 \\ 0.0480 & 0.0496 & 0.0364 & 0.0260 \\ 0.0380 & 0.0404 & 0.0496 & 0.0320 \\ 0.0392 & 0.0464 & 0.0456 & 0.0288 \end{bmatrix}$$

which leads to

$$(I-AB)^{-1} = \begin{bmatrix} 1.0607 & 0.0569 & 0.0416 & 0.0313 \\ 0.0567 & 1.0585 & 0.0441 & 0.0313 \\ 0.0464 & 0.0491 & 1.0575 & 0.3740 \\ 0.0477 & 0.0522 & 0.0534 & 1.0342 \end{bmatrix}$$

Equation (6.40) may be used to derive the following total employment vector from the basic employment vector specified in Sec 6.1.1:

$$e = [126,177,64,216]$$

The household vector may be derived from Eq. (6.41):

$$p = [102,128,101,142]$$

In reviewing the A' and the B' matrices used in this example it should be noted that they both satisfy:

$$\sum_j a'_{ij} = 1.0$$

$$\sum_j b'_{ij} = 1.0$$

or, alternatively that

$$\sum_j a_{ij} = 0.8 = \text{labor participation rate}$$

$$\sum_j b_{ij} = 0.2 = \text{service employment per household}$$

It should also be noted that the sums of the rows of the AB product matrix are all less than unity.

One of the difficulties in using the Garin-Lowry equation is that the population serving employment can only be of one broad type and be dependent upon one broad home to service travel-time function This is in contrast to the original Lowry model equation which allows for a large number of population serving employment types whose spatial distributions are dependent upon different home to service travel-time-factor functions.

6.1.7 Dynamic and disaggregated extensions

The applications of the Lowry model and the Garin-Lowry model described in the previous sections represent relatively macroscopic analyses of horizon year-type plans. A fundamental assumption in these analyses is that the spatial distribution of activities in the horizon year has reached an equilibrium condition and that no lags in the relocation of activities within the region exist. A second assumption of these analyses is that the population of the region is uniform in a socioeconomic sense in that all people have equal opportunities for employment, housing, and travel. In reality, neither of these assumptions are satisfied completely.

Two important extensions of the Lowry-type models that would improve their generality are:

The addition of a dynamic extension which reflects the lags that exist in the relocation of activities and activity linkages. This would allow a model calibrated to base-year data to be used for estimating the states of an urban system at intermediate times, rather than be restricted to some horizon-year condition of pseudoequilibrium.

The disaggregation of the model into a form that can account for differences in the travel and housing preferences of different economic groups. Disaggregation of the model would permit travel demands by mode to be estimated directly along with the demands for various types of housing in each zone.

Rogers [9], Crecine [10], and Echenique [11] have suggested a number of dynamic and disaggregated extensions of the Lowry model. It should be recalled that the Lowry models relate population and employment at one particular time horizon. The following formulation, which is based largely on Echenique's work, represents an extension of the Garin-Lowry model. The general structure of the model is retained but the accessibility matrices are changed with time producing locational adjustments as well as changing the distribution of basic employment with time.

Given the Garin-Lowry model view of urban spatial structure the following represent the potential sources of change:

1. Changes in basic employment vector due to growth, decay, or migration
2. Changes in the properties of the transport system
3. Changes in the labor participation rate due to changes in fertility rates, unemployment, or the participation of women in the labor force
4. Changes in the population density constraints of residential zones

5. Changes in the population-serving employment ratio due to increasing incomes, changes in employee productivity, etc.
6. Changes in the minimum-size constraints on zonal population serving employment magnitudes

The change in the basic employment vector during the interval t to $t + 1$ may be represented by:

$$e^b(t+1) = e^b(t)G \tag{6.42}$$

where $e^b(t+1)$ = the basic employment vector at the new time horizon
$e^b(t)$ = the basic employment vector in the base year
G = a growth matrix which projects the basic employment vector through one time period

Echenique [11] suggests that the matrix G may be considered to consist of the following:

$$G = (f - g + M) \tag{6.43}$$

where f = a diagonal matrix whose elements represent the increase in basic employment in a zone
g = a diagonal matrix whose elements represent the decay in basic employment in a zone
M = a square matrix whose elements represent the proportion of employment in zone i at time t which is in zone j at time $t + 1$

The dynamic versions of Eqs. (6.40) and (6.41) are:

$$e(t+1) = e^b(t+1)\,[I - A(t+1)\,B(t+1)]^{-1} \tag{6.44}$$

$$p(t+1) = e^b(t+1)\,[I - A(t+1)\,B(t+1)]^{-1}\,A(t+1) \tag{6.45}$$

where $A(t+1)$ represents the work-to-home accessibility matrix for the year $t + 1$, the elements $[a'_{ij}(t+1)]$ and $[a_j(t+1)]$ of the matrix $A(t+1)$ reflect the transport network characteristics, the population density characteristics, and the labor participation rate appropriate to the year $t+1$. The accessibility matrix $B(t+1)$ may be interpreted in an analagous manner.

Wilson [12] has developed a Lowry type residential location model that has been disaggregated to account for the following effects: (1) different household income groups, (2) different wage levels by location of employment, (3) different housing types, and (4) variation in house prices with location. Wilson has used his entropy-maximizing formalism to derive a residential allocation model of the following type:

$$T_{ij}{}^{kw} = A_i{}^k B_j{}^w H_i{}^k E_j{}^w \exp(-\beta^w c_{ij}) \exp\left\{-\mu^w \left[p_i{}^k - q^w (w - c'_{ij})\right]^2\right\} \tag{6.46}$$

where $T_{ij}{}^{kw}$ = the number of workers who live in zone i in house type k and who work in zone j earning wage w

$H_i{}^k$ = the number of houses of type k in zone i

$E_j{}^w$ = number of jobs in zone j offering wage w

$P_i{}^k$ = the price of type k houses in zone i

q^w = the average percentage of income (after the deduction of transport costs) that an employee of income group w spends on housing

c'_{ij} = that component of the generalized journey-to-work cost c_{ij} which is the actual money paid

$$A_i{}^k = \frac{1}{\sum_j \sum_w B_j{}^w E_j{}^w \exp(-\beta^w c_{ij}) \exp\left\{-\mu^w \left[p_i{}^k - q^w (w - c'_{ij})\right]^2\right\}} \tag{6.47}$$

$$B_j{}^w = \frac{1}{\sum_i \sum_w A_i{}^k H_i{}^k \exp(-\beta^w c_{ij}) \exp\left\{-\mu^w \left[p_i{}^k - q^w (w - c'_{ij})\right]^2\right\}} \tag{6.48}$$

Wilson has provided some extensions of this model and has also noted: "The data problems associated with calibrating a model of this type are clearly immense. However, they are not intractable: on the one hand, the development of this type of model should encourage the collection of the appropriate data; on the other hand, even in the short run, proxy variables can be constructed for indices such as house type." While it may be possible to calibrate this model to base-year data, extreme difficulties would be experienced in using the model for some horizon-year state.

The Lowry model may be disaggregated in a way that is more compatible with available data and our forecasting capabilities. The basic employment vector e^b may be disaggregated by forming a partitioned basic employment vector e^{bc}. The elements of each cell of this partitioned vector represent the number of persons in basic employment category c. The number of employees of socioeconomic type k within each industry category c may be estimated from an industry-person-type matrix. This $k \times c$ matrix shows the number of persons of type k employed in each industry category c. Some characteristics of the Canadian labor force have been presented in Chap 3. That is:

$$[e^{bk}] = [e^{kc}]\ [e^{bc}] \tag{6.49}$$

where $[e^{bk}]$ = the basic employment vector disaggregated by person type k
$[e^{kc}]$ = the person-type–industry category matrix
$[e^{bc}]$ = the basic employment vector partitioned into industry type c

The population-serving employment may be disaggregated in a manner similar to that used in Eq. (6.49) for basic employment:

$$[e^{sk}] = [e^{kr}]\ [e^{sr}] \tag{6.50}$$

where $[e^{sk}]$ = the population-serving employment vector disaggregated by person type k
$[e^{sr}]$ = person type k–service industry type r matrix
$[e^{sr}]$ = a row vector of service employment partitioned into r types

The residential locations of any socioeconomic group may be established by formulating an accessibility matrix A^k which distributes the residences of socioeconomic group k working in zone i over all zones j such that $\sum_j a_{ij}{}^k = 1$.

$$A^k = [a'^k_{ij}]\ \ [a_j{}^k] \tag{6.51}$$

where $[a'^k_{ij}]$ = a measure of the accessibility of households demanded by type k persons by the mode of travel used by type k persons in traveling between work and home
$[a_j{}^k]$ = the labor participation rate associated with type k households

The housing opportunities available to type k persons may be estimated from:

$$[o^k] = [s^{kd}]\ [g^d] \tag{6.52}$$

where $[o^k]$ = a partitioned row vector of the housing opportunities compatible with the demands of type k persons
$[s^{kd}]$ = a $k \times d$ matrix of the probabilities of type k persons living in housing opportunities in density group d
$[g^d]$ = a partitioned column vector showing the number of housing opportunities in each density group in each zone

In this approach, residential density has been used as a proxy for housing type and price, and it is one of the few variables that may be estimated for future time horizons.

The a'^k_{ij} elements of Eq. (6.51) may be estimated from Eq. (6.6) in the following way:

$$a'^k_{ij} = \frac{o_j{}^k f_{ij}{}^{wk}}{\sum_j o_j{}^k f_{ij}{}^{wk}} \tag{6.53}$$

Equations (6.49)-(6.53) may be used along with Eqs. (6.1)-(6.15) to achieve a spatial distribution of population and employment which is disaggregated by person type k.

6.2 APPLICATIONS OF THE LOWRY MODEL

Batty [8] used the formulation of the Lowry model described in Sec. 6.1.5 in the Nottinghamshire-Derbyshire region of England. Figure 6.3 shows the zone system used in this study along with some of the broad characteristics of the region. The model was calibrated both with and without constraints on population or service employment. The results of both calibrations are shown in

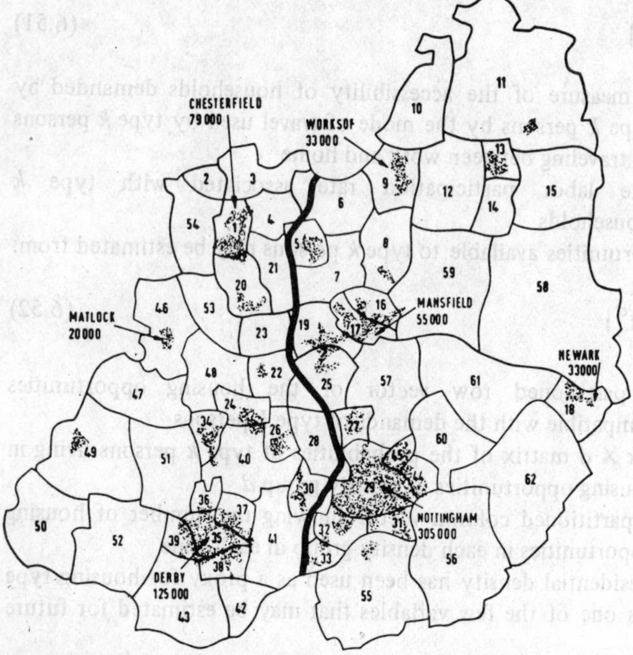

FIG. 6.3. Zone system used in Nottinghamshire/Derbyshire study. (*From Michael Batty "Design and Construction of a Sub-Regional Land Use Model," Socio-Economic Planning Sciences, Vol. 5, Pergamon Press,* 1971.)

Table 6.1. Goodness of fit of Nottinghamshire/Derbyshire model

Statistics or parameter	Calibration without constraints	Calibration with constraints
	Best value	
Residential parameter α	0.2300	0.2400
Service-center parameter β	0.1600	0.1600
Ratio of observed to predicted mean work-trip lengths	1.0755	1.0711
Ratio of assumed to predicted mean service-trip lengths	0.9389	0.9648
R^2 between log-transformed population distribution	0.9364	0.9402
R^2 between log-transformed employment distribution	0.9764	0.9802

Table 6.1. It is interesting to note from Table 6.1 that there is little change in the goodness of fit parameters for the constrained and unconstrained calibrations. Table 6.2 shows the observed and estimated population and service employment vectors for both forms of calibration of the model. Additional evidence on the validity of the model is shown in Fig. 6.4 in which the observed and predicted trip-length frequency distributions are presented. The agreement between the observed and estimated trip-length frequency distributions is not as good as between the observed and estimated activity vectors.

The American-Yugoslav project in planning studies was established as a result of the earthquake that destroyed much of Ljubljana in Yugoslavia. Figure 6.5 shows a flow diagram of the activities involved in the application of the Lowry model in this project [13].

Three policy inputs to the model were identified and these are the transport network, the pattern of industrial locations, and the densities of land development. In this study 123 zones were used and the model estimated the population, population-serving employment, and the land consumed by these activities for each zone, given the above input variables and the model structure shown in Fig. 6.5.

In this application of the Lowry model, the process shown in Fig. 6.5 was reiterated until fewer than 100 population-serving employees were added to the region. Experience with the Ljubljana region showed that this was accomplished in about 10 iterations and that 80 to 85 percent of the total population and employment were accounted for after the first iteration. After each iteration, an accounting check was made using the density data to check if a given zone had reached capacity. If the population capacity of a zone was exceeded, the excess population was reallocated.

Table 6.2. Observed and simulated population and employment vectors for Nottinghamshire/Derbyshire study

Zone no. Area	Observed values (1966)		Calibration without constraints (1966)		Calibration with constraints (1966)	
	Population	Service employment	Population	Service employment	Population	Service employment
1 Chesterfield	79,080	22,080	111,298	27,956	79,175*	26,334
2 Eckington	27,510	1,850	18,879	1,736	28,103	2,221
3 Bolsover	11,070	430	8,703	360	12,103	455
9 Worksop	33,010	8,740	35,591	8,540	33,047*	8,797
11 Gringley	11,450	1,220	6,786	656	7,059	703
16 Woodhouse	22,640	2,470	30,249	3,350	22,712*	3,349
17 Mansfield	55,610	18,050	77,194	24,778	55,799*	24,313
19 Sutton	40,840	4,200	47,445	5,201	40,985	5,227
22 Alfreton	32,050	3,410	21,297	2,715	37,035*	3,583
26 Heanor	24,130	3,410	21,607	3,242	24,297	3,771
29 Nottingham	305,050	81,410	439,397	102,293	307,930*	92,904
31 West Bridgeford	65,130	10,600	43,283	7,600	65,731*	8,470
33 Long Eaton	31,090	5,090	23,068	3,704	31,339*	4,485
35 Derby	125,900	49,340	202,644	50,940	126,782*	48,403
37 Spondon	30,430	200	24,190	163	32,642	191
39 Mickleover	22,010	3,620	13,475	1,840	23,158	2,077
41 Breaston	21,900	2,510	12,579	1,612	35,463	2,246
45 Arnold	29,840	4,130	25,735	3,697	30,113*	3,463
47 Wirksworth	8,160	1,060	5,064	475	6,225	579
52 Broughton	6,620	930	1,858	225	5,083	298
57 Bildworth	21,880	2,160	13,828	1,733	35,363	2,773
59 Ollerton	23,830	1,730	22,519	1,343	23,013	1,415
62 East Leake	8,540	21,170	2,698	406	5,854	577

*Shows zones in which the maximum density constraint on population is necessary.

Population-serving employment was subdivided into shopping-goods employment and convenience-goods employment. Shopping goods were defined as goods which are purchased only after a comparison of competing goods is made. Convenience goods were identified as those goods purchased on a daily basis for which comparisons are not made. Because of the relatively coarse zone size used in this study, convenience goods were assumed to locate in the zones where population generated the demand for them. Shopping goods were further broken down into local and regional classifications. The distinction between the two types was the distance that people are willing to travel to purchase them. It was assumed that there were no constraints on the maximum service employment in a zone.

The accessibility function used in this application of the gravity model was of the following form:

$$a'_{ij} = \left[\frac{q_j c_j (d_{ij}{}^n s_{ij})^{-1}}{\sum_j q_j c_j (d_{ij}{}^n s_{ij})^{-1}} \right] \tag{6.54}$$

where q_j = the land area available for development in zone j
c_j = an attractiveness factor for zone j
n = travel-time exponent
s_{ij} = interzonal distance

The population of a zone is calculated from:

$$p_j = \sum_i e_i a'_{ij} \tag{6.55}$$

In this application of the model, when the calculated land use for a zone exceeded the capacity of a zone by more than 10 percent, residential land was subtracted until the total land used in the zone equalled the capacity of the

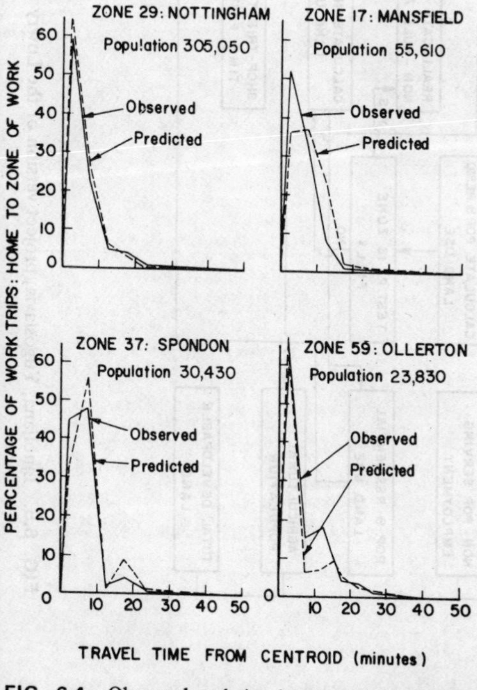

FIG. 6.4. Observed and simulated work-trip length frequency distributions.

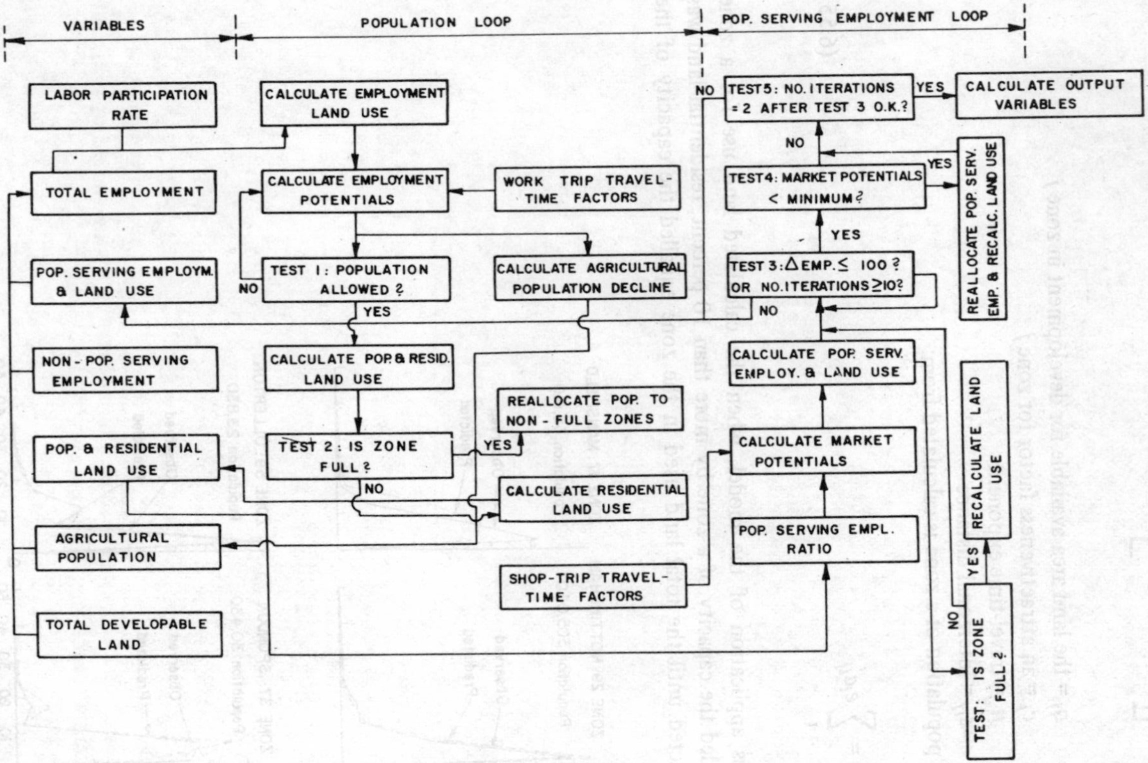

FIG. 6.5. Ljubljana, Yugoslavia, project version of the Lowry model.

zone. The population to be reallocated is pooled and reallocated to all non-full zones in proportion to their accessibilities to employment.

An accessibility function similar to that expressed in Eq. (6.54) was used to allocate service employment. In this study the non-convenience-goods population-serving employment was calculated as strictly proportional to the relative market potential for all zones, until the last two iterations, when the minimum size constraints are allowed to act and result in reallocations. The reallocation was accomplished by setting the potential for all zones not meeting the minimum size constraints to zero. The remaining potential is summed for all zones not complying with the constraints in proportion to their share of the remaining potential.

Some of the most comprehensive applications of the Lowry models have been performed at the Institute of National, Regional and Local Planning of the Swiss Federal Institute of Technology in Zurich. This form of the Garin-Lowry model, called ORL-MOD-1, has been described by Stradal and Sorgo [14]. Stradal and Hutchinson [15] have described a number of applications of this model to European planning problems.

The basic flow of activities in this model is shown in Fig. 6.6. The model incorporates interrelationships between the four basic variables used to describe a zone: basic employment, population, population-serving employees, and total employment. Besides developing a stable codistribution of input and output variables for each zone, the model also computes for each zone the relevant costs, land areas consumed, trip generation, travel times, and accessibilities.

Exponential-type accessibility functions of the type described in Eq. (4.11b) were used in this model.

ORL-MOD-1 has been calibrated to the Zurich region [14] and the parameter magnitudes yielded by this calibration are shown in Figs. 6.7 and 6.8. These figures provide a comparison of the observed and simulated trip-length frequency distributions for the work-to-home and the home-to-shop trips. The calibrated model is being used to analyze some of the probable impacts of a number of regional development proposals for the Zurich region. The alternatives being examined have been described by Stradal and Hutchinson [15].

Other applications of the Lowry model have been described by Cripps and Foot [16] and Batty [17]. Cripps and Foot have described an application to Bedfordshire and Batty has described an application of the Garin-Lowry model to the central Lancashire subregion.

SUMMARY

A weakness of the travel demand forecasting models described in Chaps. 2 to 5 is their requirement for a completely specified land-use allocation at both the production and attraction ends of trips. The Lowry family of land-use models

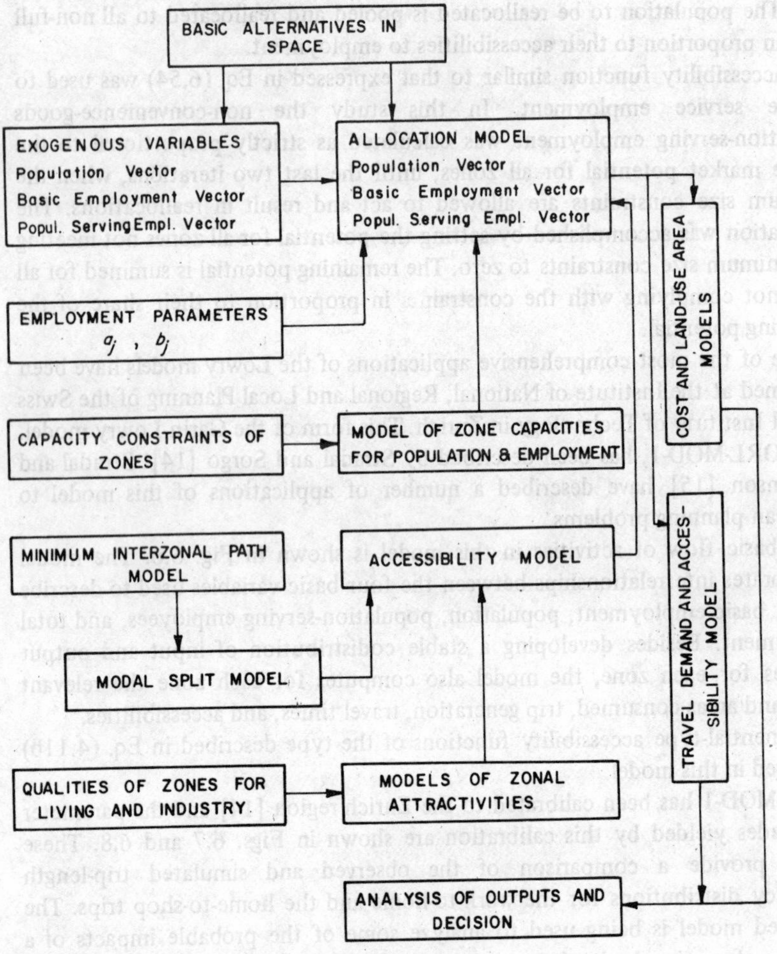

FIG. 6.6. Flow of activities in the ORL-MOD-1 version of the Garin-Lowry model.

described in this chapter require less land-use information to be specified exogenously and allow land-use allocations and the associated transport flows for work and service trips to be estimated simultaneously.

The Lowry model conceives of the major structural elements of an urban area in terms of employment in basic industries, employment in population-serving industries, and employment in households. The location of basic employment in an urban area is assumed to be independent of the population and is specified exogenously to the model. The location of population-serving employment is assumed to be dependent upon the population distribution and is calculated internally to the model. The population distribution is a function of the total employment and is calculated within the model. The population allocation function reflects both the travel-time properties of the area under consideration as well as the relative attractivities of residential zones. Travel times are incorporated in the allocation function through the travel-time factor function and residential attractivities are usually expressed by population-holding capacities. The population-serving employment allocation functions also reflect the travel-time properties of the area as well as the relative attractivities of the alternative service centers. The allocations of population and population-serving employment estimated by the model are normally subject to constraints.

With the original form of the Lowry model a stable codistribution of population and employment that does not violate the constraints is achieved by an iterative procedure. The Garin formulation of the Lowry model obviates the need for an iterative solution and allows the codistribution of population and employment to be calculated directly.

The Lowry model may be disaggregated into a form that estimates the spatial location decisions of a number of socioeconomic groups. Simple dynamic forms of the model may also be developed readily. While these extensions of the Lowry model are relatively simple from a conceptual point of view, the greatest difficulty is to assemble sufficient information to allow calibration of these extended versions.

The various applications of the Lowry model have used a procedure similar to that used for the gravity model for calibration. The travel-time factor functions have been altered in an iterative manner until the codistribution of population and employment estimated by the model agrees substantially with the observed.

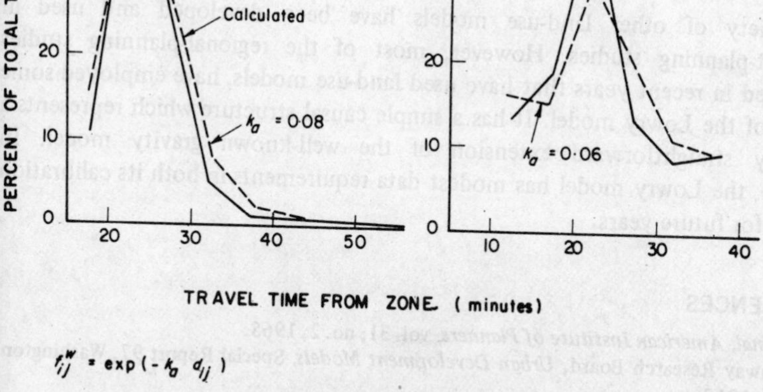

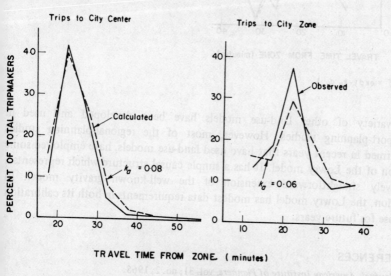

FIG. 6.7. Travel parameters for Zurich, Switzerland: Home to work.

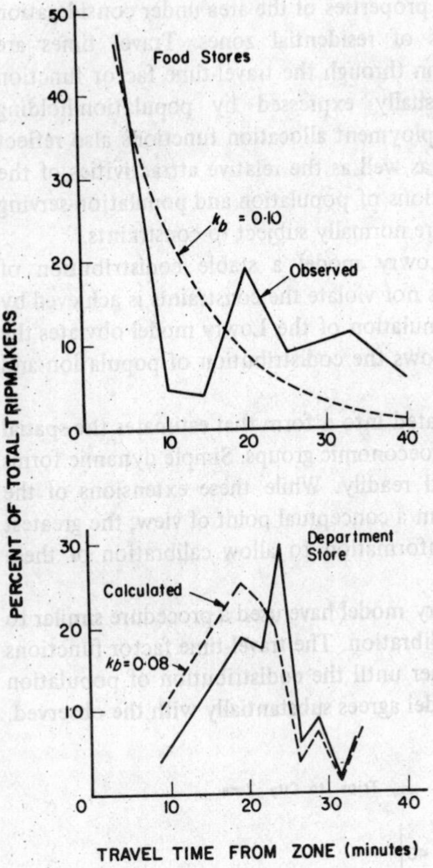

$$f_{ij}^s = \exp(-k_b\, d_{ij})$$

FIG. 6.8. Travel parameters for Zurich, Switzerland: Home to shop in city center.

A variety of other land-use models have been developed and used in transport-planning studies. However, most of the regional-planning studies performed in recent years that have used land-use models, have employed some version of the Lowry model. It has a simple causal structure which represents a relatively straightforward extension of the well-known gravity model. In addition, the Lowry model has modest data requirements in both its calibration and use for future years.

REFERENCES

1. *Journal, American Institute of Planners,* vol. 31, no. 2, 1965.
2. Highway Research Board, *Urban Development Models,* Special Report 97, Washington, D.C., 1968.

3. Irwin, N. A., *Review of Existing Land Use Forecasting Techniques,* Highway Research Record No. 88, Highway Research Board, Washington, D.C., 1965.
4. Swerdloff, C. N., and J. R. Stowers, *A Test of Some First Generation Residential Land Use Models,* Highway Research Record No. 126, Highway Research Board, Washington, D.C., 1966.
5. Lowry, I. S., *A Model of Metropolis,* Technical Memorandum RM-4035-RC, The RAND Corporation, Santa Monica, California, 1964.
6. Garin, R. A., "Matrix Formulation of the Lowry Model for Intra-Metropolitan Activity Allocation," *Journal, American Institute of Planners,* vol. 32, no. 6, pp. 361–364, 1966.
7. Batty, M. J., "Design and Construction of a Sub-regional Land Use Model," *Socio-Economic Planning Sciences,* vol. 5, no. 2, pp. 97–124, 1971.
8. Batty, M. J., "The Development of an Activity Allocation Model for the Notts./Derby. Sub-region," *Regional Studies,* vol. 4, no. 3, pp. 307–332, 1970.
9. Rogers, A., "A Note on the Garin-Lowry Model," *Journal, American Institute of Planners,* vol. 32, no. 6, pp. 364–366, 1966.
10. Crecine, J. P., *Spatial Location Decisions and Urban Structure: A Time Oriented Model,* Discussion paper, Institute of Public Policy Studies, University of Michigan, Ann Arbor, Michigan, 1969.
11. Echenique, M., *Urban Systems: Towards an Explorative Model,* Report No. CES UWP 2, Center for Environmental Studies, Regent's Park, London, 1969.
12. Wilson, A. G., *Entropy in Urban and Regional Modelling,* Pion Limited, London, 1970.
13. Stubbs, J. R., and B. Barber, *The Lowry Model: A Mathematical Method for Forecasting the Distribution of Population and Jobs in an Urban Region,* American-Yugoslav Project in Regional and Urban Planning Studies, Ljubljana, Yugoslavia, 1970.
14. Stradal, O., and H. Sorgo, *ORL-MOD-1: A Model for Regional Allocation of Activities,* Working Paper No. 25.1, Institute for National, Regional and Local Planning, Swiss Federal Institute of Technology, Zurich, 1970.
15. Stradal, O., and B. G. Hutchinson, *Notes for a Short Course on Practical Applications of Regional Development Models,* The Transport Group, Department of Civil Engineering, University of Waterloo, Waterloo, Ontario, 1971.
16. Cripps, E., and D. H. S. Foot, "A Land Use Model for Sub-regional Planning," *Regional Studies,* vol. 3, no. 3, pp. 243–263, 1969.
17. Batty, M. J., "Some Problems of Calibrating the Lowry Model," *Environment and Planning,* vol. 2, pp. 173–189, 1970.

7 URBAN TRAVEL DEMANDS

The specific spatial and temporal patterns of travel demand that are likely to occur in a given urban area are a function of the properties of that area. However, similarities in land development and travel demand have been observed in many cities throughout the world. The purpose of this chapter is to provide a summary of some of the broad trends in travel demands that have been observed in a number of cities.

An appreciation of these broad trends is useful in assessing the validity of the detailed travel demands forecast by the models discussed in the earlier chapters. Travel-demand forecasts are only as valid as the prognostications of land use that have been substituted into the models. In many transport studies land-use forecasts have been prepared without due attention to the trends in urban development. The land-use forecasts seem to be based more on the hopes of the planner and not on an objective assessment of development trends. A second reason for developing a broad understanding of urban travel demands is to assist in the initial appraisals of new transport modes.

The chapter begins by classifying urban travel into a number of broad components. Empirical evidence on the trends in each of these travel demand components is then introduced.

7.1 A CLASSIFICATION OF URBAN TRANSPORT DEMANDS

Studies of existing travel-demand patterns and those forecast in a number of transport-planning studies suggest that urban travel demands may be classified into the following broad categories.

Type 1: Radial-type travel along corridors focussed on the central business district

Type 2: Circumferential-type travel between activities located in the suburbs of cities

Type 3: Travel within residential areas where this type of travel might be between local area activities or travel at the beginning or completion of a longer trip within an urban region

Type 4: Travel within the central business district where this travel might be between activities within the central area or to and from the terminals of regional transport facilities focussed on the central area

Type 5: Travel to and from major activity concentrations not located within the central area such as airports, universities, and recreational areas

7.2 TYPE 1: RADIAL TRAVEL TO THE CENTRAL BUSINESS DISTRICT

Many observers of urban problems seem to perceive of "the urban transport problem" exclusively in terms of the work-trip travel demands to and from the central business district. The implication is that because some peak hour congestion exists on centrally focussed transport facilities at present, congestion will become intolerable with the continued growth of the metropolitan area unless massive investments are made in radial facilities.

While type 1 travel demands have created difficulties in the past, the declining relative importance of this type of travel has been observed in a number of cities. Figure 7.1 shows the generalized patterns of urban travel-demand observed and predicted for three different time horizons in Washington, D.C. [1].

7.2.1 Principal trip purposes

Figure 7.2 is a generalized relationship illustrating the proportions of various trip types to the central areas of cities of various population sizes. This diagram illustrates the dominance of the journey to work in type 1 travel in the larger metropolitan areas. Journey to shop is the second most important trip purpose.

7.2.2 Trends in travel demand

Figure 7.3 shows the trends in travel to the Toronto central business district during the peak period and throughout the day observed over a 20-year period [2]. These travel demands were obtained from annual counts of travel across a

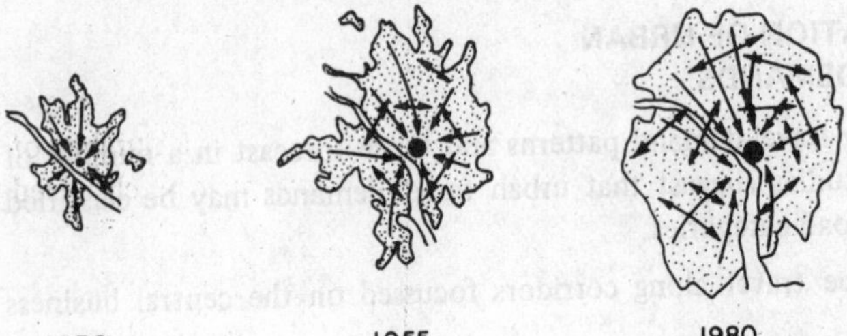

FIG. 7.1. Generalized patterns of urban travel demand in Washington, D.C. (*Adapted from Ref. 1, Chap. 7.*)

cordon line surrounding the central business district. The information presented in Fig. 7.3 shows that the peak period travel has been relatively stable despite the fact that the population of Metropolitan Toronto has been increasing at about 2.7 percent per year for the period covered by the graph. During this same time period approximately 25 miles of subway have been constructed along with a comprehensive freeway network, both of which are centrally focussed.

Figure 7.3 illustrates that total daily travel to the Toronto central business district has begun to increase in recent years. Most of this increase outside the peak travel periods may be traced to the accelerated development of entertainment facilities in the central business district during recent years.

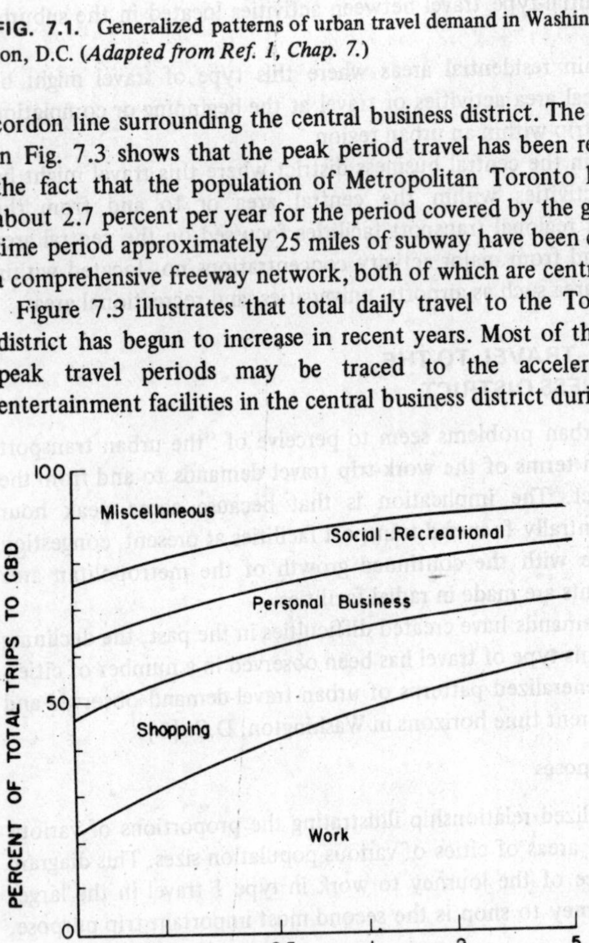

FIG. 7.2. Proportions of various trip purposes to central areas of cities of various sizes. (*Adapted from Ref. 1, Chap. 7.*)

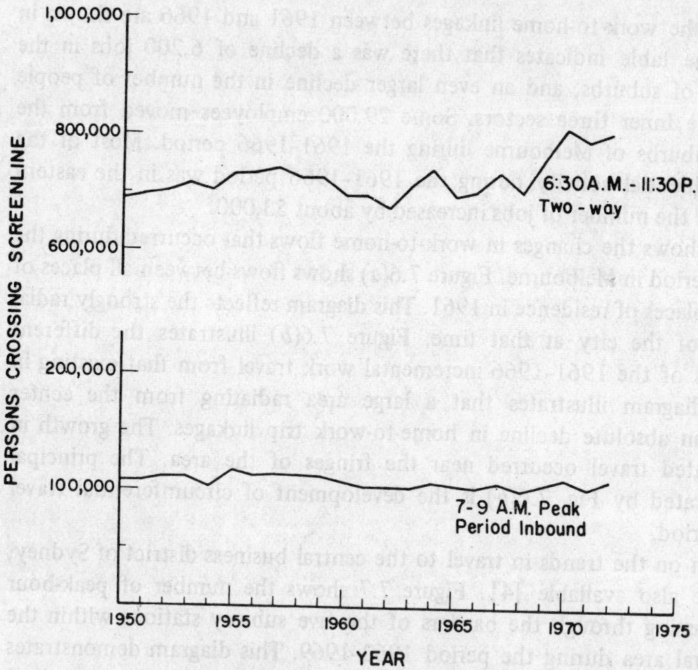

FIG. 7.3. Trends in travel to Toronto CBD throughout day and during peak period. (*Adapted from Ref. 2, Chap. 7.*)

Further evidence of the stability of travel demands to the central areas of cities is presented in Fig. 7.4 for five cities throughout the world [1]. All of the metropolitan areas represented in Fig. 7.4 have undergone rapid population growth during the period covered by the graph without experiencing significant changes in the peak-hour travel demands to their central areas.

Figure 7.5 shows the trends in the morning peak period travel to central London. The morning peak period covers the time between 7:00 A.M. and 10:00 A.M. This diagram shows that travel demands reached a maximum in about 1963 and since that time have showed a steady decline. The Department of Planning and Transportation, Greater London Council, believe that the trends in travel demand shown in the diagram are broadly representative of trends in employment in central London.

Paterson [3] has conducted a comprehensive study of the changes in work-to-home travel patterns in Melbourne, Australia, between the 1961 and 1966 census years. Table 7.1 shows the home-to-work travel between six broad geographical sectors of the Melbourne metropolitan area in 1961. This table illustrates the dominance of the central suburbs as an employment location in 1961. There were 404,900 jobs located in the central sector out of a regional total of 791,900 jobs.

Changes in the work-to-home linkages between 1961 and 1966 are shown in Table 7.2. The table indicates that there was a decline of 6,200 jobs in the central group of suburbs, and an even larger decline in the number of people residing in the inner three sectors. Some 29,000 employees moved from the inner three suburbs of Melbourne during the 1961-1966 period. Most of the growth in residential activity during the 1961-1966 period was in the eastern suburbs where the number of jobs increased by about 53,000.

Figure 7.6 shows the changes in work-to-home flows that occurred during the 1961-1966 period in Melbourne. Figure 7.6(*a*) shows flows between all places of work and all places of residence in 1961. This diagram reflects the strongly radial organization of the city at that time. Figure 7.6(*b*) illustrates the different characteristics of the 1961-1966 incremental work travel from that existing in 1961. This diagram illustrates that a large area radiating from the center experienced an absolute decline in home-to-work trip linkages. The growth in radially oriented travel occurred near the fringes of the area. The principal feature illustrated by Fig. 7.6(*b*) is the development of circumferential travel during the period.

Information on the trends in travel to the central business district of Sydney, Australia, are also available [4]. Figure 7.7 shows the number of peak-hour passengers passing through the barriers of the five subway stations within the Sydney central area during the period 1962-1969. This diagram demonstrates that the peak-hour total passenger count for all five stations has remained relatively stable throughout the period. The changes between stations reflects the changes in the spatial distribution of employment that have occurred within the Sydney central business district. Comprehensive information is not available

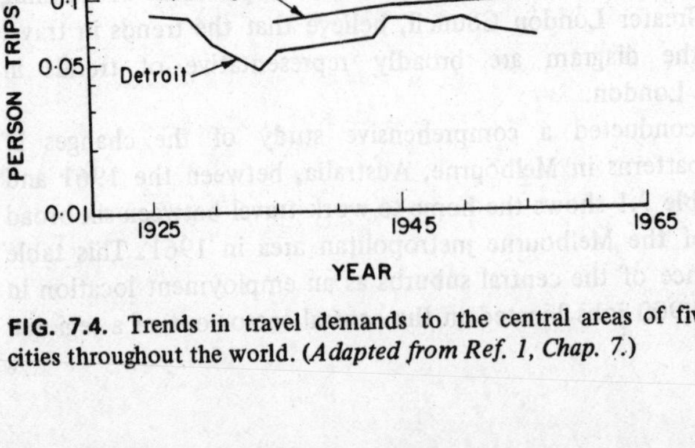

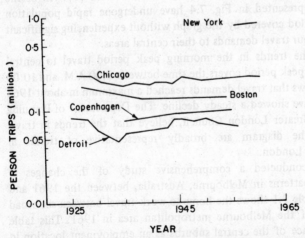

FIG. 7.4. Trends in travel demands to the central areas of five cities throughout the world. (*Adapted from Ref. 1, Chap. 7.*)

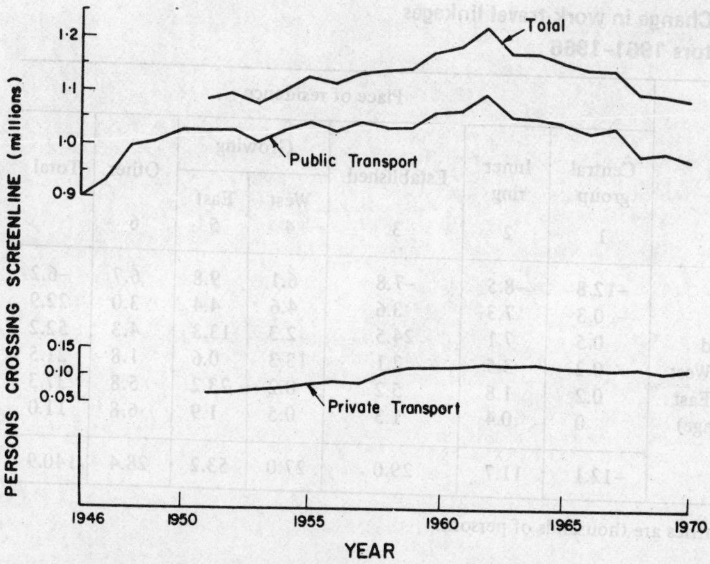

FIG. 7.5. Trends in 7 A.M.–10 A.M. person crossings of inner London cordon. Inner London cordon is bounded roughly by the Thames River on the south, Paddington and Marylebone Stations on the northwest, Euston, Kings Cross, and St. Pancras Stations on the north and Liverpool Street Station on the east. (*Source: Department of Planning and Transportation, Greater London Council.*)

Table 7.1. Work travel between individual municipalities in Melbourne, Australia, 1961

Workplace	Place of residence: Central group 1	Inner ring 2	Established 3	Growing: West 4	Growing: East 5	Other 6	Total
1. Central	85.1	139.3	113.8	24.1	32.4	10.2	404.9
2. Inner ring	10.6	99.3	35.4	16.7	8.6	3.1	173.6
3. Established	3.4	16.6	71.5	2.6	15.2	4.8	114.1
4. Growing: West	2.2	12.7	4.7	24.0	0.7	0.5	44.8
5. Growing: East	.4	2.4	6.6	0.1	25.6	3.0	38.1
6. Other (fringe)	.5	1.4	3.0	0.3	3.7	7.2	16.1
Total	102.2	271.6	235.0	67.8	86.2	28.8	791.9

NOTE:–Entries are thousands of persons.

Table 7.2. Change in work-travel linkages between sectors 1961-1966

Workplace	Place of residence						
	Central group	Inner ring	Established	Growing		Other	Total
				West	East		
	1	2	3	4	5	6	
1. Central	-12.8	-8.5	-7.8	6.1	9.8	6.7	-6.2
2. Inner ring	- 0.3	7.3	3.6	4.6	4.4	3.0	22.9
3. Established	0.5	7.1	24.5	2.3	13.3	4.3	52.2
4. Growing: West	0.2	3.5	2.1	13.3	0.6	1.8	21.5
5. Growing: East	0.2	1.8	5.2	0.2	23.2	5.8	37.3
6. Other (fringe)	0	0.4	1.3	0.5	1.9	6.8	11.0
Total	-12.1	11.7	29.0	27.0	53.2	28.4	140.9

NOTE:–Entries are thousands of persons.

for bus, ferry, and automobile transport to the Sydney central area. However, the available information suggests a similar stability in these modes.

7.2.3 Trends in central business district activities

Additional indirect evidence of the stability or low rates of growth of centrally focussed travel is provided by the limited data on central area employment available. Figure 7.8 shows the changes in employment within various geographic sectors of Melbourne, Australia, since 1951 [5]. This diagram indicates that employment in the central area of Melbourne has remained constant at about 150,000 jobs since 1951. Employment within the total region has been growing at about 2 percent per year during the same period.

Studies of trends in the functions of the central areas of cities in North America, Australia, and Europe have shown that the office and financial functions, specialized entertainment and major cultural activities, along with certain service functions, are becoming the dominant activities.

A recent study in Sydney, Australia, [4] has shown that while 34 percent of the total metropolitan employment was located in the central area in 1947 this proportion had declined to 20 percent in 1966. This study also showed that while the annual growth rate in central area employment was 0.7 percent during the 1961-1966 period, the growth rate in the tertiary sector was about 1.3 percent.

Objective evidence of the declining relative importance of the Sydney central area as a retail trade center was also provided by this study. Figure 7.9 shows the trends in retail trade in the central area and at suburban locations. The graph illustrates the spectacular growth in suburban retail sales that has occurred in Sydney and this pattern is typical of many cities.

Many observers of urban problems have refused to accept the evidence on the stabilization or low rates of growth of centrally focussed travel demands. They point to the vigorous building activity within the central areas of cities as evidence that the central business district is growing significantly: Figure 7.10 shows the trends in office development in the Sydney central area to 1973. A net addition of about 1 million square feet has been provided since about 1964. In Toronto during the 1960–1966 period the net supply of office space grew at about 2.6 percent per year.

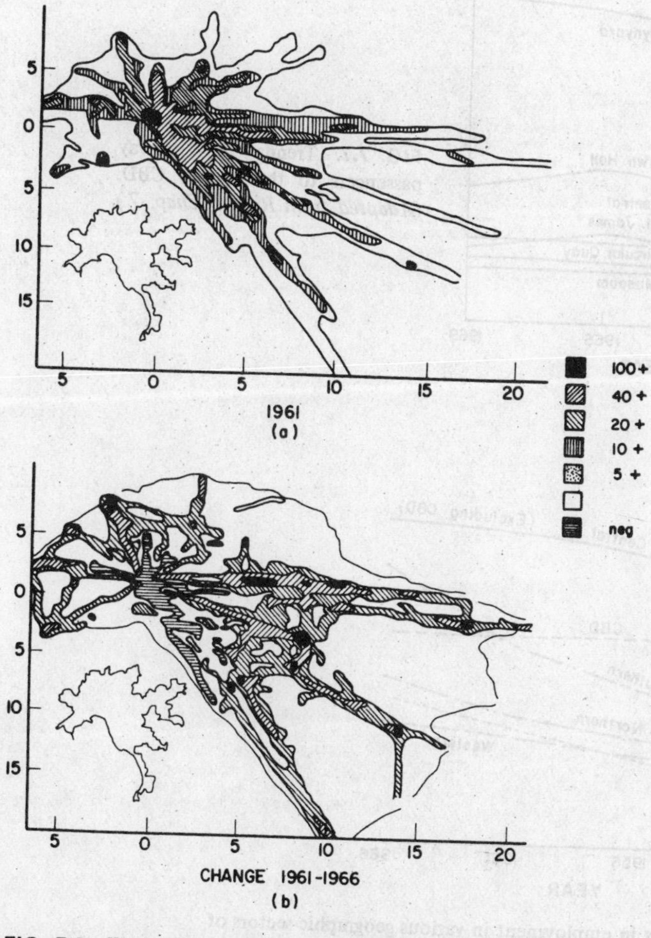

FIG. 7.6. Work-to-home linkages for (*a*) 1961 and (*b*) 1961–1966—Melbourne, Australia. (*Adapted from Ref. 3, Chap. 7.*)

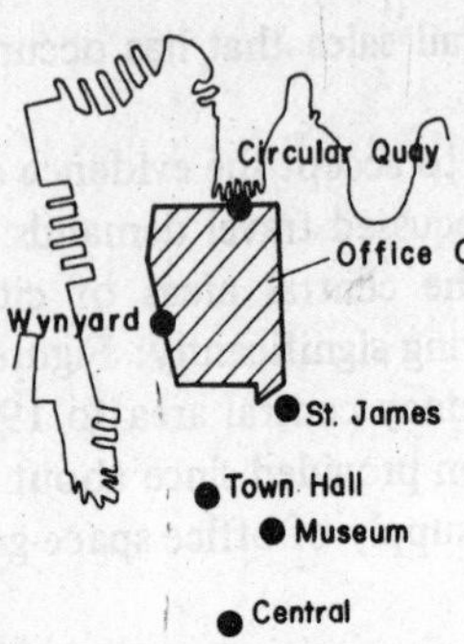

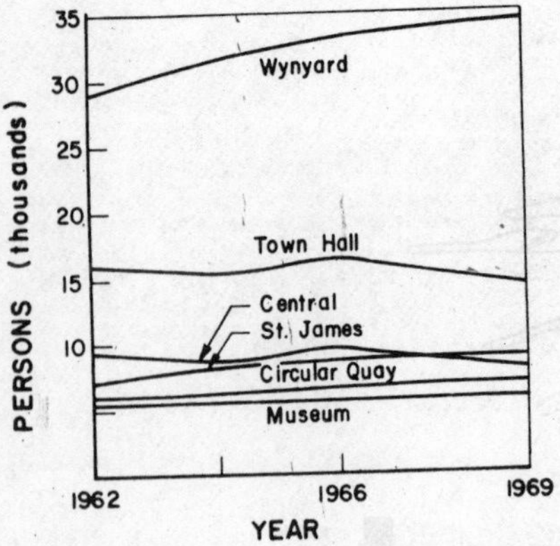

FIG. 7.7. Trends in subway passengers to the Sydney CBD. (*Adapted from Ref. 4, Chap. 7.*)

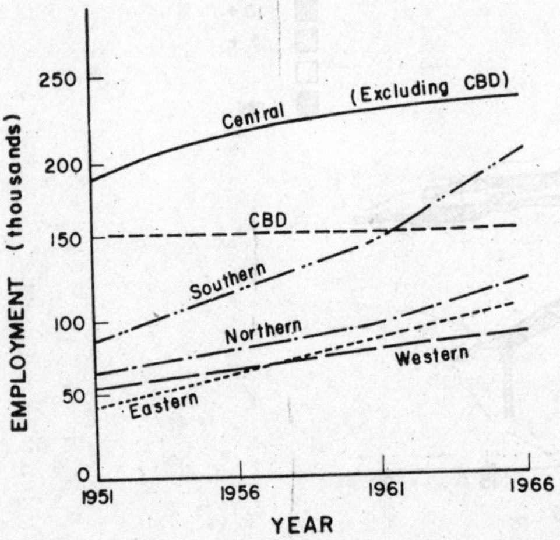

FIG. 7.8. Changes in employment in various geographic sectors of Melbourne, Australia. (*Adapted from Ref. 5, Chap. 7.*)

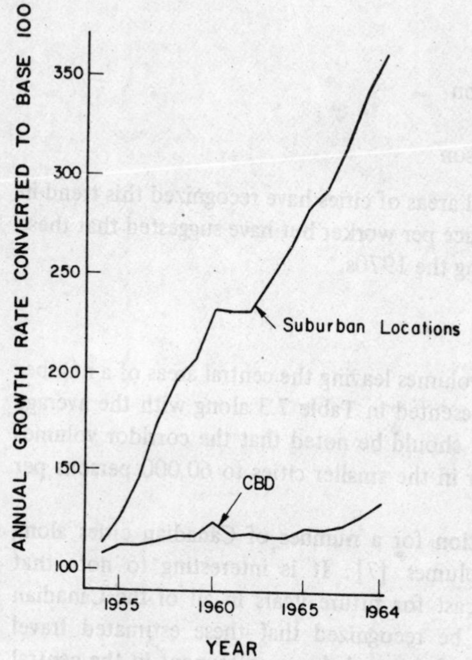

FIG. 7.9. Trends in retail trade in Sydney, Australia. (*Adapted from Ref. 4, Chap. 7.*)

This apparent enigma between a stable peak-hour travel demand and a physically growing central business district is explained by an examination of the per employee consumption of office space. In 1964 in the Toronto central area, the average office space consumption per employee was about 160 square feet. This increased to 300–380 square feet per employee in some of the office buildings constructed in 1968 [6]. A floor-space consumption study conducted in 1968–1969 in Sydney showed the following consumption indices:

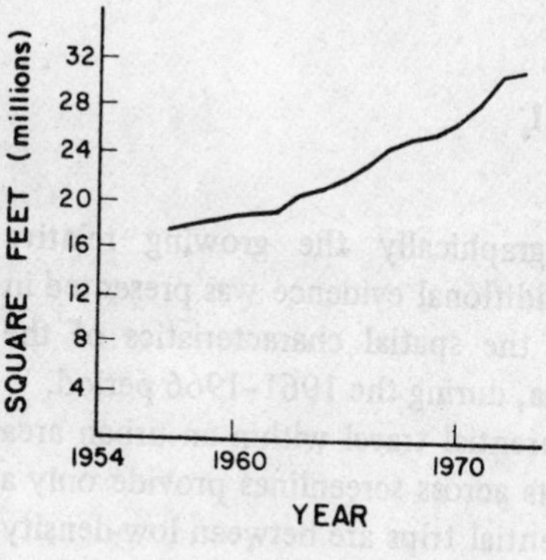

FIG. 7.10. Trends in office development in the Sydney CBD, Australia. (*Adapted from Ref. 4, Chap. 7.*)

Office: 200 square feet/person
Retail: 400 square feet/person
Warehousing: 400 square feet/person
Industry: 400 square feet/person
Miscellaneous: 240 square feet/person

A number of studies of the central areas of cities have recognized this trend in increasing consumption of office space per worker but have suggested that these increases will begin to taper off during the 1970s.

7.2.4 Radial corridor volumes

The evening peak corridor travel volumes leaving the central areas of a number of cities in the United States are presented in Table 7.3 along with the average volume in a typical corridor [1]. It should be noted that the corridor volumes range from 6,000 persons per hour in the smaller cities to 60,000 persons per hour in New York City.

Table 7.4 shows similar information for a number of Canadian cities along with estimated future corridor volumes [7]. It is interesting to note that significant increases are being forecast for future years in all of the Canadian cities listed in the table. It must be recognized that these estimated travel demands are derived from forecasts of the probable employment in the central business districts of these cities. In most of these Canadian cities the annual growth rates in centrally focussed travel required to yield these estimated horizon-year volumes are much higher than the rates of growth observed in travel to the central area in recent years. For example, in Vancouver rapid transit demands to the central business district would have to grow at from 2 to 4 percent per annum in order to yield the forecasted year 2000 corridor volumes. During the 1960–1970 period trips to the Vancouver central business district have been growing at about 1 percent per year. The large forecasted increases in travel are due to the optimistic estimates of central area employment prepared by the land-use planner.

7.3 TYPE 2: CIRCUMFERENTIAL TRAVEL BETWEEN SUBURBAN ACTIVITIES

Figure 7.1 has already demonstrated graphically the growing relative importance of circumferential-type travel. Additional evidence was presented in Table 7.2 which illustrated the change in the spatial characteristics of the work-to-home linkages in Melbourne, Australia, during the 1961–1966 period.

Time-series data on the growth in circumferential travel within an urban area are difficult to provide. Counts of movements across screenlines provide only a coarse indication of growth. Most circumferential trips are between low-density origins and destinations, and trips between locations which are separated widely

Table 7.3. P.M. Peak-hour volumes leaving central areas of major U.S. cities

CBD	No. persons leaving CBD/ peak hour	No. persons leaving CBD/peak hour in average corridor
New York, N.Y.	> 250,000	Above 60,000
Chicago, Ill.	200,000–250,000	30,000–40,000
Philadelphia, Pa. Boston, Mass. Washington, D.C.	150,000–200,000	20,000–30,000
Los Angeles, Calif. San Francisco, Calif.	100,000–150,000	13,000–20,000
Cleveland, Ohio Detroit, Mich. Atlanta, Ga. Pittsburgh, Pa. New Orleans, La. St. Louis, Mo. Baltimore, Md.	75,000–100,000	9,000–13,000
Dallas, Tex. St. Paul, Minn. Minneapolis, Minn. Providence, R. I. Forth Worth, Tex. Milwaukee, Wisc.	50,000–75,000	6,000–9,000
Miami, Fla. Cincinnati, Ohio Rochester, N.Y. Seattle, Wash. Kansas City, Mo. Denver, Colo.	Less than 50,000	Below 6,000

may occur within one corridor. This is unlike type 1 travel where at least one end of the trips is concentrated geographically.

Figure 7.11 shows time-series data for the average daily traffic volume on the MacDonald-Cartier Freeway at two locations. The locations of these counting stations within the Metropolitan Toronto area are shown in the diagram. Much of the development of Toronto has occurred in the sector within which these two stations are located. The rates of growth illustrated in this diagram should be compared with the trends in centrally oriented demands shown in Fig. 7.3.

Figure 7.12 provides time-series data for the average daily traffic volumes at points on four major circumferential routes in Sydney, Australia. The locations of these points in the Sydney metropolitan area are shown in the diagram. The

Table 7.4. Observed and forecasted CBD corridor volumes in Canadian cities

City	Maximum corridor volume	
	Base year	Horizon year
Ottawa	29,000 (1963 Pop. 500,000)	37,000 (1986 Pop. 851,000)
Hamilton	4,800 (1963 Pop. 267,700)	10,000 (1985 Pop. 454,000)
London	2,000 (1963 Pop. 173,000)	10,000 (1986 Pop. 295,000)
Winnipeg	10,500 (1963 Pop. 504,000)	12,000 (1991 Pop. 781,000)
Calgary	4,400 (1964 Pop. 335,800)	10,000 (1986 Pop. 775,700)
Edmonton	2,700 (1961 Pop. 336,000)	7,500 (1980 Pop. 660,000)
Vancouver	5,700* (1969 Pop. 665,000)	21,000* (2000 Pop. 2,200,000)

*A.M. Peak-hour inbound travel; all other entries are two-way A.M. peak-hour volumes.

spectacular growth in circumferential travel in Sydney contrasts sharply with the evidence on travel demands to the Sydney central business district presented in Fig. 7.7.

Similar evidence on the changes observed in type 2 travel demands could be presented for many cities throughout the world. These changes would not only reflect the total growth of these urban areas but also the rapid decentralization of both jobs and housing. The provision of mass transport facilities for type 2 travel demands is a relatively intractable problem when compared with type 1 travel demands. The collection and distribution of low-density origins and destinations becomes an expensive proposition.

7.4 TYPE 3: TRAVEL WITHIN RESIDENTIAL AREAS

The most important type of travel within residential areas from the viewpoint of metropolitan transport planning is travel to and from mainline public transport facilities. The studies of modal transport usage described in Chap. 3 have illustrated that public transport patronage is very sensitive to the time spent during this stage of a trip.

Some of the more practical proposals directed toward increasing public transport patronage for the journey to central areas are aimed at this end of the trip. Demand scheduled bus services are being used in a number of cities in an attempt to increase the use of public-transport services. The available information on the demand for this type of transport service is presented in Chap. 8.

7.5 TYPE 4: TRAVEL WITHIN THE CENTRAL BUSINESS DISTRICT

Very little attention has been directed toward this type of travel demand until recently. The major metropolitanwide transport facilities serving central areas cannot penetrate them completely and rely on pedestrian trips within the central business district for the terminal components of trips. In addition, most of the internal circulation within the central areas of cities must be achieved on foot in order to achieve a satisfactory downtown environment. While the amount of land consumed by pedestrian facilities is small, pedestrian circulation is playing an increasingly important role in the articulation of activities within the central business district. Modal transport choice is very sensitive to the pedestrian component of a trip. Central area retail sales are becoming more dependent upon

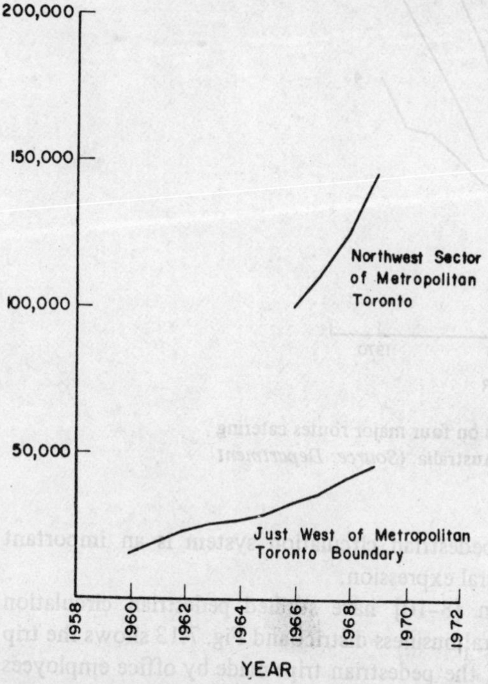

FIG. 7.11. Trends in AADT volumes at two locations on the MacDonald-Cartier Freeway, Toronto, Ontario. (*Source: Ministry of Transportation and Communications, Ontario.*)

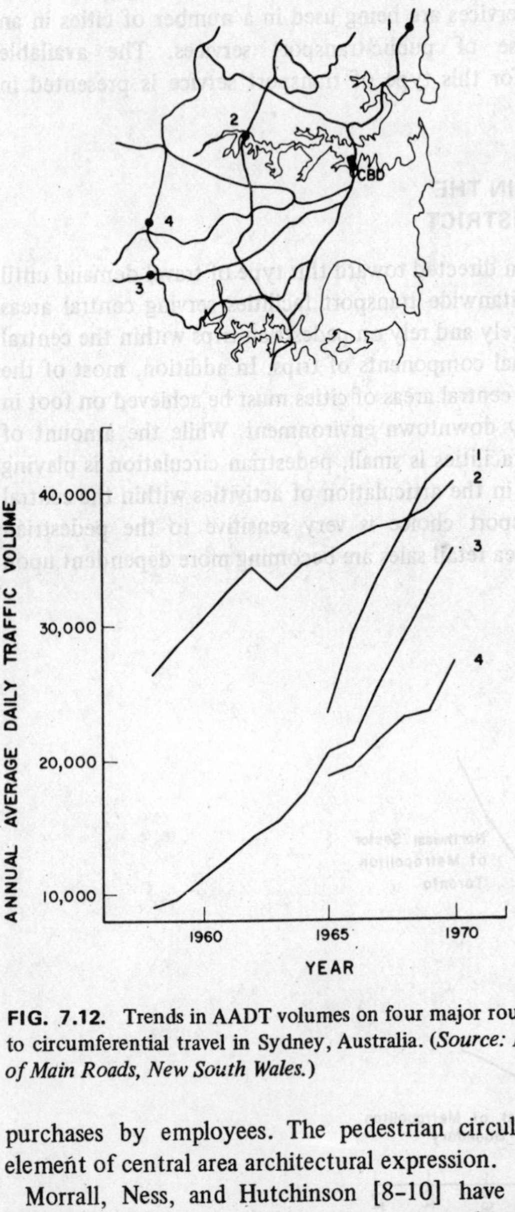

FIG. 7.12. Trends in AADT volumes on four major routes catering to circumferential travel in Sydney, Australia. (*Source: Department of Main Roads, New South Wales.*)

purchases by employees. The pedestrian circulation system is an important element of central area architectural expression.

Morrall, Ness, and Hutchinson [8–10] have studied pedestrian circulation patterns within the Toronto central business district and Fig. 7.13 shows the trip length frequency distributions of the pedestrian trips made by office employees using the various modes of transport serving the Toronto central area. This study demonstrated that the gravity model could be used to simulate employment-location to transport-terminal pedestrian trips.

Lunch-hour pedestrian trips were also simulated with the gravity model and Fig. 7.14 shows the trip-length frequency distributions observed. The survey revealed that employees leaving their offices during the lunch period made an average of 1.7 visits per head to shops, restaurants, etc. Table 7.5 shows a breakdown of these rates by purpose.

The rate at which office employees participated in lunch-hour activities varied with the accessibility of an office location to the major retail trade complexes. Figure 7.15 shows the variation in the proportion of office employees leaving a building for the Toronto central area. The rate decreases rapidly as the distance from the major retail areas increases. The retail trade implications of Fig. 7.15 cannot be appraised directly, as retail expenditures by employees were not surveyed.

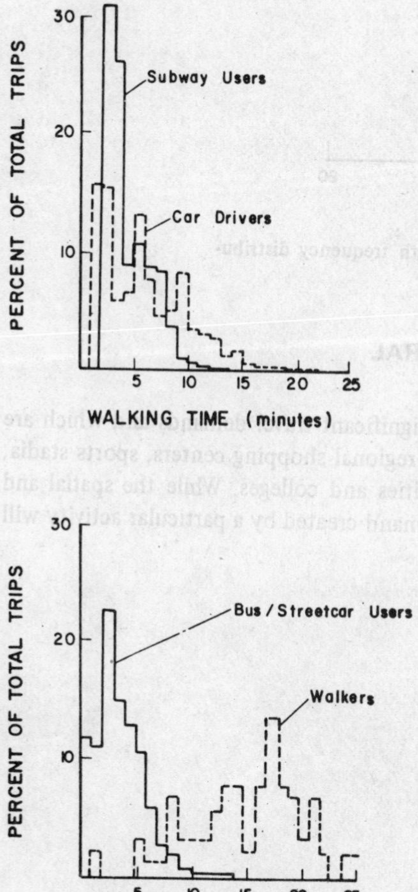

FIG. 7.13. Trip-length frequency distributions of CBD pedestrian trips. (*Adapted from Ref. 10, Chap. 7.*)

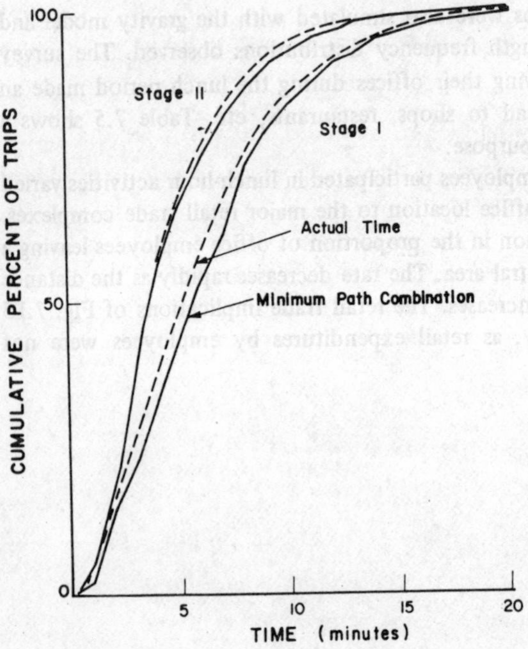

FIG. 7.14. Lunch hour pedestrian trip-length frequency distributions. (*Adapted from Ref. 10, Chap. 7.*)

7.6 TYPE 5: TRAVEL TO NONCENTRAL ACTIVITY CONCENTRATIONS

The major activities which generate significant travel demands and which are not located centrally include airports, regional shopping centers, sports stadia, and public institutions such as universities and colleges. While the spatial and temporal properties of the transport demand created by a particular activity will

Table 7.5. Pedestrian trip purpose breakdown

Activity	Visits/head
Department store	0.57
Retail shop	0.36
Restaurant	0.36
Personal business	0.29
Recreational stop	0.06
Recreational walk	0.05
Transportation	0.01
Total	1.70

be a function of the specific characteristics of that activity, some general characteristics have been observed in the studies performed to date.

7.6.1 Airports

The travel demands generated by airports serving major urban complexes tend to have spatial and temporal properties similar to the travel demands created by the central business district. Figure 7.16 shows the hourly distributions of

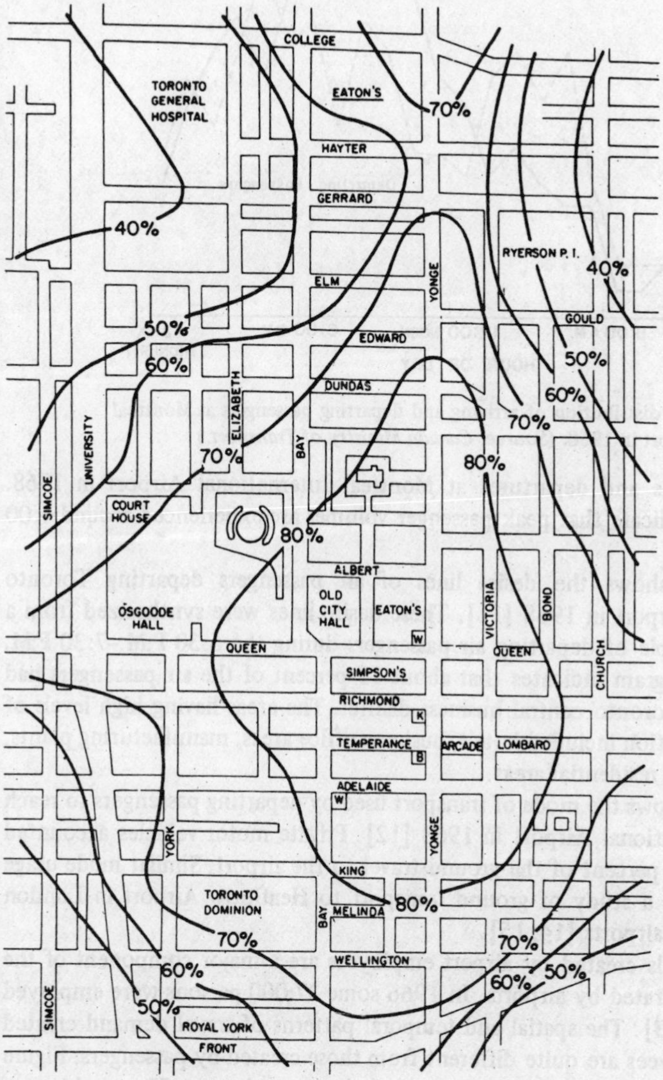

FIG. 7.15. Contours of lunch hour pedestrian trip-generation rates for Toronto, Ontario. (*Adapted from Ref. 10, Chap. 7.*)

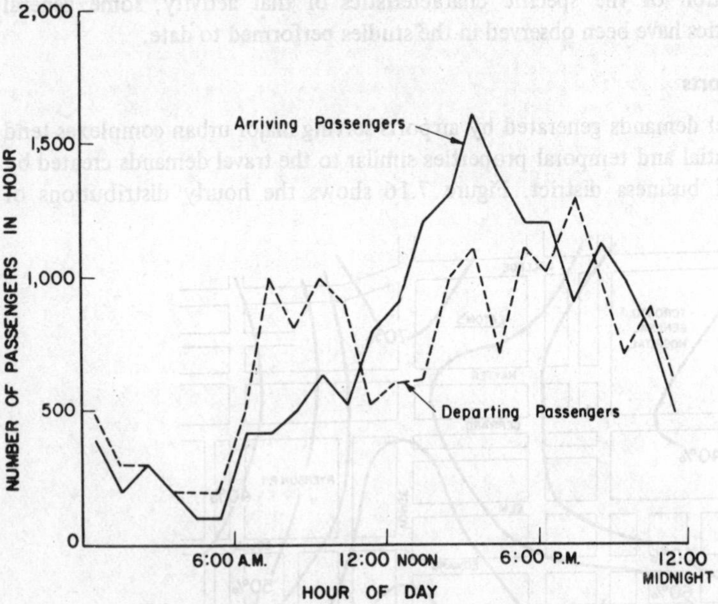

FIG. 7.16. Daily distribution of arriving and departing passengers at Montreal International Airport in 1968. (*Source: Canada Ministry of Transport.*)

passenger arrivals and departures at Montreal International Airport in 1968. These graphs indicate that peak passenger volumes are experienced around 4:00 P.M.

Figure 7.17 shows the desire lines of air passengers departing Toronto International Airport in 1968 [11]. These desire lines were synthesized from a 35 percent sample of departing air passengers during the 6:30 P.M.–7:30 P.M. period. This diagram indicates that about 15 percent of the air passengers had origins in the Toronto central business district. The areas having high levels of passenger generation included hotels, business office areas, manufacturing plants, and high-income residential areas.

Figure 7.18 shows the mode of transport used by departing passengers to reach Toronto International Airport in 1968 [12]. Private motor vehicles accounted for just over 55 percent of the ground travel to the airport. Similar mode usage was observed in a study of ground transport to Heathrow Airport in London [13], and other airports [14, 15].

Travel demands created by airport employees are a major component of the total travel generated by airports. In 1966 some 37,000 persons were employed at Heathrow [13]. The spatial and temporal patterns of travel demand created by these employees are quite different from those created by passengers. Figure 7.19 shows the hourly arrival patterns of these employees. The peaking of inbound trips during the 6:00 A.M.–9:00 A.M. period should be noted. The

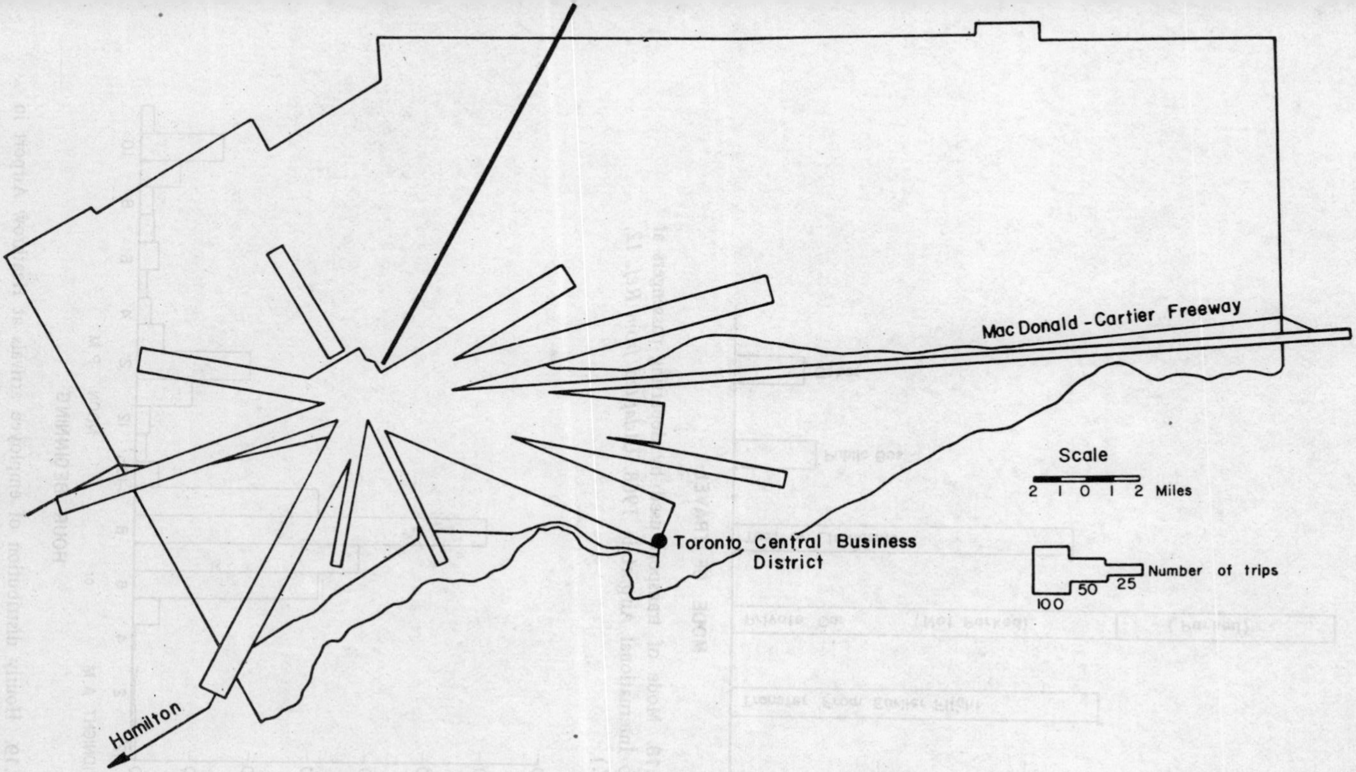

FIG. 7.17. Desire lines of air passengers departing Toronto International Airport in 1968. (*Adapted from Ref. 11, Chap. 7.*)

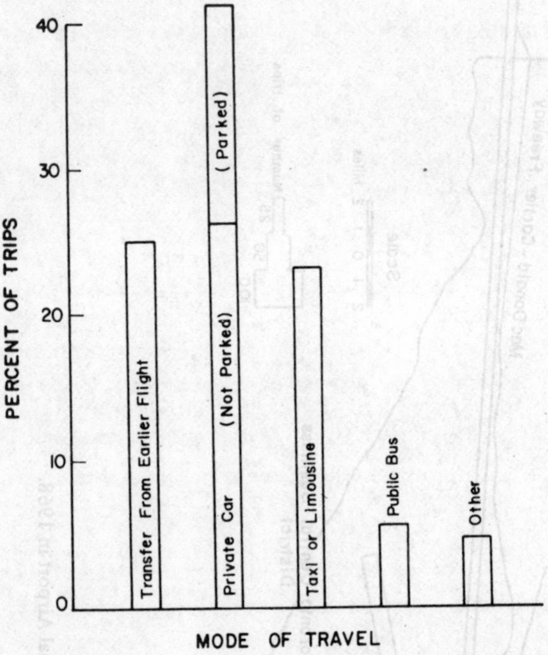

FIG. 7.18. Mode of transport used by departing passengers at Toronto International Airport in 1968. (*Adapted from Ref. 12, Chap. 7.*)

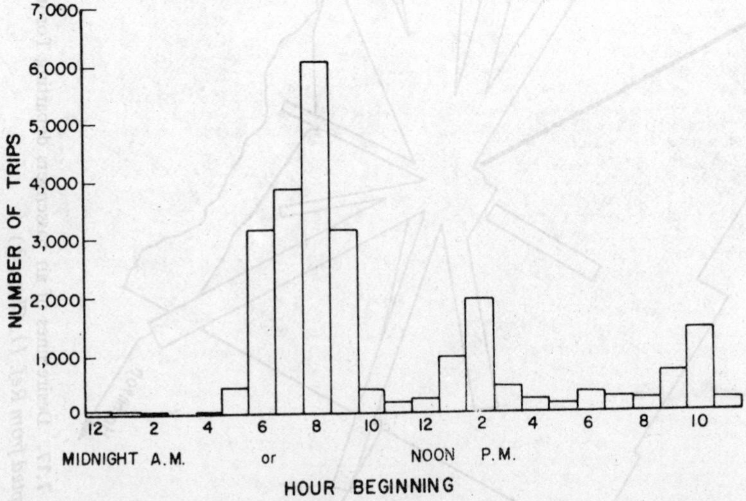

FIG. 7.19. Hourly distribution of employee arrivals at Heathrow Airport in 1968. (*Adapted from Ref. 13, Chap. 7.*)

principal component of this morning peak is travel by maintenance workers. It is interesting to note from this survey that 57 percent of the female employees used public transport for the journey to work while only 13 percent of the male employees used public transport. Figure 7.20 illustrates the spatial distribution of the households of Heathrow employees along with the proportions of employees who used car and public transport for the journey to work. It is interesting to note that the majority of the airport employees lived in areas adjacent to the airport.

While the data described above is for particular airports throughout the world it is typical of the general properties of travel demand generated by airports serving major urban complexes. A few airports throughout the world have concentrations of tourist travel and this will influence the hourly distribution of passengers, the spatial pattern of travel to and from the airport and the mode of transport used for ground travel. However, it is interesting to note from Refs. 12 and 13 that except for the differences in absolute magnitude, the characteristics of ground travel generated by Heathrow and Toronto Airports are very similar.

7.6.2 Regional shopping centers

Large regional shopping centers have developed rapidly in most cities throughout the world in which car-ownership levels are relatively high. Figure 7.9 showed the trends in the distribution of retail trade between the central

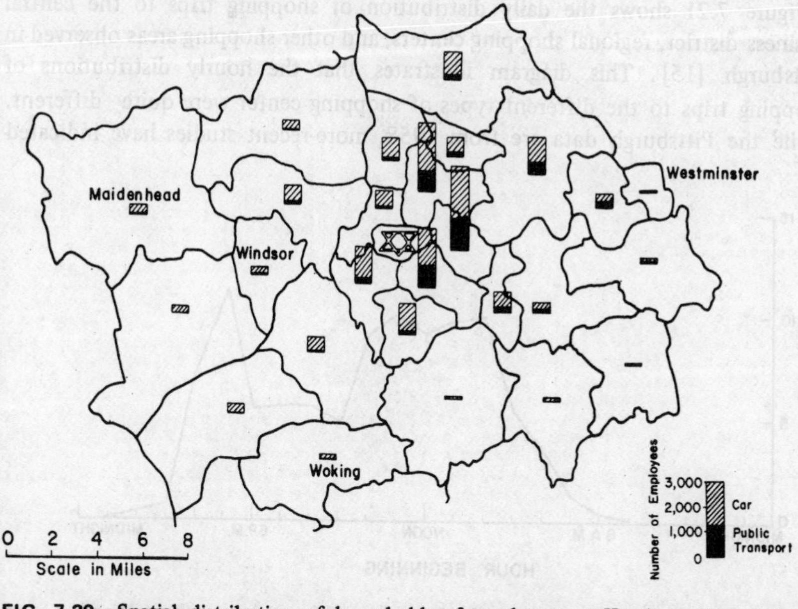

FIG. 7.20. Spatial distribution of households of employees at Heathrow Airport in 1968. (*Adapted from Ref. 13, Chap. 7.*)

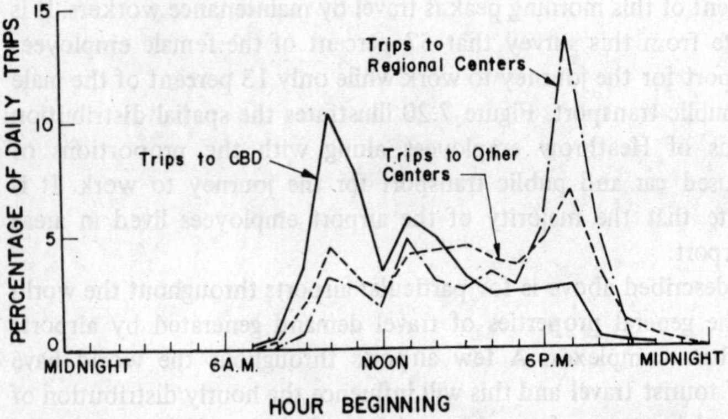

FIG. 7.21. Hourly distribution of shopping trips to various types of retail trade centers in Pittsburgh, Pennsylvania. (*Adapted from Ref. 15, Chap. 7.*)

business district and suburban locations for Sydney, Australia. The trends illustrated in Fig. 7.9 are typical of those observed in many cities. Current trends in the functions of these centers indicate their evolution toward subregional centers containing significant concentrations of offices, personal services, and entertainment facilities.

Figure 7.21 shows the daily distribution of shopping trips to the central business district, regional shopping centers, and other shopping areas observed in Pittsburgh [15]. This diagram illustrates that the hourly distributions of shopping trips to the different types of shopping center were quite different. While the Pittsburgh data are from 1958, more-recent studies have indicated

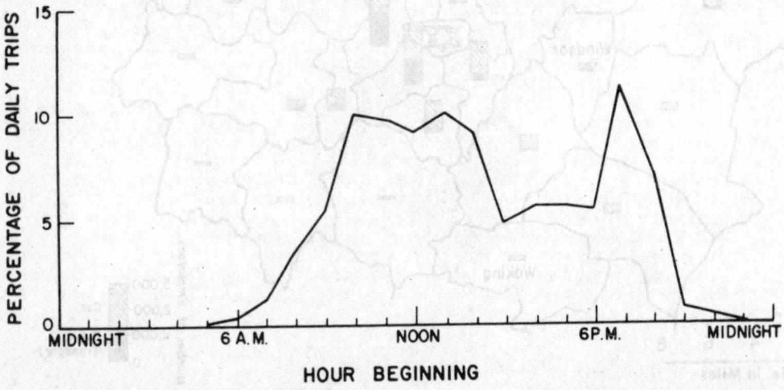

FIG. 7.22. Composite hourly distribution of car driver trips to three Miami, Florida, shopping centers. (*Adapted from Ref. 15, Chap. 7.*)

similar daily variations. Figure 7.22 shows a composite hourly distribution curve of car-driver trips to three regional shopping centers in Miami [15]. This distribution differs from that shown in Fig. 7.20 in that it also includes car trips by center employees.

Difficulties have been experienced in developing a simple relationship for estimating the trips generated by regional shopping centers. Figure 7.23 shows a relationship between the daily person shopping trips and the gross floor area for a number of regional shopping centers in the United States. This relationship has been plotted from data contained in Ref. 15. Keefer [15] attempted to develop more-refined prediction equations from the same data set but had to resort to multiple term regression equations.

Voorhees and Crow [16] have studied the parking demands generated by 270 regional shopping centers throughout the United States and Canada. Figure 7.24 shows a typical relationship of the trends in parked vehicle accumulation throughout the day for the peak day and a normal day within the Christmas shopping period. The relative importance of retail trade activities during the Christmas period is illustrated by Fig. 7.25 (17). This diagram illustrates that the peak week preceding Christmas has a daily sales volume of about 2.5 times the

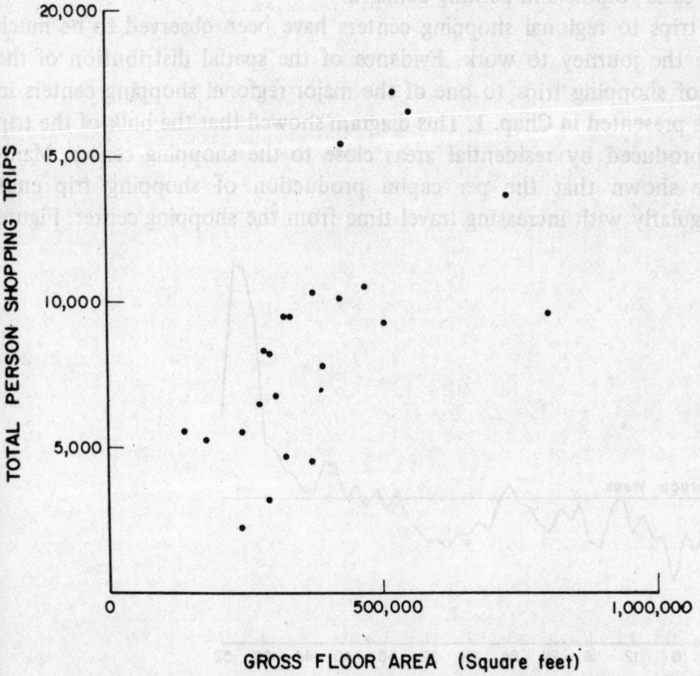

FIG. 7.23. Total person shopping trips vs. gross floor area for U.S. regional shopping centers. (*Adapted from Ref. 15, Chap. 7.*)

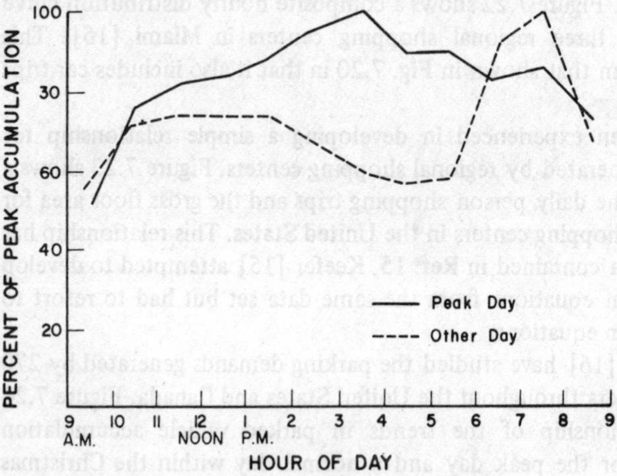

FIG. 7.24. Hourly variations in parking accumulation at a regional shopping center. (*Adapted from Ref. 16, Chap. 7.*)

average week. Reference 17 also notes that there is a high degree of correlation between the sales volume and parking demand.

Shopping trips to regional shopping centers have been observed to be much shorter than the journey to work. Evidence of the spatial distribution of the home ends of shopping trips to one of the major regional shopping centers in Toronto was presented in Chap. 1. This diagram showed that the bulk of the trip ends were produced by residential areas close to the shopping center. Many studies have shown that the per capita production of shopping trip ends decreases regularly with increasing travel time from the shopping center. Figure

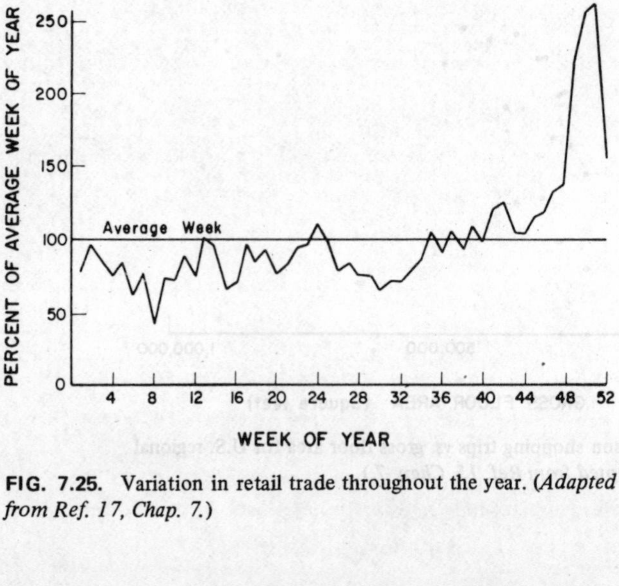

FIG. 7.25. Variation in retail trade throughout the year. (*Adapted from Ref. 17, Chap. 7.*)

7.26 shows a composite curve developed by Keefer [15]. Similar evidence has been presented for Australian conditions by Harding [18].

7.6.3 Suburban industrial parks

Trends in circumferential-type travel demands in several metropolitan areas have been presented in Sec. 7.3. Much of the growth in this type of travel demand has been generated by the growth in employment located in suburban industrial parks, as well as at airports and regional shopping centers.

Williams and Latchford [19] have conducted a comprehensive study of certain manufacturing companies in the northeast of England. Most studies of industrial trip generation have shown that plant floor areas are poor predictors of trips because of the wide variations in floor area per employee between industry types and due to the age of the plant. The best predictor of trip generation is employment, but employment is difficult to predict directly for future years and is usually derived from forecast floor areas. Figure 7.27 shows the relationship developed in Ref. 19 between daily vehicle trips generated and plant floor space. Superimposed on Fig. 7.27 is information reported by Keefer [15] for a sample of manufacturing plants in the United States. The two sets of data are not strictly comparable. The British data are expressed in terms of equivalent

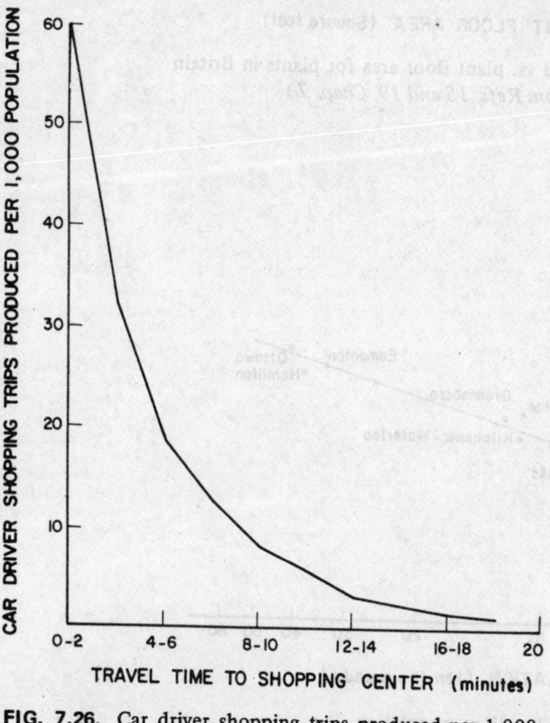

FIG. 7.26. Car driver shopping trips produced per 1,000 persons vs. travel time to shopping center. (*Adapted from Ref. 15, Chap. 7.*)

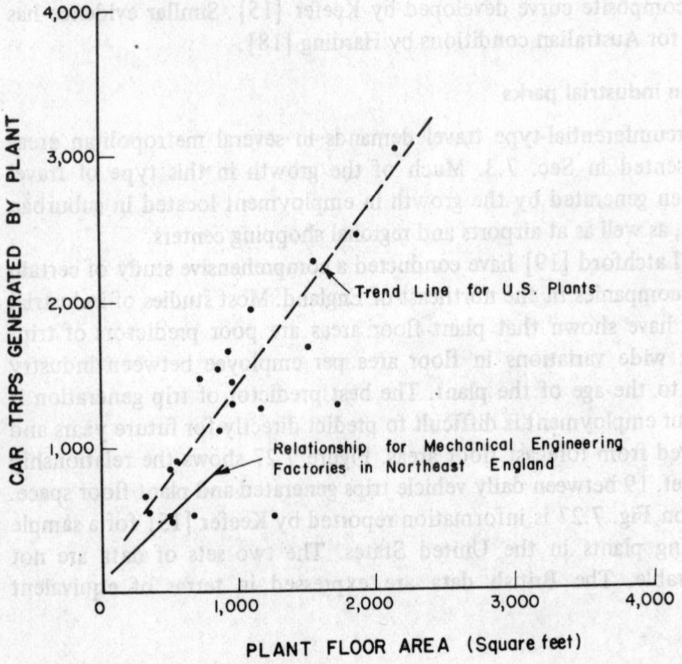

FIG. 7.27. Car trips generated vs. plant floor area for plants in Britain and United States. (*Adapted from Refs. 15 and 19, Chap. 7.*)

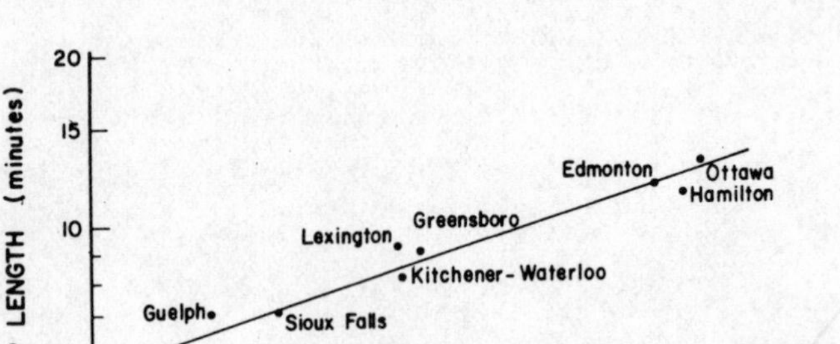

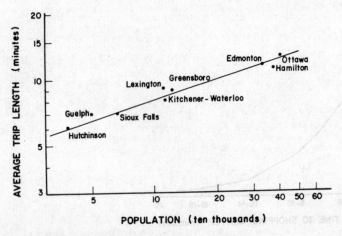

FIG. 7.28. Average work-trip length vs. population.

passenger-car units and contain car and truck movements. The rate of trip generation is still less than that for plants in the United States, but this no doubt reflects the much higher rate of public-transport tripmaking in Britain for the journey to work.

Work trips are normally the longest trips made by urban residents. Figure 7.28 shows a relationship between average work-trip length and the population of urban regions developed by Voorhees, Bellomo, and Cleveland [20]. Data for several Canadian cities have been added to the diagram [21].

SUMMARY

This chapter has summarized some of the historic data that are available on trends in various types of urban travel demand. This information has been assembled from a wide variety of sources and cannot be considered as a comprehensive treatment. Urban travel statistics of the type that are useful to urban transport planning are not available in any convenient form in most countries of the world. Information which is useful for urban transport planning and which is collected on a regular basis is discussed in detail in Chap. 13.

REFERENCES

1. Wilbur Smith and Associates, *Transportation and Parking for Tomorrow's Cities,* Automobile Manufacturers Association, Detroit, Michigan, 1968.
2. Metropolitan Toronto Planning Board, *Summary of Toronto Transit Commission Cordon Counts,* Toronto, Ontario, May, 1971.
3. Paterson, J., "The Dynamics of Urban Change," in N. Clark, (ed.), *Analysis of Urban Development,* Department of Civil Engineering, University of Melbourne, Melbourne, Australia, 1970.
4. Council of the City of Sydney, *City of Sydney Strategic Plan,* Sydney, Australia, 1971.
5. Melbourne and Metropolitan Board of Works, *Planning Policies for the Melbourne Metropolitan Region,* Melbourne, Australia, 1971.
6. Read, Voorhees and Associates, *Central Area Transportation Study,* Toronto, Ontario, 1968.
7. Thompson, G. A., *Forecasting the Long Range Potential of New Modes of Urban Transportation,* M.A.Sc. thesis, Department of Civil Engineering, University of Waterloo, Waterloo, Ontario, 1971.
8. Morrall, J. F., and B. G. Hutchinson, *A Study of the Journey to Work by CBD Employees,* Proceedings, International Symposium on Optimal Systems Planning, International Federation of Automatic Control, pp. 99–114, June, 1968.
9. Morrall, J. F., M. P. Ness, and B. G. Hutchinson, *Traffic Prediction Models for Central Business District Planning,* Proceedings, Australian Road Research Board, Melbourne, pp. 112–133, 1968.
10. Ness, M. P., J. F. Morrall, and B. G. Hutchinson, *An Analysis of Central Business District Pedestrian Circulation Patterns,* Highway Research Record No. 283, Highway Research Board, Washington, D.C., 1968.
11. Hutchinson, B. G., and P. M. Pearson, *An Evaluation of Ground Transportation Requirements for Airports,* Paper presented to Canadian Transportation Research Forum, Vancouver, British Columbia, 1968.

12. McLeod, M. G., *A Comprehensive Survey of Passengers Flying from Toronto International Airport, May-June 1968*, Tech. Note No. 141, Institute for Aerospace Studies, University of Toronto, Ontario, August, 1969.
13. Freeman, Fox, Wilbur Smith and Associates, *London Airports Traffic Study Heathrow Airport Part 1: Traffic Characteristics*, British Airports Authority, London, June, 1967.
14. Consultative Group on Transportation Research, *Air Transport and Access to Urban Areas*, Organization for Economic Co-operation and Development, Paris, June, 1971.
15. Keefer, L. E., *Urban Travel Patterns for Airports, Shopping Centers, and Industrial Plants*, Report 24, National Cooperative Highway Research Program, Highway Research Board, Washington, D.C., 1966.
16. Voorhees, A. M., and C. E. Crow, *Shopping Center Parking Requirements*, Highway Research Record No. 130, Highway Research Board, Washington, D.C., 1966.
17. Cleveland, D. E., and E. A. Mueller, *Traffic Characteristics at Regional Shopping Centers*, Bureau of Highway Traffic, Yale University, New Haven, Connecticut, 1961.
18. Harding, C. V., *Traffic Characteristics of Major Shopping Centers*, Proceedings, Australian Road Research Board, Melbourne, pp. 208–232, 1966.
19. Williams, T. E. H., and J. C. R. Latchford, *Prediction of Traffic in Industrial Areas*, Traffic Engineering and Control, London, June, 1966.
20. Voorhees, A. M., S. J. Bellomo, and D. E. Cleveland, *Factors in Work Trip Lengths*, Highway Research Record No. 141, Highway Research Board, Washington, D.C., 1966.
21. Hutchinson, B. G., "Establishing Urban Transportation Demands by Synthetic Procedures," *Engineering Journal*, June, 1971, pp. 22–26.

8 URBAN TRANSPORT TECHNOLOGY

Urban travel demands have been classified into five broad types in Chap. 7 and some evidence of the nature of these travel demands has been presented. This chapter provides a summary of the principal types of urban transport technology and examines in a broad way the capabilities of alternative technologies to serve the different types of travel demand. The specific combination of transport technologies chosen for a particular urban area must be a result of detailed studies conducted in that area. The information presented in this chapter provides only a very coarse screening of the urban transport technologies available.

During the past decade a large number of urban transport concepts have been advanced. Very few of these concepts have reached the detailed design phase and even fewer exist as working prototypes. The continued development of the majority of the recently advanced concepts is not dependent upon technological innovation, but rather on the existence of a travel market in urban areas for these technologies.

8.1 CLASSIFICATION OF URBAN TRANSPORT TECHNOLOGIES

Several classification schemes have been used to display the broad properties of urban transport technologies. In this chapter, two schemes are used to display the available transport technologies. The set of travel demands identified in Chap. 7 is used as one scheme, while the second scheme involves the broad functional properties of urban transport technologies.

8.1.1 Demand classification

Five travel-demand types were identified in Chap. 7 and it is useful to disaggregate type 1 travel demands into three subclasses based on the following volume ranges:

Type 1A: Demand volumes of greater than 20,000 persons per hour
Type 1B: Demand volumes from 8,000 to 20,000 persons per hour
Type 1C: Less than 8,000 persons per hour

8.1.2 Functional classification

The second classification factor is based on the following broad groupings of the functional properties of urban transport systems.

Mass rapid-transit systems: Transport technologies that operate on fixed guideways, have fixed on-line station locations, fixed vehicle routings, and operate on fixed schedules

Personal rapid-transit systems: Transport technologies that operate on fixed guideways, have fixed off-line station locations, and may have flexible vehicle routings and schedules

Bus systems: Transport systems that use buses that may have a range of passenger capacities and performance characteristics, and may operate on fixed routes with fixed schedules, or may be flexibly routed and demand scheduled

Dual-mode systems: Transport systems that use individual small vehicles that may be operated under manual control on the street system but provide for automatic control of the vehicles on the guideway

Table 8.1 shows the two-factor classification scheme and illustrates in a broad way those cells of the matrix in which the transport technologies and the travel-demand types are compatible.

8.2 MASS RAPID-TRANSIT SYSTEMS

Mass rapid-transit systems have been defined as those transport technologies that operate on fixed guideways, have fixed station spacings, fixed vehicle routings, and fixed schedules. The conventional steel-wheeled duorail mass transit systems that operate in many cities throughout the world are the

Table 8.1. Travel-demand type—transport technology compatibility matrix

Travel-demand type	Transport technology			
	Mass rapid transit	Personal rapid · transit	Bus systems	Dual-mode systems
Type 1–radial travel				
> 20,000 persons/hr	x			
8,000–20,000 persons/hr	x	x	x	x
< 8,000 persons/hr	x	x	x	x
Type 2–circumferential travel		x	x	x
Type 3–residential area travel			x	
Type 4–travel within CBD		x	x	
Type 5–travel to non-central activities	x		x	

most-common examples of mass rapid transit. The rubber-tired systems that operate in Paris, Mexico City, and Montreal are also examples of mass rapid transit. Many transport planning agencies have established that these high-capacity mass-transit systems are most appropriate for travel-demand corridors in which the peak hour demands exceed 20,000 persons per hour.

Various tramway and streetcar systems operate in cities throughout the world and tend to serve travel-demand corridors with peak-hour travel demands of less than 10,000 persons per hour. In recent years, increasing attention has been directed toward the development of technologies capable of serving travel demands within the 8,000–15,000 persons per hour range. Many of the European developments of this type are ususally referred to by the term *light rapid transit.*

8.2.1 General operating characteristics

The principal service features of mass transit technologies may be summarized as shown in Fig. 8.1. This diagram shows the relationship between average travel speed, station spacing, top speed of vehicle, and station stop time [1]. This relationship is based on acceleration and deceleration rates at stations of 3 miles per hour per second. It is interesting to note that the average speed of travel is not influenced greatly by increases in the top speed of a vehicle above about 50 miles per hour. Stated in another way, the average speed of travel by urban mass transit is governed essentially by the station spacing. It has been shown in Chap.

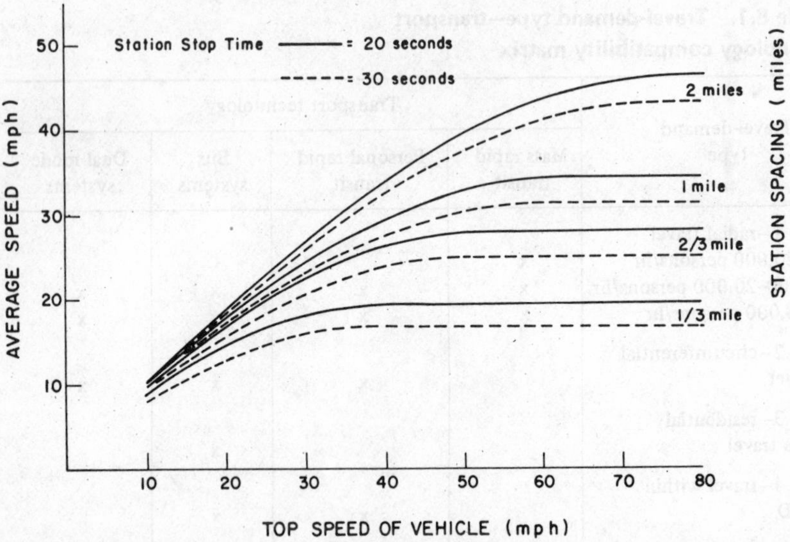

FIG. 8.1. Average speed of travel by mass transit vs. top vehicle speed, station spacing, and station stop time. (*From A. Scheffer Lang and Richard M. Soberman, "Urban Rail Transit," M.I.T. Press, Cambridge, Massachusetts,* 1964.)

3 that the average travel time of a transport mode is an important determinant of the patronage of that mode.

A second important feature of mass transit is its capacity. The capacity of a mass-transit system is normally expressed in terms of the maximum number of passengers per hour that can be moved past any point in the system. The capacity of a single mass-transit track is determined by the number of trains that can pass a given point in a unit of time and the number of passengers per train. Lang and Soberman [1] show that this capacity may be calculated from:

$$Q = \frac{60\,kL}{H} = \frac{60\,knl}{H} \tag{8.1}$$

where Q = capacity in passengers per hour on a single transit track
H = headway between trains in minutes
k = loading coefficient in passengers per foot of train length
l = length of each car in feet
n = number of cars per train
L = total train length = nl

For a headway of H and an average speed of $\bar{V}$, the distance spacing between trains is given by $H\bar{V}$. The total number of trains required per route mile, neglecting turnaround time, is given by the reciprocal of the distance spacing:

$$N = \frac{60\,n}{HV} \tag{8.2}$$

where N = the approximate number of cars required per mile of single track

The minimum safe headway for transit lines containing stations is given by:

$$h = T + \frac{L}{V} + \frac{V}{2a} + \frac{5.05\,V}{2d} \tag{8.3}$$

where h = headway in seconds
T = station stop time in seconds
V = maximum train speed in feet per second
a = rate of acceleration in feet per second per second
d = rate of deceleration in feet per second per second

Equations (8.1) and (8.3) have been used by Lang and Soberman [1] to develop the single transit track capacities shown in Table 8.2. As an example, this table shows that an increase in train length from 400 feet to 600 feet will increase the capacity from 60,000 to 83,000 passengers per hour.

Figure 8.2, which was also developed by Lang and Soberman, shows the interrelationships between the factors just described. Figure 8.2(*a*) shows the relationship between maximum speed and minimum headway for trains of various lengths, assuming a station stop time of 40 seconds. The capacities corresponding to these conditions are shown in Fig. 8.2(*b*), while the average train speeds corresponding to these conditions and a station spacing of 0.5 mile are shown in Fig. 8.2(*c*). Finally, Fig. 8.2(*d*) identifies the equipment required to satisfy the conditions specified in the earlier graphs. If an average travel speed is selected, then Fig. 8.2 may be used to estimate the equipment requirements and capacity.

8.2.2 High-capacity systems

The high-capacity mass rapid-transit system most commonly used and in use to date has been the steel-wheeled duorail system. Examples of duorail systems

Table 8.2. Single-track passenger capacities*

Running speed (mph)	Average acceleration (mph/sec)	Passengers/hr		
		L = 400 ft	L = 500 ft	L = 600 ft
20	3.0	60,600	72,400	83,200
30	3.0	56,200	68,300	79,700
40	2.65	52,100	62,300	73,200
50	2.0	44,600	55,100	65,000

Source: *(From A. Scheffer Lang and Richard M. Soberman, "Urban Rail Transit," M.I.T. Press, Cambridge, Massachusetts,* 1964.)

*For station stop time = 40 sec loading coefficient = 3.1 passengers/ft.

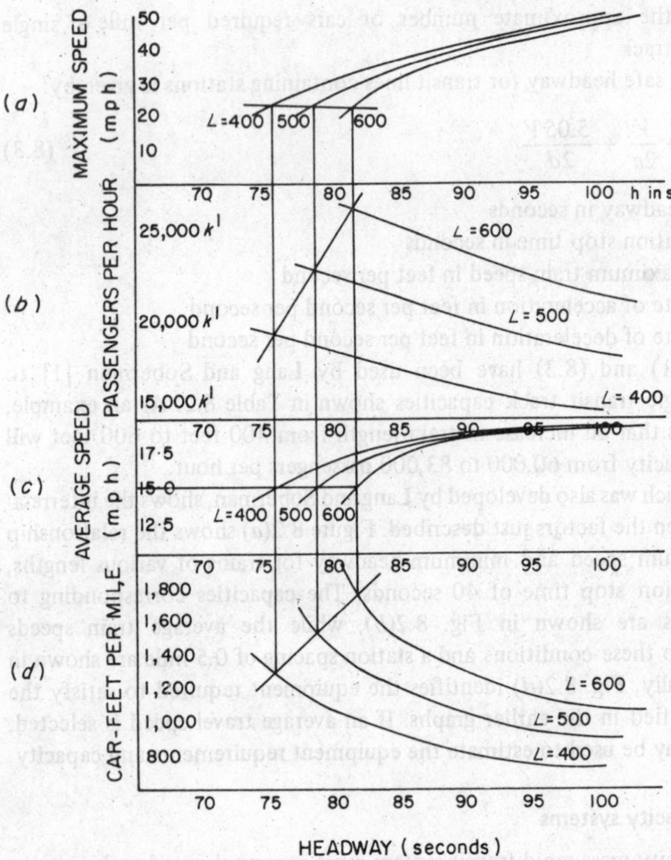

FIG. 8.2. Interrelationships of factors affecting mass-transit equipment selection. (*From A. Scheffer Lang and Richard M. Soberman, "Urban Rail Transit," M.I.T. Press, Cambridge, Massachusetts,* 1964.)

installed recently are the BART system in the San Francisco region, the Victoria Line of the London Transport underground system, and the Toronto Transit Commission subway system.

The broad technological features of most of the duorail systems are quite similar. Some of the more-recent systems, such as the BART system and the Victoria Line, are more sophisticated in that they are more highly automated than earlier systems and the carriage designs have improved through the use of lightweight materials, improved suspension systems, and air-conditioning.

Figure 8.3 shows the route structure of the Toronto subway system and indicates the year of construction and capital investment costs for each component. Table 8.3 summarizes the operating costs for the entire Toronto Transit Commission system for 1971.

A second type of high-capacity mass rapid-transit system which has been used to a limited extent is the monorail. Three types of monorail have been developed and these are: (1) the top-supported or suspended vehicle, (2) the bottom-supported vehicle, and (3) the side-supported vehicle.

One of the earliest monorail systems is that in Wuppertal, Germany, where vehicles are suspended from double-flanged wheels rolling along a single rail above the car body. The best-developed suspended monorail system available to date is the SAFEGE system developed by a French consortium. Vehicles are suspended from a bogey with four rubber-tired wheels which operates within an inverted U-shaped girder on a wooden-surface track.

Major disadvantages of suspended monorail systems include the relatively high cost of the supporting structure, difficulties with vehicle switching, and oscillations of the vehicle at high speeds and in high winds.

The Alweg system is the best-developed bottom-supported monorail system available. Each vehicle is supported by 8 rubber-tired wheels that ride on the surface of concrete girders while 24 wheels follow the sides of the beam to

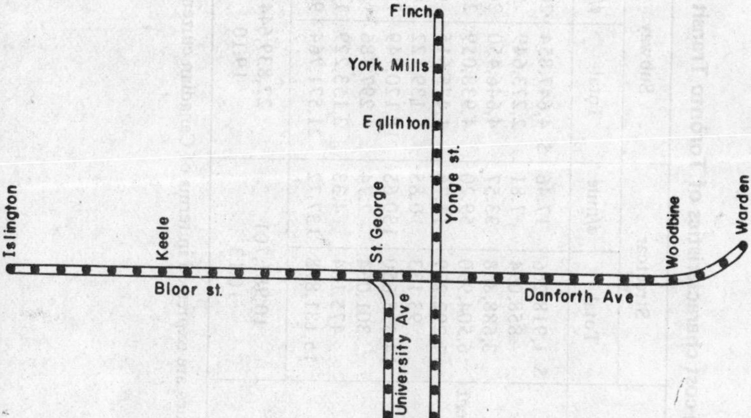

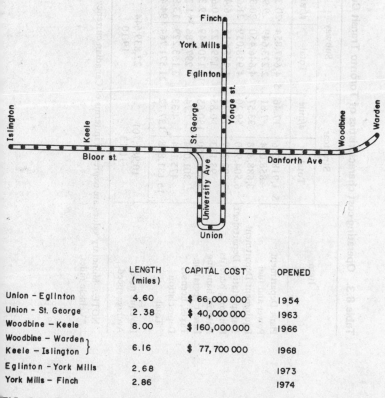

	LENGTH (miles)	CAPITAL COST	OPENED
Union – Eglinton	4.60	$ 66,000 000	1954
Union – St. George	2.38	$ 40,000 000	1963
Woodbine – Keele	8.00	$ 160,000 000	1966
Woodbine – Warden } Keele – Islington	6.16	$ 77,700 000	1968
Eglinton – York Mills	2.68		1973
York Mills – Finch	2.86		1974

FIG. 8.3. Characteristics of subway system–Toronto, Ontario.

Table 8.3. Operating cost characteristics of Toronto Transit Commission system 1971

Item	Streetcar		Subway		Trolley coach		Red bus	
	Total	¢/mile	Total	¢/mile	Total	¢/mile	Total	¢/mile
Plant Department	$ 1,918,286	17.46	$ 4,647,854	20.35	$ 330,542	8.27	$ 1,344,622	3.76
Power and fuel	858,094	7.81	2,273,649	9.95	212,350	5.32	2,518.651	7.03*
Equipment Department	3,688,868	33.57	4,646,450	20.34	897,665	22.47	6,521,414	18.21*
Transportation Department	6,504,990	59.20	4,938,059	21.63	2,492,114	52.39	18,275,491	51.06
Pensions, benefits	1,292,279	11.76	1,475,615	6.46	400,600	10.03	2,783,965	7.78
Material handling	93,133	0.85	139,122	0.61	25,956	0.65	204,450	0.57
Direct operating	14,355,650	130.65	18,120,749	79.34	4,359,227	109.13	31,648,953	88.41
Taxes, licenses	301,064	2.74	297,786	1.30	92,732	2.33	870,404	2.43*
Depreciation	475,164	4.33	3,153,229	13.81	192,960	4.83	2,788,360	7.79*
Total	15,131,878	137.72	21,571,764	94.45	4,644,919	116.29	35,307,357	98.63
Revenue miles	10,987,701		22,839,644		3,994,391		35,794,944	
Average speed	10.13		19.10		9.55		11.92	

NOTE: –Monetary values are expressed in terms of Canadian currency.

*Vehicle miles.

provide lateral stability and guidance. Bottom-supported monorails suffer from essentially the same types of disadvantages as the top-supported systems. The only significant installation of this type of monorail is that which connects Tokyo Airport with the central area of Tokyo.

The *Manchester Rapid Transit Study* [2] represents one of the few transport-planning studies in which monorail systems were considered as a viable alternative to a duorail mass-transit system. The results of the economic analysis provided by this study are shown in Table 8.4. This table demonstrates quite clearly the relative cost characteristics of duorail and monorail systems under three design capacity levels.

One radically different technology that has been proposed for the high-capacity movement of people is the Transveyor system [3]. This technique uses a moving belt along with an escalator-type device for accelerating people from normal walking speeds up to the belt speed, and vice-versa. This proposal is still under development; only insufficient technical and cost data are available.

8.2.3 Medium-capacity systems

Several medium-capacity rapid-transit systems are under active development. One of the most-developed systems is the Westinghouse Skybus system [4]. The carriages are lightweight buslike vehicles of variable size that move on an elevated concrete guideway. Traction is provided by electrically driven pneumatic tires and braking is achieved by dynamic regenération and auxiliary air brakes. Vehicle guidance is achieved by rubber wheels running along a central I-beam with the vehicles being controlled automatically from a central computer.

Table 8.4. Comparative costs of mass rapid-transit systems
***Manchester Rapid Transit Study* 1967**

Design capacity	Duorail	Alweg monoraii	Safege monorail	Westinghouse Skybus
10,000 passengers/hr				
Capital	$133,925,000	$143,875,000	$168,400,000	$136,800,000
Annual operating cost	2,025,000	2,125,000	2,350,000	2,200,000
20,000 passengers hr				
Capital	$144,1C0,000	$156,350,000	$185,925,000	$152,000,000
Annual operating cost	2,675,000	3,200,000	3,700,000	3,300,000
30,000 passengers/hr				
Capital	$152,725,000	$167,300,000	$202,775,000	$165,600,000
Annual operating cost	3,525,000	4,400,000	5,100,000	4,500,000

NOTE:–Costs are for 16-mile route, and are expressed in terms of Canadian currency. Property costs are approximately equal for each technology.

Skybus installations exist in Pittsburgh and at the Tampa and Seattle-Tacoma international airports. Additional installations are planned for Pittsburgh with a capacity of 20,000 passengers per hour achieved through the use of 10-car trains at 2-minute headways with 66 passengers per car.

In many European cities older tram systems have been upgraded in recent years. New equipment has been introduced and in many cities the tram systems operate on separate rights-of-way. These modernized tram systems are usually referred to as *light rapid transit.* Table 8.5 summarizes the characteristics of a number of the European systems [5]. The Riverside Line in Boston is one example of a light rapid-transit line constructed outside of Europe in recent years. Light rapid-transit lines have been proposed for Vancouver [6] and Edmonton [7].

One of the most extensive systems in Europe is in Gothenburg, Sweden. As newer suburbs were built in the Gothenburg region, the existing tram system was extended into these suburbs on grade-separated rights-of-way. Figure 8.4 illustrates the principal features of the Gothenburg light rapid-transit system. The sharp increase in the average speed of trams during the peak period as they move from city streets onto grade-separated rights-of-way is clearly demonstrated in Fig. 8.4.

A principal argument advanced in support of the use of light rapid-transit systems is that their capacities may be increased as the passenger demand increases. The number of carriages in a train may be expanded to increase capacity and the system may be automated gradually.

Table 8.5. Properties of some European light rapid-transit systems

City	Type of vehicle	Speed (mph)	Length (ft)	Seats	Capacity
Frankfurt (U-Bahn)	6-axle articulated	50	75	64	231
Cologne	6-axle articulated	40	69 + 46	129 + 35	213 + 145
Munich	4-axle articulated with trailer	50	55	44	158 + 177
Gothenburgh	Bogie car	45	47	36	124
Basel	6-axle articulated	40	64	46	150

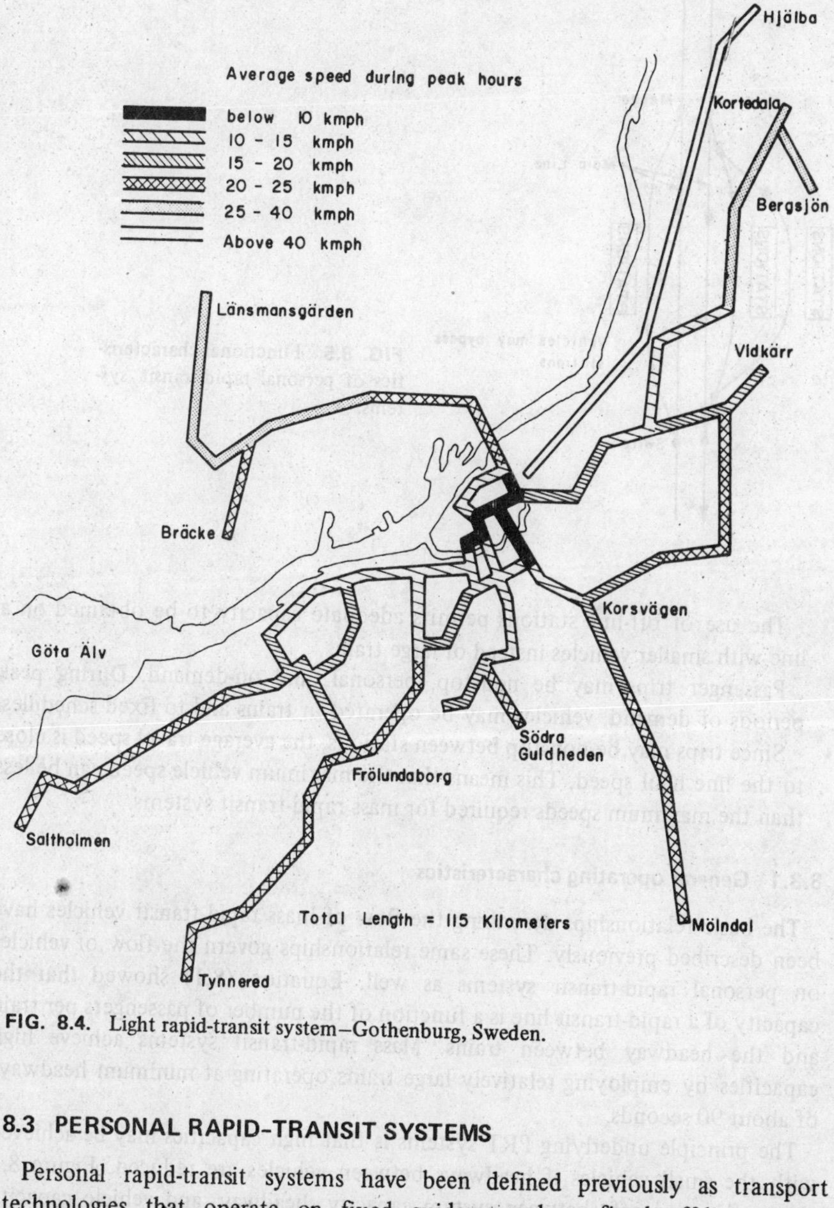

FIG. 8.4. Light rapid-transit system–Gothenburg, Sweden.

8.3 PERSONAL RAPID-TRANSIT SYSTEMS

Personal rapid-transit systems have been defined previously as transport technologies that operate on fixed guideways, have fixed off-line station locations and may have flexible vehicle routings and schedules. Figure 8.5 illustrates the major functional features of a number of personal rapid-transit systems. Anderson and associates [8] identify the following features as the most-important characteristics of personal rapid-transit (PRT) systems:

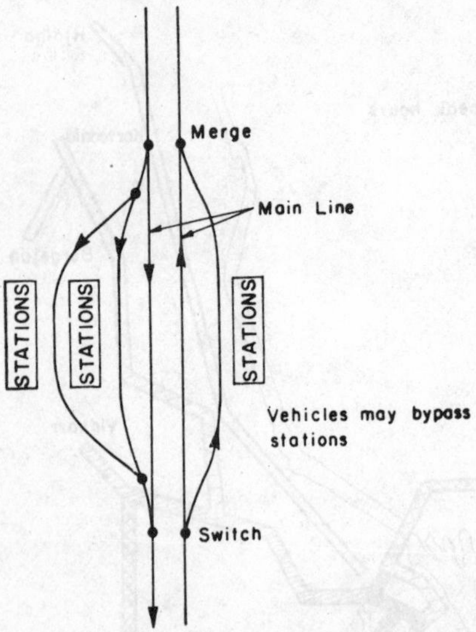

FIG. 8.5. Functional characteristics of personal rapid-transit systems.

The use of off-line stations permits adequate capacity to be obtained on a line with smaller vehicles instead of large trains.

Passenger trips may be nonstop, personal, and on-demand. During peak periods of demand, vehicles may be operated in trains and to fixed schedules.

Since trips may be nonstop between stations, the average travel speed is close to the line haul speed. This means that the maximum vehicle speed can be less than the maximum speeds required for mass rapid-transit systems.

8.3.1 General operating characteristics

The basic relationships describing the flow of mass rapid-transit vehicles have been described previously. These same relationships govern the flow of vehicles on personal rapid-transit systems as well. Equation (8.1) showed that the capacity of a rapid-transit line is a function of the number of passengers per train and the headway between trains. Mass rapid-transit systems achieve high capacities by employing relatively large trains operating at minimum headways of about 90 seconds.

The principle underlying PRT systems is that high capacities may be achieved with the small vehicles if headways between vehicles are reduced. Figure 8.6 shows the tradeoffs between system capacity, headway, and vehicle capacity [9]. Table 8.6 provides a comparison of the headways and capacities that are typical of present transport systems and PRT systems. This information demonstrates quite clearly that in order to achieve reasonable system capacities, PRT system vehicles will have to operate on short time headways.

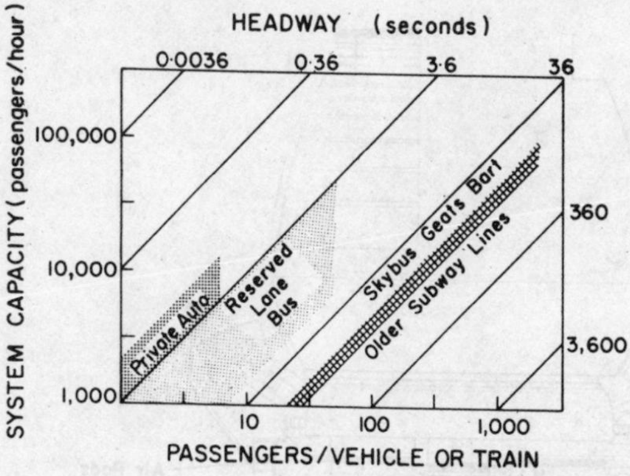

FIG. 8.6. Relation between capacity, headway, and vehicle capacity.

8.3.2 Typical PRT systems

A number of transport technologies are under development which may be classified as PRT systems. While the overall functional properties of these systems are similar, they do differ in terms of vehicle suspension, guidance, and propulsion. Two of these systems are suspended by air cushions and propelled by linear induction motors. Transport Technology Incorporated (TTI) is developing one of these systems [10], while the second is a French development known as Urbatrain [11].

The principal features of the TTI system are illustrated in Fig. 8.7. The individual cars are designed to carry from four to ten passengers, are supported

Table 8.6. Comparison of transport system capacities

System	Headway (sec)	Capacity (vehicles/hr)	Capacity (passengers/hr)
Automobile			
City street	1-2	600–800	900–1,200
freeway		1,500–2,000	2,250–3,000
Bus transit			
City street	60	60	3,000
freeway	15	240	12,000
theoretical max.	4	850	40,000
Subway			
10-car train	90	40	40,000–72,000
PRT systems	2-10	360–1,800	1,000–20,000

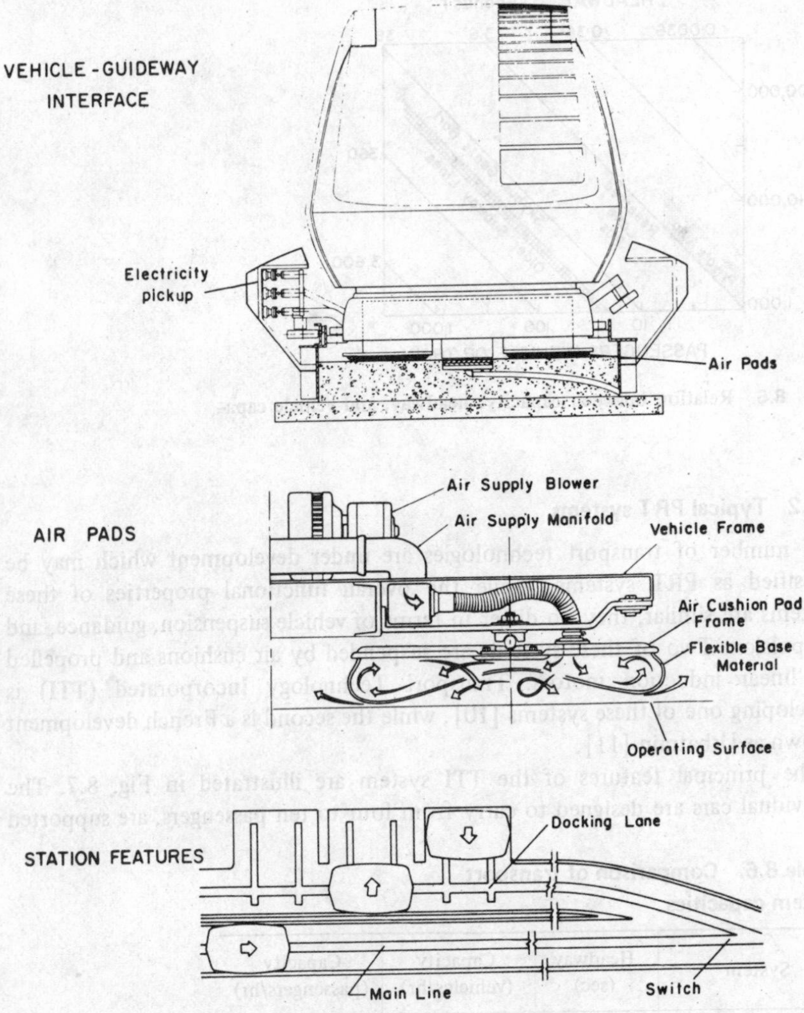

FIG. 8.7. Properties of Transport Technology Incorporated PRT system.

by an air cushion, and propelled for deceleration and braking by reversing the electromagnetic fields. The diagram shows that vehicles are diverted from the main line at stations and are moved laterally into docks from the docking lane. Switching is accomplished by on-board switches and the system is controlled by a central computer that directs the operation of the vehicles and the switches. The normal operating speed of the vehicle is about 30 miles per hour.

The main properties of the Urbatrain system are shown in Fig. 8.8. Vehicle suspension is achieved by a negative air pressure creating lift on the head within the box beam. The cabin of the vehicle is suspended from this head. The linear induction motor is mounted in the head with the primary of the motor attached to the box beam. Propulsion and braking are achieved through the linear induction motor. The individual cabins may be connected together and 8-, 30-, 42-, and 100-seat versions have been proposed. Capacities of up to 11,000 passengers per hour per direction have been claimed for this system.

The Monocab system represents a third PRT system which is under active development and is one of the four PRT systems demonstrated at Transpo '72 near Washington, D.C., in the summer of 1972.[1] Small six-passenger vehicles are suspended from an enclosed guideway. The suspension consists of pneumatic wheels that are electrically driven. Braking is achieved by dynamic regeneration and mechanical brakes. Vehicles are routed automatically to destinations with most of the control system carried on board each vehicle. The maximum operating speed of the vehicle is 50 miles per hour. The system has a capacity of about 5,000 passengers per hour per direction.

A second system demonstrated at Transpo '72 is the Dashaveyor system being developed by the Bendix Corporation [12]. The guideway is channel-shaped and stations are located on off-line sidings. Switching is achieved either by an on-board mechanism or a switching mechanism located in the guideway. Electric power is carried in the guideway and distributed to individual vehicles through a sliding brush assembly. Dashaveyor vehicles may vary in capacity from 4 to 40 passengers, and the vehicles may be operated singly or in coupled trains. Drive is

[1] Transpo '72 was an exhibition of transportation equipment organized by the U.S. Department of Transportation at Dulles International Airport.

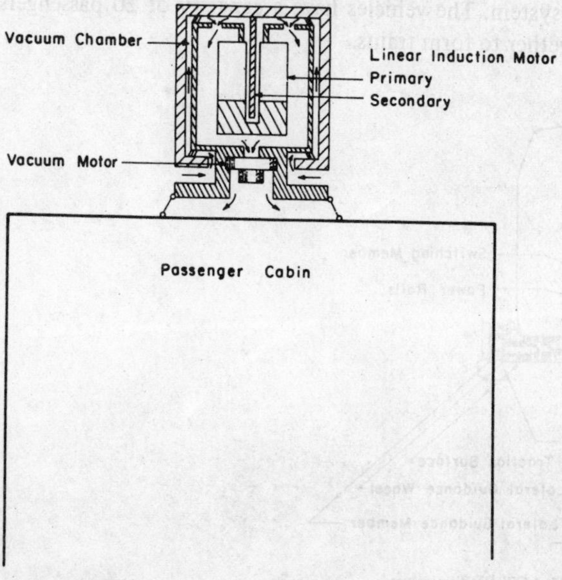

FIG. 8.8. Properties of Urbatrain PRT system.

by two electric motors driving rubber-tired traction wheels and two rubber-tired guide wheels direct the vehicles through the guideway. The driverless vehicles are routed and controlled by a centrally located computer. Maximum operating speed is 38 miles per hour with a maximum capacity of 15,000 passengers per hour per direction.

The fourth technology demonstrated at Transpo '72 is the Automatically Controlled Transportation (ACT) system being developed by the Ford Motor Company [13]. The characteristics of this system are illustrated in Fig. 8.9 and are very similar to the Dashaveyor system. The present version of the vehicles has a capacity of 30 people and propulsion is achieved by 60-horsepower electric motors driving pneumatic tires. Power is collected in a manner similar to the Dashaveyor system and guidance is achieved through the use of lateral wheels. Switching is achieved by an on-vehicle assembly which consists of a rubber-tired wheel which is extended to engage an angle mounted in the guideway. Braking is achieved by a combination of electrical regeneration and friction-type brakes. The control system consits of a combination of on-board controllers, wayside control units, and a central computer. Information is transmitted through a transmission line built into the guideway. The system operates with a 2- to 5-second headway and has a maximum capacity of 40,000 passengers per hour per direction. However, a more-practical estimate of the system capacity is 20,000 passengers per hour per direction with a headway of 4.25 seconds.

Krauss-Maffei of Germany have developed a PRT system that uses magnetically supported and guided vehicles that are propelled by a linear induction motor. Figure 8.10 illustrates the characteristics of the magnetic suspension and guidance system. The vehicles have a capacity of 20 passengers and may be assembled together to form trains.

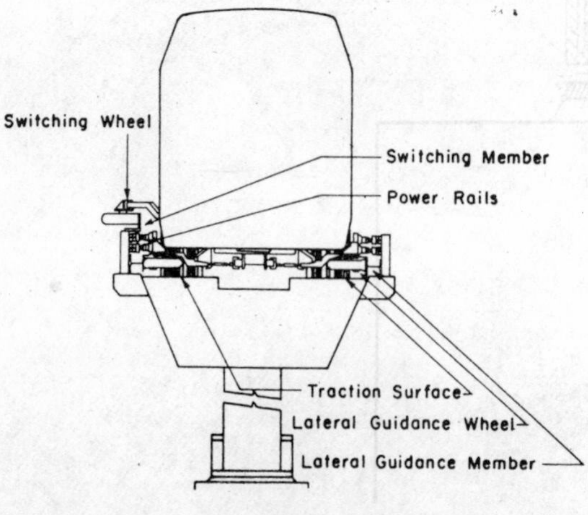

FIG. 8.9. Properties of Ford ACT PRT system.

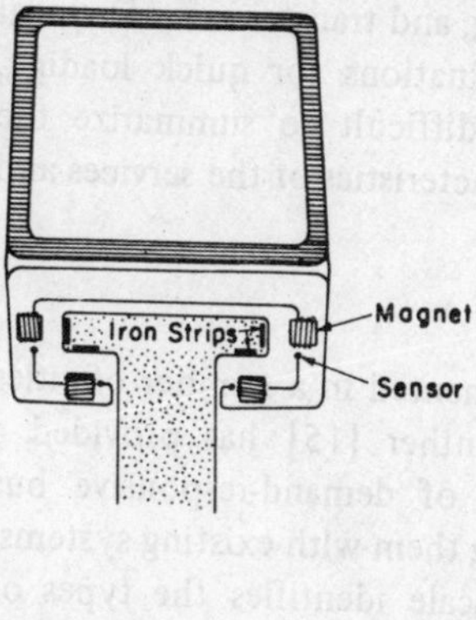

FIG. 8.10. Properties of Krauss-Maffei PRT system.

The Government of Ontario is planning to install a 2.5-mile demonstration project of this technology in Toronto which is scheduled to open in late-1974.

Additional PRT systems have been proposed and some are under active development. While these systems differ in technological detail from those described above, their broad functional and service characteristics are very similar. All of the PRT systems are at a relatively early stage of development and meaningful capital and operating cost data are not available.

8.4 BUS SYSTEMS

Buses exist in various sizes and may be operated according to a variety of schedules. They may range in size from 10–12-passenger buses to buses with 60–90-passenger capacities. Bus systems may operate as fixed-schedule systems on line haul routes or as demand-responsive systems serving as a feeder mode to line haul systems. There have been proposals for bus-train systems that operate on specialized guideways which provide mechanical guidance to the bus-trains.

8.4.1 Express bus systems

The basic feature of express bus systems is their use of exclusive bus lanes, and in some cases exclusive rights-of-way, for the line haul portion of the trip. Metro-Mode is the name given by General Motors to a system of public transport that uses buses on exclusive rights-of-way [14]. The concept is that the same vehicle is used to operate on the public road system to pick up passengers en route to a restricted use roadway. The buses then travel at relatively high speeds (50–70 miles per hour) along the exclusive roadway and exit at the chosen point to distribute passengers. Capacities of 50,000–60,000 passengers per hour are claimed for this concept.

Express bus services using existing freeway facilities have been introduced in a number of cities throughout the world. Express bus services are usually implemented in conjunction with the following types of facilities: (1) fringe parking areas where travelers may park their cars and transfer to an express bus,

(2) bus stations which provide for loading, unloading, and transfer areas for local buses and private cars, and (3) terminals at destinations for quick loading, unloading, and distribution of passengers. It is difficult to summarize the experience with express bus systems, since the characteristics of the services and patronage vary widely from route to route.

8.4.2 Demand-responsive bus systems

Demand-responsive bus systems have been implemented in a number of cities in the United States, Canada, and Europe. Guenther [15] has provided a convenient scheme for classifying the spectrum of demand-responsive bus services that have been developed and for comparing them with existing systems. Figure 8.11 shows this scheme. The horizontal scale identifies the types of routing while the vertical scale identifies the frequency of service. Four major public transport regimes are identified in the diagram; the taxi is identified as the concept with the best response to passenger demands. The diagram suggests that demand-responsive bus systems approach the service characteristics of taxi systems. The diagram identifies four versions of demand responsive systems and these are:

1. Many home origins to one destination
2. Many home origins to a few destinations

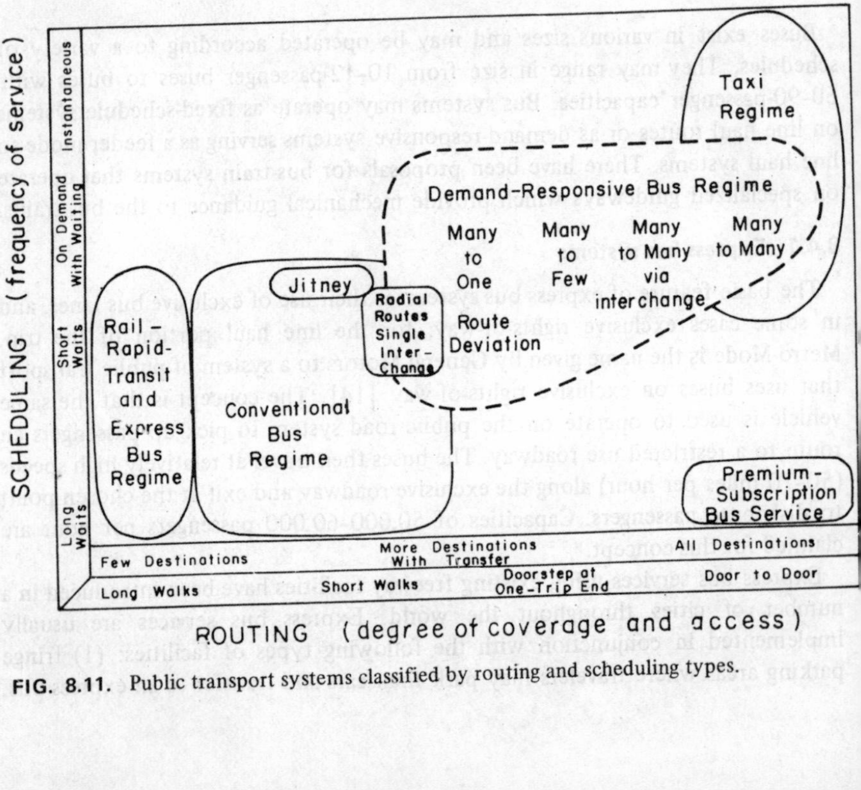

FIG. 8.11. Public transport systems classified by routing and scheduling types.

3. Many home origins to many destinations via a central interchange point
4. Many home origins to many destinations

The many-to-one version has been the demand-responsive bus concept used most commonly. A focal point exists for the service which might be a town center, a commuter rail station, an express bus stop, shopping center, or other major activity center. The many-to-few version is similar, but more focal points within an area are served. Each activity center may be served by a specific set of vehicles, or a given set of vehicles may serve several adjacent activity centers. The version with a central interchange point or points is an extension of the many-to-few version, where passengers may transfer between service areas. The fourth version is simply a modified version of the taxi which provides for pooled riding.

The many projects undertaken to date have provided the agencies involved with valuable operating experience, but systematic information on the response of tripmakers to demand-responsive bus systems is fragmentary. Ridership counts are available from most studies, but little evidence is available on the trips eligible for this type of travel.

Bauer [16] has described a theoretical study of the probable response to a demand-responsive bus system. The study is an excellent contribution in that it attempts to develop a sound estimate of the trips in the community that represented the potential market for the system.

Figure 8.12 shows the basic diversion curves developed in this study. The percentage of trips likely to switch to a demand-responsive system is shown as a function of the fare charged and the service characteristics of the system. Figure 8.13 shows hourly distributions of estimated bus patronage and total eligible trips.

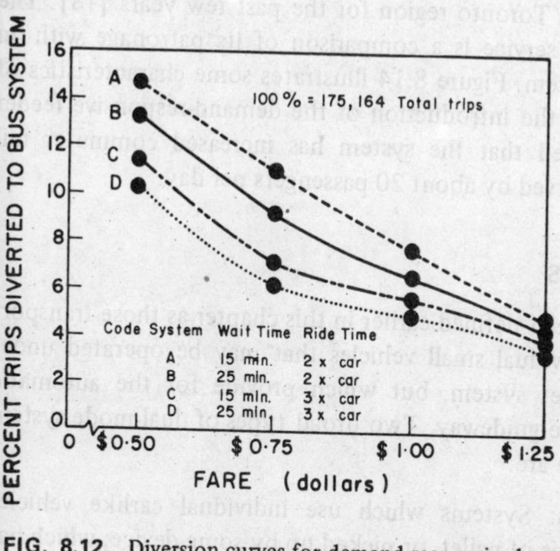

FIG. 8.12. Diversion curves for demand-responsive bus.

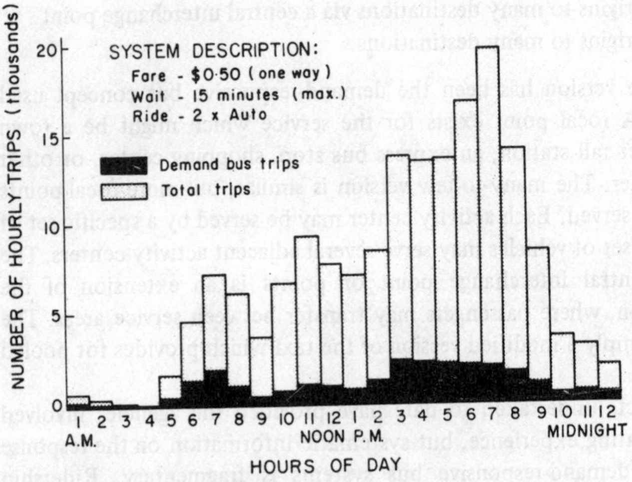

FIG. 8.13. Hourly distribution of trips diverted to bus system.

A demonstration demand-responsive bus system was started in a residential area of Regina, Saskatchewan, in September, 1971. This system acted as a feeder mode to an express bus system serving the central business district. The population of the service area was 18,000 and the average daily bus usage was about 1,200 passengers after 1 year of service. A user survey provided the information summarized in Table 8.7 [17]. It is interesting to note that about 47 percent of the passengers surveyed did not use the earlier fixed-route and fixed-schedule bus system.

A many-to-one system has been in operation as a feeder service to a commuter rail station in the Toronto region for the past few years [18]. The only basis for assessing this service is a comparison of its patronage with an earlier fixed-route feeder system. Figure 8.14 illustrates some characteristics of the change in demand since the introduction of the demand-responsive feeder service. It has been estimated that the system has increased commuter rail patronage from the station served by about 20 passengers per day.

8.5 DUAL-MODE SYSTEMS

Dual-mode systems have been defined earlier in this chapter as those transport technologies which use individual small vehicles that may be operated under manual control on the street system, but which provide for the automatic control of the vehicles on the guideway. Two broad types of dual-mode systems have been proposed and these are:

1. Dual-mode transporters: Systems which use individual carlike vehicles transported on some type of pallet, or picked up by some device, which has

its own support, suspension, guidance, propulsion, and automatic control

2. Dual-mode vehicles: Systems that use individual carlike vehicles that have the capabilities of a car but the additional capability of operating under system control and power

A number of very general concepts have been proposed that may be classed as dual-mode transporters [19]. One such system is the Magnaline system proposed by Cornell Aeronautical Laboratories. The system consists of wheel assemblies running on an overhead rail and propelled by a linear induction motor. Cars are to be attached to these overhead carriages by a roof connection and the combination would be routed throughout the network. Wilson [20] has described progress on one pallet system.

A group of dual-mode vehicle concepts have been proposed and some of these concepts have reached the prototype testing stage. The most commonly advanced concept is the automatic highway. This concept envisions the use of modified conventional cars controlled by signals from circuits embedded in the highway pavement. The Alden Starrcar [21] is based on specially designed small cars with battery-powered electric motors. The cars would be provided with additional equipment which would allow for automatic control of the vehicles on specially provided guideways. A personal rapid-transit version of the Starrcar has also been developed.

Table 8.7. Characteristics of Regina bus users

Characteristics	Percent
Trip purpose	
Work	51
School	13
Shop	14
Personal business, etc.	22
Mode used prior to demand bus	
Car driver	11
Car passenger	13
Taxi	9
Walk	10
Did not make trip	4
Walked to regular bus stop	53
Other	
Male	24
Female	76
Possess driver's license	50
Car available for trip	38

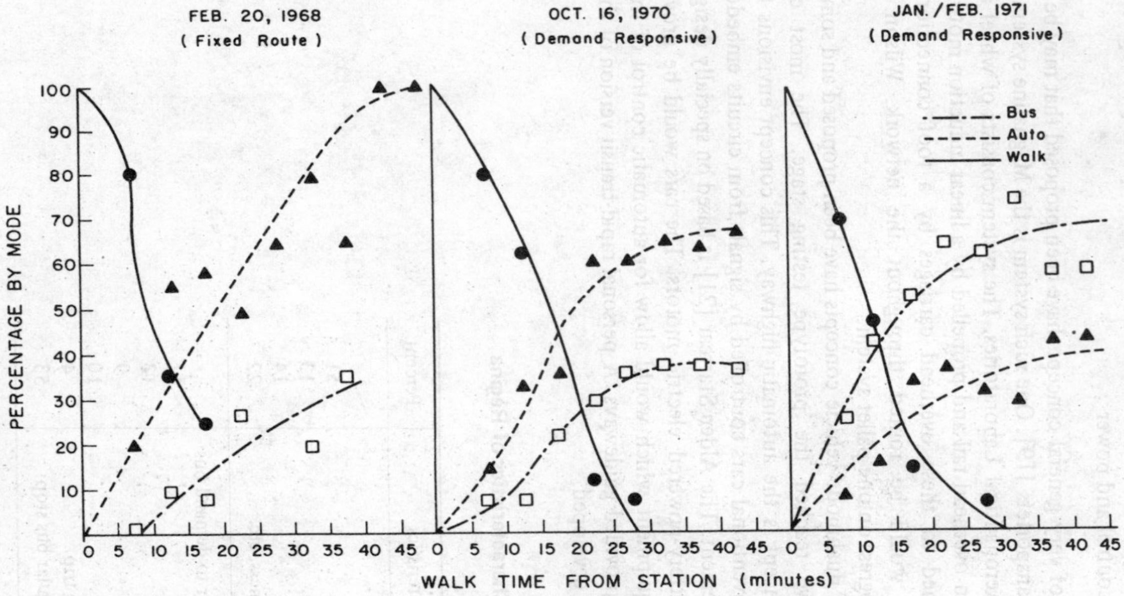

FIG. 8.14. Access mode used vs. walking time from commuter rail station.

Table 8.8. Cost characteristics of Urbmobile system

Expenses	Cost	Annual cost	Daily cost
Fixed expenses	($ × 10^6)		
Line			
New subway			
(4.1 miles @ $8 × 10^6/mile)	33		
Elevated and surface			
(13.3 miles @ $2 × 10^6/mile)	27		
Stations			
13 outer	26		
1 central	4		
Subtotal	90	6.3	
Operations			
100 station attendants,			
200 other employees		3.0	
Power supplies, maintenance		3.7	
Total		13.0	
Expenses for household Urbmobile			($)
Depreciation $3,000		390	1.07
Insurance		50	0.14
Maintenance			0.12
Road-use tax*			0.12
Total			1.45

NOTE:–Cost expressed in terms of U.S. currency.
*Fifty percent of travel to be on roads.

Other small-car dual-mode concepts have been proposed and these include the General Electric Transporter and the Urbmobile systems [22, 23]. None of the dual-mode vehicle systems are under immediate consideration for urban areas. Fichter [24] has described a study of the potential patronage and economic viability of an Urbmobile system in Rochester, New York. This study suggested that an Urbmobile system might approach financial feasibility. Table 8.8 summarizes the cost estimates of an Urbmobile system developed in this study.

SUMMARY

Four broad groups of transport technology may be identified and these are mass rapid-transit systems, personal rapid-transit systems, bus systems, and dual-mode systems.

The principal role of mass rapid-transit systems is in serving radial-type travel demands in high-demand corridors. Many transport-planning agencies in North America and Europe consider that the conventional duorail mass-transit system can be justified only in corridors with demands in excess of 20,000 persons per hour. Trends in the development of the major metropolitan areas in North America, Europe, and Australia would suggest that unless demands of this magnitude already exist, they are not likely to be realized in the future given the current trends in metropolitan development. Steel-wheeled and rubber-tired duorail systems, and several types of monorail systems are the technologies that are available to serve high-demand corridors. The few comparative studies of these technologies indicate that the conventional duorail systems are superior from both technical and economic viewpoints to the various monorail systems.

Light rapid-transit systems are being used in a number of European and North American cities in travel corridors experiencing lower travel demands. These systems represent in many cases an upgrading of older existing tram systems. The principal advantage of this technology is that its capacity may be increased if demands increase over time.

A great deal of development work is underway currently on a number of different personal rapid-transit systems. These systems have the advantage of off-line stations which allows individual vehicles, or trains of vehicles, to travel at short time headways. Most of the systems under development have the capability of automated and flexible vehicle routing allowing vehicles to bypass stations and have average speeds which approach the line haul speeds. These technologies are directed toward travel-demand corridors with expected demands of 15,000–20,000 passengers per day.

Buses exist in various sizes and may be operated according to a variety of schedules. They may operate as fixed-schedule systems on line haul routes, as demand-responsive systems serving as a feeder mode to line haul systems, and as express bus systems serving pairs of points. Recent demonstration projects with dial-a-bus and express bus services have shown that significant increases in demand may occur. The principal shortcoming of bus systems is the high-labor-cost component of their operating costs, which under North American conditions may be as high as 60 to 75 percent. Their principal advantage is their flexibility.

A number of dual-mode systems are under development but their large-scale implementation would create very serious administrative and legal problems. It seems unlikely that a viable urban dual-mode system will be available for implementation before 10 or 15 years.

REFERENCES

1. Lang, A. S., and R. M. Soberman, *Urban Rail Transit: Its Economics and Technology*, Massachusetts Institute of Technology Press, Cambridge, Massachusetts, 1963.

2. DeLeuw, Cather, and Partners, Hennessey, Chadwick, O'Heocha, and Partners, *Manchester Rapid Transit Study,* vol. 2, Manchester City Transport, Manchester, England, 1967.
3. Bouladon, G., "The Transport Gaps," *Science Journal,* vol. 3, no. 4, pp. 41–48, 1967.
4. Prytula, G., "The Transit Expressway," *Journal of the Franklin Institute,* November, 1968.
5. Walker, P. J., *The New Tramway,* Light Railway Transport League, London, April, 1969.
6. Parkinson, T. E., *A Preliminary Study of Light Rapid Transit in Vancouver, British Columbia,* Planning Department, Greater Vancouver Regional District, Vancouver, British Columbia, September, 1971.
7. University Practicum in Rapid Transit, *Light Rapid Transit: The Immediate Answer for Edmonton,* The University of Alberta, Edmonton, Alberta, 1972.
8. Anderson, J. E., et al., (eds.), *Personal Rapid Transit,* Institute of Technology, University of Minnesota, April, 1972.
9. McGean, T. J., "Some Performance Factors Relevant to the Evaluation of People Movers," in J. E. Anderson, et al. (eds.) *Personal Rapid Transit,* Institute of Technology, University of Minnesota, April, 1972.
10. Transport Technology Incorporated, *TTI at Transpo '72,* Denver, Colorado, 1972.
11. Brabyn, H., "The Inverted Hovertrain," *New Scientist,* March 14, 1968, pp. 581–583.
12. The Dashaveyor Company, *Dashaveyor Personal Rapid Transit System,* Ann Arbor, Michigan, 1972.
13. Ford Motor Company, *Automatically Controlled Transportation,* Dearborn, Michigan, 1972.
14. Canty, E. J., and A. J. Sobey, *Case Studies of Seven New Systems of Urban Transportation,* Paper No. 690038, Society of Automotive Engineers, New York, 1969.
15. Guenther, K., *Incremental Implementation of Dial-a-Ride Systems,* Special Report 124, Highway Research Board, Washington, D.C., 1971.
16. Bauer, H. J., *Case Study of a Demand Responsive Transportation System,* Special Report 124, Highway Research Board, Washington, D.C., 1971.
17. Irwin, N. A., *Transit Innovation - The Promise of Telebus,* Proceedings, Roads and Transportation Association of Canada, 1972.
18. Ministry of Transportation and Communications Ontario, *Dial-a-Bus: The Bay Ridges Experiment,* August, 1971.
19. Chilton, E. G., *Future Urban Transportation Systems: Technological Assessment MR-2,* Stanford Research Institute, U.S. Clearinghouse for Federal Scientific and Technical Information, Springfield, Virginia, May, 1967.
20. Wilson, D. G., "Pallet Systems for Integrating Urban Transportation," *Transportation Engineering Journal,* American Society of Civil Engineers, May, 1972.
21. Alden, J., "How the Starrcar Works," *Ekistics,* no. 146, 1968, pp. 11–12.
22. Hayman, R. A., et al., *Bi-Modal Urban Transportation System Study,* vol. I, Cornell Aeronautical Laboratory Report No. VJ-2431-V-2, U.S. Clearinghouse for Federal Scientific and Technical Information, Springfield, Virginia, March, 1968.
23. Notess, C. B., et al., *Bi-Modal Urban Transportation System Study,* vol. II, Cornell Aeronautical Laboratory Report No. VH-2431-V-2, U.S. Clearinghouse for Federal Scientific and Technical Information, Springfield, Virginia, March, 1968.
24. Fichter, D., *Analysis of Dual-Mode Transport,* Highway Research Record No. 367, Highway Research Board, Washington, D.C., 1971.

9 CHARACTERISTICS OF URBAN STRUCTURE

In Chap. 1 urban structure was defined as a particular articulation of adapted spaces, or land in different uses, that might exist in an urban area. It was also pointed out in Chap. 1 that the human activities that are housed by the adapted spaces interact within the context of various activity systems, such as the household-workplace subsystem. The transport and communication networks facilitate the activity system interactions.

The purpose of strategic land use–transport planning is to synthesize an urban structure which best houses the system of activities expected to develop in an urban area and which is capable of accommodating changes in these activity systems. A critical element of an urban structure plan is the configuration of the transport network, since it ties together the other components of urban structure.

This chapter introduces a set of principles that represent useful guidelines for the development of alternative transport system plans. A brief discussion of urban activity systems is followed by discussion of two notions fundamental to the development of transport-system plans: the concepts of movement hierarchical levels and concepts of an environmental area. Alternative urban structure concepts are then described as is the role of the transport network within each structure. Finally, several case studies illustrate how the concepts described in the first part of the chapter have been applied.

9.1 URBAN ACTIVITY SYSTEMS

Figure 9.1 shows the weekly activity pattern for the members of one household in Kitchener, Ontario. This diagram indicates approximately the length and location of each trip, the mode of travel used, and the number of trips made throughout the week. The travel-demand forecasting process described in Chap. 1 to 5 of this book, recognizes that urban travel demands are an aggregation of spatial activity patterns of the type shown in Fig. 9.1.

Many observers of urban areas have pointed out that the bulk of urban activities occur in ordered hierarchies. Certain activities, such as elementary schools and small neighborhood shopping centers, exist at a scale that serves only local areas. Other types of urban activities exist in larger concentrations and may serve an entire urban region. Examples of regionwide activities include major cultural facilities, post-secondary education facilities, specialized retail trade outlets, and certain types of personal services.

Figure 9.2 illustrates an idealization of the hierarchy of some of the activities located in urban areas. Two activity systems are identified in Fig. 9.2 and these are the household-workplace subsystem and the household-service-place subsystem. Service places are of a very general nature and include educational facilities, medical services, retail trade, and the like. The generalized activity patterns shown in Fig. 9.2 may be regarded as an aggregation of household-based activity patterns of the type shown in Fig. 9.1.

The community centers shown in Fig. 9.2 may be thought of as including junior high schools, medical clinics, and shopping facilities. The district centers might contain major retail trade outlets, high schools, personal services, and certain types of cultural and entertainment facilities. The activities labeled as "non-household-serving employment" in Fig. 9.2 may be regarded as being equivalent to the basic employment-type activities identified in Chap. 6. They have been shown at an hierarchical level intermediate between the district and regional centers, because industries typical of this sector are relatively large in order to achieve satisfactory economies of scale. The regional center might contain government offices, specialized retail trade outlets and personal services as well as the major cultural facilities of the region. The frequency and magnitude of the trips between households and the various activity levels will vary between the hierarchical levels. An additional hierarchical level could have been identified in Fig. 9.2 which might be referred to as the "neighborhood center" containing elementary schools and local shopping facilities.

Activity linkages also exist between the economic activities shown in Fig. 9.2. It has been pointed out in Chap. 2, however, that home-based travel demands

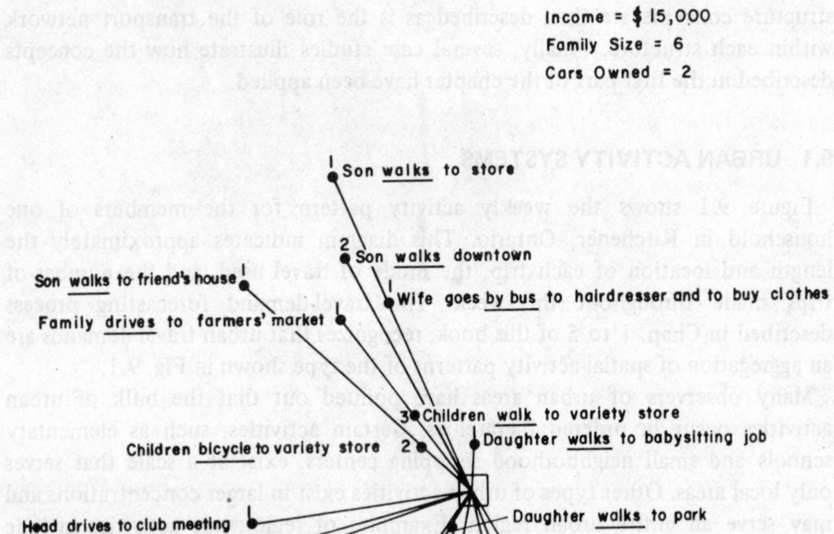

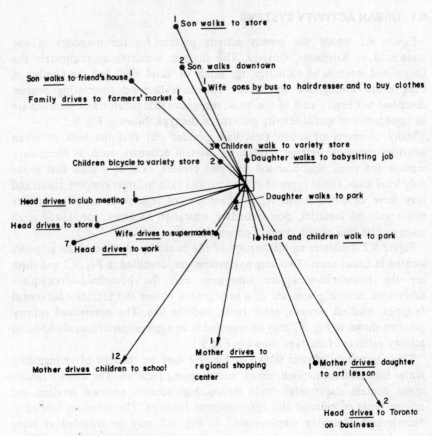

FIG. 9.1. Weekly household activity pattern.

represent over 80 percent of the total travel in urban areas. In addition, travel by commercial vehicles is normally about 12 to 15 percent of total vehicle trips within urban areas.

9.2 MOVEMENT HIERARCHIES

Transport systems provide two fundamental functions and these are movement and access to land-based activities. There is a conflict between these two functions. Figure 8.1 showed that the station spacing on rapid-transit lines is the controlling factor in the average speed of travel on these lines. In other words, as access to a rapid-transit line is increased through decreased station spacing, the efficiency of movement decreases. A similar effect for road travel has been illustrated in Fig. 5.8. The travel-time–traffic volume relationships shown in that diagram illustrated that the efficiency of travel along controlled access roads is far superior to travel along arterial and collector roads without control of access, or with limited control of access.

Figure 9.3 illustrates one hierarchical classification of roads which consists of four classes with the following properties.

Class 1: Expressways–provide for high volume and relatively fast movements to and from major activity concentrations that depend on region-wide support; traffic movements on these facilities are grade separated without direct land access and movements between different road facilities are achieved by interchanges.

Class 2: Arterials–provide for the movement of trips between freeways and collectors where ease of traffic movement is emphasized and little or no direct access to land is provided; intersections between arterials, and with collectors, are usually at grade and signalized.

Class 3: Collectors–provide for the movement of trips between arterials and locals and provide some direct access to land.

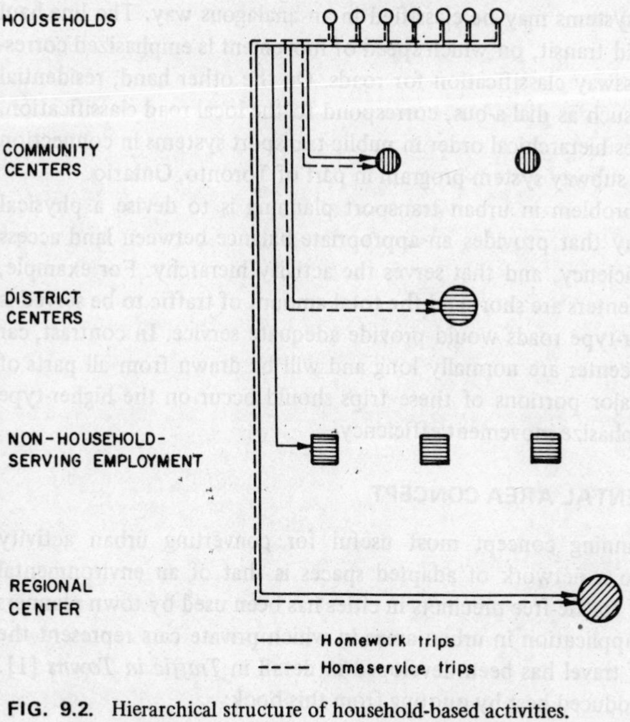

FIG. 9.2. Hierarchical structure of household-based activities.

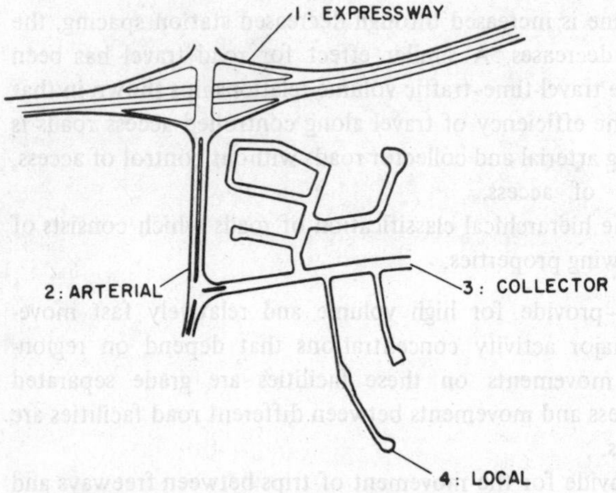

FIG. 9.3. Hierarchical classification of road types.

Class 4: Locals–provide for the distribution of traffic within activity areas where the emphasis is on the integration of the road with the land and where the speed of movement is deemphasized.

Public-transport systems may be classified in an analagous way. The line haul routes, such as rapid transit, on which speed of movement is emphasized correspond to the expressway classification for roads. On the other hand, residential feeder bus routes, such as dial-a-bus, correspond to the local road classification. Figure 9.4 illustrates hierarchical order in public-transport systems in connection with a dial-a-bus to subway system program in part of Toronto, Ontario.

A fundamental problem in urban transport planning is to devise a physical movement hierarchy that provides an appropriate balance between land access and movement efficiency, and that serves the activity hierarchy. For example, car trips to minor centers are short and the total amount of traffic to be served is small, and collector-type roads would provide adequate service. In contrast, car trips to a regional center are normally long and will be drawn from all parts of the region. The major portions of these trips should occur on the higher-type facilities which emphasize movement efficiency.

9.3 ENVIRONMENTAL AREA CONCEPT

Perhaps the planning concept most useful for converting urban activity concentrations into a network of adapted spaces is that of an environmental area. The notion of traffic-free precincts in cities has been used by town planners for centuries. Its application in urban areas in which private cars represent the dominant mode of travel has been developed in detail in *Traffic in Towns* [1]. The concept is introduced best by quoting from this book:

This is the only principle on which to contemplate the accommodation of motor traffic in towns and cities, whether it is a design for a new town on an open site or the adaptation of an existing town. There must be areas of good environment-urban rooms—where people can live, work, shop, look about, and move around on foot in reasonable freedom from the hazards of motor traffic, and there must be a complementary network of roads—urban corridors—for effecting the primary distribution of traffic to environmental areas. These areas are not free of traffic—they cannot be if they are to function—but the design would ensure that their traffic is related in character and volume to the environmental conditions being sought. If this concept is pursued it can easily be seen that it results in the whole of the town taking on a cellular structure consisting of environmental areas set within an interlacing network of distributory highways. It is a simple concept, but without it the whole subject of urban traffic remains confused, vague, and without comprehensive objectives.

This book goes on to discuss the adaptation of this notion to the organization of urban areas:

Applied to a whole town, it would produce a series of areas within which considerations of environment would predominate. These areas would be tied together by the interlacing network of distributory roads on to which all longer movements would be canalized without choice. The relationship between the network and the environmental areas would therefore be essentially one of service: the function of the network would be to serve the environmental areas and not vice versa.

Figure 9.5 illustrates the concept of an environmental area for a freeway-oriented transport plan. Major traffic movements are channeled along the boundaries of environmental areas on freeways and arterials. Direct access to the environmental areas is provided by the collector and local roads. The environmental area concept has been applied to the layout of shopping precincts, residential areas, and city centers in many countries.

Figure 9.6 illustrates an application of this concept to the design of the Dickson community center in Canberra, Australia. Stores, offices, and community facilities are grouped within a pedestrian mall and parking facilities

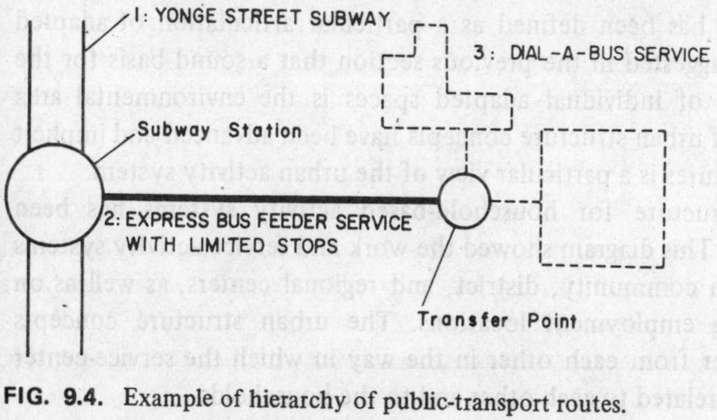

FIG. 9.4. Example of hierarchy of public-transport routes.

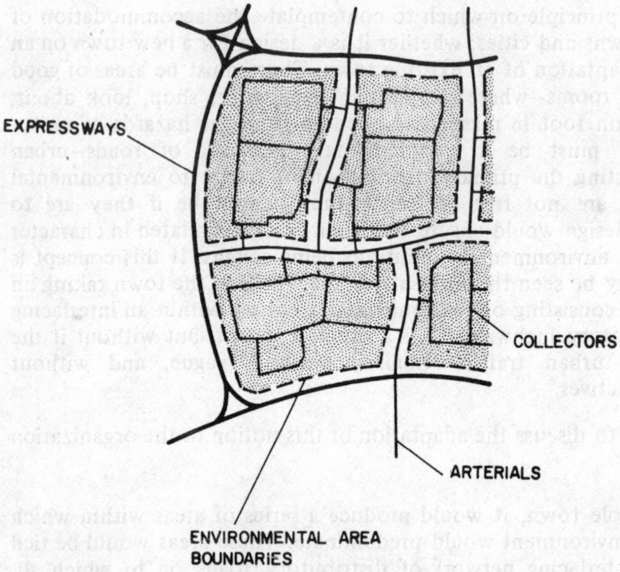

FIG. 9.5. The environmental area concept.

are restricted to the perimeter of the center with direct access to an arterial road.

Figure 9.7 shows the way in which the environmental area concept has been used in conjunction with road hierarchical levels for the layout of Västra Frölunda in Gothenburg, Sweden. The apartment blocks are located on local and collector roads connected to the nearby expressway by an arterial street with controlled access.

Antoniou [2] has described a number of applications of this concept to traffic planning.

9.4 PROPERTIES OF URBAN STRUCTURE

An urban structure has been defined as a particular articulation of adapted spaces. It has been suggested in the previous section that a sound basis for the design of the layout of individual adapted spaces is the environmental area concept. A number of urban structure concepts have been advanced and implicit to each of these structures is a particular view of the urban activity system.

An hierarchical structure for household-based activity systems has been illustrated in Fig. 9.2. This diagram showed the work and service activity systems focussing, in turn, on community, district, and regional centers, as well as on non-household-serving employment locations. The urban structure concepts described below differ from each other in the way in which the service-center hierarchical levels are related to each other and to the households.

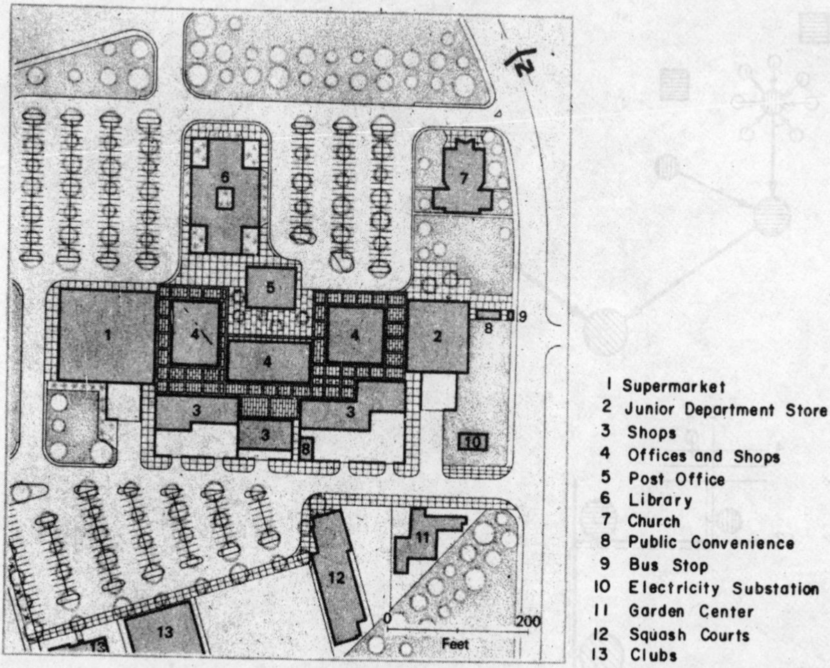

FIG. 9.6. Layout of Dickson Community Center, Canberra, Australia. (*From "Tomorrow's Canberra" by the National Capital Development Commission,* 1970. *By permission of The Australian National University Press.*)

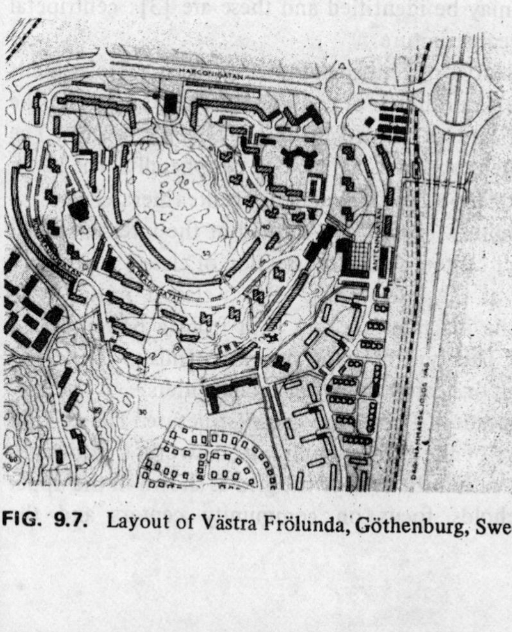

FIG. 9.7. Layout of Västra Frölunda, Göthenburg, Sweden.

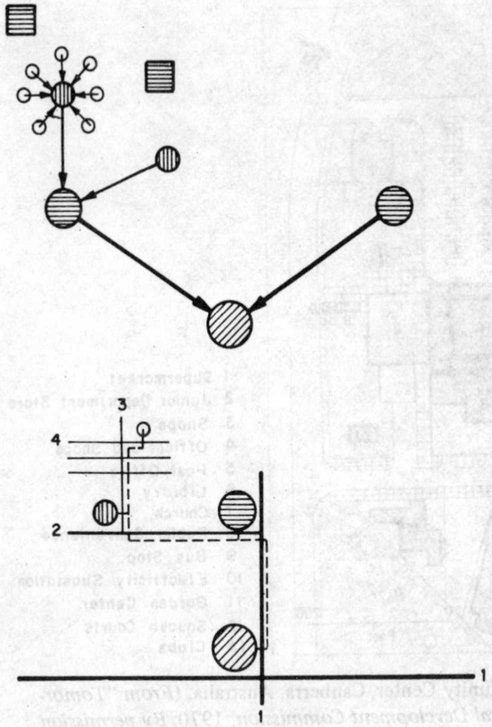

FIG. 9.8. Centripetal-type urban structure.

Three basic urban structures may be identified and these are [3]: centripetal structure, grid structure, and linear structure.

Figure 9.8 illustrates the properties of centripetal urban structure. Households focus first on community centers, a number of community centers focus on the district center, and the district centers then focus on the regional centers. The non-household-serving employment activities are located peripherally. The lower part of Fig. 9.8 illustrates the relationship of the service-center hierarchy to the transport-link hierarchy. Community centers are located at the intersection of class 3 and class 2 routes, district centers at the intersection of class 2 and class 1 routes and the regional center at the intersection of two class 1 routes. Also shown on the lower part of the diagram is a trip path from a household to service centers of various levels. This type of urban structure tends to route trips to the high-order centers through or nearby the lower order centers.

Figure 9.9 illustrates the properties of grid-type urban structure. The cells of the grid are formed by the links of the primary transport network. Community and district centers are located within the cells of the grid as shown in the upper part of the diagram. Households focus on community centers and the community centers focus on the district center. This concept differs from the centripetal structure in that the households focus independently on the regional center. The lower part of Fig. 9.9 illustrates the relationship of the service-center hierarchy to the transport-link hierarchy. Community centers are located at the intersection of two class 3 routes, district centers at the intersection of two class 2 routes, and the regional center at the location of two class 1 routes. The trip paths shown on the lower part of Fig. 9.9 illustrate that trips to the district and regional centers tend to be routed through or nearby community centers. However, trips to district and regional centers bifurcate after they have passed through the community centers.

Figure 9.10 illustrates the properties of linear-type urban structure. Service centers of all hierarchical levels are located along the same corridor. Households

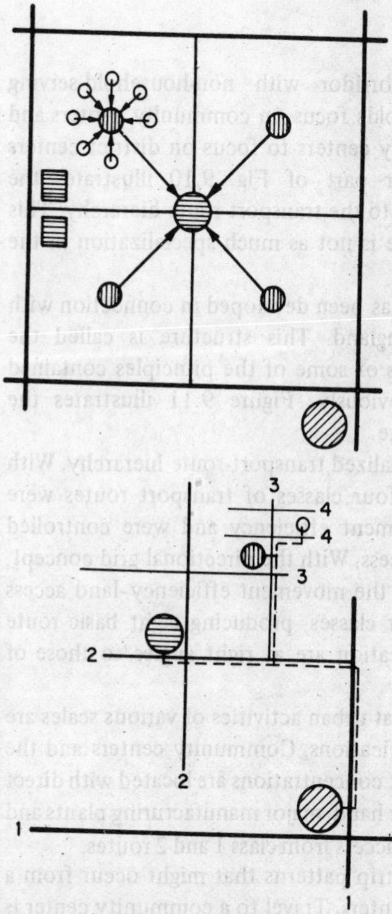

FIG. 9.9. Grid-type urban structure.

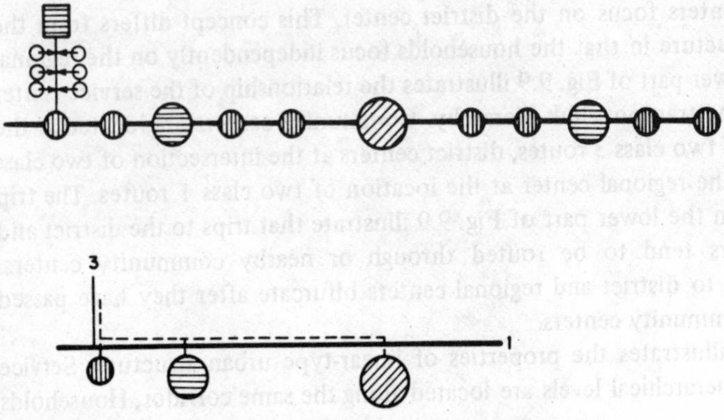

FIG. 9.10. Linear-type urban structure.

are located at right angles to the corridor with non-household-serving employment located peripherally. Households focus on community centers and the linear corridor allows these community centers to focus on district centers and on the regional center. The lower part of Fig. 9.10 illustrates the relationship of the service-center hierarchy to the transport-route hierarchy. This diagram shows that for this concept there is not as much specialization in the transport links.

An additional urban structure concept has been developed in connection with the *South Hampshire Study* [3] in England. This structure is called the *directional grid* and represents a synthesis of some of the principles contained within the three concepts discussed previously. Figure 9.11 illustrates the properties of this concept of urban structure.

The basis of this concept is a more-specialized transport-route hierarchy. With the three concepts discussed previously, four classes of transport routes were used. Classes 1 and 2 emphasized movement efficiency and were controlled access. Classes 3 and 4 emphasized land access. With the directional grid concept, four transport-route classes are used, but the movement efficiency-land access dichotomy is maintained through all four classes, producing eight basic route classifications. The routes of one classification are at right angles to those of classifications above or below it.

The upper portion of Fig. 9.11 shows that urban activities of various scales are related directly to routes of various classifications. Community centers and the smaller non-household-serving employment concentrations are located with direct access to route classes 3 and 4. On the other hand, major manufacturing plants and the regional center are provided with direct access from class 1 and 2 routes.

The lower part of Fig. 9.11 shows the trip patterns that might occur from a household to the three levels of service centers. Travel to a community center is provided by a class 4 access route. Travel to a district center is provided by a class 4 through route and then a class 3 access route. Finally, travel to the regional center is accomplished along a class 4 through route, a class 3 through route, and then a class 2 access route.

The following section describes a number of applications of these concepts to urban planning. The advantages and disadvantages of each of these concepts of urban structure will be highlighted after these case studies have been introduced.

9.5 CANBERRA

Canberra is the federal capital of Australia and occupies a separate federal area. The site of Canberra was chosen in 1908. The inner Canberra area was based on a plan developed by the American architect Walter Burley Griffin. This 1912 plan was designed to accommodate about 40,000 people and was planned in the

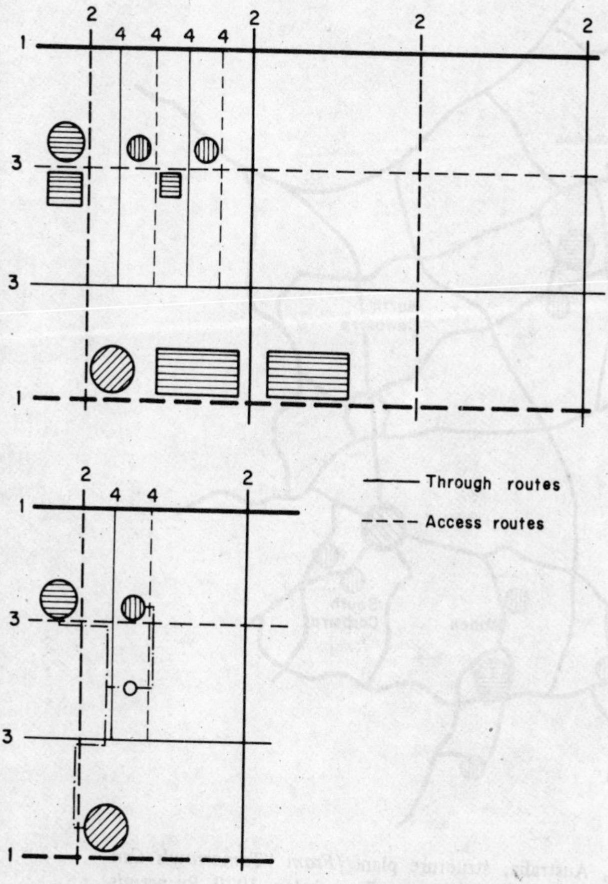

FIG. 9.11. Directional grid-type urban structure.

tradition of the garden city and city-beautiful movements. A second plan was published in 1965 for a population of 250,000 people. This plan is shown in Fig. 9.12 and might be thought of as an application of the centripetal concept, but with some features of the grid-type urban structure [4,5].

In this plan, households focus on community centers, community centers focus on district centers, and the three decentralized district centers focus on the city or regional center. However, the focus on the regional center is achieved through a network of controlled-access roads that pass along the boundaries of the districts. Table 9.1 shows the distributions of population and employment for the plan illustrated in Fig. 9.12.

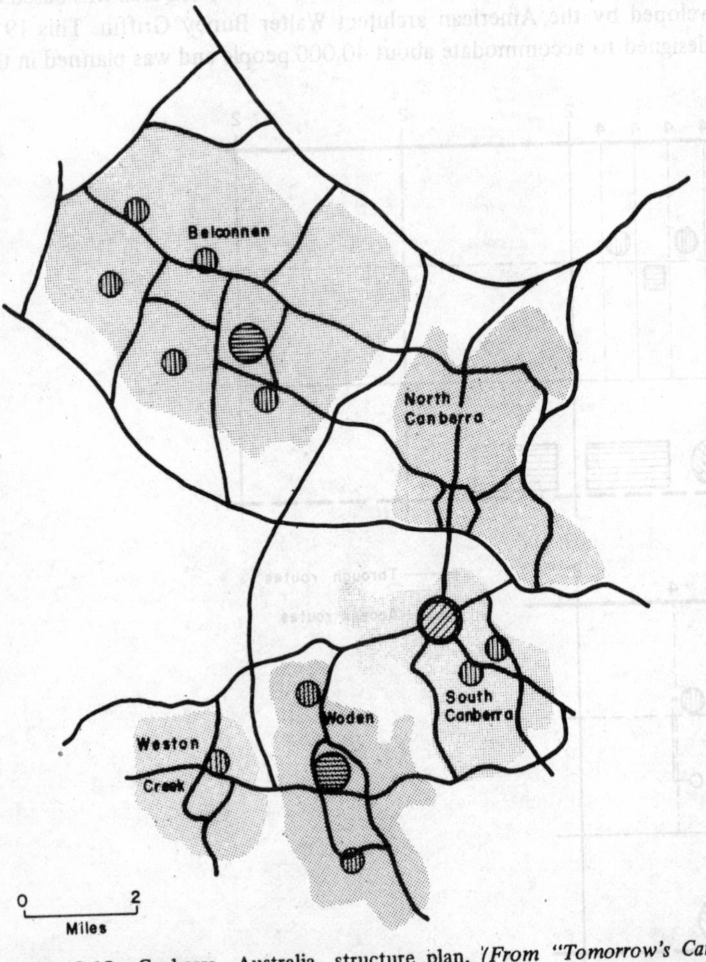

FIG. 9.12. Canberra, Australia, structure plan. *(From "Tomorrow's Canberra" by the National Capital Development Commission, 1970. By permission of The Australian National University Press.)*

Table 9.1. Population and employment distributions for Canberra, Australia

District	Population	Employment
North Canberra	58,000	45,000
South Canberra	32,000	20,500
Belconnen	55,000	6,000
Woden-Weston Creek	50,000	9,000
Majura	55,000	6,000
Total	250,000	86,500

Each district consists of a number of communities and each community contains a number of neighborhoods. Neighborhoods contain 3,000–4,000 people and the average residential density is about 12 persons per acre. Most neighborhoods are designed around an elementary school and a small shopping area catering to daily shopping needs. All households within the neighborhoods are normally within ½ mile walking distance of the shops and school.

The district centers serve as neighborhood centers for the adjoining high-density residential areas as well as the focus for district-level activities such as comparison shopping and cultural facilities. With the Canberra plan these district centers also contain significant concentrations of non-household-serving employment. Figure 9.13 shows the plan for the Woden district center of Canberra.

Reference 4 describes the Canberra plan shown in Fig. 9.12 in the following way:

> To sum up, the outline plan for a city of 250,000 accommodates people in a series of clearly defined towns (districts), each which would be relatively self-contained but which would jointly support the central area, the city centre, and the special institutional or functional zones. Transport would be by way of buses and cars using a network of major roads located within the parkland system to provide easy cross city movement with a minimum interference to other activities within the area.

9.6 STOCKHOLM

Stockholm, Sweden, has been developed around a comprehensive rapid-transit network that may be thought of as an application of the linear plan concept. Figure 9.14 illustrates the broad properties of the Stockholm plan. The central business district of Stockholm is located adjacent to the historic core of the city. This nucleus is surrounded for a distance of 3 to 4 miles by a compact area of fairly dense older residential areas containing some industry, wholesale trade, and institutions. Outside of the inner metropolitan area to a distance of about 10 miles, there are corridors of development along the rapid-transit lines that radiate from the central area.

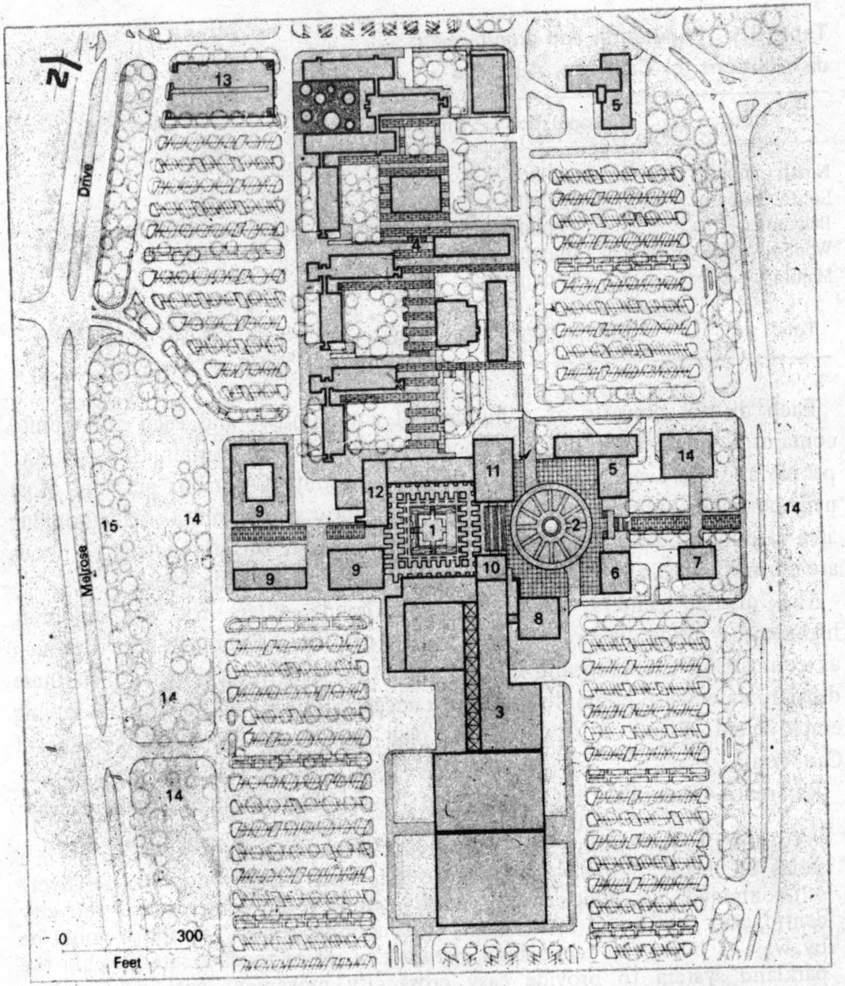

1 Town Square
2 Forecourt
3 Phased Retail Development
4 Government Office Precinct
5 Hotels
6 Police Station
7 Law Courts
8 Library
9 Offices
10 Church
11 Theater
12 Post Office
13 Parking Structure
14 Future Development
15 Pedestrian Underpass

FIG. 9.13 Woden district plan, Canberra, Australia. (*From "Tommorrow's Canberra" by the National Capital Development Commission,* 1970. *By permission of The Australian National University Press.*)

The nature of the Stockholm plan may be described as follows [6]:

> The builders of the new suburbs tried to make them as independent as possible and to make them blend with the landscape in such a way as to avoid clashes with their natural surroundings. Between the various districts they preserved green belts to provide the inhabitants with places of recreation.

In Stockholm an attempt has been made to give each of these suburban districts an individual unity, to make them relatively independent of the central districts and to provide them with some degree of commercial, cultural and social self-sufficiency.

Originally, it was planned that each of these districts should have a radius of a little under three-quarters of a mile and support a population of about 10,000 persons. At the focal point of each district, in the immediate proximity of the underground station, a centre was built designed to meet the various needs of the inhabitants.

Three and four storey blocks and apartment houses of up to fifteen storeys were erected in the immediate neighbourhood of the centre. The density of the built-up area decreased successively towards the outskirts, which are chiefly occupied by detached villas and rows of terrace houses.

The Stockholm plan recognized that district centers containing larger concentrations of commercial establishments were required and Fig. 9.14 shows the locations of commercial centers of three hierarchical types. In 1965 the basic characteristics of each of these types of commercial center were as shown in Table 9.2.

Figure 9.15 shows the Vällingby Centre which is a district-type center containing about 225,000 square feet of retail selling space. The center is built on a concrete raft that spans the underground line. This center serves about 25,000 people directly and a secondary population of about 70,000 located in adjacent communities along the rapid-transit line.

9.7 BRITISH NEW TOWNS

The British new-town program had its origins in the work of Ebenezer Howard [7] and his garden-city movement, which led to the development of Letchworth and Welwyn garden cities in 1903 and 1920, respectively. The major stimulus to new-town creation after the Second World War came with the publication of Abercombie's *Greater London Plan* in 1944 [8].

The structure of Stevenage, England, shown in Fig. 9.16 is typical of the structure of a number of the new towns built during the early post-World War II period. The basic premise was that industrial areas should be located away from the residential areas and along a regional rail or highway link. The town centers were also located adjacent to the industrial areas so that both workers and shoppers could be transported easily by a centrally focussed bus system.

There are six neighborhood residential areas in Stevenage, each containing about 10,000 persons. These neighborhoods contain subcommunity-level retail trade outlets and services as well as schools. The Stevenage plan may be regarded as an application of the centripetal type of urban structure with the exception that there is no regional center in Stevenage because of its limited population.

Two types of difficulty have been experienced with the Stevenage-type new-town structures, and both of these are related to increasing car ownership. The reduced use of bus transport for the journey to work and the concentration

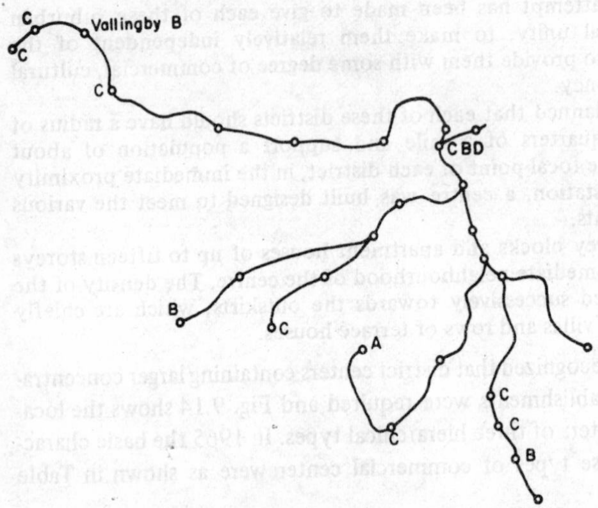

FIG. 9.14. Broad characteristics of Stockholm, Sweden, development.

of the bulk of employment at one point has created traffic congestion in and around the town center. Increased mobility has resulted in the second-level service centers being bypassed in favor of outlets in the town center. This increased mobility has also resulted in some bypassing of the town center in favor of larger regional-scale retail outlets outside of the town.

Runcorn new town represented a significant departure from the earlier new-town plans. The effects of increasing car ownership were recognized and an urban structure plan was created that attempted to encourage full use of public transport. Figure 9.17 illustrates the basic structure of Runcorn new town and this plan may be regarded as an application of the linear concept of urban structure. The primary transport service is provided by a bus loop where the buses operate on a reserved right-of-way. Residential areas are located within the bus loop and the industrial areas are located on the outside of the loop. The bus

Table 9.2. Properties of commercial centers in Stockholm, Sweden

Type of center	Basic clientele	Selling surface (sq ft)
A - Regional	150,000–400,000	> 325,000
B - District	50,000–120,000	130,000–325,000
C - Community	8,000–15,000	27,000–54,000
D - Neighborhood	4,000–7,000	< 16,000

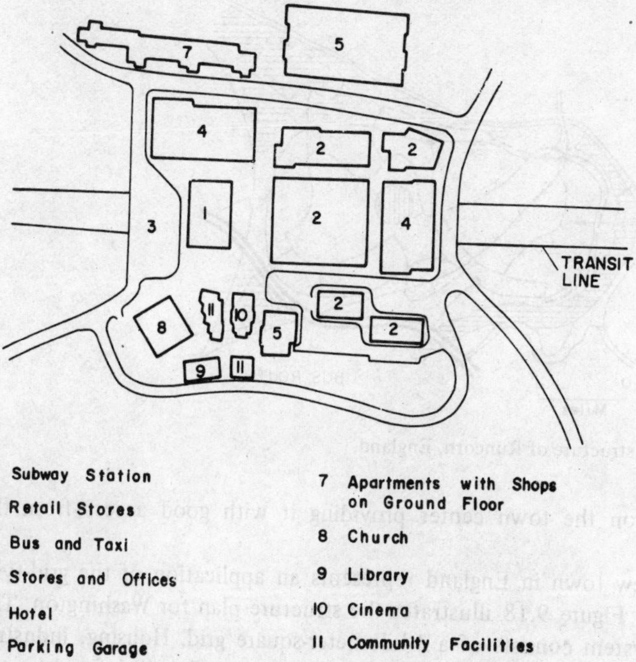

FIG. 9.15. Plan of Vällingby district center, Stockholm, Sweden.

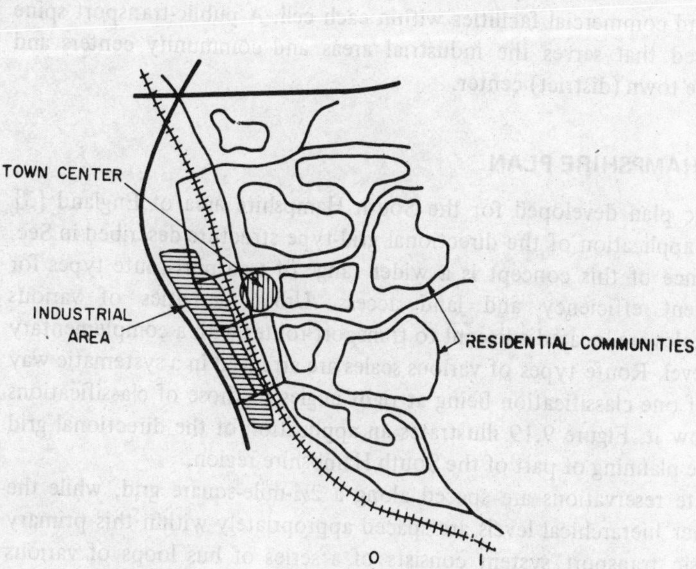

FIG. 9.16. Urban structure of Stevenage, England.

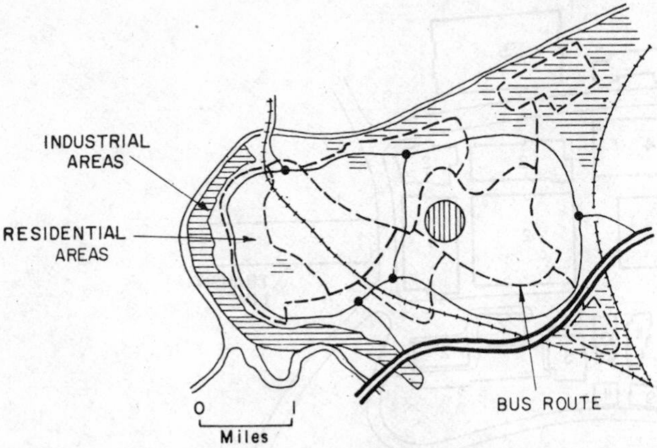

FIG. 9.17. Urban structure of Runcorn, England.

loops converge on the town center providing it with good access from the residential areas.

Washington new town in England represents an application of the grid-type urban structure. Figure 9.18 illustrates the structure plan for Washington. The primary road system consists of a 1-kilometer-square grid. Housing, industry, commercial areas, and open space are provided within each cell defined by the primary road network. This layout attempts to obtain a balance between jobs, households, and commercial facilities within each cell. A public-transport spine is also provided that serves the industrial areas and community centers and focusses on the town (district) center.

9.8 SOUTH HAMPSHIRE PLAN

The strategic plan developed for the South Hampshire area of England [3] represents an application of the directional grid-type structure described in Sec. 9.5. The essence of this concept is a wider range of transport-route types for both movement efficiency and land access. Urban activities of various hierarchical scales are located adjacent to transport routes with a complementary hierarchical level. Route types of various scales are arranged in a systematic way with routes of one classification being at right angles to those of classifications above or below it. Figure 9.19 illustrates an application of the directional grid concept to the planning of part of the South Hampshire region.

Class 1 route reservations are spaced along a 2½-mile-square grid, while the routes in lower hierarchical levels are spaced appropriately within this primary grid. The basic transport system consists of a series of bus loops of various hierarchical levels. A class 1 bus route links the area shown with the region. Along the northerly boundary it operates as an express bus service, but along the central southerly spine, limited access is provided from the bus service to district-level activities.

A class 2 access-type bus service provides transport along the central north-south corridor of the district. A class 3 bus route that provides for both access and movement efficiency operates within the central part of the district. The locations of class 4 bus routes are illustrated in the diagram.

The correspondence between shopping and educational facilities of various hierarchical levels and the route classes should be noted. The district-level shopping center is located at the intersection of the class 1 and 2 routes. It should also be noted that industrial establishments of various scales are located on transport-route classes of the appropriate scale.

9.9 CAPABILITIES OF DIFFERENT URBAN STRUCTURES

The descriptions of urban plans developed according to the various structure concepts must be regarded as ideal applications in the sense that the planning control available was atypical. A comprehensive and objective comparison of

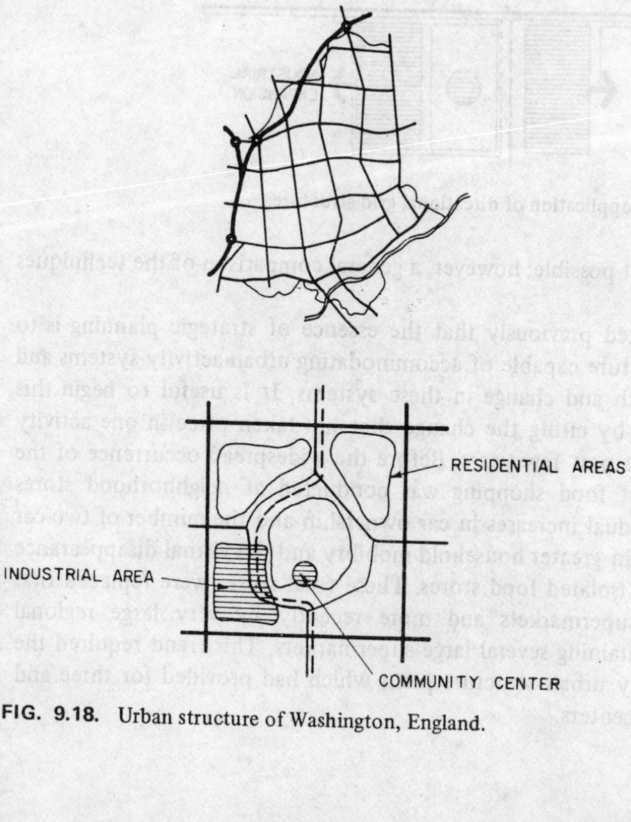

FIG. 9.18. Urban structure of Washington, England.

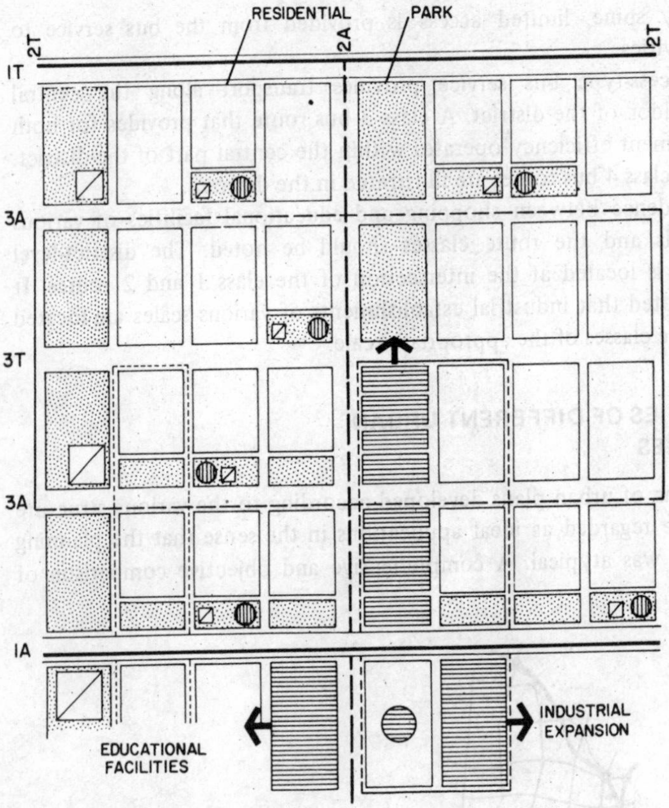

FIG. 9.19. Conceptual application of directional grid structure.

these structures is not possible; however, a general comparison of the techniques is possible.

It has been suggested previously that the essence of strategic planning is to devise an urban structure capable of accommodating urban activity systems and of adapting to growth and change in these systems. It is useful to begin this comparative analysis by citing the change that has taken place in one activity subsystem during the past few years. Before the widespread occurrence of the two-car family, most food shopping was conducted at neighborhood stores reached on foot. Gradual increases in car ownership and the number of two-car families has resulted in greater household mobility and the virtual disappearance of many smaller and isolated food stores. These food stores were replaced first by moderate-sized supermarkets and more recently by very large regional shopping centers containing several large supermarkets. This trend required the modification of many urban structure plans which had provided for three and four levels of service centers.

The extent of this change in North American cities has been expressed as follows [9]:

> A few miles to west of Houston, along the freeway circling the inner core of the metropolis, a two-year old shopping complex called the Galleria bustles with exhilarating activity from breakfast time until nearly midnight.
>
> More than just a shopping center, the Galleria is . . . an intricate and compact orchestration of mixed land uses: shopping, offices, food, lodging and entertainment. A three-level, climate-controlled shopping mall surrounds a hockey-sized ice rink topped with a barrel-vault roof of glass.
>
> The new urban form, to be sure, is the outcome of a long process that began with the invention of the automobile and gained momentum with middle-class migration to the suburbs after World War II. But it was the greater Interstate Highway program, with its freeways looping around the hearts of big cities, that made the proliferation of huge regional centers economically feasible. The freeways enabled centers to attract shoppers from much longer distances with no increase in travel time.

Figure 9.20 shows the location of the major regional shopping centers in the vicinity of Washington, D.C. The Capital Beltway which was completed in the 1960s has had an important impact on the location of these centers which serve close to 1 million people who reside along the beltway.

The centripetal and grid structures are very rigid in that the household-support areas required by various types of urban activities are tightly defined. In addition, the transport networks that serve the various activity centers lack flexibility. With the centripetal structure, trips to higher-level centers pass through or nearby centers of lower hierarchical levels. This successive focussing of trips is satisfactory if most of the travel takes place on public transport, where higher levels of service may be provided as the demand increases. If the majority of travel is by private car, then this gradual concentration of trips leads to severe

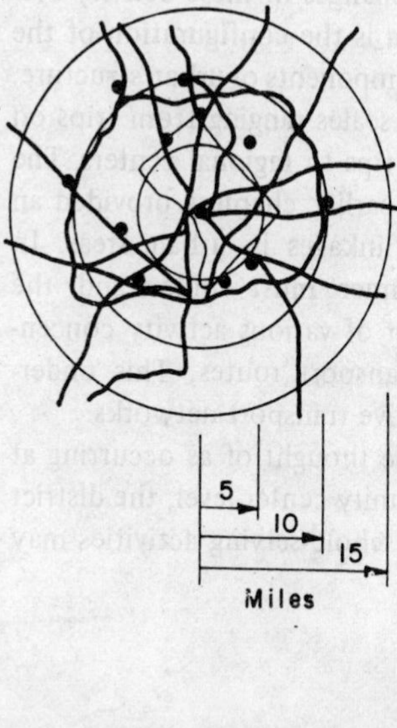

FIG. 9.20. Location of large regional shopping centers near Washington, D.C. *(Adapted from drawing originally appearing in Fortune Magazine, October* 1972. *By permission of the publishers.)*

congestion. A similar comment may be made about the grid-type structure. However, the grid does represent an improvement over the centripetal-type structure in that regional-scale trips are removed fairly directly from the interiors of the grids to the primary transport network.

The linear structure also lacks flexibility and does not provide for sufficient specialization in the transport network. This structure was conceived originally for urban areas organized along a rapid-transit facility. Access between households and the linear transport corridor was intended to be on foot. To provide adequate access to residential areas the station spacing must be relatively small which decreases the average speed of travel along the corridor. Household-based trips at the regional scale are very slow. Some improvements in movement efficiency along the corridor may be obtained by providing two levels of transport service. The higher-speed service would connect district centers and the regional center while the lower-speed service would provide the connection between community and district centers.

The directional grid structure represents an extension of the linear concept. It provides a great deal of flexibility in that various activity levels are not tied to rigid household-support levels. The greater specialization of transport routes provides for more efficient movement as well as greater access to activities. Previous reference has been made to the evolution of large regional shopping centers. Similar changes in scale are also occurring in other types of urban activities such as educational facilities and cultural facilities. An urban structure must be capable of responding to changes in all urban activity systems.

SUMMARY

The purpose of strategic land-use-transport planning is to synthesize an urban structure that best houses the system of activities expected to develop in an urban area and that is capable of accommodating changes in these activity systems. A critical element of an urban structure plan is the configuration of the transport network, since it ties together the other components of urban structure.

Household activity patterns occur at a variety of scales ranging from trips on foot to local schools and stores to car and transit trips to regional centers. The travel-demand forecasting techniques described in earlier chapters provided an aggregated view of the most important activity linkages in urban areas. In addition to this knowledge, the transport planner must understand the interrelationship between the hierarchical character of various activity concentrations and the hierarchical structure of the transport routes. This understanding is vital to the development of good alternative transport networks.

Household-serving activity concentrations may be thought of as occurring at three hierarchical levels, and these are at the community center level, the district center level, and the regional center level. Non-household-serving activities may also occur at each of these centers.

Transport systems provide two fundamental functions and these are movement of persons and goods and access to land-based activities. There is a conflict between these two functions; as access is increased from a transport route the efficiency of movement decreases. Transport routes may be classified hierarchically with some routes emphasizing movement efficiency and other routes emphasizing land access.

A concept central to the development of an urban structure plan and a complementary transport route hierarchy is that of an environmental area. In road-oriented plans the major traffic movements are channeled along the boundaries of the environmental areas on freeways and arterials. Direct access to the environmental areas is provided by collector and local roads.

Three broad types of urban structure may be identified and these are centripetal, grid, and linear structure. These concepts differ from each other in the way that the various service center levels are related to transport-route hierarchy.

With the centripetal structure, households focus on community centers, community centers focus on district centers, and the district centers focus on the regional center. This successive focussing of the trips is satisfactory if most of the travel takes place on public transport. If most of the travel is by private car, then this concentration of traffic leads to congestion. The centripetal structure is also rigid in the sense that the household-support areas required by various types of activity concentrations are tightly defined. Changes in activity pattern cannot be easily accommodated by the centripetal-type structure.

With the grid structure, households focus on community centers and the community centers then focus on district centers. Trips to a regional center are more easily accommodated by the grid structure in that these trips are removed directly from the interiors of the grids to the primary transport network. The grid structure also suffers from a rigid structuring of the household-support areas for the community and district centers.

In the linear structure, service centers of all hierarchical levels are located along the primary transport corridor. The intention of most applications of the linear concept has been that access between households and the primary transport system would be on foot. To provide adequate access to residential areas, the station spacing must be relatively small and the primary transport corridor must be long in large cities. Unless different transport-route classes are provided within the linear corridor the speed of movement along the corridor is poor.

A fourth type of urban structure, called the *directional grid,* has been proposed which represents a synthesis of some of the features of the grid and linear structures. The central feature of this concept is the greater specialization of the transport-route structure for both movement efficiency and land access. Route types of various scales are arranged systematically with routes of one classification being at right angles to those classifications above or below it. Urban activities of various hierarchical scales are located adjacent to transport routes with a complementary hierarchical level. This concept has been developed only recently and has not been applied widely to the development of urban structure plans.

Applications of the urban structure concepts described in this chapter to planning have occurred under conditions which may be classified as being atypical of the North American planning environment. However, it is essential that the transport planner be aware of these principles, as well as the expected travel demands, when alternative transport networks are being generated.

REFERENCES

1. Her Majesty's Stationery Office, *Traffic in Towns,* Penguin Books, London, 1964.
2. Antoniou, J., *Environmental Management: Planning for Traffic,* McGraw-Hill Book Company, Maidenhead, England, 1971.
3. Colin Buchanan and Partners, *South Hampshire Study,* Her Majesty's Stationery Office, London, 1966.
4. The National Capital Development Commission, *The Future Canberra,* Angus and Robertson, Sydney, Australia, 1965.
5. The National Capital Development Commission, *Tomorrow's Canberra,* Australian National University Press, Canberra, Australia, 1970.
6. Stockholm Chamber of Commerce, *Swedish Shopping Centers,* Stockholm, Sweden, 1965.
7. Howard, E., *Garden Cities of To-Morrow,* Faber and Faber Ltd., London.
8. Abercombie, *Greater London Plan,* 1944.
9. Breckenfeld, G., "Downtown Has Fled to the Suburbs," *Fortune,* vol. 86, no. 4, October, 1972.

10 THE EVALUATION OF URBAN TRANSPORT INVESTMENTS

The broad sequence of activities involved in the urban transport-planning process, as well as the systems-planning process, has been described in Chap. 1. Figure 1.5 has shown that following the generation and analysis of alternative systems, the next phase of the process involves the evaluation of the alternative systems. It is the purpose of this chapter to describe a number of methods which have been advanced for the evaluation of transport systems.

In simple terms, an urban transport system may be viewed as a production process that consumes resources in order to produce outputs which are of use to the community. The resources consumed for the construction and operation of transport systems may be expressed normally in monetary terms. The outputs of urban transport systems may be thought of as creating both benefits and disbenefits. Typical of the changes in system output which yield benefits are: decreases in travel time between points in an urban area, decreases in vehicle operating costs, and improvements in travel safety. Examples of system outputs which create disbenefits are: adverse environmental impacts such as noise and air pollution. The essence of transport-investment evaluation is to assemble both the benefits and disbenefits in order to obtain the net benefits that are likely to be produced by a transport-system investment, and to compare the net benefits with the resource costs required.

At present, generally accepted methods of evaluation are not available for transport-investment evaluation. A number of different methods have been developed and used in transport-planning studies during the past 20 years. The best that can be expected at the present time is for the reader to develop a sound understanding of economic principles, to appreciate how these economic principles have been applied in the development of the methods, and to understand some of the deficiencies of these techniques.

This chapter begins by reviewing certain principles of economic theory which are relevant to the methods of evaluation described in it. This review is supported by a more detailed treatment of these principles contained in an Appendix to this chapter.

The second part of this chapter examines the various evaluation techniques that have been proposed. The principal types of information that are available from the travel analysis of each alternative network are:

1. The travel demand between any pair of zones by each mode of transport
2. The properties of travel between any pair of zones, such as, travel distance, travel time, and trip cost
3. The volume of travel on any link of a network
4. The properties of travel on any link

The essential differences between the methods of evaluation discussed in this chapter are due to differences in the type of output information used for the evaluation.

The methods of evaluation are grouped into the following classifications for discussion: (1) traffic-systems evaluation, (2) transport-systems evaluation, and (3) transport-subsystem evaluation. The methods classed as *traffic-systems evaluation procedures* concentrate on the benefits to road-users likely to accrue from potential road investments. With these methods, the road system is viewed as a relatively independent entity having little interaction with the public-transport system and no nonuser impacts. The term *transport-systems evaluation* is used to refer to evaluation methods that also concentrate on user benefits but that attempt to isolate the optimum combination of two or more modes of transport. Methods labeled as *transport-subsystem evaluation procedures* view transport systems as having significant nonuser impacts on the community as well as user impacts.

The final part of the chapter discusses several rating frameworks that have been used for transport investment evaluation along with a discussion of the role of public participation in transport-investment evaluation.

10.1 BRIEF REVIEW OF CERTAIN ECONOMIC PRINCIPLES

The Appendix to this chapter contains a review of those aspects of welfare theory that provide the theoretical basis to benefit-cost analysis. The purpose of this section is to provide the reader with a very brief introduction to the economic principles that are discussed in detail in the Appendix.

10.1.1 Traditional benefit-cost analysis

Table 10.1 provides information on the expected capital costs and potential benefits for five freeway alternatives. The daily vehicle miles of travel produced by each alternative are shown in column 2 of this table. The annual user savings shown in column 4 are converted to a present value using a 10 percent discount rate and a 20-year life, and the results of this calculation are shown in column 5. Column 6 shows the net present value of each freeway system which is the difference between the present value of user savings and the capital costs for each alternative. Column 7 shows the difference in the net present value of the marginal user savings and the marginal capital costs. The first entry is calculated by $[(297.5 - 229.5) - (110 - 90)] = 48$.

The economic criterion used to identify the best alternative from among those examined is the maximum difference between total benefits and total costs; or, alternatively, the system for which the marginal benefits and marginal costs are equal. The benefit and cost characteristics of the alternative freeway systems given in Table 10.1 are plotted in Fig. 10.1. In the upper part of the diagram the total benefits and total costs are plotted against the daily vehicle miles of travel produced by each freeway alternative. The marginal benefits and marginal costs are plotted against the daily vehicle miles of travel produced in the lower diagram. If the relationships shown in Fig. 10.1 were continuous, then the best

Table 10.1. Traditional benefit-cost analysis of freeway alternatives

System no.	Vehicle miles* produced	Capital† cost	User† savings	PV‡ user savings	Savings-‡ costs	Δ Savings § - Δ costs
1	1.50	$ 90	$27	$229.5	$139.5	—
2	1.82	110	35	297.5	187.5	$48
3	2.11	140	39	331.5	191.5	4
4	2.30	180	41	348.5	168.5	−23
5	2.45	230	42	357.0	127.0	−41.5

NOTE: –Monetary values are expressed in terms of U.S. currency.
*Millions of vehicles miles per day.
†Millions of dollars per year.
‡Present value for 20 yr at 10% p.a. in millions of dollars.
§Marginal user savings–marginal capital costs in millions of dollars.

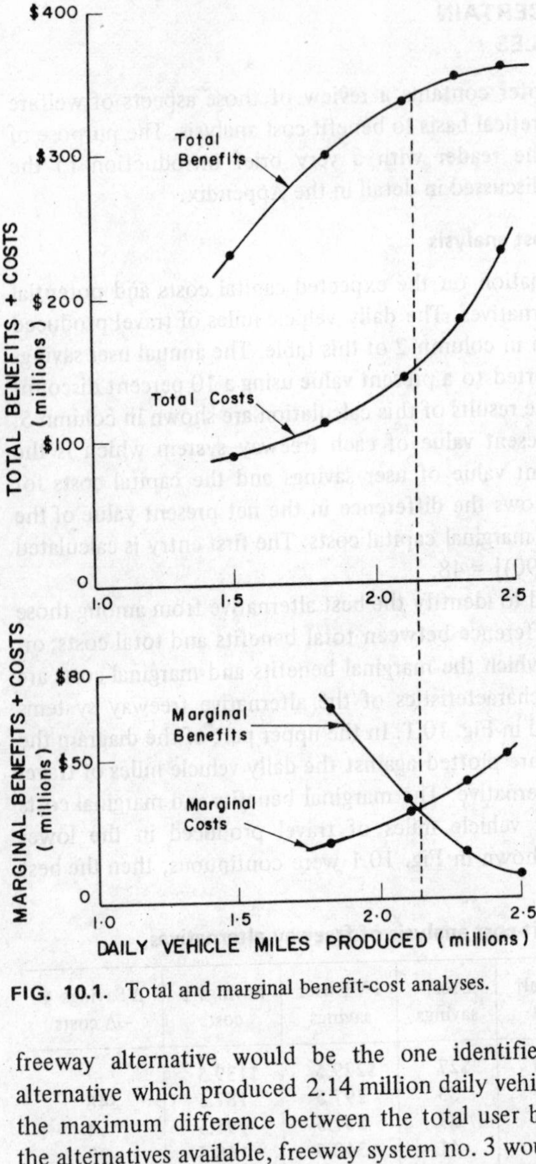

FIG. 10.1. Total and marginal benefit-cost analyses.

freeway alternative would be the one identified by the vertical line. The alternative which produced 2.14 million daily vehicle miles of travel would yield the maximum difference between the total user benefits and capital costs. For the alternatives available, freeway system no. 3 would be the best alternative.

The traditional approach to benefit-cost analysis assumes that the benefits accruing from an investment may be summed by aggregating the average benefits over all recipients of the benefits. This approach also assumes that the resource costs of an alternative may be estimated from the market values of the resources consumed for the construction and operation of the facility. The economic bases for the estimation of benefits and costs are explored in the following sections.

10.1.2 Benefit estimation

It is pointed out in the Appendix that the concept of a demand curve is central to the derviation of the benefits associated with expenditures on public projects. The theoretical basis of benefit estimation is found in the economic notion of utility. It is shown in the Appendix that a demand curve conveys a consumer's indifference between the utility of a good or service and money. This assertion is based on the assumption that the marginal utility of money is constant.

The notion of consumers' surplus is used to convert utility into monetary terms. The consumers' surplus is normally defined as the difference between the maximum amount a consumer is willing to pay for a specified quantity of good rather than go without it, and the value of the given quantity of the good at the good's market price.

Figure 10.2 shows a demand curve for travel by car along a corridor within an urban area. The price of travel used in this relationship includes not only out-of-pocket costs, but also the costs of travel time and other factors perceived by motorists as influencing their travel behavior. This diagram shows that as the price of travel decreases the demand by vehicles for travel along the corridor increases.

Assume that existing travel along the corridor is represented by *A* on the demand curve. The price of travel is 12 cents per mile and the vehicle volume is

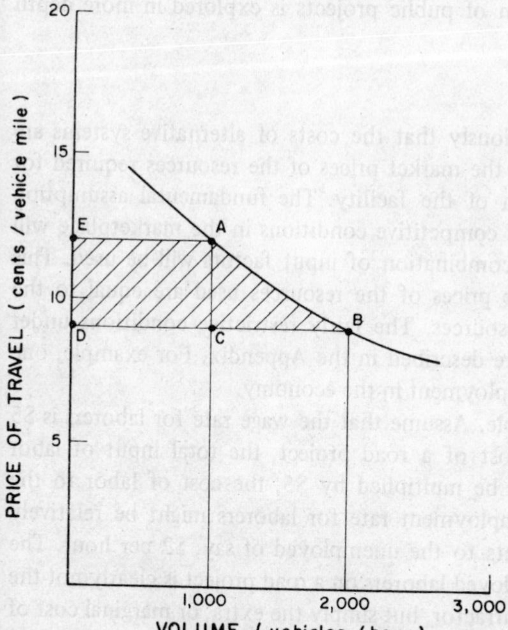

FIG. 10.2. Demand curve for travel along an urban corridor.

1,000 vehicles per hour. Assume further that additional road capacity is planned for the corridor which would reduce the price of travel to 9 cents per mile. Travel on the proposed road may be represented by *B* which would result in an increase of travel along the corridor in the peak hour to 2,000 vehicles per hour. The surplus to consumers would be equal to the hatched area in Fig. 10.2, or $[(12-9)/100]\ [(1{,}000+2{,}000)/2] = \$45$ per mile.

The surplus just calculated may be thought of in two parts which are represented by the rectangle *EACD* and the triangle *ABC* in Fig. 10.2. The area of the rectangle is $[(12-9)/100]\ 1{,}000 = \$30$, which may be regarded as the surplus, or benefits, to the 1,000 users of the original road. The area of the triangle is $\frac{1}{2}\ [(12-9)/100]\ 1{,}000 \doteq \$15$, which may be thought of as the surplus, or benefits, to the 1,000 users induced to use the new road because of the lower price of travel.

The consumers' surplus just calculated assumes that the utility functions of all of the road-users are identical. Or, in other words, the total benefit to society of the road improvement is simply the sum of the utilities, or surpluses, of the individual road-users. It is pointed out in the Appendix that this approach assumes the existence of a unique social welfare function which allows the utilities of individuals to be aggregated. This is certainly not the case, as a wide range of individual preferences have been shown to exist for road-users. For example, the value of travel time has been shown to vary significantly with the incomes of motorists. This concept of interpersonal comparisons of utility and its importance to the evaluation of public projects is explored in more depth later in this chapter.

10.1.3 Cost estimation

It has been pointed out previously that the costs of alternative systems are normally expressed in terms of the market prices of the resources required for the construction and operation of the facility. The fundamental assumption underlying this approach is that competitive conditions in the marketplace will ensure that the most-efficient combination of input factors will be used. This assumption is valid only if the prices of the resources used are equal to the marginal costs of using the resources. The fairly restrictive conditions under which this assumption holds are described in the Appendix. For example, one condition is that there is full employment in the economy.

Consider the following example. Assume that the wage rate for laborers is \$5 per hour. In estimating the cost of a road project, the total input of labor required by the project would be multiplied by \$5, the cost of labor to the contractor. However, the unemployment rate for laborers might be relatively high, requiring welfare payments to the unemployed of say, \$2 per hour. The cost to society of using unemployed laborers on a road project is clearly not the \$5 per hour paid out by the contractor, but simply the extra, or marginal cost of utilizing the unemployed laborers. The significance of the assumptions described in the Appendix to the evaluation of urban tranpsort investments is examined in greater detail later in this chapter.

10.2 TRAFFIC–SYSTEMS EVALUATION

It has been noted above that the procedures labeled as *traffic-systems-evaluation techniques* concentrate on user benefits. The principal component of these road-user benefits is the savings in travel time to road-users. The following section is devoted to a discussion of the problems of valuing travel-time savings.

10.2.1 The value of travel-time savings

The approach used most commonly to establish a value of travel-time savings relates travel time to the value of time in work. Figure 10.3 illustrates the economic concepts which underpin this approach [1]. In this diagram, income is measured along the ordinate and leisure time along the abscissa. The indifference curve shows the various combinations of income and leisure time to which individuals are indifferent. Each individual has a stock of time *OA*, and if all of this time is consumed in leisure, then an individual will have zero income.

AB illustrates the combinations of income and leisure time that an individual could have if the journey to work involved zero cost and travel time. The negative of the slope of *AB* is equal to the wage rate. Maximum satisfaction for

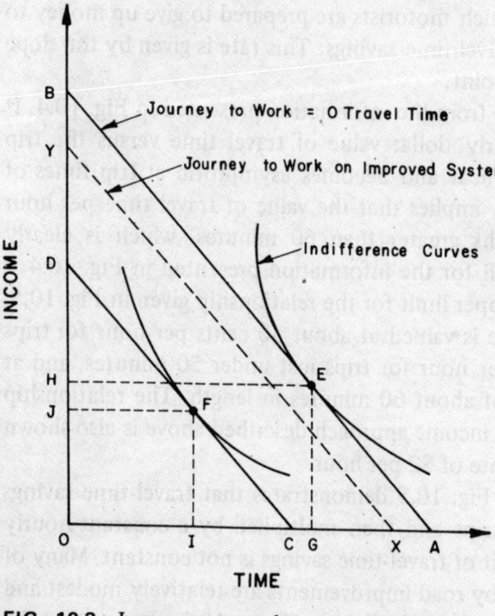

FIG. 10.3. Income approach to the valuation of travel-time savings.

the individual occurs at point *E* where *AB* is tangent to the indifference curve. At this point an individual would have *OH* income, would work *OG*, and have *GA* leisure time.

A journey to work with positive travel time and no travel cost may be represented by *CD*. The new equilibrium condition for an individual would be *F*, where the individual would have *OJ* income, would work *OI*, have *IC* leisure time, and *CA* travel time.

Transport-system improvements which reduced the work-trip travel time could be represented by a line parallel to *AB* and *CD*, somewhere in the region *ABDC*, say *XY*. The evaluation problem is to establish the value that this travel-time change has for road-users. It is pointed out in the Appendix that the spacing of indifference curves is of an ordinal nature. The difference in satisfaction of being on various indifference curves cannot be quantified directly. The assumption is usually made that travel-time savings (in this case *CX*) may be multiplied by the wage rate to yield a measure of marginal benefits equal to *DB*. This approach to the valuation of travel-time savings suffers from certain difficulties since it assumes that the marginal utility of travel-time savings is constant.

Figure 10.4 shows an indifference curve between travel cost and travel time that is typical of motorist's route-choice behavior in urban areas. This indifference curve is concave to the origin since increases in consumption are toward the origin. The nonlinear character of this relationship reflects the principle of diminishing marginal utility. The value of travel time at any point along this curve is the rate at which motorists are prepared to give up money to increase their consumption of travel-time savings. This rate is given by the slope of the indifference curve at any point.

Figure 10.5 has been developed from the information presented in Fig. 10.4. It shows the variation in the hourly dollar value of travel time versus the trip length. The relationship is nonlinear and becomes asymptotic at trip times of about 60 minutes. This diagram implies that the value of travel time per hour becomes infinite for trip lengths greater than 60 minutes, which is clearly absurd. The maximum trip length for the information presented in Fig. 10.4 is about 35 minutes which is the upper limit for the relationship given in Fig. 10.5. The graph shows that travel time is valued at about 50 cents per hour for trips just under 30 minutes, at $1 per hour for trips just under 50 minutes, and at about $2.40 per hour for trips of about 60 minutes in length. The relationship which would be produced by the income approach described above is also shown in Fig. 10.5 for an hourly wage rate of $2 per hour.

The information presented in Fig. 10.5 demonstrates that travel-time savings should not be summed for all trips and then multiplied by a constant hourly dollar value. The marginal benefit of travel-time savings is not constant. Many of the travel-time savings produced by road improvements are relatively modest and involve principally trip lengths of 20 to 40 minutes. Figure 10.5 suggests that the marginal benefit of time savings for trip lengths of this magnitude is about 50

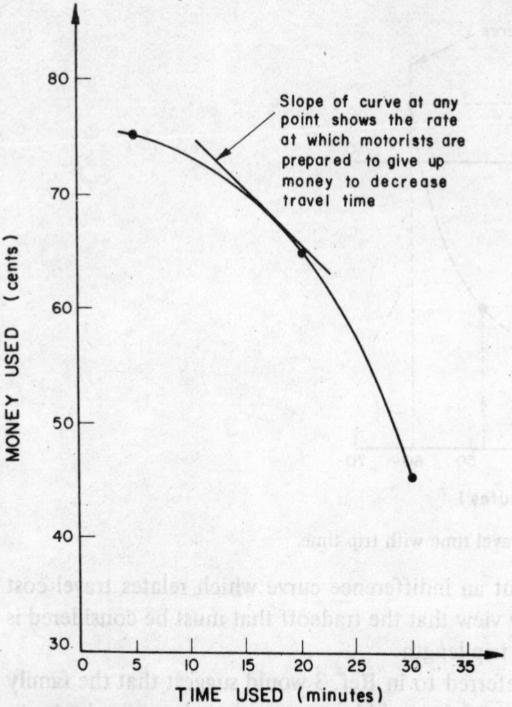

FIG. 10.4. Indifference curve for time and money used between various origin and destination pairs. Points on the curve were established by isolating routes between origin and destination pairs to which motorists were indifferent.

cents per hour. Figure 10.6 has been derived from Fig. 10.5 and shows a family of benefit curves for various trip lengths. The slope of each line is equal to the marginal benefits of travel-time savings.

While the relationships presented in Fig. 10.6 reflect the concept of diminishing marginal utility with respect to the total trip length, the marginal benefits of travel-time savings within a specific trip length are assumed to be constant. Haney [2] and Thomas and Thompson [3] have presented empirical evidence which indicates that motorists are insensitive to small amounts of time saved. They have also argued that the principle of diminishing marginal utility applies to time savings as the amount of time saved continues to increase. They have hypothesized the relationship shown in Fig. 10.7. The linear approximation to the hypothesized relation presented in Fig. 10.7 is based on the assumption of a constant marginal utility of time savings within the 5- to 20-minute range.

There are difficulties with this approach because of the assumption that the principle of diminishing marginal utility applies to trip-length savings and not to changes in total trip length. In other words, the appropriate indifference curve is

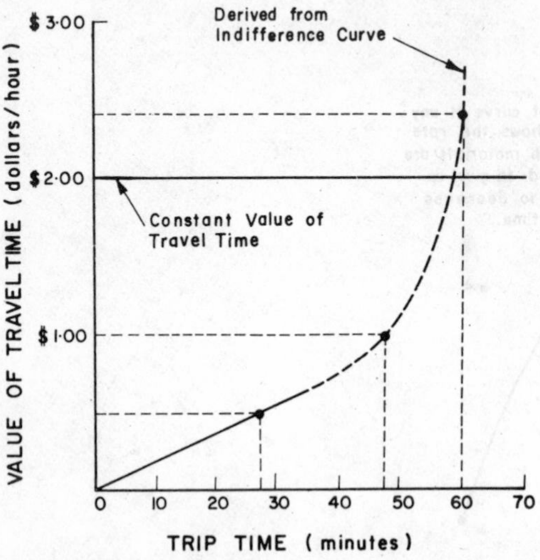

FIG. 10.5. Variation in value of travel time with trip time.

not that given in Fig. 10.4, but an indifference curve which relates travel cost and travel-time savings. It is my view that the tradeoff that must be considered is between money costs and total trip length.

The empirical observations referred to in Ref. 3 would suggest that the family of relationships presented in Fig. 10.6 should be truncated at about 5 minutes to produce the functions shown. Whether the marginal benefits taper off with

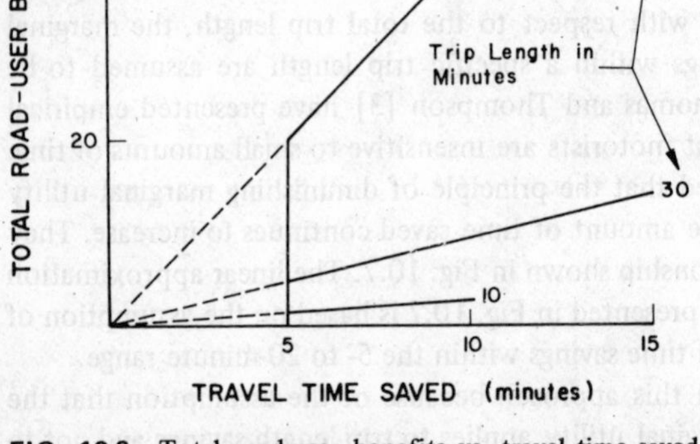

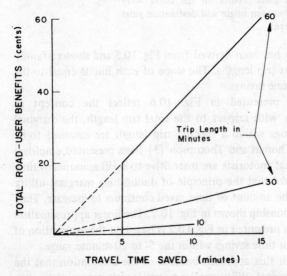

FIG. 10.6. Total road-user benefits vs. travel time saved and trip length.

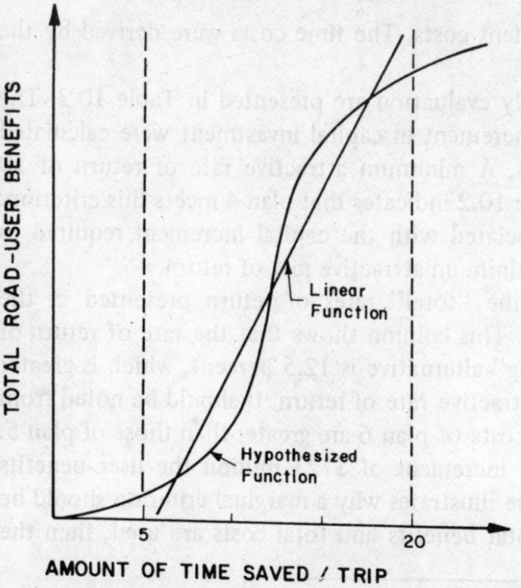

FIG. 10.7. Total road-user benefits function hypothesized by Thomas and Thompson.

increasing travel-time savings is essentially a theoretical issue since transport improvements in most urban areas yield relatively modest travel-time savings of much less than 15 minutes.

10.2.2 Methods of evaluation

One of the earliest attempts at urban traffic-systems evaluation was that performed in connection with the Chicago Area Transportation Study [4]. The transport-system objectives established for this study were: (1) greater speed, (2) increased safety, (3) lower operating costs, (4) economy in new construction, (5) minimized disruption due to new transport facilities, and (6) promotion of better land development.

The extent to which each of the first four objectives was fulfilled by each of the alternative transport systems developed in the Chicago study was measured in dollar values. The impacts of the alternatives on the other two objectives were assessed subjectively. In this study the proposed freeway alternatives and public-transport proposals were evaluated independently.

The output of the freeway system isolated in this study was the average speed on each link of the network. The average user cost in cents per vehicle mile was then estimated for each link from the information contained in Fig. 10.8, multiplied by the link traffic volume, summed for all links to yield the total annual user cost. Inspection of Fig. 10.8 indicates that the user cost includes vehicle operating, time, and accident costs. The time costs were derived by the income approach discussed earlier.

The results of the Chicago study evaluation are presented in Table 10.2. The marginal user benefits for each increment in capital investment were calculated from the decreases in user costs. A minimum attractive rate of return of 10 percent was established and Table 10.2 indicates that plan 4 meets this criterion. The marginal rate of return associated with the capital increment required to construct plan 5 falls below the minimum attractive rate of return.

It is instructive to examine the "total" rates of return presented in the right-hand column of Table 10.2. This column shows that the rate of return of plan 6 relative to the "do nothing" alternative is 12.5 percent, which is greater than the 10 percent minimum attractive rate of return. It should be noted from Table 10.2 that the annual user costs of plan 6 are greater than those of plan 5. That is, for a capital investment increment of $723 million the user benefits decrease by $11 million. This case illustrates why a marginal criterion should be used in economic analyses. If total benefits and total costs are used, then the

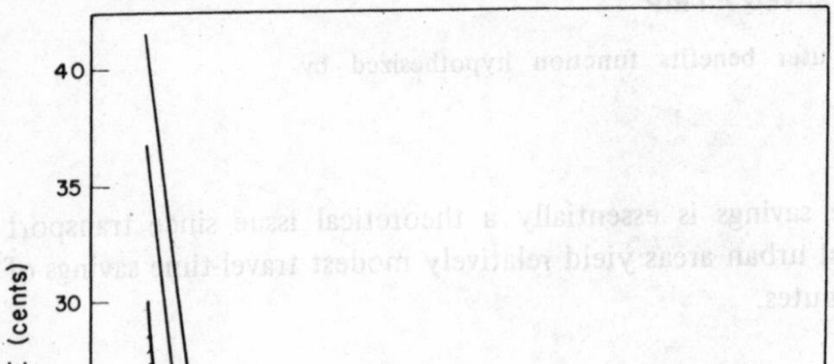

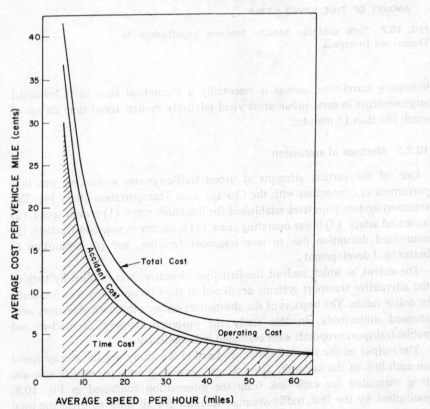

FIG. 10.8. Average travel costs per vehicle vs. link average speed.

Table 10.2. Chicago Area Transportation Study evaluation method

Variable	Plan no.					
	1	2	3	4	5	6
Miles of expressway	288	327	466	520	681	986
Capital cost (in millions)	$907	$1,274	$1,797	$2,007	$2,457	$3,180
Annual travel cost (in millions)	$2,097	$1,982	$1,864	$1,826	$1,786	$1,797
Average weekday speed (mph)	28.1	29.9	33.0	34.0	34.4	33.1
Average weekday accidents	504	450	378	359	346	416
Increment in capital cost (in millions)*	–	$367	$523	$210	$450	$723
Increment in travel savings (in millions)*	–	$115	$118	$38	$40	–$11
Marginal rate of return (percent)	–	29.3	22.5	17.8	7.5	–
Rate of return relative to 1 (percent)	–	29.3	25.7	24.5	19.9	12.5

NOTE:–Monetary values are expressed in terms of U.S. currency.
*Increment with respect to the immediately previous alternative.

decision criterion should be the maximization of the difference between benefits and costs.

A principal deficiency of this approach is that all capital investments were assumed to take place in the horizon year and the user benefits are expressed as an annual rate of return on the capital investments. This approach leads to difficulties in which the optimality of alternatives is sensitive to the time profile of investments throughout the planning period. The significance of project timing is discussed later in this chapter.

The estimation of user benefits in this method of evalution is also deficient. User benefits were determined from differences in user travel costs aggregated for each system. The greatest proportion of the user benefits between alternative networks was derived from differences in the aggregate travel times on both networks. In effect, these benefits were derived from short travel-time savings summed over millions of trips. The deficiencies of this approach have already been discussed in Sec. 10.2.1.

Wohl and Martin [5] have suggested an alternative approach to the derivation of the user benefits associated with road projects through the introduction of the concept of a demand curve for travel along a road. Figure 10.9 illustrates the manner in which Wohl and Martin have proposed that benefits be measured. A hypothetical demand curve for travel along a road link is shown along with supply curves for an existing road and a proposed road improvement. The perceived user price per trip includes user time, operating, accident, and inconvenience costs as perceived by road users.

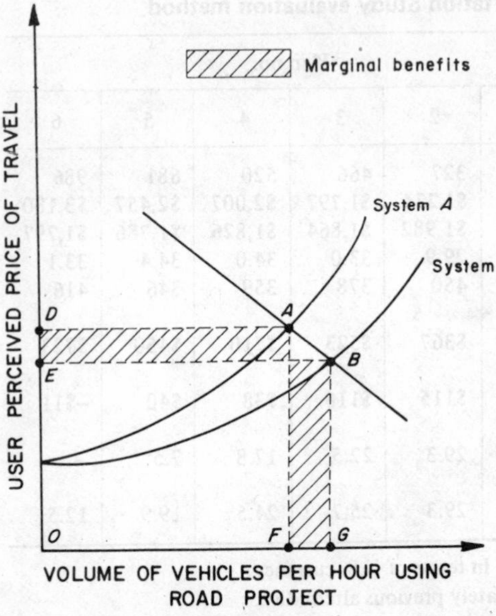

FIG. 10.9. Measure of marginal user benefits proposed by Wohl and Martin. (*From Martin Wohl and Brian V. Martin, "Traffic System Analysis for Engineers and Planners," McGraw-Hill Book Company, New York,* 1967.)

It has been suggested in Sec. 10.1.2 that the change in consumers' surplus, the area *EDAB* in Fig. 10.9, is the appropriate measure of marginal benefits. Wohl and Martin [5] have rejected the increment in consumers' surplus as the appropriate measure of marginal benefits. The basis of their argument is best conveyed by quoting directly from Ref. 5:

> The additional value or benefit (over and above the price paid) termed consumer surplus by the economist, is not unique to public projects, but will generally be manifested in any private or public situation and with the same result. An individual will usually be willing to pay a little more than he was actually charged (or than his payments in time, effort and expense) and thus will receive a little extra value or net benefit. With a uniform single-price policy, this surplus to the consumers would not be relevant to the economic analysis of a private firm, since it does not represent revenue or benefit to the firm or its owners, but accrues only to its customers. Importantly, if consumer surplus is not considered and is not included in analyzing the economy of private investments, then to include it in those for the public sector would mean that expenditures could more easily be justified in the public sector.

Wohl and Martin suggest that the appropriate measure of benefits is the imputed revenue generated by the amount of travel consumed. The revenue is calculated from the product of the imputed price and the amount consumed, the rectangles *ODAF* and *OEBG* in Fig. 10.9. The marginal benefit associated with system B is then *OEBG–ODAF*, or the difference of the two hatched areas shown in Fig. 10.9. It should be remembered that the measure of marginal benefit used by most analysts is the area *EDAB*.

The error in the approach suggested by Wohl and Martin may be illustrated by the following simple example. Assume that a community has an annual budget for transport services of $1,200 and that the prices for the two available goods are bicycles, $100 each, and roller skates, $5 per pair, with the budget allocated equally between the two goods. A capital investment is being considered by the community which would reduce the price of bicycles to $50 each and the community is interested in the potential benefits that would be obtained from this investment. It should be assumed further that consumers have a unitary price elasticity of demand for bicycles.

The increment in consumers' surplus due to the price reduction to $50 is equal to $50(6+12)/2 = $450. Or alternatively, the extra benefit is six extra bicyles with an average value of $75.

If the revenue approach of Wohl and Martin is used, then the "before" revenue = 6 × $100 + 120 × $5 = $1,200, and the "after revenue = 12 × $50 + 120 × $5 = $1,200 = annual budget for transport services. The marginal benefits due to the capital investment in bicycle manufacturing facilities would be 0 according to this approach.

The economic evaluation conducted in connection with the *London Transport Study* [6] contained some innovations which had to do with the way in which the road-user benefits were estimated. Table 10.3 categorizes the costs and benefits included in this economic evaluation. The rate-of-return equation presented at the foot of Table 10.3 shows that the major components of the benefits are the savings in time and operating costs and the increases in tax revenue to the central government.

It should be recalled from Chap. 4 that trip-distribution models assume that the trip matrix changes with changes in the travel-time properties of the networks being tested. In the London study a variable trip matrix was used. A second feature of this study was the assessment of some form of trip restraint aimed at reducing the potential demands for use of some alternative networks to the capacity of those networks.

The evaluation proceeded by isolating three main sources of trips:

1. Trips between the same origin-destination pair as in the previous alternative
2. Newly generated trips due to reductions in transport costs
3. Redistributed trips due to differential changes in the costs of travel between origin-destination pairs

Figure 10.10 illustrates these trip sources along with the benefits that were associated with them. With all trips combined the following expression for user benefits may be developed:

Table 10.3. Categories of benefits and costs used in the *London Transport Study* evaluation method

Item	Whether included in calculations
Initial costs	
a. Capital cost of motorways	Yes
b. Capital cost of new railway lines	Yes
c. Capital cost of ancillary roads to motorway	No
d. Capital cost of delays, etc., due to construction	No
e. Capital cost of providing new parking spaces	Yes
Benefits to individual transport users	
f. Changes in operating costs of vehicles to existing users	Yes
g. Changes in parking costs to existing users	No
h. Changes in fares paid by existing public transportation users	No
i. Changes in restraint tax	No
j. Changes in time costs of existing users	Yes
k. Benefit received by generated traffic	Yes
Benefits to public transport operators	
l. Changes in operating costs of public transport	Not for road plans
m. Changes in receipts from existing passengers	No
n. Changes in receipts from gen. or degen. passengers	Not for road plans
o. Changes in receipts received by car park operators	No
p. Changes in costs of operating parking spaces	No
Benefits to central or local governments	
q. Change in tax received from private + goods transport	Yes
r. Change in tax received from public transport	No
s. Change in level of tax received from restraint tax	No
Other costs and benefits	
t. Accident costs	No
u. Changes in quality of environment	No

NOTE:–Rate of return for 1981 = $\dfrac{(f+j+k)+(l+n)+q}{(a+b+e)} \times 100\%$

$$\text{Benefit} = V_{XY}(c_1 - c_2) + V_{XZ}(d_1 - d_2) + 0.5S_{XY}(c_1 - c_2) + 0.5S_{XY}(d_1 - d_2) + 0.5\,R(c_1 - c_2 + d_1 - d_2) \qquad (10.1)$$

where the symbols are all defined in Fig. 10.10.

Figure 10.11 illustrates the components of benefits contained in the rate-of-return formula shown in Table 10.3. The numerator contains the consumers' surplus derived by road-users from the road improvements plus a component which represents the increase in taxes received by central and local governments. The inclusion of the increment in taxation receipts as a marginal benefit is a controversial issue. Many analysts [7] would argue that taxation merely represents a redistribution of wealth between travelers and the government, since resources are not really consumed. In the London study it was argued that this extra taxation should be included as a benefit for the following reasons:

> Generated traffic is generated just because sufficient benefit will be derived from a trip to more than cover all the costs incurred on the journey and this includes the cost of taxation which is a cost to the individual but not to a Central Government. Consequently when a new trip is generated both the individual and the Government gain some benefit, notwithstanding in the travellers case the existence of indirect taxation, and the benefit to both should be separately calculated.

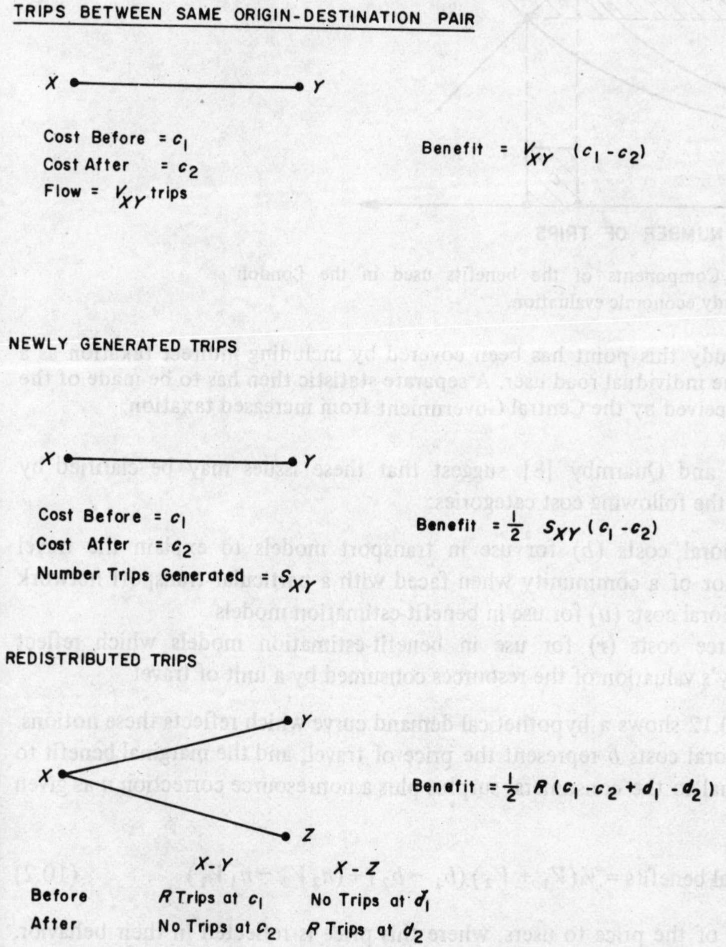

FIG. 10.10. Classes of user benefits identified in London Transport Study.

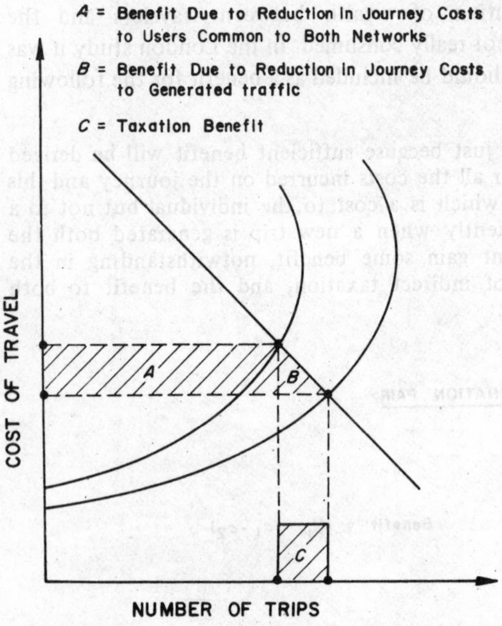

FIG. 10.11. Components of the benefits used in the London Transport Study economic evaluation.

In this study this point has been covered by including indirect taxation as a cost to the individual road user. A separate statistic then has to be made of the benefit received by the Central Government from increased taxation.

McIntosh and Quarmby [8] suggest that these issues may be clarified by identifying the following cost categories:

1. Behavioral costs (b) for use in transport models to explain the travel behavior of a community when faced with a particular transport network
2. Behavioral costs (u) for use in benefit-estimation models
3. Resource costs (r) for use in benefit-estimation models which reflect society's valuation of the resources consumed by a unit of travel

Figure 10.12 shows a hypothetical demand curve which reflects these notions. The behavioral costs b represent the price of travel, and the marginal benefit to users is equal to the consumers' surplus plus a nonresource correction n as given by:

$$\text{Marginal benefits} = \tfrac{1}{2}(V_1 + V_2)(b_1 - b_2) + (n_2 V_2 - n_1 V_1) \tag{10.2}$$

Some part of the price to users, where this price is reflected in their behavior, does not represent a consumption of resources but is additional surplus transferred to the community as a whole; n may be equal to the gasoline tax levied by many governments.

McIntosh and Quarmby point out that since $n = b - r$ Eq. (10.2) may be rewritten as:

$$\begin{aligned}\text{Marginal benefits} &= \tfrac{1}{2}(V_1 + V_2)(b_1 - b_2) + V_2(b_2 - r_2) - V_1(b_1 - r_1)\\ &= \tfrac{1}{2}(V_1 + V_2)(b_1 - b_2) + (V_2 b_2 - V_1 b_1) - (V_2 r_2 - V_1 r_1)\end{aligned} \tag{10.3}$$

Equation (10.3) states that the marginal benefits are equal to the changes in consumers' surplus plus the increase in costs to users minus the increase in resource costs. If n is a gasoline tax, then $n_1 = n_2$, and the nonresource correction will be equal to the amount of gasoline tax transferred to the government which is equal to $(V_2 - V_1)n_2$.

It is interesting to note that the measure of marginal benefits suggested by Wohl and Martin [5] and described previously is equal to $V_2 b_2 - V_1 b_1$, the increase in the aggregate costs to users.

A second contribution of the evaluation method developed for the *London Transport Study* was the approach to the problem of traffic restraint. Some of the traffic systems evaluated in the London study would require suppression of some of the estimated demand in order to maintain acceptable minimum travel speeds. Figure 10.13 shows a hypothetical demand curve along with supply curves for three traffic-system plans. The price of travel is shown as consisting of

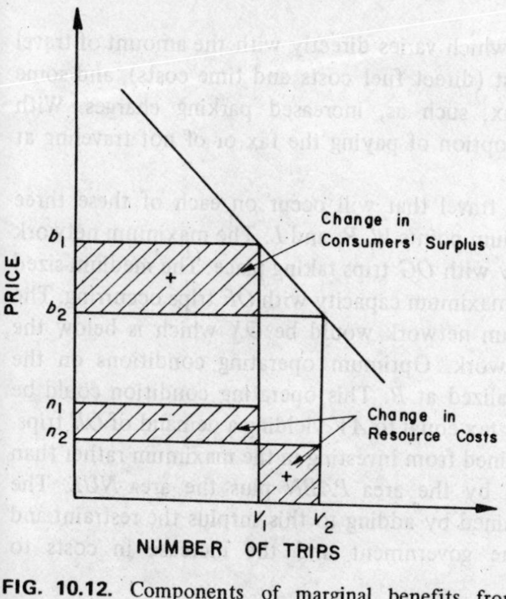

FIG. 10.12. Components of marginal benefits from transport investment.

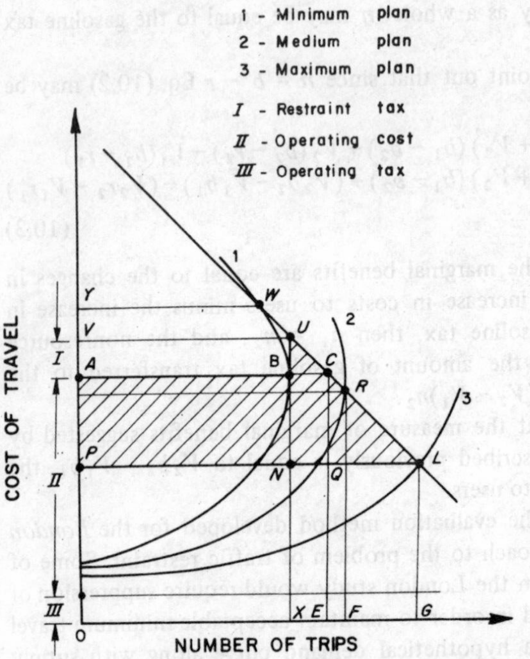

FIG. 10.13. Measurement of marginal user surplus where minimum system has restraint tax imposed.

three components: the taxation which varies directly with the amount of travel (gasoline tax), the operating cost (direct fuel costs and time costs), and some form of additional restraint tax, such as, increased parking charges. With the restraint tax, users have the option of paying the tax or of not traveling at all.

The quantity of unrestrained travel that will occur on each of these three networks is given by the equilibrium points *W*, *R*, and *L*. The maximum network is not being used to full capacity with *OG* trips taking place. The medium-sized network is just being used at its maximum capacity with *OF* trips occurring. The number of trips on the minimum network would be *OX* which is below the maximum capacity of the network. Optimum operating conditions on the minimum network would be realized at *B*. This operating condition could be achieved by imposing a restraint tax equal to *AV* yielding a demand of *OE* trips.

The marginal user surplus obtained from investing in the maximum rather than the minimum network is given by the area *PABN* plus the area *NUL*. The marginal benefits would be obtained by adding to this surplus the restraint and gasoline tax transferred to the government and the increase in costs to users.

10.2.3 Deficiencies of methods

Perhaps the major deficiency of the methods of evaluation discussed above has to do with the validity of the transport-system output variable used in the methods. The method used in the Chicago study and the procedure advocated by Wohl and Martin use link volumes as a measure of the economic good consumed by urban tripmakers. The London study, the work of McIntosh and Quarmby, and the criticism of the London study presented by Beesley and Walters [7] are all developed in terms of the trip magnitudes between origin and destination pairs. While the use of trip-interchange magnitudes between origin and destination pairs is a more-meaningful measure of the underlying economic good than link volumes, this measure is still imperfect. Transport demand is the joint consequence of land-development patterns and the transport system. The interaction between land use and transport has been discussed in Chap. 6 and it seems clear that the real economic good of interest to an urban community at the level of strategic planning is the broad accessibility properties of a region.

A second deficiency of these methods is the assumption that all capital investments will occur in the horizon year and that annual user benefits may be expressed as a rate of return on this investment. The methods ignore the impact of the timing of investments. Wohl and Martin introduce the concept of a changing demand curve over the planning period but do not indicate how these demand curves can be estimated.

Transport investments, like investments in most public sectors, are subject to budgetary constraint. The principles of evaluation under budgetary constraint are well described in the literature. Under budgetary constraint the variations in the scale of a project have to be compared with each other and with the other projects available.

Finally, the methods described above have used a constant monetary valuation of time based in one way or another on the hourly wage rates of tripmakers. The difficulties of this approach have been discussed in Sec. 10.2.1.

10.3 TRANSPORT-SYSTEMS EVALUATION

The methods of evaluation discussed in Sec. 10.3 were concerned with road-traffic systems. Most transport-planning studies are concerned with the development of a transport plan consisting of a road system in conjunction with one or more modes of public transport. A critical issue in many urban communities is the identification of the optimum combination of transport modes.

Rahman and Davidson [9] have advanced a procedure for examining the implications of intermodal investments. Person miles of travel produced during the peak hour was identified as the significant output of the transport system. In this method the modes of transport are considered as input factors to the production of person miles of travel during the peak hour.

Figure 10.14 shows the production function concept which underlies this approach. Production isoquants of 100,000, 150,000, and 200,000 person miles of travel during the peak hour are shown as a function of various combinations of bus and car vehicle miles of input. The line *AB* represents the isocost line of the community where the slope of this line is given by the ratio of the unit prices of the two inputs. These unit prices include the annual cost per mile of capital, operating, maintenance, and social costs of each mode. The optimum combination of input factors would be *OP* bus vehicle miles and *OQ* car vehicle miles. If the price ratio changed and the new isocost line was *DE*, then the equilibrium conditions would be represented by point *F*. At *C* (and at *F*) the marginal rate of substitution of public for private transport services equals the cost ratio as viewed by the community. Figure 10.15 shows a production function developed by Rahman and Davidson for 1964 conditions in Brisbane, Australia. Methods of estimating the demand curves for person miles of travel during the peak hour are also discussed in Ref. 9.

10.4 TRANSPORT SUBSYSTEM EVALUATION

The methods of evaluation presented in the previous sections dealt only with the benefits accruing to road- or transport-system users. The evidence presented in Chap. 1 suggested that in many urban areas a major transport-related issue was the conflict between the provision of accessibility and the quality of the urban environment.

The broad goals of urban transport investment might be identified as follows:

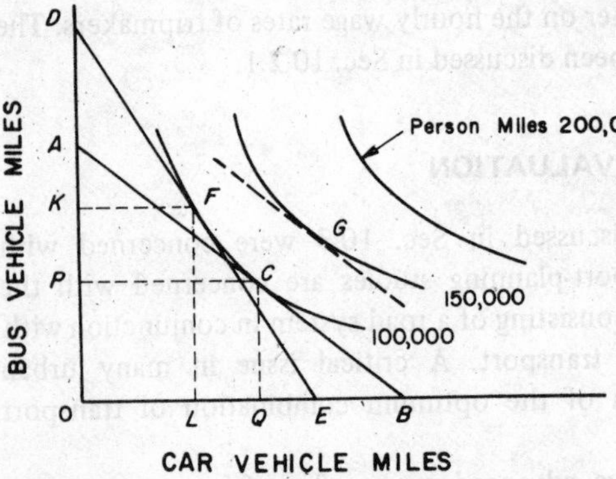

FIG. 10.14. Urban transport production functions proposed by Rahman and Davidson.

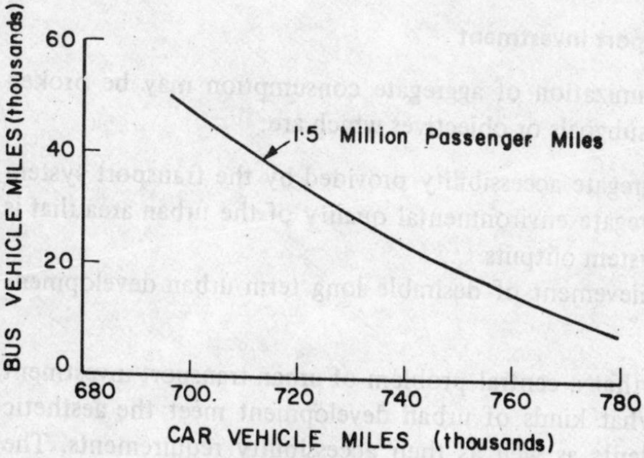

FIG. 10.15. Production function for Brisbane, Australia.

1. To maximize the aggregate consumption of the community
2. To assist in the realization of an equitable real-income distribution among members of the community

It should be recalled from Chap. 1 that planners of public systems must be concerned with both the economic and distributional efficiencies of potential investment policies.

In the Appendix it is pointed out that economic efficiency is usually defined in terms of the Pareto optimum. An allocation of resources to a system is said to be economically efficient if there is no other allocation of resources that would make anyone better off without making someone else worse off. The marginal conditions which must be fulfilled to yield economic efficiency are described in the Appendix.

An allocation of resources to a system may be said to be efficient in a distributional sense if the distribution of real income corresponds to the distribution desired by the community. The question as to whether a particular urbanwide distribution of travel opportunities is efficient in the distributional sense is a value judgment that must find expression through the political process.

The concept of distributional efficiency in urban transport systems is illustrated by the following quotation from Thompson [10]:

> Simultaneously with the decline of mass transit, manufacturing, retailing and other activities have been suburbanizing. With suburban densities far too low to support the extension of the lines of even a healthy mass transit system, the elderly, those financially unable to own a car, those unable to drive, and others, find that dependence on the central city mass transit system has narrowed their employment opportunities very appreciably. Clearly, growing affluence has led to greater mobility for most, but less mobility for a significant group, both in their roles as consumers and producers. A wide range of choice, the great virtue of the large city, is more the prerogative of some than others.

10.4.1 Objectives of transport investment

The broad goal of maximization of aggregate consumption may be broken down into three groups of subgoals or objectives which are:

1. To maximize the aggregate accessibility provided by the transport system
2. To maximize the aggregate environmental quality of the urban area that is related to transport-system outputs
3. To maximize the achievement of desirable long term urban development patterns

These objectives suggest that a central problem of urban transport investment analysis is to determine what kinds of urban development meet the aesthetic preferences of urban residents as well as their accessibility requirements. The orientation of investment implied by these objectives is quite different from the previous approaches to evaluation which have been concerned primarily with the evaluation of potential changes in movement impedance.

Experience with urban transport investments in many countries has demonstrated that to a large extent the objectives of accessibility and environmental quality are competitive. Much of the recent investment in transport facilities has been in roads which has encouraged the increased penetration of urban land uses by motor vehicles, which has in turn decreased the environmental quality of these land uses.

A great deal of evidence has been accumulated which shows that the spatial distribution of activities in an urban area is related to the properties of the transportation system. However, urban land development is influenced by many other factors and the third objective identified above cannot be related exclusively to accessibility. The importance of this third objective has been discussed by Harris [11]:

> The bland assumption of the economists that a competitive optimal allocation of resources coincides with a social optimum may lead to serious pitfalls. In part, these can be avoided by a consideration of externalities, but this will lead to a consideration of policies. This will happen because it will be discovered that the externalities of locational decisions are not covered in a system of economic rents, and consequently do not adequately influence the behaviour of decision makers. There is also a deeper question of the same nature having to do with the development patterns and optimization over time. Even if present externalities are accounted for in the behavioural system and the related objective functions, the effects of current decisions are frozen in capital works. As time passes and conditions change, these decisions not only may be no longer optimal but they may generate new externalities as their effects are propagated through the system. It is almost certain that the institutional arrangements which might equate individual and social optimization at one point in time, would require drastic modifications to equate individual optimization with long run social optimization.

As capital is not instantaneously convertible from one use to another, dynamic development patterns depend not only on instantaneous pressures but upon the whole history of the system.

It is clear that the third objective cannot be incorporated in a formal evaluation framework, given our present imperfect knowledge of the urban development process. At present the evaluation methodology must be restricted to a shortrun equilibrium analysis of the other two objectives.

10.4.2 Transport-system outputs

Comments were made in Sec. 10.2.3 about the validity of the transport-system output variables used in traffic-systems evaluation. While most would agree that "accessibility" is the output of principal interest to the community there is little agreement on an appropriate measure of accessibility. One definition of accessibility that has been used frequently is that derived from the gravity model:

$$ACC_i = \sum_{j=1}^{n} a_j f_{ij} \tag{10.4}$$

where ACC_i = the accessibility of zone i relative to all n zones of an urban region
a_j = a meaure of attractiveness of the other zones
f_{ij} = a measure of the effect of travel time on the perception of the attractiveness of a zone

The definition and measurement of environmental quality has not received as much attention as accessibility. The Buchanan report [12] and other studies in Britain [13] provide the major sources of information. It is generally agreed that the two major factors which influence the transport-related environmental quality of an urban zone are: (1) the volume of vehicles using a transport network link, and (2) the visual intrusion of parked vehicles and their rights-of-way.

Motor vehicles affect the environmental quality through their emission of noise, exhaust fumes, and vibration, and through their interference with pedestrian circulation and safety. Figure 10.16 shows a relationship developed by the Wilson Committee [14] in Britain which relates mean noise level to traffic volume. In the absence of additional information on environmental quality, the average (or peak-hour) vehicle volume on a road link would seem to represent the transport-system output which relates most directly to environmental quality.

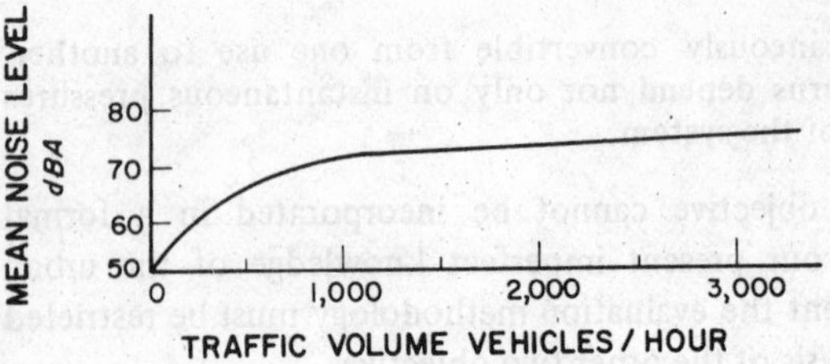

FIG. 10.16. Mean noise level vs. traffic volume.

The environmental impacts of transport technologies other than motor vehicles are also noise and visual intrusion. These characteristics vary greatly with the type of technology and cannot be summarized easily.

10.4.3 Community willingness to pay for outputs

The community-demand curve is the economic concept that is available for expressing the community willingness to pay for various levels of system output. The use of the demand curve to derive measures of consumers' surplus has been described earlier in this chapter and in the Appendix to this chapter.

Neuburger [15] has used the gravity model to derive a measure of the consumers' surplus associated with changes in accessibility in an urban area. Neuburger has derived the following function for estimating consumers' surplus:

$$S = \frac{1}{\beta} \sum_i \sum_j \left[t_{ij} \log \frac{t_{ij}}{p_i a_j} - t_{ij}) + t_{ij} d_{ij} \right] \tag{10.5}$$

where $p_i a_j$ = measures of the trip production and attraction forces inherent in a zone which are independent of the accessibility of a zone

β = the index of the f_{ij} function assumed which is equal to $1/e^{\beta d_{ij}}$

d_{ij} = the interzonal travel time

Neuburger suggests that Eq. (10.5) is a measure of the correlation between the number of trips originating from a zone and the accessibility of that zone to desirable destinations. This interpretation is reasonable if p_i represents the desirability of zone i as a residential location and a_j is a measure of the desirability of zone j as an employment location. Equation (10.5) may be used to derive measures of changes in consumers' surplus for each zone i which would result from changes in accessibility within an urban area. Neuburger argues that changes in accessibility may be achieved from changing travel times or from the rearrangement of land use.

Hutchinson [16] has argued that measures of the changes in consumers' surplus may be derived from studies of urban land values. Kain [17] has assumed a linear relation between land values and straight line distance from the central business district, while Berry et al. [18] have observed a negative exponential relation between land values and distance from the central business district.

Theoretical frameworks of the type developed by Wingo [19] and Alonso [20] appear to offer some promise. The basic structure of the approach proposed by Wingo is reviewed below in order to demonstrate one possible approach. Figure 10.17 shows the transport function isolated by Wingo for an urban region. This transport function has then been used to derive a spatial structure of position rents of the type shown in Fig. 10.18. The notion embodied in Fig. 10.18 is that the householder at *i* enjoys a premium in transport costs with respect to a householder located at the margin *m*. This locational advantage invites competition from all households located at a distance greater than *i* from the center. A household at the margin can offer a position rent for *i* equal to the difference in the transport costs between the two locations. In this way, a locational equilibrium is established where each household's location costs are constant.

Wingo has then demonstrated how density and unit rent profiles of the type shown in Fig. 10.19 may be derived from certain assumptions about space consumption and the position rent relation of Fig. 10.18. Changes in the density and unit rent profiles due to changes in the transport function are shown by the broken lines in Fig. 10.19 and 10.17, respectively.

Limited empirical studies of the variations in the selling prices of houses in the Metropolitan Toronto area have been conducted at the University of Waterloo.

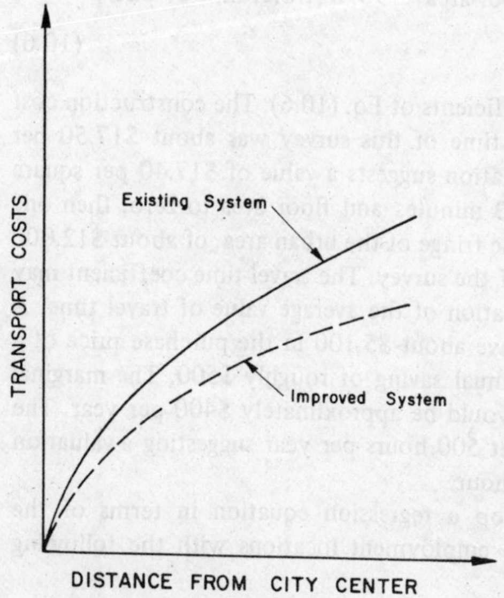

FIG. 10.17. Urban transport function assumed by Wingo. (*From L. Wingo, "Transportation and Urban Land," The Johns Hopkins University Press,* 1961. *By permission of Resources for the Future, Inc., Washington, D.C.*)

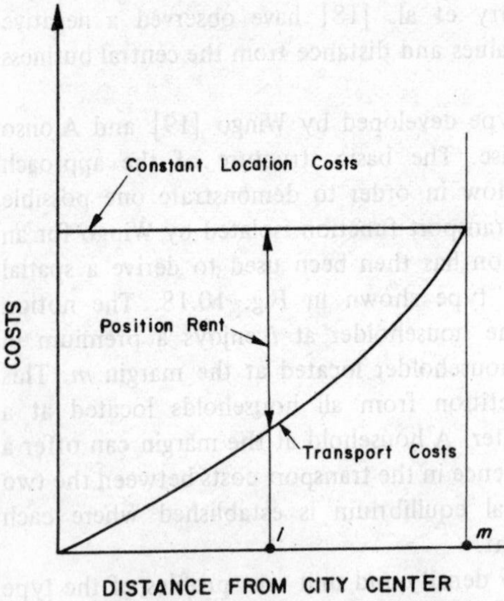

FIG. 10.18. Spatial structure of position rents. (*From L. Wingo, "Transportation and Urban Land," The Johns Hopkins University Press,* 1961. *By permission of Resources for the Future, Inc., Washington, D.C.*)

A regression analysis of the selling prices of single-family dwelling units yielded the following equation:

$$\text{Selling price} = 17{,}648 + 17.4\,(\text{floor area}) - 95.6\,(\text{travel time to CBD})$$

$$R^2 = 0.516 \qquad (10.6)$$

It is interesting to examine the coefficients of Eq. (10.6). The construction cost of new housing in Toronto at the time of this survey was about $17.50 per square foot and this regression equation suggests a value of $17.40 per square foot. If the travel time is set to 60 minutes and floor area to zero, then one obtains a selling price, for a lot at the fringe of the urban area, of about $12,000 which was reasonable at the time of the survey. The travel-time coefficient may also be used to derive a rough valuation of the average value of travel time. A householder at the margin would save about $5,100 in the purchase price of a house which is equivalent to an annual saving of roughly $500. The marginal transport costs from this location would be approximately $400 per year. The aggregate travel time would be about 500 hours per year suggesting a valuation of travel time of about 20 cents per hour.

An attempt was made to develop a regression equation in terms of the accessibility of residential zones to employment locations with the following results:

$$\text{Selling price} = 6{,}400 + 19.5\,(\text{floor area}) + 0.29\,(\text{accessibility})$$
$$R^2 = 0.585 \tag{10.7}$$

where the accessibility of a zone was calculated from Eq. (10.4). However, the coefficient of accessibility was found to be significant only at the 20 percent level of significance.

Wabe [21] has developed the following regression equation from an analysis of the selling price of houses in London, England:

$$\begin{aligned}\text{Selling price} = {} & 3{,}236 - 20.38T - 18.74P + 3.47SC \\ & - 23.08PD + 276.46GB + 3.59A \\ & + 16.29\,D - 285.87CH\end{aligned}$$
$$R^2 = 0.900 \tag{10.8}$$

where T = average journey time in minutes by train from the borough to central London
P = average price in pence (predecimalization) for a single journey by train to central London
SC = number of persons per thousand in the upper socioeconomic groups
PD = population density of borough in persons per acre
GB = a dummy variable indicating access to green belt
A = average floor area of houses sold in borough
D = date at which houses were built
CH = availability of central heating

There are some difficulties with the interpretation of Eq. (10.8) since some of the independent variables are collinear. It would be expected that T and P would

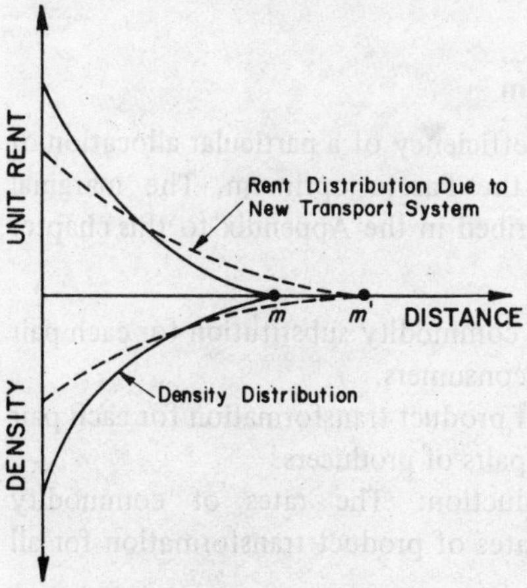

FIG. 10.19. Density and unit rent profiles for existing and improved transport systems. (*From L. Wingo, "Transportation and Urban Land," The Johns Hopkins University Press,* 1961. *By permission of Resources for the Future, Inc., Washington, D.C.*)

be collinear because rail and underground fares in London vary with distance. The simple correlation matrix presented in Ref. 21 shows a simple correlation coefficient of 0.89 between T and P.

Additional empirical studies of land values and the calibration of simple models of residential rent models should lead to the development of appropriate measures of the consumers' surplus likely to be derived from accessibility changes.

10.4.4 A decision criterion

Marglin [22] has proposed a decision criterion for water resource systems which may be stated as follows:

A proposed system $A1$ is economically more efficient than a system $A2$ if those affected by $A1$ are willing to pay those affected by $A2$ a sum sufficient to persuade them to agree to the construction of $A1$.

Willingness to pay for a system may be subdivided into those who are made better off by a system A and those who are made worse off:

$$W(A) = E(A) - C(A) \tag{10.9}$$

where $W(A)$ = aggregate willingness to pay for system A

$F(A)$ = willingness to pay of those who benefit from system A rather than have no system at all

$C(A)$ = willingness of those who are made worse off by system A, to pay not to have the system at all

Marglin has pointed out that the decision criterion given in Eq. (10.9) will provide a transitive ordering of systems only if the amount which the beneficiaries of one system are willing to accept as compensation to do without their project is equal to the amount that they are willing to offer as compensation to the beneficiaries of other systems to persuade them to do without their projects.

10.4.5 Marginal conditions for an optimum

It has been pointed out above that the efficiency of a particular allocation of resources may be judged in terms of the Pareto optimum. The marginal conditions for a Pareto optimum are described in the Appendix to this chapter and these are:

1. Efficiency in exchange: The rates of commodity substitution for each pair of commodities must be equal for all consumers.
2. Efficiency in production: The rates of product transformation for each pair of commodities must be equal for all pairs of producers.
3. Efficiency in exchange and production: The rates of commodity substitution must be equal to the rates of product transformation for all pairs of commodities.

Figure 10.20 illustrates a hypothetical transformation function that might be developed for an urban transport system. It shows the combinations of accessibility and environmental quality that can be achieved for a fixed monetary input. That is, points along the transformation function represent transport systems consisting of various amounts of public-transport and road facilities. The transformation function is the locus of the "best" transport systems for a fixed monetary input. The marginal conditions for efficiency in production require that a system must fall on this transformation function, or production-possibility frontier.

A line *AB* may also be plotted on Fig. 10.20 which shows the combinations of accessibility and environmental quality that are of constant value to the community. The equilibrium condition is given by the point of tangency between the price line and the transformation function. *C* identifies the best combination of outputs that can be achieved for a fixed input. An expansion path is also shown on Fig. 10.20 which represents the locus of the points of tangency.

It is shown in the Appendix that the rate of product transformation (as shown by the transformation function) must be equal to the rate of commodity substitution for all pairs of products in order to achieve a Pareto optimum. At *C*, then, the following conditions must hold:

Rate of commodity substitution = commodity price ratio
= commodity marginal cost ratio
= rate of product transformation

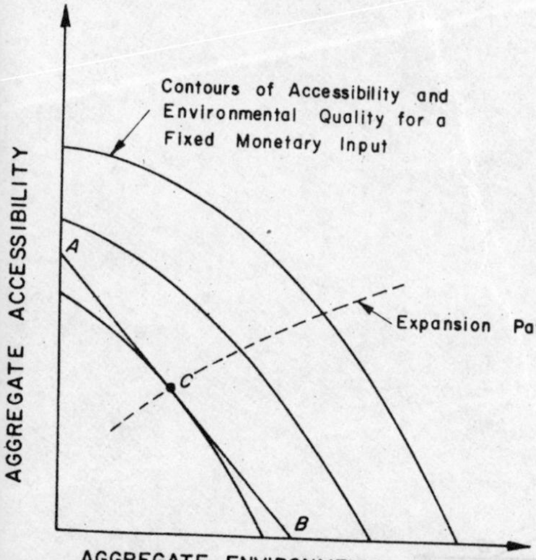

FIG. 10.20. Hypothetical product transformation function for urban transport systems.

These marginal conditions are concerned with identifying economically efficient allocations of resources. These conditions must be modified to reflect the second goal of urban transport investment which is concerned with distributional efficiency.

A fundamental assumption of welfare theory is that the initial distribution of real income in a community is satisfactory and that the gains and losses to individuals are small in relation to income levels. Evidence has been presented earlier in this book that demonstrates that all socioeconomic groups within the community do not have equal access to community facilities.

Assume that urban households may be classified into car owning (*CO*) and non-car owning (*NCO*). Assume further that *NCO* households tend to be segregated geographically and that these households lack adequate travel opportunities. The distributional efficiencies of alternative urban transport systems may be examined in terms of Fig. 10.21.

In Fig. 10.21 the aggregate accessibility of *CO* households is plotted as the ordinate and the aggregate accessibility of *NCO* households is plotted as the abscissa. The transformation function shows the locus of "efficient" transport systems. Community welfare functions may be plotted on Fig. 10.21 which shows the relative weights that the community places on these two objectives. The equilibrium condition is point *C*, where the slope is equal to the slope of *AB*. The slope of *AB* implies that the marginal rate of transformation between the accessibilities of the two sets of households is equal to the marginal premium

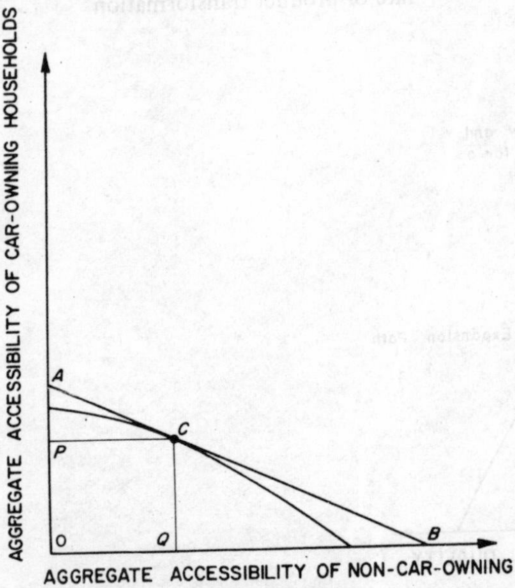

FIG. 10.21. Distributional efficiency of urban transport system.

placed on *NCO* household accessibility. The alternative represented by *C* will contribute *OP* to *CO* household accessibility and *OQ* to *NCO* household accessibility.

10.5 WELFARE ECONOMICS AND TRANSPORT SYSTEM EVALUATION

This chapter has described in detail a selection of the methods that have been advanced for the benefit-cost analysis of urban transport investments. The basic aim of benefit-cost analysis is extremely simple and that is to identify that alternative which maximizes the difference between benefits and costs. In Sec. 10.1 it was mentioned briefly that the translation of this aim into practice leads to many theoretical and practical difficulties.

The theoretical foundations of benefit-cost analysis are found in the principles of welfare economics which are outlined in the Appendix. The Paretian concept of welfare changes in a society is the central notion of welfare theory. The marginal conditions for a Pareto optimum are described in the Appendix and have been used in varying degrees in the evaluation methods described previously in this chapter.

It is pointed out in the Appendix that the analysis of community welfare in terms of Pareto optimality leaves a great deal of indeterminancy in the solution since there are an infinite number of states that are Pareto optimal. This indeterminancy is the result of the Paretian assertion that an increase in welfare is unambiguously defined if an improvement in one individual's satisfaction is not accompanied by a deterioration in the satisfaction of another.

The general form of a social welfare function is:

$$W = W(U_1, U_2, \cdots, U_i, \cdots, U_n) \tag{10.10}$$

where U_i = the utility of the *i*th consumer

The utility function is not a unique function and its form depends on the value judgments of the person for whom it is a desirable function. It expresses one set of views concerning the effect that the utility level of the *i*th consumer has on the welfare of the society. Figure 10.21 provides one example of the types of value judgments that are necessary to define a social welfare function for an urban transport system. Other criteria which have been proposed are discussed in the Appendix.

Value judgments of the type required by a social welfare function usually find expression through the political process. The role of public participation in transport planning and its relationship to the economic principles described in this chapter are discussed in subsequent sections. Reference [23] provides a useful discussion of welfare theory and its application to public-systems evaluation.

In many practical benefit-cost analyses it has been argued that it is impossible to fulfill all of the marginal conditions and, therefore, it is better to satisfy at least some of these conditions. This approach is rejected by the so-called *theory of the second-best.* This theory demonstrates that the marginal conditions of a Paretian optimum are not valid criteria of an increase in welfare in a situation in which they are not all satisfied simultaneously. The following quotation from Winch [24] summarizes effectively the principal implications of this theory:

> In general, while the Paretian conditions constitute a simple statement of the necessary first-order conditions of a first-best, there is no corresponding set of rules for the achievement of a second-best, or even a better, position in a world where the first-best is unattainable. Piecemeal welfare economics based on achievements of the Paretian conditions in a partial equilibrium context may well lead to recommendations that would result in a reduction in welfare when viewed in a general equilibrium context of sub-optimality.
>
> The importance of this principle in most areas of applied welfare economics is difficult to overestimate. It is not true, for example, that public utilities or nationalized industries should price at marginal cost when other industries do not. Repeal of an apparently distorting marginal tax might reduce welfare if other marginal taxes remain in force.
>
> The general conclusion about optimization in an imperfect world is clear. While the first-best conditions are straightforward and rigorous, the corresponding conditions of a second-best optimum are complex in even the simplest model. The real world is an imperfect second-best world of far greater complexity than our simple models. In such a world there are no simple a priori rules for establishing a second-best optimum, nor even rigorous criteria of whether a particular change would constitute an improvement even if not an optimum. The rules of first-best optimality, coupled with the caveat of second-best, do however, constitute part of the fund of guidelines from which good, if not perfect, policy might be formulated.

10.6 RATING FRAMEWORKS

The methods of evaluation described in the previous sections are based on the notion of a simple competitive market. There are difficulties in assembling the necessary empirical data for these methods because simple competitive markets do not exist for the outputs of urban transport systems. A group of methods have been advanced which attempt to replace the concept of a simple competitive market by some form of rating scheme. Hill [25], Schimpeler and Grecco [26], and Falk [27] have proposed methods which are typical of the rating frameworks.

10.6.1 Basic structure

While the methods do differ in detail, the conceptual structure that underlies all of these techniques is essentially the same. The method proposed by Schimpeler and Grecco [26] is described in this section. Figure 10.22 illustrates

ALTERNATIVE PLAN	COMMUNITY OBJECTIVES G_1	G_2	.	.	G_j	.	.
P_1	e_{11}	.	.	.	.	.	.
P_2	.						
P_l	e_{l1}	.	.	.	e_{lj}		
.	.	.	.	.	.	.	.

$$U_l = \sum_{j=1}^{n} e_{lj} \ u_j$$

FIG. 10.22. Effectiveness matrix for rating evaluation framework.

the concept of an effectiveness matrix which is central to this procedure and where the symbols used have the following meanings:

G_j, $j = 1, \ldots, n$ = the community objectives which are being used to assess alternative plans.

P_i, $i = 1, \ldots, m$ = the set of alternative plans under consideration.

u_j, $j = 1, \ldots, n$ = a numerical utility value associated with each community planning objective where each utility measure must comply with the constraint [Eq. (10.11)] that follows.

$$\sum_{j=1}^{n} u_j = 1 \tag{10.11}$$

e_{ij} = a measure of the probability that objective j can be achieved if plan i is adopted.

U_i = a measure of the total utility of plan i based on the evaluation of plan i relative to all objectives where the total utility is given by Eq. (10.12).

$$U_i = \sum_{j=1}^{n} e_{ij} u_j \tag{10.12}$$

Schimpeler and Grecco [26] suggested two methods for determining the utilities u_j. The first method is based on a ranking technique in which each member of the evaluation panel was asked to rank each objective in decreasing order of importance from 1 to n. Each objective was then assigned a converted rank where $n-1$ was assigned to the objective receiving a raw rank of 1, and a converted rank of 0 to the objective receiving a raw rank of n. The composite rank R_j for objective j was determined by summing the converted ranks of all r judges:

$$R_j = \sum_{k=1}^{r} R_{kj} \tag{10.13}$$

where R_{kj} = the converted rank given by judge k to objective j

The utility magnitudes were obtained from:

$$u_j = \frac{R_j}{\sum_{j=1}^{n} R_j} \tag{10.14}$$

The rating scale approach was used to establish utility magnitudes in the following way:

$$v_j = \sum_{k=1}^{r} V_{kj}$$

$$u_j = \frac{V_j}{\sum_{j=1}^{n} V_j} \tag{10.15}$$

where V_{kj} = the rating between 0 and 10 assigned by judge k to objective j

10.6.2 Principles of rating scale construction

The central feature of the rating-type evaluation procedures is some form of subjective rating procedure. Although the manner in which humans gauge the potential impacts of alternative plans is necessarily an empirical problem, the known facts of psychophysics set valuable guidelines. It is well established that psychological experiences are measurable but all psychophysical quantities are subject to bias and potential distorting factors. The fact that an observer can be influenced in what he reports does not mean that psychological impressions are not quantifiable, but merely that the task of measurement is difficult. An observer is sensitive not only to the stimulus that he is trying to measure but also to a large number of other factors that can distort his judgment to varying degrees.

Measurement is concerned with the rationale involved in the construction of a measuring scale as well as with the properties that can be attributed to measurements executed with that scale. Measurements are normally expressed in terms of the real number system and the real number system possesses certain fundamental properties of which the most important are order and additivity. The order of numbers is given by convention. Additivity refers to the fact that the operation of addition (used in the completely general sense) gives results that are internally consistent. In other words, equal differences can be determined from the numbers, such as $7 - 5 = 4 - 2$, as well as equal ratios, such as $8/4 = 6/3$.

If it is possible to assign numbers to the properties of objects, so that the properties of objects designated by the various numbers have the same characteristics as the number system, then the number system may be used as a mathematical model of the properties of the object. It is of great analytical advantage if this isomorphism can be established. The principles and manipulations of mathematics applicable to the number system may then be used to manipulate the properties of the objects themselves.

Measurement exists in a variety of forms depending on the extent to which the properties of the number system are reflected in the scale of measurement. Measurement scales are classified into four basic types and the classification described by Stevens [28] and given in Table 10.4 is generally accepted. Each of the four scale types reduces the arbitrary element in the assignment of numbers to property magnitudes to a different degree. Table 10.4 contains a brief description of the empirical rule or operation invoked in the measurement operation, the transformations under which each scale type remains invariant, an example of each scale type, and the mathematical operations allowable on the measurements. Inasmuch as the arbitrary element in the assignment of numbers to properties is restricted to a different degree for each scale type, the characteristics of the numbers that are available for meaningful use as a model of object properties are likewise restricted.

Table 10.4. A classification of scales of measurement

Scale	Basic empirical operation*	Allowable transformations	Example
Nominal	Determination of equality	Any one-to-one substitution	"Numbering" of football players
Ordinal	Determination of greater or less	Any increasing monotonic function	Moh hardness scale of minerals
Interval	Determination of equality of intervals	Any linear transformation	Temperature (°F)
Ratio	Determination of equality of ratios	Any linear transformation retaining natural origin	Length, density, temperature (°K)

*The basic operations needed to create a given scale are those listed down to and including the operation listed opposite the scale.

The utility functions described in Sec. 10.6.1 required a ranking of objectives in the one case, and a subjective rating in the second case. The derivations of the utility functions and their use in Eq. (10.12) involves multiplication operations. The information presented in Table 10.4 indicates that numbers must represent at least an interval scale measurement status to allow this type of mathematical manipulation. It is generally considered that subjective rating procedures achieve the measurement status of ordinal scales and only approach the status of interval scales under closely controlled conditions [28-30]. This would indicate that the results obtained from the arithmetical manipulation of the rankings and ratings required by the method described in Sec. 10.6.1 are invalid.

10.6.3 Deficiencies of rating methods

The major deficiency of the rating-based methods of evaluation has been described in the previous section. A second major deficiency of these methods has to do with the difficulty in communicating the magnitudes of the impacts of alternative plans to the raters. Borland [31] used a paired comparisons technique in an attempt to assess the relative desirabilities of alternative urban freeway alignments as viewed by the community. This comparison involved an existing freeway and a hypothetical realignment of the freeway. Borland concluded that it was not possible to convey to the sample population how much the various impacts under consideration differed between the alternative and existing alignments. In the survey of the alternative facility, the unsatisfactory impacts of the existing facility continued to be associated with the alternative facility in spite of significant improvements in the impacts.

Rating methods require raters to formulate a consistent set of objectives along with statements about the relative importance of these objectives. A number of studies have demonstrated that raters cannot develop a consistent set of objectives in the abstract but can only judge between tangible alternatives.

10.7 PUBLIC PARTICIPATION IN PLAN EVALUATION

Real public concern has developed about the extent to which the electorate is having an influence on government decisions particularly those made by the executive arms of governments. In many communities, decisions that had to be made about locating urban freeways have served to focus these frustrations. Bouchard [32] has argued that this public concern seems to arise from the apparent inabilities of elected officials at all levels of government to oversee effectively the vast bureaucracies which constitute the machinery of government.

It seems clear that if democratic rule is thought of as no more than a majority rule decision process, then formal evaluation of alternatives has little role to play. If, instead, democracy is considered as a method of reaching agreement through informed debate, then the principles by which decisions are reached become relevant.

The methods of evaluation discussed in previous sections relied on money as a measure of value or utility. A review of urban transport-investment decisionmaking in recent years would suggest that the use of market values, or imputed market values, has met with little success. It seems that if any real progress is to be made in evaluation, then the basis of the method should be some consistent theory of democratic group decisions.

10.7.1 Models of the political process

Normative models of the democratic state have been proposed by several investigators and Fig. 10.23 shows a flow diagram of the main components of one such model [33]. While this model developed by Maass is based on the American federal system of government, it is general enough to represent broadly the process of government found at federal, state, and municipal levels of many countries.

The principal structural characteristic of this model is its classification of components into either the community or the state. The underlying premise of this model is that man is capable of debating and identifying the standards by which he wishes to live in a community with others. The unique role of the community is to promote a process of community debate which will result in agreement on community goals, along with a desire to reexamine these goals.

The major functions of the state are seen to be:

1. To guarantee individual economic and political freedom in order to facilitate community debate
2. To place before the community pertinent information about the state of the community in order that community debate will be constructive and meaningful
3. To provide the institutional means whereby the community goals can be focussed to become the basis of specific courses of action

Figure 10.23 indicates that there are three institutionalized government processes which provide the means for translating the broad goals of the community into specific objectives for planning and design. These are the electoral process, the legislative process, and the administrative process.

The electoral process takes over from the broad discussion within the community and its groups. The principal aim of the electoral process is to select community representatives who are capable of carrying the discussion of community goals to a more definitive stage. The legislative process follows the electoral process and translates into rules of law the general goals endorsed by the electorate. The legislators are involved effectively in a process of mutual enlightenment and accommodation of the diverse points of view within the community that they represent. An assumption of this model is that the

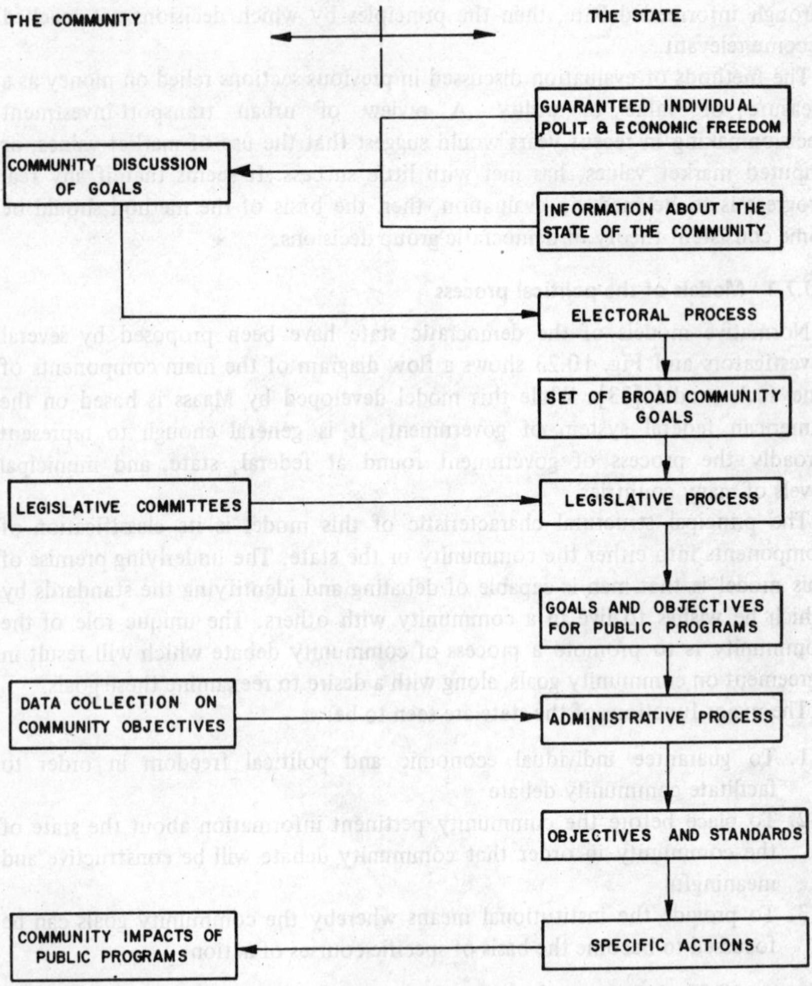

FIG. 10.23. A model of the principal elements of the constitutional form of democratic government.

legislature is a much more specialized body than the electorate and is capable of more effectively using information on the state of the community. This model assumes that this information is used to discriminate between the alternative sets of goals and objectives and that a set of goals and objectives is embodied eventually in the legislative acts.

The third institutionalized government process is the administrative process. This process translates the goals and objectives embodied in the legislative acts into more specific objectives, and sometimes standards. These objectives and standards must be in a form that is immediately useful to the development of specific courses of action by the state through its instrumentalities. Figure 10.23

indicates that the administrative process requires more detailed information on the state of the community in order to explore alternative courses of action.

A principle embodied in this model is that both leadership and accountability are provided for in each phase of government. The model incorporates the principle of the division of labor which assigns a deliberative function to each phase and in this way provides multiple opportunities both for leadership and accountability. The model is structured in such a way that it attempts to ensure that the progression from the broad community goals through to the formulation of specific objectives and standards in the administrative process is consistent. It is assumed that a division of labor of the following type will promote consistency between these phases:

1. The principal role of the legislature is to oversee the legislative and administrative processes and to educate the community on the important issues facing it; the legislature should be oriented toward broad issues and the discussion of community goals and objectives.
2. The principal role of the chief executive is to initiate the legislative and administrative processes and to ensure their coordination.

Another fundamental principle embodied in this model of the democratic state is the concept of the division of government power. There are three principal modes of dividing government power and these are by process, function, and constituency. These divisions of government power may be combined with capital and areal divisions of power to yield the six general classes shown in Table 10.5. The principal reason for the division of government power is to ensure that the diverse objectives of society are realized. This last assertion is conditional on the following assumptions holding in a particular society:

Table 10.5. Divisions of government power

Divisions	Capital	Areal
Process	Legislative process assigned to one body, administrative process assigned to a second, and the judicial process to a third	Legislative process assigned to the central government and the administrative process assigned to decentralized units of the same government
Function	Functions may be divided among agencies and departments of the same government which possess a significant degree of independence from each other	Functions may be divided among the central, provincial, and municipal governments
Constituency	Upper chamber of the federal legislature elected from one electoral base and the lower chamber from another base	Upper chamber elected from a provincewide constituency and the lower chamber elected from proportional representation

1. The electoral process selects legislators who, as a group, are broadly representative of the community, where the community is viewed as a pluralist political association seeking agreement on objectives.
2. The division of government power which results from the electoral process and, therefore, based on constituency, when appraised along with divisions of power based on process and function, should fully reflect the community goals and objectives.
3. The community social structure is such that with the institutional arrangements that foster it, the community will search for consensus through discussion.
4. The institutional arrangements, including government divisions of power, can be developed which will encourage the process of discussion.

That is, assumptions 3 and 4 imply that there is a reciprocal relation between the division of government power and the social structure of the community.

A rather different approach to modeling the democratic system of government has been developed by Downs [34]. Downs attempts to develop a behavioral theory of government in which votes are viewed as a type of currency. A set of propositions is then developed about the behavior of voters, political parties, and governments. These propositions are based on the assumption that politicians are motivated by self-interest in a manner analogous with the search for profits which is usually taken as the prime objective of business.

Democracy is defined as a governmental system in which there is one man, one vote; in which voters have a real choice; and in which legality prevails. Government is defined as the locus of ultimate power in society in that it can coerce all other groups into obeying its decisions, whereas they cannot similarly coerce it. Political parties are defined as coalitions of men seeking to control the governing process by legal means, and the voters are offered a choice between at least two parties at fixed intervals of time.

A vote is considered to be exchangeable for only one commodity, a party in power. Downs suggests that the government's objective is to maximize political support and it carries out those acts of spending that gain the most votes by means of those acts of financing that lose the fewest votes. A set of propositions is then developed from this model about political behavior in a two-party system. Many of these behavioral propositions seem to agree with available empirical evidence.

An important conclusion of this behavioral theory of government is that it may be politically impossible to effect an arrangement that is Pareto optimal because the required change from the status quo involves unpopular redistributive effects for which compensatory arrangements are impractical.

Buchanan and Tulloch [35] have also attempted to develop a behavioral theory of government, based on the orthodox economic theory of markets. They view collective decisionmaking as a form of human activity through which mutual gains are made possible. The basic concept is that collective decisionmaking activity, like market activity, is a genuinely cooperative endeavour in which all parites stand to gain. This view is in contrast to much of the current sociopolitical thought which is based on the view that collective decisions involve a partisan struggle in which beneficiaries of actions secure gains solely at the expense of others.

Meyerson and Banfield [36] have provided a useful conceptualization of the political process that was derived from a study of public-housing decisions in Chicago. The basic premise of this framework is that politics is concerned with actors (persons, organizations, groups) and that each of these actors is attempting to achieve a particular set of objectives. An issue is said to exist when there is a conflict between sets of objectives of different actors, or within the objective set of a single actor. A settlement consists of the set of objectives made on the basis of action that terminates an issue. Politics is defined as the activity by which an issue is agitated and settled by a mode of agitation such as negotiation, argument, or dictation.

The simplest unit of politics is described as one which involves two actors with a single issue, and this unit of politics may be described in terms of four components:

1. A description of those objectives of each actor which are relevant to the issue
2. The respects in which the objectives of the two actors are in conflict
3. The nature of the activity by which the issue is agitated and settlement is reached
4. The terms of the settlement

Meyerson and Banfield [36] have suggested that modes of agitation may be classified into four principal groups which are:

1. Co-operation: This involves the selection of a shared set of objectives, or some procedural principle mutually agreed upon, whereby an objective set is selected as the basis of choice among the objectives at issue; that is, actors engage in a cooperative search for that settlement implied by the objectives or principles which they agree ought to be decisive.
2. Contention: Actors mutually endeavor to make their objectives prevail over those of the other actors by the exercise of power; that is, each actor attempts to bring the issue to settlement on the terms most favorable to him.
3. Accommodation: One actor freely chooses to make the objectives of the other actor his own, thus ending the conflict.
4. Dictation: A settlement is reached by one actor stating the terms of settlement and compelling the other actor to accept those terms.

An issue is said to be settled on its own merits if the settlement is logically implied by some standards of equity that are deemed relevant to the issue.

The models of the political process described above are broadly representative of the constructs that are currently available. While this review cannot be considered exhaustive, it does provide sufficient background for exploring the potential contributions of existing models to the development of an improved transportation-evaluation framework.

10.7.2 Modes of public participation

Before exploring the potential roles of the models of the political process in transport evaluation it is instructive to review the modes of decision that have been used during the past decade. During this period most transport-policy decisions were made by elected representatives on the advice of transport planners with only cursory attention being paid to other interest groups within the community.

The methods of evaluation reviewed earlier in this chapter have illustrated that evaluation was based on an aggregated view of the impacts of these investments and a concentration on those impacts associated with the movement of private motor vehicles on the road system. Investment costs were measured generally in terms of the capital costs of construction and the market prices of land required for the rights-of-way. Few attempts were made to reflect in these analyses the costs arising from the displacement of people and businesses, the opportunity costs of the land consumed, or the environmental impacts of these investments.

During the past decade of transport planning, some attempts were made to reconcile the desires of the various interest groups within the community through the mechanism of the public hearing. Most public hearings have simply provided a forum for focussing the negative reactions of groups affected adversely by transport plans. A major deficiency of this mode of public participation has been the lack of any real communication between planners, elected representatives, and electorates. Transport planners have failed to communicate the real impacts of alternative proposals on the various interest groups within the community, or to consider alternatives that attempt to provide equitable impacts on all interest groups.

The greatest conceptual deficiency of most public hearings has been the failure of planners to highlight the real issues to be resolved by the community. It has been suggested throughout this book that the conflict between the provision of accessibility and environmental quality is perhaps the dominant transport-related issue. Very few transport-planning studies have explored the variations in these two outputs between alternative plans and the differential impacts of these outputs on the various interest groups.

A fundamental assumption of Maass's model of the democratic state is that there is a reciprocal relation between the social structure of the community and the divisions of government power. The model assumes that the community social structure is such that with the institutional arrangements which foster it, the community will search for consensus through discussion. That this assumption is violated seems to be reflected in the widespread belief that elected representatives are no longer truly representative of all segments of the community. Many urban communities are experiencing a demand by the electorate for an additional process, or a completely new process, that will reflect public concerns on issues such as transport investment. The freeway design team concept which has evolved in the United States is one response to this demand for increased public participation.

Meyerson and Banfield's unit of politics provides a simple concept for structuring certain principles about public participation. The first step involves the identification of the actors along with the objectives of each of the actors. Manheim et al. [37] have noted that most actors are unable to articulate a consistent set of objectives in the absence of a set of tangible alternative plans. Maass's model indicates that the formulation of consistent objectives by the community requires that information on the state of the community must be placed before it. A major issue in many public hearings on freeways has had to do with the validity of the demand forecasts prepared by transport planners. Park [38] has noted in connnection with the freeway route planning process that:

> Unless the community is convinced of the validity of the transportation demand projection, no amount of community interaction efforts can be assured of success. The objective is to jointly make the demand analysis on a particular corridor based on anticipated regional and local land use developments, evaluate what the most appropriate transportation modes are to meet the demand, and also assess the future consequences of having no freeway facility improvements.

Park [38] has identified the following interest groups with respect to freeway location along with the dominant impacts perceived by the interest groups:

1. Owners and occupants of properties displaced by freeway:
   a. dislocation of families and businesses and separation from established neighborhood social patterns
   b. need for replacement housing, relocation technical assistance, and monetary payments
   c. problems in disposing of property and possible property-value depreciation during period from route adoption to acquisition
   d. nonmaintenance of properties despite assurance of compensation as reflected in fair market value
2. Owners and occupants of properties left adjacent to freeway:
   a. impact of noise, air, and dust pollution
   b. difficulty of disposing of freeway-adjacent properties at full value due to environmental impacts
   c. redefinition of neighborhood boundaries and establishment of new neighborhood edges to freeway
   d. impact on lifestyles of increased mobility and environmental impacts

3. Neighborhood or area adjacent to freeway:
   a. severance of neighborhood from larger community and from schools and other community facilities
   b. change in vehicle and pedestrian circulation patterns including new and increased traffic flow
   c. proliferation of new freeway-related uses resulting in possible conflict with existing uses
   d. overall effects on neighborhood cohesiveness and stability
4. School district:
   a. impact of noise, air, and dust pollution on school facilities
   b. change in pupil load resulting in possible disruption to facility plans and changes in operating efficiency
   c. change in school attendance boundaries and reduction of school district revenue
5. City and country:
   a. short term change in economic base and impact on tax revenues
   b. local traffic reorientation
   c. pressure for accelerated land-use change with possible conflict on orderly growth plans and budget programs
   d. potential conflicts and confrontation between various community interest groups and elected officials

Issues of the type identified by Park can only really be identified and articulated by the various interest groups if specific alternatives are proposed and debated. In the process of public participation proposed by Manheim et al. [37] the second stage, referred to as *issue analysis*, is described as follows:

> The objective of this stage is to develop, for both the location team and the interest groups affected, a clear understanding of the issues. The major thrust is on developing a range of alternatives which represent different assumptions about the objectives to be achieved, and which when presented to various interest groups help them to clarify their own objectives. Ideally, all parties concerned are seeking to develop their understanding of the advantages and disadvantages of various alternatives.
>
> In this stage, the location team starts to develop location alternatives. Perhaps none of these will be selected; the purpose is to get a wide range which shows the spectrum of possibilities. The team also engages in a program of direct interaction with formal and informal community groups. By presenting information about the alternatives and their impacts to various groups, the location team helps to learn about the issues and demonstrates the trade-offs which might be possible.

The third element of Meyerson and Banfield's model is the identification of a mode of agitation by which the issues between actors are resolved. A fundamental tenet of democracy is that agreement is reached through informed debate. Meyerson and Banfield identify cooperation as that mode of agitation involving the selection of a shared set of objectives, or some procedural principle which is mutually agreed upon, whereby an objective set is selected as the basis of choice among the objectives which are at issue.

The basic value judgment of welfare economics is that welfare is increased if at least one person is made better off and no one worse off. This assertion has been extended by the compensation principle which argues that if the aggregate benefits exceed the aggregate costs so that it would be possible for the gainers to compensate the losers, then an action would yield a net increase in welfare. The model developed by Buchanan and Tulloch [35] suggests that if full side payments are allowed to take place, any decisionmaking rule for collective action will lead to positions that may be classified as Pareto optimal. They show, in fact, that only if full side payments are introduced is there any assurance that majority-rule decisionmaking will lead to positions that may be classified as Pareto optimal.

In addition, the following decision criterion was introduced in Sec. 10.4.4 to ensure transitivity in the ordering of alternative systems:

A proposed system $A1$ is economically more efficient than a system $A2$ if those affected by $A1$ are willing to pay those affected by $A2$ a sum sufficient to persuade them to agree to the construction of $A1$. It was pointed out that this criterion would provide a transitive ordering of systems only if the amount which the beneficiaries of one system are willing to accept as compensation to do without their project is equal to the amount that they are willing to offer as compensation to the beneficiaries of other systems to persuade them to do without their projects.

This criterion may be rephrased in the following way to reflect the issue created by many urban freeway location projects:

The amount which those losing from a freeway location $A1$ are willing to accept as compensation to agree to the construction of $A1$ must be equal to the amount that they are willing to offer as compensation to those losing from a freeway location $A2$ to persuade them to agree to the construction of $A2$.

The development of an institutional framework within which transport-related issues might be resolved is, at the present time, an empirical problem. Manheim et al. [37] have observed:

> Fundamental to this approach (of public participation) is the premise that there is no single political/institutional mechanism through which all interest groups potentially affected by a highway decision can make their voices heard effectively. If there were such a mechanism, then the role of the highway team would be to serve as professional staff supporting it, and to assist it in developing and analyzing alternative courses of action.
>
> The kind of process which the location team executes must provide a focus not only for the interaction of formal political institutions, but also for the participation of those groups who do not find effective representation through these institutions.

The final element of the unit of politics proposed by Meyerson and Banfield [36] is the nature of the settlement. Recent experience in the United States demonstrates that a settlement in freeway location projects may involve compensation through a package of community facilities and programs not related directly to transport or the transport facilities. The compensation and willingness to pay implied by the decision criterion described previously must be thought of in a broader way than simply monetary terms.

SUMMARY

Urban transport systems consume resources in order to produce outputs which are of use to the community. The essence of transport-system investment evaluation is to assemble both the benefits and dis-benefits likely to be produced by a system in order to establish the net benefits, and to compare the net benefits with the resource costs required. The economic criterion used to identify the best alternative is the maximum difference between net benefits and costs, or, equality of marginal benefits and marginal costs.

The methods of evaluation which have been proposed may be grouped into the following classes: (1) traffic-systems evaluation, (2) transport-systems evaluation, and (3) transport-subsystems evaluation.

The methods of evaluation, classed as traffic-systems evaluation, concentrate on the benefits to road-users likely to accrue from potential road investments. With these methods of analysis, the road system is viewed as a relatively independent entity having little interaction with the public-transport system and no nonuser impacts. The essential difference between the methods is in the way in which the properties of the alternative traffic systems are expressed. Some of the methods use link-traffic volumes as a measure of the economic good consumed by tripmakers. Other methods use the trip-interchange magnitudes between origin-destination pairs as the measure of the underlying economic good. The most appropriate measure seems to be the accessibility of points in the study area since traffic-system demands are the joint consequence of land development patterns and traffic-system properties.

The changes in utility of the users is measured by the changes in consumers' surplus with respect to the particular output variables used. The price of travel is usually obtained from a summation of out-of-pocket costs, travel-time costs, and accident costs. The methods normally assume that the marginal value of travel, the critical component of the trip price, is invariant with respect to both the amount of time saved and the length of the trip for which the travel-time savings accrue. Empirical evidence indicates that this assumption is not valid and that the value of travel-time savings is overestimated significantly. User benefits are also influenced by the road-pricing regime under which a road network will operate. The principal practical difficulty in applying these methods of evaluation is in defining the location of the demand functions throughout the period of analysis.

The methods of evaluation, classed as transport-systems evaluation, recognize that transport systems consist of more than one modal network and address themselves to the problem of the optimum combination of transport modes. The different transport modes are viewed as factors of production which yield in different combinations, different levels of transport capability. The optimum combination of transport modes to produce a specified transport capability may be identified by the point of tangency between the transport-production function and the isocost line.

The methods of evaluation, classed as transport-subsystems evaluation, view the transport system as having both transport and nonuser outputs. The general application of the relevant economic principles to this type of evaluation are outlined in this chapter. Little empirical evidence to support the application of this approach is available currently.

The theoretical foundations of benefit-cost are found in the principles of welfare economics. The methods of evaluation described in this chapter reflect these principles to varying degrees. The Paretian concept of welfare changes in a society is the central notion of welfare theory. With this concept, an increase in welfare occurs if an improvement in one individual's satisfaction is not accompanied by a deterioration in the satisfaction of another. This is not a satisfactory criterion since there are an infinite number of states that are Pareto optimal. This deficiency may be rectified through the definition of a social welfare function which requires explicit interpersonal comparisons of utility to be made. The value judgments required by a social welfare function usually find expression through the political process.

Because of the difficulties of expressing benefits and costs as market values, a group of evaluation methods have been proposed which are based on some form of rating scheme. The methods calculate some aggregate utility measure for each alternative, where this utility has been derived from subjectively determined utility measures for each system output. Rating scales of the type used in these evaluation methods yield, at best, ordinal scale measurements which cannot be manipulated mathematically in the ways required by the evaluation techniques.

Public participation in urban transport-planning studies has become widespread in North America. Public participation may be viewed as a way of obtaining the interpersonal comparisons of utility required by the social welfare function. Some of the theoretical work on conceptual models of the political process provides a useful basis for structuring public participation in transport-planning studies.

A generally accepted method of evaluation for urban transport projects does not exist at the present time. The material presented in this chapter must be regarded simply as a statement of the current capabilities. However, a clear understanding of the relevant economic principles will allow the transport planner to structure better the decisions that have to be made by elected representatives.

REFERENCES

1. Moses, L. N., and H. F. Williamson, "Value of Time, Choice of Mode and the Subsidy Issue in Urban Transportation," *Journal of Political Economy,* vol. 81, no. 3, June, 1968.
2. Haney, D. G., *The Value of Time for Passenger Cars,* vol. I: *A Theoretical Analysis and Description of Preliminary Experiments,* PB 175 653, Stanford Research Institute, Menlo Park, California, May, 1967.
3. Thomas, T. C., and G. I. Thompson, *The Value of Time for Commuting Motorists as a Function of their Income Level and Amount of Time Saved,* Highway Research Record No. 314, Highway Research Board, Washington, D.C., 1970.
4. Chicago Area Transportation Study, *Study Report,* vol. 1–3, Chicago, Illinois, 1969.
5. Wohl, M., and B. V. Martin, *Traffic System Analysis for Engineers and Planners,* McGraw-Hill Book Company, New York, 1967.
6. Freeman, Fox, Wilbur Smith and Associates, *London Transportation Study,* Chap. 20, London, November, 1968.
7. Beesley, M. E., and A. A. Walters, "Some Problems in the Evaluation of Urban Transport Investment," *Applied Economics,* vol. I, no. 4, pp. 241–257, 1970.
8. McIntosh, P. T., and D. A. Quarmby, *Generalized Costs and the Estimation of Movement Costs and Benefits in Transport Planning,* Presented at 51st meeting, Highway Research Board, Washington, D.C., 1972.
9. Rahman, W. M., and K. B. Davidson, *A Model for the Analysis and Evaluation of Urban Transport,* Proceedings, Australian Road Research Board, Melbourne, pp. 135–152, 1968.
10. Thompson, W. R., *A Preface to Urban Economics,* Johns Hopkins Press, Baltimore, Maryland, 1965.
11. Harris, B., *Problems in Regional Science,* Papers and Proceedings, Regional Science Association, vol. 21, 1968.
12. *Traffic in Towns: The Specially Shortened Edition of the Buchanan Report,* Penguin Books Ltd., Harmondsworth, Middlesex, England, 1963.
13. Greater London Council, *Kensington Environmental Management Study,* London, 1966.
14. Her Majesty's Stationery Office, *Noise: Final Report, Sessional Papers,* London, 1963.
15. Neuburger, H., "User Benefit in the Evaluation of Transport and Land Use Plans," *Journal of Transport Economics and Policy,* vol. 5, no. 1, pp. 52–75, January, 1971.
16. Hutchinson, B. G., *An Approach to the Economic Evaluation of Urban Transportation Investments,* Highway Research Record No. 314, Highway Research Board, Washington, D.C., 1970.
17. Kain, J. F., *A Multiple Equation Model of Household Location and Trip Making Behavior,* RM-3086-FF, the RAND Corporation, Santa Monica, California, 1962.
18. Berry, B. J. L., J. W. Simmons, and R. J. Tennant, "Urban Population Densities: Structure and Change," *Geographical Review,* vol. 53, no. 3, pp. 389–405, 1963.
19. Wingo, L., *Transportation and Urban Land,* Johns Hopkins Press, Baltimore, Maryland, 1961.
20. Alonso, W., *A Theory of the Urban Land Market,* Papers and Proceedings, Regional Science Association, Philadelphia, vol. 6, 1950.
21. Wabe, J. S., "A Study of House Prices as a Means of Establishing the Value of Journey Time, The Rate of Time Preference and the Valuation of Some Aspects of Environment in the London Metropolitan Region," *Applied Economics,* vol. 3, pp. 247–255, 1971.
22. Marglin, S. A., "Economic Factors Affecting Systems Design" in A. Maass (ed.), *Design of Water Resource Systems,* Harvard University Press, Cambridge, Massachusetts, 1966.

23. de Neufville, R., and J. H. Stafford, *Systems Analysis for Engineers and Managers,* McGraw-Hill Book Company, New York, 1971.
24. Winch, D. M., *Analytical Welfare Economics,* Penguin Books Ltd., Harmondsworth, Middlesex, England, 1971.
25. Hill, M., *A Method for the Evaluation of Transportation Plans,* Highway Research Record No. 180, Highway Research Board, Washington, D.C., 1967.
26. Schimpeler, C. C., and W. L. Grecco, *Systems Evaluation: An Approach Based on Community Structure and Values,* Highway Research Record No. 238, Highway Research Board, Washington, D.C., 1968.
27. Falk, E. L., *Measurement of Community Values: The Spokane Experiments,* Highway Research Record No. 229, Highway Research Board, Washington, D.C., 1968.
28. Stevens, S. S., "On the Theory of Scales and Measurement," *Science,* vol. 103, no. 2684, pp. 677–686, 1946.
29. Torgerson, W. S., *Theory and Methods of Scaling,* John Wiley & Sons, Inc., New York, 1960.
30. Hutchinson, B. G., *Principles of Subjective Rating Scale Construction,* Highway Research Record No. 46, Highway Research Board, Washington, D.C., 1964.
31. Borland, L. R., *A Method for Optimizing the Functional Design of an Urban Expressway,* M.A.Sc. thesis, Department of Civil Engineering, University of Waterloo, Waterloo, Ontario, 1970.
32. Bouchard, R. J., *Community Participation: How to Get There from Here,* Presented at 51st meeting, Highway Research Board, Washington, D.C., 1972.
33. Maass, A., "Systems Design and the Political Process: A General Statement," in A. Maass (ed.), *Design of Water Resource Systems,* Harvard University Press, Cambridge, Massachusetts, 1966.
34. Downs, A., *An Economic Theory of Democracy,* Harper & Row, Publishers, New York, 1957.
35. Buchanan, J. M., and G. Tulloch, *The Calculus of Consent,* Michigan University Press, Ann Arbor, Michigan, 1962.
36. Meyerson, M., and E. C. Banfield, *Politics, Planning and the Public Interest,* Free Press, Glencoe, Illinois, 1955.
37. Manheim, M. L., J. H. Suhrbrier, A. T. Reno, and E. Bennett, *Community Values in Highway Location and Design,* Report No. 71-5, Urban Systems Laboratory, Massachusetts Institute of Technology, Cambridge, Massachusetts, December, 1971.
38. Park, K. S., *Achieving Positive Community Participation in the Freeway Planning Process,* Presented at 51st meeting, Highway Research Board, Washington, D.C., January, 1972.

APPENDIX

A REVIEW OF WELFARE THEORY

A.1 THE DEMAND CURVE

The concept of a demand curve is central to the derivation of the benefit associated with expenditures on public projects. A demand curve illustrates the way in which the quantity of good or service consumed varies with the unit price of a good or service. Figure A.1 illustrates a hypothetical demand curve *DD*. D_1 on this demand curve illustrates that at price p_1, q_1 units of the good will be consumed. Demand curves are usually assumed to possess a negative slope as illustrated in the diagram.

Demand curves depict the reaction of consumers to prices for a particular set of incomes and prices for the other goods and services available to consumers. Changes in income, or the prevailing prices for other goods and services, may change the demand curve. For many goods and services the demand curve may be determined empirically.

Economic theory attempts to explain the nature of the demand curve in terms of a theory of consumer behavior. The utility of an economic good or service may be defined as the subjective benefit which a consumer receives from the consumption of that good or service. The theory of consumer behavior described below relies on an ordinal interpretation of utility. Consumers need only state which of two goods is preferred without attempting to report the absolute magnitude of the strengths of these preferences.

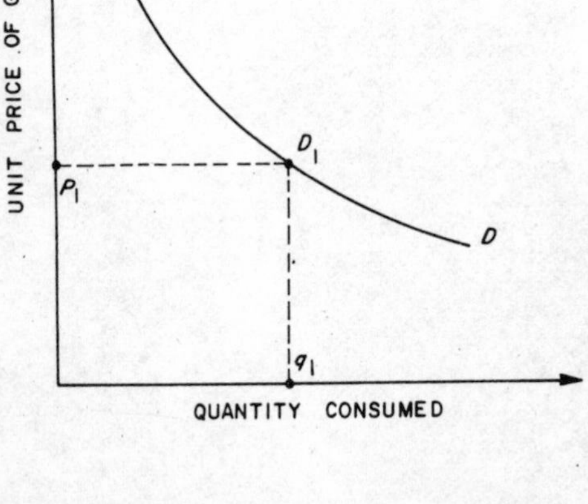

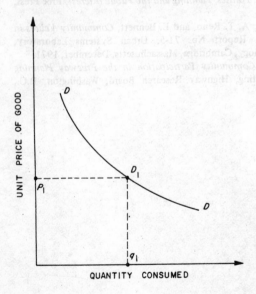

FIG. A.1. A hypothetical demand curve.

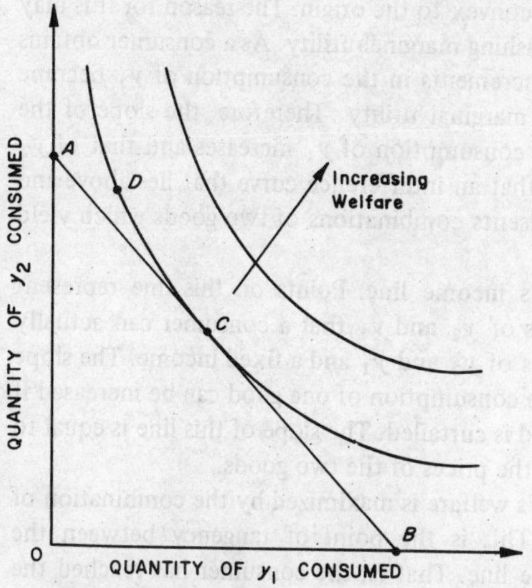

FIG. A.2. A consumer indifference curve.

A consumer is assumed to have a set of preferences and to allocate a limited income in such a way as to maximize his well-being or welfare. A consumer is said to be in equilibrium when a particular allocation of his income yields a level of welfare that cannot be exceeded by any other allocation of income.

Consumer behavior is developed in terms of an indifference curve. A hypothetical indifference curve is shown in Fig. A.2. Points along the curve identify the combinations of the quantities of y_2 and y_1 consumed to which the consumer is indifferent. OA is the maximum amount of y_2 that could be purchased if all the available income was used for its purchase; OB is the maximum amount of y_1 that could be purchased if all the available income were devoted to its purchase.

$$OA = \frac{\text{income}}{p_{y_2}} \tag{A.1}$$

$$OB = \frac{\text{income}}{p_{y_1}} \tag{A.2}$$

where p_{y_2}, p_{y_1} = the unit prices of y_2 and y_1, respectively

The slope of the indifference curve at any point, say D, shows the rate at which a consumer is prepared to give up his consumption of y_1 to increase his consumption of y_2, while retaining a constant level of welfare. The absolute magnitude of the slope is called the consumer's marginal rate of substitution of y_1 for y_2. It may be regarded as the consumer's subjective rate of exchange between the two goods.

The indifference curve is always convex to the origin. The reason for this may be found in the principle of diminishing marginal utility. As a consumer obtains more of y_1 and less of y_2, these increments in the consumption of y_1 become less valuable to him, or have less marginal utility. Therefore, the slope of the indifference curve decreases as the consumption of y_1 increases and that of y_2 decreases. It is shown in Fig. A.2 that an indifference curve that lies above and to the right of another curve represents combinations of two goods which yield greater welfare.

AB is known as the consumer's income line. Points on this line represent combinations of the consumptions of y_2 and y_1 that a consumer can actually purchase given the prevailing prices of y_2 and y_1 and a fixed income. The slope of *AB* shows the rate at which the consumption of one good can be increased if the consumption of the other good is curtailed. The slope of this line is equal to the negative inverse of the ratio of the prices of the two goods.

In terms of Fig. A.2, a consumer's welfare is maximized by the combination of consumption represented by *C*. This is the point of tangency between the indifference curve and the income line. That is, the consumer has reached the highest indifference curve yet remaining within his income. *C* is said to have the property that the marginal rate of substitution in consumption is equal to the price ratio.

At *C* the consumer has arranged his consumption of each good so that each is providing him with marginal utility proportional to the prices. The following relationship, then, expresses consumer equilibrium:

$$MRS_{y_1 \text{ for } y_2} = \frac{p_{y_1}}{p_{y_2}} = \frac{MU_{y_1}}{MU_{y_2}} \tag{A.3}$$

The consumer indifference curve may be used to derive an individual's demand curve for a particular good. Figure A.3 shows how the demand curve for y_1 may be constructed in principle from the indifference curve. The income line *AB* varies with each price change in y_1. The points of tangency between the indifference curves and the expenditure lines define a price-consumption curve. The amounts of y_1 consumed DD^1 may be projected on to the lower graph along with the corresponding prices to define the demand curve.

A demand curve represents the results of two sets of forces, the desires of consumers and their willingness to pay to satisfy these desires. A community demand curve for a good may be derived by summing the individual demand curves. Figure A.4 shows that the community willingness to pay for the consumption of an amount Q is given by the area under the demand curve. This aggregate willingness to pay represents the aggregate, or total benefit to the community of the consumption of an amount Q.

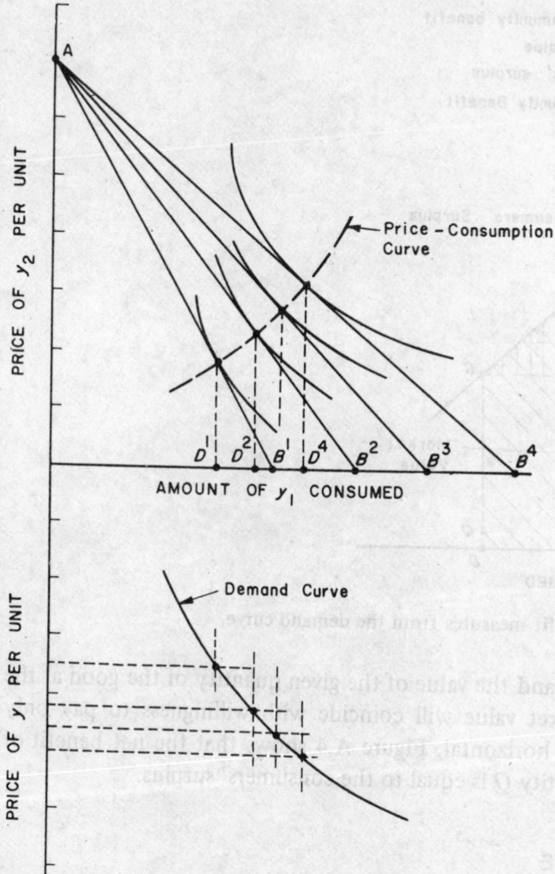

FIG. A.3. Derivation of a demand curve from an indifference map.

The willingness to pay consists of two subareas, the triangle *BAC* and the rectangle *OBCD.* At price p the total amount actually paid by the community for an aggregate amount of consumption Q is equal to pQ, the area of the rectangle. Because of the law of diminishing marginal utility the earlier units of consumption are worth more to the community than those units in the vicinity of Q. The earlier units are worth more since the community is willing to pay more for them. The community pays p for all units of consumption and therefore enjoys a surplus of benefit on the earlier units equal to the area of the triangle *BAC.*

The consumers' surplus is normally defined as the difference between the maximum amount consumers are willing to pay for specified quantity of a good

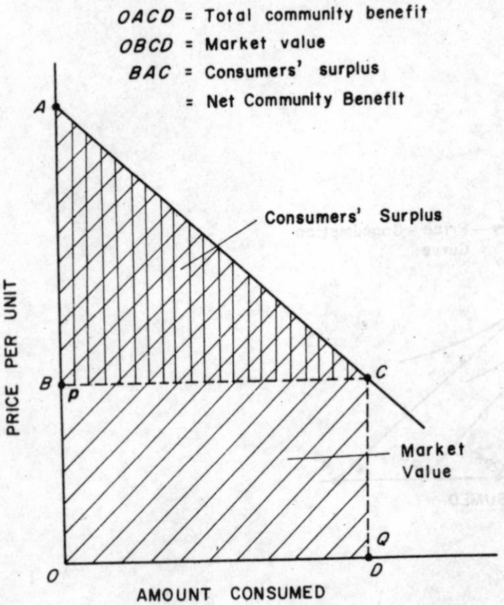

FIG. A.4. Derivation of benefit measures from the demand curve.

rather than go without it, and the value of the given quantity of the good at the good's market price. Market value will coincide with willingness to pay only when the demand curve is horizontal. Figure A.4 shows that the net benefit of the consumption of a quantity Q is equal to the consumers' surplus.

A.2 THE SUPPLY CURVE

A supply curve shows the amounts of a good that producers are willing to supply at various prices. Each producer is faced with some combination of fixed and variable costs which contribute to the total cost of each level of output. The fixed costs are those costs which the producer has to incur even with zero output. The variable cost is zero when the output is zero and it increases as the output increases. The marginal cost of an increase in production is the increment in the total cost that comes from each increment in output of a producer. Figure A.5(a) illustrates the concepts of average and marginal costs.

The average cost per unit of production is equal to the total cost divided by the total output. The average cost relationship is also shown in Fig. A.5(a). It should be noted that the marginal cost curve cuts the average cost curve at its minimum value. In some cases the marginal cost curve intersects the average cost curve in two places. In these cases the minimum average cost is the point where the rising marginal cost curve cuts the average cost curve.

In a perfectly competitive market a firm can sell as much or as little as it likes at a fixed price per unit. The marginal revenue of a firm is equal to the extra income it receives for each extra unit of production that it sells. A marginal revenue curve is illustrated in Fig. A.5 (*a*). It should be noted that the marginal revenue curve intersects the marginal cost curve at an output of 9 units.

The total revenue and the total cost characteristics of the firm represented in Fig. A.5(*a*) are illustrated in the lower part of the diagram [Fig. A.5(*b*)]. The region in which the firm makes a profit is shown by the hatched area. This diagram illustrates that maximum profit occurs at a production of 9 units.

The relationships illustrated in Fig. A.5 demonstrate that a firm maximizes its profit if it produces up to the point where the marginal revenue equals the marginal cost. That is, the amount of a good or service that a competitive firm will choose to supply at each price is the amount at which the price (i.e., marginal revenue) equals the marginal cost. Therefore, the marginal cost curve represents the shortrun supply curve.

The objective of profit maximization may be illustrated in an alternative way with the aid of Fig. A.6. The conditions illustrated in this diagram differ slightly from the case analyzed in Fig. A.5. The market is no longer perfectly

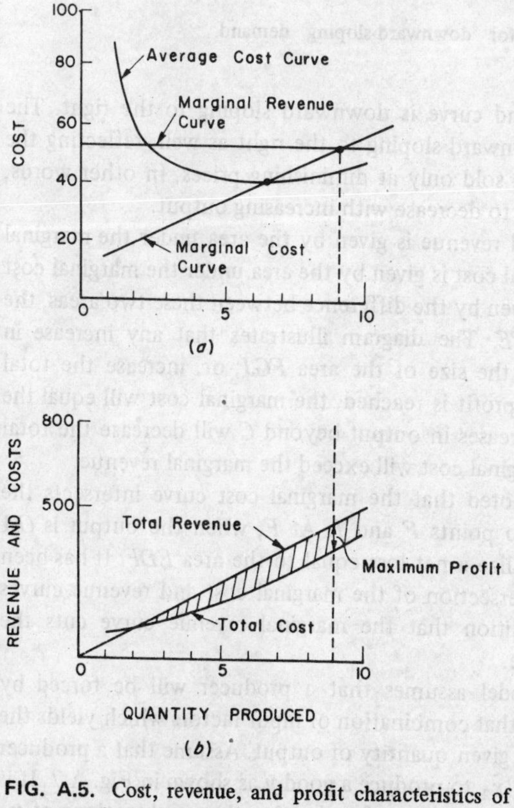

FIG. A.5. Cost, revenue, and profit characteristics of a firm; (*a*) average and marginal costs and revenue, (*b*) total revenue and total cost characteristics.

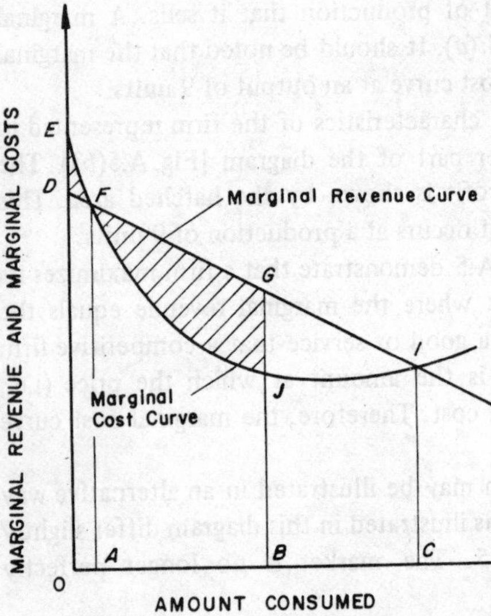

FIG. A.6. Profit maximization for downward-sloping demand curve.

competitive in that the demand curve is downward sloping to the right. The marginal revenue curve is downward sloping to the right as well, reflecting the fact that larger outputs can be sold only at diminishing prices. In other words, the marginal revenue continues to decrease with increasing output.

At any output, say *OB*, total revenue is given by the area under the marginal revenue curve *OBGD*. The total cost is given by the area under the marginal cost curve *OBJE*. Total profit is given by the difference between these two areas, the area *FJG* minus the area *DFE*. The diagram illustrates that any increase in output up to *C* will increase the size of the area *FGJ*; or, increase the total profit. At *C*, when maximum profit is reached, the marginal cost will equal the marginal revenue. Further increases in output beyond *C* will decrease the total profit, since beyond *C* the marginal cost will exceed the marginal revenue.

In Fig. A.6 it should be noted that the marginal cost curve intersects the marginal revenue curve at two points *F* and *I*. At *F*, when the output is *OA* units, the firm would only realize a net loss equal to the area *EDF*. It has been noted previously that the intersection of the marginal cost and revenue curves must comply with the condition that the marginal revenue curve cuts the marginal cost curve from above.

The simple competitive model assumes that a producer will be forced by competitive conditions to use that combination of input factors which yields the least cost of production for a given quantity of output. Assume that a producer uses two input factors x_1 and x_2 to produce a good y as shown in Fig. A.7. It is possible to plot isoquants of production of y showing the combinations of x_1

and x_2 required for the production of this constant amount of output. Isoquants of different levels of output are shown in Fig. A.7.

The standard economic assumption influencing the shape of the production isoquant is the principle of diminishing marginal productivities of input factors. That is, as more of an input is employed with all other inputs being held constant, a point will be reached where additional quantities of input will yield diminishing marginal contributions. The slope of the production isoquant at any point shows the rate at which one input factor has to be increased as the input of the second factor is decreased.

The line *AB* may be plotted on Fig. A.7 from a knowledge of the prices of x_1 and x_2. This line represents the combinations of x_1 and x_2 which yield an equal total cost. *AB* is usually referred to as the *isocost line* and its slope is equal to the ratio of the prices of the input factors. The equilibrium condition for a given cost is given by the point of tangency between the isocost line and the highest production isoquant. In the case illustrated in Fig. A.7 the least-cost combination of inputs would be *OE* of x_2 and *OD* of x_1.

Point *C* is said to have the property that the rate of input factor substitution at this point must equal the slope of the isocost line. The production function reflects the existing technology of production. A change in this technology will change the interrelationship between the inputs and the outputs.

Figure A.7 illustrates the expansion path for a firm. The expansion path is the locus of points of tangency between isocost lines and the isoquants with increasing input budgets. The expansion path describes how the firm's optimal input combination varies when the size of the input budget varies. If the expansion path is linear then a production process is said to exhibit constant

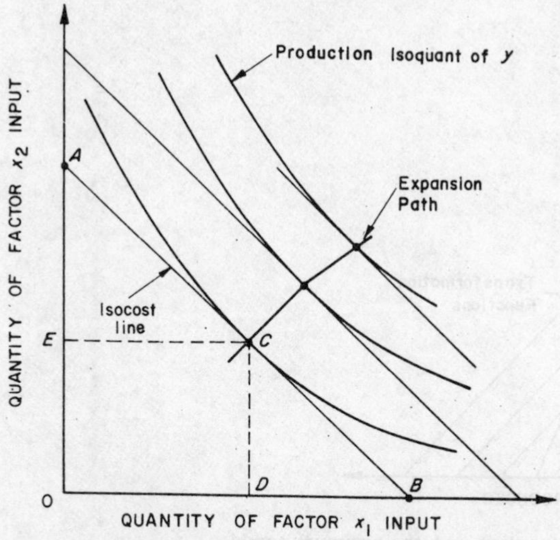

FIG. A.7. A firm's production function and expansion path.

returns to scale. This means that given the prices of its inputs, the optimal proportion of the inputs will not change with the size of the firm's input budget. Firms may also exhibit increasing and decreasing returns to scale.

The previous discussion has been concerned with the characteristics of a firm that produces one commodity. The production function was the concept used to relate the quantity of a good produced to the amount of each input factor used in production. For firms which produce two or more commodities it is necessary to introduce the concept of a production-possibility curve, or a transformation function. Figure A.8 illustrates the nature of a transformation function for a two-product firm. The quantities of goods produced are plotted along the two axes. The transformation function shows the combinations of outputs that can be produced for a fixed production budget. For example, as the production of y_2 is increased the production of y_1 must be curtailed, and the transformation function shows the rate of substitution.

A set of isorevenue lines may be plotted on Fig. A.8. Points along any one of these lines represent combinations of outputs that would yield the firm constant revenue. The equilibrium condition for the firm is given by C. At this point the firm is receiving maximum revenue for a fixed production budget. The locus of the points of optimum combination of outputs may be defined for increases in the production budget.

The slope of the transformation function at any point shows the rate at which the production of y_2 must be given up to produce more of y_1 without varying

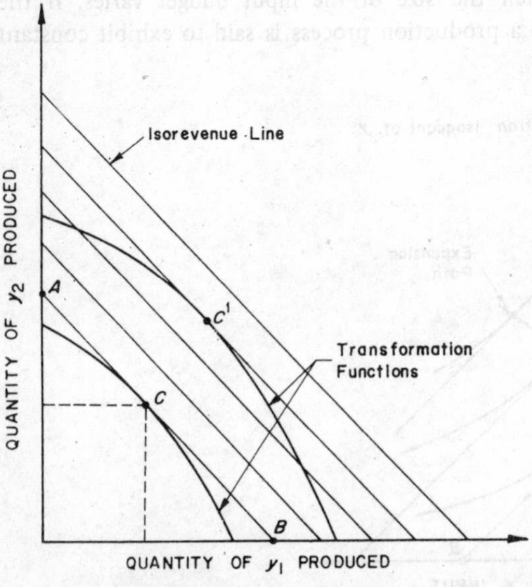

FIG. A.8. The transformation function and the optimum combination of outputs for a two-product firm.

the input of resources. The slope is usually called the *rate of product transformation.* The slope of the isorevenue line is equal to the ratio of the marginal revenues for the products. For a profit-maximizing firm the marginal revenue must equal the marginal cost for each product. Therefore the slope of *AB* is also equal to the ratio of the marginal costs of the two products. Thus at *C* the rate of product transformation equals the ratio of the marginal costs of the two products.

A.3 DEMAND–SUPPLY EQUILIBRIUM

Equilibrium between demand and supply is defined by the point of intersection between the demand and supply curves. This condition is illustrated in Fig. A.9. At *C* an amount *Q* will be purchased at price *p*. The equilibrium price *p* is the only price that can last since it represents a balance between the willingness of consumers to pay for a quantity *Q* and the willingness of producers to supply a quantity *Q*.

A.4 CONDITIONS FOR GENERAL EQUILIBRIUM

The earlier sections in this Appendix identified the conditions which determined the equilibrium positions of consumers and producers. In this section the conditions that yield welfare maximization are identified. The welfare of a society depends in the broadest context upon the satisfaction levels of all of its consumers, where these satisfaction levels derive from the amounts of goods and services consumed by individuals. Welfare economics is concerned with the determination of the appropriate distribution of inputs among the various goods to be produced and of the appropriate distribution of outputs among consumers.

Economic efficiency, often called *Pareto optimality* is defined in the following way. The distribution of goods among consumers is efficient if every possible reallocation of goods among consumers results in the reduction of the satisfaction of at least one consumer. Production is efficient if every feasible reallocation of inputs among producers decreases the output level of at least one firm. It is shown in this section that the equilibrium conditions for a perfectly competitive market satisfy the conditions of Pareto optimality.

The Pareto optimality conditions may be stated in another way. It may be undesirable to increase the production of one product because the necessary concomitant decrease in the production of the second product is more valuable to society. The optimal allocation of resources to the production of the two goods is a matter of the relative urgency of the demands for them and their relative costs of production. The optimal level of production of a good cannot be determined in isolation but only in comparison with the production of other goods with which it competes for society's limited resources.

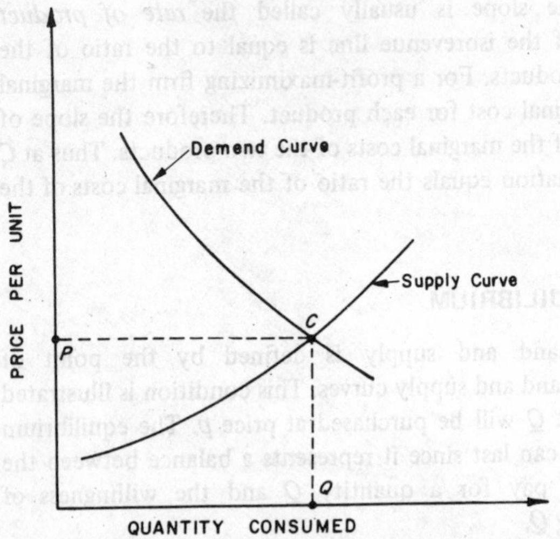

FIG. A.9. Equilibrium between demand and supply curves.

A.4.1 The consuming sector

The utility function of the ith consumer is:

$$U_i = U_i(y_{i1}, y_{i2}, \ldots) \tag{A.4}$$

where $y_{i_1}, y_{i_2}, \ldots$ = the quantities of the goods $y_1, y_2, \ldots$ consumed by the ith consumer.

Let these goods have market prices $p_{y1}, p_{y2}, \ldots$ and assume that the consumer has an income of M_i to devote to the purchase of these goods. The consumer must comply with the following budget constraint equation:

$$M_i = y_{i1} p_{y1} + y_{i2} p_{y2} + \cdots \tag{A.5}$$

The equilibrium of the ith consumer may be obtained from the maximization of Eq. (A.4) subject to the constraint equation (A.5).

The following Lagrangian expression may be formed from Eqs. (A.4) and (A.5):

$$L = U_i(y_{i1}, y_{i2}, \ldots) + \lambda(y_1 p_{y1} + y_2 p_{y_2} + \cdots - M) \tag{A.6}$$

The conditions for first order maximization of Eq. (A.6) are:

$$\frac{-dy_{i2}}{dy_{i1}} = \frac{p_{y1}}{p_{y2}} \tag{A.7}$$

Equation (A.7) states that the satisfaction of the ith consumer will be maximized if the rate of commodity substitution in consumption between any pair of goods equals the inverse of their price ratio.

Assume a simple economy in which there are two consumers A and B and that there is a fixed supply of two goods y_1 and y_2. The indifference maps of the two consumers are shown in Fig. A.10 where O_A is the origin of A's indifference map and O_B is the origin of B's indifference map. The sides of the box are equal to the amounts of y_1 and y_2 available for consumption. Thus O_AC and DO_B are equal to the quantity of y_1 available for consumption and O_AD and CO_B are equal to the quantity of y_2 available for consumption.

Suppose that the initial allocation of goods between the two consumers is that represented by P. A would then possess O_AE of y_1 and O_AG of y_2. B would possess O_BF of y_1 and O_BH of y_2. At P, A's marginal rate of substitution in consumption of y_2 for y_1 is high as shown by the slope of MM'. In contrast, B's marginal rate of substitution is low as indicated by the slope of RR'. Individual A is willing to exchange a larger amount of y_2 per unit of y_1 than is necessary to induce B to make an exchange. The situation at P is such that an exchange involving A trading some of y_2 to B in return for some of y_1 is indicated.

From this suboptimal point P there are an infinite number of ways to achieve an improvement in the welfare of the individuals. At one extreme an exchange of goods between the individuals could take the parties from P to P_1. In this case the increase in welfare would all accrue to B, since A would move along the same indifference curve and B would be on a higher indifference curve. At the other extreme A would obtain the entire benefit if the exchange led from P to P_3. In this case, B would remain on his original indifference while A moved from I_A to III_A.

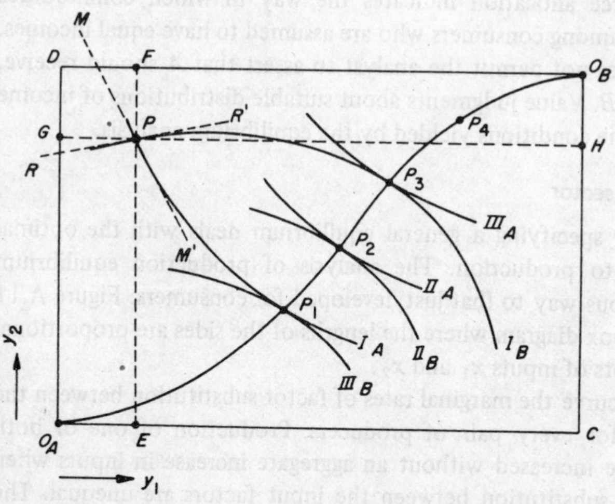

FIG. A.10. Edgeworth box diagram for two consumers.

A movement by the exchange of goods from P to P_2 represents one of many intermediate states in which both parties would benefit from the exchange. The principle governing the equilibrium positions in Fig. A.10 is that the marginal rate of substitution between every pair of goods must be the same for every pair of consumers. If it is not then the exchange can benefit one or both participants. Figure A.10 shows the locus of equilibrium points which defines all possible allocations of the available amounts of y_1 and y_2 that equalize the marginal rates of substitution of consumers A and B. The curve is usually called the *contract curve.*

The contract curve shows all of the possible allocations of goods between the two consumers that are optimal in the following sense. Any allocation which is represented by a point not on the curve is inferior to any infinite number of attainable allocations on the curve in that one or both parties are made better off while neither party suffers.

On the other hand, any point on the contract curve is not necessarily superior to a point not on the curve. For example, while points P_1, P_2, and P_3 are all preferable to P, one cannot judge between points P and P_4. At P_4, B is worse off than at P but to judge between points such as P and P_4 requires a statement of the importance that is to be attached to each member of the consuming community.

Equation (A.7) may be stated more generally as:

$$\left[\frac{\partial U_{ij}/\partial y_i}{p_{y_j}}\right] = \text{constant for all } i \text{ and } j \tag{A.8}$$

This rule for resource allocation indicates the way in which commodities should be distributed among consumers who are assumed to have equal incomes. Economic analysis does not permit the analyst to assert that A should receive, say, twice as much as B. Value judgments about suitable distributions of income must be tacked onto the conditions yielded by the equilibrium analysis.

A.4.2 The producing sector

The second rule for specifying a general equilibrium deals with the optimal allocation of inputs to production. The analysis of production equilibrium proceeds in an analagous way to that just developed for consumers. Figure A.11 shows an Edgeworth box diagram where the lengths of the sides are proportional to the available amounts of inputs x_1 and x_2.

Along the contract curve the marginal rates of factor substitution between the two inputs is equal for every pair of producers. Production of one or both outputs can always be increased without an aggregate increase in inputs when the marginal rates of substitution between the input factors are unequal. The locus of points of equilibrium shows the optimal output of each commodity

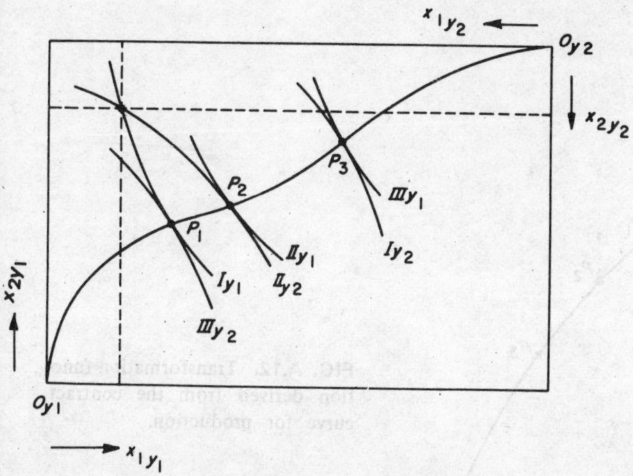

FIG. A.11. Edgeworth box diagram for the producing sector.

corresponding to every possible allocation of x_1 and x_2 between y_1 and y_2. The transformation function shown in Fig. A.12 may be developed by plotting the output pairs corresponding to each point of tangency in the Edgeworth box diagram of Fig. A.11.

A production function may be expressed as follows:

$$y = f(x_1, x_2) \tag{A.9}$$

where y is the output of the production process and x_1 and x_2 are the inputs.

For movements along the production isoquant y = constant and $dy = 0$; the following expression may be developed from Eq. (A.9):

$$dy = \frac{\partial f}{\partial x_1} dx_1 + \frac{\partial f}{\partial x_2} dx_2 = 0 \tag{A.10}$$

which yields:

$$\frac{-dx_1}{dx_2} = \frac{\partial f/\partial x_2}{\partial f/\partial x_1} \tag{A.11}$$

$-dx_1/dx_2$ is the slope of the production isoquant and represents the marginal rate of substitution in production of x_1 for x_2. The terms $\partial f/\partial x_2$ and $\partial f/x_1$ are known as the marginal products of x_2 and x_1, respectively. The marginal products indicate the change in output that is achieved by a unit change in inputs. The following expression may be written:

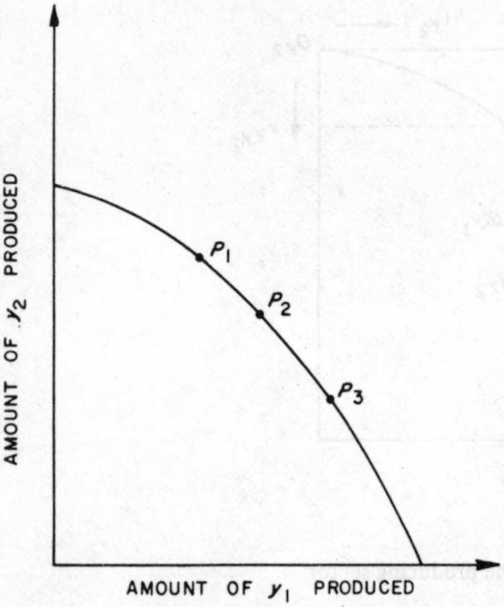

FIG. A.12. Transformation function derived from the contract curve for production.

$$MRS_{x_1 \text{ for } x_2} = \frac{-dx_1}{dx_2} = \frac{MP_{x_2}}{MP_{x_1}} \tag{A.12}$$

Consider the following production function $y = f(x_1, x_2)$ and budget constraint $C = p_{x1}x_1 + p_{x2}x_2$ of a firm. The following lagrangian expression may be formed in order to determine the equilibrium conditions for output maximization:

$$L(x_1, x_2) = f(x_1, x_2) + \lambda(p_{xi}x_1 + p_{xi}x_2 - C) \tag{A.13}$$

and differentiation of Eq. (A.13) yields the following conditions for maximization:

$$\frac{\partial f/\partial x_1}{\partial f/\partial x_2} = \frac{p_{x_1}}{p_{x_2}} \tag{A.14}$$

Equation (A.14) states that the ratio of the marginal products must be equal to their price ratio.

A transformation function has been defined as a locus of output quantity combinations that can be secured for a given input x. The negative of the slope of the transformation function is defined as the rate of product transformation *RPT*:

$$RPT = \frac{-dy_2}{dy_1} \tag{A.15}$$

The characteristics of a producer with a single input factor x and a pair of outputs y_1 and y_2 may be expressed as:

$$x = f(y_1, y_2) \tag{A.16}$$

The total differential of Eq. (A.16) is given by:

$$dx = \frac{\partial f}{\partial y_1} dy_1 + \frac{\partial f}{\partial y_2} dy_2 \tag{A.17}$$

For movements along the transformation function $dx = 0$ which yields from Eqs. (A.15) and (A.17):

$$RPT = \frac{-dy_2}{dy_1} = \frac{\partial f/\partial y_1}{\partial f/dy_2} \tag{A.18}$$

The rate of product transformation may also be expressed in terms of the marginal products:

$$\frac{\partial y_1}{\partial x} = \frac{1}{\partial f/\partial y_1} \text{ and } \frac{\partial y_2}{\partial x} = \frac{1}{\partial f/\partial y_2} \tag{A.19}$$

and Eqs. (A.18) and (A.19) yield:

$$RPT = \frac{-dy_2}{dy_1} = \frac{\partial y_2/\partial x}{\partial y_1/\partial x} \tag{A.20}$$

Equation (A.20) states that the rate of product transformation equals the ratio of the marginal product of x in the production of y_2 to the marginal product of x in the production of y_1.

If there are two inputs x_i and x_j used in the production of y_1 and y_2 then it can be shown that:

$$\frac{MP_{x_{i1}}}{MP_{x_{j1}}} = \frac{MP_{x_{i2}}}{MP_{x_{j2}}} \tag{A.21}$$

Equation (A.21) states that the ratio of the marginal physical products of inputs x_i and x_j in the production of y_1 must be the same as in the production of y_2.

A.4.3 Amount of output

The final conditions that must be established for general equilibrium relate to the determination of the optimum output levels. If a producer sells his output in a perfectly competitive market then the marginal revenue is constant and the total revenue is given by:

$$\text{Total revenue} = q f_1(q) \tag{A.22}$$

A demand curve may be expressed in the following way:

$$p = f_1(q) \tag{A.23}$$

Let $C = f_2(q)$ be the total cost function, then profit is given by the following expression.

$$p = q f_1(q) - f_2(q) \tag{A.24}$$

and profit maximization is given by $dp/dq = 0$.

$$\frac{dp}{dq} = f_1(q) - f_2'(q)$$

that is

$$f_1(q) = f_2'(q) \tag{A.25}$$

where $f_2'(q)$ = the marginal cost

Equation (A.25) states that profit maximization is obtained by the level of output at which marginal revenue is equal to marginal cost. If resources are to be allocated optimally between any two outputs y_1 and y_2 then it may be shown that the ratio of the marginal revenue to the marginal cost of y_1 must be equal to the corresponding ratio for y_2.

A.4.4 Interrelation of consuming and producing sectors

It has been shown above that the consumers' rates of commodity substitution between y_k and y_j must be equal to the price ratio p_j/p_k. The price ratio is also equal to the producers' rates of product transformation between y_k and y_j. Therefore, the rates of commodity substitution must equal the rates of product transformation for all consumers, producers, and consumers.

Figure A.13 illustrates this concept and shows that for two commodities y_1 and y_2 the two curves are tangent to each other at the point representing the optimum combination of outputs.

Equation (A.7) showed that: consumers' maximize their satisfaction if the rate of commodity substitution (*RCS*) between any pair of goods equals the price ratio.

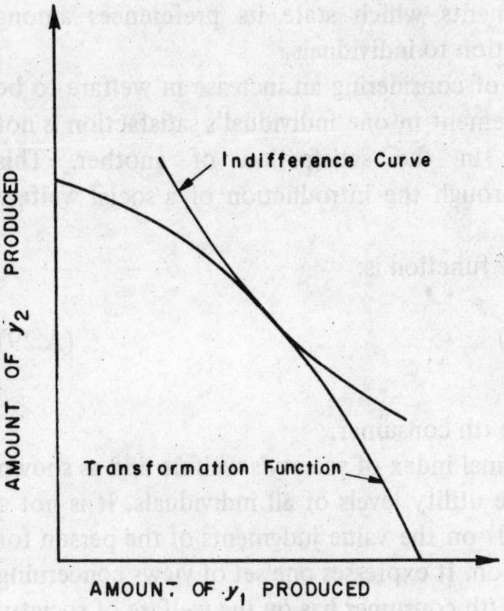

FIG. A.13. Community indifference curve and transformation function.

$$RCS = \frac{p_j}{p_k} \tag{A.26}$$

If there is perfect competition between producers then equation (A.12) showed that:

$$p_j = \frac{r}{MP_j} \quad \text{and} \quad p_k = \frac{r}{MP_k} \tag{A.27}$$

where r is the price of factor x and MP_j and MP_k are its marginal products in producing y_j and y_k.

From Eqs. (A.26) and (A.27) the following may be developed:

$$RCS = \frac{p_j}{p_k} = \frac{r/MP_j}{r/MP_k} = \frac{1/MP_j}{1/MP_k}$$

$$= \frac{\text{marginal cost of } y_j \text{ in terms of } x}{\text{marginal cost of } y_k \text{ in terms of } x}$$

$$= RPT \tag{A.28}$$

A.4.5 Social welfare functions

The analysis of community welfare in terms of Pareto optimality leaves a great deal of indeterminancy in the solution since there are an infinite number of points in the Edgeworth box diagram that are Pareto optimal. In order to judge the relative social desirability of alternative points on the contract curve, society must make additional value judgments which state its preferences among alternative ways of allocating satisfaction to individuals.

This indeterminancy is the result of considering an increase in welfare to be unambiguously defined if an improvement in one individual's satisfaction is not accompanied by a deterioration in the satisfaction of another. This indeterminancy may be removed through the introduction of a social welfare function.

The general form of a social welfare function is:

$$W = W(U_1, U_2, \ldots, U_i, \ldots, U_n) \tag{A.29}$$

where U_i = the utility index of the ith consumer.

A social welfare function is an ordinal index of society's welfare and as shown by Eq. (A.29) it is a function of the utility levels of all individuals. It is not a unique function and its form depends on the value judgments of the person for whom it is a desirable welfare function. It expresses one set of views concerning the effect that the utility level of the ith consumer has on the welfare of society.

In terms of the Edgeworth box diagram shown in Fig. A.10 the social welfare function is equivalent to ranking all points on the contract curve from the viewpoint of social preference. This means that the welfare optimum is completely defined as a result of the introduction of distributional value judgments in the form of a social welfare function.

Economists have proposed several criteria by which one can judge whether a given change in an economy is preferable socially to an existing state. The main features of some of these criteria are listed below.

1. The Kaldor criterion: A state A is socially preferable to a state B if those who gain from A can compensate the losers and still be in a better position than at B.
2. The Hicks criterion: A state A is socially preferable to a state B if those who lose from A cannot profitably bribe the gainers into not making the change from B to A.
3. The Scitovsky criterion: A state A is socially preferable to a state B if the gainers can bribe the losers into accepting the change and simultaneously the losers cannot bribe the gainers into not making the change.

A.4.6 Summary of conditions for general equilibrium

The aim of welfare economics is to assess the desirability of alternative allocations of resources. The Pareto criterion considers a reallocation of resources to be an improvement in welfare if at least one person is made better off without making anybody worse off.

The previous sections of this Appendix have shown that the following conditions must be fulfilled for Pareto optimality:

1. The rates of commodity substitution for each pair of commodities must be equal for all consumers.
2. The rates of product transformation for each pair of commodities must be equal for all producers.
3. The rates of commodity substitution must be equal to the rates of product transformtion for all pairs of commodities.

Perfect competition results in the fulfillment of these conditions for Pareto optimality and it is in this sense that perfect competition represents a welfare optimum. The Pareto criterion results in a degree of indeterminancy in the analysis. Every point on a contract curve is Pareto optimal and one cannot choose among them without the additional restrictions introduced by a social welfare function.

BIBLIOGRAPHY

J. deV. Graaff, *Theoretical Welfare Economics,* Cambridge University Press, London, 1957.
E. J. Mishan, *Welfare Economics,* Random House, London, 1964.
D. M. Winch, *Analytical Welfare Economics,* Penguin Books, Harmondsworth, Middlesex, England, 1971.

11 A STRATEGIC TRANSPORT PLANNING PROCESS

It has been suggested in Chap. 1 that transport planning is a continuous process involving an interaction between government and the community. It was also suggested in Chap. 1 that planning activities occur in ordered hierarchies with different issues being addressed at the various levels of planning. Table 1.2 provided examples of the types of decision that need to be made within the various hierarchical levels.

One major deficiency of many of the urban transport-systems studies conducted in the past has been the failure to relate this level of planning to the other levels of planning and design that both precede and follow the systems-planning level. The tendency to use the transport-systems-planning process at levels of planning and design for which it was not intended has been mentioned previously.

A number of investigators [1-3] concerned with improving the transport-systems-planning process have suggested that it should be thought of in a context similar to that shown in Fig. 11.1. The labeling of the phases in Fig. 11.1 is different from that used in Fig. 1.14 simply to reflect the terminology used in many parts of North America.

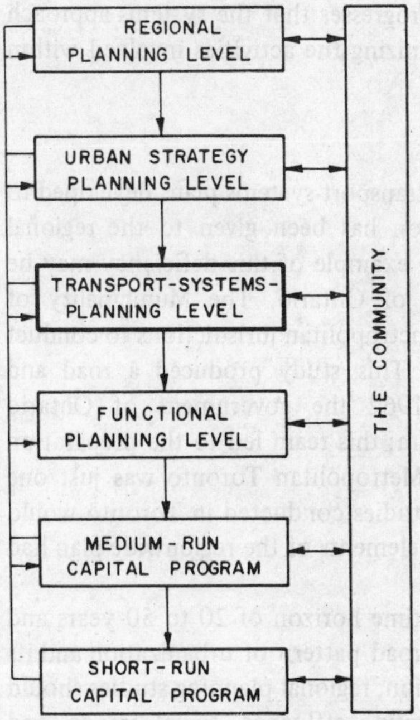

FIG. 11.1. Phases of planning.

Figure 11.1 suggests that with each planning phase there is interaction with the community as well as an interaction between all levels of planning. Recent community disenchantment with plans produced by the transport-systems-planning process have already been noted in Chap. 1. The rejection of innercity freeway plans has occurred in many cities in spite of the fact that general community agreement may have been obtained earlier, during the transport-systems-planning phase. This rejection at the program level may have been due to a change in community attitudes, or to the accumulated empirical experience of the deleterious impacts of constructed freeway sections. Transport projects rejected at the program level may be such key components of the systems plan, that the entire systems plan may have to be rejected. Rejection of a transport systems plan may also require rejection or significant modification of an urban strategic development plan.

This chapter describes each of the phases of planning shown in Fig. 11.1 in general terms and then details the urban strategy planning and systems planning levels. The overriding aim of this chapter is to demonstrate how the material introduced in Chaps. 2 to 10 might be applied in an integrated way to urban strategy planning and to transport-systems planning.

11.1 LEVELS OF PLANNING

The systems-engineering morphology was identified in Chap. 1 as being a useful technique for organizing the process of government-community interaction. It will be seen as this chapter progresses that the systems approach provides an appropriate framework for organizing the activities involved within each level of planning.

11.1.1 Regional planning level

A major weakness of many of the urban transport-systems plans developed to date has been that inadequate consideration has been given to the regional setting of the urban area being studied. An example of this deficiency may be drawn from the Toronto-Centred Region of Ontario. The Municipality of Metropolitan Toronto was one of the first metropolitan jurisdictions to conduct a major transport-systems-planning study. This study produced a road and public-transport plan for the area. In 1962 the government of Ontario established a regionwide transport-study team; this team led to the preparation of a regional development plan in which Metropolitan Toronto was just one component. The initial transport-planning studies conducted in Toronto would have been far more effective if the principal elements of the regionwide plan had been established first.

Regional planning studies should have a time horizon of 20 to 50 years and their principal emphasis should be on the broad pattern of urbanization and its impact on the natural environment. In addition, regional planning studies should explore the longrun implications of increasing affluence, social trends, and technological change. For example, in the Toronto-Centred Region planning study [4] it was noted that the relationship of the population to the region's resources and space would be altered by three types of change:

1. Expected tripling of family incomes by the end of the century
2. Increasing leisure time due to considerably shorter workweeks and longer vacations
3. Significant increases in mobility

Some indication of the scale of regional planning studies may be obtained by recognizing that the Toronto-Centred Region study area encompasses 8,600 square miles of primary interest and an area of total interest of 15,000 square miles. This is in contrast to the original transport systems planning area of about 700 square miles.

A number of goals have been established for this region of Ontario and these include the following: (1) to preserve the unique attributes of the regional landscape, (2) to minimize the urban use of productive agricultural land, (3) to minimize the pollution of water and the atmosphere, (4) to facilitate and maintain a pattern of identifiable urban communities, (5) to provide essential transportation, water, and sewer facilities at minimum cost consistent with overall benefit, (6) to develop in a manner consistent with emerging and probable future technological innovations, and (7) to develop in a manner consistent with the needs arising from social changes resulting from future economic and technological developments such as changing patterns of leisure.

Six alternative regional development proposals were prepared for the region. Two of these were trend-type plans which differed from each other in terms of the density of residential development that might occur. The other four plans involved specific structurings of urban development within the region. Broad public reaction to the development concepts was elicited and Fig. 11.2 shows the urbanized portion of the regional development plan chosen eventually by the Government of Ontario in 1970.

It is expected that the concept shown in Fig. 11.2 will accommodate 5.7 million of the area's 8 million people by year 2000. The population distribution targets shown in Fig. 11.2 would require a significant reduction in the rate of growth of Metropolitan Toronto, as well as a significant shift of the thrust of development from the west and southwest to the east.

The Toronto-Centred Region study is fairly typical of a number of broad long range regional studies performed in recent years. The major output of a regional planning study should be a set of parameters for each of the constituent urban areas along with the public policy set required to achieve the particular regional development structure selected. The parameters for each urban area should include population targets, appropriate types and levels of employment, and the probable type and phasing of regionwide services such as public utilities and transport facilities. These parameters then serve as the principal inputs to the urban strategy planning level.

11.1.2 Urban strategy planning level

A weakness of the transport systems planning process cited in Chap. 1 was its failure to reflect adequately the interaction between transport investment, land development, and the other public utilities systems plans. The principal objective of urban strategy planning is to specify alternative urban development concepts in detail sufficient to allow their transport and servicing implications to be examined. For example, the following objectives were set for a strategy planning study in Hamilton, Ontario, which is at the southwestern end of the Toronto-Centred Region plan shown in Fig. 11.2 [5]:

> The immediate requirement in the establishment of the transportation planning process is to carry out a strategic planning study to evaluate the alternative choices available to the City in terms of possible transportation systems, their interrelationships with future development patterns, and the expansion of the water and sewerage systems. The . . . study will be aimed at presenting the transportation and servicing implications of several development alternatives as a basis for public discussion and policy consideration.

In the Hamilton strategy study the alternative urban structures were developed in terms of the spatial locations of households, manufacturing, service, and retail employment. Alternative urban structures were expressed in terms of committed development and floating development. The committed development was

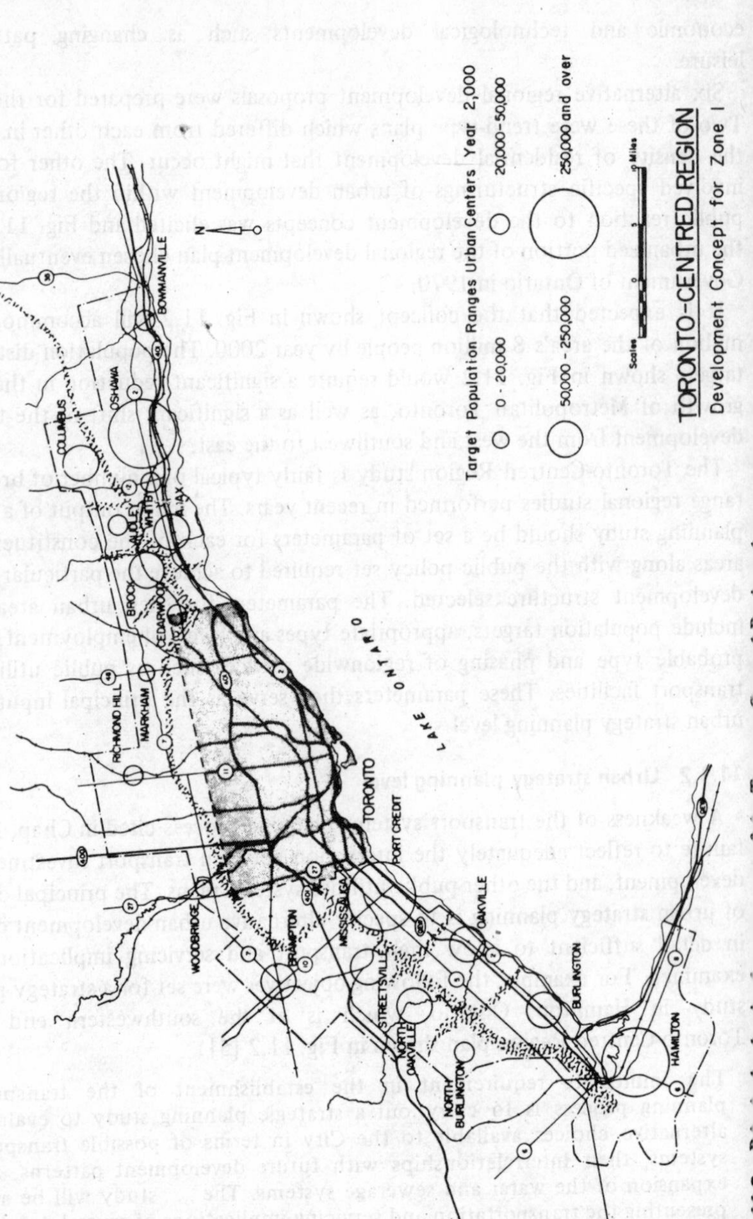
TORONTO-CENTRED REGION
Development Concept for Zone I
Target Population Ranges Urban Centers Year 2,000
0 - 20,000
20,000-50,000
50,000 - 250,000
250,000 and over
Scale
Miles
N
LAKE ONTARIO
TORONTO
PORT CREDIT
MISSISSAUGA
OAKVILLE
BURLINGTON
HAMILTON
NORTH BURLINGTON
NORTH OAKVILLE
STREETSVILLE
BRAMPTON
WOODBRIDGE
RICHMOND HILL
MARKHAM
BROCK
CEDARWOOD
AJAX
WHITBY
OSHAWA
COLUMBUS
BOWMANVILLE

defined through an analysis of the amount and location of land which was being developed or which was almost certain to be developed in the future because of existing commitments. About two-thirds of the development required for the 30-year population and employment estimates was considered to be committed development.

Eleven alternative development strategies were generated in this study and Fig. 11.3 illustrates the nature of one of these alternatives. The principal inputs to the generation of alternatives were the constraints imposed by topographic and environmental considerations. The transport implications of each alternative were estimated using a simplified version of the gravity model and the servicing implications were estimated subjectively. More-formal analyses of the Hamilton development strategies are introduced later in this chapter. The alternative concepts are then to be discussed publicly and a particular urban development strategy is to be selected.

A second example of urban strategy planning is provided from a study conducted in Canberra, Australia, in 1966 [6, 7]. Reference has been made in Chap. 9 to the urban structure plan developed for Canberra to accommodate a population of 250,000. The 1966 strategy study had the following overall objective: "To provide guidelines for the preparation of the Canberra Region of a long range development plan which will minimize the probability of significant

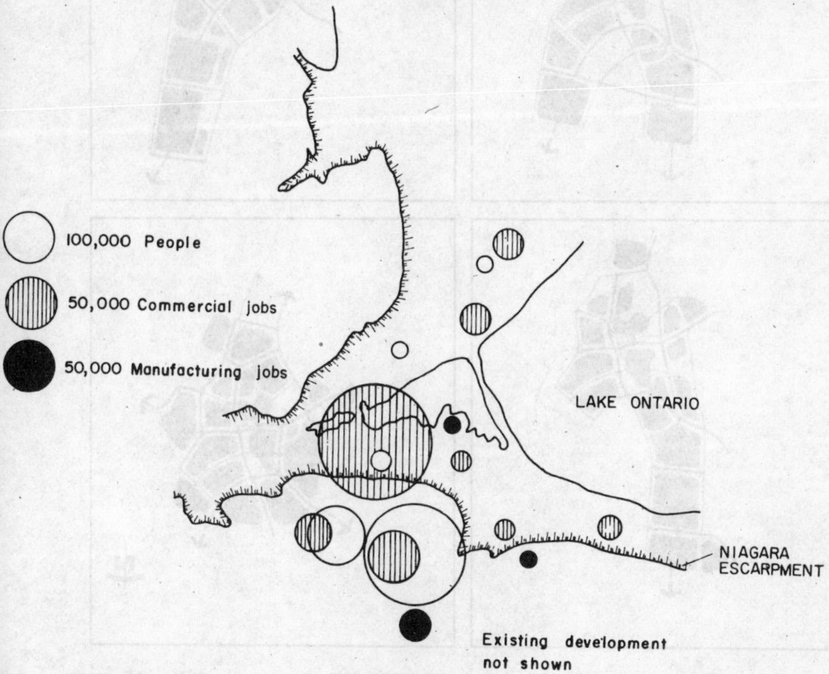

FIG. 11.3. One urban strategy concept–Hamilton, Ontario.

traffic congestion occurring as the region grows to serve populations of 500,000 persons and more."

In the Canberra study, six alternative development strategies were generated and the broad structures of four of these alternatives are shown in Fig. 11.4. The district concept described in Chap. 9 was used as the basic unit of subregional organization for each strategy. Figure 11.4 illustrates that the different alternatives were created by assembling these districts of 50,000–150,000 persons into different metropolitan structures.

The work-trip implications of each alternative development strategy were estimated using the gravity model and a simplified traffic assignment analysis. A second phase of the analysis involved a retail trade market analysis which was directed toward the identification of a viable system of district level retail trade

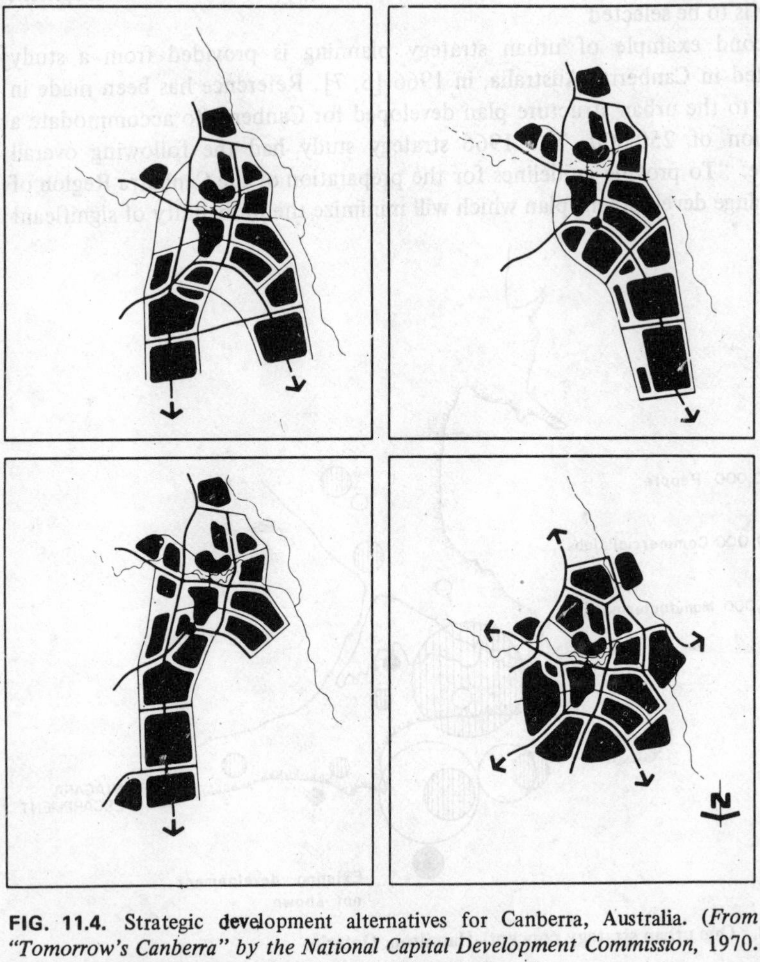

FIG. 11.4. Strategic development alternatives for Canberra, Australia. (*From "Tomorrow's Canberra" by the National Capital Development Commission,* 1970. *By permission of The Australian National University Press.*)

centers. These two analyses were carried out in an independent manner. It has been shown in Chap. 6 that the Lowry model may be used to assess these two characteristics of urbanization in a simultaneous way. Applications of the Lowry model to this type of urban strategy planning problem are described later in this chapter.

The major output of an urban strategy planning study should be a statement of the spatial distributions of population and employment in sufficient detail to allow the systems planning to proceed. The study should have accounted for the first-order interactions between the spatial distribution of development and the properties of the transport and utilities systems. The analysis of the alternatives should have proceeded to the extent that the travel and other servicing demands can be handled by feasible systems. The urban strategy concept should be accompanied by a statement of the public policy set necessary to create the intended spatial distribution of activities.

11.1.3 Transport-systems-planning level

Transport-systems plans are developed normally for 20-year periods and updated at about 5-year intervals. Transport-systems plans, as well as plans for other public systems, should be developed to the level of detail that can provide direct input to the functional planning and design studies necessary for the preparation of a 10-year capital program. It has been noted previously that much of the transport planning conducted since the 1950s has been at this level. The content of the transport-systems-planning level is developed in detail later in this chapter.

11.1.4 Functional planning and capital program levels

The output of the transport-systems-planning level is a transport plan showing the locations and capacities of the primary road and public transport networks. The purpose of the functional planning level is to break up the transport system into a number of projects and to develop the design of these projects to the extent that detailed design and construction may begin.

Capital investment programs should be prepared for a 10-year time horizon and updated annually. Most transport agencies require a capital program horizon of this length in order to complete functional and detailed designs, conduct public hearings, acquire any property, and to advertise and let contracts. In addition, the construction of primary transport facilities usually involves a sequence of projects over a 5- to 10-year period before a component of a network can function fully. Annual revision of the capital program is necessary because of budget constraints, delays in property acquisition, and so on.

11.2 URBAN STRATEGY PLANNING

The aims of urban strategy planning have been established previously; they include estimating the servicing implications of alternative development strategies, exploring the viability of certain key spatial elements of the strategies, and examining the probable impact of the different strategies on the existing urban area. The approach to urban strategy planning developed in this section is structured according to the systems approach described in Chap. 1.

11.2.1 Typical objectives

In Chap. 1 it was emphasized that the objectives set for a system provide a basis for the generation of alternative plans as well as for their evaluation. The basis for the setting of these objectives are the planning issues that exist in a particular community. During the 1960s there was a belief within the various planning professions that comprehensive objectives could be set and that these objectives could provide a basis for the formal evaluation of the alternative systems studied by planning teams.

A number of urban strategy planning studies have demonstrated that such an approach is not feasible. A useful approach, however, is for the planning team to generate a range of alternative concepts and to explore the implications of these alternatives through technical analyses and public participation and debate. An important contribution to this procedure is the articulation of a common set of objectives to guide the planning team.

Objectives at this level of planning can be specified only in very general terms and a typical set of objectives for an urban strategy study might be:

1. To minimize the adverse impacts of future development on the existing urban area; e.g., street widenings and innercity freeway construction.
2. To minimize the deleterious effects of future development on the natural environment; e.g., stream pollution and the destruction of valued natural features.
3. To ensure that basic employment is located properly throughout the urban area in order to obtain suburban area compatibility between employment and housing.
4. To ensure that a viable system of population-serving employment centers develops that is compatible with the distribution of population.
5. To ensure that future development can be serviced adequately and economically.

Figure 11.5 shows the broad flow of activities involved in urban strategy planning and illustrates the role that objectives of the type just mentioned play in this process. The objectives are used along with estimates of future population and employment to generate a number of alternative sketch plans which are then subject to more-formal analyses. An important input to the development of the alternative sketch plans are any constraints that might be created by the natural environment.

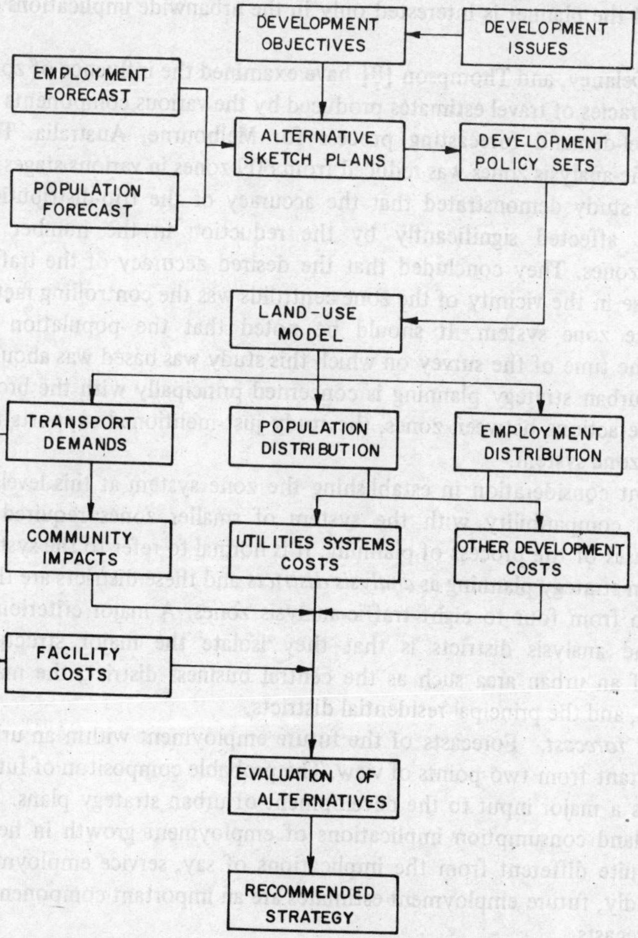

FIG. 11.5. Activities involved in urban strategy planning.

11.2.2 Strategy inputs

Figure 11.5 suggests that the principal inputs to the strategy concepts are the expected population and employment totals that must be accommodated by any strategy plan. An important consideration at this stage of strategy planning is the scale of the zone system to be used for the study.

Size of analysis zones. A relatively coarse analysis zone system is used for urban strategy planning. The Hamilton strategy study referred to previously used a 28-zone system for an horizon-year population of 1 million. The Canberra strategy study used a 14-zone system for a target population also of 1 million. The principal reason for using a small number of analysis zones in strategy planning is that at this stage, development policies may be expressed only in broad terms and the planner is interested only in the urbanwide implications of these policies.

Wildermuth, Delaney, and Thompson [8] have examined the influence of zone size on the accuracies of travel estimates produced by the various components of the urban travel-demand forecasting process for Melbourne, Australia. The number of traffic-analysis zones was reduced from 609 zones in various stages to 40 zones. This study demonstrated that the accuracy of the trip-distribution phase was not affected significantly by the reduction in the number of traffic-analysis zones. They concluded that the desired accuracy of the traffic assignment phase in the vicinity of the zone centroids was the controlling factor in selecting the zone system. It should be noted that the population of Melbourne at the time of the survey on which this study was based was about 2 million. Since urban strategy planning is concerned principally with the broad urban scale interactions between zones, the study just mentioned supports the use of a coarse zone system.

One important consideration in establishing the zone system at this level of planning is its compatibility with the system of smaller zones required in subsequent phases of the process of planning. It is normal to refer to the system of zones used in strategy planning as *analysis districts* and these districts are then subdivided into from four to eight traffic-analysis zones. A major criterion in establishing the analysis districts is that they isolate the major structural components of an urban area such as the central business district, the major industrial areas, and the principal residential districts.

Employment forecast. Forecasts of the future employment within an urban area are important from two points of view. The probable compositon of future employment is a major input to the development of urban strategy plans. The location and land consumption implications of employment growth in heavy industries is quite different from the implications of say, service employment growth. Secondly, future employment estimates are an important component of population forecasts.

In estimating future employment it is important to maintain the dichotomy between basic employment and service employment introduced in Chap. 6. The following equation has been introduced in Chap. 6:

$$e = e^b + e^s \tag{11.1}$$

and Eq. (11.1) may be rewritten as follows:

$$e = \frac{e^b}{1 - (e^s/e)} \tag{11.2}$$

where Eq. (11.2) represents the traditional expression of economic base theory.

The form of Eq. (11.2) is based on the notion that the ratio e^s/e is constant, or at least may be forecast. That is, Eq. (11.2) is based on the idea that a constant proportion of total employment is absorbed by nonbasic industries. If this assumption holds, or if the trend in this ratio is regular, then the problem of estimating total employment is reduced to one of estimating the basic employment magnitude.

Many arguments have been advanced to suggest that this forecasting process is too simplistic. It has been argued that an urban region may continue to grow even if its exports do not increase. Changes in productivity, changes in consumption patterns, private and government investment activity in an urban area, may all create employment growth without increasing the exports from a region. However, most of these arguments may be refuted on the basis of their extremely narrow interpretation of exports. For example, universities do not create a measurable flow of exports to areas outside of the communities within which they are located. However, with most universities the resources required to support faculty, staff, and facilities are derived from sources external to the communities within which they are located.

Table 11.1 shows the relationship between basic employment and population-serving employment developed in a number of communities in several countries. Some of the variations between the ratios reported in Table 11.1 are due to differences in the definitions of basic and service employment between studies.

In many employment studies the future employment magnitudes have been developed subjectively. Each economic sector is examined separately and probable trends in employment in that sector are estimated.

Some progress has been made with the use of input-output tables and other econometric techniques for estimating the regional shares of employment

Table 11.1. Components of employment

Area	Year	Employment			e^s/e
		Total	Basic	Service	
England					
Reading	1963	63,000	33,000	30,000	0.476
Stevenage	1966	27,000	19,600	7,400	0.274
Hook	2000	44,000	25,800	18,200	0.414
Milton Keynes	2000	120,000	72,100	47,900	0.400
Australia					
Canberra	2000	370,000	265,000	105,000	0.284
Canada					
Hamilton	1961	125,500	72,860	52,640	0.419
	2000	472,450	278,700	193,750	0.410

estimated for larger regions such as provinces and states. However, many difficulties still exist in using these techniques directly. Forecasts of future employment in a region may be converted to population estimates by multiplying by the inverse of the labor participation rate expected for the future time horizon.

Population forecast. The change in population in an urban area depends on three principal factors which are: the birth rate, the death rate, and the net migration to or from the area.

A number of population forecasting methods exist and these include: trend projection methods, ratio and correlation methods, and the cohort-survival method.

Trend projection methods involve an extrapolation of population with time and the differences between the methods occur in the structure of the equation either fitted to the data, or implied by the subjective extrapolation of the data. Typical functions that have been used are linear, exponential, and logistic functions. Figure 11.6 shows the growth in population that has occurred in Waterloo County, Ontario, since 1901. The population of the County increased steadily from the early 1800s, when the area was settled by the Pennsylvania Dutch, until about 1951. In 1951 there was an acceleration in this rate of growth due to industrial expansion and university growth. Linear and quadratic growth functions have been fitted to the observed data from 1946 and these

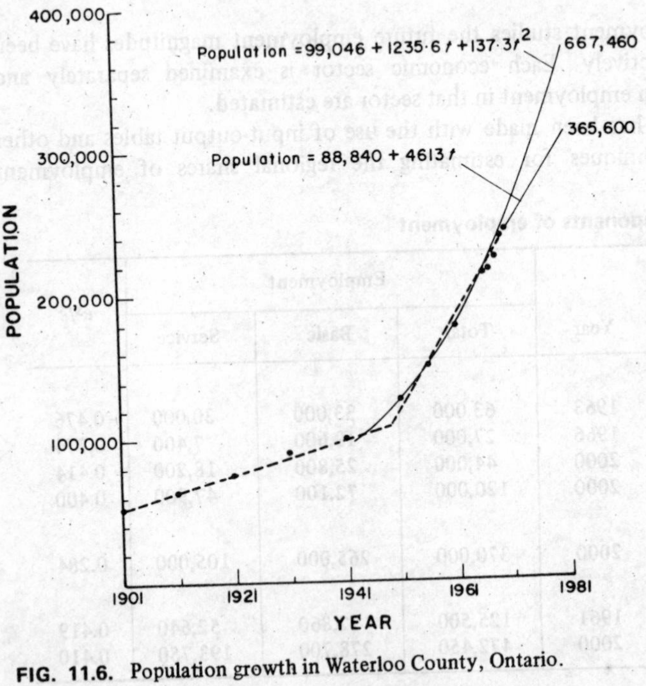

FIG. 11.6. Population growth in Waterloo County, Ontario.

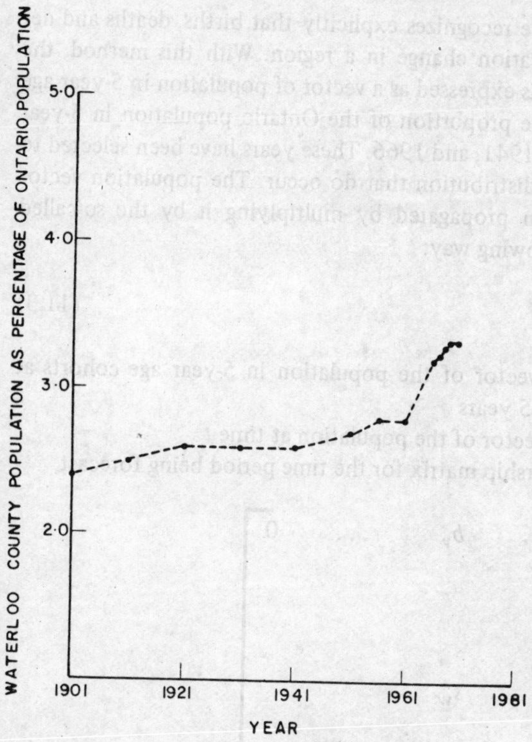

FIG. 11.7. Trend in ratio of Waterloo County population/Ontario population.

relationships are shown in Fig. 11.6. This diagram illustrates the dangers of population extrapolation where a difference of some 300,000 in the 1981 population is obtained through the use of the two forecasting equations.

The principal weakness of the trend projection approach is the assumption that the determinants of past population change will operate with the same intensity over the forecast period. The population history shown in Fig. 11.6 provides an excellent illustration of these dangers.

Ratio and correlation methods rely on the assumption that there is a relatively stable relationship between the population of an urban area and the region within which the area is located. The ratio of the population of the area and the region is estimated for future years, and this ratio is then used along with the population estimated for the region in order to estimate the future urban area population. Figure 11.7 shows the trend in the ratio of the Waterloo County population to the Ontario population. The pre-1961 variation is not quite as stable as is suggested by the graph since only the 10-year points are shown. There is a similar difficulty in identifying the appropriate ratio to use as there is to the identification of a suitable trend function.

The cohort-survival technique recognizes explicitly that births, deaths and net migration influence the population change in a region. With this method, the existing population of an area is expressed as a vector of population in 5-year age cohorts. Figure 11.8 shows the proportion of the Ontario population in 5-year age cohorts by sex for 1911, 1941, and 1966. These years have been selected to illustrate the changes in age distribution that do occur. The population vector for a given base year is then propagated by multiplying it by the so-called *survivorship matrix* in the following way:

$$p(t+5) = p(t)S \tag{11.3}$$

where $p(t+5)$ = a column vector of the population in 5-year age cohorts at time t plus 5 years
$p(t)$ = a column vector of the population at time t
S = the survivorship matrix for the time period being forecast

$$S = \begin{bmatrix} 0 & 0 & \cdots & b_v & \cdots & 0 \\ s_1 & & & & & \\ & s_2 & & & & \\ & & \ddots & & & \\ & & & s_w & & \\ & & & & \ddots & \\ & & & & s_n & 0 \end{bmatrix}$$

where b_v = the age-specific birth rate for the vth age cohort
s_w = the age-specific probabilities of survival for the wth age cohort

That is, the survivorship matrix has zeros everywhere except in those elements of the first row which represent the childbearing-age cohorts, and along the subdiagonal.

Figure 11.9 shows trends in the age-specific fertility and mortality rates for selected age cohorts in Ontario. The sharp drop in the fertility rates for the 20–24 and 30–34 age cohorts that began in 1963 should be noted. The significant decline in the infant mortality rate that has occurred since 1921 should also be noted in Fig. 11.9.

A critical component of the population forecast for an urban area is the net migration. This is an extremely difficult factor to forecast and is related closely to the system of economic opportunities that exists in an entire nation. Rogers [9] and others have explored the problems of multiregional population change but it is beyond the scope of this book to explore this information. Population forecasting methods are discussed in detail in Refs. [10–12].

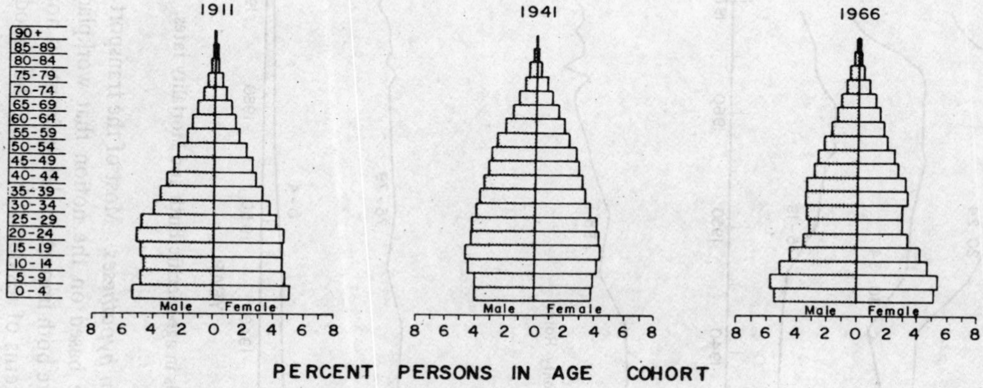

FIG. 11.8. Age distribution profiles for selected years–Ontario.

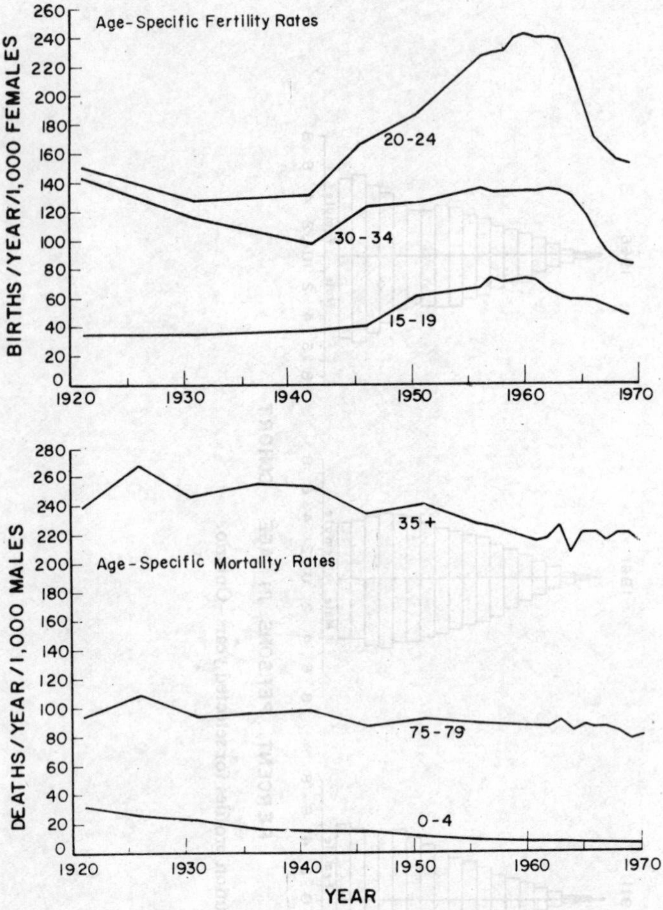

FIG. 11.9. Ontario trends in age-specific Birth and Mortality rates.

Urban activity system hypotheses. Most of the transport and land-use models developed to date are based on the notion that workplace location, and the overall rate of work, are both important determinants of household location and the urban activity patterns of residents. In using these models to analyze future states it is normal to assume that urban activity patterns will remain essentially invariant over the planning horizon. It has been mentioned previously in connection with the Toronto-Centred Region plan that both affluence and leisure time would increase significantly by year 2000.

In developing alternative urban strategy plans, explicit judgments must be made about the probable urban activity systems that might operate in future years. Changes in affluence and leisure time might have an important influence on city structure and the relationships between the elements.

11.2.3 Output information required

In the introduction to this section the aims of urban strategy planning were established as estimating the servicing requirements of alternative development strategies, as exploring the viability of certain key spatial elements of the strategies and of examining the probable impact of different strategies on the existing urban area. It is essential at this stage, that the planner have a clear understanding of the output information required from the analysis phase of urban strategy planning.

The first set of information required are the spatial distributions of population and employment that are likely to result from the adoption of a particular public policy set. These activity distributions may then be converted to peak period transport demands in the principal corridors of the area. The demands for water supply and sewage disposal are also related directly to the distributions of population and employment and the densities of these activities.

The probable impacts of the peak period travel demands in each corridor must then be assessed. This may be accomplished by a simplified traffic assignment to facilities in a corridor along with an assessment of the traffic-related environmental capacities of the corridors. The spatial distributions of demands for each of the utilities may be used to design feasible trunk services systems and to estimate the costs of these systems.

Finally, the analysis should provide an indication of the viability of the proposed system of district-level population-serving centers as well as the regional center. The example introduced later in this section will indicate how each of these groups of output information may be derived for each urban strategy alternative.

11.2.4 Generation of alternatives

The activities involved in urban strategy planning, which have been illustrated in Fig. 11.5, suggest that the specification of the development objectives, and the population and employment forecasts, may be used to generate a set of alternative sketch plans. This same diagram also indicates that the pertinent features of these sketch plans must be formulated as a set of development policies that can be manipulated by urban governments in some way. That is, there is little point in suggesting a particular spatial distribution of population unless an urban government has the leverage to obtain this population distribution.

The Lowry model has been advanced in Chap. 6 as a useful technique for estimating some of the probable spatial properties of urban areas. Figure 11.10 illustrates the broad groups of policies that may be tested by the Lowry model and these include:

1. The locations of employment in basic industries such as industrial parks, major institutions, etc.

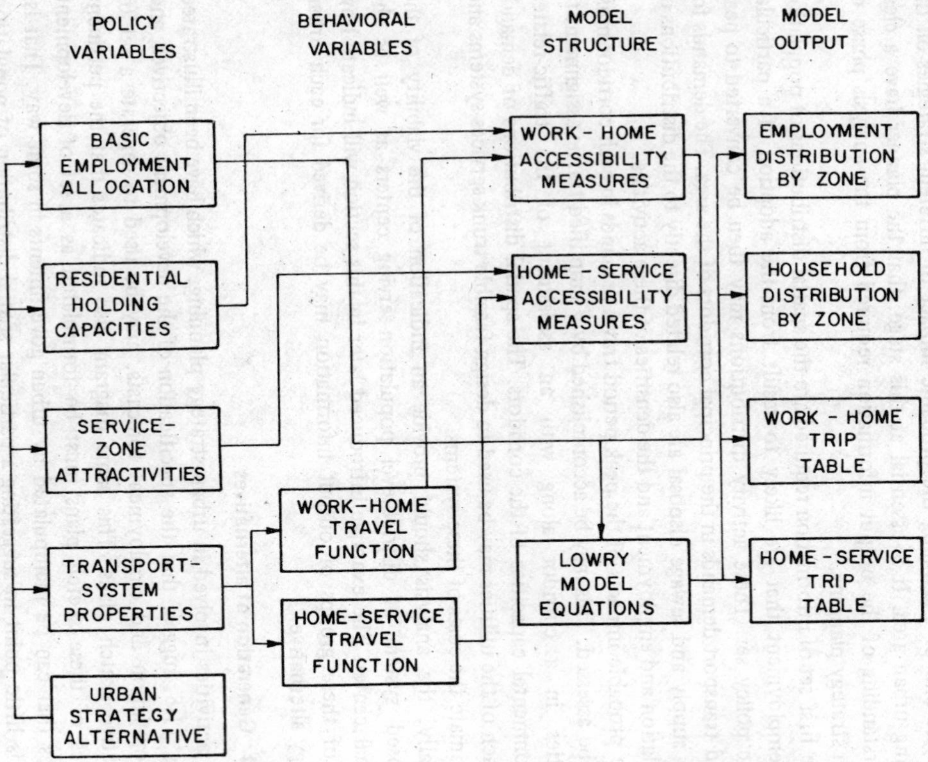

FIG. 11.10. Use of Lowry model to analyze urban strategy alternatives.

2. The locations of major residential areas along with alternative development densities for these areas
3. The locations at which the principal aggregations of service employment are to be allowed to develop
4. The locations of the primary transport-system components

It is sufficient to reiterate in connection with Fig. 11.10 that the Lowry model will estimate for each alternative set of development policies the locations of service employment and households, the homebased work- and service-trip matrices. The public policy variables just mentioned have been used in many urban areas to manipulate the pattern of urban development. Many municipalities have developed industrial parks and through this have had an important impact on the location of new industries as well as the relocation of older industries. Residential development locations and densities are controlled through the location and phasing of public utilities systems and zoning. In addition, the locations of major shopping centers are controlled carefully in many municipalities to ensure that a viable system of centers develops. Finally, the location of primary transport system components such as freeways and transit facilities has an important influence on land development. The importance of transport investment on urban development varies significantly between jurisdictions depending on the extent to which the other public policy variables are used.

11.2.5 Analysis of alternatives

Figure 11.3 has illustrated one of the urban development strategies proposed for Hamilton, Ontario. If the Lowry model is to be used to explore some of the spatial implications of this strategy, then the way in which this sketch plan had to be expressed as a public policy set was outlined in the previous section. Table 11.2 shows the allocations of population, basic employment, and service employment that are desired under this development strategy. It is the purpose of this section to describe the way in which the Lowry model may be used to explore the implications of this development concept.

Lowry model formulation. The Lowry model equations have been introduced in Chap. 6 and in the analysis described in this section a version of the model with constrained population allocations to residential zones is used. The relevant equations from Chap. 6 are:

$$p = eA \tag{6.1}$$

$$e^s = pB \tag{6.2}$$

$$e = e^b + e^s \tag{6.3}$$

Table 11.2. Desired population and employment distributions

Zone no.	Employment		Population
	Basic	Service	
1	26,040	26,990	91,470
2	3,370	2,750	25,370
3	3,890	1,350	18,690
4	540	320	4,740
5	400	230	5,180
6	400	720	11,840
7	50	100	2,980
8	2,430	820	10,930
9	340	770	13,100
10	5,840	5,430	18,370
11	10,270	2,930	24,100
12	51,250	60,550	68,560
13	7,660	9,370	47,930
14	11,660	16,150	156,560
15	28,350	0	0
16	5,800	8,390	43,770
17	5,350	7,110	32,900
18	3,720	4,540	39,840
19	13,650	18,880	161,220
20	31,610	330	4,780
21	5,730	7,730	53,340
22	17,990	12,880	60,760
23	160	360	5,200
24	30,480	1,100	25,220
25	3,300	3,200	55,710
26	10,180	340	7,640
27	70	170	3,200
28	160	220	6,600
Total	280,690	193,730	1,000,000

$$a_{ij}^* = \frac{h_j^* f_{ij}{}^w}{\sum_j h_j^* f_{ij}{}^w} \qquad (6.10)$$

$$h_j^* = h_j \frac{h_j}{p_j} \qquad (6.11)$$

$$b_{ij}' = \frac{s_i f_{ij}{}^s}{\sum_i s_i f_{ij}{}^s} \qquad (6.7)$$

It has been pointed out in Chap. 6 that the above set of equations may be iterated until a stable codistribution of population and employment is obtained. The home-based work- and service-trip tables may be obtained from:

$$T^w = WA' \tag{6.14}$$

$$T^{sr} = RB^{r'} \tag{6.15}$$

Example. The population targets shown in Table 11.2 may be interpreted as population-holding capacities for the purposes of this example. The assumption is that the appropriate servicing policies and zoning regulations will be adopted to produce the spatial distribution of residential opportunities given in Table 11.2. The h_j of Eq. (6.11) was set equal to the populations of Table 11.2. In the initial run of the model, s_i of Eq. (6.7) was set equal to the population-serving employment magnitudes shown in Table 11.2. In subsequent iterations of the equation set, s_i was set equal to the population-serving employment magnitudes allocated in the prior iteration. The travel times used in the analysis were derived from the regionwide facilities that are expected to exist in the horizon year. The travel-time factor functions used were derived from an earlier calibration of the Lowry model to base-year conditions.

Figure 11.11 illustrates the population allocated to residential zones on the basis of the travel-time properties of the region only, without regard to the population-holding capacities of the zones. Zones 14 and 19 are the zones in

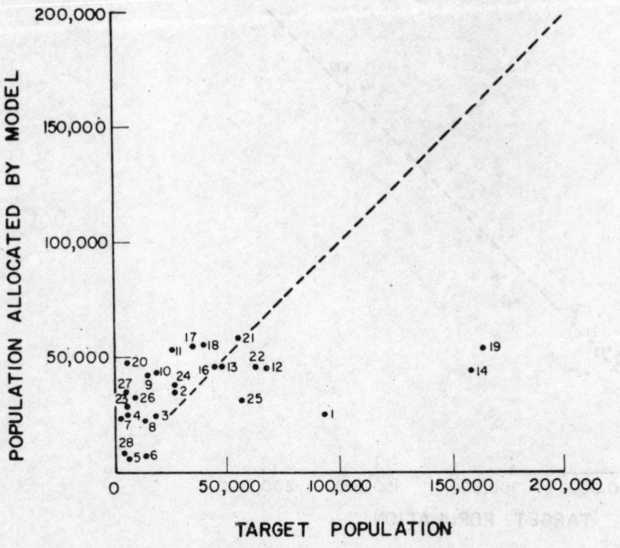

FIG. 11.11. Model allocated vs. target populations for allocations on travel-time properties only.

which major population growths are desired and Fig. 11.11 indicates that the population targets for these zones are drastically underallocated. This is simply a reflection of the fact that these zones are located on top of the Niagara Escarpment and access is rather circuitous. One approach to this problem would be to explore alternative transport policies directed toward improving the accessibilities of these zones. A second approach would be to examine alternative distributions of basic employment geared to increasing the population demand in these zones. That is, in terms of Fig. 11.10 the policy set could be revised by making the assumption that population will allocate in an unconstrained way and that basic employment locations and transport-system variables must be manipulated in order to achieve the target population allocations.

Figure 11.12 shows the population allocation achieved by three iterations of the population allocation constraint technique defined in Eqs. (6.10) and (6.11). Figure 11.13 shows the distribution of service employment demand produced by the population allocation shown in Fig. 11.12. The residential constraint procedure had the effect of redistributing the excess demand for location in inner residential areas to the peripheral residential areas where population could still be accommodated. The information presented in Fig. 11.13 demonstrates that the population-serving employment targets expressed in the development strategy being explored would not likely be realized under natural market forces. This observation suggests that the population-serving employment location policy contained within the strategy being studied should be revised. A

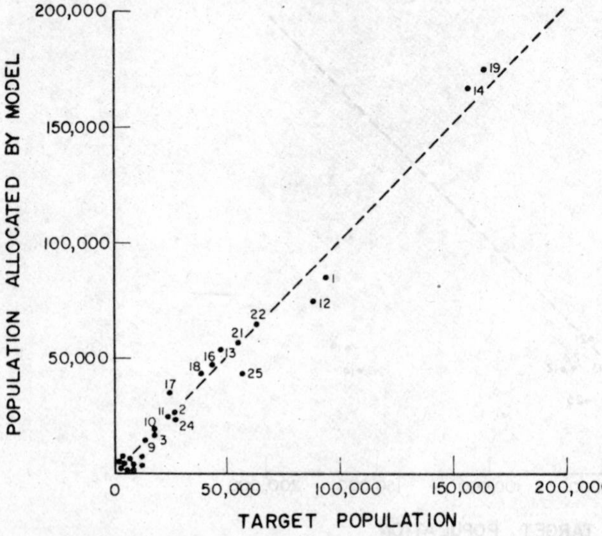

FIG. 11.12. Model allocated vs. target population for allocations constrained to holding capacities.

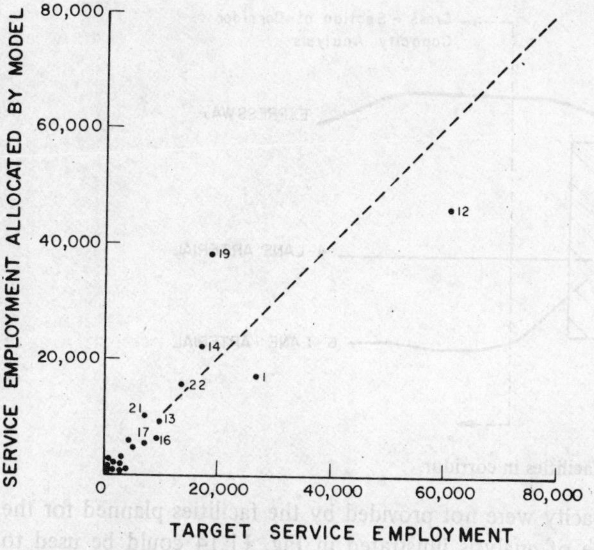

FIG. 11.13. Model allocated vs. target service employment for constrained population allocations.

more-refined analysis of the system of population-serving employment centers could be conducted by disaggregating service employment into a number of categories such as institutional, personal service, convenience, comparison goods shopping, and so on. However, at the urban strategy planning level it is difficult to justify other than a very coarse analysis.

The trip matrices for the home-based work and service trips are provided directly by the above analysis through the use of Eqs. (6.14) and (6.15). The home-based work-trip matrix may be used for corridor analyses of the probable impacts of peak-period travel demands. Consider the corridor in Fig. 11.3 which runs from the east between Lake Ontario and the Niagara Escarpment to the central area of Hamilton. Figure 11.14 shows the principal road facilities that are expected in this corridor. The peak-hour inbound demand that has been estimated in this corridor is just less than 6,000 vehicles per hour. This volume was obtained by converting the appropriate entires of the home-based trip matrix to peak-hour demands and deducting from this estimate the probable trips by public transport.

Figure 11.15 shows the travel-time–traffic-volume relationships for each of the three facilities at the cross-section indicated in Fig. 11.14. The peak-hour volumes that might be expected on each of these facilities may be estimated by assigning traffic to each facility in such a way that the average speed on each facility is equal. Figure 11.15 indicates the distribution of traffic volumes that would satisfy the inbound corridor demand and demonstrates that the average speed of travel along the corridor is likely to be about 20 miles per hour.

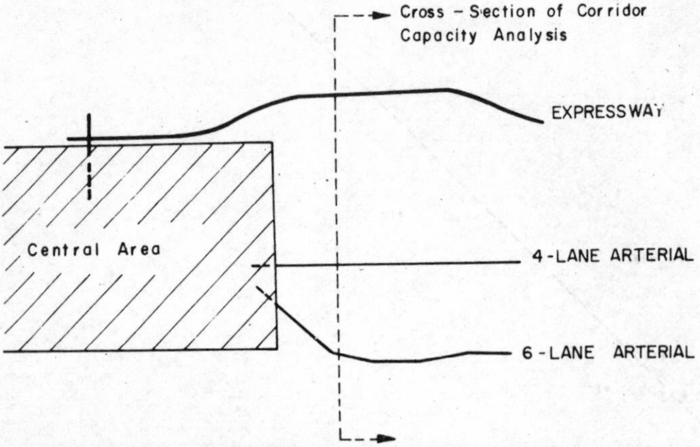

FIG. 11.14. Major road facilities in corridor.

If adequate road capacity were not provided by the facilities planned for the corridor, then the type of analysis illustrated in Fig. 11.14 could be used to determine the combinations of road capacities required to satisfy the expected demands. Or alternatively, the increase in public-transport patronage that would be required to provide sufficient corridor capacity if additional road capacity was not to be provided.

A second stage of the corridor analysis is to explore the likely environmental impacts of the traffic volumes assigned to the mix of facilities within the corridor. Sharpe and Maxman [13] have outlined an approach for the calculation of the environmental capacities of road networks. This approach followed the tradition of the earlier British studies in that noise, air pollution, and pedestrian safety were identified as the critical environmental factors. Table 11.3 illustrates the traffic volume-related environmental capacities of roads with different abutting land uses. The environmental capacity is shown in terms of the average daily traffic volume and the controlling environmental impact factor is also identified in the table.

A corridor-by-corridor analysis of the travel demands created by each urban strategy alternative is an essential phase of this level of planning. If adequate capacity cannot be provided within each corridor, then the feasibility of a development strategy is compromised severely. Reference has already been made to the fact that transport-system plans have had to be abandoned, because adverse public reaction prevented the construction of a key element of a systems plan.

11.2.6 Evaluation of alternatives

It has been suggested earlier that at the urban strategy planning level the evaluation of alternative strategies cannot be carried out formally. The planning team can highlight the principal findings of the analyses but the evalution must

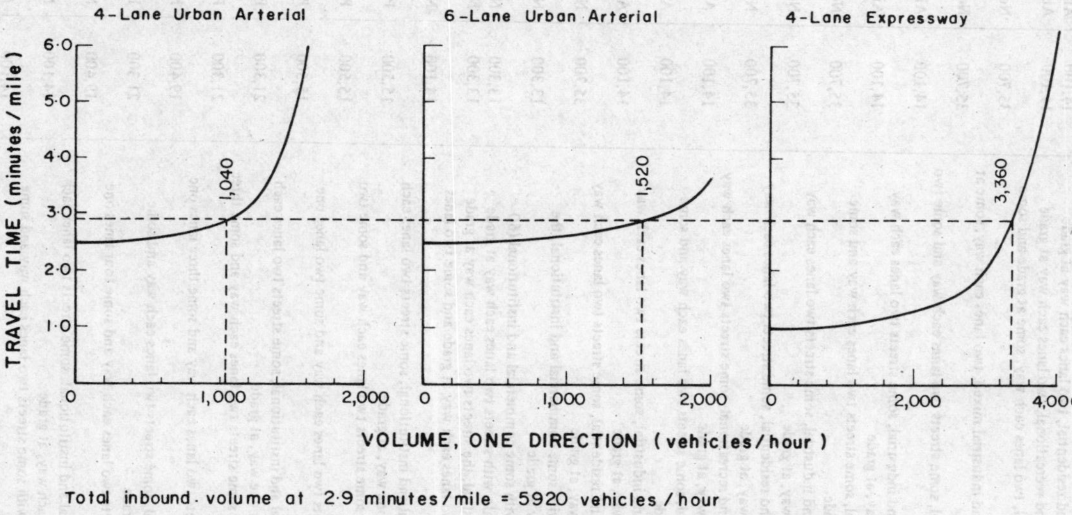

FIG. 11.15. Assignment of traffic to facilities within corridor to produce equal speeds. Total inbound volume at 2.9 minutes/mile = 5,920 vehicles/hour.

Table 11.3. Environmental capacities of streets

Prototype characteristics	Environmental capacity (ADT)*	Controlling environmental factor
Commercial and institutional, two lanes each way at grade	14,100	Air pollution
Commercial, institutional, and industrial mixed, two lanes each way at grade	35,700	Noise
Commercial, institutional, and residential, two lanes each way at grade	14,100	Air pollution
Commercial, institutional, and recreational, two lanes each way at grade	14,100	Air pollution
Commercial and institutional, two lanes each way, some at grade and some elevated	35,700	Noise
Commercial, institutional, and industrial mixed, two lanes each way, some at grade and some elevated	35,700	Noise
Commercial and institutional, some streets two lanes each way and some two lanes one way, at grade	14,100	Air pollution
Commercial, institutional, and industrial, some streets two lanes each way and some two lanes one way, at grade	14,100	Air pollution
Commercial and institutional, some streets two lanes each way and some three lanes one way, at grade	35,700	Noise
Commercial, institutional, and industrial, some streets two lanes each way and some three lanes one way, at grade	35,700	Noise
Commercial, institutional, and residential, some streets two lanes each way and some three lanes one way, at grade	35,700	Noise
Commercial, institutional, and recreational, some streets two lanes each way and some three lanes one way, at grade	14,100	Air pollution
Commercial and institutional, some streets two lanes each way and some four lanes one way, at grade	14,100	Air pollution
Commercial, institutional, and industrial, some streets two lanes each way and some four lanes one way, at grade	14,100	Air pollution
Commercial, institutional, and residential, some streets two lanes each way and some four lanes one way, at grade	35,700	Noise
Predominantly residential with some commercial and institutional, the streets two lanes each way at grade	13,300	Noise
Predominantly residential with some commercial and institutional (60 percent or more residential), with streets two lanes each way at grade	13,300	Noise
Residential with some industrial, the streets two lanes each way at grade	13,300	Noise
Residential, some streets two lanes each way at grade and some two lanes each way elevated	14,100	Noise
Residential with commercial and institutional, some streets two lanes each way and some two lanes one way, at grade	15,500	Public safety
Residential with industrial, some streets two lanes each way and some two lanes one way, at grade	15,500	Public safety
Residential with some streets two lanes each way and some two lanes one way, at grade	15,500	Public safety
Residential with commercial and institutional, some streets two lanes each way and some three lanes one way, at grade	21,300	Public safety
Residential with industrial, some streets two lanes each way and some three lanes one way, at grade	21,300	Public safety
Residential with some streets two lanes each way and some three lanes one way, at grade	19,400	Noise
Residential and recreational, some streets two lanes each way and some three lanes one way, at grade	21,300	Public safety
Residential with most streets two lanes each way and some four lanes one way, at grade	19,400	Noise
Residential with commercial and institutional, some streets two lanes each way and some one lane each way, at grade	14,100	Noise
Residential and industrial with some streets two lanes each way and some one lane each way	14,100	Noise
Residential with most streets two lanes each way and some one lane each way	14,100	Noise
Residential with streets two lanes and three lanes each way, at grade	13,300	Noise
Residential with some commercial and institutional, the streets two lanes each way at grade and three lanes each way elevated	21,300	Public safety
Residential with industrial, the streets two lanes each way at grade and three lanes each way elevated	21,300	Public safety

*Average daily traffic (volume).

involve comprehensive public debate. Desjardins [14] has noted in connection with the Hamilton strategy study that the following factors were the most important during the evaluation phase:

1. Social implications: Disruption of existing neighborhoods was established as the most-important factor and was measured by the number of families that would have to be displaced in a particular corridor to accommodate the travel demands created by a particular strategy.
2. Environmental implications: Air and noise pollution and the potential conflict with unique environmental features such as conservation areas and the Niagara Escarpment were the indicators used to convey the environmental implications of each strategy.
3. Economic implications: The capital, operating, and maintenance costs of the public systems required by each strategy were used to describe the relative economic implications of each strategy.
4. Accessibility implications: An important issue in this strategy study was the maintenance and enhancement of the Hamilton central business district as the regional center; the peak-hour travel times to the central area from the various parts of each of the strategies were used as the indicator of central area accessibility.

Some of the principles derived from models of the political process which have been described in the latter part of Chap. 10 may be used to assist in the structuring of public debate and participation. Of particular importance is the education of the public as to the nature of the issues to be resolved, and secondly, the potential tradeoffs between the issues that have to be made through public debate.

11.3 URBAN TRANSPORT-SYSTEMS PLANNING

The information provided by the urban strategy planning phase is an internally consistent spatial allocation of population and employment for a chosen public policy set. This public policy set includes some broad statements about the properties of the transport system largely in terms of expected travel times between various parts of the urban area. The travel-demand analysis conducted at the urban strategy level is relatively crude and is developed to an extent just sufficient to assess the probable impacts of future travel demands in each of the principal corridors of the existing urban area.

The purpose of urban transport-systems planning is to dimension the transport systems properties to the point where they may be used as a basis for functional planning and design and for long range capital programming. Creighton Hamburg [15] have defined urban strategic transport planning in the following way: "Strategic transportation planning for urban areas is defined as the process of determining a recommended long range level of investment in transportation, the division of investment between major modes of travel (i.e., between expressways, arterials and transit), the location of corridors for expressways and rail rapid transit facilities (or in smaller urban areas the locations of arterials) and the general timing and sequence of investments."

The urban transport-planning process which has been used in most studies has been described in Chap. 1 and the transport analysis methods imbedded in this process have been outlined in Chaps. 2 to 5. It has been suggested earlier in this book that these analysis methods may be regarded as conditional forecasting methods in that they require as input information a completely specified spatial allocation of land use. This section examines an adaptation of the Lowry model for transport systems planning. It represents a natural extension of the analyses conducted at the urban strategy planning level.

11.3.1 Transport-system objectives

Urban transport systems have three broad classes of impacts that must be reflected in the objectives set for the system and these are: the impact on land development patterns, the environmental impacts, and the impacts on transport-system users.

The first-order impacts of transport services and other public utilities on land development are accounted for at the urban strategy planning level. However, there are second-order impacts of transport on urban activity patterns that must be accounted for and these effects become apparent when an urban area is disaggregated into a number of socioeconomic groups. Kassoff and Deutschman [16] have noted in connection with the New York metropolitan region that:

> The concentration of low-income households in the core areas of the nation's cities, coupled with a growing trend towards dispersion of employment opportunities, particularly in the unskilled and semiskilled categories, is resulting in a growing spatial mis-match of low-income residential areas and the location of available jobs. The problem is compounded by the general reliance of poverty-level households on public transport systems that typically do not provide adequate access to outlying suburban areas.

The environmental impacts of transport facilities were also assessed in a relatively coarse way in the urban strategy planning level. The environmental impacts of transport facilities must be explored in more detail. It has been suggested in Chap. 9 that a concept useful for transport systems planning is the environmental area concept. With this concept, environmental standards are set.

The impacts of transport investment normally perceived by the user are the changes in operating costs, travel safety, and travel time. The nature of these impacts has been discussed in some detail in Chap. 10.

Objectives typical of those which might be set during the transport systems planning phase include:

1. To develop a transport system with a range of services that caters to all socioeconomic groups in an urban area, and which is compatible with the

residential, employment and other urban opportunities available to these groups
2. To create a transport system that has satisfactory environmental impacts and which is compatible with the planning principles embodied in the land-use plan
3. To ensure that operating, accident, and time costs of the transport-system users are minimized
4. To ensure that the resource costs necessary for the construction, operation, and maintenance of the system are minimized

11.3.2 Transport-system inputs

The land-use arrangement selected at the urban strategy planning level is specified in terms of a relatively coarse system of zones. While some evidence has been introduced previously to show that the use of a coarse zone system has little impact on the accuracy of trip distribution estimates, the number of zones was shown to influence the accuracies of other phases of the travel analysis. A finer zone system must be used at the transport systems level and activity estimates must be developed for each zone.

Size of analysis zones. The following guidelines are used in establishing a system of traffic analysis zones for the typical transport systems planning study:

1. Zone boundaries should be compatible with census tract boundaries in order that census information can be used easily.
2. Principal geographic and physical barriers to travel and land development such as rivers, escarpments, rail lines, canals, freeways, etc., are useful zone boundaries.
3. Major arterial streets do not always provide reasonable zone boundaries as the types of land use on either side of the streets are usually similar and should be contained within the same zone.
4. The physical location of the zone centroid should be identifiable as travel times are measured from centroids.
5. The central area zone or zones should contain only those activities which are truly CBD-type activities and not those activities which are typical of the CBD frame such as warehousing.
6. The traffic-analysis zone system should be compatible with the strategy planning zone system.

Ideally, information used for transport systems planning should be geocoded which permits the data to be aggregated into different zone systems. The principles of geocoding and the normal sources of urban data are discussed in Chap. 13.

The work of Wildermuth, Delaney, and Thompson [8] has been referred to in Sec. 11.2.2, "Size of analysis zones," in connection with the effect of zone size on the accuracy of travel analysis results. It was pointed out in that section that traffic assignment was the controlling factor. In this study of travel in Melbourne they checked the output of the traffic assignment phase against observed traffic volumes on the links at 16 check-lines using both a multiple-path technique and an all-or-nothing technique. Table 11.4 shows the results of this analysis in which the root mean square error is shown for each zone system. This table indicates that the number of zones could be reduced to less than half of the original number before the error increased. Table 11.4 also shows that the error for the multipath assignment technique was slightly less than that for the all-or-nothing assignment.

Wildermuth, Delaney, and Thompson concluded: "For major route planning purposes, adequate traffic assignements should be obtained from zone plans with an average of 10,000 to 15,000 trip ends per zone. For predictions of traffic growth within transportation corridors or segments of urban areas, zone plans with as many as 30,000 trip ends per zone should yield traffic assignments with sufficient accuracy."

Trip types. It has been noted in Chap. 2 that the trip types of interest to transport systems planning studies vary with the type of transport planning issue under study. The dominance of the home-based work-trip of both daily and peak-period travel has been noted previously. The second most important trip type from the viewpoint of transport-facility design is the shopping trip. In many urban areas increases in affluence and leisure time have resulted in significant growth of weekend recreational travel demands. Figure 11.16 shows the variation in the average daily traffic volume over the months of the year for one major highway leading from Toronto to the summer recreational areas located in the Canadian Shield.

The movement of goods in urban areas has assumed importance in many urban areas. The movement of urban goods is discussed in Chap. 14.

Land-use information. The type of land-use information required for urban transport systems planning varies with the approach used to estimate urban

Table 11.4. Change in assignment error with zone size

Number of zones	Root mean square error	
	Multipath assignment	All-or-nothing assignment
607	7,022	7,596
263	7,047	7,494
144	7,454	8,940
136	8,722	8,635
056	9,618	10,553
040	12,510	12,255

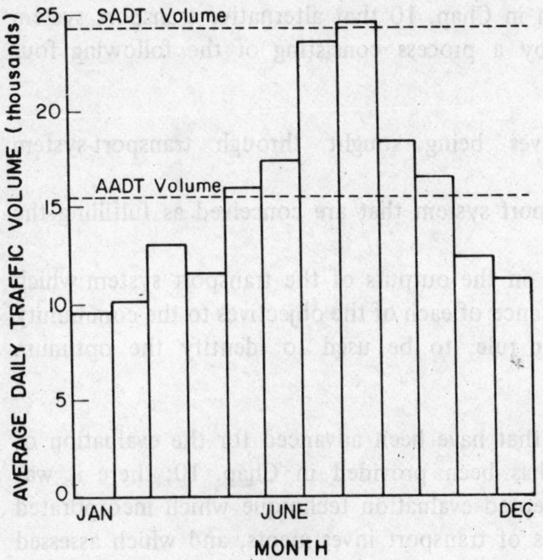

FIG. 11.16. Monthly variations in average daily traffic volume on recreational route north of Toronto, Ontario.

travel demands. If the traditional travel forecasting process is used then population and employment magnitudes must be specified completely for each traffic-analysis zones. If a land-use model of the Lowry type is to be used, then far less detailed land-use information is required. More specific statements about land-use information are presented in Sec. 11.3.5.

11.3.3 Output information required

Typical of the output information required from the analysis of alternative transport systems are the following:

1. Peak-hour (or period) travel volumes on the principal links of the road and public transport networks
2. Link-travel volumes during other critical time periods
3. The properties of travel along any link of the network such as average speed
4. The spatial distributions of residences and jobs for each socioeconomic group with evidence such as the trip-length frequency distributions for each group
5. Various secondary outputs, such as environmental impacts, that may be derived from the link volume information

11.3.4 Value functions

It has been emphasized in Chap. 1 that the objectives set for a transport system form the basis for the evaluation of the alternative systems. It was suggested in Chap. 1 and again in Chap. 10 that alternative transport system proposals may be evaluated by a process consisting of the following four components:

1. The community objectives being sought through transport-system investment
2. The outputs of the transport system that are conceived as fulfilling the investment objectives
3. The weights to be placed on the outputs of the transport system which reflects the relative importance of each of the objectives to the community
4. The decision criterion, or rule, to be used to identify the optimum investment alternative

A review of the techniques that have been advanced for the evaluation of alternative transport systems has been provided in Chap. 10; there it was concluded that a generally accepted evaluation technique which incorporated both user and nonuser impacts of transport investments, and which assessed investments from a multimodal viewpoint, was yet to be developed. The best approach at present seems to be to assess road and transit-system investments separately where this assessment is limited to user impacts. This would ensure that the alternative transport systems selected for final evaluation would be efficient from a user point of view. Intergroup comparisons and the assessment of nonuser impacts should then be carried out through debate in the public and political arenas.

The treatment of the road and public-transport networks separately, while not strictly correct, is acceptable in most urban areas since the patronages of the road and transit systems are essentially independent of the relative levels of service provided on each network. The evidence presented in Chap. 3 would suggest that this assertion is not correct for certain corridors in large cities where comprehensive rapid-transit facilities exist and significant parking charges are levied on private cars.

The objectives of urban transport-systems investment may be rephrased for each of the constituent modal subsystems as:

1. To maximize the benefits to transport-system users
2. To minimize the resource costs required for the construction, maintenance and operation of the system
3. To ensure that adequate environmental standards are maintained in all communities of the urban area
4. To ensure that the transport-system proposals support the land development proposals

This set of objectives leads one to decide on the following rule for identifying the optimum transport system from a user point of view: *To maximize the difference between user benefits and resource costs subject to a set of environmental constraints or standards.*

Figure 11.17 illustrates the nature of these objectives and the decision rule. Alternative transport plans are developed within the constraints imposed by the environmental area concept and other planning considerations. Changes in the user movement costs are then compared with the resource costs required for the construction and maintenance of the movement channels. The following evaluation approach is developed for road networks, but an analagous method may be formulated readily for the public-transport network.

It was suggested in Chap. 10 that the relevant economic good provided by transport systems is the accessibility provided at each point within an urban area. Transport investment alternatives can only be evaluated relative to a fixed set of policies in the other public policy sectors. As the relative travel times in an urban area are changed the trip interchange magnitudes between pairs of zones will change. It has been shown in both Chaps. 4 and 6 that the trip-interchange magnitudes are functions of the relative ease of movement between zones.

The ease of movement between any centroid pair may be expressed in terms of a trip distance, a trip time, and, therefore, an average speed. Studies of the

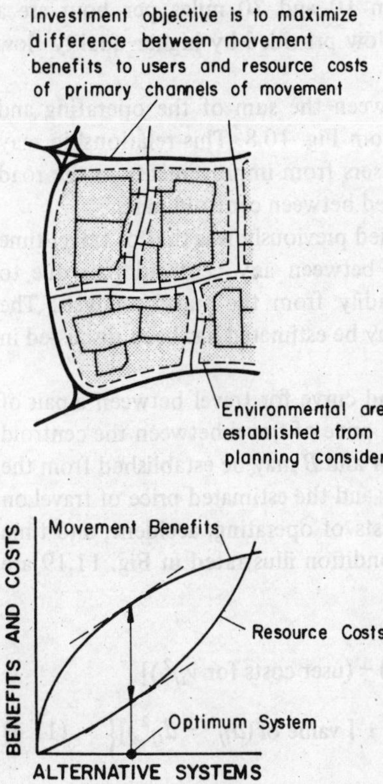
Investment objective is to maximize difference between movement benefits to users and resource costs of primary channels of movement
Environmental areas established from planning considerations
Movement Benefits
Resource Costs
Optimum System
BENEFITS AND COSTS
ALTERNATIVE SYSTEMS

FIG. 11.17. Transport-system evaluation procedure.

operating costs of vehicles in urban areas have shown that the operating costs are related to the average speed on a link. Figure 10.8 has shown the relationship established in the Chicago Area Transportation Study between vehicle operating costs and the average speed of travel on links. The diagram showed that operating costs decrease with average speed increases to 40 miles per hour and then begin to increase with increases in average speed. The initial reductions in operating costs are due to reductions in vehicle delays which occur at high link volumes and, therefore, at low average speeds. After about 40 miles per hour, increased fuel consumption begins to outweigh the savings due to reductions in delay, and the operating costs increase.

The Chicago study also found that the accident cost per vehicle mile varied inversely with the average speed on a link. Accident rates of 14.3 per million vehicle miles were observed on arterials and 2.8 per million vehicle miles on expressways. Studies of accident costs, including a monetary valuation of deaths, yielded an accident cost rate of 18.6 cents per mile on arterial roads, and 0.38 cents per mile on expressways. Figure 10.8 has shown the relationship developed between accident cost and average speed. Figure 10.8 illustrates that large decreases in accident costs occur between 10 miles per hour and 30 miles per hour with decreases in accident costs beginning to level off at about 60 to 70 miles per hour. The large savings between 10 and 30 miles per hour are a reflection of the improvements in traffic flow provided by higher quality flow on arterials and expressways.

Figure 11.18 shows the relationship between the sum of the operating and accident costs and average speed derived from Fig. 10.8. This relationship may be used to estimate the benefits to road-users from improvements in the road system which increase the average travel speed between centroid pairs.

The third element of user benefits identified previously was that of travel-time minimization. Changes in the travel time between any centroid pair due to transport network changes is available readily from the travel analysis. The manner in which the value of travel time may be estimated has been discussed in Chap. 10.

Figure 11.19 shows a hypothetical demand curve for travel between a pair of centroids as a function of the user-perceived price of travel between the centroid pair. The two points on the demand curve A and B may be established from the trip-interchange magnitudes for two systems and the estimated price of travel on the two systems. The price of travel consists of operating, accident, and time costs. The marginal user benefits for the condition illustrated in Fig. 11.19 are given by

$$\Delta B = \tfrac{1}{2}(t_{ij}^1 + t_{ij}^2)\Big\{[(\text{user costs for } \bar{v}_{ij}^1) - (\text{user costs for } \bar{v}_{ij}^2)] + [\text{value of}(d_{ij}^1 - d_{ij}^2)]\Big\} \qquad (11.4)$$

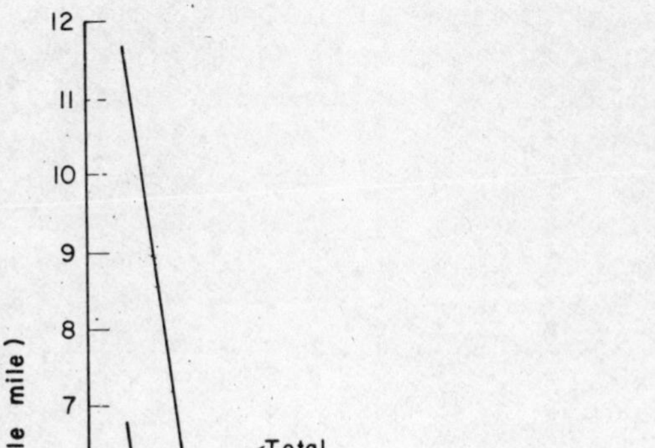

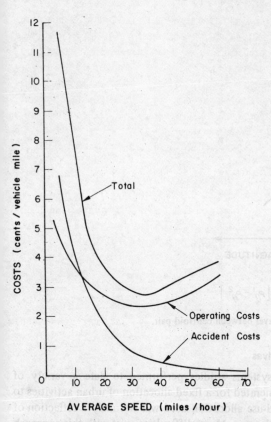

FIG. 11.18. Operating and accident costs vs. average speed.

where ΔB = marginal user benefits for time period under consideration

$\bar{v}_{ij}$ = the average speed of travel between i and j and the superscripts identify the two systems under study

d_{ij} = the travel-time savings between zones i and j

The total marginal user benefits for any urban area may be estimated by summing Eq. (11.4) over all centroid pairs and integrating it over all time periods throughout a year which are judged to create user benefits. User benefits may be transformed to a present value and compared with the resource costs. The alternative which yields the maximum difference between benefits and costs is the most efficient from the viewpoint of the users. It should be noted in connection with Eq. (11.4) that for certain centroid pairs there will be an increase in velocity and travel time. These increases will yield decreases in user benefits. Equation (11.4) should be summed algebraically in order to produce the net change in benefits.

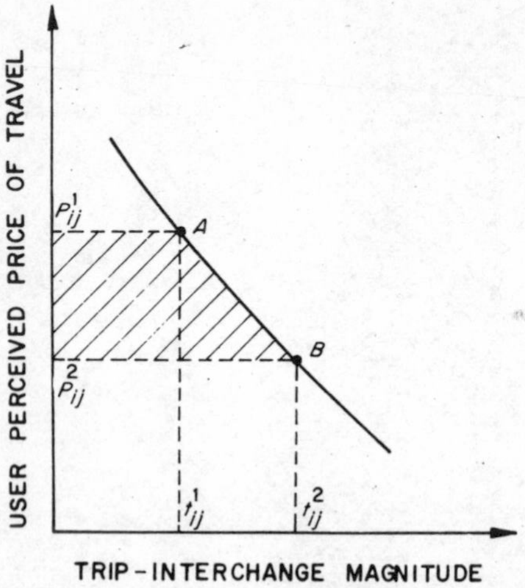

$$\text{Marginal Benefits} = \frac{t_{ij}^1 + t_{ij}^2}{2}\left[P_{ij}^1 - P_{ij}^2\right]$$

FIG. 11.19. Demand curve for travel between centroid pair.

11.3.5 Generation of alternatives

In most of the transport systems studies performed to date a variety of alternative plans have been generated for a fixed allocation of urban activities to traffic-analysis zones. The land-use allocation used was normally a reflection of the official or master plan for the area. Many difficulties exist with this approach including the following:

1. A great deal of effort is involved in allocating population and employment to each of the traffic-analysis zones.
2. There are interactions between the spatial distributions of activities and the properties of the transport system; when there are significant changes in the properties of the transport systems being tested then new equilibrium distributions of urban activities must be allowed to occur.
3. The interaction referred to in (2) becomes even more critical when the activity distributions and their interactions are disaggregated by socioeconomic group.

Three concepts have been introduced in Chap. 9 which are central to the generation of alternative plans at this level of planning and these are the concepts of urban structure, of hierarchical transport-route structure, and of an environmental area. These three concepts may be used along with the broad development policies isolated at the urban strategy level in order to develop alternative land-use and transport systems plans.

Four public policy variables were identified for urban strategy planning and these were the locations of basic and service employment, residential areas, and the primary transport network. These policy variables must be developed to a much finer scale for this level of planning. A typical set of development policies for the transport systems planning level would be:

1. The locations of the primary concentrations of basic employment by industry category; it has been noted previously that different industry categories have different characteristic employee income distributions.
2. The locations planned for the primary aggregations of population-serving employment of various types such as convenience and comparison shopping, entertainment, secondary and post-secondary education, and so on.
3. The locations planned for residential areas where the proportions of each area to be devoted to the various residential density groups are specified.
4. The locations of the primary freeway network, major arterial roads, and the primary public transport network.

A large number of variations are possible within each of the four broad classes of development policy just mentioned.

A particularly important part of any alternative concept are the proposals for the already developed portions of the study area. Antoniou [17] has proposed an interesting approach to plan formulation for developed areas. The elements of this approach are illustrated in Fig. 11.20. The essential element of this approach is the environmental area concept.

11.3.6 Analysis of alternatives

Figure 11.21 outlines the elements of a transport systems analysis process which is consistent with the approach advocated in this chapter. The development policy set selected at the urban strategy level is converted to a more-detailed set of land development and transport-system proposals. These policies are then used with a version of the Lowry model which is disaggregated by socioeconomic group to estimate the land development and transport implications of the policy set. The spatial pattern of travel demands estimated by the land-use model is then analyzed further using the techniques described in Chaps. 3 to 5.

Land-use-trip-distribution analysis. The following disaggregated version of the Lowry model may be introduced, part of which has already been described in Chap. 6.

$$[p^k] = [e^k] A^k \tag{11.5}$$

$$[e^{sr}] = pB^r \tag{11.6}$$

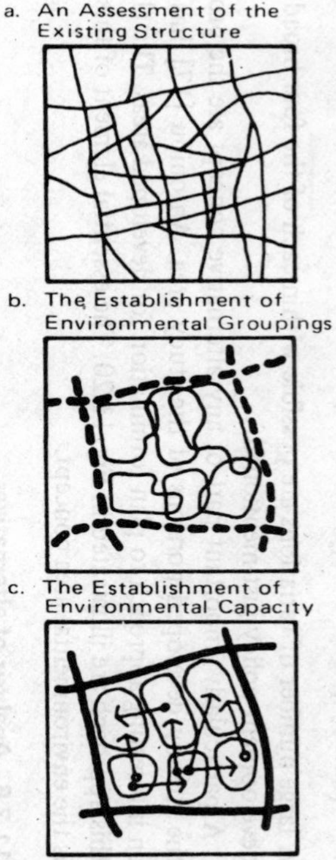
a. An Assessment of the Existing Structure
Layout arrangements
Traffic characteristics
Land use and activities
Density and building form
Visual image
Environmental conditions
b. The Establishment of Environmental Groupings
Possible routes to carry through traffic
Homogeneous land use areas
Catchment areas
Areas of architectural and landscape value
Areas having high potential for improvement
c. The Establishment of Environmental Capacity
Degree of vehicular movement characterization
Availability of parking and garaging
Age, condition, and layout of buildings
Pattern of pedestrian movement
Groups of architectural and landscape value

d. Environmental Standard at the Periphery of Environmental Areas

Development of network of high standards by the implementation of traffic engineering techniques: high speeds predominate routes, upgraded by either limitation or prohibition of access to existing junctions.

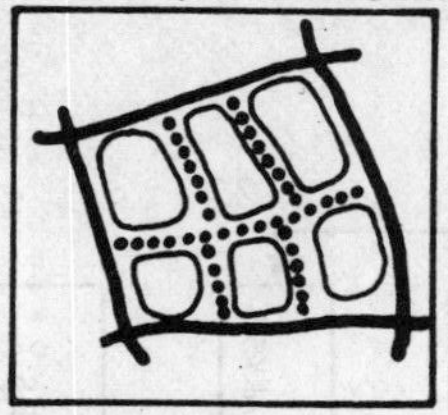

Degree of acceptability of existing frontages

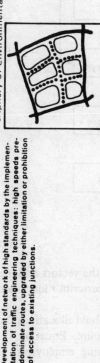

e. Environmental Standard within Environmental Area

Discourage through traffic, but not prevent free movement of local traffic
Limitation of on-street parking
Provision of off-street parking and garaging
Provision of loading bays
Integrate public transport services

Consideration of vehicular/pedestrian conflict
Degree of discomfort by reason of noise, fumes, vibration and visual intrusion
Disturbance by reason of undesirable parked vehicles and their ancillary uses
The creation of a continuous, uninterrupted pedestrian network, based on the nature and extent of awareness of existing uses, public transport access points, view points, urban landscape, visual image, etc.

f. Visual Treatment

The provision of a visual sequence for the driver in motion

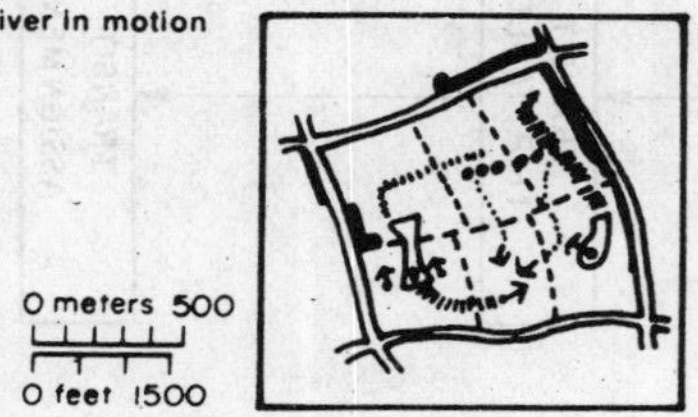

Skilful attention to the urban landscape
The functional treatment of external space

FIG. 11.20. Principles of plan formulation for developed areas. (*Reproduced from Jim Antoniou "Environmental Management Planning for Traffic," McGraw-Hill Book Company (U.K.) Limited,* 1971.)

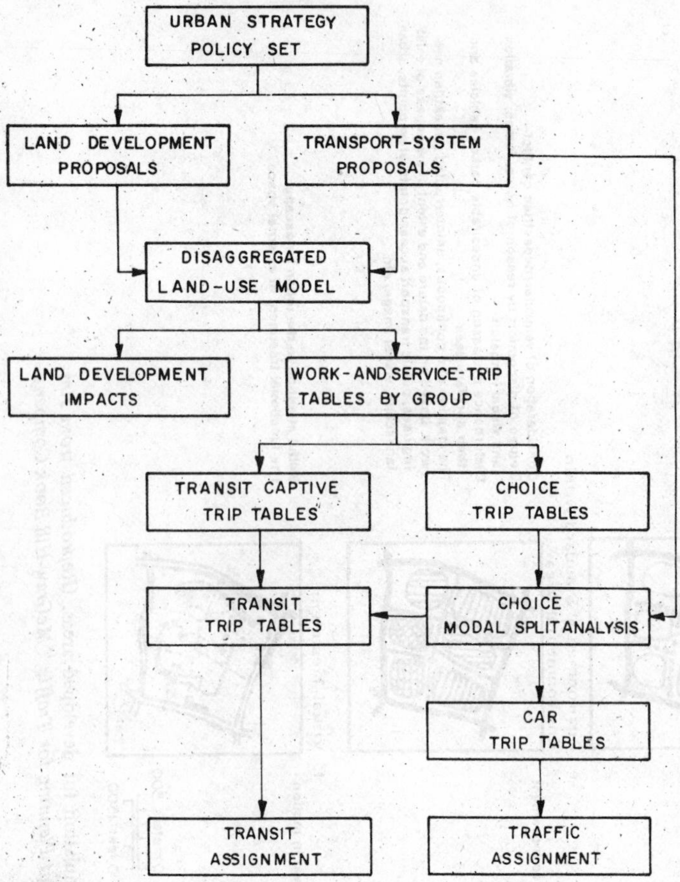

FIG. 11.21. Transport-systems analysis process.

$$[e^k] = [e^{bk}] + [e^{sk}] \tag{11.7}$$

In Eqs. (11.5) to (11.7) the superscript k indicates that the vectors and matrix are disaggregated by socioeconomic group k, and the superscript r identifies the various types of population-serving employment.

Equation (11.5) suggests that the employment to household allocations should be conducted separately for the k socioeconomic groups. Equation (11.6) indicates that the demand for type r population-serving employment is a function of the spatial distribution of the total population rather than for the k groups separately.

It has been shown in Chap. 6 that the terms on the right-hand side of Eq. (11.7) may be calculated in the following way:

$$[e^{bk}] = [e^{kc}]\ [e^{bc}] \tag{11.8}$$

$$[e^{sk}] = [e^{kr}]\ [e^{sr}] \tag{11.9}$$

where $[e^{kc}]$ = $k \times c$ person type–basic employment industry category matrix
$[e^{kr}]$ = $k \times r$ person type–service employment industry category matrix
$[e^{bc}]$ = the basic employment vector partitioned by industry category c
$[e^{sr}]$ = the service employment vector partitioned by industry category r

Characteristic income distributions for various industry types have been provided in Chap. 3. Table 11.5 shows more detailed income distributions observed for both the New York metropolitan area and Hamilton, Ontario. The person type–industry category matrices required by Eqs. (11.8) and (11.9) may be derived from information of the type presented in Table 11.5.

It was also suggested in Chap. 6 that the residential locations of socioeconomic group k may be estimated from:

$$A^k = [a_{ij}'^k]\ [a_j^k] \tag{11.10}$$

where the terms have been defined in Chap. 6.

The accessibility elements required by Eq. (11.10) may be estimated from:

$$a_{ij}'^k = \frac{o_j^k f_{ij}^{wk}}{\sum_j o_j f_{ij}^{wk}} \tag{11.11}$$

where the term o_j^k has been defined as the residential opportunities available in zone j which are compatible with the preferences of socioeconomic group k.

The housing opportunities available to type k persons may be estimated from:

$$[o^k] = [s^{kd}]\ [g^d] \tag{11.12}$$

where $[s^{kd}]$ = a $k \times d$ matrix of the probabilities of type k persons living in density group d
$[g^d]$ = a partitioned column vector showing the number of housing opportunities in each density group planned for each zone

The residential area capacity balancing procedure described in Chap. 6 may be used if necessary.

Table 11.6 shows the effect of household income on the housing type occupied for Hamilton, Ontario. As would be expected, the lower income households tend to occupy the higher density residential areas.

The service location decisions of the population may be estimated from:

Table 11.5. Household income by industry distribution of household heads

Household income range	Construction	Manufacturing	Utilities, communication, transport	Wholesale	Retail	Finance, insurance, real estate	Professional and service	Public administration	Total employed
< $4,000	3.4*	30.2	4.7	2.6	15.2	7.8	31.9	4.2	434,000
$4,000–10,000	7.1	31.5	11.7	4.7	13.4	6.0	17.7	7.9	1,552,000
> $10,000	6.3	30.4	8.7	6.2	10.5	8.9	23.4	5.6	1,057,000
All	6.5	31.1	10.2	4.8	12.8	6.9	20.7	7.0	3,043,000

*Percentage of total in income range.

Table 11.6. Income-housing-type probability distribution, Hamilton, Ontario, 1961

Income range	Housing type		
	Single detached	Single attached	Apartment
< $2,000	0.0591	0.1417	0.1369
$2,000–3,000	0.0678	0.1544	0.1527
$3,000–4,000	0.1569	0.2579	0.2337
$4,000–5,000	0.2577	0.2682	0.2270
$5,000–6,000	0.2178	0.1299	0.1438
$6,000–7,000	0.1047	0.0479	0.0597
$7,000–10,000	0.0973	0.0	0.0386
> $10,000	0.0389	0.0	0.0077

*In terms of Canadian currency.

$$B^r = [b_{ij}'^r]\ [b_j^r] \tag{11.13}$$

where $b_{ij}'^r$ = home to service employment type r accessibilities, and
b_j^r = service employees of type r demanded per person for households in zone j

The accessibility elements required by Eq. (11.13) may be estimated from:

$$b_{ij}'^r = \frac{s_i^r f_{ij}^{sr}}{\sum_i s_i^r f_{ij}^{sr}} \tag{11.14}$$

where the term s_i^r has been defined as the attractivity of zone i for type r services.

The home-based work and home-based service trip matrices may be estimated from:

$$[t_{ij}^{wk}] = [w^k]\ [a_{ij}'^k] \tag{11.15}$$

$$[t_{ij}^{sr}] = [\dot{r}]\ [b_{ij}'^r] \tag{11.16}$$

where $[w^k]$ = an $n \times n$ diagonal matrix of the work-trip-generation rate per employee for the time period of interest
$[r]$ = an $n \times n$ diagonal matrix of the service-trip generation rate per household to type r service employment for the time period of interest.

The trip rates required by Eqs. (11.15) and (11.16) may be established by the techniques described in Chap. 2.

SUMMARY

Transport-systems planning must be considered as just one activity in a multilevel process of development planning. Transport-systems planning should be preceeded by the regional and urban strategy planning levels and followed by the functional planning and capital program levels.

Regional planning studies should have a time horizon of 20 to 50 years and their principal emphasis should be on the broad pattern of urbanization and its impact on the natural environment. The major output of a regional planning study should be a set of parameters for each of the constituent urban areas, such as population and employment.

Urban strategy planning studies should have a time horizon of 20 to 30 years and their major aim is to specify alternative urban development concepts in sufficient detail to allow their transport and servicing implications to be examined. The principal output of an urban strategy planning study should be a statement of the desired spatial distribution of population and employment along with the public policy set necessary to achieve the particular spatial structure of development.

Transport-system plans should have a time horizon of 20 years and the objective of this type of study is to develop a plan of road and public-transport investment in sufficient detail that it may be used for functional planning and capital programming.

Urban strategy plans may be developed and analyzed in terms of a relatively coarse system of zones or districts. The Lowry model provides a useful tool for analyzing the land development and transport implications of various urban strategy policy sets. Coarse analyses of corridor travel demands may be conducted to determine the feasibility of serving the future travel demands created by a particular strategic development alternative.

A wide range of urban land-use-transport-system plans may be developed within the broad development guidelines established in the urban stragegy planning level. A version of the Lowry model which is disaggregated by socioeconomic group may be used to test rapidly the land development implications and travel-demand patterns of any policy set. The travel demands estimated by the Lowry model may be analyzed in detail through the use of a two-stage modal split model and a traffic-assignment procedure.

Comprehensive and formal evaluations of transport-system plans are not possible at this time. The user impacts of transport investments may be assessed in quasi-formal way. However, the assessment of the land development impacts and the intergroup comparisons required for intermodal investment evaluation must be developed through public debate.

REFERENCES

1. Boyce, D. E., N. D. Day, and C. MacDonald, *Metropolitan Plan Making,* Monograph Series No. 4, Regional Science Research Institute, Philadelphia, Pennsylvania, 1970.

2. Organization for Economic Cooperation and Development, *The Urban Transportation Planning Process,* Paris, 1971.
3. Hutchinson, B. G., and J. H. Shortreed, *New Requirements of Urban Transport Planning,* International Conference on Transportation Research, Bruges, Belgium, 1973.
4. The Government of Ontario, *Design for Development: The Toronto-Centred Region,* Toronto, Ontario, 1970.
5. Kates, Peat, Marwick and Company, *Hamilton Transportation Strategy Study: Study Approach,* Toronto, Ontario, 1972.
6. Alan M. Voorhees and Associates, Inc., *Canberra Land Use Transportation Study: General Plan Concept,* McLean, Virginia, 1967.
7. Hansen, W. G., and I. W. Morison, *Canberra: A Study of Land Use and Transport,* Proceedings, Australian Road Research Board, Melbourne, pp. 44–61, 1968.
8. Wildermuth, B. R., D. J. Delaney, and K. E. Thompson, *Effect of Zone Size on Traffic Assignment and Trip Distribution,* Highway Research Record No. 392, Highway Research Board, Washington, D.C., 1972.
9. Rogers, A., *Matrix Analysis of Inter-regional Population Growth and Distribution,* University of California Press, Berkeley, 1968.
10. Keyfitz, N., *Introduction to the Mathematics of Population,* Addison-Wesley, Publishing Company, Inc., Reading, Massachusetts, 1968.
11. McJunkin, F. E., "Population Forecasting by Sanitary Engineers," *Journal, Sanitary Engineering Division,* American Society of Civil Engineers, August, 1964.
12. Wilson, A. G. (ed.), "Special Issue on Mathematical Demography," *Environment and Planning,* vol. 5, no. 1, 1973.
13. Sharpe, C. P., and R. J. Maxman, *A Methodology for Computation of the Environmental Capacity of Roadway Networks,* Highway Research Record No. 394, Highway Research Board, Washington, D.C., 1972.
14. Desjardins, R. J., *The Hamilton Transportation Strategy Study: A New Direction in Urban Transportation Planning,* Reference paper, Roads and Transportation Association of Canada, 1973.
15. Creighton Hamburg, *Data Requirements for Metropolitan Transportation Planning,* National Cooperative Highway Research Program Report 120, Highway Research Board, Washington, D.C., 1971.
16. Kassoff, H., and H. D. Deutschman, *Transportation: The Link Between People and Jobs,* Highway Research Record No. 322, Highway Research Board, Washington, D.C., 1970.
17. Antoniou, J., *Environmental Management,* McGraw-Hill Book Company, London, 1971.

12 SEQUENTIAL-TYPE PLANNING PROCESS

An horizon-year–type transport-planning process has been described in Chap. 11. With that process, some future horizon-year state is forecast (usually 20 years ahead) and transport plans are developed for that state. It has been pointed out in Chap. 1 that there has been some disenchantment with the deterministic character of the horizon-year–type planning process.

Perhaps the dominant characteristic of large urban transport-system investments is that they are made sequentially over a relatively long time period. The transport planner has the opportunity of monitoring the performance of implemented projects and of using this information to reappraise future investments. This concept of performance monitoring has found formal expression in several transport demonstration projects in North America. The high-speed rail project in the Northeast corridor of the United States and the government of Ontario demonstration projects in the Toronto region provide typical examples.

A second trait of transport investments is that they are made under conditions of uncertainty with respect to future demand and the costs of construction and operation. Planning and design studies are conducted to generate information about probable demand and costs, but there is no rationale for assessing the optimal scale of information to be generated. Demand information-generating activities may range from rather informal assessments, through the traditional transport study, to full-scale demonstration projects. The transport planner requires a rationale that permits improvements in demand, cost, and impact forecasts to be traded off against the costs of attaining the information in order to select the appropriate type of study.

The importance of the uncertainties associated with transport investment is emphasized in a report on transport planning, published by the Organization for Economic Cooperation and Development [1];

> Foremost among the obstacles to orderly innovation (in urban transport services), however, has been the element of uncertainty and risk which surrounds the introduction of major changes in transportation systems.
>
> Risk is always present in ushering innovative ideas, but it is particularly acute in the field of transportation. Massive resources will be required for research and development to carry new transportation systems from concepts to operational prototypes, to test them, refine their design and produce working operational systems. As with any untried technology, there will be uncertainty about actual construction and operation costs, and engineering performance. There will be uncertainties about the new systems' environmental side effects, their effects on property values and their compatibility with existing transportation networks. Most importantly, there will be uncertainties about the degree of public acceptability, passenger response and the resulting magnitude of the market for the new transportational service.

It is the purpose of this chapter to describe an approach to transport planning, sequential in nature, and which provides for a formal treatment of uncertainty as well as the value of information obtained from planning studies.

12.1 ELEMENTS OF STATISTICAL DECISION THEORY

Three deficiencies of the existing transport-planning process, that have been identified above are:

1. The inadequate treatment of uncertainty
2. The absence of any formal analysis of the value of information obtained from planning studies
3. The lack of any formal recognition that transport plans are implemented sequentially

This section reviews certain principles of statistical decision theory which can be used to provide an approach to the three deficiencies just identified.

12.1.1 Elements of a decision problem

Statistical decision problems are defined in terms of the following components [2]:

1. The alternative terminal decisions open to a decisionmaker $d_1, d_2, \ldots$

2. The possible states of nature, $\theta_1, \theta_2, \ldots$
3. The possible experiments (or analyses) $e_0, e_1, \ldots$, that may be performed prior to the selection of a terminal decision in order to generate information about the probability of occurrence of the states of nature
4. The possible experimental outcomes $z_1, z_2, \ldots$, that may be observed for each of these experiments
5. The values or utilities u which represent the decisionmaker's preferences for all e, z, d, θ combinations relative to his objectives
6. The probabilities which the decisionmaker assigns to the joint probability distribution of z, θ for each of the potential experiments or analyses

The interrelationships of these six components of a decision problem are most readily visualized in terms of a decision tree. Figure 12.1 shows such a decision tree. The upper branch of the decision tree shows the sequence of the activities involved when a terminal decision is taken without any prior experimentation and is referred to as the prior branch. In this branch e_0 and z_0 identify a dummy experiment and a dummy outcome to that experiment simply to make the flow of activities compatible with the posterior branch in which experimentation actually occurs.

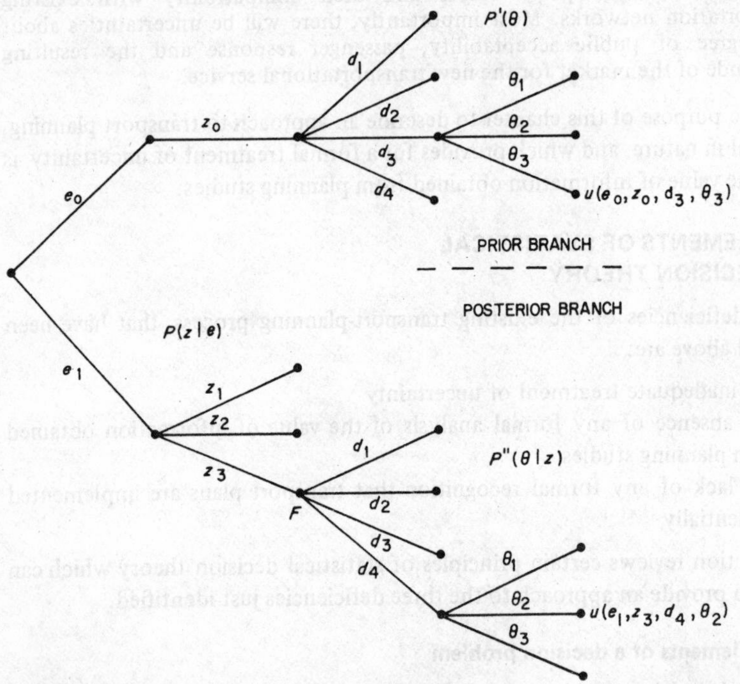

FIG. 12.1. Components of an elementary decision tree showing the prior and posterior branches.

In this particular decision tree there are four potential terminal decisions and three states of nature that may occur after a terminal decision has been selected. This results in 12 potential outcomes which must be evaluated. The uncertainty regarding the states of nature is expressed in the prior probability distribution $P'(\theta)$. The expected utility or value of each of the four possible terminal decisions may be calculated from these probabilities and utility of each outcome.

In the posterior branch, an experiment e_1 is performed; three potential outcomes z_1, z_2, and z_3 provide additional information on the probability of occurrence of each of the states of nature. When an outcome has been observed, the decisionmaker may then select a terminal decision that will interact with the state of nature that occurs resulting in an outcome. Before the experiment is performed there are three potential outcomes of the experiment, for each outcome there are four potential decisions, and for each decision there are four possible states of nature resulting in $3 \times 4 \times 3 = 36$ potential decision paths. The uncertainty associated with the states of nature after the new information has become available from the experiment is expressed in the posterior probability distribution $P''(\theta|z)$.

Two basic modes of analysis have been formulated for this decision problem [2]. One mode of analysis is concerned with the choice of a terminal decision after an experiment had been performed and its outcome observed. This mode of analysis is referred to as *posterior analysis.* The second mode of analysis, called *preposterior analysis,* is concerned with the identification of the most valuable experiment to be performed before the selection of a terminal decision.

The central problem of both forms of analysis is to assign either directly or indirectly a joint probability measure $P(\theta, z|e)$ to the joint distribution of θ, z for each of the potential experiments. The joint probability measure expresses information on the extent to which the occurrence of a particular experimental outcome is favorable to the occurrence of a particular state of nature.

The joint probability measure determines four other probability measures. These are:

1. The marginal probability measure $P'(\theta)$ on the states of nature that the decisionmaker would assign to θ prior to knowing the outcome z of the experiment e
2. The conditional probability measure $P(z|e,\theta)$ on the space Z of the experimental outcomes for a given experiment e given that θ is the true state of nature
3. The marginal probability measure $P(z|e)$ on the space Z for all θ and a specified e
4. The conditional measure $P''(\theta|z,e)$ on the space Θ of the states of nature for a given e and z, which the probability measure that the decisionmaker would assign to the state space posterior to knowing the outcomes z for experiment e

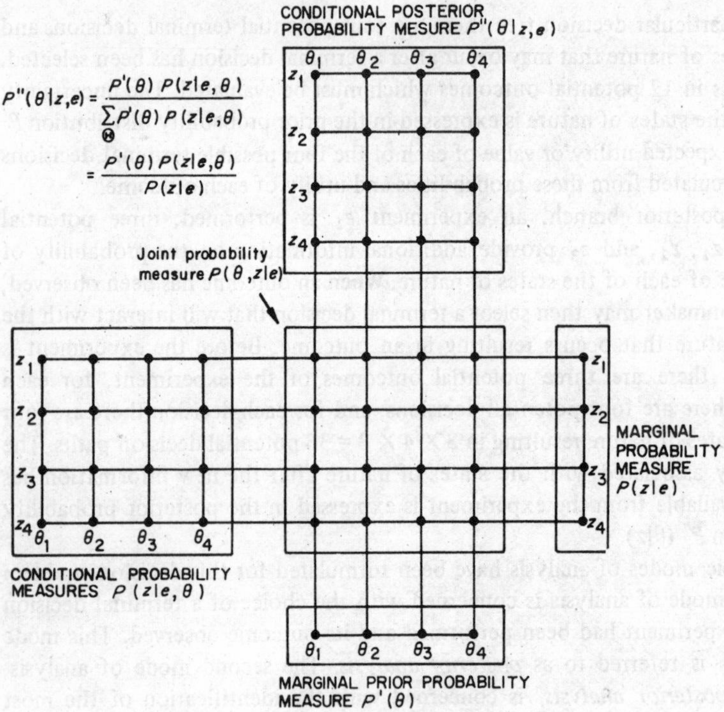

FIG. 12.2. Interrelationship of the probability measures in a Bayesian decision problem.

The interrelationships of the five probability measures are illustrated graphically in Fig. 12.2. The method of analysis described below requires that three of these probability distributions be estimated. These are the prior measures $P'(\theta)$, the posterior measure $P''(\theta|z,e)$ and the marginal measure $P(z|e)$. There are several separate ways in which these probability distributions can be estimated and two of these methods are:

1. The prior measure $P'(\theta)$ and the conditional measure $P(z|e, \theta)$ may be estimated directly, and the marginal measure $P(z|e)$ and the posterior measure $P''(\theta|z,e)$ may be calculated from:

$$P''(\theta|z, e) = \frac{P'(\theta) \cdot P(z|e, \theta)}{\sum_{\Theta} P'(\theta) \cdot P(z|e, \theta)} \tag{12.1}$$

$$P(z|e) = \sum_{\Theta} P'(\theta) \cdot P(z|e, \theta) \tag{12.2}$$

Equation (12.1) is known as *Bayes theorem*.

2. The marginal measure $P(z|e)$ and the posterior measure $P''(\theta|z,e)$ may be estimated directly and substituted in Eqs. (12.1) and (12.2) to derive the prior and conditional measures.

12.1.2 Preposterior mode of analysis

The preposterior mode of analysis mentioned above is of central interest to this chapter. This method of analysis proceeds by working backwards from the right-hand extremity of the decision tree to its origin. Assume the following probabilities $P'(\theta)$, $P''(\theta|z,e)$, and $P(z|e)$ are known. The analysis begins by determining the terminal decision that should be selected if an experiment had been performed and its outcome observed; that is at point F of the posterior branch. Since the state of nature is a random variable until after the terminal decision has been selected, only the expected utility associated with each terminal action may be computed.

$$u^*(e, z, d) = E''_{\theta|z}[u(e, z, d, \tilde{\theta})] \tag{12.3}$$

In Eq. (12.3), $E''_{\theta|z}$ means the expectation of the random variable identified by the tilde within the brackets with respect to the probability distribution $P''(\theta|z)$. The asterisk is used as a superscript to u to identify it as an expected utility.

The optimal terminal decision is given by that decision with the maximum expected utility:

$$u^*(e, z) = \max_d u^*(e, z, d) \tag{12.4}$$

The outcome of each experiment is a random variable and the expected utility of an experiment may be calculated from:

$$u^*(e) = E_{z|e}[u^*(e, \tilde{z})] \tag{12.5}$$

where the expectation of z is with respect to the probability distribution $P(z|e)$.

The experiment with the maximum expected utility can be readily selected and the expected utility associated with the optimal strategy identified:

$$u^* = \max_e u^*(e) = \max_e E_{z|e} \{\max_d E''_{\theta|z}[u(e, z, d, \tilde{\theta})]\} \tag{12.6}$$

A useful concept which may be derived from the preposterior analysis is the value of information obtained from experimentation. The d' may be defined as the terminal decision which is optimal under the prior distribution of $\theta, P'(\theta)$, and it may be identified in the following way:

$$E'_{\theta}[u_t(d', \tilde{\theta})] \geqslant E'_{\theta}[u_t(d, \tilde{\theta})] \tag{12.7}$$

for all d where the subscript t identifies u as a terminal utility; Equation (12.7) states simply that the expected value of terminal decision d' is equal to or greater than the expected value of any other terminal decision.

The d_z may be defined as the terminal decision which is optimal under the posterior distribution of θ which has been determined after the outcome z of experiment e has been observed:

$$E''_{\theta|z}[u_t(d_z, \tilde{\theta})] = \max_d E''_{\theta|z}[u_t(d, \tilde{\theta})] \tag{12.8}$$

If instead of choosing the optimal prior decision d' directly, the decisionmaker performs an experiment e, observes an outcome z, and then chooses d_z, the terminal utility is increased by:

$$v_t(e, z) = E''_{\theta|z}[u_t(d_z, \tilde{\theta})] - E''_{\theta|z}[u_t(d', \tilde{\theta})] \tag{12.9}$$

and $v_t(e,z)$ is termed the *conditional value of sample information.* Equation (12.9) states that the conditional value of sample information is the expected value of the optimal terminal decision under the posterior distribution less the expected value of the optimal prior decision under the posterior distribution.

Equation (12.9) can only be evaluated conditionally after a particular z has been observed. However, before z has been observed, the expected value of sample information can be calculated from:

$$v_t^*(e) = E_{z|e}[v_t(e, \tilde{z})] \tag{12.10}$$

The economic significance of $v_t^*(e)$ is that the expected terminal utility of a particular experiment is the expected utility of an immediate terminal decision augmented by the expected value of sample information which is:

$$u_t^*(e) = u_t^*(e_0) + v_t^*(e) \tag{12.11}$$

The expected net gain of experimentation is defined to be the expected value of sample information less the cost of obtaining it:

$$v^*(e) = v_t^*(e) - c_s \tag{12.12}$$

If $v^*(e)$ is positive then the cost of performing an experiment is justified.

12.1.3 A numerical example

In 1967 the Government of Ontario began a demonstration commuter rail project in one of the major CBD-oriented demand corridors not served by the existing subway system [3]. The objective of this demonstration project was to provide additional information on commuter rail demands which would assist the government in deciding whether to adopt commuter rail provision as a general policy for several radial corridors in the Toronto region. This demonstration project provides a vehicle for illustrating the application of the above principles of statistical decision theory. Using the notation of the previous section it is possible to define the following components of the problem.

d_1 = adopt a commuter rail provision policy
d_2 = reject a commuter rail provision policy, implying a continuation of the current freeway building policy
e_1 = conduct a standard transport-planning study for cost c_1
e_2 = conduct a more-detailed transport-planning study which includes detailed market studies for cost c_2
e_3 = conduct a commuter rail demonstration project in corridor A for cost c_3
z_i = the set of experimental outcomes that are possible for each of the experiments
θ_n = the transport demand levels and modal splits that may occur in the future (say 3 demand levels X 2 modal split proportions yielding 6 states of nature)
$u(\ )$ = the values of each of the potential outcomes that can result from the e,z,d,θ sequences

A basic assumption of decision theory is that the state of nature that actually obtains in the future is independent of the terminal decision selected. In this example, the action of acceptance or rejection of the commuter rail subsidization policy is independent of the future state of nature that actually occurs. This is not to say that if a commuter rail service is actually implemented it will not influence the demand.

The best source of information for establishing a prior probability measure over the states of nature is the existing evidence on demand and modal split behavior. In this particular example the corridor of interest is a relatively well-developed corridor and the total demand within a CBD-oriented corridor and the modal split change slowly. Chapter 7 has provided a great deal of evidence on the stability of CBD-oriented travel demands in a number of cities.

In this particular example, the future travel demand is assumed to be equal to the existing level and three modal split proportions are isolated: $\theta_1 = 65\%$, $\theta_2 = 60\%$, and $\theta_3 = 50\%$. Further, assume that on the basis of the existing trends in modal split the following prior probabilities are reasonable: $P'(\theta) = 0.2, P'(\theta_2) = 0.5$, and $P'(\theta_3) = 0.3$.

The second probability distribution that is required is the conditional measure $P(z|e,\theta)$, which is a measure of the reliability of the experimental technique in forecasting the true states of nature. In other words, this conditional probability measure is the sampling distribution. One would expect that a demonstration project would be an extremely reliable predictor of the response to the introduction of commuter rail services in other corridors, relative to, say, a standard transport study. The reliability of an experimental or analytical forecasting technique must be established from experience with the technique. For example, the reliability of the standard transport-planning process could be established by comparing demand and modal split forecasts with those actually observed. For other experiments and analyses with which there is little experience, the reliabilities would have to be estimated subjectively.

For the purpose of this example three experimental techniques for estimating the future modal split to commuter rail services have been identified above. These potential experiments have been labeled e_1, e_2, and e_3 and the reliabilities assumed for these techniques are given in Table 12.1. The information presented in Table 12.1 indicates that the reliabilities increase from the standard transport-planning study through to the demonstration projects. The posterior probability measures can now be derived using Eq. (12.1) and these measures are presented in Table 12.2.

The elements of the problem are illustrated in Fig. 12.3. The letters *A* to *F* shown on the diagram are used to label the key features of the decision analysis. *A* identifies the prior probability measures which have been assigned to the three possible states of nature. The probabilities shown in the posterior branch of the diagram are those which are listed in Table 12.2.

B identifies the terminal utilities (in this case present values of costs) that are associated with each strategy-state-of-nature combination. The number 380 indicates that the net present worth of the costs associated with strategy d_1 if θ_2 is the true state of nature is $380 million. This amount includes the capital, operating, and social costs. In the e_3 branch these terminal costs are reduced by $5 million since the demonstration project is assumed to have a capital outlay of $5 million which will be part of any terminal strategy, except the all-freeway strategy.

The expected cost of each strategy within each branch is entered at *C* and is obtained from the sum of the products of the probabilities and the terminal costs; the expected cost of selecting d_1 in the prior branch is $405 million. The

Table 12.1. Conditional probability measures

Experiments	Conditional probabilities	States of nature		
		$\theta = \theta_1$	$\theta = \theta_2$	$\theta = \theta_3$
$e = e_1$	$P(z_1 \mid e,\theta)$	0.6	0.2	0.2
	$P(z_2 \mid e,\theta)$	0.2	0.6	0.2
	$P(z_3 \mid e,\theta)$	0.2	0.2	0.6
$e = e_2$	$P(z_1 \mid e,\theta)$	0.2	0.2	0.1
	$P(z_2 \mid e,\theta)$	0.2	0.7	0.1
	$P(z_3 \mid e,\theta)$	0.1	0.1	0.8
$e = e_3$	$P(z_1 \mid e,\theta)$	0.90	0.05	0.05
	$P(z_2 \mid e,\theta)$	0.05	0.90	0.05
	$P(z_3 \mid e,\theta)$	0.05	0.05	0.90

Table 12.2. Posterior probability measures

Experiments	Posterior probabilities	Experimental outcomes		
		$z = z_1$	$z = z_2$	$z = z_3$
$e = e_1$	$P''(\theta_1 \mid z,e)$	0.43	0.10	0.125
	$P''(\theta_2 \mid z,e)$	0.36	0.75	0.314
	$P''(\theta_3 \mid z,e)$	0.21	0.15	0.561
$e = e_2$	$P''(\theta_1 \mid z,e)$	0.52	0.09	0.06
	$P''(\theta_2 \mid z,e)$	0.37	0.84	0.16
	$P''(\theta_3 \mid z,e)$	0.11	0.07	0.78
$e = e_3$	$P''(\theta_1 \mid z,e)$	0.82	0.021	0.032
	$P''(\theta_2 \mid z,e)$	0.11	0.950	0.082
	$P''(\theta_3 \mid z,e)$	0.07	0.029	0.886

expected costs entered at D represent the minima of the expected costs of the two possible terminal decisions. For branches e_1, e_2, and e_3, these expected costs are conditional expectations and must be expected with respect to the marginal probability distribution $P(z\ e)$, as shown in Eq. (12.5), to yield the expected cost at E. The cost of performing the experiment must be added to the expected cost to yield the total expected cost of pursuing each of the experimental branches.

Inspection of the expected costs at E shows that the posterior branch e_3 has the minimum expected cost of \$395.2 million. That is, the best course of action is to carry out a demonstration project and to observe the outcome of this experiment. If the outcome is z_1 or z_2 then the optimal terminal strategy is to implement a continuing commuter rail policy. If the outcome is z_3 then the optimal terminal policy decision is to embark on a freeway building policy.

It is interesting to note for this example that if the prior distribution was assumed to be $P'(\theta_1) = 0.1$, $P'(\theta_2) = 0.7$, and $P'(\theta_3) = 0.2$, then the best course of action would be to select an immediate terminal decision d_1 without first performing a survey or a demonstration project. Stated in another way, the cost of generating additional information on modal split in the corridor would not be justified; or, the uncertainty associated with the estimates of modal split in the corridor was not great enough to justify the cost of obtaining the additional information.

Returning to the example presented in Fig. 12.3, the value of information yielded by the demonstration project may be calculated using Eq. (12.11)

$$\begin{aligned} v_t^*(e_3) &= u_t^*(e_3) - u_t^*(e_0) \\ &= (389.2 - 405.0) \times 10^6 \\ &= \$15.8 \times 10^6 \end{aligned}$$

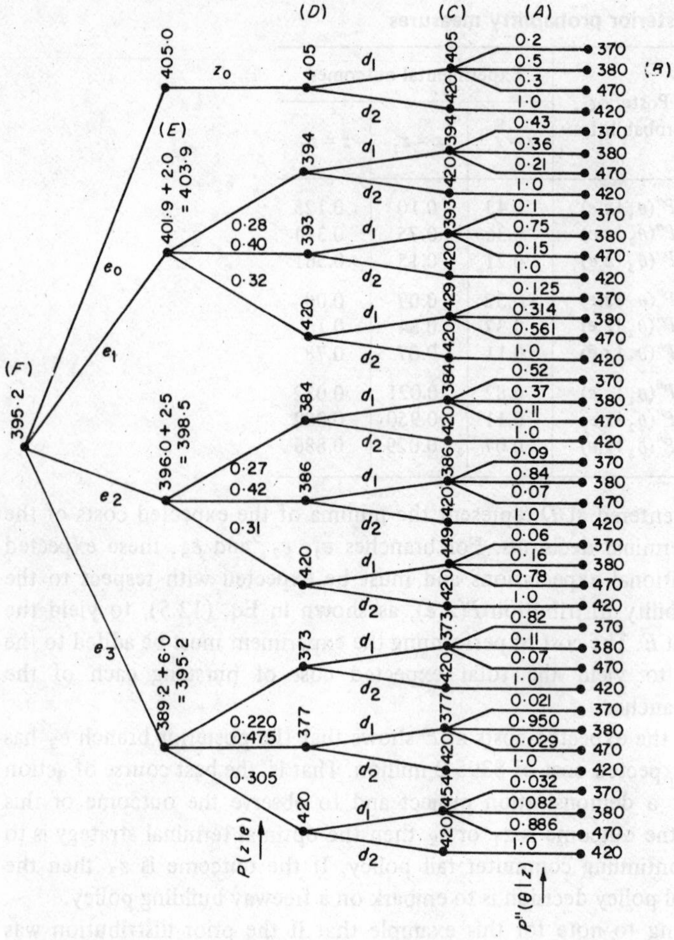

FIG. 12.3. Elements of a corridor transportation policy decision.

The cost of the demonstration project is $\$6 \times 10^6$, so the net gain from the information generated by the demonstration project is $\$9.8 \times 10^6$.

12.2 A SEQUENTIAL PLANNING FRAMEWORK

The implementation of long range strategic transportation plans involves the construction of a sequence of projects over a relatively long time period. Table 12.3 shows the sequence of projects involved in the construction of the Toronto subway system. A similar table could be prepared to show the sequence of freeway projects in the Metropolitan Toronto region in order to illustrate the relatively long period of time over which the freeway system has been developed. In this period of development there have been large changes in the size and character of the Toronto region that were not forecast precisely in the original planning activities.

Transport planning may be thought of as a sequence of "experiments" in which components of some horizon-year plan are introduced into an urban area with changing conditions. The actual performance of implemented projects can then be used to assess the validity of implementing future components of the planned transport system. This approach to transport planning has been referred to as *adaptive planning.*

In the report on the status of transport planning prepared by the Organization for Economic Cooperation and Development [1], referred to earlier in this chapter, the following statement has been made with respect to adaptive planning:

> Transportation planning takes place in a context of continuous evolution in demand, in technology, in people's preferences and in objectives. Since there are significant time lags in the implementation of transportation systems, the planner must build into his plans an opportunity to review and revise his strategy to accommodate changing conditions.
>
> Consider a comprehensive long-range transportation development plan for a metropolitan region. We can expect that even by the end of the first five years things will have changed. Demand patterns will have evolved as a result of urban growth; new technologies and new ways of using existing technologies will have developed as a result of research and development efforts; behavioural research and data collection activities will have produced new insights into people's needs and wants, which in turn will have altered the planner's view of community goals and objectives. The conditions would no longer correspond to the planner's initial set of assumptions, and therefore may call for a modified plan of action.
>
> If changes have been relatively minor, the actions to be implemented in the subsequent stages of the planning strategy may be the same; more likely, however, the later stages of the plan will likewise have to be revised because of further changes in critical conditions.

Table 12.3. Sequence of projects involved in Toronto subway system construction

Project	Length (miles)	Year opened
Yonge Street	4.6	1954
University Avenue	2.4	1963
Bloor-Danforth	8.0	1966
Bloor-Danforth extensions	6.2	1968
Yonge Street extension	2.7	1973
Yonge Street extension	2.3	1974

The planning process described above involves an iterative or sequential approach: the transportation plan is conceived as a sequence of staged actions; at the conclusion of each stage, the planning strategy is reviewed and possibly modified in the light of fresh data and information acquired through observation and appropriate demonstrations.

The approach to urban transport planning suggested by the above may be formalized through the use of the statistical decision principles discussed earlier. The numerical example given in Sec. 12.1.3 was concerned only with a two-stage process in which there was a demonstration project followed by a transport policy decision. This same approach could easily be extended to an *N*-stage process in which a set of projects was identified. A long range plan for some horizon year may be identified using the transport-planning process described in Chap. 11. Statistical decision theory can then be used to articulate the possible sequences of project investment.

Additional sources of uncertainty may be incorporated into the decision tree. For example, the final capital cost may be a source of uncertainty. The states of nature may then be expressed as a doublet with one dealing with the probable modal split (or an alternative demand variable) and the second dealing with the capital cost.

Uncertainties with respect to the community's objectives, and the weighting of these objectives could be incorporated in the decision tree in a similar manner. The probable outcomes of various actions could be mapped into the objectives using different utility functions. It would be necessary for the analyst to define a probability distribution over these utility functions.

Khan [4,5] has discussed the application of statistical decision theory to transport-policy planning in more detail than the illustrative example provided in Sec. 12.1.3.

REFERENCES

1. Organisation for Economic Cooperation and Development, *The Urban Transportation Planning Process*, Paris, 1971.
2. Raiffa, H., and R. Schlaifer, *Applied Statistical Decision Theory*, Division of Research, Harvard Business School, Boston, Massachusetts, 1960.
3. Cowley, R. D., *A New Look for Commuters in Canada,* Proceedings, Canadian Good Roads Association, Ottawa, Ontario, pp. 192–210, 1966.
4. Khan, A. M., "Cost-Benefit Analysis of Information Acquisition in Transportation Planning," *Environment and Planning,* vol. 3, no. 3, pp. 327–342, 1971.
5. Khan, A. M., "Transport Policy Decision Analysis: Recent Developments in the Techniques of Investment Planning," *High Speed Ground Transportation Journal,* vol. 6, no. 1, pp. 7-26, 1972.

13 URBAN INFORMATION SOURCES

The transport-planning techniques introduced throughout this book require relatively detailed information for their calibration and use. An expensive and time-consuming part of any transport-planning study is the collection and coding of land-use and travel information. In many studies the cost of data collection and coding has been as high as 50 to 60 percent of the total study costs. There are two principal ways in which data collection costs may be reduced significantly and these are: (1) by using data on population, employment, etc., that are collected on a regular basis by other agencies, and (2) developing valid relationships between travel behavior and urban activities in order to minimize the need for special travel surveys.

Large amounts of data are collected by a variety of organizations but most of this information is not at the spatially disaggregated level required by urban transport-planning studies. However, recent innovations in the U.S. Census of Population and Housing allow population and employment observations to be reported at the traffic analysis zone level.

This chapter provides the reader with a broad understanding of the types of urban information that are available nationally in both Canada and the United

States. Information is also collected at the state, provincial, and municipal levels. As it is difficult to provide an exhaustive treatment of the data available at these levels, because of the variations in sampling methods and reporting of the variables measured, references are made to indices of these data sources. The principal concern of the chapter is with the information provided by the U.S. and Canadian censuses of population and housing.

13.1 GEOGRAPHICAL CODING OF INFORMATION

Decennial population censuses have been conducted for many years in both the United States and Canada. The U.S. Census of Population and Housing is conducted in the years ending with a zero and the Canadian population census in the years ending with a one. Censuses of more limited scope are conducted in both countries in the mid-decade years. One of the principal organizational problems of a census is to select a series of geographic codes for reporting summarized data.

13.1.1 Census geographic codes

The basic unit of observation for the population census is the dwelling. Statistics Canada defines a dwelling "as being structurally separated from any other living or business unit and either having direct access either from outside or from a common hall, lobby, vestibule or stairway within the building. If access can be achieved only by passing through some other living quarters, the unit is not considered to be a separate dwelling." A similar definition is used by the U.S. Bureau of the Census.

The group of persons occupying a dwelling unit are defined as a household. Thus, the individual members of a household are not necessarily related by marriage.

In Canada the organization of the census survey is based on the delineation of enumeration areas (enumeration districts in the United States). An enumeration area normally represents the workload for one enumerator. In the 1971 census of Canada the following six criteria were used to delineate enumeration areas:

The maximum population is 200 households or 100 farms.

The boundaries are recognizable in the field in that they are defined by such tangibles as rivers, railroads, and streets.

The socioeconomic characteristics of the population within the areas are reasonably homogeneous.

An enumerator has ready access to each part of the area.

The boundaries of other statistical or administrative areas are respected.

Since 1941, Canadian metropolitan areas and other cities of 50,000 or more have been divided into small statistical areas called *census tracts.* Each census

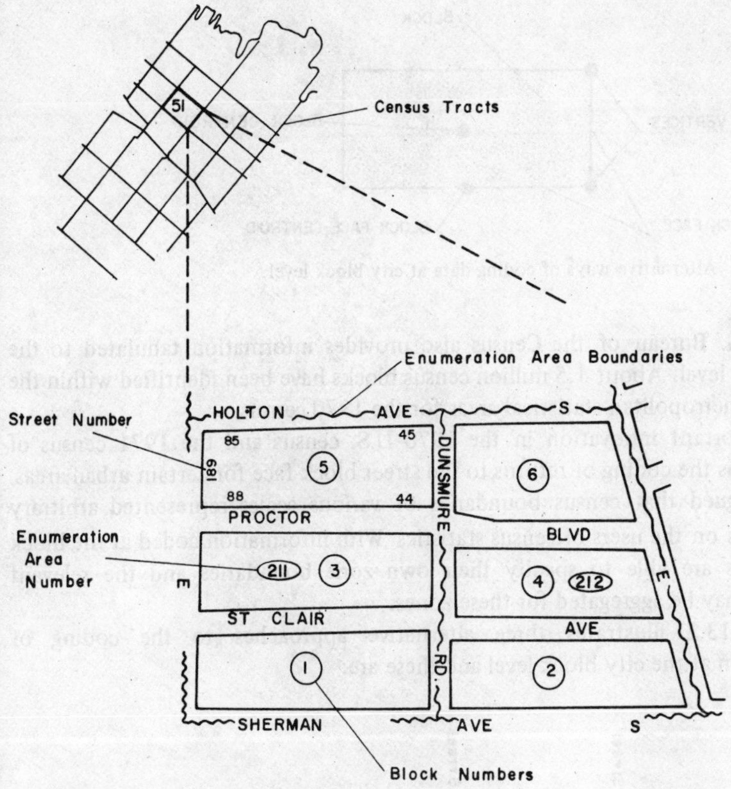

FIG. 13.1. Enumeration areas and census tracts–Hamilton, Ontario, 1971.

tract contains a number of enumeration areas. Figure 13.1 illustrates the interrelationship of census tracts and enumeration areas in Hamilton, Ontario, for the 1971 census of Canada.

In the United States census tracts are established in each of the metropolitan statistical areas and there were 233 of these areas in 1970. The U.S. Bureau of the Census describes census tracts in the following way [1]:

"Census tracts are small, permanently established, geographical areas into which large cities and their environs have been divided for statistical purposes. Tract boundaries are selected by a local committee and approved by the Bureau of the Census." In the 1970 U.S. census there were about 35,000 census tracts.

Census tracts normally contain about 2,000 to 5,000 people and are established in order to achieve some uniformity of population characteristics, economic status, and living conditions. The census tract is normally the smallest geographic area for which comprehensive population and housing characteristics are published on a routine basis.

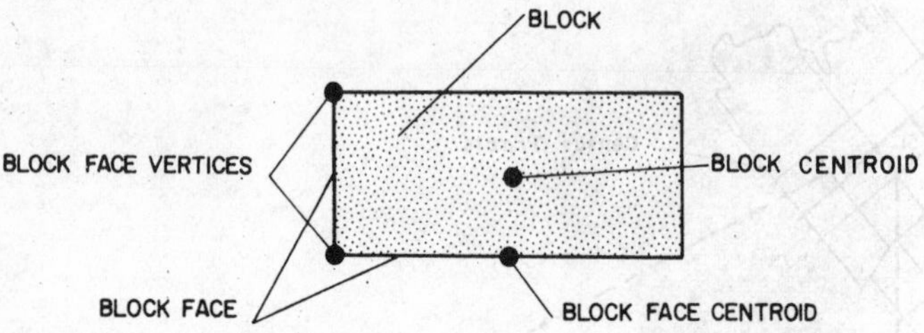

FIG. 13.2. Alternative ways of coding data at city block level.

The U.S. Bureau of the Census also provides information tabulated to the city-block level. About 1.5 million census blocks have been identified within the standard metropolitan statistical areas for the 1970 census.

An important innovation in the 1970 U.S. census and the 1971 census of Canada was the coding of returns to the street block face for certain urban areas. It was argued that census boundaries of various scales represented arbitrary constraints on the users of census statistics. With information coded at the block face, users are able to specify their own zone boundaries and the relevant statistics may be aggregated for these zones.

Figure 13.2 illustrates three alternative approaches to the coding of information at the city block level and these are:

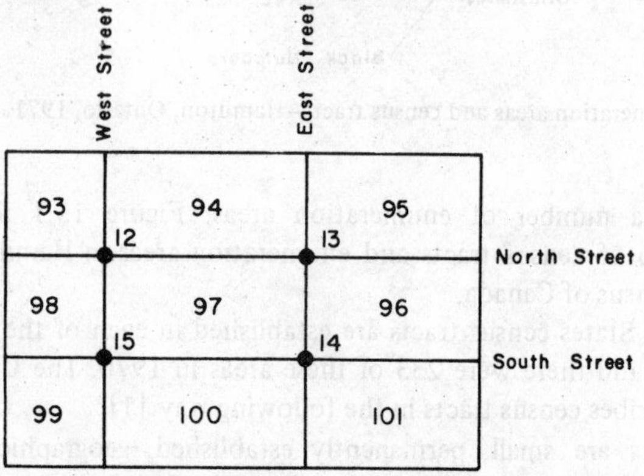

SEGMENT NAME	NODES FROM	NODES TO	BLOCK NUMBER LEFT	BLOCK NUMBER RIGHT	ADDRESS LEFT LOW	ADDRESS LEFT HIGH	ADDRESS RIGHT LOW	ADDRESS RIGHT HIGH
North Street	12	13	94	97	133	229	134	230

FIG. 13.3. Form of segment records in a DIME file.

1. Assigning geographic coordinates to a centroid for an entire block
2. Assigning geographic coordinates to a centroid for each block face
3. Assigning geographic coordinates to each end of each block face

Coding of block face centroids was selected for the 1971 census of Canada in 14 cities. Outside of these 14 urban areas the coding unit is still the enumeration areas. Centroids are described by the grid coordinates of the 6° Universal Transverse Mercator Grid System. The principles of geocoding are discussed briefly in the section that follows.

The U.S. Bureau of the Census selected the third coding alternative just mentioned. This approach is much more powerful in that the network properties of an area are recorded and are not simply a series of points on various parts of the network. The system used is illustrated in Fig. 13.3 and is known as the *DIME system** [2]. A DIME file is composed of segment records (a segment is defined as a length of street or other feature between two distinct vertices). Each segment is coded separately with three basic codes that are shown in Fig. 13.3. Vertices are then assigned coordinates according to the State Plane Coordinate System.

13.1.2 Geocoding

The geocoding of a point may be defined as the assignment of x and y coordinates to that point in a cartesian coordinate system. A coordinate system is a grid of lines that defines blocks where the size of the blocks is dependent upon the scale of the coordinate system. The location of a block is defined by the x,y coordinates of its lower left-hand corner. If a very fine coordinate system scale is used, then the blocks become small and may approach points. Figure 13.4 illustrates how a grid system may be used to reference points, lines, and areas.

The Universal Transverse Mercator Grid divides the earth's surface into zones 6 degrees of longitude wide and extending north from the equator to the 84th parallel of latitude in Canada. Zones are numbered from west to east and the Detroit-Toronto region is located in zone 17 as illustrated in Fig. 13.5. Since the width of a zone varies with the degree of latitude, a rectangular grid is superimposed on each zone. The ordinates of this grid are parallel to the central meridian of a zone and the abscissae are perpendicular to the central meridian. Measurements on this grid are made in meters. Northings begin at 0 at the equator. The central meridian of a zone is assigned a magnitude of 500,000 meters and eastings are measured from the central meridian.

Figure 13.6 shows part of Hamilton, Ontario, recorded on a Universal Transverse Mercator Grid of 1,000 meters at a scale of 1:25,000. The Hamilton City Hall is located at an easting of 591,450 meters and a northing of 4,789,650 meters in zone 17. Its coordinates would be expressed as 17/591,450/4,789,650.

*DIME = Dual Independent Map Encoding.

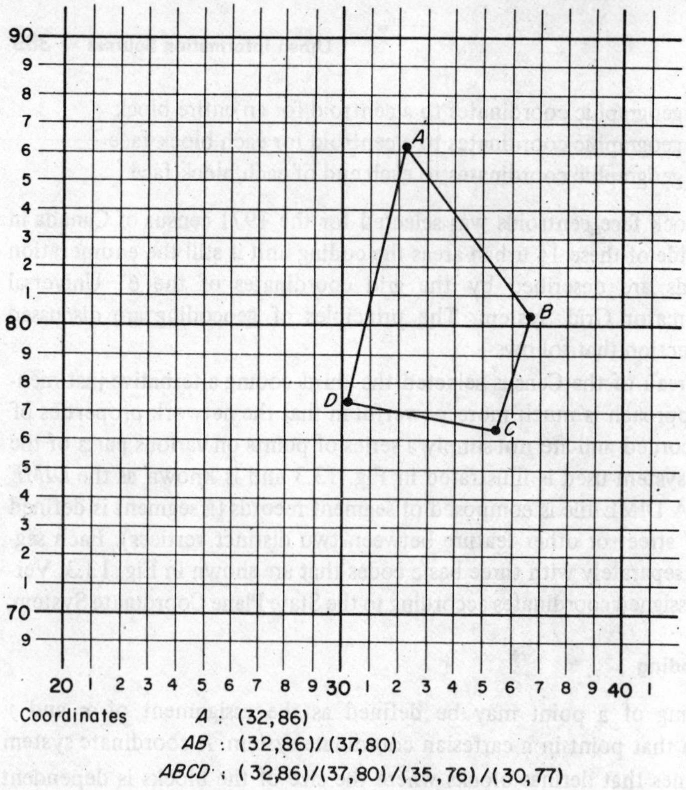

FIG. 13.4. Geocoding with cartesian coordinate system.

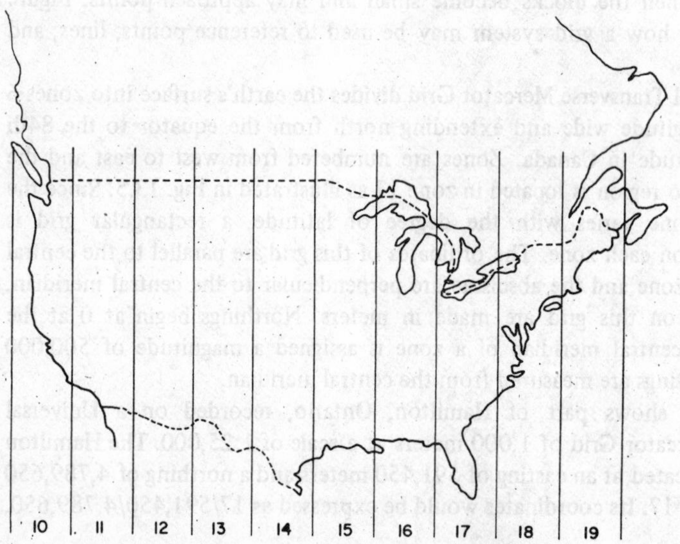

FIG. 13.5. Universal transverse Mercator grid zone system.

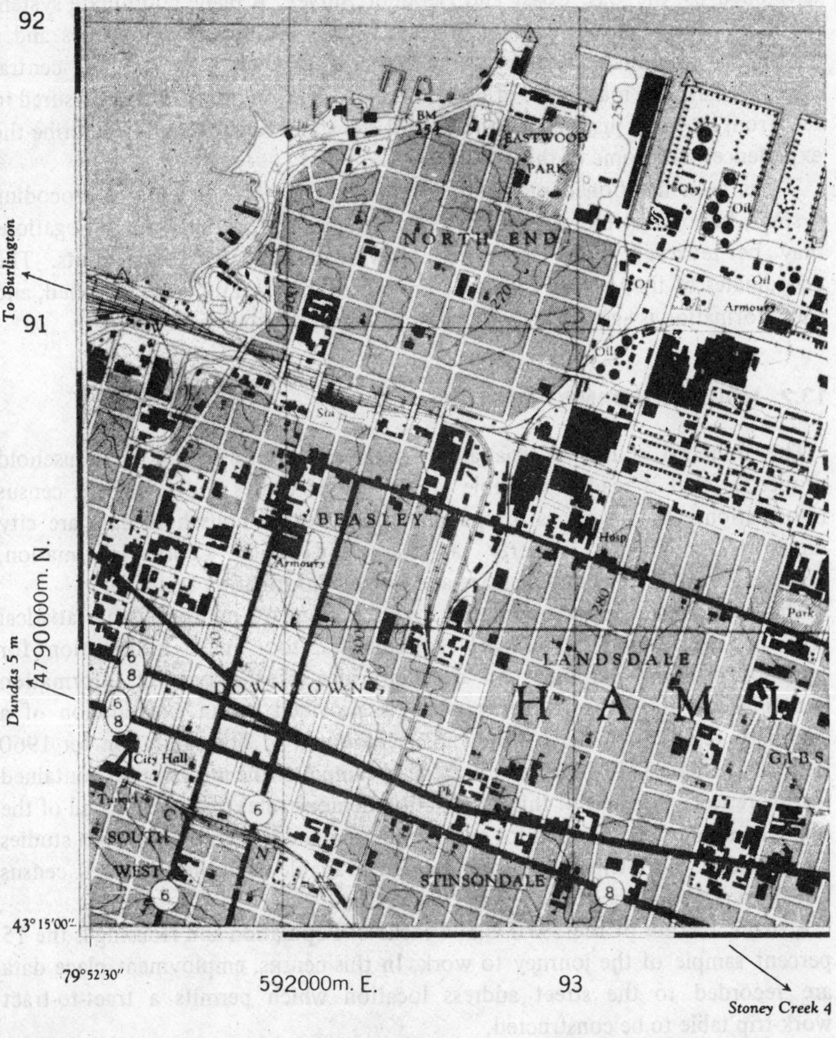

FIG. 13.6. Geocoding of Hamilton City Hall with 1,000-meter universal transverse Mercator grid. (Compiled 1961–1962 by the Army Survey Establishment, R.C.E., from air photographs taken in 1960.)

Other grid systems are used which are based on other types of map projections. In addition, many local grid systems have been established for coding data. For example, the system used originally for the Chicago Area Transportation Study was a ½-mile grid system skewed to fit the existing street system and focussed on the intersection of State and Madison Streets in the Chicago CBD. This system has been revised and points are now identified by the coordinates of the state plane system. The State Plane Coordinate System was developed by the U.S. Coast and Geodetic Survey. A plane coordinate system has been developed for each U.S. state. States are divided into zones and a rectangular coordinate system is superimposed on each zone with the central meridian having a magnitude of 500,000 feet. The y coordinates are measured in feet from an origin just outside the base of the state. References 3-5 describe the experiences with some of these systems.

It has been mentioned previously that one of the advantages of a geocoding system, in contrast to a zone-type referencing system, is that data aggregations may be retrieved with respect to individually specified areal units. The coordinates of the vertices of the perimeters of the areal units are specified, and the information is aggregated for all points within the zone boundaries.

13.2 HOUSEHOLD INFORMATION

The principal source of spatially disaggregated information on household properties that is readily available in the United States and Canada is census information. Other sources of spatially disaggregated household data are city directories, municipal property tax files, and so on. Census information, however, is the most comprehensive and reliable information available.

The census tract reports available for each standard metropolitan statistical area in the United States [6] contain far too much information for transport-planning purposes. An excellent idea of the type of information contained in the census tract reports is provided by an examination of a summary report prepared by the U.S. Department of Transportation for 1960 U.S. census data [7]. Table 13.1 provides a sample of the information contained in this report. A review of this information demonstrates that virtually all of the socioeconomic data required for trip production and trip end modal split studies are provided. Work-trip distribution data are available from the 1960 U.S. census but the work end is coded to a very coarse scale.

A major feature of the 1970 U.S. Census of Population and Housing is the 15 percent sample of the journey to work. In this census, employment place data are recorded to the street address location which permits a tract-to-tract work-trip table to be constructed.

A second important feature of the 1970 census is the development of a set of census-processing programs by the Federal Highway Administration. Normal traffic-analysis zones are smaller than the census tract. With the geocoding used in the 1970 census, data summaries may be provided at the urban traffic-zone level. The data summaries contain a work-trip table along with tabulations of the properties of zones of residence, the zones of employment, and certain areawide properties. The tabulations at the zone of residence include person characteristics, household-head characteristics, household characteristics, and housing properties. The tabulations at the zone of employment include workers by occupation and industry. The tabulations at the areawide level include cross-classifications of household characteristics, housing characteristics, and mode of transportation to work.

This information will be very useful for individual planning agencies. A longer-term benefit will be the generalized relationships that may now be developed between work-trip travel and household and employment characteristics for a large number of cities. While generalizations have been developed in the past from data collected in transport-planning studies, these attempts have suffered because of differences in the survey and analysis techniques between study areas.

Information collected in the census of Canada is very similar to that obtained in the U.S. census. This information is reported in a similar

Table 13.1. Example entries from U. S. Department of Transportation planning data

Standard location area		
Total population	9,065	12,617
Total no. households	2,459	3,859
Total housing units	2,564	4,068
% Renter-occupied housing	9.4	41.2
Workers as % population	38.3	37.8
Auto per household	1.6	1.1
Persons per auto	2.3	2.9
Workers per auto	0.9	1.1
Persons per household	3.7	3.3
Workers per household	1.4	1.2
% Workers making work trip by		
Auto	92.0	82.6
Rail	2.0	0.7
Bus	4.1	14.0
% Households with		
0 auto	0	15.4
1 auto	46.4	56.3
2 auto	46.6	27.3
3+ auto	7.0	1.0
% Families earning		
< $5,000	14.6	37.8
$5,000–8,000	35.1	28.2
$8,000–15,000	45.0	21.6
> $15,000	5.4	2.3
Median income	8,025	5,774

Population, household, and family characteristics by census tracts, Census Metropolitan Area of Hamilton, 1966

No.	Characteristics	Metropolitan area — Zone métropolitaine	Hamilton, c. Total	1	2	3	4	5	6	7	8	9	10	11	12
1	POPULATION, 1966	449,116	298,121	5,205	9,748	3,066	4,026	4,132	6,058	4,335	3,672	3,183	3,907	3,076	2,133
2	" , 1961	395,189	273,991	5,363	7,880	3,066	4,089	3,983	6,264	4,436	3,416	3,060	3,443	2,411	1,997
	AGE GROUP:														
3	Males	223,638	147,542	2,428	4,813	1,493	1,981	1,960	3,129	2,125	1,813	1,539	1,882	1,206	1,014
4	0- 4 years	24,479	15,183	137	488	106	210	182	329	231	221	173	141	30	78
5	5- 9 "	25,291	15,512	175	410	124	206	183	341	225	180	139	106	19	49
6	10-14 "	22,033	13,705	208	357	104	162	168	243	199	124	128	112	31	36
7	15-19 "	18,777	12,140	236	357	137	173	172	269	194	146	101	123	60	56
8	20-24 "	15,944	11,307	187	530	140	197	138	174	126	184	168	228	184	128
9	25-34 "	28,414	18,994	216	759	127	259	199	407	259	250	235	360	203	161
10	35-44 "	32,439	21,099	245	592	166	225	233	462	301	211	185	231	146	139
11	45-54 "	24,787	16,502	321	550	228	233	272	349	213	184	158	201	149	99
12	55-64 "	16,545	11,936	366	433	195	156	191	246	181	140	135	175	156	109
13	65-69 "	5,694	4,307	132	139	74	50	69	119	69	66	41	75	85	59
14	70 years and over	9,235	6,857	205	198	92	110	153	190	127	107	76	130	143	100
15	Under 1 year	4,668	2,962	23	110	18	36	36	47	49	51	34	39	7	20
16	" 18 years	83,119	51,640	656	1,449	412	681	632	1,078	774	606	492	430	107	188
17	" 21 "	94,043	58,915	801	1,700	504	794	726	1,219	885	708	562	530	165	242
18	Females	225,478	150,579	2,777	4,935	1,573	2,045	2,172	2,929	2,210	1,859	1,644	2,025	1,870	1,119
19	0- 4 years	23,103	14,411	140	438	88	208	161	312	210	166	143	131	48	64
20	5- 9 "	24,197	14,821	172	418	95	190	197	333	207	145	124	88	19	32
21	10-14 "	21,213	13,115	187	359	86	193	151	305	191	146	102	94	28	24
22	15-19 "	18,461	12,282	228	357	125	155	176	221	175	156	125	133	85	100
23	20-24 "	16,396	11,685	191	503	112	133	154	192	172	169	166	214	201	156
24	25-34 "	28,801	18,801	199	683	133	223	204	392	271	231	239	243	197	118
25	35-44 "	32,599	21,278	312	633	206	269	273	410	283	229	195	229	204	113
26	45-54 "	23,583	16,112	403	591	252	239	275	266	221	190	182	249	245	123
27	55-64 "	17,238	12,815	431	483	238	178	246	228	225	180	160	218	329	138
28	65-69 "	6,679	5,144	186	177	89	91	112	110	77	88	56	138	165	77
29	70 years and over	13,208	10,115	328	293	149	166	223	160	178	159	152	288	349	174
30	Under 1 year	4,388	2,765	23	89	16	45	34	61	41	31	32	30	22	18
31	" 18 years	79,231	49,308	634	1,410	339	678	606	1,091	706	543	441	371	127	160
32	" 21 "	90,509	57,159	763	1,654	422	766	716	1,209	811	659	521	492	214	254
	MARITAL STATUS:														
	Males:														
33	Single, total	112,068	72,912	1,074	2,137	654	1,019	933	1,642	1,077	895	749	902	475	490
34	" , 15 and over	40,261	28,508	554	882	320	441	400	729	422	370	309	543	395	327
35	Married	106,537	70,784	1,290	2,576	788	917	966	1,375	965	850	740	904	662	466
36	Widowed	4,307	3,270	61	89	49	41	54	96	70	58	41	62	51	45

	Females:														
37	Single, total	100,743	65,354	1,094	1,921	549	884	944	1,334	987	767	666	767	727	442
38	" , 15 and over	32,227	23,004	595	706	280	293	435	384	379	310	297	454	632	322
39	Married	107,219	71,398	1,309	2,574	794	927	975	1,346	975	866	769	917	710	464
40	Widowed	16,373	12,896	363	407	210	221	240	234	234	210	200	308	393	194
41	OCCUPIED DWELLINGS (HOUSEHOLDS)	123,352	84,540(1)	1,672	3,167	1,065	1,199	1,247	1,434	1,213	1,177	1,057	1,598	1,653	856
42	Owner-occupied	84,119	53,343	1,410	1,773	782	757	947	845	693	450	453	394	272	90
43	Tenant-occupied	39,233	31,197(1)	262	1,394	283	442	300	589	520	727	604	1,204	1,381	766
44	Single attached	6,971	5,289	13	28	24	55	14	470	215	118	50	91	26	42
45	Single detached	83,576	52,106(1)	1,421	1,788	789	704	855	597	579	395	337	364	84	63
46	Apartments, flats	32,693	27,142	238	1,351	252	440	378	367	418	664	670	1,143	1,543	751
	By number of persons:														
47	1	12,269	10,047	218	371	184	180	163	117	178	218	194	531	773	345
48	2-3	52,325	37,343	853	1,713	566	545	601	534	517	568	560	762	780	389
49	4-5	41,409	26,010	484	852	246	319	347	431	337	254	204	224	75	80
50	6-9	16,583	10,620(1)	113	228	67	146	130	321	170	128	87	77	24	38
51	10 or more	766	520	4	3	2	9	6	31	11	9	12	4	1	4
52	Persons per household	3.6	3.4(1)	3.1	3.1	2.9	3.3	3.3	4.1	3.5	3.1	3.0	2.4	1.8	2.2
	By number of families:														
53	0	16,990	14,020	311	517	234	251	250	189	240	296	285	686	948	426
54	1	102,963	67,847(1)	1,339	2,597	820	925	974	1,102	933	848	755	897	702	418
55	2 or more	3,399	2,673	22	53	11	23	23	143	40	33	17	15	3	12
56	Households with lodgers	7,159	6,012	75	115	43	71	58	218	93	77	89	109	77	63
57	FAMILIES	110,005	73,374(1)	1,383	2,705	842	973	1,020	1,404	1,016	919	793	932	712	462
	By age of head:														
58	Under 25 years	6,076	4,384	25	215	32	54	34	62	51	89	74	79	67	53
59	25-34 years	23,735	15,245(1)	133	628	94	211	153	306	202	201	183	222	103	90
60	35-44 "	30,241	19,269	229	573	155	204	210	354	266	196	170	155	94	92
61	45-54 "	23,344	15,238	315	561	220	224	259	266	187	169	147	169	107	69
62	55-64 "	15,022	10,658	362	431	191	146	173	181	158	122	125	151	144	77
63	65-69 "	4,733	3,516	137	131	74	49	71	86	54	60	30	56	67	38
64	70 years and over	6,854	5,064	182	166	76	85	120	149	98	82	64	100	130	43
	By number of children:														
65	0	33,238	24,109	588	1,069	364	312	368	443	335	369	320	456	497	249
66	1-2	47,467	31,515	552	1,160	348	415	425	559	399	354	319	367	190	174
67	3-4	23,474	14,168(1)	211	407	111	183	179	296	228	151	125	85	20	29
68	5 or more	5,826	3,582	32	69	19	63	48	106	54	45	29	24	5	10
	Children in families, by age:														
69	Under 6 years	57,314	35,588(1)	338	1,077	232	512	410	791	531	451	351	307	88	152
70	6-14 years	81,807	50,375(1)	680	1,378	362	649	621	1,069	699	525	445	359	84	119
71	15-18 "	27,615	17,686	349	524	213	246	259	373	273	199	147	142	71	76
72	19-24 "	17,569	11,628	345	426	179	182	225	206	153	117	106	126	98	47
73	Persons per family	3.7	3.5(1)	3.3	3.2	3.2	3.6	3.5	3.7	3.6	3.4	3.3	3.0	2.4	2.8
74	Children per family	1.7	1.6(1)	1.2	1.3	1.2	1.6	1.5	1.7	1.6	1.4	1.3	1.0	0.5	0.9
75	Number of lodging families	1,050	918	—	8	3	1	3	75	8	7	1	5	2	22

(1) Includes census tract No. 58 for which figures are not shown to ensure anonymity.

FIG. 13.7. Information contained in Statistics Canada census tract bulletins.

Table 13.2. City directory accuracy check

Number of individuals checked	Incorrect address	Incorrect employer	Not listed in directory	Listed but not as worker	All entries correct
217	15	5	67	73	57

manner at the census-tract level and Fig. 13.7 provided an example of the information contained in the census-tract reports published by Statistics Canada [8].

A fundamental difficulty in using census information for transport planning is the conflict between the small geographic scale of zones used for transport planning and the disclosure rules governing the release of census information. Normally, traffic-analysis zones are at the scale of enumeration areas. At this scale, only relatively coarse information may be revealed, such as total population, number of households, and so on. The transport models discussed in early chapters frequently require cross-classifications of information at a level that violates census disclosure rules. For example, the number of households within each income range cross-classified by the number of employees per household at the enumeration-area level would contain many cells which would violate disclosure constraints.

Areawide cross-classifications are provided, however. The use of areawide averages is not too restrictive since many of the analytical tools use areawide averages. Examples of the use of areawide crossclassifications are provided in Chaps. 3, 6, and 11.

A large variety of other sources of household information exist for many municipalities. For example, city directories are compiled and marketed by private firms [9]. Andrews [10] has conducted a check on the validity of the entries contained in the *Kitchener-Waterloo City Directory.* The data in the directory included name, address, employer, occupation, and sex. A sample of the directory entries was compared with the personnel records of a major industrial firm in the area. The results of this accuracy check are illustrated in Table 13.2. The most important error revealed by this check was that the directory listed slightly less than 50 percent of the workers.

13.3. EMPLOYMENT DATA

It has been pointed out previously that the 15 percent journey-to-work sample contained in the 1970 U.S. census allows the location of employment by occupation and industry to be estimated. Employment data are also collected in the Census of Business, the Census of Manufactures, the Annual Census of Manufactures, and the Census of Governments. Unfortunately, most of the information collected in these surveys is not available at the disaggregated spatial scale required by transport-planning studies. The finest scale of data availability on a routine basis is normally the city or county scale.

Statistics Canada conducts a similar surveys and these include the Census of Merchandising and Service Businesses. The census covers all retail, wholesale, and service businesses with some exceptions such as door-to-door selling, establishments in which retailing represents a minor activity, services relating to health and welfare, education, finance, and so on. Data available at the census-tract level includes the total number of stores, total sales, and sales by six groups of stores where the classifications are food, general merchandise, automotive, apparel, and accessories, hardware, and home furnishings and other. Many entries are suppressed because of the census disclosure constraints. Detailed breakdowns of sales and employees are provided at coarser levels of aggregation. Similar information is available for the service trades and wholesale trade. Similar information is tabulated for the Census of Manufactures. However, it is difficult to obtain employment estimates at the census tract level other than by using areawide averages to convert sales levels to employment. It is virtually impossible to derive employment levels for the normal traffic-analysis-zone scale. Reference [11] provides a systematic listing of employment and economic activity data available in the United States.

Reference [12] provides some useful discussions of the use of the 1970 U.S. census data for urban transport-planning purposes.

13.4 EXTENDED USES OF CENSUS DATA

It has been suggested above that the wider use of basic census data is possible with the development of relationships between travel-related variables and the basic small area census variables of population, household structure, and so on, that are expressed as totals or averages. An example of the type of relationship that might be developed is shown in Fig. 13.8 in which the percentage of

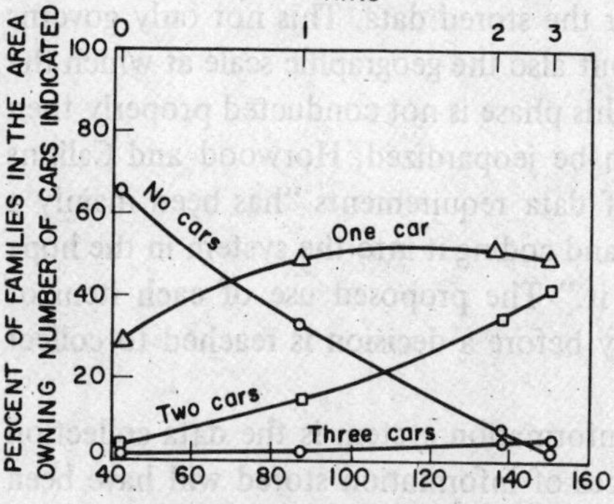

FIG. 13.8. Relation between car-ownership distribution and average car ownership.

car-owning families in various categories is plotted against the average number of cars per 100 families in an area [13]. That is, given the relationship shown in Fig. 13.8, the number of families without a car in an area could be predicted from a knowledge of the average car ownership of a zone.

Other relationships have been established between average age of household head and income distribution, average years of education of household head and income distribution, and so on. As additional relationships of the type shown in Fig. 13.8 are developed, it will be possible to extend census records to build up a very detailed picture of urban social and economic structures.

13.5 URBAN INFORMATION SYSTEMS

Horwood and Calkins [14] have provided the following definition of an urban information system:

"An urban and regional information system is one involving the sequence of steps in the synthesis of information from diverse data inputs by the use of automation to bear on the definition, display and solution of the set of problems relating to planning, political and management decisions in urban affairs."

Information systems have been developed and used in most of the major transport-planning studies. These information systems have been developed to collect, store, and retrieve data required by the transport-planning process. These systems were designed and implemented over a short period of time and in many cases were not used after the completion of the transport-planning study. In recent years many municipalities and other levels of government have attempted to establish information systems to serve a variety of purposes. These attempts have not all been successful, since the broad role of the information system could not be defined clearly. In planning an urban information system six broad phases must be considered and these are: (1) the proposed use of the data, (2) the collection of the data, (3) the updating of data, (4) the storing of the data, (5) the retrieving and display of the data, and (6) the analysis of the data.

The most fundamental issue to be resolved by an agency is to identify clearly and systematically the uses planned for the stored data. This not only governs the type of information to be stored, but also the geographic scale at which the data are to be recorded and stored. If this phase is not conducted properly then the efficiency of the entire system can be jeopardized. Horwood and Calkins [14] have noted that the definition of data requirements "has been mainly a process of grabbing what was available and coding it into the system in the hope that something useful would come of it." The proposed use of each item of information must be examined carefully before a decision is reached to collect it.

A critical element of the cost of an information system is the data collection procedure to be used. Many of the pieces of information stored will have been collected by other agencies. An important component of the data collection procedure must be the mechanisms to be used for the maintenance and regular updating of the information files.

A principal concern in the storing of information has to do with the geographic referencing of the data. The advantages of some form of geocoding system which allows information to be assembled for various spatial scales has been mentioned earlier in this chapter.

The way in which data are retrieved is related closely to the way in which data are used for decisionmaking in the agency concerned. Very frequently the format of the data output has been governed largely by the designer of the information systems, rather than by a systematic assessment of the utility of the output to the person or agency using it. Horwood [15] has discussed the requirements of a good query system for transport planning and has stated that "a data handling procedure designed for ease of use is the single most important element of an information system."

The final phase identified above is related closely to the first-mentioned phase. Most observers suggest that the design of the information system should be geared closely to the analytical and modeling capability within a planning agency.

Worrall [16] has described the design of a planning information system developed for the Denver Regional Council of Governments. The system recommended contained six interrelated file-sets which are: land use, population, employment, housing, transportation, and environmental systems. Data were coded to the 1970 census tract system for the study area.

The proposed content of the population file-set is listed to illustrate the type of information stored:

1. Total regional and tract-level population and household counts
2. Tract-level populations stratified by sex, race, age, industry of employment, occupation, education, school attendance, and residence in group quarters
3. Tract-level household numbers stratified by race, size, income, persons employed, marital status of household head, presence of children, period of residence, and home and automobile ownership

SUMMARY

Large amounts of information on urban areas is collected and published by a variety of public and private agencies. However, much of this information is not reported at the spatially disaggregated scale required by urban transport-planning studies. Geographic coding innovations used in the 1970 U.S. census and the 1971 census of Canada allow much of the recorded census information to be aggregated at a much finer spatial scale. The journey-to-work question contained in the 1970 U.S. census allows work-trip tables and some information at the employment end to be assembled.

Other data are available from government and private sources but the reliability of much of this information is unknown in most cases. The greatest potential for the more-comprehensive use of census data rests with the development of generalized relationships that allow zone averages to be converted into distributions by finer categories.

Continuing transport-planning studies require an efficient information system for storing the relevant data. To be effective, information systems must be carefully designed in conjunction with the tasks to be performed by a particular agency. The most-important phase of the design of information system is the identification of the end use of each item of information planned for collection.

REFERENCES

1. Bureau of Census, *Census Tract Manual,* 4th ed., U.S. Government Printing Office, Washington, D.C., 1958.
2. Bureau of Census, *Census Use Study: The DIME Geocoding System,* U.S. Government Printing Office, Washington, D.C., 1970.
3. Vance, J. A., *Geographical Data Coding Grid,* Proceedings, Canadian Good Roads Association, Ottawa, Ontario, pp. 265–278, 1966.
4. Crawford, R. J., *Utility of an Automated Geocoding System for Urban Land Use Analysis,* Research Report No. 3, Urban Data Center, University of Washington, Seattle, 1967.
5. Haack, H., "Geocoding at CATS - A Before and After Review," in J. E. Rickert and S. L. Hale (eds.), *Urban and Regional Information Systems: Past, Present and Future,* Center for Urban Regionalism, Kent State University, Kent, Ohio, 1970.
6. Bureau of the Census, *Census of Population and Housing: 1970 Census Tracts,* U.S. Government Printing Office, Washington, D.C., 1972.
7. Department of Transportation/Federal Highway Administration, *Transportation Planning Data for Urbansized Areas - Based on 1960 Census,* U.S. Government Printing Office, Washington, D.C., 1970.
8. Statistics Canada, *Census Tract Bulletin 1971 Census of Canada,* Ottawa, Ontario, 1973.
9. Vernon Directories Limited, *Kitchener-Waterloo City Directory,* Hamilton, Ontario, 1969.
10. Andrews, M. G., *Travel Characteristics of Selected Manufacturing Industries in Kitchener-Waterloo,* M.A.Sc. thesis, Department of Civil Engineering, University of Waterloo, Waterloo, Ontario, 1972.
11. Department of Commerce/Bureau of Public Roads, *The Role of Economic Studies in Urban Transportation Planning,* U.S. Government Printing Office, Washington, D.C., August, 1965.
12. Highway Research Board, *Use of Census Data in Urban Transportation Planning,* Special Report 121, Washington, D.C., 1971.
13. Wickstrom G. C., "Use of Census Data in Urban Transit Planning," in Highway Research Board, *Use of Census Data in Urban Transportation Planning,* Special Report 121, Washington, D.C., 1971.
14. Horwood, E. M., and H. W. Calkins "Perspectives on Where we Have Been in Urban/Region Information Systems," in J. E. Richert and S. L. Hale (eds.), *Urban and Regional Information Systems: Past, Present and Future,* Center for Urban Regionalism, Kent State University, Kent, Ohio, 1970.

15. Horwood, E. M., *Urban Information Systems and Transportation Planning,* Highway Research Record No. 194, Highway Research Board, Washington, D.C., 1967.
16. Worrall, R. D., "Information Systems for Regional Planning Agencies: A Pragmatic View," in J. E. Rickert and S. L. Hale (eds.), *Urban and Regional Information Systems: Past, Present and Future,* Center for Urban Regionalism, Kent State University, Kent, Ohio, 1970.

14 URBAN GOODS MOVEMENT

Little attention has been directed toward the problem of urban goods movement in past transport-planning studies. Trucks represent only a very small proportion of the vehicles in urban areas and do not represent a particularly important factor in road design. Increasing attention has been directed toward urban goods movement problems in recent years. An important event in this regard was the Conference on Urban Commodity Flow sponsored by the Highway Research Board in 1970 [1]. This conference brought together people with a broad range of interests in commodity movements. It included transport planners, freight carriers, shippers, and persons from a number of regulatory agencies.

A principal conclusion of this conference was that there is a wide spectrum of goods movement problems. These range from a broad concern about the spatial patterns of goods movement demand created by different land-use arrangements, to the design of truck-loading facilities in the central areas of cities. In fact, four broad types of problem may be isolated and these are:

1. The interaction between commodity flows and the spatial arrangement of land uses.

2. The general efficiency and economy of goods movement in urban areas.
3. The environmental problems of noise and air pollution created by truck movements.
4. The provision for truck movement and loading in zones of concentrated land use such as the central business district.

This chapter identifies the broad types of goods movement that occur in urban areas and describes current knowledge on methods for estimating the magnitudes of these movement demands. The chapter is directed toward the strategic planning level as opposed to the design of freight terminals and loading facilities and it concentrates on the forecasting of freight demands; it does not explore potential solutions to freight movement problems. The reason for this is that adequate definitions of the various urban freight movement subproblems have yet to be developed.

14.1 BROAD CLASSES OF URBAN GOODS MOVEMENT DEMANDS

One of the findings of the Highway Research Board Conference on Urban Commodity Flow referred to previously, concerned the estimation of goods movement demands. The needs in this area were stated as follows:

> Forecasts of urban goods movement should include consideration of (*a*) changing patterns of urban development and structure; (*b*) locations of terminals and transfer points; (*c*) land use patterns; (*d*) changing economics and costs of the goods movement industry; (*e*) labor practices within the industry; (*f*) potential technological innovations in goods movement; (*g*) effects of governmental policy, financial aid, and regulation on the movement of goods; and (*h*) social and environmental considerations. Demand forecasting should portray the inter-relationships among industry location, inter-industry transactions, terminal interfaces, freight flow, mode choice and packaging, and urban transportation network.

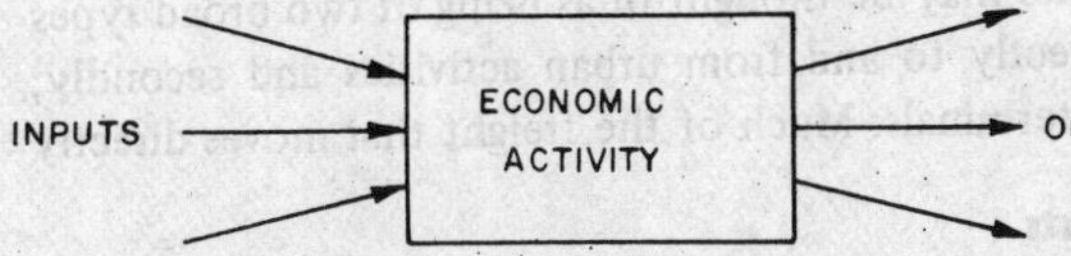

FIG. 14.1. Simple conceptualization of economic activities.

Goods movement demands are created by the economic activities of production and consumption. A convenient way of thinking about urban goods movement problems is to identify the principal economic units in an urban area and to develop an understanding of their internal structures and their associated commodity movement demands.

Each unit of economic activity may be thought of in the manner shown in Fig. 14.1. A unit receives certain types of commodity as input and dispatches other types of commodity as output. A manufacturing plant receives inputs of raw materials and semifinished products and dispatches semifinished and finished products for other destinations. Households receive food and other consumer products and dispatch garbage for disposal. Freight terminals receive goods that are either consolidated into larger consignments for external locations, or goods that must be separated into smaller consignments for distribution within the urban area.

The person travel-demand techniques discussed earlier in this book demonstrated that the determinants of person travel demands are relatively straightforward. The factors which generate many goods movement demands are more complex. One example of this is provided in Table 14.1 in which are shown the tons of commodity per employee per year that were required as input to a number of industrial sectors in Ontario in 1967. The commodity input requirements ranged from 0.2 tons per employee for fabric glove manufacturers to 232 tons per employee for distilleries. A second example has to do with the sizes of consignments within one commodity type. A manufacturer of consumer products might use a small truck to deliver local orders but might ship only container loads to destinations 1,000 to 2,000 miles away. For any one commodity type there may be several trip types that are distinguished from each other by the size of the consignment. Another complicating factor is the frequency at which consignments are received and shipped. The bulk of person travel is quite regular and stable. Goods movement does not have the temporal stability of person travel.

The first broad classification of urban goods movement that may be made is the spatial pattern of demand. The broad groups that may be identified are:

1. Goods movements between urban areas and external locations
2. Interindustry goods movements within an urban area
3. Household-based goods movements within an urban area

Figure 14.2 illustrates this broad grouping of urban commodity movements. External-type goods movements may be thought of as being of two broad types and these are movements directly to and from urban activities and secondly, movements via urban freight terminals. Much of the freight that moves directly

Table 14.1. Commodity inputs per production employee, 1967

Industry sector	Inputs/tons/ employee
Breakfast cereals	127
Steel pipe mills	186
Tobacco products	23
Cardboard boxes	51
Fabric gloves	0.2
Distilleries	232

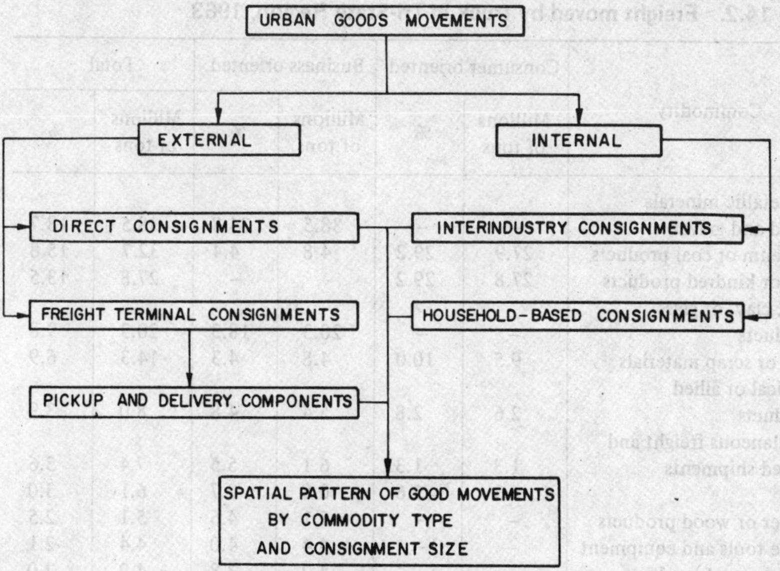

FIG. 14.2. Broad classification of urban goods movements.

to and from urban units is carried by truck, although some plants have rail sidings. Freight that moves via a freight terminal will involve a pickup- or delivery-truck trip within the urban area. Freight terminals may cater to one external mode, or in some cases may serve two or more modes.

Interindustry movements of goods within an urban region are virtually all accomplished by trucks of various sizes. These movements involve the distribution of semifinished products between plants, the distribution of finished products to warehouses and retail establishments, and so on.

Residential-based goods movements usually involve the delivery of consumer goods, maintenance and service vehicles, and public vehicles such as garbage trucks. Table 14.2 shows the broad tonnages of different commodities moved in the Tri-State Region centered on New York City in 1963 [2]. It shows the estimated split in these tonnages between consumer-oriented uses and business-oriented uses and demonstrates that the split is about equal.

A second level of goods movement classification that may be established is by commodity type. The most useful classification system is the standard industrial classification system, or some aggregation of this system [3,4]. A third level of classification is consignment size which is usually expressed in terms of the weight of a consignment. Each broad type of economic unit will create different spatial pattern–commodity-type–consignment-size implications for urban goods movement. Movement mode, time of movement, truck size, and so on varies with each of the combinations just mentioned. The following sections outline some of the current knowledge on each commodity movement type.

Table 14.2. Freight moved by truck in Tri-State Region, 1963

Commodity	Consumer oriented		Business oriented		Total	
	Millions of tons	%	Millions of tons	%	Millions of tons	%
Nonmetallic minerals (sand and gravel)	–	–	38.5	34.8	38.5	18.7
Petroleum or coal products	27.9	29.2	4.8	4.4	32.7	15.8
Food or kindred products	27.8	29.2	–	–	27.8	13.5
Stone, clay, or glass products	–	–	20.3	18.3	20.3	9.8
Waste or scrap materials	9.5	10.0	4.8	4.3	14.3	6.9
Chemical or allied products	2.6	2.8	5.4	4.8	8.0	3.9
Miscellaneous freight and mixed shipments	1.3	1.3	6.1	5.5	7.4	3.6
Coal	5.3	5.6	0.8	0.7	6.1	3.0
Lumber or wood products	–	–	5.1	4.6	5.1	2.5
Service tools and equipment	–	–	4.4	4.0	4.4	2.1
Primary metal products	–	–	4.2	3.8	4.2	2.0
Pulp, paper, or related products	4.1	4.4	–	–	4.1	2.0
Farm products	3.8	4.0	–	–	3.8	1.8
Fabricated metal products	–	–	3.5	3.2	3.5	1.7
Machinery, except electric	–	–	2.6	2.3	2.6	1.3
Printed matter	1.6	1.7	1.0	0.8	2.6	1.2
Transportation equipment	2.4	2.6	–	–	2.4	1.2
Furniture or fixtures	2.0	2.1	0.4	0.3	2.4	1.2
Basic textiles	–	–	2.2	2.0	2.2	1.1
Workers	–	–	2.2	2.0	2.2	1.1
Electrical machinery	–	–	2.2	2.0	2.2	1.1
Laundry and dry cleaning	2.0	2.1	–	–	2.0	1.0
Containers, returned empty	–	–	1.7	1.5	1.7	0.8
Apparel or related products	1.6	1.6	–	–	1.6	0.8
Miscellaneous products of manufacturing	1.0	1.1	–	–	1.0	0.5
All other commodities	2.2	2.3	0.7	0.6	2.9	1.4
Total	95.1	100.0	110.9	100.0	206.0	100.0

14.2 EXTERNAL COMMODITY MOVEMENTS

The classification of goods movements presented in Fig. 14.2 suggested that commodity movements to and from external locations are of two broad types that have been referred to as *direct consignments* and *consignments via a freight terminal.* The majority of the direct consignments are made by truck, and consignment via freight terminals involves pickup and delivery components by

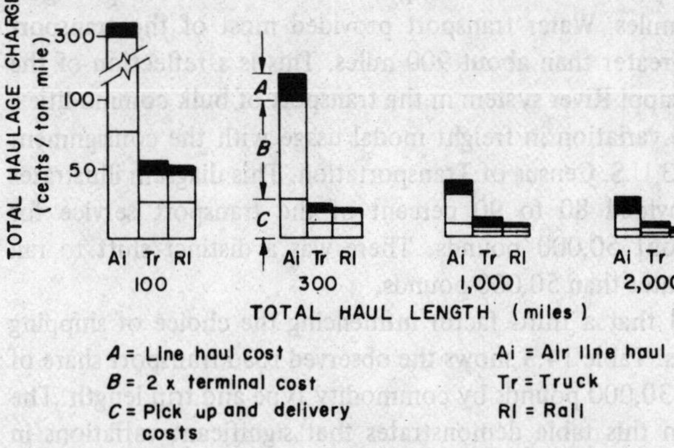

FIG. 14.3. Components of haulage charges–Canada, 1967.

truck. The proportion of direct consignments and the modes used for terminal-type consignments are a function of the freight pricing regime that exists external to the urban region under consideration.

It is generally recognized that the costs of intercity goods movement consist of the pickup and delivery costs, the terminal handling costs, the line haul costs, and the ownership and packaging costs of the goods while they are in transit. Wallace [5] has conducted a study of goods movement costs in Canada for 1967. Figure 14.3 summarizes a few of the results of this study. It should be noted that ownership and packaging costs are not included. The important characteristic to be noted from Fig. 14.3 is the relative unimportance of line haul costs except for the very long trip lengths.

The net effect of cost characteristics of the type illustrated in Fig. 14.3 is shown in Fig. 14.4 where the variation in freight modal usage with haul length observed in the 1963 U.S. Census of Transportation [6] is given. This diagram shows that for trip lengths up to about 300 miles the dominant mode of

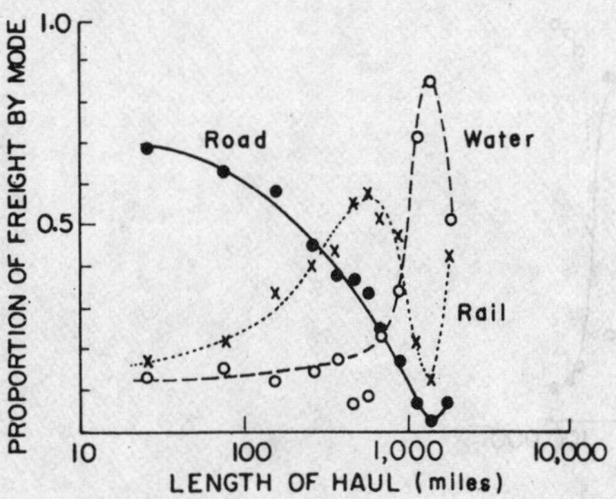

FIG. 14.4. Mode usage vs. haul length–United States, 1963.

shipping was road transport, with rail transport dominating for trip lengths between 300 and 900 miles. Water transport provided most of the transport service for trip lengths greater than about 900 miles. This is a reflection of the importance of the Mississippi River system in the transport of bulk commodities.

Figure 14.5 shows the variation in freight modal usage with the consignment size observed in the 1963 U.S. Census of Transportation. This diagram illustrates that road transport provided 80 to 90 percent of the transport service for consignments up to about 50,000 pounds. There was a distinct shift to rail service for shipments greater than 50,000 pounds.

Church [6] has noted that a third factor influencing the choice of shipping mode is commodity class. Table 14.3 shows the observed road transport share of shipments of 10,000 to 30,000 pounds by commodity type and trip length. The information presented in this table demonstrates that significant variations in modal usage occurred when both consignment size and trip length were held constant. The distribution of truck freight that was shipped directly to and from final origins and destinations, and via freight terminals was not reported by Church.

Surti and Ebrahimi [7] have also conducted analyses of the data collected in the 1963 U.S. Census of Transportation. The data were sorted so that only highway and rail freight movements were analyzed. Figure 14.6 shows the proportion of road transport used for intercity consignments as a function of haul length and consignment weight for selected commodity group.

Buhl [8], Surti and Ebrahimi [7] have shown that there is an inverse relationship between the size of the manufacturing plant and the relative use of road transport for outbound shipments. Table 14.4 summarizes the data obtained in the 1963 U.S. Census of Transportation. The average haul tends to increase with increasing plant size and with the more-specialized products.

Wood [2] has provided some limited evidence on the size of external shipments to and from a 1-square-mile area of central Brooklyn and this

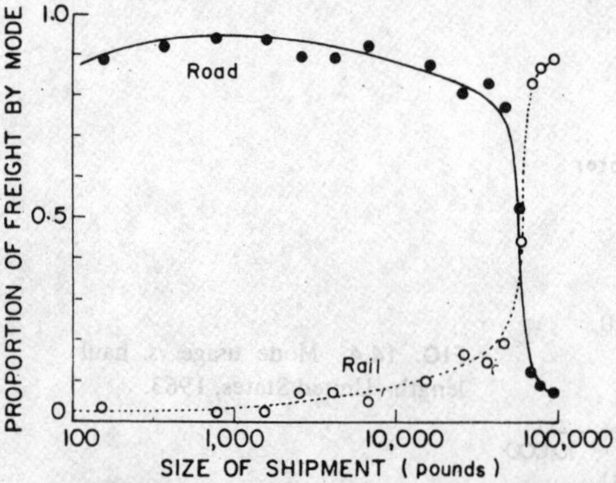

FIG. 14.5. Mode usage vs. shipment size–United States, 1963.

Table 14.3. Highway share of 10,000- to 29,999-lb shipments by commodity code and mileage block

TCC code	Commodity	Percent of total tons originated				
		Under 200 miles	200–399 miles	400–599 miles	600–999 miles	1,000 miles and over
228	Thread and yarn	100	100	98	100	85
307	Miscellaneous plastics products	96	92	90	97	80
356	General industrial machinery and equipment	87	93	95	91	68
361	Electrical transmission and equipment	100	97	79	86	82
265	Containers, boxes, and related products	92	83	69	45	36
349	Miscellaneous fabricated metal products	75	77	92	91	49
322	Glass and glassware	99	95	86	82	6
208	Beverages and flavoring extracts	99	92	94	72	47
382	Measuring and controlling instruments	100	100	100	78	95
284	Soap, detergents, etc.	98	80	89	83	64
345	Bolts, screws, rivets, washers, etc.	84	72	54	87	6
335	Nonferrous metal basic shapes	99	97	94	78	76
343	Plumbing fixtures and heating apparatus	89	98	67	68	35
367	Electronic components or accessories	65	100	72	28	27
201	Meat and poultry (fresh or frozen)	89	95	78	62	49
233	Women's and infants' clothing	100	–	–	–	–
365	Radio and television receiving sets	89	86	42	39	18
339	Miscellaneous primary metal products	99	98	100	98	71
301	Tires and innner tubes	79	84	81	68	74
282	Plastics materials and plasticizers	96	99	96	97	79
289	Miscellaneous chemical products	100	98	76	74	46
331	Steel works and rolling mill products	97	93	95	92	60
354	Metal working machinery and equipment	100	69	68	67	73
363	Household appliances	50	53	17	7	4
262	Paper (exc. building paper)	94	60	67	67	5
204	Grain mill products	97	69	43	50	23
	Median	96	93	86	78	49

information is presented in Table 14.5. The average weight of consignments within the urban region was 177 pounds for inbound shipments and 236 pounds for outbound shipments. In contrast, the external shipments averaged 13,429 pounds for inbound shipments and 23,833 pounds for outbound shipments.

A number of investigators have attempted to construct micromodels of individual shipper mode selection decisions and Refs. [9-12] provide some examples. These methods are based on a total transport-cost approach including factors such as inventory costs, shipment reliability, and so on. Studies of the shipping decisions of individual companies in Ontario have demonstrated that

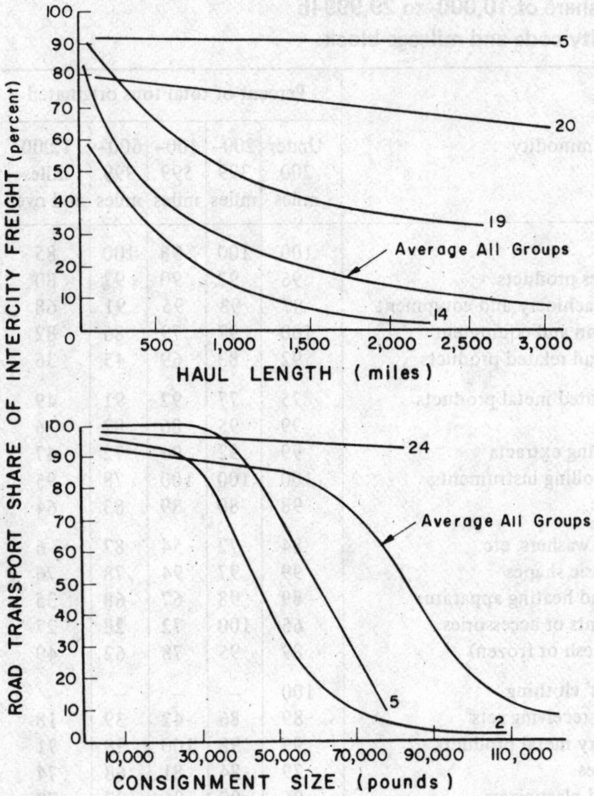

FIG. 14.6. Road transport share vs. haul length, consignment size, and commodity type.

the mode choice for a given commodity type and trip length varies over relatively short periods of time. In many cases the choice of a shipping mode depends on the day-by-day variations in transport rates and other factors.

14.3 INTERINDUSTRY CONSIGNMENTS

Some general evidence of the factors that influence shipping-mode choices for external commodity movements has been presented in Sec. 14.2. For the 1963 U.S. Census of Transportation the bulk of manufactured goods moved by truck for trip lengths of 300 to 500 miles, with the proportion varying with the commodity type being shipped and the size of the plant. Table 14.1 showed that the tons of commodity input per production employee per year varied widely between industry types. Similar variations occur in the tons of commodity per employee produced by industrial plants. The development of a commodity flow prediction process for external trips and for interindustry movements within

Table 14.4. Average haul length by shipper type and plant size

Shipper type	Average haul in miles by plant size (no. of employees)			
	Less 20	20–100	100–500	500 and over
1 - Meat, dairy products	140	320	370	590
2 - Other food products	270	300	430	510
3 - Candy, beverages, tobacco products	102	200	320	390
4 - Textile mill and leather products	390	440	420	620
5 - Apparel and related products	330	576	550	620
6 - Paper and allied products	210	190	320	570
7 - Chemicals, plastics, fibers	210	310	410	540
8 - Drugs, paints	210	280	390	650
9 - Petroleum and coal products	419	170	370	800
10 - Rubber and plastic products	470	480	430	580
11 - Lumber and wood products	150	540	780	999
12 - Furniture, fixtures	230	310	460	690
13 - Stone, clay and glass products	90	130	160	220
14 - Primary iron and steel products	340	390	300	270
15 - Primary non-ferrous metal products	290	310	590	620
16 - Fabricated metal products	140	300	350	520
17 - Metal cans	130	300	420	360
18 - Industrial machinery	570	380	520	470
19 - Machinery	410	430	630	640
20 - Communications products	999*	560	640	650
21 - Electrical products and supplies	680*	420	500	530
22 - Motor vehicles and equipment	480*	320	460	460
23 - Transportation equipment	200	470	480	420
23 - Instruments, photographic, watches	630*	780	710	710

*Based on a very small sample.

urban areas requires that the economic characteristics of various industry types be understood clearly.

14.3.1 Input-output table

A useful tool for highlighting the economic structure of industry is the input-output table. The use of the input-output table for commodity flow estimation has been proposed by several investigators [13-15]. Figure 14.7 shows part of the direct requirements matrix of the Ontario input-output table. Each column of the direct requirements matrix shows the dollar value of inputs that the industry named at the top of the column requires from other industries in order to produce a dollar of total output. For example, industry no. 28—metal stamping, pressing, and coating requires 39.6 cents of input from iron and steel mills in order to produce $1 of output; and 20.4 cents in salaries and

Table 14.5. Characteristics of for-hire truck shipments to and from downtown Brooklyn, New York

From and to	Inbound		Outbound	
	Number trucks	Mean consignment size (pounds)	Number trucks	Mean consignment size (pounds)
Internal*	412	177	304	236
External	7	13,429	12	23,833

*Internal to the Tri-State Region.

wages, and 14.5 cents of input from capital facilities, to produce $1 of output. In contrast, the printing and publishing industry requires 0 cents input from iron and steel mills but 39.5 cents of labor input. The published version of the Ontario input-output table [16] contains 49 industrial sectors (130 and 250 sector tables exist but these are confidential because of census disclosure constraints).

The input-output table format may be extended readily to include other important urban sectors such as warehousing, retailing, commercial, and so on. The necessary technical coefficients required to connect these additional sectors to other sectors of the input-output table would have to be established by survey. Artle [17] has described an input-output table for Stockholm, Sweden, which includes a variety of urban industry sectors not shown as separate sectors

INDUSTRY SECTOR	INDUSTRY Nº					
	24	25	26	27	28	29
24 – Printing, Publishing	0·034451	0·000144	0·000030	0·0	0·000629	0·000515
25 – Iron, Steel Mills	0·0	0·185166	0·047004	0·358441	0·396149	0·158633
26 – Other Primary Metals	0·000457	0·019122	0·327892	0·005927	0·056476	0·130246
27 – Fabr. & Struct. Metals	0·000342	0·0	0·0	0·0	0·0	0·013028
28 – Metal Stamping, Etc.	0·000034	0·000031	0·004292	0·0	0·000036	0·006945
29 – Other Metal Fabric Ind.	0·002897	0·003131	0·039306	0·035729	0·056490	0·077058
50 – Wages & Salaries	0·394777	0·203510	0·238601	0·252745	0·203964	0·258327
51 – Other Value Added	0·150277	0·294799	0·111362	0·247984	0·145281	0·127002

FIG. 14.7. Part of the direct requirements matrix of the 1965 Ontario input-output table.

Table 14.6. Part of input-output table for Stockholm, Sweden

Input sector	Output sector										
	Construction		Wholesale trade						Retail trade		
	Building	Other than building	Hardware, lumber, construction materials	Fuels	Shop and office fittings	Machinery, equipment, and supplies	Pulp, paper, and paper products	Other	Motor vehicles	Other consumers' durables	Department and variety stores
Wholesale trade											
Hardware, lumber, construction materials	25.1	9.8	5.0							0.2	
Fuels	0.7	0.5		1.2							
Shop and office fittings											
Machinery, equipment, and supplies						0.2					
Pulp, paper, and paper products							1.9				
Other kinds of business	0.7	0.5						14.0	3.6	14.9	0.3

NOTE: –Entries are millions of Swedish crowns in 1950.

in the usual interindustry input-output table. Table 14.6 shows part of this table.

Input-output tables provide a coarse view of the average economic characteristics of various industry sectors. Estimates of the annual inputs by commodity type to a particular zone may be obtained from:

$$a_j^e = [a_{ef}]\, p_j^e \tag{14.1}$$

where a_j^e = a column vector of the cash value of the annual consumption by commodity-type e by industries in zone j

$[a_{ef}]$ = the direct-requirements matrix of the input-output table for the e input industries and the f output industries

p_j^e = a column vector of the cash values of the annual production of commodity type e in region j

These cash values may be converted to physical units by the use of producers' prices. For future conditions the annual productions by commodity type by zone would have to be estimated from a knowledge of the types and intensities of manufacturing activities that are likely to locate within each zone.

Leontief and Strout [14] have proposed the following gravity-type expression for estimating interregional commodity flows:

$$t_{ij}^e = \frac{p_i^e a_j^e}{\sum_j a_j^e}\, q_{ij}^e \tag{14.2}$$

where t_{ij}^e = the cash value of the annual flow of commodity e from region i to region j

q_{ij}^e = an empirically determined coefficient which characterized the interregional flows of commodity e

Leontief and Strout have pointed out that in the case where base-year statistics comprise information not only on regional productions and consumptions, but also on regional flows, then the q_{ij}^e terms may be derived directly. They have also outlined an approach to estimating the q_{ij}^e magnitudes when the interregional flows are not available and this technique is described in Ref. 14.

Wilson [18] has suggested the following modifications of the Leontief-Strout commodity flow model:

$$t_{ij}^e = \frac{p_i^e a_j^e \exp(-\mu^e c_{ij})}{\sum_j a_j \exp(-\mu^e c_{ij})} \tag{14.3}$$

where μ^e = a parameter that expresses the importance of transport costs c_{ij} on the distribution patterns of commodity type e

Other investigators have suggested that the distribution of commodities may be accomplished by a linear programming approach. These approaches have been applied at the regional level but have not been applied as yet to a comprehensive estimation of urban commodity flows.

14.3.2 Truck trip-generation equations

Since the majority of intraurban interindustry commodity consignments are carried by truck, the daily truck trip-generation characteristics of various industry types are of interest for some types of transport-planning problems. Truck trip-generation rates tend to be cyclical and are not stable from day to day as are the bulk of person trips. It is difficult to establish reliable trip-generation equations from data collected over short time periods. Kardosh and Hutchinson [19] have described the results of a truck trip-generation study conducted in Metropolitan Toronto. One-day inventories of the truck movements at about 240 manufacturing industries were taken. In addition, a number of characteristics of the industries were recorded such as employment by type, annual value of production, and so on.

Table 14.7 shows the total number of trucks of four classes observed in this study. This table indicates that some 70 to 80 percent of the truck movements recorded involved two-axle trucks. Wood [2] has suggested that the major trip patterns may be classified as: (1) single-shipment loads that tend to be large often taking up the entire capacity of a truck, (2) single origin with multiple deliveries and vice versa, and (3) simultaneous pickup and delivery at each stop. Wood has noted that for the Tri-State Region in 1963 single-shipment loads accounted for 21 percent of the vehicle miles but almost 70 percent of the tonnage. Multiple-stop loads generated about 55 percent of the vehicle miles and 30 percent of the tonnage. Smaller trucks accounted for about 90 percent of the truck trips.

Table 14.8 shows the truck trip-generation equations developed for Toronto for all industry types combined. A number of alternative regression equations were examined and the number of private trucks owned was found to be the

Table 14.7. Proportions of truck types observed

Truck size	Truck trip production		Truck trip attraction	
	Number of trucks	Percent of total	Number of trucks	Percent of total
2 axles–single tires	603	24.4	679	32.2
2 axles–dual tires on rear	1,310	52.8	1,019	48.3
3 axles	173	7.0	124	5.9
4 or more axles	391	15.8	287	13.6
Total	2,477	100.0	2,109	100.0

Table 14.8. Truck trip generation equations

Truck trip productions
Daily trips produced = 11.4 + 1.53 (Total private trucks owned)
$r^2 = 0.807$
Truck trip attractions
Daily trips attracted = 12.5 − 0.86 (Total private trucks owned)
$r^2 = 0.532$

independent variable that explained most of the observed variation in tripmaking. It has been observed in a number of studies that industries which produce many truck movements tend to own truck fleets. Other industries tend to rely on common carriers. The Toronto sample contained a number of heavy-truck trip generators such as food and beverage companies, newspapers, and ready-mixed concrete plants. The causal basis to the trip attraction equation shown in Table 14.8 seems to be that plants which produce many truck trips also attract a larger than normal number of truck trips because of their higher commodity throughput.

There are difficulties in using the equations given in Table 14.9 for predictive purposes because of the problems of estimating the magnitudes of the independent variables. Table 14.9 shows the regression equations developed for four groups of industries aggregated to the two-digit level of the standard industrial classification code. A number of the equations are not particularly valid and it should be noted that the number of private trucks owned is still a dominant independent variable. Employment variables did enter some of the equations. However, difficulties still exist in using the equations shown in Table 14.9 for predictive purposes. Suitable equations could not be developed in terms of employment variables alone.

Smith [20] has provided the following information on truck trip characteristics:

1. Retail shops generate about 11 truck trips per day per 1,000 square feet of floor area and convenience shops generate about 5 truck trips per day per 1,000 square feet.
2. Destinations of urban truck trips are oriented toward the city center with about 80 percent of truck trips being attracted to zones within 6 miles of the central business district.

14.3.3 Daily truck-movement profiles

The truck trip-generation equations described in the previous section are for trips over a 24-hour period. A useful set of information obtained in the Toronto

Table 14.9. Truck trip generation equations

Industry group	Equations
01 - Food and beverage	$\log_e YP = 2.62 + 0.33 \log_e$ (Private trucks) $R^2 = 0.656$ $YA = 2.24 + 0.10$ (Male manufacturing) $+ 0.39$ (Private trucks) $R^2 = 0.715$
10 - Paper and allied products	$\log_e YP = 0.74 + 0.43 \log_e$ (Total office) $+ 0.22 \log_e$ (Private trucks) $R^2 = 0.600$ $YA = 7.03 + 0.07$ (Male manufacturing) $R^2 = 0.293$
11 - Printing, publishing	$\log_e YP = 1.05 + 0.28 \log_e$ (Male manufacturing) $+ 0.51 \log_e$ (Private trucks) $R^2 = 0.883$ $\log_e YA = 2.29 + 0.26 \log_e$ (Private trucks) $R^2 = 0.418$
14 - Machinery	$\log_e YP = 1.11 + 0.32$ (Total office employees) $R^2 = 0.190$ $YA = 4.54 + 0.13$ (Total office employees) $+ 1.50$ (Private trucks) $R^2 = 0.751$

NOTE: – YP = daily truck trips produced;
YA = daily truck trips attracted.

survey referred to previously was the daily time distribution of truck movements. Figure 14.8 shows the hourly distribution of truck movements for all manufacturing industries for both trip productions and trip attractions. Trucks involved in the movement of raw materials had two peak periods with the major peak at 10:30 A.M. and a minor peak at 2:00 P.M. Trucks involved in the movement of finished products had peaks at 8:00 A.M., 10:30 A.M. and 3;00 P.M., with the dominant peak at 3:00 P.M.

Figure 14.9 shows a 24-hour time profile of trucks involved in delivering finished products for each of the four truck types. This graph demonstrates that the largest number of two-axle single-tire trucks are generated at about 8:00 A.M. The remaining truck types tend to move generally throughout the normal 8:00 A.M. to 5:00 P.M. period with peaks at midmorning and midafternoon.

Figure 14.10 shows the daily time profiles of trucks involved in the delivery of raw materials. These distributions tend to have the same characteristic shape as those presented in Fig. 14.9 with the exception of a peak at about 8:00 A.M. for two-axle single-tire trucks. Figure 14.11 shows the 24-hour distribution of truck trip origins observed in the Tri-State Region in 1963 [21]. This distribution is

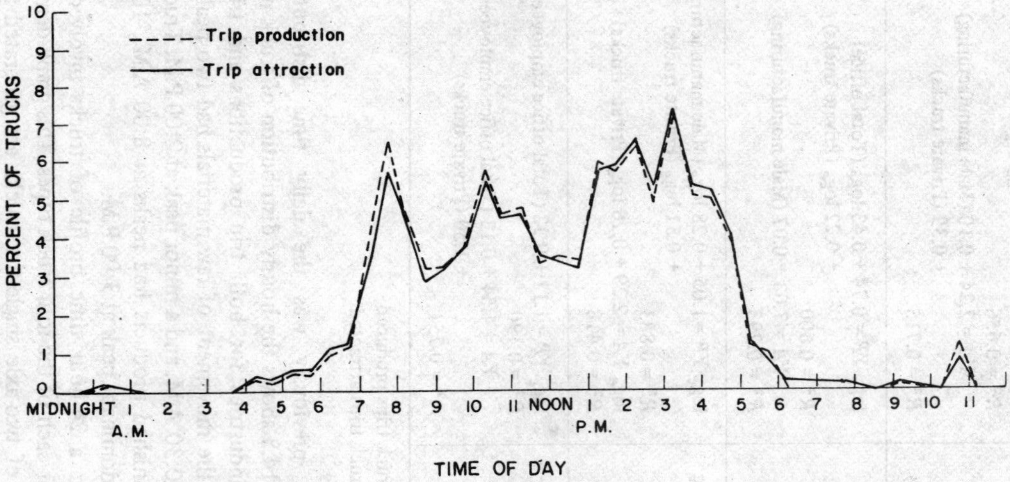

FIG. 14.8. Twenty-four hour distribution of truck movements for all manufacturing industries.

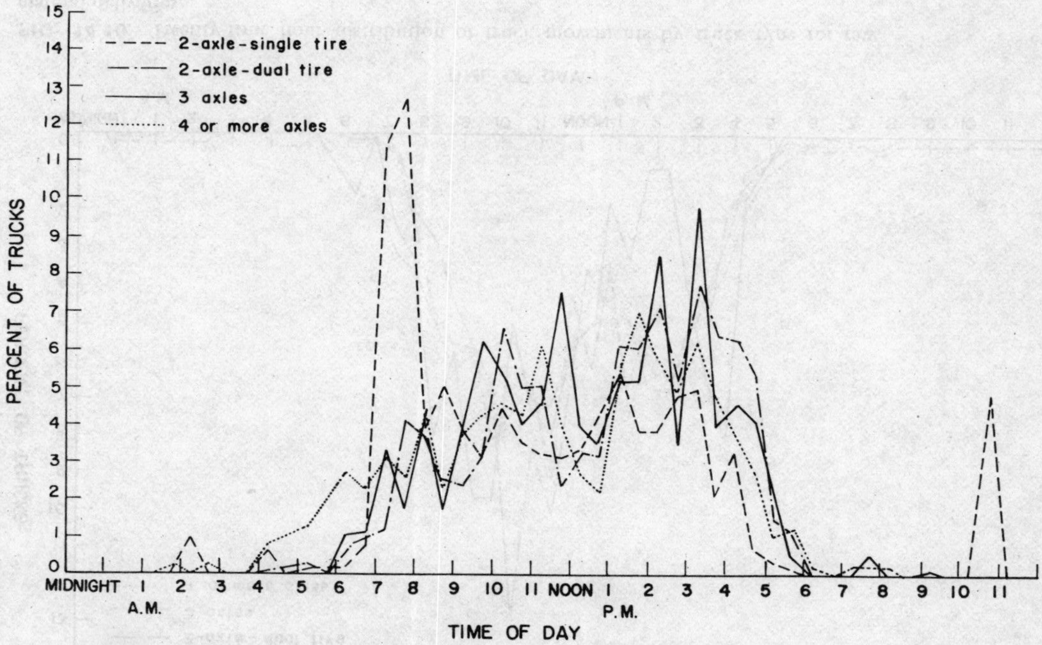

FIG. 14.9. Twenty-four distribution of truck movements by truck type for finished product deliveries.

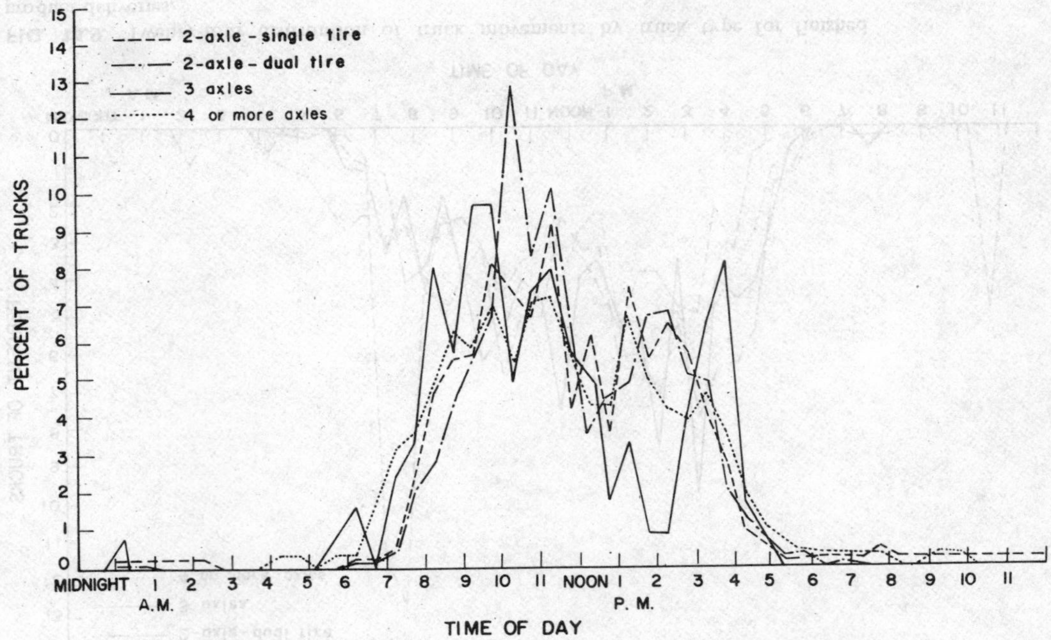

FIG. 14.10. Twenty-four hour distribution of truck movements by truck type for raw material deliveries.

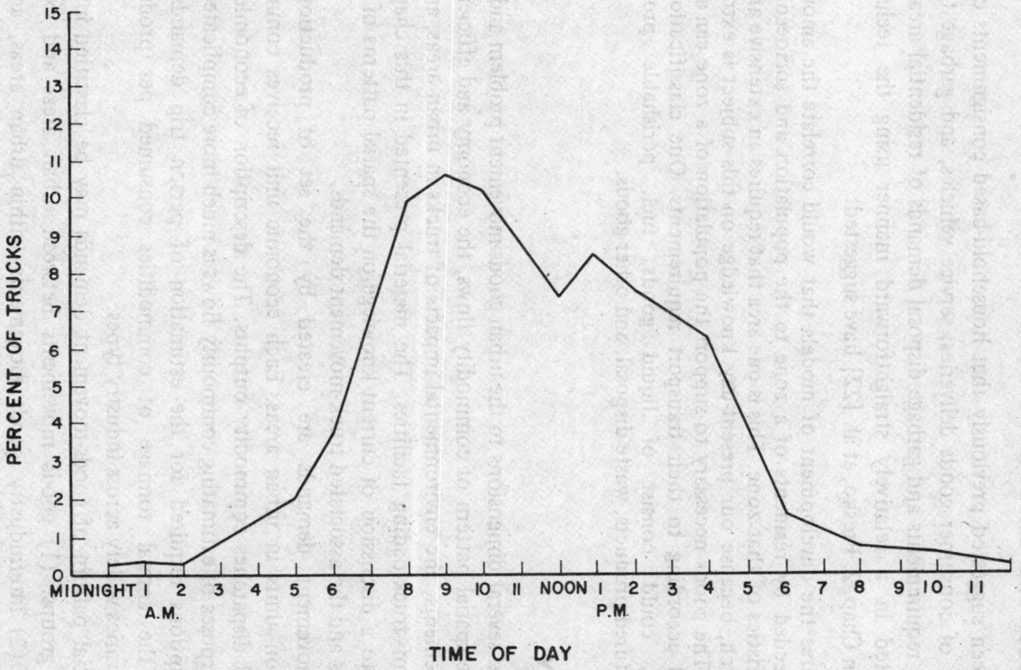

FIG. 14.11. Twenty-four hour distribution of truck trip origins in Tri-State Region.

similar to that shown in Fig. 14.8 for Toronto with the exception that not as many secondary peaks were observed.

14.4 HOUSEHOLD-BASED CONSIGNMENTS

It has been suggested previously that household-based consignments consist principally of consumer goods deliveries, service vehicles, and garbage trucks. The goods requirements and garbage disposal demands of residential areas may be estimated in a relatively straightforward manner using the techniques discussed in Chap. 2. Fresko, et al. [22] have suggested:

> . . . requires the development of models that would correlate the amount of goods needed by residents of a zone to the population and socioeconomic characteristics of that zone. This is one area that requires an extensive amount of research, because our present-day knowledge on this subject is extremely limited. The goods necessary to support the population of a zone can also be classified according to their transport requirements. One classification, for example, could consist of liquid goods, fuel, perishable products, manufactured products, waste disposal, and other goods.

SUMMARY

There are several dimensions to the urban goods-movement problem and these include the spatial pattern of commodity flows, the economy and efficiency of these movements, the environmental impacts of trucks in urban areas, and the provision of truckloading facilities. The material presented in this chapter is restricted to a discussion of current knowlege on the spatial patterns of goods movements and the associated truck-movement demands.

Goods-movement demands are created by the set of production and consumption units in urban areas. Each economic unit receives commodity inputs and dispatches commodity outputs. The description of economic units for the purposes of estimating commodity flows is much more complicated than the descriptions required for the estimation of person trip demands. For example, the annual tonnage of commodities consumed per production employee varies widely across industry types.

The spatial pattern of goods-movement demands may be classified into the following groups: (1) goods movements between urban areas and external locations, (2) interindustry goods movements within urban areas, and (3) household-based goods movements within an urban area. Goods movements may also be classified by commodity type and consignment size. This three-level classification of spatial pattern, commodity type, and consignment size seems to be adequate for the purposes of urban goods-movement estimation.

External goods movements may be classified as either direct consignments or consignments via a freight terminal. Most direct consignments are by truck as are the pickup and delivery components of the terminal-based trips. An understanding of the freight modal split regime external to an urban region is required in order to predict the intraurban truck movement components of these external trips. The principal factors influencing shipping-mode choice are commodity type, haul length, consignment size, and plant size.

A number of investigators have suggested that the input-output table concept provides a useful approach to the estimation of interindustry commodity movements. The input-output table allows the commodity input and output requirements of broad industry types to be estimated. The spatial distributions of commodity flows may be estimated by a gravity model or a linear programming approach. The industry sectors of the traditional input-output table may be modified to reflect sectors which are important in urban areas such as warehousing, wholesale and retail trade. Household-based goods-movement requirements may be approached in the tradition of person-movement studies.

Urban truck trip-generation rates are of interest in urban road planning. Truck trip movements tend to be cyclical and are not stable from day to day as are the bulk of person trips. It is difficult to establish valid truck trip-generation equations from information collected over daily observation periods. When all industries are viewed together, the variable which best explains truck trip generation is the number of private trucks owned. Companies that generate large volumes of truck movements, such as food and beverage distributors, tend to own truck fleets rather than use common carriers.

Movements by two-axle trucks have been observed to account for 70 to 90 percent of the total truck movements in urban areas. The individual consignments carried by these trucks tend to be small and account for only 20 to 30 percent of the total tonnages of freight moved by trucks in urban areas. Urban truck movements tend to peak just prior to the morning person trip peak period and again in the midafternoon period.

The current knowledge on urban commodity movements is extremely primitive. Theoretical and empirical studies are required to develop urban commodity flow demand models which are sensitive to both land-use variables, transport variables, and public-policy variables.

REFERENCES

1. Highway Research Board, *Urban Commodity Flow,* Special Report 120, Washington, D.C., 1971.
2. Wood, R. T., "Structure and Economics of Intraurban Goods Movement," in Highway Research Board, *Urban Commodity Flow,* Special Report 120, Washington, D.C., 1971.
3. Bureau of the Budget, *Standard Industrial Classification Manual,* U.S. Government Printing Office, Washington, D.C., 1956.
4. Statistics Canada, *Standard Industrial Classification Manual,* Ottawa, Ontario, 1960.
5. Wallace, R. S., *A Domestic Multi-Modal Goods Distribution Model with Emphasis on Air Cargo,* Ph.D. thesis, Department of Civil Engineering, University of Waterloo, Ontario, 1971.

6. Church, D. E., *Impact of Size and Distance on Intercity Highway Share of Transportation and Industrial Products,* Highway Research Record No. 175, Highway Research Board, Washington, D.C., 1967.
7. Surti, V. H., and A. Ebrahimi, "Modal Split of Freight Traffic," *Traffic Quarterly,* October, 1972, pp. 575–588.
8. Buhl, W. F., *Intercity Highway Transport Share Tends to Vary Inversely with Size of Plant,* Highway Research Record No. 175, Highway Research Board, Washington, D.C., 1967.
9. Bayliss, B., *Modal Split in Freight Transport,* Proceedings, Conference on Freight Traffic Models, Planning and Transport Research and Computation Company Limited, London, 1971.
10. Noortman, H. J., and J. Van Es, "Modal Split Models in Freight Transport," in B. Bayliss, *Modal Split in Freight Transport,* Proceedings, Conference on Freight Traffic Models, Planning and Transport Research and Computation Company Limited, London, 1971.
11. Roberts, P. O., "The Logistics Management Process as a Model of Freight Traffic Demand," in B. Bayliss, *Modal Split in Freight Transport,* Proceedings, Conference on Freight Traffic Models, Planning and Transport Research and Computation Company Limited, London, 1971.
12. Baumol, W. J., and H. D. Vinod, "An Inventory Theoretic Model of Freight Transport Demand," *Management Science,* vol. 16, no. 7, 1970.
13. Goss, D. N., et al., *Urban Goods Movement Demand,* Battelle Memorial Institute for U.S. Department of Housing and Urban Development, October, 1967.
14. Leontief, W., and A. Strout, "Multi-Regional Input-Output Analysis," in T. Barna (ed.), *Structural Interdependence and Economic Development,* St. Martin's Press, London, 1963.
15. Hutchinson, B. G., *Forecasting Inter-Regional Commodity Flows,* Proceedings, NATO Conference on The Application of Operational Research to Transport Problems, Sandefjord, Norway, August, 1972.
16. Frank, R. H., S. M. Batrik, and D. Haronitis, "The Input-Output Structure of the Ontario Economy," *Ontario Economic Review,* vol. 8, no. 1, 1970.
17. Artle, R., *Studies in the Structure of the Stockholm Economy,* Columbia University Press, New York, 1965.
18. Wilson, A. G., *Entropy in Urban and Regional Modelling,* Pion Limited, London, 1970.
19. Kardosh, R., and B. G. Hutchinson, *Truck Trip Generation Characteristics of Manufacturing Industries in Metropolitan Toronto,* Transport Group Working Paper, Department of Civil Engineering, University of Waterloo, Waterloo, Ontario, December, 1972.
20. Smith, W., "State of Research and Data on Urban Goods Movements and Some Comments on the Problem," in Highway Research Board, *Urban Commodity Flow,* Special Report 120, Washington, D.C., 1971.
21. Chappell, C. W., and M. T. Smith, "Review of Urban Goods Movement Studies," in Highway Research Board, *Urban Commodity Flow,* Special Report 120, Washington, D.C., 1971.
22. Fresko, D., G. Shunk, and F. Spielberg, "Analysis of Needs for Goods Movement Forecasts," *Journal, Urban Planning and Development Division,* American Society of Civil Engineers, vol. 98, no. UP1, pp. 1–16, July, 1972.

15 FURTHER DEVELOPMENT OF THE PLANNING PROCESS

It has been emphasized in Chap. 1, and again in Chap. 11, that to be efficient, transport systems planning should be conducted in the context of a multilevel process of development planning. An approach to this problem of multilevel planning has been outlined in Chap. 11. There are a number of deficiencies in the available techniques that inhibit the effective implementation of this multilevel process. This chapter explores some of the current developments that might lead to an improved transport systems planning process.

For the purposes of this chapter, the components of the above-mentioned process that are directly relevant to transport systems planning are:

1. The estimation of the land development patterns within an urban area that are likely to result from a particular set of public-policy decisions and consumer preferences
2. The estimation of detailed travel demands for a broad development concept and a range of specific transport system proposals
3. The evaluation of alternative transport system proposals
4. The development of a staged investment program to achieve the horizon-year plan selected

With current transport-planning practice these four broad types of activity are carried on in a quasi-independent manner. Travel times are used in each of the land-use and transport submodels, but the relative importance of these travel times varies between the analysis activities. For example, most land-use allocation and trip distribution studies have shown that tripmakers are relatively insensitive to travel times within the range 0–15 minutes in their choice of destinations. In contrast, choice modal split studies demonstrate that the selection of public transport is very sensitive to excess vehicle travel time which, in turn, is valued differently to in-vehicle travel times. The value of travel time is an important component of the economic evaluation of transport investments. However, the values of travel time used in most economic studies have normally been different to the time values used in the travel-demand models.

In transport-planning studies, the alternative transport system selected is usually specified as an horizon-year configuration, and not as a sequence of projects that will eventually yield the desired endpoint. The benefits realized from alternative systems are not simply a function of the horizon-year configuration, but of the specific time sequence of project investments. The methods of project investment staging which have been developed to date permit an optimum project investment schedule to be identified for a specific horizon-year system. However, different sequences of projects will have different impacts on land development and travel demands. Optimal project staging cannot be considered independently of the other phases of planning.

A number of investigators have recognized these and other deficiencies of urban transport planning. This chapter introduces the reader to some of the current efforts in transportation research that are directed toward overcoming some of the shortcomings mentioned previously.

15.1 MODELS OF DEVELOPMENT

The land-use and transport models described in the earlier chapters of this book are based heavily on the notion that workplace location, and the role of work, are both important determinants of household locations and the lifestyles of urban residents. The land-use allocations prepared for most studies performed in the 1950s and 1960s represented simple extrapolations of development trends and consumer behavior that existed at that time.

The transport and land-use models are calibrated to base-year conditions and the parameters estimated from the calibration procedure are assumed to remain invariant throughout the planning period. While the land-use models described in Chaps. 6 and 11 provide for some relaxation of the land-use inputs, a dominant factor in these models is still the work-to-home linkage.

Hutchinson and Shortreed [1] have suggested that the behavioral hypotheses implicit in existing models may be expressed in the following general way:

$$p_i(t), lu_i(t), e_i(t) = f\{p_i(t-1), lu_i(t-1), e_i(t)\} \tag{15.1}$$

where $p_i(\ )$ = the population of urban area i at the particular time horizon
$lu_i(\ )$ = the demands for land-use consumption at a particular time horizon
$e_i(\ )$ = the employment of urban area i at a particular time horizon

The principal assertion expressed in Eq. (15.1) is that the employment expected in the horizon year is the central factor influencing the total amount of development, and in turn, the magnitudes of transport demands. Equation (15.1) suggests that the population in the horizon year t is related closely to the amount of employment and the base-year labor participation rates. Finally, the spatial distribution of population is determined by employment locations and the base-year preferences for land-use consumption.

As certain societies enter the postindustrial era, increasing affluence and the shorter workweek will have important influences on the residential locations and activity patterns of individuals. Deman [2] has made the following comments in connection with future work and leisure patterns;

> No one can be in any doubt that by the year 2000 the contemporary world will have undergone profound changes—changes which, as time goes by, will be increasingly inter-related.
>
> Thus . . . changes in the structure of the working population, and in the time devoted to work or to leisure will be very closely linked with one another. Added to this, changes of equal importance in material living conditions and the way people live their lives will certainly affect their behaviour, the manner in which they achieve adulthood and develop their personalities, to say nothing of their relationships one with another within their own family circles and within their own particular groupings in society at large.

Hutchinson and Shortreed [1] have suggested that more-appropriate behavioral hypotheses than those expressed in Eq. (15.1) might be:

$$p_i(t), lu_i(t), e_i(b) = f\{p_i(t-1), lu_i(t-1), e_i(t), ct_i(t-1), cl_i(t-1), av_i(t), wr_i(t), ct_n(t-1), cl_n(t-1), av_i(t-1), wr_n(t-1)\} \quad (15.2)$$

where $ct_i(t-1)$ = cost of transport in urban area i at $t-1$
$cl_i(t-1)$ = cost of land rents and taxes in urban area i at $t-1$
$av_i(t-1)$ = value of environmental quality, urban amenities, etc., of urban area i at $t-1$
$wr_i(t-1)$ = job opportunities and wage rates i at $t-1$
n = an index which indicates that the above terms are for all other urban centers in the region

Equation (15.2) suggests that population and land-use consumption and employment forecasts for a city should not be developed in isolation but as a function of the relative attractiveness of a particular urban area to other urban areas within a region. For example, if transport and land costs are high in the principal regional city relative to other cities in the region, then employment and population activities will tend to shift to these other cities. The attractivity of these cities will be a function of the employment opportunities, wage rates, and general amenities in these cities.

Figure 15.1 outlines the broad structure of the approach suggested by Eq. (15.2). The allocation function required by Eq. (15.2) would have to be solved iteratively since for any urban area ct_i, cl_i, and av_i are all consequences of a land-use-transport plan based on $p_i(t)$, $lu_i(t)$, and $e_i(t)$.

The hypotheses contained in Eq. (15.2) are supported in a general way by recent evidence of a declining rate of growth of the New York metropolitan area and the absolute decrease in population of Greater London, along with increasing growth rates for medium-sized provincial towns. Figure 15.2 shows the trends in population observed for the Greater London area between 1801 and 1971. In contrast, the population of the southeast region of England has been growing steadily.

Equation (15.2) has been introduced to emphasize that urban land-use-transport models must operate in conjunction with population and employment allocations that are determined dynamically. For example, the *London Transportation Study* [3] used the traditional urban transport-planning techniques and produced a transport plan estimated to cost £ 2 billion. It is clear that if such a plan is not implemented, and the horizon-year population and employment forecasts are realized, then the travel cost component of Eq. (15.2)

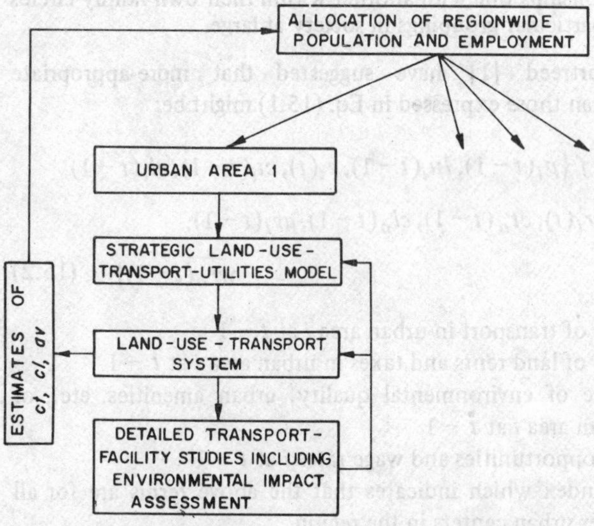

FIG. 15.1. Regional system model and its relationship to strategic land-use-transport planning.

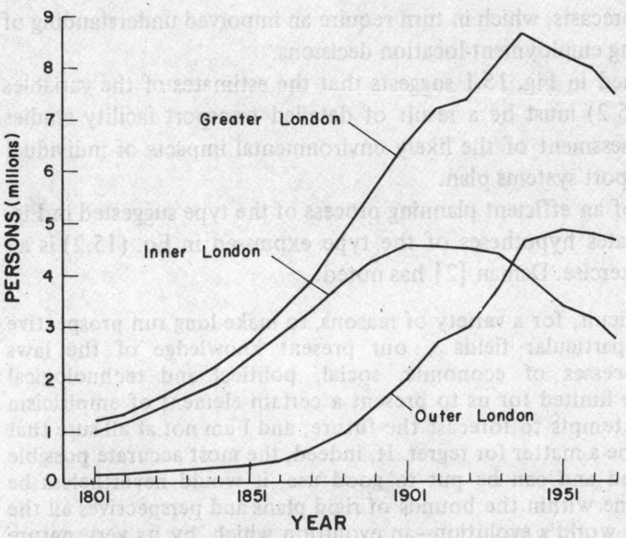

FIG. 15.2. Population trends for Greater London.

would become very high and the environmental quality component very low. If the plan were implemented, the land cost component of Eq. (15.2) would become very high due to increased taxes. In either case, the changes in the components of Eq. (15.2) would become so high, that the population and employment estimates input originally to the transport models will in fact, not occur.

The mechanism suggested by Eq. (15.2) may be observed in the growth of many metropolitan areas during the post-World War II period. Evidence has been presented in Chap. 7 which illustrates the rapid decline in the relative importance of the central business district as an employment center. The stability, or decline, in central area employment has been observed in many rapidly growing metropolitan areas. Population has shifted to suburban areas because of cheaper land costs and improved environmental quality. Employment has also decentralized because of high central area land costs and decreased accessibility to population.

An additional factor influencing the differential rates of growth of cities and towns is the composition of the employment opportunities. In the early part of the postwar period, employment in secondary industries grew rapidly. Many of these industries located in the large regional centers for a number of reasons including lower transport costs, availability of labor, and proximity to other industries. In recent years, the tertiary sector has been growing rapidly. Many of the tertiary industries have a broader range of location choices since these industries are not as sensitive to factors such as transport costs, labor force mobility, and so on. A critical input to the approach suggested in Eq. (15.2) are valid employment forecasts, which in turn require an imporved understanding of the factors influencing employment-location decisions.

The process outlined in Fig. 15.1 suggests that the estimates of the variables contained in Eq. (15.2) must be a result of detailed transport facility studies which include an assessment of the likely environmental impacts of individual elements of the transport systems plan.

The development of an efficient planning process of the type suggested in Fig. 15.1 which incorporates hypotheses of the type expressed in Eq. (15.2) is an extremely difficult exercise. Deman [2] has noted:

> It is extremely difficult, for a variety of reasons, to make long run prospective outlines in these particular fields . . . our present knowledge of the laws governing the processes of economic, social, political and technological development is too limited for us to present a certain element of empiricism from dominating attempts to forecast the future, and I am not at all sure that this should in fact be a matter for regret. If, indeed, the most accurate possible forecasts are desired and can be put to good use, it would nevertheless be impossible to confine within the bounds of rigid plans and perspectives all the complexities of the world's evolution–an evolution which, by its very nature and the speed with which it is taking place continually modifies its own premises.

15.2 DIRECT DEMAND MODELS

Central to the urban transport-systems-planning process described throughout this book is the availability of a set of transport-demand models with a sound conceptual basis. The transport-demand submodels used in the five-stage analysis process described in earlier chapters of this book are quasi-independent in character. Tripmaker decisions about choice of destination, choice of mode, and choice of route within a mode are modeled in a sequential way.

This sequential-type approach to transport demand estimation has been criticized by many who argue that the decision to make a trip involves the simultaneous choice of destination, móde, and route. For example, a report by the Organization for Economic Cooperation and Development on the status of the urban transport-planning process states [4]:

> In practice, the existing system of models makes a number of simplifications, resulting in a segmented series of computations with internal consistencies.
>
> No wholly satisfactory system of models exists that (*a*) analyzes multi-modal systems (particularly with new technologies); (*b*) tests a wide range of operating, financing and pricing policies as well as network alternatives; (*c*) takes into account the influence on consumer choice of transportation mode and route attributes other than total trip time and cost (such as reliability, number of transfers, privacy, flexibility, and other difficult to measure aspects of quality of services: or (*d*) considers explicitly alternative time sequences of investment and uncertainty.

Brand and Manheim [5] have noted in connection with travel demand models that:

> Travel forecasting procedures must have a basis in behaviour if planners and decision-makers are able to have confidence in the results of the forecasts . . . we must confront squarely the validity of our theories describing relationships between people and their locations on one hand, and travel on the other. This involves consideration in particular of how people view the transportation system which connects or potentially connects the origins and destinations of their journeys.

A number of so-called *direct demand models* have been proposed [6-9] which are directed toward the development of travel-demand models with an improved conceptual basis. Quandt [10] has described direct-demand models in the following way: "Consumers are assumed to have available various destinations and/or modes of travel which may be regarded as economic goods each with its own price and among which the consumer chooses so as to maximize, either implicitly or explicitly, some index of satisfaction."

One of the earliest direct demand models to be introduced was that developed by Quandt and Baumol [6]. This model has been introduced already in Chap. 4 as a multiterm gravity model. The abstract mode model introduced in Chap. 4 has the following form:

$$t_{ij}^m = ap_i^b p_j^c q_i^e q_j^f f(d_{ij}^m) f(z_{ij}^m) \tag{15.3}$$

where t_{ij}^m = the number of trips between zones i and j by mode m
p,q = characteristics of zones i and j such as population and employment which are determinants of travel demand
d_{ij}^m = the travel time by mode m between zones i and j
z_{ij}^m = the generalized cost of travel by mode m between zones i and j

In terms of the economic theory of behavior this model attempts to estimate travel demands by mode through a consideration of the utility functions of individuals. Tripmakers are considered to derive utility from the various attributes of modes such as speed, cost, convenience, and so on. Quandt [10] has noted in connection with the abstract mode model that "Their (the demand functions) precise mathematical form is somewhat ad hoc and is not derived in detail from attribute-oriented utility theory, except for the simple observation that the demand for travel from i to j by mode m, t_{ij}^m, must depend in some sense on both the attribute content of the mth mode relative to other modes and on the attribute contents of all modes relative to the consumer's income."

Manheim [11] has attempted to introduce a unified method of classification for travel-demand models. He has introduced a so-called *general share model* of the following form:

$$t_{ij}^{mp} = \alpha(y)\beta_i(y)\gamma_{ij}(y)\delta_{ij}^m(y)\omega_{ij}^{mp}(y) \tag{15.4}$$

where y = some function of the urban activity system and the transport-level-of-service variables in a region

$t \quad = \alpha(y)$
$\quad = $ total amount of travel in a region
$p_i \quad = $ the proportion of the total travel that originates in zone i
$\quad = t\beta_i(y)$
$t_{ij} \quad = $ the proportion of the travel that originates in zone i and is destined for zone j
$\quad = p_i\gamma_{ij}(y)$
$t_{ij}^m \quad = $ the proportion of the t_{ij} travel that uses mode m
$\quad = t_{ij}\delta_{ij}^m(y)$
$t_{ij}^{mp} = $ the proportion of the t_{ij}^m travel that uses path p
$\quad = t_{ij}^m \, \omega_{ij}^{mp}(y)$

Manheim has suggested that the term, share model, is appropriate for Eq. (15.4) since each of the terms α, β, γ, δ, and ω splits the total amount of travel into successive shares of the total travel in a region. Manheim has shown how the various direct demand models, as well as the sequential-type demand models, may be derived from the structure of the general share model.

For example, the following model is derived from the general share model:

$$t_{ij}^m = \left\{\left[\sum_i x_i \left(\sum_j x_j z_{ij}^a\right)^b\right]^c\right\} \left\{\frac{x_i(\sum_j x_j z_{ij}^d)^e}{\sum_i x_i(\sum_j x_j z_{ij}^d)^e}\right\} \times \left\{\frac{x_j z_{ij}^f}{\sum_j x_j z_{ij}^f}\right\} \left\{\frac{z_{ij}^m}{z_{ij}}\right\} \qquad (15.5)$$

where x = some measure of the activities in zones which generate transport demands
z_{ij} = the generalized cost of travel between zones i and j which represents the combined effect of all modes
z_{ij}^m = the generalized costs by a specific mode
a,b,c,d,e,f = parameters that must be estimated from empirical data.

Four sets of braces { } have been used to partition Eq. (15.5). The terms inside the first set of braces estimate the total number of trips generated in the region. The terms inside the second set of braces partition the total trips generated among each of these zones, while the terms inside the third set of braces distribute the trips between origins and destinations. The final set of terms partitions the trip interchanges between zones among competing modes. Inspection of the terms inside of the first set of braces indicates a structure similar to the abstract mode model described in Eq. (15.3). The x_i and x_j represent measures of the transport-generating activities in origin and destination zones and z_{ij} is a measure of the separation of these zones. Since the expressions contained in the other three sets of braces are all normalized they represent share probabilities of trip generation, trip distribution, and modal split, respectively. It is interesting to note from Eq. (15.5) that the only real difference between its structure and the sequential-type models introduced in earlier chapters is the introduction of the exponents *a,b,c,d,e,* and *f*.

While many of the investigators who have advanced direct demand models argue that these models have a sound behavioral basis, it is useful to recall Quandt's statement introduced earlier in this section which is that the precise mathematical form of the demand functions "is somewhat ad hoc and is not derived in detail from attribute-oriented utility theory."

Manheim [11] has suggested that the theoretical results derived from his general share model lead to the following directions in the design of a new generation of urban transport models:

1. A model system should treat the transportation system of a region as a single multimodal system, taking each trip from door to door through any possible mix of transport facilities.
2. A model system should allow explicit treatment of any number of market segments and should allow each market segment to have different behavior patterns.
3. A model system should have the capability for including explicitly any desired set of level-of-service variables.
4. A model system should have a valid procedure for computing equilibrium of supply and demand within the network, considering the interaction of all market segments.

These recommendations would suggest that a very refined travel-demand forecasting model is required for transport systems planning. However, there is no systematic empirical evidence that supports the pursuit of the degree of sophistication in demand modeling advocated above. In addition, current capabilities in the other activities involved in urban transport planning are not compatible with the refinements in demand modeling suggested. To be effective, travel-demand models must be integrated fully with the techniques used for land-use estimation and the evaluation of alternative systems.

15.3 EVALUATION OF ALTERNATIVES

Chapter 10 has provided a review of certain principles of economics along with examples of the application of these principles to the economic evaluation of alternative transport systems. It was concluded in Chap. 10 that a generally accepted method of evaluation for urban transport projects does not exist. The principal reason for this deficiency is because of the difficulties of expressing benefits and costs in some quantitative way.

It was pointed out in Chap. 10 that the theoretical foundations of benefit-cost analysis are found in the principles of welfare economics. The paretian concept of welfare changes in a society is the fundamental notion in this approach. With this concept, an increase in welfare occurs if an improvement in one individual's satisfaction is not accompanied by a deterioration in the satisfaction of another. This criterion was recognized as being unsatisfactory; a social welfare function must be defined in order to provide an improved criterion of welfare changes. The final point made in Chap. 10 was that public participation in the planning process may be thought of as a way of obtaining the interpersonal comparisons of utility required to define the social welfare function.

A second theme has been introduced in Chap. 12 which has to do with the sequential nature of transport-plan implementation, the uncertainty under which transport system decisions are made, and with the role of information in reducing the uncertainty characteristics of planning decisions. A very fruitful area of research appears to be the integration of the two themes just mentioned. Transport-planning studies and project implementation may be regarded as sequences of experiments that provide information for decisions in the next stage. Some of the information will be about the demand for and behavior of different transport concepts. Other information will be on the utilities of the alternative systems as perceived by the community.

Steger [12] has noted in connection with citizen participation that:

> Until community participation and involvement is afforded as well accepted set of functional roles in a revised urban transportation planning process, its status will continue to be that primarily of an ad hoc, opportunistic resource, perhaps assisted by an advocacy planning orientation. What is clearly lacking is a sound theoretical basis, not merely for the increased democratization of the process—surely, an emotionally appealing virtue—but for the enhancement of overall goal achievement which community involvement can help bring about.

Steger [12] goes on to note that:

> There is much left to study, given the economist's view about community involvement. It is a cost effective view, . . . in that it is designed to help in determining what the system should be and, given that the interest group trade-offs are well reflected in the design, the system is likely to achieve substantial net benefits for most of the community. Researchable questions which remain, given this viewpoint, include:
>
> 1. How best can obtained data be utilized in developing programmatic strategies?
> 2. What are the most effective ways to determine public-preference functions?
> 3. To what extent does the degree to which a system of complete information exists affect the net benefits observed through alternative transportation investments and service levels?

A problem closely related to that of systems evaluation is the scheduling of the sequence of projects necessary to yield the horizon-year network. A number of investigators have proposed techniques for scheduling projects. Some of the earlier attempts used a linear programming approach [13–15] to identify the optimum sequence of project investments. Most of the procedures were directed towards the identification of the project sequence which minimized the sum of the investment and user costs subject to certain budgetary constraints. More-recent attempts have been based on dynamic programming formulations [16,17] with similar objective functions. The principal weakness of all of these methods is their concentration on only one small part of the transport-planning problem and this is the supply of road capacity.

The staged decision process described in Chap. 12 provides a technique for enumerating alternative project sequences. The number of potential project combinations in most urban transport plans is relatively small and in many cases the project sequence is constrained by a variety of factors. The decision theoretic framework of Chap. 12 provides a potentially important basis for the development of improved evaluation procedures.

REFERENCES

1. Hutchinson, B. G., and J. H. Shortreed, *New Requirements of Urban Transport Planning,* Paper presented at International Conference on Transportation Research, Bruges, Belgium, 1973.
2. Deman, C., *The Future is Tomorrow - Introduction to Section 4,* Martinus Nijhoff, The Hague, Netherlands, 1972.
3. Freeman, Fox, Wilbur Smith and Partners, *London Transportation Study,* vols. I–III, London, England, 1964–1968.
4. Organization for Economic Coöperation and Development, *The Urban Transportation Planning Process,* Paris, France, 1971.
5. Brand, D., and M. L. Manheim, *Directions for Research in Travel Forecasting,* Paper presented at International Conference on Transportation Research, Bruges, Belgium, 1973.
6. Quandt, R. E., and W. J. Baumol, "Abstract Mode Model: Theory and Measurement," *Journal, Regional Science,* vol. 6, no. 2, pp. 13–26, 1966.
7. Domencich, T. K., G. Kraft, and J. Valette, *Estimation of Urban Passenger Travel Behaviour: An Economic Demand Model,* Highway Research Record No. 238, Highway Research Board, Washington, D.C., 1968.
8. Billheimer, J. W., *Segmented Multi-Modal, Inter-City, Passenger Demand Model,* Highway Research Record No. 392, Highway Research Board, Washington, D.C., 1972.
9. Ben-Akiva, M., *A Disaggregate Direct Demand Model for Simultaneous Choice of Mode and Destination,* Paper presented at International Conference on Transportation Research, Bruges, Belgium, 1973.
10. Quandt, R. E., *The Demand for Travel: Theory and Measurement,* Heath Lexington Books, D.C. Heath and Company, Lexington, Massachusetts, 1970.
11. Manheim, M. L., *Practical Implications of Some Fundamental Properties of Travel Demand Models,* Highway Research Record No. 422, Highway Research Board, Washington, D.C., 1973.
12. Steger, W. A., *Reflections on Citizen Involvement in Urban Transportation Planning: Towards a Positive Approach,* Research Report No. 4, University of Toronto–York University Joint Program in Transportation, Toronto, Ontario, April, 1972.
13. Garrison, W. L., and D. R. Marble, *Analysis of Highway Networks: A Linear Programming Formulation,* Proceedings, Highway Research Board, Washington, D.C., vol. 37, pp. 1–14, 1958.

14. Morlok, E., "A Goal Directed Transportation Planning Model," *Transportation Research,* vol. 4, no. 2, pp. 199–213, 1970.
15. Funk, M. L., and F. A. Tillman, "Optimal Construction Staging by Dynamic Programming," *Journal of Highway Division,* American Society of Civil Engineers, vol. 94, no. HW2, pp. 255–265, 1968.
16. de Neufville, R., and Y. Mori, "Optimal Highway Staging by Dynamic Programming," *Transportation Engineering Journal,* American Society of Civil Engineers, vol. 96, TE1, pp. 11–24, 1970.
17. Chapman, L. D., "Investing in Regional Highway Networks," *Transportation Engineering Journal,* American Society of Civil Engineers, vol. 99, TE2, pp. 353–362, 1973.

NAME INDEX

SUBJECT INDEX